MW00994288

MIRACLES, MISSIONS, AND AMERICAN PENTECOSTALISM

Gary B. McGee

ORBIS BOOKS

Maryknoll, New York 10545

Founded in 1970, Orbis Books endeavors to publish works that enlighten the mind, nourish the spirit, and challenge the conscience. The publishing arm of the Maryknoll Fathers and Brothers, Orbis seeks to explore the global dimensions of the Christian faith and mission, to invite dialogue with diverse cultures and religious traditions, and to serve the cause of reconciliation and peace. The books published reflect the opinions of their authors and are not meant to represent the official position of the Maryknoll Society. To obtain more information about Maryknoll and Orbis Books, please visit our website at www.maryknollsociety.org.

Library of Congress Cataloging in Publication Data

McGee, Gary B., 1945-2008
    Miracles, missions, and American Pentecostalism / Gary B. McGee ; foreword by Byron Klaus.
        p. cm. — (American Society of Missiology series ; # 45)
    Includes bibliographical references (p.   ) and index.
    ISBN 978-1-57075-854-6 (pbk.)
    1. Pentecostal churches—Missions—History. 2. Missions, American—History.
I. Title.
BV2565.M38   2010
266'.994—dc22

                                                                    2009034310

Rev. Walter and Frances Black and Jennie Glassey

In memory of Jennie Glassey
of Cuba, Missouri,
missionary to Palestine
who stayed the course

Contents

PART 1
PENTECOSTAL POWER AND MISSIONS

PART 2
APOSTOLIC POWER AND MISSIONS

Preface to the American Society of Missiology Series

The purpose of the American Society of Missiology Series is to publish—without regard for disciplinary, national, or denominational boundaries—scholarly works of high quality and wide interest on missiological themes from the entire spectrum of scholarly pursuits relevant to Christian mission, which is always the focus of books in the Series.

By *mission* is meant the effort to effect passage over the boundary between faith in Jesus Christ and its absence. In this understanding of mission, the basic functions of Christian proclamation, dialogue, witness, service, worship, liberation, and nurture are of special concern. And in that context questions arise, including, How does the transition from one cultural context to another influence the shape and interaction between these dynamic functions, especially in regard to the cultural and religious plurality that comprises the global context of Christian life and mission?

The promotion of scholarly dialogue among missiologists, and among missiologists and scholars in other fields of inquiry, may involve the publication of views that some missiologists cannot accept, and with which members of the Editorial Committee themselves do not agree. Manuscripts published in the Series, accordingly, reflect the opinions of their authors and are not understood to represent the position of the American Society of Missiology or of the Editorial Committee. Selection is guided by such criteria as intrinsic worth, readability, coherence, and accessibility to a range of interested persons and not merely to experts or specialists.

The ASM Series, in collaboration with Orbis Books, seeks to publish scholarly works of high merit and wide interest on numerous aspects of missiology—the scholarly study of mission. Able presentations on new and creative approaches to the practice and understanding of mission will receive close attention.

The ASM Series Committee
Jonathan J. Bonk
Angelyn Dries, O.S.F.
Scott W. Sunquist

Foreword

Byron Klaus

The publishing of *Miracles, Missions, and American Pentecostalism* allows the late Dr. Gary B. McGee a final "download" of keen insights to those of us who have come to revere his life and legacy. While the scholarship that is offered in this volume will easily provide us with seminal knowledge about the essence of incipient Pentecostal missionary efforts, readers would miss a full-orbed experience if they did not at least have a brief awareness of the essence of who Gary B. McGee was.

In the memorial service for Gary McGee at the Assemblies of God Theological Seminary, I offered my remarks as president through the lens of an Old Testament text that I had actually used at my own father's funeral. Second Samuel 3:38 records the lament of David at the death of a man named Abner. In response to Abner's death, David queries to all who would listen, "Do you not realize that a prince and a great man has fallen in Israel this day? And today, though I am an anointed king, I am weak." That's the way I felt that day as I presided over a memorial service of a bereaved community. A "prince" had fallen in the land, and frankly it left me weak. The stature of this man was evident in his scholarship, but became most clear in human encounters that revealed the purity of a self-less character shaped by a long obedience to Christ that showed most clearly in the shadow of death that was Gary's experience in the last month of his life.

I actually gained my greatest insight into Gary McGee during that last month of life. When he fell ill and was hospitalized, we realized that there were literally hundreds, even thousands of people globally who would want to have a regular update on Dr. McGee's health. Our seminary Web site became a focal point for daily updates on his health and the welfare of his family. We created an opportunity on the Web site for people to leave a message for Dr. McGee and the family. During the month that he lingered before passing into the presence of our Lord, we received over 11,000 hits on the McGee Web link and people left over 800 messages. We printed these messages and gave them to the family. Many of these poignant words were read to Gary as he lay unconscious in the hospital. Invariably, they recalled an incident or encounter that was brought to the writer's remembrance to reveal the truest essence of Gary McGee as a person. Descriptors like encourager or listener were frequent; stories that were long forgotten by Gary were indelibly imprinted on the person who brought the remembrance to the light of day. I was reminded, with each account, that Gary's influence was deep and wide, broad and varied; leaving "forever" reminders of a man whom we would all miss.

The McGee "clan" came into the Pentecostal movement through Gary's maternal grandmother, who was introduced to the Pentecostal message through an evangelistic campaign in Canton, Ohio, led by Aimee Semple McPherson. The family became faithful members at Bethel Temple Assembly of God in Canton where Gary, the second oldest of five children, grew up. McGee's life calling as a historian began to emerge early in life. He actually met many of the people he wrote about throughout his career. They were not just historical figures and subjects of research, but people who had influenced his family.

Gary McGee's reputation as a teacher developed over the years. He began his career teaching at the Open Bible College in Des Moines, Iowa, in 1967. He continued at his alma mater, Central Bible College, in Springfield, Missouri, from 1970 to 1984 when he joined the faculty of the Assemblies of God Theological Seminary (AGTS). At the time of his death, he was the Distinguished Professor of Church History and Pentecostal Studies and was approved as professor emeritus (posthumously) in October 2009 by the AGTS board of directors.

His students saw him as a stern taskmaster, with their research papers turned back looking like a Christmas tree with "to be" verbs circled and connected through their papers. Students even begged Gary's young daughters to talk to their father about his stern measures in grading papers. While he admitted to being technologically challenged, his content needed little help to be clear and profound. Though the student grapevine would forever describe McGee as a hard grader whose expectations were exceedingly high, the fear of his red pen gave way to the recognition that Dr. McGee was connected to his Lord in a profound way. His personal piety was not on display for admiration, but as a humble expression of a life lived with Christ at its center. He strategically and intentionally desired that encounters with students would be filled with the extending of human dignity. Those who served with him as teaching assistants were encouraged to call him Gary, but admitted that calling him Gary was akin to calling the pope "bro." The respect he deserved was returned to students in abundant proportion, with a desire to pour honor and dignity into lives that too often had received scant human recognition in their young lives.

As a church historian McGee saw it as his duty to introduce his students, many of whom had little experience outside their Pentecostal tradition, to the broader world of Christian traditions. He had a love for icons and statues. One of his prize possessions was his bust of Martin Luther. He loved that bust; and whether it was used as a fixture in his office or a prop for his lectures, the bust of Luther was a reminder that he saw the larger-than-life characters of church history as real people, not mere objects of abstract conjecturing. He loved cathedrals and churches, the tinkling bells and smoking scepters of high church liturgy and joyfully introduced his "Spirit-led" students to experience the beauty of those unique contributions made by the larger Christian family.

You could not be around McGee without realizing he was a teacher who loved the local church. He had the spiritual gift of teaching and you did not need to be in his presence long to know he was born to that calling. He told those students aspiring to be teachers that the best place to sharpen their teaching skills, on a regular basis, was to lead a Sunday school class. A small volume he wrote, entitled *How Sweet the Sound*, testified to a passion for hymns and gospel songs sung in local churches that he felt never grew old. He taught his courses by starting each session with prayer and the singing of a song. For countless students, their introduction to the hymns and gospel songs that shaped the Pentecostal tradition and beyond were heard for the first time as Gary sang them. Church history courses included lessons in the chapel where students sang while Gary accompanied at the piano, giving voice to the heart of the church in hymns that had been sung for centuries by countless Christians.

As a scholar, McGee certainly had a wide variety of interests. What the reader will see in this volume is a final testament to a dominant set of assumptions that developed throughout his life's scholarly work. He believed that the emergence of the Pentecostal movement in the twentieth century was all about missiology. He did his research, becoming increasingly convinced that to understand Pentecostals at their core, one had to realize that they were constantly reflecting on the question of how the world could be evangelized in the "last days" before the imminent return of Christ. He further believed that to understand Pentecostals, an observer had to comprehend that the reasonable response to the need for world evangelism was a passionate desire for the resurgence of the dynamic work of the Holy Spirit, which had accompanied the ministry of the disciples in the book of Acts.

In the late 1990s, he coined a descriptor that, I would suggest, is arguably the single most enduring contribution he made to the understanding of the Pentecostal movement historically. He wrote an article entitled "The Radical Strategy in Modern Mission: The Linkage of Paranormal Phenomena with Evangelism."[1] He traced historically the role of the Holy Spirit and what some would term "spiritual warfare" in Christian world mission. While acknowledging a missiological perspective shared in varying degrees by a broad set of Christian tradition, he continued on to posit the emergence and significant of this *radical strategy* as a critique of the Great Century of missions represented in the nineteenth century. McGee clearly affirmed the historical continuity between previous missionary strategies and Pentecostalism. Still, he argued for historical discontinuity between the Great Century's strategy of *Christianization by civilization* and the *radical strategy* espoused by the missionary efforts of early Pentecostals. This DNA of Pentecostalism personified in the radical strategy was, to McGee, the clear mark of a new era, with a fresh theological reflection and strategic critique offered by these early pioneers. The missiological quandary that faced the late nineteenth century, as groups like the Student Volunteer Movement championed reaching the world in their generation, was how this effort could be accomplished more rapidly and effectively, given present mission strategy? The

1. Gary McGee, "The Radical Strategy in Modern Mission: The Linkage of Paranormal Phenomena with Evangelism," in *The Holy Spirit and Mission Dynamics*, ed. C. Douglas McConnell (Pasadena, CA: William Carey Library, 1997), 69-95.

growing passion among this deeply committed cadre of mission-minded people was to seek the restoration of the Spirit's power as taught and illustrated in the New Testament. McGee argued that this earnest questioning was the historical and spiritual cauldron in which a blueprint for "end-time" evangelism emerged. This *radical strategy* was a uniquely pneumatological approach to mission that affirmed a belief in the need for a subsequent spiritual empowerment that sent the recipient toward a destiny connected to the continuing redemptive mission of Jesus Christ. The empowerment was for the purpose of world evangelism, and the soon return of Christ made it necessary to "work while it is day" (John 9:4). This work, empowered by the Holy Spirit, was accompanied by "signs and wonders," thus energizing missionary efforts and hastening the return of Christ. While the evaluation of whether or not commitment to the radical strategy is still alive in Pentecostal ranks, McGee's key insight into the nature of incipient Pentecostalism stands as obvious.

The second valuable contribution of Gary McGee is not unique among historians. However, a signature of McGee's scholarly work is his affirmation of a historiographical method that takes human narratives seriously. His seminal work, *People of the Spirit*,[2] which chronicles the story of the Assemblies of God, uses this methodology with powerful effect. The story we read is of colorful characters whose pioneering spirit is clothed with triumph as well as a patchwork of human tragedy and feet of clay. Some would view such a stark picture of the prime characters in the history of this large church organization as uncomfortable, somehow replacing perceived piety with human frailty. McGee affirmed that in human stories or "testimonies," as Pentecostals would call them, was the reality of simple people led by the Spirit who had done extraordinary exploits through the power and strength of God. He believed that younger generations needed to hear these stories of ministry and blessing, warts and all, to provide inspiration for the contemporary expressions of Pentecostal life.

As I write this short foreword for Gary McGee's final work, I am reminded that the final memorial service at AGTS was held in the William J. Seymour Chapel. The seminary's chapel was named in honor of Bishop Seymour and his significant contribution to the Pentecostal movement. While realizing that the life experiences of Seymour and McGee are separated by decades of time and wide social chasms, their lives do have some commonalities of no small significance. They were both humble men who did their work not for recognition but for the sheer joy of being obedient to their Lord. They both are remembered with fondness, not for their overpowering personalities or human strength, but for their faithfulness to serve those God had placed within their sphere of influence. They both died too early in life, leaving us to wonder what might have been possible with more years of health to undergird their deep spirituality.

The Seymour Chapel at AGTS was a place that the character of Gary McGee would show itself regularly. In the middle of vibrant Pentecostal worship, McGee's voice would invariably rise with a clear prophetic utterance. His prophetic gift was well known, and his clear voice of encouragement, challenge, or

---

2. Gary B. McGee, *People of the Spirit* (Springfield, MO: Gospel Publishing House, 2004).

comfort would come forth with the strength of heaven itself. Gary's voice was trusted because we all knew the pure life that God was using.

This book is the final chapter of research that had been on Gary's front burner for a while. In 2006, Gary presented his inaugural lecture as Distinguished Professor of Church History and Pentecostal Studies and gave us a small glimpse of what would become his *magnus opus*. For this celebratory event, Gary was ensconced in academic regalia, and the boy from humble beginnings was being recognized as the eminent Pentecostal historian that he was. Among the guests were the Catholic bishop of the local archdiocese and special envoys from the Vatican. These special guests had come to honor Gary's work and thank him for his role in official Catholic-Pentecostal dialogues. Seymour, McGee, and Vatican are not words usually used in the same sentence in the Pentecostal tradition, but to Gary McGee the picture of that very special day was what the Kingdom of God looks like.

Gary's friend and colleague of many years, Bill Burrows, says that he became a great admirer of Gary and his work as a historian and interpreter of the world-wide Pentecostal movement. Bill—for twenty years managing editor at Orbis Books and a past president of the American Society of Missiology—says that Catholics around the world knew Gary's work, including his work in official Catholic-Pentecostal dialogues. He stressed that as much as they relied on him to interpret Pentecostalism and as much as they respected his scholarship, they felt even closer to him because they detected in him the same Spirit than animates the entire church of God. Reflecting on that sweet spirit, Bill recalls, "There was no one whose counsel and wisdom was more esteemed than Gary's."

What you read in this volume is the story of people passionate for Christ's Kingdom and willing to endure considerable sacrifice on that journey. They are people who are "frail creatures of dust," who, in the words of William Carey, "expected great things from God and attempted great things for God." How ironic that a story of Pentecostal missionary efforts would be published by a Catholic missionary society! Gary is smiling and I think I can even hear that infectious cackle we all recognized and loved.

Acknowledgments

I wish to thank the following for their help and advice at various stages in the research and writing of this book. Without them, it would have never come into being: Byron Klaus; James R. Goff, Jr.; Myron Houghton; Timothy Murray; Warren and Annette Newberry; Anthony Palma; Gloria Robinette; Darrin Rodgers; Grant Wacker; the librarians and staff—Assemblies of God Theological Seminary, Central Bible College (Springfield, Missouri); the Carl and Marie Hyllberg Memorial Fund (which funded research travel, books, and materials); and my students in the course *Early Pentecostal Missions*—spring 2008, who provided valuable research and interaction that influenced the final product.

Gary B. McGee

POSTHUMOUS ACKNOWLEDGMENTS

As the reader will realize, Gary McGee died before this book was put into production by the publisher. It was my privilege to coordinate the last stages of getting this book of my dear friend and colleague ready for copyediting. I could not have done it without the help of others.

Thus, I want to especially acknowledge Byron Klaus for writing the foreword, and my wife, Annette Newberry, for the introduction. Gary's daughter Catherine spent hours laboring over and sorting a tall stack of photocopied articles looking for missing citations and critically reviewing the entire manuscript for errors. Darrin Rogers was extremely helpful in discovering things we missed or were unaware of.

A very special appreciation goes to Orbis Books in general and to Catherine Costello and Bill Burrows in particular for publishing Gary's manuscript posthumously.

On behalf of the McGee family, Alice, Angela, and Catherine, I thank you all.

Warren B. Newberry

Introduction

Annette Newberry

In the latter part of the nineteenth century, the radical evangelical Protestant missions movement longed for the restoration of apostolic power before the imminent return of Christ. The attention given to pneumatology by the Wesleyan and Keswickian wings of the Holiness movement inspired people to seek the fulfillment of Joel's prophecy (Joel 2:28-29) to supply the spiritual energy necessary to bring about societal reform and evangelization of the world. *Miracles, Missions, and American Pentecostalism* contends that Pentecostalism arose out of this nineteenth-century groundswell of interest and the missional concerns of leaders such as A. T. Pierson, A. B. Simpson, and A. J. Gordon, who worked to quickly spread the gospel message to the uttermost parts of the earth in what they considered to be the closing days of time. Emerging from this background and the heightened interest in the person and work of the Holy Spirit, Pentecostalism represented a new renewal movement that began shortly after the turn of the twentieth century and rapidly gained followers all over the world.

In the midst of complaints that modern missions methods had failed to accomplish the desired goals, the rebirth of awareness among the radical evangelicals in the possibility of the restoration of apostolic power in signs and wonders to expedite gospel proclamation fostered new hope that Christ's command to his followers in Matthew 29:19-29 could be fulfilled before the rapture of the church. The first Pentecostal missionaries rushed to the mission field giving little thought to mission theory or strategic planning. They firmly believed preaching the gospel to be their prime responsibility and aimed to accomplish the task quickly to usher in the end-time events (Matt. 24:14). When missionaries arrived on the mission fields and the reality of the task before them set in, they settled down to day-to-day missions work: discipling converts, building churches, starting Bible institutes, and ministering to the pressing needs of the people around them. While their daily routine may have appeared mundane, the Pentecostal message was not. Their proclamation of a supernaturally wrapped package resonated well with the worldviews of peoples to whom they ministered. In areas where people lived daily with an acute awareness of the spirit world, men and women came to the Christian faith because of the wonder-working power in the name of Jesus and empowerment of the Holy Spirit to overcome spirits, drive out demons, and provide deliverance from their physical problems. The immanent power and gifts of the Spirit were far more relevant for their lives than church creeds of any tradition.

Following the somewhat disorganized early period of Pentecostal missions, order gradually prevailed through the formation of mission agencies and the adoption of strategies, particularly in regard to the development of indigenous churches according to the "New Testament pattern." Missionary personnel focused their efforts on training indigenous leaders and engaging in ministries of compassion. Though differentiated by the *glossolalia* plank in their theological platform, Pentecostals exhibited much of the same behavior and doctrinal convictions of the holiness and evangelical missionaries without neglecting the traditional Pentecostal view of evangelism with signs and wonders. This view continued through the efforts of missionaries, healing evangelists, independent charismatic leaders, and especially through the work of Christians in the former mission lands who found it indispensible in their frequent power encounters with "the powers of darkness."

A SUMMARY OF
MIRACLES, MISSIONS, AND AMERICAN PENTECOSTALISM

While the historiography of Pentecostal expansion is emerging from its infancy and several significant studies have been published, *Miracles, Missions, and American Pentecostalism* differs from some of the most recent works in that it more closely examines the historical, theological, and missiological context of the American Pentecostal movement and how the expectancy of miracles fit into the early-twentieth-century mission landscape. Gary McGee, who feels that required texts in Bible colleges, universities, and seminaries often overlook or evade reports about supernatural phenomena and extraordinary experiences, generously sprinkles his book with terminology such as miracles, signs and wonders, healings, visions, revivals, spiritual gifts, power encounters, and exorcisms.

Even though the precedent for miracles in missions dates from the time of the apostles, acceptance of the possibility of miracles beyond the initial establishment of Christianity has long generated debate. McGee tackles what he considers to be an awkward position needing a more comprehensive explanation—the attempt to explain the apostolic nature of mission without the possibility of miraculous signs and wonders included in the explanation. The author identifies and probes five attitudes among Protestant missionaries and their home-base supporters regarding the issue of miracles—ranging from full-blown cessationism, the liberal theological view, to wholehearted acceptance and anticipation of the full restoration of miracles and spiritual gifts, the view of radical evangelicals, who declared like Paul, "Our message of the gospel came to you not in word only, but in power and in the Holy Spirit and with full conviction" (1 Thess. 1:5). McGee believes that many authors and mission studies have too long disregarded the full range of opinions, choosing to ignore the latter radical evangelical view in favor of the first more liberal idea—a fact that he tries to remedy in this book. Showing his propensity for discovering pertinent data, he delved deeply into the subject, mining a wealth of information from hundreds of Catholic, Protestant, and Orthodox sources including patristic writings, missions periodicals, personal letters, secular newspaper articles, religious journals, church histories, missionary society papers and reports, denominational reports and minutes, missionary manuals, personal diaries, theses, and unpublished papers. Even when fighting the effects of an illness, he continued to search through dusty tomes in stuffy archives and little-known libraries, tirelessly turning the brittle pages of old journals and vintage newspapers for every hint of information about miracles, missions, and Pentecostalism. The combined results, skillfully woven together in a very readable volume, represent his legacy to the fields of church history and missiology. Over 1,700 citations will serve as a springboard for launching further in-depth research into this fascinating subject.

The book, which is divided into two main sections, examines the early background of the Pentecostal movement, how Pentecostals understood empowerment in the Spirit, how they went about the work of mission, and how in a little over a century Pentecostalism has become a global force in Christianity. Chapter 1 covers the expectation of miracles in missions from the time of the ancient church to the "modern missions" of the nineteenth century whole explaining beliefs concerning the supposed decline of supernatural gifts. Chapter 2 explores the concept of the outpouring of the Spirit in relation to missions from the Protestant Reformers to the Edinburgh Missionary Conference in 1910; the tenor and affect of nineteenth-century revivals in the mission lands; and the influence of the Wesleyan and Keswick streams of the Holiness movement. Chapter 3 probes nineteenth-century radical evangelical expectations of signs, wonders, and miraculous happenings in missions including faith healings, exorcisms, and cosmic spiritual warfare (Mark 16:17-18). Chapter 4 concentrates on the anticipation of languages supernaturally endowed without instructional assistance—a divinely supplied shortcut to language preparation for missionary preaching, thus enabling missionaries to skip the time-consuming hurdle of language study before launching into immediate world evangelization. Chapter 5 presents developments in early Pentecostal missions and spotlights diverging ways in which radical evangelical, mainline evangelical, liberal, and Pentecostal missionaries perceived the Spirit's work up to the 1910 World Missionary Conference in Edinburgh, Scotland.

The second part of the book, "Apostolic Power and Missions," turns to the meaning of glossolalia for empowerment for evangelization, the changes that took place in understanding this issue, and the exegetical challenge resident in the insistence of tongues for Spirit baptism. Chapter 6 examines how radical evangelicals, mainstream evangelicals, and theological progressives all registered interest in what the Holy Spirit might accomplish in church and missions even though they had conspicuously different expectations. It also considers how the earliest twentieth-century Pentecostal revivals influenced some of the earliest missionaries and details some of their experiences.

Chapter 7 investigates the emergence of Pentecostal mission agencies and missionary networks, faith missionaries working under the direct guidance of the Holy Spirit, and the widespread missional influence of the Christian and

Missionary Alliance. Chapter 8 covers the characteristics of some early missionaries, their struggles with limited resources and challenges of living abroad, the necessity for missionary training, and the development of mission strategies including the Three Selfs—building self-governing, self-supporting, and self-propagating churches. This chapter also highlights the contributions of women as founders, administrators, and teachers in missionary education and the substantial part they played in shaping Pentecostal mission strategies.

Chapter 9 tackles the decline of the expectancy of miracles in missions among evangelicals in the early 1920s, an attitude fostered partially because of advances in medical science and partially because of evangelical rejection of Pentecostalism. While evangelicals prioritized the spiritual aspect of salvation above physical healing, Pentecostals saw them as inextricably linked together in ministering to the whole person, a fact illustrated by revival movements in China and the post–World War II surge in salvation/healing campaigns in North America which had a spillover effect on world missions.

The book concludes by summarizing the apostolic faith as it stands in the third millennium and how interest in the miraculous has changed the landscape of modern missions. In the miraculous power of the Holy Spirit, Pentecostalism not only survived but expanded to become a vibrant force in Christianity. Chapter 10 identifies the present-day cadre of missionaries as better prepared, more adequately supported, higher educated, and better organized than the first early zealots who rushed to the mission fields at the beginning of the twentieth century. Third-millennium missionaries think more about the theology of missions, work with the established indigenous churches, look positively at teamwork and strategic planning, and make substantial contributions to evangelism, education, and compassion ministries. Yet, with all the advances and advantages, they maintain the same commitment to mission as the early pioneers.

Several challenges face the third-millennium corps of Pentecostals. First, Pentecostalism must no longer be viewed through a single North American frame, and vital lessons must be learned from the insights of Pentecostals living in other regions of the world. Pentecostal theology must maintain focused on Spirit baptism as its chief theological distinctive while allowing for a diversity of nuances and interpretations from among its worldwide adherents. Second, North American Pentecostalism must recognize and face an existing identity crisis. In many cases, a North American Pentecostal church's charismatic characteristics are hidden in the conformity of success needing a sign to announce its pneumatological leanings rather than its practicing beliefs in signs and wonders.

Third, Pentecostals, who have been known for their quick actions, need to reflect and theologize more. Fourth, since a more holistic approach to ministry has been tucked under the apostolic banner, Pentecostals must continue to bring reconciliation among groups across racial, cultural, social, and class barriers and contend for deliverance from poverty, hunger, and the damaging effect of systemic evils in the world today. Fifth, Pentecostals must continue to retain their evangelistic fervor while grappling with other issues such as the need for renewal, Christian unity, and the quest for spiritual power.

Modern Pentecostalism came as a jolt to the Western church world in the twentieth century. Insistent that the Holy Spirit wants to baptize every believer with spiritual power for mission, Pentecostals told of how it enabled them when witnessing for Christ, praying for the sick, ministering in the charismatic gifts (1 Corinthians 12), and casting out demons. Their heightened emphasis on the supernatural element of the Christian faith scandalized Christians who were more accustomed to traditional decorum in worship, comfortable with a rational spirituality that rules out mystical experiences such as speaking in tongues, and convinced that divine sovereignty severely restricts the possibility of miracles. Finding more compatible audiences in the Majority World (Africa, Asia, Latin America, Oceania), Pentecostal missions have thrived to become a substantial force in the Christian world movement.[1]

The wave of the Spirit's renewal that began in the early days of the twentieth century has steadily increased in proportion and scope, rising into a giant swell of charismatic Christianity breaking on the shores of many countries and traditions. A study of the past such as this reveals a substantial Pentecostal/charismatic fortitude when it comes to wrestling with the challenges and difficulties. History proves that the movement has successfully juggled the tensions of obeying the voice of the Spirit and doing what it takes to get the job done—successfully balancing the relationship of renewal to institutionalization. This suggests bright hope for the future and the promise of a new chapter in the history of world Christianity.

IN MEMORY OF JENNIE GLASSEY OF CUBA, MISSOURI

The dedication of *Miracles, Missions, and American Pentecostalism* to Jennie Glassey, an independent faith missionary to Palestine, may seem strange to some people, but it represents the lengths to which Gary McGee went to discover what made early missionaries tick, forsake all that life had to offer in the United States of America, and sail into the unknown regions beyond with only God's promise of his continuing presence and the power for witnessing. Glassey represents hundreds of other missionaries, some unknown and unnamed, who took God seriously when he promised that if they believed in him, they would be able to perform greater works that those witnessed by the disciples (John 14:12).

Glassey was converted in the Presbyterian Church of Cuba, Missouri, in a revival held by John Stewart and Walter Black, who preached that miracles were still possible if people exercised true faith in God. Shortly after her conversion, she received a missionary call from God. Even though she pleaded with God about her general lack of all things necessary for this type of ministry—finances,

---

1. When Gary McGee died, this book was in its final stages and the manuscript completed except for the preface and introduction. I was chosen to write the introduction because Gary was my mentor and I had worked closely with him on other writing projects. I have tried to complete the introduction as he would have. While going through his manuscript and papers, this one paragraph, the beginning thoughts for his introduction, was found. I have chosen to include the author's last words here to give the reader the complete McGee experience. I would also like to add that my friend, Gary, "… fought the good fight, … finished the course, and …kept the faith" (2 Tim. 4:7).

language skills, and knowledge of missions work, God assured her that it was a package deal—with his call came his provision.

While her family protested, the seventeen-year-old young woman packed her bags and left for St. Louis to receive Bible training while boarding with Walter and Frances Black. There she received the promised empowerment from God and began a journey that would take her as a missionary to Palestine. The Blacks with their infant daughter and Glassey sailed to Liverpool, England, as independent faith missionaries in January 1896. They planned to book passage for Africa but were delayed by insufficient funds.

Two years later, and for unknown reasons, they joined Frank Sanford on his missionary expedition to Jerusalem. Sanford's stay in the Holy Land was short lived, and the Blacks returned to Canada after a few years. Glassey, however, remained faithful to her missionary calling and continued to evangelize Muslims with the help of a Palestinian woman. Little is known about what she endured or accomplished, but the Christian and Missionary Alliance recognized her for faithfulness and service in a difficult area.

The tenacity of this courageous young woman inspired Gary McGee to visit Cuba, Missouri, to investigate her life from the local newspaper archives and locate her grave. Her life and testimony fueled at least part of the interest in writing this book about other missionaries who dared to trust God for the possibility of the miraculous in connection with their missions calling. Today, a charismatically inclined spirituality predominates in the larger sector of Majority World Christianity, due in part to the contributions of Pentecostal and charismatic missionaries like Jennie Glassey who stayed the course.

Abbreviations
(not including newspapers)

Adva	*Advance*
Agora	*Agora*
AW	*Alliance Weekly*
Amer	*America*
AM	*American Magazine*
AQ	*American Quarterly*
AE	*Apostolic Evangel*
AF	*Apostolic Faith*
AL	*Apostolic Light*
AT	*Apostolic Truth*
AJPS	*Asian Journal of Pentecostal Studies*
AGH	*Assemblies of God Heritage*
BA	*Baptist Argus*
BHH	*Baptist History and Heritage*
BMR	*Baptist Missionary Review*
BS	*Bibliotheca Sacra*
BGBA	*Bombay Guardian and Banner of Asia*
BCHL	*Brethren in Christ History and Life*
BM	*Bridegroom's Messenger*
CTJ	*Calvin Theological Journal*
CML	*Canadian Missionary Link*
Char	*Charisma and Christian Life*
CR	*Chinese Recorder*
CA	*Christian Alliance*
CAFMW	*Christian Alliance and Foreign Missionary Weekly*
CAMW	*Christian Alliance and Missionary Weekly*
CMAW	*Christian and Missionary Alliance Weekly*
CB	*Christian Beacon*
CC	*Christian Century*
CE	*Christian Evangel*
CF	*Christian Fundamentalist*
CP	*Christian Patriot*
CT	*Christianity Today*
CH	*Church History: Studies in Christianity & Culture*
CMI	*Church Missionary Intelligencer*

CMIR	Church Missionary Intelligencer and Record
CMRev	Church Missionary Review
CMR	Church Missionary Record
CWPI	Cloud of Witnesses to Pentecost in India
Comm	Commonweal
Conf	Confidence
CCW	Congregationalist and Christian World
CPCR	Cyberjournal for Pentecostal/Charismatic Research
DJMT	Dialogue: A Journal of Mormon Thought
DACB	Dictionary of African Christian Biography
DAC	Dictionary of Asian Christianity
DPCM	Dictionary of Pentecostal and Charismatic Movements
Dnya	Dnyanodaya
EM	Eclectic Magazine
Econ	Economist
Enri	Enrichment: A Journal for Pentecostal Ministry
Eter	Eternity
EMes	Evangelical Messenger
EQ	Evangelical Quarterly
EG	Everlasting Gospel
ET	Expository Times
FS	Faithful Standard
FF	Flames of Fire
FR	Fortnightly Review
FGMH	Full Gospel Missionary Herald
HF	Harvest Field
IA	India Alliance
IER	Indian Evangelical Review
IW	Indian Witness
IM	Intercessory Missionary
IBMR	International Bulletin of Missionary Research
IRM	International Review of Missions
JAH	Journal of American History
JES	Journal of Ecumenical Studies
JEPTA	Journal of the European Pentecostal Theological Association
JRH	Journal of Religious History
LRE	Latter Rain Evangel
LH	Leaves of Healing
Life	Life
LD	Literary Digest
LT	Living Truths
MCMR	Madras Church Missionary Record
Mara	Maran-Atha
Miss	Missiology: An International Review
MF	Missionary Forum
MH	Missionary Herald

MRW	*Missionary Review of the World*
MS	*Mission Studies*
MW	*Mission World*
MM	*Mountain Movers*
MPB	*Mukti Prayer Bell*
NA	*New Acts*
NIDPCM	*New International Dictionary of Pentecostal and Charismatic Movements*
NZCR	*New Zealand Christian Record*
PA	*Pentecostal Advocate*
Pent	*Pentecost*
PE	*Pentecostal Evangel*
PHA	*Pentecostal Holiness Advocate*
PP	*Pentecostal Power*
PT	*Pentecostal Testimony*
Pneuma	*Pneuma: The Journal of the Society for Pentecostal Studies*
PR	*Presbyterian Review*
PTR	*Princeton Theological Review*
Pulse	*Pulse*
RCW	*Record of Christian Work*
RT	*Redemption Tidings*
RB	*Regions Beyond*
RAC	*Religion and American Culture*
RJ	*Renewal Journal*
RH	*Review and Herald*
SMJ	*Southern Medical Journal*
TC	*The Christian*
TCFSC	*The Christian Fundamentals in School and Church*
TEW	*The East and the West*
TGAL	*The Gospel in All Lands*
TP	*The Pentecost*
Time	*Time*
TPE	*Today's Pentecostal Evangel*
TFire	*Tongues of Fire*
Trans	*Transformation*
TF	*Triumphs of Faith*
Trust	*Trust*
Watch	*Watchword*
WE	*Weekly Evangel*
WT	*Whole Truth*
WWit	*Word and Witness*
WW	*Word and Work*
WWW	*The Word, the Work and the World*
WP	*World Pentecost*
YMI	*Young Men of India*
WTJ	*Wesleyan Theological Journal*

Part I

PENTECOSTAL POWER AND MISSIONS

1

The Nagging Comparison

The apostles performed many miraculous signs and wonders among the people. . . .[1]

Acts 5:12

Missionaries of the Church of Scotland have been sent forth . . . in the absence of miracles.[2]

Missionary to India Alexander Duff, 1839

We talk a great deal about apostolic methods. Shall we attempt to do exactly as the apostles did? That would require us to travel on land with camels and donkeys, and on the sea with sail-and-oar ships. Is it precise apostolic methods that we want, or the apostolic spirit in the use of modern methods?[3]

Unnamed missionary quoted in *Missionary Review of the World*, 1892

Is it part of God's plan that such mighty manifestations of the Spirit's power among the heathen as are recorded in the Acts of the Apostles should be as much a thing of past ages, as those mighty manifestations of animal energy which we wonder at in the gigantic skeletons at the British Museum? This position is often maintained.[4]

Niger missionary Graham Wilmot Brooke, 1892

The study of missionary biography reveals a true and remarkable "apostolic succession." . . . This grand succession has continued, without one break or missing link in the chain.[5]

Mission promoter and editor Arthur T. Pierson, 1894

[Missionaries have done] an infinite amount of harm in China without making a single convert. . . . They [are], and always [have] been, the greatest liars on the face of the earth.[6]

Inventor of the Maxim Gun, Sir Hiram Maxim, 1910

3

When applied to God's mission through the church in the world, church leaders, theologians, historians, and missiologists have employed the term "apostolic" to refer variously to the faith and actions of the apostles, the spectacular growth of early Christianity, patterns of ecclesiastical authority, unity among churches, and the missionary task. In regard to the latter, it has included the means of fulfilling that responsibility through the displays of divine power that accompanied gospel witness and the planting of churches in the Acts of the Apostles and afterward. Ironically, the church fathers who met at Constantinople in A.D. 381 and expanded the Nicene Creed to emphasize their belief in "one, holy, catholic, and apostolic Church," could not have imagined the controversies that would swirl around those four attributes for centuries to come.[7] Although it remains outside the purview of this study to explore all the attendant issues, one feature has remained constant in regard to the apostolic nature of mission: attempts to lay claim to the term apostolic without the possibility of the "miraculous signs and wonders" that characterized the ministries of the apostles and their followers has invariably created an awkwardness, a need for explanation, or a defensive posture. In the nineteenth century, in the midst of charges that modern missions had failed, a resurgence of interest in the possibility of miracles among radical evangelicals offered hope that the Great Commission (Matt 28:19-20) might be achieved through the restoration of apostolic power before the imminent return of Christ. Allied with the supernaturally charged spirituality of Christians in the mission lands, this development would change forever the face of global Christianity.

APOSTOLIC POWER AND MISSIONS

Jesus, the apostles, and their successors established the precedent for miracles in missions—the expectancy of paranormal displays of power in evangelism. Many observers believed this dynamic had assisted in the rapid growth of ancient Christianity. However, the credibility of miraculous claims has long generated disagreement because of philosophical, historical, and theological considerations. Thomas Aquinas in the medieval "Age of Faith" offered an inclusive definition of a miracle—"Something altogether wondrous, i.e. having its cause hidden absolutely and from everyone. This cause is God."[8] But by the eighteenth-century Age of Enlightenment, philosophers like David Hume contended that supernatural interventions would violate the laws of nature and, hence, could not occur.[9] Deists certainly had no room for miracles, as when Thomas Jefferson removed all traces of the supernatural from his rearrangement of the four Gospels in the *Jefferson Bible: The Life and Morals of Jesus of Nazareth* (1820). Questions about sources, as well as the obvious ideological agendas of the authors that controlled the evaluation of evidence, have naturally troubled modern historians.[10]

Theological presuppositions, naturally influenced by philosophical and historical considerations, have been of paramount importance in the debate within the church world, especially within the churches that grew from the Protestant

Reformation. The issue has centered in part on whether miracles fulfilled their purpose in the first century. "No transition in the history of the Church [was] so sudden, abrupt, and radical as that from the apostolic to the post-apostolic age," wrote the nineteenth-century Reformed church historian Philip Schaff. "God himself . . . established an impassable gulf. . . . The apostolic age is the age of miracles."[11] Presbyterian theologian Benjamin Warfield concurred. In his judgment, the extraordinary "gifts of power" of the apostles had served to authenticate them as the "authoritative founders" of the church. In turn, they conferred this capability on their own disciples. But as the church became established and the early leaders passed off the scene, so did the demonstrations of miraculous power.[12] Despite Anglican attempts to defend the occurrences of miracles into the patristic age, he would have none of it. In his estimation, the "great harvest of miracles" that came with the evolution of Roman Catholicism grew from the tares of "heathendom."[13] These assumptions, however, coming from Western Christians in the modern era, have served to obscure the important place that miracles once held in the expansion of the faith.

Nonetheless, miracles continued to be sighted on the trails of Christian missionaries in the post-apostolic era and ostensibly played an important part in drawing people to the faith.[14] As the early church historian Eusebius noted, "The Holy Spirit . . . wrought many wonders as yet through [the 'preaching evangelists'], so that as soon as the gospel was heard, men voluntarily in crowds, and eagerly, embraced the true faith with their whole minds."[15] Neither the Western and Eastern church fathers, nor those of the Oriental Orthodox churches suggested that miracles and the charismata had been intended only for the New Testament church. Even the "charisms" of the Holy Spirit, the gifts of tongues, interpretation, and prophecy among them—viewed later as "extraordinary gifts"—were sought for and received during the rites of Christian initiation (baptism, confirmation, Eucharist), with evidence provided by witnesses from around the Mediterranean seaboard dating from the end of the second to the eighth century.[16]

More directly related to missions, records tell of unusual demonstrations of power in the progress of Christianity, with some analogous to phenomena found in the Old and New Testaments.[17] For instance, Basil of Cappadocia lauded the remarkable number of conversions in the ministry of the third-century missionary bishop in Asia Minor, Gregory Thaumaturgus ("wonder-worker"). "By the superabundance of gifts, wrought in him by the Spirit in all power and in signs and marvels," he reported, Gregory "was styled a second Moses by the very enemies of the Church."[18] In Egypt, the famous desert father Antony became legendary for prevailing in conflicts with demons and working miracles. Revealing the seismic doctrinal struggle of the time between orthodox Christianity and the growing popularity of Arianism, his biographer, Athanasius, a stalwart defender of the orthodox position on the Godhead, skillfully trumped the spiritual authority of his Arian opponents by attributing the feats and successes of Antony in converting non-Christians in Alexandria to his fidelity to Nicene Christology.[19]

In the same era, a slave girl named Nino taken captive to the Caucasus region and afterward canonized by the Orthodox Church of Georgia as an "equal to the apostles," prayed for the healing of Queen Nana. In turn, this contributed to the conversion of King Mirian and the nation.[20] The connection of a physical healing or some other kind of miraculous incident to the conversion of an individual, tribe, or nation can be found elsewhere, from that of the Ethiopian eunuch in the book of Acts (8:26-40); to the third-century King Trdat of Armenia; to the fourth-century Emperor Constantine; to the fifth-century Clovis, king of the Franks; to the eight-century Boniface who felled the sacred oak of Thor; to the ninth-century Nestorian missionary Elias, who cut down the sacred oak of Yazd, prayed for the sick, and cast out demons on the plain of Moqan, west of the Caspian Sea; and to Stephen of Perm's burning of the sacred birch tree of the Komi Permyaks in eastern Russia in the fourteenth century.[21] A hundred years earlier to the south in Ethiopia, the miracles of the Orthodox monk Takla-Haymanot reputedly assisted in the conversion of non-Christians.[22]

The reliability of these stories has been much discussed and such accounts were sometimes transformed into fantastic tales. This happened in the case of Patrick of Ireland. Though he himself credited his escapes from captivity and calling to evangelize to the influence of voices and dreams, later accretions distorted aspects of his actual ministry.[23] Medieval reports reflect the same problem. In Britain, the Venerable Bede, the father of English history, recorded miracles that took place during the evangelization of England led by Augustine of Canterbury. Healings, exorcisms, calming of the sea, raising the dead, signs in the heavens, and other unusual occurrences lay sprinkled throughout his *History of the English Church and People*.[24] Responding to reports about the evangelistic endeavors of Augustine and his fellow monks among the Anglo-Saxons, Pope Gregory the Great (reigned A.D. 590-604) praised their achievements and said they stood "resplendent with such great miracles . . . that they seem to imitate the powers of the apostles in the signs which they display."[25] Given the prefigurement of the church in the Old Testament and inauguration in the New Testament, Bede's *History* had simply added more pages to the ongoing story of the church.[26] While both Gregory and Bede doubted the possibility of such miracles in normal church life, they recognized their continuing importance for the missionary advance.[27] Even so, widespread stories of miracles among Christians performed through the intercession of the saints pressed church leaders to regulate the process of canonization, evidence of the continuing role of supernatural happenings in grassroots life and piety.[28]

MIRACLES AND THE TRUE CHURCH

As Catholic missions flourished in the Reformation and post-Reformation eras, only Catholic missionaries seriously entertained the possibility of paranormal phenomena occurring.[29] In fortress Rome, threatened still in the late sixteenth century by the growing hordes of Protestants to the north, Cardinal Robert Bellarmine declared that the "glory of miracles" served two purposes: "First they are necessary for new faith or for extraordinary missionary persuasion. Secondly they are efficacious and sufficient because . . . they cannot be among the adversaries of the true church and [show] that the true church is among us."[30] Interestingly, the unexpected but timely discovery of more catacombs under the city, whose relics testified to the blood of the early martyrs and their spiritual vigor, confirmed that the city sat atop holy ground, further evidence of the authority of the papacy and the truth of Catholic teachings.[31] The continuance of miracles in the lives of the saints from the time of the ancient church became an important component in Catholic apologetics.

The theological combat had naturally crossed over into the realm of missions, with the worldwide extension of the faith bringing comfort to Catholics in the face of the Protestant schism. Catholics pointed to the miracles performed by Francis Xavier in India and the remarkable number of conversions that followed.[32] Even the defenders of the notorious Synod of Diamper, called in 1599 to Latinize the St. Thomas Christians of Malabar, appealed to the miraculous ending of a monsoon rain to permit a public procession to celebrate the ecclesiastical triumph of Archbishop Aleixo de Meneses as evidence of divine sanction.[33] In an age of Catholic and Protestant polemics, Catholic leaders such as Bellarmine saw such happenings as not only upholding the integrity of the Roman Church, but also demonstrating the authenticity of its apostolic character.

In the citadels of the Protestant revolt, Martin Luther and John Calvin doubted the probability of miracles happening after the New Testament period, and by so doing shaped Protestant views on the miraculous dimension of the faith for centuries to come.[34] For the Reformers, miracles had been required to sow the seeds of the new faith and thereby convince the first generation to accept the redemptive claims of Jesus of Nazareth. Weaning the church from the "mother's milk" of miracles, God now fed his people the spiritual meat of Holy Scripture.[35] "We are . . . retaining that very gospel whose truth all the miracles that Jesus Christ and his disciples ever wrought serve to confirm," wrote Calvin in his *Institutes of the Christian Religion*. Expectancy of additional miracles, a false hope concocted by the "sheer delusions of Satan," would only "draw the people away from the true worship of their God."[36]

Seventeenth-century Lutheran and Reformed scholastic theologians perpetuated this outlook. The Basel Reformed theologian Johannes Wollebius found no contemporary need for miracles since they had been "given for the confirmation of the gospel, and they have passed away now that the gospel has been spread and preached among the nations." To thump Catholic claims, he added, "The apostles promised neither more miracles nor more prophecies, but rather made boasting about prophecies and miracles a mark of the antichristian 'church.'"[37] Free of the "superstitions" and "idolatry" of Catholicism, Protestants confidently saw their faith as being in harmony with the emerging forces of modernity: reason and science.[38] For theologians and many church leaders, miracles and even foreign missions,[39] so characteristic of ancient and medieval Christianity, had both lost their relevance.[40]

Against this backdrop at the close of the eighteenth century, William Carey wrote his influential *Enquiry into the Obligations of Christians, to Use Means for the Conversion of the Heathens* to contest the prevailing view "that because the apostles were extraordinary officers and have no proper successors, and because many things which were right for them to do would be unwarrantable for us, therefore [the Great Commission] may not be immediately binding on us . . . though it was so upon them."[41] For those like Carey who ventured abroad in mission, the absence of miraculous expectancy sometimes left them perplexed as to why the results of their efforts seemed to pale when compared to the "apostolic missions" of the early church.[42] A later Baptist missionary serving in Calcutta (Kolkata), George Rouse, confessed that "in the great work which God has given us to do in this land, that of bringing it from the darkness of heathenism and estrangement from God to the enjoyment of the light which Christ alone can give, we cannot help now and again casting our eyes back to the records of the early triumphs of the Gospel." Unfortunately, the "result is generally a feeling of sadness, almost, at times, of despondency, because our success seems so much less than that of the Apostles and their contemporaries."[43]

A skirmish between Catholic and Protestant writers in the nineteenth century over the miracles attributed to José de Anchieta (1534-1597), a pioneer Jesuit missionary to Brazil, captured the awkwardness of the Protestant position.[44] When Protestant writers referred to the "pretended miracles" of Anchieta,[45] the British Catholic mission historian Thomas Marshall shot back, "Who dreams of an Anglican miracle, or a Wesleyan prophet, or a Presbyterian saint?" Contrasting the apostolic endeavors of Catholic missionaries with those of Protestants in India and Burma, he queried, "Who can imagine [Thomas] Middleton [the first Anglican bishop of Calcutta] bidding a stream spring forth in the plains of Bengal? or [Claudius] Buchanan respected by panthers? or [the Baptist Adoniram] Judson transfigured? or [Bishop Reginald] Heber raising the dead?"[46]

Appealing to Scripture, Marshall pointedly asked what Jesus meant when he said to his disciples—"the first missionaries"—that "Ye shall do greater things than these!" (John 14:12 [AV]). "When did He who gave that promise recall it, or when did He first begin to send forth apostles without the gifts of apostles?" He then demanded: "And what new God is this, who has neither the will nor the power to interfere in human affairs, and who is hopelessly fettered by the 'laws of nature' as a plant or an insect?" Could it be that "Protestants [have] agreed to accept the definition of the Creator . . . current among the Hottentots, who considered Him 'an excellent man, who dwells far beyond the moon, and does no harm to anyone'?"[47] In fact, those who profess the Christian faith, but deny the possibility of miracles, "know neither God nor themselves." Consequently, they wouldn't believe a miracle if they saw one, because "what they *fear* in them is their exhibition of Divine power, what they *hate* is their testimony to the Catholic faith."[48]

Despite Marshall's belief in the miraculous dimension of Catholic missions, the later Catholic historian Joseph Schmidlin observed that while "striking answers to prayer and evidence of grace" could be found in post-Enlightenment Catholic missions, "they show no clearly demonstrable miracles in the strict sense, at least not of the same number and importance as formerly."[49] Even so, he may have overstated his case; only in recent years have historians and missiologists placed more attention on the popular reception of the faith. Spiritual dynamics in Catholic contexts included claims of various kinds of miracles with some related to evangelism.[50] In the labors of the Redemptorist, Jesuit, and Paulist missionaries in the United States, when holding "parish missions" (the equivalent of revivals) in Catholic parishes for the "re-evangelization" of the thousands of Catholic immigrants, prayers for the sick and healings held an important place. "For forty years," wrote Francis Weninger, S.J., one of the outstanding Catholic evangelists of the nineteenth century, "cures followed cures without interruption."[51]

THE LEVER OF PROVIDENCE

Marshall handily exploited what he considered to be a glaring weakness in the Protestant belief in the cessation of miracles, namely, the absence of definitive scriptural support. Whether one turns to the words of Jesus in Mark 16:17–18 ("And these signs will accompany those who believe: In my name they will drive out demons; they will speak in new tongues; they will pick up snakes with their hands; and when they drink deadly poison, it will not hurt them at all; they will place their hands on sick people, and they will get well")[52] or in John 14:12 ("Very truly I tell you, all who have faith in me will do the works I have been doing, and they will do even greater things than these"), the New Testament did not confine the extraordinary wonder-working acts of God to first-century Christianity. "For Protestants, who had made Scripture the supreme—indeed nearly the sole—religious authority," noted historian D. P. Walker, "this lack was a very grave defect."[53]

Notwithstanding the claimed cessation of miracles, the Protestant mindset on supernatural manifestations involved more complexity than the discussion thus far has revealed.[54] To rule out miracles entirely would have placed limits on the sovereignty and omnipotence of God, the keystone in the Protestant—especially the Calvinist—arch of theology. Not only does God uninterruptedly govern the lifeless, as well as the living parts of the creation, but all aspects of the world of humankind. Divine interventions could bestow gifts of benevolent care to individuals and even specific groups as the actions of the Almighty based on his foreknowledge and according to his eternal purposes. For example, those who heard about the restoration of eyesight to a Greenlander who had been prayed for by the Norwegian Lutheran Hans Egede would have considered it a providential act and, at the same time, have casts doubts on whether such an unusual mercy could be promised to others who were vision impaired.[55] While the line between acts of "special providence" and miracles remained fuzzy in the classrooms of theological orthodoxy,[56] confidence in the possibility of miraculous happenings often characterized popular piety.[57]

With some exceptions, Protestants yoked the Christian faith to the fortunes of their respective countries, especially during the colonial expansion of the nineteenth century.[58] Thus, Sheldon Dibble, an early missionary of the American Board of Commissioners for Foreign Missions serving in the Sandwich Islands (Hawaiian Islands),[59] knew with rock-solid confidence that the United States had been "planted by God, enriched by his providence, nourished by his Holy Spirit, and brought to the strength of manhood in this solemnly momentous time . . . to have committed to her in a special manner the work of the world's evangelism."[60] As divine providence seemed to guide the relations among nations and the development of the colonial empires, Western "Christian" powers grabbed for the lion's share of God's blessing and got it. The speech by Lieutenant-Colonel Herbert Edwardes before the delegates at the 1860 Conference on Missions in Liverpool in which he asserted that God had given Britain control of India to effect her Christianization and even helped her crush the recent "mutiny" met with repeated cheers and rounds of applause.[61]

Eighteen years later at another international missionary conference on British turf, the potentially volatile complications of providence bubbled to the surface again when August Wilhelm Schreiber announced that Christians and churches in his homeland had received a new impulse to mission due to the recent surge in Imperial German colonization: "The heathen have been brought nearer to their heart by becoming their fellow subjects, and the duty of making the way of salvation known to them is dawning more and more upon the minds of all who wish to do God's will and to be led by His guidance."[62] Not surprisingly, skeptics chuckled at such assertions, quipping, "Providence sides with the biggest battalions."[63]

Missionaries also looked for the role of God's handiwork in particular contexts and personal aspirations. They had little difficulty in telling how the "lever of Providence" had guided their activities and even prepared particular nations or tribal groups to receive the gospel.[64] After William Carey and his family reluctantly moved from the interior of Bengal to the Danish colony of Serampore in 1799 to join his labors with those of the newly arrived missionaries, Joshua Marshman and William Ward, he wrote, "We see that the divine Hand was in it, and are convinced that this is the very place where we ought and are best advantaged to be."[65] Over four decades later, Lutherans attributed to the work of God the circumstances that led to the selection of Guntur in India for the mission work of John Heyer.[66]

More dramatic episodes included the calling of John Stewart, an American of mixed European and African descent. While living in Virginia, he heard the voice of a man and then of a woman "from the sky" say to him, "Thou shalt go to the Northwest and declare my counsel plainly." Afterward, a "peculiar halo" became visible and filled the western horizon.[67] Traveling to the northwest region of Ohio, he began preaching to the Wyandot Indians with great success in 1816. As a result, Stewart's example helped inspire the establishment of the Methodist Missionary Society four years later, an agency whose personnel eventually circled the globe. Far away in the mountains of Burma, Jonathan and Deborah Wade got lost on their journey and came upon a Karen house. An elderly man sitting on the verandah gazed on them for a few moments in silence and then called out, "The teacher has arrived; the teacher has arrived!" Soon a crowd from the neighborhood gathered, for they had received a prophecy telling them that "the teacher is in the jungle, and will call on you. You must . . . listen to his precepts."[68] As a result, the gospel gained a warm reception, converts received baptism, and the missionaries established a permanent mission station. This account became one of the best-known illustrations of the providential preparation of a people group to receive the Christian faith.

Stories like these multiplied in the course of the nineteenth century. Arthur Pierson, editor of the influential *Missionary Review of the World*, found scores of similar happenings to include in his four books entitled *The Miracles of Missions: Modern Marvels in the History of Missionary Enterprise*s (1891-1902). Even outside the corridors of conventional evangelicalism, missionaries told of acts of special providence, notably in the journeys of Seventh-Day Adventists.[69] Yet, the notion that the signs and wonders of the apostles, which included the raising of the dead (Acts 5:12; 9:36-42), exorcism of demons, speaking in tongues, and physical healings (Mark 16:17-18), could occur in modern missions remained beyond the pale of likelihood. In India, Baptist missionary John Clough lamented the downright disadvantage under which missionaries labored: "Many apparently forget that the Apostles were possessed of power not given to the modern missionary."[70]

In spite of that, virtually all missionaries—Protestants, Catholics, and Orthodox alike—hoped that non-Christians would receive the "great miracle" of salvation through Christ, the spiritual grace that would release them from the darkness of heathenism into the light of Christianity.[71] Reflecting widely shared sentiments, the Synod of Pittsburgh convened in 1831 for "calling into action the slumbering energies of the Presbyterian Church in the great work of sending the gospel of salvation to the perishing heathen."[72] A Quaker missionary to Madagascar, Henry Clark, framed it this way: "Christ . . . established His Church as a Church of witnesses, as a Church of testimony; and the Church can only be in a prosperous state when she is extending the knowledge of her Saviour throughout the world."[73] Likewise, Methodist bishop James Thoburn advised delegates at the General Missionary Conference at Allahabad, India, that though "we appear before the people as witnesses for Christ . . . in the absence of visible miracles," missionaries should passionately share their own "hearts' experience . . . that this living Jesus has appeared to us, that we know him, love him, commune with him in our hearts, and through him find the peace that flows from forgiveness, and the purity which the Holy Spirit imparts."[74] Hopefully, their converts would become "real Christians," gathering in spiritually vibrant churches, in marked contrast to the nominal Christianity found in Europe and North America.

THE NAGGING COMPARISON

No self-respecting minister or missionary in the eighteenth and nineteenth centuries would have admitted their work was less than apostolic in character, though some did not hesitate to poke at the shortcomings of others. Edward Irving's three-and-a-half-hour sermon at the anniversary conference of the London Missionary Society (LMS) in 1824 both wearied and flabbergasted the delegates by contending that missionaries would be more effective if they pursued the pattern of the "apostolical school" in depending on God's provision for their financial needs instead of relying on their salaries (Matt 10:9-10).[75] On the other side of the Atlantic, the Congregationalist Rufus Anderson, secretary of the American Board, decried the policy of some church organizations that placed their missionaries under the authority of "missionary bishops," whom they considered to be "successors of the apostles." According to 2 Corinthians 12:12, such officers could not be apostles "since they lack the 'signs, and wonders, and mighty deeds,' which St. Paul . . . declares to be the needful 'signs of an apostle.'"[76] To Anderson, the "apostolic example" meant simply "to plant and multiply self-reliant, efficient churches, composed wholly of native converts, each church complete in itself, with pastors of the same race with the people."[77] Still, the issue could not be so briskly resolved; the spiritual enablement required to achieve apostolic success long challenged the missionary community. Hence, the discontinuity between first-century and nineteenth-century mission dynamics drew considerable attention in mission circles, prompting addresses at conferences, lectures in seminaries, articles, and books.

Many discussed the advantages of the early Christian missionaries. The first, and perhaps the most obvious, centered on the extraordinary power of working miracles that the apostles possessed. "If . . . we could convince [the Indians] that we come with weighty credentials, as shown by our power to work miracles," mused George Rouse, "if they saw the lame walk, or the blind see, or the dumb speak, or the dead made alive . . . their interest would be excited, their attention aroused, and they would listen to the preacher as to one whose message was indeed from another world."[78] But, he lamented, "We have no such power."[79] Robert Mather of the London Missionary Society bemoaned that missionaries had been left to acquire "all qualifications needful for their office . . . by the exercise of their own natural powers, quickened and directed by those spiritual influences only which are free to all, in all times, and in all countries."[80]

Second, early Christian evangelism benefited from factors already set in place to encourage acceptance of the gospel and expedite its expansion. God had providentially "prepared the soil . . . for the reception of the good seed" through the Jewish diaspora, according to William Miller, a Free Church of Scotland educator at Madras Christian College.[81] Paul's status as a rabbi gave him an obvious advantage by opening the doors of synagogues in the cities he visited, providing him with audiences that shared his worldview. Fortunately, he did not have to worry about the scandalous behavior of nominally Christian fellow countrymen, a deeply troubling problem created by Euro-Americans in the modern era that caused "grievous impediments" to the advancement of God's kingdom.[82] With their knowledge of God, many Jews readily understood and expressed interest in the preaching of the apostles, in marked contrast to the hostile reception to the gospel message among peoples steeped in the darkness of the non-Christian religions. "We preach to people who know nothing of the true God, who are enslaved to the most polluting and licentious idolatry, who have scarcely a religious idea in common with us," remarked Rouse.[83]

Other benefits included the Roman road system, protected by the *Pax Romana*, which offered the early evangelists relatively safe avenues of travel. Furthermore, the prevalence of the Greek language in the empire, coupled with the use of the Septuagint (Greek) translation of the Old Testament, freed them from the time-consuming delay of language study and the toil of Bible translation.[84] Robert Stewart told his Presbyterian colleagues at a conference in Sialkot, India (now in Pakistan), that their predecessors also worked under more favorable social conditions. In three lectures entitled "Apostolic and Indian Missions Compared," he observed that apart from the Jews, "no impassable barrier between tribes and classes, as to association, marriage, eating, and drinking" existed. This gave preachers a boost in the spread of the gospel since "profession of faith in Christ did not then necessarily break the ties of marriage, or family, or community. . . . Persecution there might be . . . but not persecution and separation of the same character as that we have in India."[85]

A third advantage centered on the superior fervor and preparation of the early disciples. American Board missionary Herman Barnum described them as being in "dead earnest" about their evangelistic work, which made their message irresistible. Yet, the effectiveness of the modern church, though blessed with unlimited resources and unrestricted access to most countries, regrettably remained "hampered by selfishness, by worldliness, [and] by indifference."[86] Robert Mather contended the preparation of the disciples had been enhanced by the bestowal of languages on the Day of Pentecost "to communicate the truth to heathen foreigners in their own idiomatic speech, and with all the forcibleness of those to whom the speech was native."[87] Even more importantly, the "apostles enjoyed a special degree and kind of illumination with regard to the questions involved in the founding of the church which has not been granted since their day," said Thailand missionary Chalmers Martin in lectures presented at Princeton Theological Seminary.[88]

Consequently, the disciples stood far in advance of the indigenous workers under the tutelage of modern missionaries. Not surprisingly, a gathering of missionaries in India in 1879 resolved: "This Conference, while convinced of the great importance of promoting by every judicious means the self-support and self-government of the Native Church, desires to place on record its conviction that the Native Church is in no part of it as yet in a position to dispense with European guidance and support." As if to warn any enterprising missionary of the risks involved in allowing their workers to take the reins of ecclesiastical leadership, the resolution added that "any premature step in this direction would be highly injurious to [the Native Church's] healthy development and ultimate stability."[89]

Despite the perceived advantages of the early Christians, nineteenth-century promoters of missions and missionaries recurrently expressed enthusiasm about the apostolic integrity and remarkable successes of their own endeavors. The advances and advantages of Western civilization, prompting the seemingly unquenchable optimism of the age in which they lived, made up for whatever shortcomings they had when compared with their predecessors.[90] Pierson addressed the incongruity by reinterpreting the nature of miracles with the proposal that the "signs of an earlier age may have given place to the signs of a later age." Though no less effective than those of the first century, miracles had now "passed from a lower to a higher sphere; from the world of nature to the world of spirit."[91] In other words, "miracles change their form and type because their mission changes; but God never ceases working."[92] Thus, Albert Wenger of the Basel Mission, a locksmith and mechanic by trade, could say, "We are not able to make the lame man walk as Peter and John did, but it may be in our power to teach him work, so that he need no more sit at the temple door and beg."[93] Evidence of God's supernatural involvement now appeared in a variety of ways: the miracles of "soul-healing and transformation," the providential opening of doors to the gospel message, and the means to uplift the welfare of the people they encountered.[94]

This allowed Pierson and others, such as the Methodist medical missionary Walter Lambuth, to applaud the rise of medical missions as a modern application of the "gift of healing" in the ministry of the church. "The special provision of miraculous power for the apostolic age has been succeeded by skilled achievement scarcely less wonderful," Lambuth told the volunteers at the third international convention of the Student Volunteer Movement for Foreign Missions in 1898. "The highest achievements of modern surgery, which are scarcely less miraculous than the works of healing of the apostolic age, may be justly claimed for Christ and the extension of His kingdom, for they are the products of Christianity—never being found among heathen nations."[95]

No one could deny that modern missions had prospered from improved means of transportation, better communications, and the protection afforded by colonial administrators.

Progress appeared in the establishment of churches, schools, orphanages, hospitals, and clinics, as well as in Bible translations and positive changes in the social order. Even the worldwide postal system was celebrated: "We have the mighty power of the press and a complete postal system, instead of Paul's sole resort to manuscript letters sent by personal friends," wrote the jubilant Frank Ellinwood, corresponding secretary of the Presbyterian Board of Foreign Missions (U.S.A.).[96] In fact, the material and social culture carried by the missionaries themselves provided a modern substitute for traditional miracles. "What need was there, after all, for spectacular displays of tongues, healings, or resurrections," observed missiologist Jonathan Bonk, "when a missionary's way of life was itself marvelous beyond belief—houses, clothing, labor-saving devices, modern medicine, vehicles, boats, money, and the presumed backing of powerful organizations and governments?" Such stunning accoutrements— surely signs of divine favor—seemed to authenticate the credibility of the gospel before some non-Christian audiences. "So Spirit-infused were the institutions and material culture of Western society as to make recourse to the paranormal redundant and unnecessary," though perhaps more in the minds of the missionaries than their audiences.[97]

With all these advantages in mind, Frederick Trestrail, secretary of the Baptist Missionary Society, triumphantly told the delegates at the Liverpool missionary conference in 1860: "Divest the Apostles of miraculous power, and the gift of inspiration . . . and you have the *modern missionary*, a true successor of the Apostles."[98] Joseph Angus, principal of Regent's Park College in London, even insisted that "Christians of the nineteenth century are more able to preach the Gospel to the whole world than the Christians of the first century were to preach it to the world of their day."[99] In fact, the accomplishments of apostolic times had simply been surpassed, as the Presbyterian Royal Wilder noted: "We are constrained to feel that the triumphs of the Gospel in the achievements of modern missions eclipse all that is recorded of Apostolic times."[100] While the disciples had begun with a "little company of 120 in the upper room," crowed statistician James Johnston, "we can boast of 120,000,000 professing Protestant Christians, covering Britain, her Colonies, America, and parts of the continent."[101] In the march to the Christian conquest, and breathing the same air of confidence, one hundred college and university students at Dwight Moody's Mount Hermon (Mass.) Conference in the summer of 1886 accepted the challenge of "the evangelization of the world in this generation."[102]

Finally, some found comfort in the supposed weakness and decline of the non-Christian religions before the forces of Christianity. In *The Living Christ and Dying Heathenism*, Johannes Warneck, a Rhenish missionary serving in Indonesia, rhapsodized that "thousands, nay millions of heathen in the most diverse stages of civilization have renounced idolatry and entered into fellowship with the living God."[103] In Calcutta, Rouse contended that the combined influence of "European morality, civilization, [and] education" had begun to cripple the power of Hinduism.[104] With the same overflowing hope, John Ross, a pioneer Scottish missionary in Manchuria, said that while in the past, "Buddhism was a light in Asia, it had truth in it, but the light has long ago become extinguished; it has no light in it now." What's more, "the candle which filled the candlestick has burnt down to the socket, and the candlestick is now waiting for Christianity."[105] But if the candles of "heathendom" had flickered at all, it was but momentary.

THE GREAT FAILURE

The modern Protestant missionary movement, traced back to the beginning of the eighteenth century, never lacked for critics, either from within or without. Complaints ranged from the sending of monies overseas to support missionaries instead of keeping them at home for needed church endeavors, to the slow pace of conversions, frustration over endless fundraising initiatives, nostalgic longing for the "simplicity" of apostolic missions, problems between mission executives and their respective policies with missionaries, potential interference with commerce, all the way to whether or not non-Christians even needed to be converted. The cacophony of voices grew louder decade after decade. Even those who supported missions could roundly condemn the methods employed as in the case of Irving who bewailed—as early as 1824—the "lame and partial success which hath attended modern missions in the way of conversion, compared with those of former times."[106] With a more foreboding message, Oxford scholar Max Müller publicly challenged the integrity of the "controversial missionary" who felt impelled to attack the faith of non-Christians. Better that Christians and members of another religion "live together in peace, abstaining from all direct attempts at conversion" to achieve the "greatest blessing to both."[107]

At the home base, the faithful often had a romanticized notion of success, perhaps assuming that vast multitudes would be converted after the initial preaching of the gospel. But in the trenches on the foreign fields, missionaries usually struggled with the slow pace of progress, caused variously by communication and cultural barriers, climate, financial needs, and resistance to their message, from both indigenous populations and European colonists. Bartholomäus Ziegenbalg suffered imprisonment during his work in the Danish colony of Tranquebar (Tharangambadi), India,[108] while the later Robert and Mary Moffat in southern Africa continually struggled to overcome the opposition and slander of unsympathetic colonists.[109]

Many faced the "arduous task" that confronted American Board missionaries Gordon Hall and Samuel Newell in Bombay (Mumbai): "There lay before them nothing but severe and continuous toil, relieved by scarcely a gleam of success. No surprising incidents, no romantic adventures, no [marvelous] achievements . . . [caught up] in one continuous struggle against a power that frowned sullen defiance . . . without any prospect of immediate reward."[110] In East India, Carey waited nearly seven years to see the first Bengali convert;[111] and at the conclusion of twenty-seven years in China, Robert Morrison saw no more than ten converts.[112] They were more fortunate than George Bowen of Bombay who reportedly evangelized for twenty-five years before gaining a single convert.[113] Still, hardships and challenges aside, successes came to the missionary movement. Unfortunately, they did not come fast enough to silence the critics and squelch the charges of failure. "It is hardly possible to glance over the columns of a newspaper, or to overhear a conversation in society, where the subject is discussed, without encountering some expression of impatience at the slow progress of modern missions; and not infrequently it will be stated that they are an acknowledged failure," lamented Anglican Canon J. B. Lightfoot in an address before the annual meeting of the Society for the Propagation of the Gospel in 1873.[114]

In the late 1880s, the flares of faultfinding again lit the skies over the mission lands, exposing the enterprise to even more intense scrutiny. The complaints stung the large majority of missionaries who strenuously worked to plant churches, train native workers, and establish hundreds of institutions for the betterment of humankind out of Christian compassion.[115] This came at an awkward time, particularly now with the fresh winds of premillennial expectation blowing in the sails of many mission efforts; its prediction of blatant wickedness in the end-times (2 Tim 3:1-5) and a decline in zeal among Christians added a strong sense of urgency to evangelism.[116] Premillennialists could hear the final chimes of the Clock of Time—the countdown to the Second Coming had begun: The gospel would be preached in the whole world and then Christ would "rapture" his church away to heaven; seven years of intense tribulation on the earth would precede the return of Christ in judgment on the wicked, to be followed by a literal thousand years of peace. With the course of human history scheduled to end abruptly (Matt 24:12-14), little time remained to do God's work.[117] Thus, after examining the "findings of devout students of prophecy and history, as to the time of the end," Arthur Pierson sounded the alarm to the readers of the *Missionary Review of the World* that "some great crisis lies between the years 1880 and 1920, or thereabouts."[118]

Nonetheless, charges of failure affected the entire missionary community, whether those with a premillennial persuasion or not. One reply to the "most persistent critics" came from the pen of a leading Congregational pastor in New Haven, Connecticut, with ties to the American Board, Theodore Munger, who pointed to the damaging opinions of tourists and statisticians.[119] His observation was not wide of the mark.[120] Tourists would find in every port a "handful of missionaries, and behind them the great, black mass of untouched heathenism." For them, it seemed incomprehensible that "this speck of whiteness [could ever] overcome this mass of blackness."[121] Into this category fell W. T. Caine, a member of the British Parliament who visited the least successful regions of Baptist endeavors in India and groused about the meager results of Baptist missions in general.[122] The tourist "finds the missionary is a common and uninteresting man, that often his converts are chiefly retainers, that lapses are frequent, and that his methods have apparently little relation to the ends most to be desired," wrote Munger. He then proceeds to eat the "missionary's bread, as a god from Olympus might sup with mortals . . . and goes away damning the cause with faint praise of the worthy man's zeal."[123] Presbyterian missionary B. C. Henry, serving in Canton (Guangzhou), China, concurred, complaining that the home churches depended too much for information on "the reports of those who have made journeys, more or less hasty, through the lands where . . . missions are established. These travelers come in great numbers every year, and, in many cases, barely glance at the cities and countries passed, and then consider themselves authorities on all subjects pertaining to them."[124]

Still, the insights of one "tourist," Edward Blyden, a West Indian-born African American who later served as an educator and diplomat for the Republic of Liberia, could not be so easily dismissed; he had firsthand knowledge of conditions in West Africa. His observations convinced him that the religion of Muhammad had accomplished more for the elevation of Africans than Christianity. "It is not too much to say that the popular literature of the Christian world since the discovery of America, or, at least for the last two hundred years, has been anti-Negro," he declared in a stinging critique of the Christian West. In contrast, "the Mohammedan Negro has felt nothing of the withering power of caste. There is nothing in his colour or race to debar him from the highest privileges, social or political, to which any other Muslim can attain." Finally, "the slave who becomes a Mohammedan is free."[125]

Statisticians and their findings quickly came to the forefront in these discussions. Civil servants, industrialists, merchants, scientists, and missionaries collected information from their respective fields of labor, parading the great interest in numerical data that had arisen in Europe early in the century. Missionaries and their agencies readily used statistics to serve their purposes, forming a marriage of interests illustrated by the selection of James Johnston, F.S.S., to serve as secretary of the Centenary Conference on the Protestant Missions of the World that met in London in 1888. Author of *A Century of Christian Progress* and other books, he sported his credentials as a Fellow of the Statistical Society—"F.S.S."—founded in 1834.

Ironically, the widespread utility and interpretation of statistics proved to be a double-edged sword. With one side of the blade, numbers could be used to cut through the apathy of home constituencies by pressing the need to financially and prayerfully support missionaries as they carried the gospel to the vast populations of non-Christians. William Carey himself bolstered the case for missions by citing statistics in his *Enquiry*, published in 1792.[126] Twenty-six years later, Hall and Newell told of 600 million people who had not yet heard about Jesus Christ in their appropriately, if cumbersomely, titled book *The Conversion of the World: Or the Claims of Six Hundred Millions and the Ability and Duty of the Churches Respecting Them*. Moreover, they projected that American and European Protestant churches had the capability of providing sixteen thousand new missionaries every seven years. In strategizing how the initial projected contingent of four thousand Americans could be funded, they calculated that if every Christian in the republic contributed four dollars, the accumulated sum after two years would be $2.4 million, enough to provide the new missionaries with a yearly income of $600 for seven years. Consistent giving would then sustain the needs of the next two contingents.[127]

Closely related to fundraising, statistics confirmed the achievements and importance of missions. Fiji served as a showcase of progress: "With only 9 white missionaries, we have 3,505 *native preachers*," reported John Calvert, "56 ordained, who take full part in the work of the ministry with the English missionary, 47 catechists, 983 head preachers, with 1,919 ordinary local or lay preachers . . . 1,268 chapels . . . [and] 27,097 full native church members." He then cheerfully added, "Fifty years previously there was not a Christian in all Fiji; then not an avowed heathen left!"[128] Looking at the larger scene, following the mission census of 1900, Presbyterian mission executive Robert Speer lauded the 7,319 mission stations, 14,364 organized churches, and the more than 1.5 million converts to Protestant Christianity in the mission lands.[129]

With the other edge of the blade, however, less sympathetic observers employed statistics to skewer the enterprise. In China, where no more than two hundred thousand Protestants could be found out of a population of well over a quarter of a billion people in 1890, one cynic quipped, "More die here every minute than are converted in a century."[130] Three years before, the Church Missionary Society had baptized only 167 adults.[131] But an especially painful attack came from a purported "friend" of missions, Isaac Taylor, Canon of York Cathedral and well-known philologist. His address at the Wolverhampton Church Congress in 1887, published in *Fortnightly Review* in England, along with later comment in *Eclectic Magazine* in America, startled both his audience and the larger church world.[132] In looking at population figures, Taylor discovered that "unfortunately the lower races multiply faster than those higher in the scale. Negroes, Chinese, Hindus, and Japanese are extremely prolific." Comparing the annual increase in Christian converts (60,000) with the annual population growth of the Non-Christian world (11 million), he indicated "it would take the mission societies

183 years to overtake the increase of the non-Christian population in a single year." With this came his disparaging remark that Christian efforts at evangelization resembled a "tortoise racing with a railway train; the longer the race continues the further the tortoise is left behind."[133]

As with Blyden, the missionary zeal and success of Islam intrigued Taylor. Unlike the shameful attempts of European missionaries to turn Asians and Africans into "middle-class English Philistines," he contended that "Islam succeeds better than Christianity largely because it leaves the people, [Asians] or Africans, undisturbed in all the outward circumstances of their lives."[134] Furthermore, it helped in ridding the "Dark Continent" of the evils of human sacrifice, cannibalism, devil worship, drunkenness, illiteracy, and bad hygiene. A religious belief halfway between Judaism and Christianity, Islam might become a steppingstone to the acceptance of a superior type of Christianity.[135] Obviously common sense could not support the notion that Muslims needed to be converted.

Such opinions fueled discussions about the wisdom of churches sending large sums of money overseas to support futile attempts at converting non-Christians. Newspapers from the *New York Times* to the *Daily Northwestern* in Oshkosh (Wisconsin) to the Atlanta *Constitution* covered the debate,[136] with the editorial in the latter concluding: "It must be admitted that Canon Taylor has said enough to dampen the ardor of the most enthusiastic believer in foreign missions."[137] Supporters of missions swiftly took issue with Taylor and exposed the weaknesses in his arguments.[138] Edwin Bliss, a representative of the American Bible Society in the Middle East and later editor of the *Encyclopedia of Missions* (1891), spoke of Taylor's "absolute ignorance of his topic" and emphasized that "the object of sending foreign missionaries to any community is not merely the conversion of a certain number of individual souls, but the development of a Christian community, founded upon solid Christian character."[139] Other missionaries pointed to the limited perception of Islam held by Taylor and Blyden, calling attention, among other things, to the evils of the Arab Muslim slave trade in Africa.[140]

Despite the labors of its defenders and the positive reports of a different stripe of tourists,[141] severe damage had been inflicted; and for many Christians in the West, the noble aspirations of the mission movement had failed, and for some it had served its purpose. Yet, for the time being, the movement thrived, with no less a personage than President William McKinley paying a rich tribute to missionaries at the 1900 Ecumenical Missionary Conference in New York City: "Wielding the sword of the Spirit, they have conquered ignorance and prejudice. They have been among the pioneers of civilization . . . illumined the darkness of idolatry and superstition with the light of intelligence and truth . . . [and] been messengers of righteousness and love." After ending his address with the triumphant hope that a ready supply of heralds would "carry on the task— the continuous proclamation of His gospel to the end of time!"—the audience stood and solemnly sang "My Country, 'Tis of Thee."[142]

But with their eyes fixed on the hourglass, premillennialists fretted over how the Great Commission could be completed in the brief time left before the "voice of the archangel and . . . the trumpet call of God" would be heard and Christ returned for his church (1 Thess 4:16).[143] Convinced that world conditions would worsen and hostility to the gospel increase, many urgently prayed for the promised "outpouring of the Holy Spirit" to renew the church with supernatural power to finish the task. For an increasing number of radical evangelicals looking at the blueprints of the end times, the restoration of apostolic Christianity with its signs and wonders would enable "Spirit-filled" Christians to bring in the final harvest of souls. In their estimation, the "impassible gulf"—the widely held assumption about the permanent severance from the visibly miraculous dimension of the faith—plainly had been the handiwork of unbelief among Christians; it never represented God's intent. Could it be that if the followers of Jesus had the requisite faith, they might do "even greater things than these?" (John 14:12).

From Topsham, Maine, another traveler went around the world in 1890-1891, the Free Baptist pastor Frank Sandford. As in Munger's caricature of a tourist, he returned home disillusioned with what he found and solemnly pronounced the "utter hopelessness of ever evangelizing this world by any method of Christian work then in existence." The seemingly pedestrian practices of Christian missions had failed; the Great Commission still awaited its objective; something new needed to be done. Like other radical evangelicals who believed the miraculous power of primitive Christianity could be restored, Sandford determined he would follow apostolic methods.[144] There were many like him on the outskirts of the Protestant mission establishment: rebels with an iconoclastic bent, short on patience, and long on determination.

2

The Great Outpouring

The Spirit and the gifts are ours,
Through Him who with us sideth.[1]
Martin Luther, *A Mighty Fortress Is Our God* (1529)

Of 13 August, Christian David wrote: "It is truly a miracle of God that
out of so many kinds and sects as Catholics, Lutheran, Reformed, Sepa-
ratist, Gichtelian and the like, we could have been melted together into
one."... 13 August, Zinzendorf concluded, "was a day of the outpouring
of the Holy Spirit upon the Congregation"; it was "its Pentecost."[2]
Eyewitness reflections of the "Moravian Pentecost,"
August 13, 1727

God, by Joel, promised to pour out his Spirit in the latter days; these are
the latter days. Has not the Spirit come?[3]
Query by a student at an American Board
mission school in South India, ca. 1860

Christ and self-control are almost synonyms. . . . Self-control, therefore,
being a result of the Spirit's unhindered working, such leadership in a
revival as will best secure that object is legitimate and necessary. . . . And
the Hindu who takes on Christian teaching does not all at once shed his
old beliefs, nor does he quickly acquire the equapoise of his missionary
teacher. He is still Hindu, untaught in self-control, subject still to his pas-
sions and emotions, swayed and rocked under excitement. No marvel that
there are these excesses in times of spiritual strain and excitement.[4]
J. R. Stillwell at the Conference of
the Canadian Baptist Missions, 1906

Why should not the Holy Spirit have liberty to work among Indian Chris-
tian people, as he has among Christians of other countries? And why
should everything that does not reach the high standard of English and
American civilization be taken as coming from the devil?[5]
Indian Christian leader Pandita Ramabai, 1907

"What room is there for discussion on such a topic? Are we not all agreed on it already? Do we not all feel its importance? Are we not all engaged already in prayer for this as *the* blessing which is recognized as the essential pre-requisite to success in our great work?" asked American Presbyterian missionary John Morrison in his keynote address before the General Missionary Conference at Allahabad, India, in 1872.[6] The consensus? The urgent need to pray for the "out-pouring of the Holy Spirit," an ancient biblical metaphor for rain before the harvest to increase the yield, used to describe renewal and growth.

Five years later at the Shanghai Missionary Conference, the Welsh Congre-gationalist Griffith John echoed Morrison when he called his hearers to seek for the "abiding presence of the Spirit, and through the Spirit, such a full baptism of power as will perfectly fit each one of us for the special work which God has given him to do."[7] Though interest in the eschatological outpouring of the Holy Spirit predated these conferences, that both speakers could assume widespread conviction about its necessity reflected the spiritual interconnectivity of the mis-sionary movement, theological developments in the home churches, and grow-ing anticipation of how the ministry of the Spirit related to mission.

If missionaries hoped first for the great miracle of salvation among non-Christians, they prayed for the second miracle of renewal or revival to empower them and their indigenous Christian constituencies to propel the church for-ward.[8] "The most conspicuous seal of God upon the mission work of the cen-tury is found in the *spiritual quickenings* which have, at some time, visited with the power of God *every field of labor* which has been occupied by the Church," wrote Arthur Pierson.[9] It is to the nature of these "quickenings" that we now turn: What did the missionaries at Allahabad and Shanghai expect to occur in an outpouring of the Spirit? What was the "the full baptism of power"? What surprises awaited them?

THE HOLY SPIRIT AND MISSION

The spotlight on the person and work of the Holy Spirit in mission reflected the widespread interest that had been mounting for some time. "More books, booklets, and tracts on the Holy Spirit have been published during the last eighty years than in all previous time since the invention of printing," remarked Cyrus Scofield in 1889, best remembered for his annotated *Scofield Reference Bible* and founding of the Central American Mission. Though hardly a cheerleader for this unprecedented interest, he grumbled that "along with this good is much evil."[10] Others, however, had fewer misgivings. Looking for a term to describe the new attention to the Spirit and the persons and institutions that promoted it, Pierson simply dubbed it the "Pentecostal Movement" when writing about it in 1899, tracing the origins and aims to what had occurred on the Day of Pentecost.[11]

To understand this theological and missiological development, it is necessary to glance at the teachings on the Spirit's outpouring in regard to mission from the Protestant Reformers to the revivalists of the nineteenth century. In their clarification of the nature of the gospel, the Reformers addressed the issue of justification by faith, in addition to human depravity, biblical authority, and the doctrine of the church. They explored the Spirit's activity in prevenient and saving grace, and the agency of the Spirit in the ongoing means of grace through Word and sacrament. "The Holy Spirit has called me through the Gospel," wrote Martin Luther in his *Small Catechism*, "enlightened me with his gifts, and sanctified and preserved me in true faith, just as he calls, gathers, enlightens, and sanctifies the whole Christian church on earth and preserves it in union with Jesus Christ in the one true faith."[12] In the same vein, John Calvin said the Spirit "so breathes divine life into us that we are no longer actuated by ourselves, but are ruled by his action and prompting."[13] With salvation secured for the elect through God's sovereign grace as revealed in the written word of God, the Bible, both Reformers denounced the religious enthusiasm of the radical Anabaptists wherein the inward voice of the Spirit took priority over the external word of Scripture, as well as their apocalyptic speculations about the end times.[14]

To the Reformers, the Day of Pentecost represented the inauguration of the church in the redemptive mission of the Savior. The coming of the Spirit—like the "blowing of a violent wind" upon the 120 disciples present, and the concomitant speaking in other languages—marked the fulfillment of Joel's prophecy, as stated by the apostle Peter (Acts 2:17-21; cf. Joel 2:28-32a). Calvin believed the Spirit's conferral of power and gifts would endure through the entire course of the "kingdom of Christ, from the beginning to the end," in other words, the whole era from Pentecost to the close of human history.[15] Moreover, at the Spirit's coming, wrote Luther in his lectures on the book of Joel, "All will be teachers and priests of God." "Therefore it was especially necessary for this kingdom, so clearly different from that earlier one [Israel]—to be established and confirmed by obvious signs and by an open revelation, . . . or outpouring of the Spirit."[16] After the preaching of the gospel and the initial expansion of the church, the signs lost their relevance.[17] Hence, neither Reformer envisioned a later and greater outpouring of the Spirit at the end of the church age to bring in a final harvest of souls.[18]

Though the Reformers and most of the theologians who followed in their wake maintained that the Great Commission had been completed in the apostolic age,[19] others strongly objected, notably the Dutch Reformed theologian Adrian Saravia,[20] Lutheran pioneer missionary Justinian von Welz,[21] certain Anabaptist writers,[22] and of course, Roman Catholics.[23] But with the commercial and territorial expansion of the Protestant states outside of Europe and especially the emergence of evangelical revivalism ("pietism") in the late seventeenth and eighteenth centuries, "missions struck their first deep roots," wrote the German missiologist Gustav Warneck. "The vision of the religious condition of the world beyond Europe . . . made the assumption of a . . . previously diffused knowledge of Christianity ever more untenable, and so corrected the old expositions of Scripture and the old interpretation of history."[24] With colonial exploration came firsthand knowledge of the vast populations of the world and the magnitude of non-Christian peoples who had yet to hear the gospel. This discovery not only accelerated the mission movement, but eventually undermined the European-dominated principle of Christendom.[25]

Spiritual awakenings in Europe and America brought new attention to the relationship of the Holy Spirit to the mission of God, especially the relevance of Joel's prophecy for the churches in the time before the return of Christ. Indeed, though not leaving room for the "extraordinary gifts," the Puritans and the Pietists went well beyond the Reformers in spotlighting the Spirit's role in mission, in this regard preparing the way for radical evangelicalism and the Pentecostal movement.[26] "It is more than certain that Joel's prophecy has yet to be fulfilled," penned the New England Puritan Cotton Mather in 1717 in a letter to the Danish-Halle missionaries Heinrich Plütschau and Bartholomäus Ziegenbalg, serving in Tranquebar, India. "It is also probable that that pouring out of the Holy Spirit by which the Christian Church was founded is to be viewed merely as a matter of some drops, whereas at the end of the age, when the fulfillment of this prophecy will come, there will be a much more abundant rain."[27]

For American clergy and laity, the "abundant rain" would purify the cultural and national aspirations of the country, inaugurate the rule of Christ on the earth, and usher in a millennium of peace; this future scenario also significantly entrusted Anglophone peoples with a special responsibility for the evangelization of the world.[28] Convinced that the time had arrived when *"all nations, through the whole habitable world, should embrace the true religion, and be brought into the church of God,"* Mather's contemporary, Jonathan Edwards, as well as the succeeding "New Divinity" theologians in New England, such as Samuel Hopkins, looked to the universality of Joel's prophecy and other related Old Testament predictions. "It is evident from the Scripture," contended Edwards, "that there is *yet remaining* a great advancement of the interest of religion and the kingdom of Christ in this world, by an abundant outpouring of the Spirit of God, far greater and more extensive than ever yet has been."[29]

The millennial age would not come about through a cataclysmic happening, but through natural means and the force of the Spirit's enablement shown in teaching, preaching, social reform, the sending of missionaries, religious and benevolent activities, and the spread of democratic institutions at home and abroad. In this way, Edwards bonded revivalism with an optimistic eschatology. The "disinterested benevolence" of Christians in unselfish acts of love and compassion for the glory of God and the building of his kingdom, as proposed by Hopkins,[30] then "acted like a motivational detonator," according to historian David Kling. "When wired to the dynamite of revival, it set off an explosion of vast human energy, at home and abroad."[31] Hence, over a lengthy period of time, the words of the prophet Isaiah would come to realization: "For the earth will be filled with the knowledge of the Lord as the waters cover the sea" (Isa 11:9b). Though shorn of miraculous expectancy in the traditional sense, Edwards and the New Divinity theologians shaped the theology of mission that dominated nineteenth-century American missions.

Without discounting the complexity of perspectives in the eighteenth century about the Spirit's role in the renewal of the church,[32] the evangelization of the world, and the coming millennium, clearly an increasing number of Christians—from Puritans to Pietists, Moravians, and Methodists—had begun to view the time in which they lived as an epoch in which the Holy Spirit would play the lead part in the final act of the drama of redemption, however long that might take.[33] In his *Enquiry*, the Baptist William Carey—strongly influenced by Edwards and the New Divinity[34]—looked forward to the coming age when the heathen would be converted and the kingdom of God established on earth.[35] He then appealed for "fervent and united prayer," declaring that "if a temple is raised for God in the heathen world, it will not be *by might, nor by power*, nor by the authority of the magistrate, or the eloquence of the orator; *but by my Spirit, saith the Lord of Hosts*" (Zech 4:6). Predating the calls to prayer at Allahabad, Shanghai, and elsewhere, Carey stood in the vanguard of nineteenth-century missionaries when he wrote, "We have the greatest reason to suppose, that the glorious outpouring of the Spirit, which we expect at last, will be bestowed."[36] An ancient hope indeed, and one now heralded with new urgency in a far larger arena of non-Christian peoples, but not without hesitations.

THE OUTPOURING OF THE SPIRIT

Judging by the comments of John Morrison and Griffith John, the Spirit's outpouring would bring about the fulfillment of the Great Commission and cure virtually all the ailments of the mission enterprise. Morrison believed it would raise up from among the missionaries, the churches, and the converts, a "mighty army of his servants to go forth with the everlasting Gospel, conquering and to conquer the nations of the earth."[37] John said the Spirit's power would enable missionaries to "do battle with the powers of darkness, to save men from sin, and conquer China for Christ,"[38] along with uniting them together for the common task of evangelism, advancing an indigenous clergy, and transforming the churches into being self-governing, self-supporting, and self-propagating (the "Three Selfs").[39] From another vantage, Anglican mission strategist John Whiting looked to the impact on the home base in his address before the Liverpool missionary conference: "Revival will speedily multiply the zeal, the self-denial, the money, the men, the missionary prayers and thanksgivings, which indicate the existence of a spirit of aggressive Christianity in a church, and in individual disciples of the Redeemer."[40] Revival could prod the churches to better support world evangelization since it had remained consistently low on their list of priorities. But all of this would require God's people to engage in united and intense prayer.

Jonathan Edwards recounted that modern missions had been born in the "united and extraordinary applications to the God of all grace," when Scottish ministers gathered in October 1744 to pray that "[God] would . . . manifest his compassion to the world of mankind, by an abundant effusion of his Holy Spirit on all the churches, and the whole habitable earth, to revive true religion in all parts of Christendom, and to deliver all nations from their great and manifold spiritual calamities and miseries, and bless them with the unspeakable benefits of the kingdom of our glorious Redeemer, and fill the whole earth with his glory."[41] From this came the monthly "Concert of Prayer," a day set aside each month for Christians to unite in prayer for the outpouring of the Spirit on churches both at home and abroad.

Others looked back to the "Moravian Pentecost" seventeen years earlier on August 13, 1727 in Herrnhut, Germany, as the birthday of modern missions. On that occasion the quarreling Moravians were galvanized by the Spirit into a united and vibrant community devoted to mission; within twenty-five years, more than one hundred missionaries would be sent out, representing the first great global expansion of Protestant missions. Just as the Concert of Prayer proved to be enduring and influential, the revival at Herrnhut inaugurated a prayer meeting—the Hourly Intercession with relays of men and women involved in intercessory prayer—that lasted for one hundred years.[42] These emphases on united prayer led to a myriad of significant initiatives, including the Haystack Prayer Meeting in 1806, which inspired the beginning of the American foreign missionary movement; the Prayer Meeting Revival (1857-1859), the news of which sparked revivals well beyond the United States, and has been viewed by many as the most significant revival of the century. It also prompted the Week of Prayer (1860); another Week of Prayer (1878), sponsored by the Lambeth Conference; World Day of Prayer (1887); in addition to special days of prayer in particular countries, prayer leagues, prayer unions, prayer circulars, prayer cycles, and many other such plans.[43] Across the aisle, calls to prayer could be heard in the Roman Catholic Church for the renewal of the church and its recently revived foreign missions.[44]

The passionate desire for the Spirit's empowerment readily surfaced in conferences and gained important coverage in mission publications, because human resources by themselves could never substitute for divine assistance in facing the daily challenges of life and work. Missionaries, such as the American Baptist Eliza Jones, experienced the crushing effect of cross-cultural adjustment and the frustration of not seeing quicker results. "All is *reality* now," she mused after her arrival in Burma. "The fleecy, golden tipped clouds of enthusiasm and romantic zeal, through which the missionary enterprise is often contemplated by those who sit around home's cheerful fireside, have vanished, and left the mighty work naked to the gaze of the trembling volunteer."[45] Without doubting her calling, she confessed, "I, as well every other missionary, am entirely dependent on the influences of the Holy Spirit, to keep my heart faithful to the end; to guide my steps aright; and to make any of my efforts successful."[46]

Encamped faraway on the plains of Mongolia, another pioneer, James Gilmour, recorded in his diary: "Oh that God would give me more of His Spirit, more of His felt Presence, more of the spirit and power of prayer, that I may bring down blessings on this poor people of Mongolia."[47] Years later, at the Centenary Conference in London, John Hewlett from Benares, India, expressed the longing of his contemporaries: "May the Christian Church be stirred up fervently to pray that the native workers so trained may receive a Pentecostal baptism of the Holy Ghost, in order to reproduce within them the apostolic character, to make them successful in bringing many of their countrymen from the power of Satan to the kingdom of God's dear Son."[48]

Whether among Calvinists or Wesleyans, Lutherans, Moravians, Baptists or Plymouth Brethren, the importance placed on prayer for the fullness of the Spirit denoted recognition of the essentially spiritual nature of their work and the indispensable need of divine involvement. In his discussion on methods and aims, Rufus Anderson, secretary of the American Board, summed up what the Spirit's outpouring upon Christians and their leaders would accomplish: "Vastly higher will be their aims; vastly broader their plans; and vastly greater their ability to feel, pray, and consecrate their all to him."[49]

REPORTS OF REVIVALS

At the close of the nineteenth century, Arthur Pierson looked back at twenty-five memorable "quickenings" that had noticeably advanced evangelization. Reserving the word "revival" for renewal among Christians who had lapsed into spiritual indifference, he preferred "quickenings" for those movements of non-Christians coming "out of a state of absolute spiritual death."[50] The list begins with events in Tahiti in 1815-1816 and then extends to other mission lands, Germany and France, Native Americans, the evangelistic campaigns of Dwight Moody in the British universities, and concludes with happenings in Uganda beginning in 1893. In most instances, he lists particular missionaries—all men, with one exception (Fidelia Fiske in Persia)—who were key figures in the events.

To Pierson, who mentions that many other quickenings could have been added to the list, these instances—all "marked by peculiar swift and sudden outpourings of spiritual power"—showed the diverse ways in which God works in the non-Christian world: "In some cases rewarding toil by rapid and sudden visitations of the Spirit, and in quite as many other by slower but equally sure growth and development."[51] Like other interpreters of revival movements, he found them usually the result of a particular "principle" or "law" through which "God's bestowment of blessing is exhibited and exemplified."[52] The careful observer could detect "laws," lessons, or values from the revivals to adhere to, ranging from the importance of the simple preaching of the gospel, to Bible translations and scripture reading, Christian schools, organization of native churches on the basis of the Three Selfs, the pivotal role of prayer in bringing about spiritual blessing, and the self-surrender of missionaries to the power of the Holy Spirit.[53]

Unlike Pierson, missionaries usually referred to spiritual awakenings under the more familiar rubrics of revival or outpouring of the Spirit.[54] Most would have agreed that revivals had born positive results and proved to be crucial turning points in the progress of the faith; and they likely would have concurred with the lessons he cited. In their estimation, such happenings carried the freight of apostolic power, crossing the long bridge from the early church to their own day.[55] At the same time, revivals had a fragile character and required discernment and oversight.

In recent years, historians and missiologists have offered valuable insights into the multifaceted dimensions of these events.[56] By their very nature, they encouraged expressions of experiential piety, centering on confession of sin and repentance that led to changed behaviors among those spiritually renewed, as well as the newly converted. Their impact could be local, regional, or even affect the religious aspirations of an entire country, as the following examples demonstrate as seen through the eyes of missionaries.

In Shensi, China, the Scottish Baptist Janet Duncan told of a revival at her school for girls, where "night after night, they prayed, sometimes till midnight, for themselves and each other, with the result that most if not every one of the 40 [or more] professed conversion."[57] At the Uduvil Female Boarding School in Ceylon (Sri Lanka), American Board missionary Harriet Winslow recalled that during an afternoon prayer meeting, the "Holy Spirit came down with power, such as probably none of us ever felt or witnessed before, and filled all the house where we were sitting," reminding her of what took place on the Day of Pentecost (Acts 2:2).[58] Vibrant prayer meetings soon occurred at all the mission schools with students confessing their sins. These "visitations of the Spirit" had been preceded "by a deep sense of deficiency in the missionaries, which led them to humble themselves before God; and were accompanied throughout with a spirit of prayer; a pleading—a wresting for souls."[59] Days of prayer and fasting followed. The results included conversions and "an unusual seriousness [about the Christian faith] at all our stations."[60]

At the annual Methodist conference in Liberia that opened on January 29, 1885, "the Lord wonderfully poured out His spirit, and there was a gracious revival," reported Amanda Berry Smith. "Sinners were converted, backsliders reclaimed, believers sanctified. Oh, what a tidal wave swept over us! So the Conference convened in the midst of the flood-tide of revival." William Taylor, who had been appointed the bishop for Africa in the preceding year and was likely the first truly "world evangelist," preached at all the services; three days later on Sunday, he ordained ten deacons and nine elders into the Methodist ministry. The emphasis on revival in the churches, culminating in the events at the gathering, was not lost on Smith: "It was a wonderful day. Such had not been seen in Monrovia before."[61]

Major revivals led to tens of thousands of converts in Fiji and the Sandwich Islands (Hawaiian Islands), significantly altering their religious terrains.[62] To these can be added other noteworthy stirrings, including ones in South India, Japan, Uganda, and the Caribbean. Following on the heels of revivals in America and Northern Ireland, "a very remarkable revival of religion" took place in Jamaica in 1860 that affected the entire island.[63] Lengthy prayer services that set aside fixed liturgical practices, seekers being "stricken" or prostrated on the ground presumably by the might of God, and public confessions of sin marked the awakening. Impressive results ensued: Many "rum-shops" and gambling houses closed, separated spouses reconciled, wayward children returned to their parents, ministers grew in spiritual zeal, sinners were converted, churches became crowded, and the demand for Bibles exceeded supplies. According to Richard Lovett, historian of the London Missionary Society (LMS), "a movement of this kind among a dense population of semi-civilized, excitable negroes was certain to produce extravagances and much that was repugnant to quiet, unemotional people," an allusion to unsympathetic missionaries and other Euramerican residents. But, continued Lovett, "the testimony of men of sober judgment is that at least 20,000 souls were savingly awakened at this period. The missionaries on the spot believed it to be a special outpouring of the Holy Spirit in response to prayer."[64]

For Duncan, Winslow, Smith, Taylor, and other missionaries, the renewed vitality of Christians under their direction brought the mission enterprise closer to its goals, particularly when they increased the native clergy. The disruption of the normal schedule of activities seemed only a small price to pay for the benefits. Revivals could suddenly bring about inward changes that the mechanical aspects of mission work had not been able to achieve, but only lay the foundation for their occurrence. From the missionary standpoint, the Spirit's work of transformation would hopefully keep the conventional relationship between missionary and understudy intact.

THE EVANGELISTIC BAPTISM

Winslow told of a "deep sense of deficiency" among the missionaries and herself before the revival began in Ceylon. She spoke for many in her own time and later when she wrote to her parents in 1830: "During nearly the whole of this year we have been, I think, more strongly convinced than ever, that without the Spirit of God all is vain; and we have been led more earnestly to seek his divine aid, with anxious desire to have every hindrance in ourselves removed."[65] Her confidence in the benefit of an outpouring of the Spirit grew from her own reading of Scripture and the backdrop of evangelical revivalism.

Early in the nineteenth century, missionaries like Winslow might speak of *an* outpouring in a local context or outpourings in various places, and still envision *the* outpouring as an eschatological event. But by 1877 when Griffith John called for Christians to receive the "full baptism of power" within the framework of the Spirit's outpouring, an important transition had arisen from several influences: Wesleyan holiness perfectionism, Oberlin perfectionism, and the Keswick conferences, all of which reflected the legacy of eighteenth-century revivals.[66] Interrelated historically and theologically, the proponents of each movement taught that believers should seek for and receive a second work of grace following conversion—the baptism with the "Holy Spirit and fire" (Matt 3:11), an act of faith, frequently with an experiential dimension that enhanced holiness of character, a life fully devoted to God, and ultimately reformation of society.

Wesleyan-holiness advocates championed the second work as "entire sanctification" for subduing the influence of "inbred sin" in the life of the believer. "What could be plainer than this that the baptism of the Holy Ghost was a purifying work and that in that baptism God bore witness [to the early disciples] to the sanctified state of their hearts," declared holiness leader Edward Wells. "With that mighty baptism [at Pentecost] came the sanctifying, purifying power and with it the witness of the Spirit to the work wrought."[67] Thus, when returning home to America from Inhambane, Mozambique, on furlough, the Free Methodist G. Harry Agnew began a quest for greater spiritual vitality in his life, having wondered why his spiritual experience compared so poorly with that of other Christians. "I saw I had not holiness of heart," he concluded. Attending a service conducted by Vivian Dake, founder of the Pentecost Bands of the World, a holiness mission agency, he recalled the "witness came from heaven that the work was accomplished, and I said: 'It is done.' I felt all through my being that at last 'the old man' was 'crucified with Christ.' . . . A mighty baptism of the Holy Ghost and fire went all through my being." He then spoke of receiving "perfect peace" and later of new effectiveness as a missionary.[68]

But to the "Oberlin perfectionists" Asa Mahan and Charles Finney, professors at Oberlin College in Ohio, Spirit baptism brought about submission to the will to God for the changing of the individual believer, evangelistic outreach, and the improvement of society.[69] Closely related in emphasis, speakers at the annual conferences in Keswick, England, said it ushered the seeker into the "Higher Christian Life," stressing the consecrated life, the fullness of the Holy Spirit, and accentuating its utility for Christian service, especially empowerment for evangelism and missions.[70] "All Christians by virtue of their relation to Christ," wrote Finney, "may ask and receive this enduement of power to win souls to him."[71] Echoing these sentiments, Dwight Moody contended that believers who sought for the "victorious life" in Christ, in which they would walk daily in the power of the Holy Spirit, could be "anointed and qualified to do the work that God has for us to do."[72]

In British East Africa, George Pilkington, a layman serving with the Church Missionary Society, had mastered the Luganda language and worked on the translation of the Bible. Despite such successes, the "dearth of spiritual results" among the people drove him to despair. He discovered from reading a book by the Tamil evangelist David Vadakunoo Devesagayam ("Tamil David"), a Church of England convert in India whose theology had been influenced by Keswick, that "my life was not right, that I had not the power of the Holy Ghost. I had consecrated myself hundreds of times, but I had not accepted God's gift. I saw now that God commanded me to be filled with the Spirit." This prompted him to go on a personal retreat to Kome Island on Lake Victoria that changed his life. "If it had not been that God enabled me, after three years in the mission field, to accept by faith the gift of the Holy Spirit, I should have given up the work," he confessed at a later student gathering in Liverpool. "Then I read, 'All things whatsoever ye pray and ask for, believe that ye have received them, and ye shall have them,' and, claiming this promise, I received the Holy Spirit," more specifically, the "Baptism of the Holy Ghost."[73] His spiritual transformation contributed to a widespread revival in Uganda in 1893-1894.[74]

Like other seekers who wanted "something more" in their relationship with God, Agnew and Pilkington testified to receiving the "fullness" of the Holy Spirit, though their understanding of the experience diverged in some respects. As it happened, the Keswick emphasis on Spirit baptism that Pilkington championed became the prevailing view in the larger missionary community as evidenced in the discussions on the Holy Spirit and calls for renewal at regional and international missionary conferences.[75] "We are living in the latter days of Pentecostal blessing," reported Hessie Newcombe of the Zenana Missionary Society to the Missionary Conference of the Anglican Communion in 1894.

Weaving the spiritual pilgrimage of convert Guang Sing of Kucheng, China, into the Keswick tapestry, Newcombe observed: "Consecration and heart cleansing were very definite experiences with her . . . she accepted by faith the filling of the Holy Spirit for service, and from that day she has become a burning and a shining light. She lives for the salvation of souls, she breathes the atmosphere of prayer, she feeds upon the Bible; wherever she goes souls are converted."[76] At Christian student conferences on the Indian subcontinent, Robert Wilder, a leader in the Student Volunteer Movement and Presbyterian missionary in India, also heralded the Keswick view when he challenged his audiences to seek for this "power from on high," and rhetorically asked: "Shall we let Him turn us upside down in order that He may through us turn the world upside down?"[77]

Interest in the baptism of power had not come too soon, insisted James Gall, a Free Presbyterian minister in Scotland. In *The Evangelistic Baptism: Indispensable to the Church for the Conversion of the World*, he blamed the Reformers and ultimately the Roman Catholic Church for the continuing ignorance in the churches of the "Baptism of the Holy Ghost." The book was published in 1888, the same year as the Centenary Conference and the appearance of Edward Blyden's *Christianity, Islam and the Negro Race* in the bookstores. Both publications added fuel to the fiery debate over the "failure of missions," with Gall complaining that "evangelical Christianity cannot be said to be making any great progress."[78]

While he took exception to certain aspects of Keswick teaching, the Higher Life orientation appears in his notion of spiritual power, which rested on the assumption that the "baptism of the Holy Ghost was the distinguishing feature of the New Testament dispensation."[79] Though less known than other books on Spirit baptism such as *The Tongue of Fire* (1858) by William Arthur and *The Baptism with the Holy Spirit* (1895) by R. A. Torrey, the title, *The Evangelistic Baptism*, encapsulates the Higher Life view of Spirit baptism, even as the content reveals the uncertainty in sectors of evangelicalism about the progress of missions.

INDIGENOUS CHRISTIANS AND THE SPIRIT

Not everyone celebrated the coming of revivals or encouraged believers to seek for Spirit baptism. Some missionaries disagreed strongly with the notion of a second work of grace after conversion; in their estimation, there could only be "one baptism" (Eph 4:5)—the baptism into the death and resurrection of Jesus Christ, bringing about conversion (Rom 6:3-4). Members of the missionary community also flinched when outbursts of experiential piety—seemingly unrestrained "excitement"—disrupted normal church life,[80] challenged established patterns of ecclesiastical authority, and, as the Reformers greatly feared, seemed to supplant the external word of Scripture with the inward voice of the Spirit. Even Pierson, who ordinarily encouraged revival, exhibited wariness about how far human feelings could be trusted as valid demonstrations of faith: "Nowhere in the Word of God is feeling [addressed], and for good reason: if God made feeling an evidence or test, we should depend on it, and our confidence would vacillate as often as our feelings do. . . . What we call feeling is often largely at the mercy of digestion and other physical conditions which do not affect *faith* or *choice*."[81] However, this tidy distinction between faith and feeling said more about Pierson's own background than what he knew about the nature of religious psychology in other cultures.

Missionaries strongly urged upon their converts the importance of self-discipline, and referred to them in mission periodicals as "people unaccustomed to exercise self-control."[82] Notwithstanding, their attempts to preserve some semblance of a wall separating an imported, rationally inclined faith from the emotion innate to the spirituality of Christians outside of North Atlantic countries often crumbled before their eyes because "when the Spirit moved" the Africans and Indians would start praying out loud, have visions, and dance, and the Japanese would weep and cry out to God. "[The Zulus] do not seem to be able to pray silently," observed an astonished missionary in South Africa; "at their homes they often go into the bush and pray aloud. So in these meetings, when they pray, they pray aloud—40 or 50, perhaps, at the same time. . . . It is fearful confusion and discord to one accustomed to quiet."[83]

When Heinrich Ritter, the learned German pastor who wrote a history of Protestant missions in Japan, reviewed the revival happenings there in the 1880s, he grimaced over the accounts of "passionate emotion." He noted that when revival came to the Doshisha school in Kyoto, the students spent hours, sometimes late into the night, in tears, prayer, and praise. "The missionaries had to quiet the excitement in order to avoid excesses."[84] While the positive results of the revival could not be denied, he attributed the attending problems to the English and American missionaries, whose denominations all have a "more or less . . . Methodistic trait," and then preened that "hardly would German missionaries of whatever tendency—a few recently developed sects excepted—have called forth a similar movement."[85]

Maintaining control could be a major challenge. At a Nyasaland (Malawi) conference sponsored by missionaries of the United Free Church of Scotland, revival erupted when the English Methodist evangelist Charles Inwood asked "those who were willing to receive the fullness of the Spirit to stand"; a time of confession of sin followed. "And then suddenly there came the sound as of a mighty rushing wind," reported Donald Fraser. "Two thousand five hundred were praying aloud, no man apparently conscious that any other was there. Some began to cry aloud in uncontrollable agony. And the physical excitement became so dangerous that we had to sternly close the service, and carefully dismiss the great congregation." Despite the attempts of the staid Scottish missionaries to preserve order by bringing the services quickly to a close to arrest the "dreadful emotion," the people returned to their villages "full to overflowing, in the company of God the Holy Ghost."[86]

American Board missionary William Wilcox, serving in KwaZulu-Natal, South Africa, reported the missionaries there had been spiritually renewed at the Keswick convention held in Durban in 1897. The dramatic revival that followed among the missionaries and the Zulu Christians led to confessions and repentance, increased attendance in church meetings, peace and unity within the congregations, increased giving, significant additions of converts, and the restoration of backsliders. "Never in my life have I seen such exhibitions of [God's] power," he observed; but neither did he "overlook the fact that while the Spirit of God has been with us the devil has been present too . . . in the counterfeiting of the experience of some who have received the Spirit."[87]

Though Ritter did not coin the term "excess" to describe unwanted emotional and physical manifestations in revival meetings, it already had become a code word for the downside of experiential piety among both opponents and proponents of revivals. An excess not only included what some considered unwarranted outbursts (for example, shaking, shouting, speaking in tongues, falling down), but departure from Western decorum in worship.[88] Even so, some missionaries looked beyond their own cultural prejudices to the potential of what revival could achieve: "[In times of revival,] the Eastern in them responds, and wherever we Westerners have kept our hands off this movement it has swept souls to the Savior's feet," wrote Amy Carmichael at the Dohnavur Mission in South India. "God save us lest we civilize the Holy Spirit out of our churches. There is more to fear from stagnation than excitement where the things of God are concerned."[89]

Missionaries sometimes hesitated to mention controversial phenomena in reports sent to home constituencies for fear of negative reactions, preferring instead to concentrate on the fruitfulness of revivals. But for indigenous Christians, outpourings of the Spirit brought powerful personal encounters with God and in varying degrees liberated them from the liturgical routines and cultural prohibitions of Western missionaries, leading in the short term to the formation of independent churches or to the gradual elevation of indigenous clergy in the mission churches.[90] In regard to the latter, when celebrating the 1905-1906 "Jubilee Revival" among the Methodists in India, which was marked by enthusiastic worship and unusual spiritual happenings including manifestations of the gift of prophecy, Bishop Frank Warne observed: "The fact that over three hundred of the choicest young men in our educational institutions have consecrated their lives to the work of the ministry, believing that they are called by the Holy Spirit, and that even a larger number of the young women have pledged themselves to Christian work, is one fruit of the revival that has given us great joy."[91]

The problems often centered more on cultural differences than satanic intrusions, as some eyewitnesses astutely noted, revealing the limited ways in which the Christian faith had been contextualized. Missionaries naturally worried that converts would be drawn back to their former religious practices. "How far these manifestations of feeling should be allowed or controlled is a question of some difficulty," wrote William Brown in his *History of the Propagation of Christianity among the Heathen since the Reformation*, published early in the nineteenth century. "If restraint is imposed upon them, it may interfere with the natural and healthy movements of the convicted and enquiring soul; while, on the other hand, a latitude may be allowed which may give rise to wild extravagance and disorder."[92]

A missionary editor in India, recalling that physical manifestations had long been associated with revivals, deftly analyzed the emotional make-up of his colleagues who struggled to accept such happenings, portraying them as "men of a calm and deliberate temperament and of fastidious taste . . . frequently inclined to criticize or doubt or even oppose." In contrast, "those of a warmer and more enthusiastic spirit rejoice in them and in the great results which they produce."[93] In Japan, the missionaries overcame the hurdle of fear and success-fully set boundaries on behavior to prevent the enthusiasm of the students from precipitating their fall backward into the quagmire of heathen behavior. But as the personnel of the Church Missionary Society (CMS), London Missionary Society, the missionary community in India, and others knew, the worst example of revival excesses had occurred in Tiruneveli (now part of Tamil Nadu State) in the early 1860s and particularly in Travancore (now part of Kerala State) in the mid-1870s. Events in both locations showed that the work of the Holy Spirit required considerable guidance and correction. As time would show, like Uzzah in the Old Testament (2 Sam 6:6), missionaries reached out their hands to "steady" the Ark of God.

PROPHETS AND SCHISM

Queen Victoria would have blinked had she received the intended telegram from one of her subjects in South India, containing the "Divine Proclamation":

It is hereby proclaimed with certainty that there remains an interval of only six years more (from May 1875) till the glorious coming of King Jesus of Nazareth on the fiery cloud. And he is going to appear suddenly in the seventh year to be seen by all,
"Repent ye all, for the kingdom of heaven is at hand."
The proclamation made by his servant is as revealed by the Holy Ghost of King Jesus.

Justus Joseph, Pastor C.M.S., Kannit[94]

One can only wonder what Joseph expected the queen to do, given her posi-tion as supreme governor of the Church of England. Though nationalist senti-ments and apocalyptic expectations about the end of British rule among the Christians of Travancore had predated the "Divine Proclamation," its forthright declaration that Christ would return on October 2, 1881 added a new sensation to the already volatile atmosphere.[95]

The telegram would have arrived at the peak of a celebrated and controver-sial revival in central Travancore in the southern tip of the Indian subcontinent. Reports indicated it had begun in July 1873 in the village of Mankuri when a woman in the local Anglican church had a dream in which "she thought a dark cloud rested on her neck and a voice said to her 'except you repent you will per-ish.'" Another woman, the wife of an evangelist, had a similar dream. Both of them began to speak and pray with others about their need for salvation. Conse-quently, people who heard their message repented of their sins and displayed the physical phenomena that have sometimes marked the course of revivals, such as "flinging the arms in the air, shaking in every limb, violent contortions, bitter weeping, falling on the ground, and rolling about."[96]

TIRUNEVELI

Despite the story of the two women and their visions, the origins of the revival in Travancore reveal a complex set of factors that created its uniqueness; among them the prior awakening in the nearby state of Tiruneveli (known earlier as "Tinnevelly") after news reached India of revivals in the United States, England, and Ulster. Furthermore, it came on the heels of the Sepoy Rebellion (the "Mutiny") of 1857 and 1858 in North India, a failed revolt against the colonial rule of the British East India Company. Perhaps just as significantly, the revival began in the same year that a CMS committee rejected the establishment in the area of a sub-diocese of the Anglican diocese of Madras (Chennai), but which noted that "the healthy development of the native church of [Tiruneveli] was . . . so far advanced as to bring into the question the remote, but yet most important contingency, of a native bishop for the native church."[97]

When the Tiruneveli revival commenced in 1860, the number of Christians associated with the CMS numbered approximately 30,000. The missionary community welcomed the revival because of the large increase of 2,600 converts in the older districts of the mission during the first year and the revival movement among Christians in "North Tinnevelly."[98] Missionaries perceived it as a direct result of the Week of Prayer, first inaugurated in India in 1860 under the leadership of John Morrison, and the printing and distribution of a prayer for the outpouring of the Holy Spirit.[99] Revival also arose in the churches and schools of the American Board in Madurai and elsewhere, "not the result of any special methods of labor or particular exertions by any missionaries," but rather, "it was of God."[100]

The most controversial aspects occurred in North Tinnevelly where the seeds can be traced in part to the ministries of Karl Rhenius, a Prussian missionary sent out in 1814 by the CMS; Anthony Groves, an independent Plymouth Brethren missionary from England who arrived in 1833; and John Christian Arulappan (sometimes "Aroolappen").[101] Rhenius emphasized the principles of self-support and self-propagation for the Indian churches, and he ordained Indian catechists, which led to his discharge from the CMS. With Groves came an egalitarian concept of ministry, disenchantment with religious establishments, as well as belief in the imminent return of Christ and the futurist premillennial interpretation of the Old Testament prophetical books and the book of Revelation, according to which they contained information about unfulfilled future events such as the literal one-thousand-year reign of Christ.[102] Arulappan, an independent Tamil minister and the most visible leader in the revival, received training as an Anglican catechist from Rhenius and was an understudy of Groves.

In chronicling the story of the revival, he recorded in his diary for August 8, 1860: "In the month of June some of our people praised the Lord by unknown tongues, with their interpretations. . . . My son and a daughter and three others went to visit their own relations, in three villages, who are under the Church Missionary Society, they also received the Holy Ghost. Some prophesy, some speak by unknown tongues with their interpretations."[103] Other happenings included intense conviction of sin among nominal Christians, conversions of unbelievers, prayer for the sick, concern for the poor, visions, and people falling down. The appearance of spiritual gifts long believed to have been reserved for the early church—claims to supernatural interventions well beyond what both Rhenius and Groves[104] would have expected—clearly indicated Arulappan's open-ended approach to the interpretation and contemporary application of at least two key Pauline passages: Ephesians 4:11 (the gifts of the risen Savior to the church include apostles, prophets, evangelists, pastors, and teachers) and 1 Corinthians 12:8-10 (the gifts of the Holy Spirit include wisdom, knowledge, faith, gifts of healing, miracles, prophesy, discernment, speaking in tongues, interpretation).[105]

From the outset, the revival took an indigenous course: "I am thankful to the Lord, who is pleased to pour His Spirit upon poor sinners without distinction of white or black, and rich or poor," wrote Arulappan.[106] Evangelists, notably women and men, following the pattern of New Testament apostles and evangelists as modeled by Arulappan, traveled extensively on "faith" (without salary or pledged support) and set their own itineraries.[107] Ashton Dibb, a CMS missionary and observer, reported that in Arulappan's church "there was a baptism of the Holy Spirit which filled the members of this church with a holy enthusiasm; and caused them to go everywhere preaching the gospel, in demonstration of the Spirit and of power."[108]

Not surprisingly, the customary control of "native" churches and their clergy by mission societies left little room for the dispensing of the Spirit's gifts apart from the decision-making processes of church hierarchies. On one occasion, a missionary complained when several believers announced they had seen visions in which appeared the names of twelve persons to be appointed as apostles and evangelists, and seven as prophets.[109] (Interestingly, the names of missionaries did not appear on the lists.) For this reason, as well as for the physical demonstrations in the meetings—illustrating the perceived problem that Indian Christians had in maintaining self-control—missionaries had reservations from the beginning and deplored the "bodily contortions and pretended miracles," as well the "needless animal excitement" that was exhibited.[110] Nonetheless, others stood in awe of their evangelizing initiatives and the subsequent flood of conversions. "It does certainly seem to have the merit of being the *first entirely indigenous effort of the native church at self-extension*," reported Dibb.[111]

Missionaries expressed relief that the unusual features occurred primarily in the earlier period of the revival and that it had largely ebbed by 1865. The controversial elements also confirmed the lack of fitness of the Anglican churches of Tiruneveli to be governed by indigenous leaders.[112] However, they did not anticipate the effect the itinerant activities of Arulappan and his followers would have in neighboring Travancore, especially on a converted Brahmin family.[113]

TRAVANCORE

One of the singular events of 1861 occurred with the conversion of an entire Tamil Brahmin family living in Travancore.[114] CMS missionary Joseph Peet baptized the father, Venkateswara Bhagavathar, who then took the Christian name Justus Cornelius; his wife and six sons also changed their names. The eldest received the name Justus Joseph and prepared for the Anglican ministry at the Cambridge Nicholson Institution (founded in 1859) in Kottayam.[115] Given their social status, the family immediately became celebrities. "The news of their baptism has rung throughout the length and breadth of Travancore," wrote one Indian Christian. "I think such an event . . . has no parallel in the history of the Travancore Mission."[116]

Their spiritual formation, however, took an unexpected turn when they were visited in 1872 by several disciples of Arulappan from Tiruneveli who "came . . . and labored amongst both Christians and heathens with much effect in stirring up the people to prayer and earnestness."[117] In addition to zeal, their luggage contained the eschatology and ecclesiology of the Plymouth Brethren as taught to Arulappan by Groves, along with the expectancy of charismatic gifts.[118]

The revival began in 1873 and led to awakenings in churches affiliated with the CMS and LMS, and particularly in the Reformed Syrian congregations (Malankara Mar Thoma Syrian Church), a prized achievement of Anglican efforts to bring renewal and reform to the historic Syrian Orthodox community of South India.[119] It had many beneficial effects, including the conversion of non-believers, a jump in the sale of Bibles, increased concern to preach the gospel, sorrow for sin, restitution of property taken illegally, and significantly the disregard of caste in church meetings.[120] Two of Cornelius's other sons, Matthai and Chakko, composed lyrics and sang them as they evangelized, and became known as the "Moody and Sankey" of Travancore.[121]

Despite the positive elements, "excesses," "extravagances," "heresies," "pretended miracles," and unwarranted displays of "human excitement" were not hard to find. Missionaries who had been eyewitnesses of the revival in Tiruneveli immediately noticed the similarities, but while the "outward and emotional had soon passed away," such was not the case in Travancore.[122] The list of misdeeds grew as the revival continued, as Reformed Syrian congregations began to embrace the novelties, and as the frustrations of the missionaries rose to a boil. Capping them all, the Indian Syrian Christian prophet Koodarapallil Thomman received in 1875 a "Divine Revelation . . . that in six years . . . the Lord Jesus would appear in the clouds of heaven to judge the world."[123] The prophet then informed Joseph of his divine commission from the Holy Spirit to be the herald of Christ's coming.[124] Thomman, Joseph, and their adherents were subsequently called the "Six Years' Party." (A similar prophetic movement, the "Eighty-one Years' Party," led by Samuel Nadan, also spread from Tiruneveli into Travancore and predicted that the Lord's return would be on September 30, 1881.[125])

Missionaries detected serious problems in the teaching of the new prophets that needed correction. For example, CMS missionary W. J. Richards accused

Joseph of denying the doctrine of justification by faith because he claimed that
in a vision, "the Lord appeared to him, pointing to his sacred wounds, and
declaring that these were caused by the sins of professing Christians, and charging his servant to announce that pardon could only be obtained on the condition
of public and precise confession of every sin, in the presence of the congregation."[126] Consequently, according to Richards, the evangelists commanded their
listeners: "Believe in the 'Six Years,' and confess your sins one by one and aloud,
and thou shalt be saved."[127] Intense sorrow and sobbing for sins committed,
especially that of breaking the Seventh Commandment ("You shall not commit
adultery"), followed in many congregations with penitents sensationally reciting names and dates. As they traveled from church to church, they repeated their
stories before wide-eyed audiences.[128] Further problems arose with the prohibition of eating meat, abolishment of the Lord's Supper, a new creed, and new
Ten Commandments, as well as an altered version of the Lord's Prayer.[129]

LMS missionary Samuel Mateer and others compared the Six Years' Party to
the "Irvingites," followers of Edward Irving in England and Scotland, because
of their belief that the extraordinary gifts of the Holy Spirit such as speaking in
tongues and prophesy, had been restored.[130] Richards dismissed the few expressions of tongues that he heard as "nothing more than a word or two from Sanskrit, English, and Greek."[131] Other unusual gifts included the appointment of
apostles, prophets, and prophetesses, as well as the "four-and-twenty elders and
four living creatures, [and] the 'beasts' of the Book of Revelation."[132] With an
abundance of prophets and prophetesses, local congregations and their pastors
set aside the normal liturgy to follow their directives. However, attempts to perform miracles like raising the dead and turning water into wine failed.[133] Worse
yet, said an Indian CMS pastor, "women were allowed to leap up and down, to
dance, to beat whom they liked, and to speak what they pleased even within the
holy precincts."[134]

Particularly galling for the missionaries was the considerable influence of
Joseph among the Reformed Syrians. "He exuded a charisma," wrote the Indian
missiologist Joseph Kurundamannil, and "many of the people he attracted were
the Syrian Christians, some of them well to do, with responsible positions. His
all around learning, proficiency in music and . . . dexterity in Malayam, Tamil
and Sanskrit endeared him even to the non-Christians."[135] Nevertheless, the
missionaries noticed the Syrians' lack of grounding in Scripture and doctrine,
which accounted for their defections to the Six Years' movement. Indeed, it was
all "a master-stroke of Satan to destroy a good work," lamented Archdeacon
Caley of Kottayam.[136] One missionary described the Syrian Christians—"these
poor Christians"—as "uninstructed in Church history and in the philosophy of
the human mind" to explain why they had been deceived so easily. The "influences of the Holy Spirit were, no doubt, desired and felt by many; but they
were, unhappily, unable to distinguish between the ordinary gifts of the Spirit
in enlightening, renewing, comforting and sanctifying souls, and his extraordinary gifts granted to the Apostles and other believers at a special time and for a
special purpose."[137]

While the entire Bible had been translated and published in Malayam (the language of Travancore) by 1841, the missionaries recognized the need for a biblical commentary in the language, which would discourage "private interpretations" of difficult passages in the Bible, a strategy that would permit a certain form of Western Protestant tradition to govern the interpretation of Scripture.[138] Among other things, this would presumably correct unwarranted eschatological speculations, expectancy of supernatural gifts, and the claim that "the promise of the Holy Ghost to lead the disciples into all truth would be sufficient to lead them into knowledge kept even from the Twelve."[139] Reflecting his theological training, Joseph insisted in response to one critic: "The holy scriptures contain everything that is needed for salvation. . . . I did not say that we should not read . . . commentaries. . . . [But] does one commentator agree with another [?] Which is our guide? The Bible or the commentaries? Fortunately we have the Bible. If we use it prayerfully the truth shall be revealed."[140]

While the broader revival undeniably had gained dividends for Protestant Christianity in the region, the fortunes of Joseph and the revivalists who followed him declined after 1875, the same year he announced the Divine Proclamation.[141] More unfulfilled claims and especially the failure of the prophecy for 1881 pushed them off the stage and into sectarian obscurity. Many of the Christians they influenced eventually returned to their former churches.

SIGNIFICANCE OF THE INDIAN REVIVALS

The machinery to deal with the aberrations struggled to label the errors. "Heresy" and "Irvingism" could not encapsulate what the new movements were all about. Even the charge of being a "Plymouthist," a disparaging reference to the Plymouth Brethren, proved to be inadequate since the revivalists went well beyond what teachers such as John Nelson Darby and Groves believed about the gifts of the Holy Spirit in the church.[142]

Unlike the social dynamics of other revival movements that arose primarily among the poor and ostracized, the Six Years' movement in Travancore also thrived in the upper reaches of the culture. Showing the depth of their new religious commitment, some amazingly disregarded caste, a social barrier and perennial problem among India's Christian communities.[143] Its charismatic leaders spoke with great authority and urgency as apostles and seers, fluent in the language, and as children of the culture. From their reading of the New Testament, the primitive church could be restored in its fullness, both spiritually and in terms of leadership, in stark contrast to the views of the missionaries who had come with their own preconceptions of what a renewed church should look like.

Throughout the century, missionaries and their supporters prayed for the outpouring of the Holy Spirit to empower Christians to evangelize the world and assumed that renewal would reaffirm the cultural and theological forms of Western Christianity. The distance between indigenous Christians, perceived as coming from degraded cultures founded on superstitious teachings that barred the way to rational thinking and self-control, and the more highly civilized Western Christians meant the latter could expect nothing less. Two decades after the revival in Travancore, "apostles" appeared in Madagascar and Indonesia. Missionaries on location expressed hesitations about their claims to supernatural powers (prayer for the sick, exorcism of demons), just as their colleagues had done in India. Predictably, they neither grasped their cultural relevance, nor could they persuade the new apostles that "they made too much of signs and wonders."[144] As historian Philip Jenkins noted, the development of Christianity in the majority world has shown that "the Bible as a whole offers ample ammunition for the use of outsiders, and for the dismay of the established and comfortable."[145]

Radical restoration movements in the mission lands emerged with expectations of the Spirit's outpouring that would have dismayed Jonathan Edwards and William Carey. In the course of time, they challenged Western missionaries to the limits of their tolerance, transformed the mind-set of some of them, and birthed remarkable movements and applications of the faith outside the walls of Christendom.[146]

3

Expectant Faith

*Many minds are still exercised about the miraculous gifts being the neces-
sary warrant to go and preach to the heathen or Mohammedan nations.
I cannot but feel the help they might be; but that they are not needed is
plain; for all who have been converted during the last 1500 years, at least,
have been converted without them.*[1]

Missionary to India Anthony Norris Groves, 1834

*It is written, "The prayer of faith shall save the sick." That does not mean
a prayer which says, "If it be Thy will," or which says, "Perhaps the Lord
will answer me"; but it is a prayer that knows the Lord's will beforehand.*[2]

Elizabeth Baxter at the International Conference on
Divine Healing and True Holiness, London, 1885

*During the past month [missionaries] have had a good deal of opposition
[in the marketplace] from two Mohammedan [teachers] who have taunted
them, saying: "If Jesus can heal, why do Christian people take medicine?
Why do they not cast out devils?"*[3]

Missionary to India Jennie Fuller, 1893

*We are a supernatural people, born again by a supernatural birth; we wage
a supernatural fight and are taught by a supernatural teacher, led by a
supernatural captain to assured victory.*[4]

J. Hudson Taylor at the Ecumenical Missionary Conference, 1900

*If there is to be any hope of our working like the Church of Pentecost, we
must have a new era in our missions. There must be a real restoration of
the pentecostal life and power in the Church at home.*[5]

South African Dutch Reformed pastor Andrew Murray, 1901

*If this [revival] is the work of the Holy Spirit, why do you not speak with
new tongues, heal the sick, cast out devils and work miracles?"*[6]

Query by Christians in India to missionary Minnie Abrams, ca. 1906

"*Unbelief* is the final and the most important reason for the retrogression of miracles," wrote the German theologian and missiologist Theodore Christlieb in his influential book *Modern Doubt and Christian Belief*, published in 1874. "But when this fact is once admitted, it follows that the miraculous is constantly possible."[7] Along with other nineteenth-century premillennialists, he knew that the era in which he lived teetered on the brink of prophetic fulfillment. "What is our position today as regards all these prophecies?" asked H. Grattan Guinness, director of the London-based Regions Beyond Missionary Union. "They are nearly all fulfilled. The millennial age lies in the near future."[8] With the virtually "zero hour" eschatology of premillennialism and the approaching end of the century, many like Christlieb and Guinness wondered aloud about how every tribe and nation would hear the gospel in the short time left.[9] Indeed, mission leaders such as Guinness, Arthur Pierson, A. J. Gordon, and A. B. Simpson saw the days in which they lived as a "crisis of missions": With God providentially opening doors for evangelism around the world, would Christians take the challenge?[10] How could they accomplish the Great Commission in such circumstances?

The answer would come with the anticipated supernatural infusion of divine power in the church—another Pentecostal outpouring of the Holy Spirit—to broadcast the gospel and bring about the great end-time harvest of souls. This naturally raised a question about the best methods to use in missions. Should a missionary employ the "modern" methods of missions with their burdensome institutional orientation and slow pace of conversions, or attempt to recapture the "old methods"—the purportedly more effective apostolic methods, the veritable "golden keys" that would speedily expedite the mission enterprise?[11] Many shared the frustration expressed by the American Baptist pastor and mission leader A. J. Gordon at the first international convention of the Student Volunteer Movement: "Why is it that . . . the Church of Jesus Christ exhibits such deplorable weakness [?] Have we forgotten that there is a Holy Ghost, that we must insist upon walking upon crutches when we might fly?"[12]

Those whom historians label as "radical evangelicals"—the disquieting children of the mainstream evangelicals—stood as a vibrant, if not controversial force in the mission movement and lived together in the same neighborhood. Among them, Wesleyan-holiness believers who held membership in the Methodist Episcopal Churches (North and South), Free Methodist Church, Wesleyan Methodist Church, Pilgrim Holiness Church, Salvation Army, and an array of Churches of God and independent congregations.[13] By the end of the century, many of them had shifted from the postmillennial outlook on eschatology to premillennialism.[14] Meanwhile, a disruptive new movement known as the Fire-Baptized Holiness Association (later Fire-Baptized Holiness Church) had arisen among the Wesleyan-holiness faithful in the Midwest and the South, bringing new conflict into the neighborhood. Led by evangelist Benjamin Irwin, it emphasized healing, premillennialism, and most importantly the "baptism of fire" for spiritual empowerment, an experience in the life of the believer to be sought subsequent to their receiving the "second blessing" of sanctification.[15] From his School of the Prophets in Beniah, Tennessee, he announced: "We are sending forth true and tried missionaries, fire-baptized and dynamited . . . to Cuba and to Africa; and we expect to send others to South America, the Philippines, and to other portions of the earth. . . . We expect to see this gospel of the kingdom spread like a forest fire over the face of the whole earth."[16] Prominent holiness leaders condemned the new movement as the "third blessing heresy." Even so, Irwin helped lay the theological foundation for the Pentecostal movement.[17]

Reformed evangelicals of a revivalist persuasion (Oberlin perfectionists and Keswick teachers) lived in the neighborhood as well, variously represented in Baptist, Congregational, and Presbyterian circles, as well as the Christian and Missionary Alliance and like-minded groups with an affinity to the Reformed tradition. To a great extent, the rank and file of Wesleyan-holiness and Reformed evangelicals would have been indistinguishable in many respects since they often blended their understanding of purity and power.[18] More importantly, they shared a supernatural perspective that embraced the absolute authority of the Bible, the need for holiness of character, and held a range of opinions from cautiously expectant to enthusiastic about the possibility of miracles, healing for the body, and the need to confront satanic forces at work in the world, with all affirming the soon coming of Christ. "Most basically," writes historian Grant Wacker, "the worldviews of the two proved to be virtually identical: ahistorical, supernaturalist, primitivist, apocalyptic, biblicist, and pious."[19] These specifications zoned them into the neighborhood. Two persons, at the far left end, even assumed the title and role of the last-days "Elijah, the Restorer" (Mal 4:5-6); others talked about the divine appointment of new apostles and prophets, and proposed unusual strategies for foreign missions.

We now turn to the radical evangelicals and how their confidence in certain New Testament passages prepared the way for Pentecostal missions. With their heightened supernaturalism, they pinned their hopes on Scriptures such as Matthew 10:9-10 ("Do not get any gold or silver or copper to take with you. . . ."); Mark 9:23 ("Everything is possible for one who believes"); Mark 16:17 ("These signs will accompany those that believe . . ."); Acts 1:8 ("You will receive power . . ."); and Acts 2:4 ("All of them were filled with the Holy Spirit . . .").

THE LAST DAYS' AGENDA

With their eyes on the closing curtain of human history, radical evangelicals squabbled over the order and nature of the climactic events scheduled on the end-time calendar. For example, over whether all the prophetic signs, necessary before the Lord could return, had been fulfilled. One church in England even sponsored the "Conference on Unfulfilled Prophecy" to help believers "avoid the errors and contradictions into which many who had occupied themselves with prophetic studies had fallen."[20] The culprits? Premillennialist neighbors who had strayed from or never arrived at the "correct" interpretation of certain prized passages of Scripture.

For other radical evangelicals, the nearness of Christ's return required that missionaries concentrate all their efforts on preaching the gospel to non-Christians and avoid establishing schools, clinics, and other institutions as the older mission societies did. "Let it be understood," thumped the independent missionary E. F. Baldwin, "that the simple preaching of the Gospel alone is the fulfilling of the [Great] commission."[21] Strategically this meant it would be completed when the last tribe had heard the gospel message, a position based on the words of Jesus in Matthew 24:14: "And this gospel of the kingdom will be preached in the whole world as a testimony to all nations, and then the end will come." Proclamation and geography took center stage, but doubts emerged about the number that actually might be converted. Cyrus Scofield, one of the best-known dispensational premillennialists, declared, "The Gospel has never anywhere converted all, but everywhere has called out some."[22] After the church age, evangelization would presumably continue during the millennial reign of Christ on earth. These speculations, however, proved less than convincing to others, among them the Southern Baptist missiologist William Owen Carver who wrote: "Such an idea is so unworthy of God and so utterly at variance with God's declared desire that all might come to repentance and salvation, and Christ's declaration that He has not come to condemn the world but to save it, that one wonders greatly that good men should ever have thought of witnessing in this light."[23] A missionary then could not afford to wait for large numbers of conversions, but had to move quickly ahead to proclaim the gospel to unreached peoples. When the last tribe had heard the message, Christ would return, an approach deplored by the Presbyterian Ashbel Green as attempting to fulfill the Great Commission "by *evangelizing*, not by *converting*, the world."[24]

An angry letter sent to the *Missionary Review of the World* in 1892 illustrated the increasing disagreements over eschatology and mission practice. The unnamed writer, possibly a postmillennialist who felt comfortable with the methods of the major agencies, charged that the editor, Pierson, and his close friend Gordon, held that "the sole duty of missionaries is to *preach*, without any reference to conversion or the establishment of churches . . . with education, the development of literature, etc."[25] Pierson rejoined that their brand of premillennialism did not exclude the importance of setting up churches, schools, printing presses, and clinics. Rather, "our Lord's purpose and plan are that we should not wait in any one field for the full results of our sowing to appear in a thoroughly converted community before we press on to regions beyond, where as yet the name of Christ has not been spoken." Once the simple gospel message had been preached, then "it may everywhere be followed up with every other agency that helps to transform a community."[26] Nonetheless, a year later, Gordon castigated the establishing of institutions of higher education for the hopeful prospect of converting non-Christian students. "We look in vain, in the history of the ancient and modern mission, for examples of the heathen being slowly prepared, to and through cultures, for the acceptance of Christianity," he charged, "while conversely there is no lack of examples that the systematic way through civilization to evangelization has been not only a circuitous but a wrong way."[27] Certainly, the urgency to evangelize expressed by Pierson and Gordon left little time for any other activity to be "followed up."

FAITH AND UNLIMITED POSSIBILITIES

At the core of radical evangelical thinking stood not only the Lord's soon return, but the concept of expectant faith, a rock-solid confidence that God would empower believers and answer their prayers, whether for money, provisions, physical healing, or sundry other needs. In regard to the financial operation of missions, while virtually all agency leaders and missionaries agreed on the importance of faith in raising funds, many radical evangelicals pressed the issue farther by advocating faith for God's direct provision as the intended norm. In his sermon before the anniversary conference of the London Missionary Society (LMS) at George Whitefield's Tottenham Court Road Chapel in 1824—an important occasion for raising the organization's budget—Edward Irving, one of England's foremost preachers, described "faith" and "prudence" as opposite poles within the human soul, "the one attracting to it all things spiritual and divine, the other all things sensual and earthly."[28] Spirit-filled believers would always choose faith over prudence (human expediency).

When he looked at the mission enterprise, Irving bemoaned, "Money, money, money, is the universal cry. Mammon hath gotten the victory."[29] Why should God's work depend on human ingenuity and financial solvency? Indeed, at the time, mission agencies such as the LMS resembled joint stock companies in their operation with boards of directors, fundraising programs, payrolls, and annual accounts. Unlike the "cloud of witnesses" in the book of Hebrews, "who through faith conquered kingdoms, administered justice, and gained what was promised; who shut the mouths of lions, quenched the fury of the flames, and escaped the edge of the sword; and who became powerful in battle and routed foreign armies" (Heb 11:33-34), mission leaders and missionaries appeared far less heroic, though well-meaning in their intentions. They simply had accommodated themselves to the absence of supernatural means, preferring "to work in a reasonable, prudent way."[30] Others expressed reservations about fundraising practices as well, with one later observer groaning about the "flogging of the congregations to get at their money, and the men, like Judas, going about holding the bag."[31]

In contrast, the life of faith could enlarge the capacity "to brave contempt, to defy power, to bear persecution, and endure the loss of all things." It could overthrow the idol of prudence and bring far greater success to the mission movement because of divine approval and blessing.[32] Therefore, missionaries should embrace the instructions of Jesus in Matthew 10 as the divinely certified method for mission and evangelism, especially verse 9: "Do not get any gold or silver or copper to take with you in your belts—no bag for the journey or extra shirt or sandals or a staff, for workers are worth their keep." They would go to the mission lands utterly dependent on God to provide for their needs, thereby rising above the confines of human structures and financial guarantees. (Accordingly, through their prayers other persons of prayer—perhaps even strangers—would be prompted by the Spirit to send them money.) In this way, they joined the "apostolical school" of the early disciples, filled with the Holy Spirit and unrestrained by worldly interests and occupations. "The nobleness of the missionary character, its independence of all natural means, and indifference to all human patronage, its carelessness of all earthy rewards, and contempt of the arithmetic of visible and temporal things," would then correct the "lame and partial success" of the established agencies, presumably including that of his host, the London Missionary Society. This constituted God's chosen plan for mission; only "the sensual man, and those spiritual men in whom the sensual man still struggles for the ascendancy" would question the strategy outlined in Matthew 10.[33] "Irving's trust in the power of the Lord alone in missionary work passed straight into otherworldly premillennial doctrine . . . in his reaction against any notion of mission—indeed of Christianity—conceived in terms of some this-worldly success," observes historian Sheridan Gilley.[34]

This frontal assault on the existing system of finances predictably triggered a storm of outrage. But Irving and his colleagues in the Albury Circle[35] remained undaunted in their conviction of total dependence on divine provision for the mission enterprise, an indication of their confidence in what they perceived to be the literal interpretation of the Bible, as well as the influence of romanticism on their thinking in regard to missions. Their vision would endure to capture the imagination of succeeding generations.[36]

Although the faith concept in missions preceded Irving's sermon, his noto-riety and the context for its presentation put his revolutionary proposal on the marquee. Reflecting on the sermon years later, the famous British preacher Charles Haddon Spurgeon chided, "The object . . . was to prove that we were all wrong—that we ought to send out our missionaries without purse or scrip [a small bag, satchel], giving them nothing!" Then dryly adding, "Edward never volunteered to go himself! If he had done so at the end of the sermon, we might have endorsed his philosophy."[37] It would fall to others to test the theory.

MODELS OF THE FAITH LIFE

More than anyone else, the preacher and philanthropist George Müller mod-eled the idealized faith life. Prussian by birth, he had a conversion experience in 1825 during a prayer meeting while enrolled at the University of Halle in Germany. Four years later he moved to England, initially as a missionary to the Jews. But increasingly uncomfortable with the constraints of the London Soci-ety for Promoting Christianity amongst the Jews, he left to become a pastor in Teignmouth, Devon, and later in Bristol. Influenced by Anthony Groves and the Plymouth Brethren in Dublin, he became an early member.

His idea of the "life of faith" had been inspired in part by the models of August Hermann Francke and the institutions he established at Halle; the German mis-sion leader Johannes Evangelista Gossner, founder of the Gossner Mission, who took Philippians 4:19 as his motto: "My God will meet all your needs according to the riches of his glory in Christ Jesus"; and Groves.[38] Thus, he decided to minister without a fixed salary, preferring freedom to any human pressures on his preach-ing and ministry that might be based on finances. Without telling their needs to parishioners or other persons, he and his wife, Mary, literally accepted the "vol-untary poverty" recommended by Jesus in Luke 12:33: "Sell your possessions and give to the poor. Provide purses for yourselves that will not wear out, a treasure in heaven that will never fail, where no thief comes near and no moth destroys. For where your treasure is, there your heart will be also."[39] For a time at Bethesda Chapel in Bristol, supporters placed their voluntary donations in offering boxes at the rear of the church; even this was discontinued within a few years. Gifts had to be given to them personally or in another way.

Müller's fame grew with his founding of an orphanage in Bristol in 1835, an effort that would eventually expand to five orphanages and the care of two thousand children.[40] At a time when confidence in the supernatural claims of Christianity had declined in the popular mind, he looked for miracles to verify Christian belief. "I set about the work for the glory of God . . . that there might be visible proof, by God supplying, *in answer to prayer only*, the necessities of the orphans, [to prove] that He is the *living* God," Müller wrote. "And [he is] most willing, even in *our* day, to answer prayer and that, therefore, He would be pleased to send supplies."[41] Indeed, for many people, his accounts of miraculous provision supplied the "visible proof."

The story of Müller became widely known through the successive editions of his autobiographical *Narrative of the Lord's Dealings with George Müller* (1837), extensive preaching tours in England and overseas, and the popular biography *George Müller of Bristol* (1899), written by Pierson. All of this placed him in a Christian hall of fame that would inspire millions to the present time.[42] His concept of prayer and faith became so popular that some applied it in ways that would have surprised and perhaps even disappointed him.

It would be his brother-in-law, Anthony Groves, who would model Irving's proposal as a missionary. The publication of his own *Christian Devotedness* (1825) in the same year that Irving's sermon *For Missionaries after the Apostolical School* (1825) went to press explained the rationale for engaging in mission work completely reliant on God's resources. "The true servant of God knows, better than any man, the real value of money, the value of time, the value of talent of whatever order," wrote Groves. "He is accordingly the most assiduous in his vocation, the most parsimonious of his time, the most anxious to improve his talents so far as they are subservient to the interests of Christ's Kingdom."[43]

Despite his idealism, Groves struggled to find success as a missionary. He spent four discouraging years in Baghdad and then worked in India for twenty years where his sectarian view of the church undermined his efforts to work with other missionaries. To be workable as a strategy, his definition of faith living had to be modified to allow for a predictable source of income. He chose to earn support through secular employment, following the example of the Apostle Paul in earning money to provide for his needs.[44] For a time in Madras (Chennai), Groves returned to his practice of dentistry. John Christian Arulappan, his best-known disciple in India, followed this pattern by pursuing an independent ministry, relying on God for support, and farming to keep food on the table and pay his taxes.[45] Neither teacher nor student seemed able to correct the fundamental contradiction involved between theory and practice, but then they didn't bank their faith on rational calculations.

Müller, the icon of faith living, and Groves, a trailblazer of the faith life in missions, inspired many others, most notably J. Hudson Taylor, founder of the China Inland Mission (CIM). Faith mission agencies such as the CIM became known for several distinctive approaches to their work. First, premillennial eschatology tied them to a single-minded strategy of gospel proclamation in evangelization, ideally free of the encumbrances of medical and educational institutions. The faith missions originally had intended to complement the work of the denominational mission boards, not to take their place. Second, they maintained an independent and undenominational posture. Third, they refused to announce their financial needs, preferring to ask God for his benevolent provisions to be given through his people.[46] Monies received were distributed regularly to missionaries, but with no guarantee of their adequacy. Both agency officials and missionaries had to place their trust in God's compassionate care. Still, many individuals without any organizational connections went to the mission lands to practice strictly the instructions of Matthew 10:9 and were sometimes derisively called "Matthew X missionaries."

In practice, denominational and faith missionaries had similar concerns about income. Both engaged in fundraising, but through different means. If denominational missionaries and their agencies directly asked for money, faith missionaries had to help God's people understand at some point where their money should be spent. This might be achieved through prayer, but letters, preaching tours, or mission periodicals proved indispensable for describing the activities, challenges, and triumphs of missionary activities. As a method, it fell just short of directly asking for money. In any event, when the funds arrived, God received all the credit. Hence, faith missionaries professed an overtly supernatural approach to the ways in which God would meet their expenses, yet pragmatically had to raise cash, a dilemma illustrated by one missionary who stated: "We believe that, if we do the work, which God has called us to, He will move the heart of His children to supply the money. If God sends out workers, he will also send supplies. There is no limit to the measure, in which God can work on Christian hearts to move His children to give for those, who have gone forth to seek the Kingdom of God." Then tweaking the faith principle in desperation, he announced: "We need 8000 Dollars to keep our accounts balanced, and we ask all to pray, that these things may be added to us. Has any Pastor forgotten to take the collection?"[47]

Faith missions never lacked for opponents who quickly cited the stresses and disadvantages it created for missionaries and the hardships suffered by their families. They also recognized their *de facto* approach to fundraising. When William Bainbridge, pastor of Central Baptist Church in Providence, Rhode Island, made a world tour of the missions, he visited a group of eight missionaries serving with the China Inland Mission in Wuchang. Seeking to compliment their organization's "beautiful, enterprising, and largely circulated paper," *China's Millions*, he remarked that "beyond all question, it was the most admirably adapted of all the publications of all the societies as *a soliciting agency*." The missionaries were taken aback by the remark—"I shall never forget the holy horror manifested upon [their] countenances."[48] Bainbridge would have agreed with Frank Ellinwood of the Presbyterian Board of Foreign Missions on the communal and public character of faith found in the New Testament: "If the world is to be evangelized, the burden of duty must rest upon all those who go and those who stay."[49]

Acknowledging that some dismissed the faith mission as the "Vagabond Mission" and the "Free Lance," the often-caustic Robert Needham Cust of the Church Missionary Society admitted, "It is one of those enterprises of which no thoughtful man can approve, but which no God-fearing man will oppose, lest haply he should be found fighting against God."[50]

SIGNS WILL FOLLOW

If "Matthew X missionaries" stirred debate, so did the further application of faith in regard to the "promises" found in Mark 16:17-18: the ability to drive out demons, speak in new tongues, pick up snakes without injury, drink poison without harm, and heal the sick. The increasing attention given to these verses by a sector of radical evangelicals reveals both the divergence of opinion in the neighborhood about the scope of miracles and directives of the Holy Spirit in missions, as well as the escalating supernaturalism among them.

Missionaries and their supporters at the home base held various perspectives about miracles, ranging from outright rejection to hesitation to unbridled anticipation. On the one hand, those with a progressive or liberal theological persuasion blurred the definitions of "natural" and "supernatural." Since the exorcism of demons, healings, and other such experiences mentioned in Mark 16 and elsewhere in the New Testament stretched their credulity, they identified divine workings with natural processes. "The supernatural may be seen everywhere," penned Robert Hume in *Dnyanodaya*, the Anglo-Marathi newspaper published by the Ahmednagar Mission in India. "The signs which reveal a Power supreme in nature and in history [direct] the universe toward an end. The supernatural is nothing else but the spiritual working through the medium of physical nature."[51] Another editorial said that if "competent physicians and specialists in nervous diseases" had examined the "cases of supposed 'demoniacal possession' which have taken place in India within the last few years," they would have recognized them as "forms of disease well-known and described in medical books."[52] The progress of medical science would inevitably lead to a better understanding of Jesus' ministry of healing and signal an advance over the traditional conceptions of New Testament miracles.

Radical evangelicals, on the other hand, who affirmed the time-honored view of the biblical miracles held diverging perspectives on the possibility of miracles. Some had little faith in their prolongation after the period of the early church, though they believed that God answered prayer and acted providentially in human affairs. Even Irving, who called for missionaries to follow the instructions of Matthew 10:9 and pray for miraculous provision for their needs, ignored the previous verse, where Jesus commanded the disciples to "heal the sick, raise the dead, cleanse those who have leprosy, drive out demons," a curious deficit in his argument noted by Samuel Taylor Coleridge, to whom Irving had dedicated the published sermon.[53]

While falling short of a full-scale cessationism, some discounted the relevance of miracles for evangelism and missions. Typical of this perspective, Mrs. H. Grattan [Fanny] Guinness, who with her husband could be labeled as radical evangelicals because of their advocacy of premillennialism and faith missions, editorialized in *The Regions Beyond*: "What use would supernatural powers, such as were committed to the twelve and to the seventy, be to the modern missionary among the heathen? Miracles cannot enlighten their dark minds, or soften their hard hearts." Speaking for the majority of missionaries, she added, "Our aim is to enlighten, not to astonish."[54]

Still, others compared the first-time proclamation of the gospel in non-Christian countries to the experience of the first-century church. Theodore Christlieb said that "in the last epoch of the consummation of the Church . . . she will again require for her final decisive struggle with the powers of darkness, the miraculous interference of her risen Lord, and hence the Scriptures lead us to expect miracles once more for this period."[55] As evidence, he cited stories, including one from the life of Hans Egede, who arrived in Greenland as a missionary in 1721. Before mastering the language of the natives, he gave a pictorial presentation of the miracles of Christ. "His hearers, who, like many in the time of Christ, had a perception only for bodily relief, [urged] him to prove the power of this Redeemer of the world upon their sick people." Egede took the challenge and with many "sighs and prayer" laid hands on the sick, after which several testified to being healed. "The Lord could not reveal Himself plainly enough to this mentally blunted and degraded race by merely spiritual means," Christlieb added, "and therefore bodily signs were needed."[56]

Another radical evangelical, A. J. Gordon, agreed: "The rigid logic which is supposed to fence out miracles from modern Christendom, does not seem to have been careful to include heathendom in its prohibition."[57] If miracles belonged to the original planting of Christianity, then modern missions should be marked by the same. Christlieb and Gordon did not stand alone in their conviction about the dynamics that could occur in front-line evangelism. Johannes Warneck, who would not have identified himself with radical evangelicals, saw no further need for miracles after the successful introduction of Christianity on a foreign field. A missionary to the Dutch East Indies (now Indonesia) with the Rhenish Mission, he recorded that from the 1860s the Christian community increased after the coming of sensational phenomena, including dreams, visions, signs in the heavens, and several instances where missionaries (for example, Ludwig Nommensen) unwittingly consumed poison in their food given by their enemies and remained unharmed.[58] But, he contended, such miracles "have nothing more than a preparatory significance," and "lead no further than to the door of the gospel." Convinced they had "fulfilled their purpose of pointing the stupefied heathen to the gift of the Gospel," he saw "the power of working signs and wonders" as simply temporary, just as they had been in early Christianity. Nonetheless, "we must not banish such experiences to the realm of fable. They are too well attested; and they are met with everywhere among animistic peoples with considerable regularity."[59] Warneck thus allowed for a limited continuation of miracles and extraordinary spiritual manifestations.

No one publicized the occurrences of miracles in the mission enterprise more than Pierson, who between 1891 and 1902 wrote four books entitled *The Miracles of Missions: Modern Marvels in the History of Missionary Enterprise*.[60] He discovered a broad range of divine interventions in human affairs: exceptional circumstances leading to conversions; amazing answers to prayer as in the case of financial needs; deliverances from danger; opened doors for ministry; and the "miracles" of medical missions, advancing technology, and transportation. Pierson elsewhere related the healing of a Chinese epileptic after prayer by C. T. Studd, Stanley Smith, and other members of the famous "Cambridge Seven,"[61] and told of his own healing from an ear problem.[62]

The story of W. J. Davis, the Methodist "missionary Elijah," just as easily could have been included. In a Bantu-speaking part of South Africa during the late 1840s, a severe drought caused the soil to dry up and cattle began to die. Fears of famine led the tribal chief to employ the services of professional rain-makers. When unsuccessful, they blamed their failure on the presence of missionaries. Realizing the danger to his family, Davis knew he had to act quickly. Riding on his horse into the chief's village and interrupting ceremonies in progress, he announced that the rainmakers and the sins of the people were the real culprits. Emulating the prophet Elijah in challenging the prophets of Baal to a test on Mt. Carmel (1 Kgs 18:16–46), he proposed to his startled hearers, "Come to chapel next Sabbath, and we will pray to God, who made the heavens and the earth, to give us rain, and we will see who is the true God, and who are His true servants, and your best friends." After the chief accepted his offer, Davis and his fellow-believers spent the next day in fasting and prayer. On Sunday and without a cloud in the sky—"even of the size of a man's hand," the chief and his retinue entered the church. Sometime after the service began, as Davis and the congregation knelt in prayer, "they heard the big rain drops begin to patter on the zinc root of the chapel. . . . The whole region was so saturated with water that the river nearby became so swollen that the chief and his mother could not cross it that night, and hence had to remain at the mission station till the next day."[63]

Ironically, William Taylor, the pioneer Methodist bishop in Africa who also qualified as a radical evangelical or a "radical holiness" believer because of his view of sanctification and insistence that missionaries operate on faith and be self-supporting,[64] doubted the miracle's enduring value in his *Christian Adventures in South Africa* (1880). While it "seemed to produce a great impression on the minds of the chief, his mother, and the heathen party in favor of God and His missionaries, . . . signs, wonders, and even miracles, will not change the hearts of sinners." Taylor's opinion stemmed from his admitted disappointment that the chief's family did not convert.[65] Although conceding that the Africans now considered the missionary to be a rainmaker, he failed to understand the implications of Davis's transformed status as a shaman or how the tribe's perspective on Christianity might have changed.

Turning the cessationist hourglass upside down, the most ardent radical evangelicals anticipated that the full restoration of miracles and spiritual gifts could be normative in the life of the churches and in missions in the last days. With what appeared to some as reckless abandon of traditional perspectives and limitations on the work of the Spirit, they became the rowdiest kids in the neighborhood and received the sternest reprimands. In examining Mark 16:17-18, their attention focused on the supernatural signs of healing, exorcism (and satanic influence in the world), and speaking in tongues (discussed in the next chapter).

Predictably, they defended the Markan authorship of the disputed verses (16:9-20), called into question by the recently published English Revised Version of the New Testament (1881) and the American Standard Version (1901).[66]

PRAYING FOR THE SICK

"I find an insidious evil creeping in, which is called 'faith healing,'" grumbled Robert Needham Cust before the Centenary Conference in London in 1888. "Should it not be opposed entirely by all reasonable men? Is it not something, in heathen countries, very like the medicine man and witchcraft?" It seemed to be entering the mission lands largely through American missionaries. "I think it is one of the most dangerous and insidious errors that can be," he sniffed. "It stultifies the medical man if a person can pray over the sick, and trust that by a miracle he can be healed."[67] Nothing could have appeared less scientific in the modern era than faith healing, perhaps with the exception of exorcising demons.

"Faith healing," often pegged the "faith cure," became popular in the earlier part of the nineteenth century in Switzerland, Germany, England, and America. Virtually all the proponents appealed to James 5:14-15a: "Is anyone among you sick? Let them call the elders of the church to prayer over them and anoint them with oil in the name of the Lord. And the prayer offered in faith will make them well; the Lord will raise them up." Many also claimed that physical healing was a privilege available to every believer through the atoning work of Christ as interpreted from Isaiah 53:5 (partially quoted again in Matt 8:17): "But he was pierced for our transgressions, he was crushed for our iniquities; the punishment that brought us peace was on him, and by his wounds we are healed." A. B. Simpson, president of the Christian and Missionary Alliance, said that Isaiah's announcement of the "suffering servant," the Messiah, constitutes "the great Evangelical vision, the gospel in the Old Testament, the very mirror of the coming Redeemer." Furthermore, it offered the "strongest possible statement of complete redemption from pain and sickness by His life and death, and the very words which the Evangelist afterwards quotes, under the inspired guidance of the Holy Ghost (Matt 8:17) as the explanation of His universal works of healing."[68] For some, healing in the atonement—a guarantee for those who had entered the sanctified or Higher Life—meant the promise of immediate physical healing; others, however, considered that one's faith could be increased through a gradual healing.[69]

Positions varied from the more cautious Gordon, who strongly believed in healing but admitted that "God acts sovereignly and according to his own determinate counsel," to John Alexander Dowie, who had no misgivings about God's declared intention.[70] "The gifts of healings are one of the gifts of God which are the constant possession of the Church in the Holy Ghost," he charged in the first issue of his *Leaves of Healing* magazine. "And oh, what miserable substitutes have been presented for divine healing by the allopath, the hydropath, the psychopath, the homeopath and all the other paths that lead to the grave."[71] Faith healing usually carried an anti-medical stance.

Transatlantic connections played a crucial role in the worldwide dissemination of the practice of healing by faith. Important advocates included Dorothea Trudel and Samuel Zeller (Switzerland), Johann Christoph Blumhardt (Germany), Otto Stockmayer (Germany and Switzerland), Elizabeth Baxter and Charlotte Murray (England), John Alexander Dowie (Australia and later the United States),[72] and Simpson, Gordon, Ethan Otis Allen, Edward and Sarah Mix, Charles Cullis, William Boardman, Carrie Judd Montgomery, R. Kelso Carter, and Maria Woodworth-Etter (United States), among many others.[73] The movement quickly crossed denominational and confessional lines since people of many backgrounds badly needed relief from major illnesses, which medical science at the time could not adequately treat.

At the Faith Convention in 1882 at Old Orchard Beach in Maine, sponsored by the Boston physician Charles Cullis, Episcopalians, Methodists, Baptists, Presbyterians, and Quakers sought for "the fullness of the blessings of the Gospel of Christ." According to one report, "The doctrine taught at this convention was, that it is possible for the believer to enter upon a life of complete faith in a keeping Saviour, giving up the life and will wholly to Him and trusting to give the victory over every temptation." Then, denoting Higher Life teaching, "the baptism of power for the conversion of souls was eagerly sought by the Christian workers present, and great results in this line may be looked for during the coming year from those who obtained the blessing."[74] Finally, demonstrating the close harmony of holiness and healing, the convention affirmed that "Christians may claim from God the fulfillment of the promise in the Epistle of James, to the effect that when certain conditions are fulfilled the prayer of faith shall save the sick."[75] So many people asked for prayer that a special service had to be added to the schedule. Driven by confidence in the "prayer of faith," the faithful flocked to the conventions at Old Orchard and to established centers for prayer—called "faith homes"—across the United States (for example, Berachah Home in New York City; Divine Healing Homes in Chicago) that were modeled on European institutions (Elim Institution in Männedorf, Switzerland; Bethshan Healing Home in London).[76]

The movement gained widespread attention at the International Conference on Divine Healing and True Holiness held in London in 1885. In "The Call" to the Conference, the well-known holiness writer William Boardman rejoiced that "our hearts are full of the fact that God is about to bring forth the fulfillment of the prophecy of Joel, in these last days, on a grander scale than the world has ever seen," showing the bond of faith proponents to premillennial eschatology.[77] More than six hundred leaders registered at the conclave, with seventy overseas delegates in attendance. The speakers included those who addressed topics on healing, in addition to many who shared their testimonies of recovery from a variety of ailments.

In countries where the rudiments of health care barely existed, missionaries celebrated the benefits of medical missions, usually considering the work of doctors, nurses, clinics, and hospitals as a continuation of Jesus' ministry of healing, albeit just short of the miraculous. At the Liverpool Conference on Missions in 1860, William Lockhart, the first British medical missionary and stationed in Shanghai at the time, reported that medical missions began with the "various Missionary Societies in England and America, in imitation of the example of Him 'who went about doing good,' and 'healing all manner of sickness and disease among the people.'"[78] Another medical missionary observed: "Although physicians now are not endued with supernatural power, they possess means of relieving suffering of which heathen nations are destitute, and it is as much a Christian duty to relieve bodily suffering as to minister to spiritual necessities."[79] Not surprisingly, medical missions grew in popularity as their help to native peoples became evident in country after country.[80]

Nonetheless, missionaries such as M. C. Mason, serving in Assam (northeast India), still wondered "if it is not because of our lack of faith and consecration, that God cannot do many mighty works among us." In reference to the promised gifts to the church mentioned by Paul in 1 Corinthians 12:28 (for example, miracles, gifts of healing), "some of our respected brethren"—American Baptists at the home base—"are calling upon us to consider if these gifts are not among our modern mission methods."[81] Mason brought the subject to the attention of his co-workers gathered for the Jubilee Conference in Nowgong in 1886, a clear indication of the growing influence of faith healing in the broader mission movement. In response, they debated the relationship of prayer for the sick to the benefits of medical missions. Missionary Ella Phillips testified to her own healing in answer to prayer, while Mason and T. J. Jones reported that God had already demonstrated his miracle-working power among the Garos and Khasi tribes.[82] Far away in Mexico City, Mrs. S. G. Weems told of similar happenings because "God does not disregard the cry of the humblest of His creatures."[83]

For many radical evangelicals, the promotion of medical missions with its heavily institutional orientation, as well as the founding of schools and other charitable institutions, though laudable, required too much time and side-tracked progress toward the ultimate goal.[84] "We have degenerated from apostolic methods," warned Simpson in 1890. "While we are waiting to give men a finished education, millions of heathen are dying."[85] Then, while not discounting the importance of having "scholars and men to translate the Scriptures, and to build up the churches," the "crying need" called for missionaries to go to the regions beyond. Brushing off the criticisms aimed at premillennialists including him, Simpson wanted evangelists "who would sweep around the globe proclaiming, as heralds, the simple story of the cross."[86] Indeed, at the International Conference he connected healing with missions: "And this gospel of healing is inseparably linked with the evangelizing of the world. God has given it to us as a testimony to the nations, and God's work wants thousands and thousands of men and women to go to Africa, and China, and India, and live Him there, and show these simple-hearted people, that His Word is as true as ever before."[87]

More than other advocates of healing, he and his fellow leaders in the Alliance, for sometime the most important of the American faith missions, linked prayer for the miraculous with its mission strategy. "The need . . . for these supernatural evidences among the heathen is as great as ever. The Brahmins of India can reason as wide as we. The intellects of China are as profound as ours; the literature of heathen nations is full of subtlety and sophistry that can match all our arguments," admitted Simpson. Because of the lack of supernatural power, missionaries could only "produce conviction upon the minds of the heathen very largely by purely rational and moral considerations and influences." Demonstrations of divine power would quicken the pace of conversions, since "in the touch of God there is something that man cannot answer nor explain away." Non-Christians would be moved to accept the gospel if they saw diseases cured and other unusual answers to prayer take place, just as they had in New Testament times.[88] Though disease took a heavy toll on Alliance missionaries,[89] Simpson and other like-minded evangelicals marched ahead of their Western missionary colleagues in perceiving the potential role of paranormal phenomena in bringing people to the healing Christ portrayed in the Gospels.[90]

CONFRONTING THE DEVIL

"It may not be realized by those who live in Christian lands that we meet with people in our work who are fully possessed with the devil, similar to those we read of in the time of our Saviour," wrote Grace Stephens, superintendent of the Methodist Episcopal Zenana Mission in Madras, but "we know for a certainty."[91] A minority of missionaries agreed with Stephens and recognized the importance of exorcisms, while most put demon possession in the same box of heathen superstition with witchcraft, amulets, ancestral worship, and idolatry, hoping that the light of science and education eventually would eliminate such misconceptions.[92] Missionary conferences discussed the more pressing matters of how to preach to non-Christians, train native workers, develop self-supporting churches, and ways to improve education, women's work, and medical missions. What to do about demons never made it to the agendas.

Still, interest in how Christians should address the dark side of spirituality steadily grew. In Germany, the Lutheran pastor at the village of Möttlingen in the Black Forest of Württemberg, Johann Christoph Blumhardt, exorcised demons from Gottliebin Dittus and her sister Katharina in 1843. Gottliebin's cry, "Jesus is victor! Jesus is victor!" convinced him of the triumph of Christ over all manifestations of evil.[93] News of this encounter gained international attention, paralleling the interest of others such as Theodore Christlieb and the Anglican missionary bishop Robert Cardwell in understanding "demonolatry, devil dancing, and demoniacal possession."[94]

In China, Presbyterian missionary John Nevius pursued a study of demon possession despite the fact that most missionaries who entered the country doubted such a possibility, with one new recruit condescendingly surprised that "missionaries should spend their time in such an enquiry or allow native Christians connected with them to talk about or believe in 'possessions' as an existing fact." Though missionaries who spent their time stationed at the coastal ports seemingly could remain aloof from such things, those who served in the inland areas faced the ardent belief of Chinese Christians in the reality of demons.[95] Probably the best-known exorcist was Pastor Hsi Shengmo ("demon overcomer"), who worked with personnel of the China Inland Mission.[96]

"The attitude of missionaries generally may . . . be correctly stated by saying that a few believe that the so-called demon-possessions are not really such, but only a delusion," reported Nevius. But by means of an extensive correspondence, he gauged that "a larger number believe them to be real; while a still larger proportion of the whole missionary body [is] in a state of uncertainty, unprepared to express a positive opinion on one side or the other."[97] Unfortunately, this placed the missionary in an awkward position: the denial of demon possession or hesitation to exorcise a demon produced an impression of powerlessness before Chinese audiences, giving "the impression that he had a limited experience, narrow views, and was not wholly to be relied upon as a religious teacher."[98] Because they lacked a theology to account for supernatural manifestations such as exorcisms, missionaries labored at a considerable disadvantage when dealing with people who appeared to be demonically possessed.

Beyond the conflicts of demon possession, some like Alfred Street advanced the strategy of contending through prayer with satanic powers in the heavenlies to prevail over their hindrance to effective evangelism. A Presbyterian missionary on the left end of the radical neighborhood, he arrived in Hainan, China, in 1892 and engaged in linguistic work on the Hainanese dialect.[99] Apart from this, others knew him as author of the pamphlet *Intercessory Foreign Missionaries: Practical Suggestions from a Missionary to Earnest Christians*, first published by the Student Volunteer Movement. Street defined an "intercessory foreign missionary" as a "'laborer' who cannot go in person to the foreign field, but who has set himself apart to pray for the definite details of the foreign missionary work."[100] Through prayer, this kind of "missionary" would work in the invisible realm of the heavenlies.

In his analysis of Paul's statement in Ephesians 6:12 ("For our struggle is not against flesh and blood, but against the rulers, against the authorities, against the powers of this dark world and against the spiritual forces of evil in the heavenly realms"), Street—like many others past and present—found an organized and graded hierarchy of rulers over invisible kingdoms of darkness that afflicted humanity. Specific information about them also came from Daniel 10:13-20, a famously difficult passage for biblical scholars to interpret, which speaks of the "prince of Persia" and the "prince of Greece," with the former coming into conflict with Michael, one of the "chief princes" of God.

Through prayer, an intercessor could counter the evil forces of Satan over particular countries. While a missionary on the ground shared the gospel face to face with Chinese people, an intercessory missionary could "strike the spiritual prince of China only by way of the place 'above, where Christ is' ever living to make intercession."[101] This would require consistent prayer for a particular country; praying for "individual heathen" by name (if possible) for their salvation; learning the names and needs of missionaries on location, and praying they would receive "fresh fillings of the Holy Spirit." It also meant praying for revival, the development of an adequate native ministry, and for more missionaries and money to complete the Great Commission.[102] Street added that "experience has repeatedly shown that the believing prayer of one humble intercessor at home can bring about a revival on the foreign field and save thousands."[103]

Apprehension about his notion of spiritual combat bubbled to the surface among some evangelicals, notably Arthur Pierson. Instead of reprinting the pamphlet entirely, it was abridged in the *Missionary Review of the World*, notably excluding Street's interpretation of Daniel 10 and reference to the "prince of China."[104] Pierson and his staff may have feared a negative reaction from their readers that the author had unduly mixed the function of prayer with startling speculation, perhaps even superstition.

From the same end of the neighborhood, Frank Sandford presented an even more dramatic strategy for evangelization.[105] A star athlete while a student at Bates College in Lewiston, Maine, he became pastor of the Free Baptist Church in Topsham after graduation. Considering the need for church representatives to visit and report on their growing number of missionaries serving overseas, leaders of the denomination decided to send Sandford, by now pastor of a congregation in Great Falls, New Hampshire, and Thomas Stacy, corresponding secretary for the organization, to Japan, China, Malaysia, India, Egypt, Palestine, and Europe in 1890-1891. This introduced them to the larger missionary community, contemporary mission methods, and the challenges of living in the mission lands.[106] Perhaps more significantly for Sandford, it "demolished all my sermons on the world's speedy evangelization."[107] "God showed me plainly that [it] would never be accomplished by men. It would be God, and God only, who with 'signs, wonders and mighty deeds' would ever call the attention of the nations to the reality of His existence."[108]

Formative influences on Sandford included his reading of Hannah Withall Smith's holiness classic, *The Christian's Secret of a Happy Life* (1875), Higher Life teachings on Spirit baptism, the faith healing theology of Simpson, and the premillennial eschatology taught at the popular Niagara Falls Prophecy Conferences. At the 1888 Mount Hermon (Massachusetts) conference, sponsored by evangelist Dwight Moody, he signed the pledge of the Student Volunteer Movement ("It is my purpose, if God permit, to become a foreign missionary"). Later in the summer when he attended a Niagara Falls conference, he walked along the shore below and observed the debris coming over the falls and being swallowed up in the plunging water and then disappearing. He visualized it as the horror of hell: "Oh God, help me to do my part in keeping a poor lost world from the terrible rapids of sin, and that terrible fall which breaks over the edge of time and plunges the sinner into eternity."[109]

Leaving the Free Baptists in 1893, Sandford became an independent evangelist with his wife, Helen, who had served as the first Alliance missionary to Japan; they gave away all their money and started to practice the faith life.[110] As they evangelized in northern New England, he gained a following of loyal supporters and his vision broadened. A year later, he started a ministerial training school called the "Holy Ghost and Us Bible School" (Acts 15:28) and began publication of *Tongues of Fire from the World's Evangelization Crusade on Apostolic Principles*. The name identified not only his growing movement, but its restorationist spotlight on "signs and wonders": prayer for the sick, raising of the dead, exorcism of demons, and even speaking in tongues—as known human languages—"to enable preachers to proclaim this gospel to every nation, tongue and people."[111]

Sandford established his headquarters near Durham, Maine, on a sandy hill—christened "Beulah Hill"—overlooking the Androscoggin River. "Shiloh," as it became known, eventually housed a large community of supporters, the Holy Ghost and Us Bible School, and a hospital devoted to faith healing, among other institutions. It also served as a convention center and drew radical evangelical speakers such as Alliance members George Peck, M.D., Minnie Draper, and missionary F. H. Bickford from Bombay; also, Emma Whittemore of the Door of Hope Mission in New York City.[112] Sandford's wider connections notably included Elizabeth Sisson, a former American Board missionary to India and Holiness evangelist,[113] as well as Elizabeth Baker, who with her sisters had opened Elim Faith Home in Rochester, New York.[114] Sisson, Baker, and Draper would figure prominently in the growth of Pentecostalism in the Mid-Atlantic states and well beyond.

Sandford's status as an apostle and prophet had been declared by 1898 when he recorded that God now had commissioned him to "remove the covering" over the earth, based on Isaiah 25:7: "On this mountain he will destroy the shroud ('covering' [AV]) that enfolds all peoples, the sheet that covers all nations; he will swallow up death forever." Among others things, this meant that Shiloh would become a center of perpetual prayer for the evangelization of the nations; a 24-hour prayer chain began early in the year in the seven-story turret of Shiloh proper and continued without interruption until May 11, 1920 when the institution ceased operation.[115] God's call required that the uncovering begin during a time of prayer in Jerusalem to herald the inauguration of Christ's kingdom on earth. In the summer of 1898, Sandford and an associate sailed for the Middle East; on their stop in Liverpool, they met the independent faith missionaries Walter and Frances Black and Jennie Glassey, who then accompanied them to Palestine.[116]

"Removing the covering"—a territorial concept of evil influences that kept humanity in the various geographical regions of the world from understanding and accepting the gospel—would consume the resources of Sandford and his prayer warriors. A crucial part of the removal process centered on the work of the "Kingdom Fleet"—the yacht *Coronet* and the barkentine *Kingdom*—on a global expedition. Based on the scriptural premise that "this world is going to be filled with the glory of God as the waters cover the sea, that Jesus Christ is going to have dominion 'from the River to the ends of the earth,' that evil spirits are going to be 'driven out of the land,' and that God's Son is going to rule over it all from Jerusalem," Sandford and thirty followers ventured on a lengthy world cruise (1907-1911).[117] "[God] was sending us forth to go about those and all other lands in the name of the Lord," he noted in his journal, "that the redemption of His purchased possession might take place, and the 'salvation ready to be revealed in the last time' might have its final and glorious fulfillment."[118]

As they sailed along the coasts of the continents, Sandford and thirty followers beseeched God to repulse the forces of Satan so others could effectively evangelize the nations. "They literally prayed their way from island to island, harbor to harbor, continent to continent, ocean to ocean—all the way around the world," wrote biographer Frank Murray. "And while some of the prayer was for guidance and safety, the great burden of it was for the salvation of souls and for the freeing of this globe from the chains the devil had forged around it."[119] Though the voyage marked a spiritual and missiological triumph for Sandford and the faithful, it ended with a human tragedy when several crew members died from scurvy.[120]

Like John Alexander Dowie, who was vilified and his death celebrated by the newspapers, Sandford's unusual activities came under intense scrutiny from the press.[121] Both Sandford and Dowie considered themselves as prophetic figures, claimed the title "Elijah, the Restorer" (Mal 4:5) in 1901, and dominated their respective communities. But while Dowie centered his attention on faith healing and the community of Zion City (now Zion), Illinois, Sandford focused on the millennial restoration of the kingdom of God.[122] His imprisonment for manslaughter in the deaths of crew members reversed the growth of the movement, but left a faithful remnant to continue his vision of holy living and spiritual warfare.

Alfred Street, Frank Sandford, and many other radical evangelicals fell prey to the popular notion that contemporary missions had failed, an assumption reinforced by the urgency of their eschatology and the steady stream of data supplied by the "merchants of numbers," the growing cadre of statisticians. Desperate concern for rapid evangelization before the swiftly approaching end of human history made them skeptical of the seemingly ineffective mission methods of the day and led them to reach beyond the human factor to an apocalyptic scenario of supernatural interventions to keep things running on the divine schedule. Yet, as they and other premillennialists would discover, perhaps to their chagrin, "God has been in no hurry over the process of redemption," as historian Andrew Walls wryly observed.[123]

Unlike Isaac Taylor, Max Müller, and Edward Blyden, who expressed doubt about the ultimate claims of Christianity in relation to those of the non-Christian religions, Street and Sandford stood for the "old-time religion," but were sourly pessimistic about the achievements of the mission movement. Yet, long after their deaths, their theories of how victory over evil in the spiritual realm could affect evangelism on the ground resurfaced in modified forms among late-twentieth-century radical mission strategists to whom they would have been complete strangers.[124]

PIOUSLY HEADSTRONG MISSIONARIES

When Bainbridge and his family visited China on their two-year world tour in the early 1880s, they were embarrassed by the attitudes of the missionaries they met who were associated with the China Inland Mission.[125] Without doubting their piety, consecration, or hard work, he described their intellectual and cultural level as beneath that of missionaries from the leading mission societies.[126] Headstrong in their opinions, these faith missionaries held a low view of church organizations. Equally irksome, "they only understand the deep meaning of God's Word. They only are led directly and intimately by His Spirit. Their sanctification only is genuine."[127]

While their knowledge of God's Word impressed him, they unfortunately lacked expertise in the proper methods of biblical interpretation, a problem demonstrated by the propensity to read their own experiences into the text. No group of Christians could be "farther astray" in this regard than the CIM missionaries, those of the Regions Beyond Missionary Union (another faith mission), the Plymouth Brethren, and "Higher Life" Christians. To make matters worse, "they . . . feel led from day to day by Providence,"[128] and have an apparent freedom to roam: "They have *felt* like going to a certain place to preach; and now they *feel* like going to some other place, and that settled it. The feeling is God's command."[129] Already struggling to learn Mandarin Chinese, "their confusion in the language is increased by their moving around so much among the different dialects."[130]

They also embraced the faith life and faith healing; and he noticed that their Keswick view of the Higher Christian Life "seems to be peculiarly censorious."[131] With the aplomb of a respectable Baptist pastor from New England, he admitted that from time to time in church history, such "extreme movements" have positively helped "to arrest attention and to lead to consideration," though he chose not to elaborate on what this meant.[132] In his estimation, faith missionaries marched to the beat of a different drummer, regrettably one that took them in another direction from that of the larger mission movement.[133] But from their standpoint, Bainbridge probably represented the kind of stuffy evangelicalism they had left behind.

Had he been in China a decade later, he would have been equally shocked by the arrival of "Franson's floods," the scores of unprepared missionaries sent to China by the Scandinavian-American mission leader Fredrik Franson.[134] Responding to J. Hudson Taylor's call for a thousand missionaries at the Shanghai Conference in 1890,[135] he accepted this as a personal challenge; a year later, he sent to Shanghai the first party of thirty-five men and women of the Scandinavian Alliance faith mission based in Chicago. On his travels around the world, he "carried neither purse nor scrip," wrote one historian, but only a Bible, a suitcase, umbrella, and a few changes of clothes. "Property in a world about to pass away was only an encumbrance that would slacken his mad pace to bring the gospel to the people of every land before the imminent crack of doom."[136] The CIM missionaries that Bainbridge encountered and Franson's missionaries all came from a common cloth embroidered with premillennial stitching.

Bainbridge just as easily could have been describing early Pentecostal missionaries: pious, headstrong, fiercely independent, censorious, usually less educated than denominational missionaries, confident of supernatural "signs and wonders," anticipating the return of Christ at any time, and tattooed with a strongly experiential dimension to their faith from which directives of the Lord could be received on a daily basis. They came from the same subculture of popular evangelicalism, shared the same eschatology, the same faith theology, and the same distrust of the prevailing mission practices. But the impending division of the neighborhood would come as a result of a controversial proposal for the solution of learning languages, one that would be uniquely associated with Spirit baptism: "Those who believe . . . will speak in new tongues" (Mark 16:17).

4

The Shortcut to Language Preparation

The miracle [on the Day of Pentecost] was not in the ears of the hearers . . . , but in the mouth of the speakers. And this family praising God together, with the tongues of all the world, was an earnest that the whole world should in due time praise God in their various tongues.[1]
Founder of the Methodist movement, John Wesley, 1754

The gift of tongues was not designed as a means by which the apostles or others might preach the gospel to communities whose vernacular tongue was different from their own.[2]
Sometime secretary of the American Board of Commissioners for Foreign Missions, David Greene, 1865

If a servant of God were under the necessity of acquiring in the ordinary way a knowledge of languages, a large portion of his time would be unprofitably occupied. While he was spending years to learn the language of a people sufficiently accurate to preach the glad tidings of salvation unto them, thousands would be perishing for the want of knowledge.[3]
Mormon apostle Orson Pratt, 1884

The disappearance of the gift of tongues has occasioned no little disquiet in the minds of many, especially those who have supposed that this gift was originally bestowed for missionary purposes.[4]
Methodist bishop for India and Malaysia, James Thoburn, 1894

We have longed for the "gift of tongues," and the Lord has given us the equivalent. Here is our good Joel, who teaches English, Zulu, Xosa, Sesuto, and Dutch, and here is Muti, who speaks the East Coast languages, Sheetswa, Ngitonga, and Sityopi, besides Zulu and English.[5]
American Board missionary Herbert Goodenough, 1900

"The power to acquire a foreign language in such a degree as to make the student a powerful speaker before a native audience is, undoubtedly, 'a gift of

God,'" according to an article entitled "The Gift of Tongues for Missionary Service," published a decade before Charles Parham and his students at Bethel Bible School in Topeka, Kansas, testified to the divine bestowal of at least seventeen languages in January 1901. "It cannot be produced by the severest application, and therefore stands upon the same basis as any endowment of a high order. The possession of this gift does not, indeed, exempt the holder from making great efforts, but it facilitates and makes possible the use of a 'strange tongue' with oratorical power."[6] To the author, achievement of fluency in another language entailed more than the memorization of vocabulary words and the wizardry of pronunciation, it involved some measure of God-given enablement. But how much? The author had barely opened the door for this discussion before abruptly turning to the problems faced by missionaries in language study, such as finding tutors.[7]

At the first international meeting of the Student Volunteer Movement (SVM) in 1891, Ellen Cushing, a veteran missionary to Burma, offered this advice to the volunteers who might be "in a hurry to go quickly to their field of work": "Remember that if you are to evangelize the world in this generation, there are a great many unlearned, unwritten languages for you to dig out. You must have the ability to dig out the language, construct an alphabet, translate the Bible, make a dictionary, do all the preparatory work, before your brothers with less preparation can come and be evangelists in that language."[8] Whether among the college and university volunteers who attended this convention or the thousands of other women and men dedicating their lives to missions, there were many young missionaries "in a hurry to go quickly" and Cushing's advice reminded them of the slow road ahead.[9] Following a twenty-month tour of overseas missions and observing the long delay that new missionaries faced in preaching caused by their having to learn difficult languages, Congregational pastor Edward Lawrence noticed that "some have been disposed to pray for the gift of tongues."[10]

Others, however, pointed to the possibility of God instantaneously conferring the necessary proficiencies, fashioning Mark 16:17 ("And these signs will accompany those who believe . . . they will speak in new tongues") into a virtual guarantee for the applicant with sufficient faith. Both desperation to master foreign languages and particularly the premillennial urgency to encircle the globe with the gospel message encouraged this expectancy. For those racing to beat the Clock of Time, delays were best avoided.[11]

Nineteenth-century discussions about the restoration of the gift of tongues as known human languages for missionary preaching proved to be of critical importance for the rise of Pentecostalism. Although a few stories from this period tell of missionaries receiving divine assistance in their language studies,[12] this chapter concentrates on the anticipation of languages supernaturally endowed without instructional assistance.

EXPECTANCY OF MARK 16:17

The possibility that apostolic labors could be facilitated by the gift of tongues in the early modern era gained some credence from sixteenth-century legends that grew from the activities of Louis Bertrand, a Dominican missionary to South America, and Francis Xavier, the first Jesuit missionary who was declared patron of Catholic missions after his death and canonization. Predictably, earlier Catholic writers argued for the credibility of the stories, while Protestants contested them. The question of the occurrence of miracles, along with the reappearance of tongues, sprouted again in an eighteenth-century debate between two Church of England theologians, Conyers Middleton, who charged that the gift of tongues had not been experienced since the apostolic era, and William Dodwell; the Catholic apologist John Milner responded later and defended the miraculous reports about Xavier.[13] By the early twentieth century, only a few Catholic authors and a battery of popular Pentecostal apologists would defend the credibility of his using this miraculous gift in South India and Japan.[14]

The "missionary use" of tongues surfaced again in 1792 when William Carey met with the clergy of the Northampton Baptist Association to urge them to create a foreign mission society. In his famous rebuke of Carey, the elder John Ryland stated: "Young man, sit down, sit down. You're an enthusiast. When God pleases to convert the heathen, He'll do it without consulting you or me. Besides, there must first be another Pentecostal gift of tongues!"[15] At the time of this encounter, England already had begun to acquire an empire with peoples of many cultures and languages. Books on the voyages of Captain James Cook mesmerized English readers with stories of newly discovered islands and peoples. The task of learning the myriad of unfamiliar and strange sounding languages must have seemed overwhelming.

Claims to the actual reception of languages for missionary evangelism can be traced back to Mary Campbell in the West of Scotland Revival in 1830, an event influenced in part by the teachings of the controversial Presbyterian preacher Edward Irving.[16] Having hoped to become a missionary, she told of receiving the Turkish and Palauan languages, the latter spoken in the Palau Island group in the Pacific Ocean. Revealing the radical orientation of the revival, Campbell remarked, "If God has promised to furnish his servants with every necessary qualification, what have they to do but step into the field, depending on Him for all?"[17] Though her newfound proficiencies remained untested, the dream of such a miracle stayed alive. Through the bestowment of languages, the gospel in its New Testament purity—without the cultural vestments of the Western churches—could be proclaimed around the world in every language, allowing the newly empowered missionaries to transcend the particular dynamics of local cultures and even give them instantly the correct pronunciations and accents. For many radical evangelicals, the "prayer of faith" had virtually no limits.

A major effort to utilize the promised languages of Mark 16:17 occurred with the arrival of Mormon missionaries in the Sandwich Islands (Hawaiian Islands). Though outside the camp of orthodox Christianity, the Church of Jesus Christ of Latter Day Saints rested its beliefs and subsequent missionary expansion on the premise that the gifts of the Spirit, especially that of prophecy, had been restored. At mid-century, "swarms of Mormon missionaries were sent without purse or scrip to China, Japan, Australia, South Africa, [and elsewhere], and finally hoped that helped by the gift of tongues they could speak foreign languages without learning them," explained Delavan Leonard, an "authority on the Mormon question," to the Colorado Springs *Daily Gazette*. "But within five years most that survived had returned baffled and disgusted."[18]

American Board missionary Titus Coan recalled meeting Mormons on the island of Hilo. "'You are a good man,' said they, 'and have done what you could; but we have come to teach you the way of God more perfectly, and if you will unite with us and come into this new light, your people will all soon be born again.'" After water baptism by immersion and the laying on of hands in prayer, they would then receive the gift of the Holy Ghost and all the "signs" would follow: exorcism of demons, speaking in tongues, healing the sick, and miracles. When Coan asked if they could speak in tongues, they responded, "Oh, yes, we can at Utah." Then he queried, "And why not here, where you need the gift more? And why do you ask for a teacher of the native language?"[19] In the latter half of the nineteenth century, newspapers in America carried accounts of Mormons speaking and singing in tongues; their own publications told of instances where their missionaries had miraculously received and utilized the languages for preaching, though presumably not mentioning the failure on the Hawaiian Islands.[20]

In a startling account printed in 1881, the *New Zealand Christian Record* told how an evangelical missionary, Miss C. M. Reade of the South Arcot Highways and Hedges Mission, had received Hindustani as a "gift of tongues" for preaching, and through this gift she also gained revelatory insight into the Islamic religion that would assist her in preaching to Muslims.[21] "One month she was unable to do more than put two or three sentences together; while the next month, she was able to preach and pray without waiting for a word. Those who heard her could only say with herself, 'It was a gift from above.'"[22] Nevertheless, the fact that she appears to have had some familiarity with the Hindustani language should be taken into consideration, a factor that sets her apart from later persons who said they hoped to be given languages of which they had no knowledge.

In the same year, the potential restoration of tongues attracted a much wider audience with the publication of A. J. Gordon's *Ministry of Healing: Miracles of Cure in All Ages*. Not surprisingly, Mark 16:17-18 merited special attention.[23] While the main interest centered on praying for the sick and he fails to explain how tongues would function, his examination of Mark 16 and 1 Corinthians 12-14 led him to conclude that the "gifts of tongues and of prophecy . . . do not seem to be confined within the first age of the church."[24] The popularity of the book undoubtedly prompted evangelicals to put more stock in the "promises" of Mark 16, thus adding to a growing and far-reaching anticipation of supernatural interventions.[25]

The appeal to these verses did not escape the watchful eye of New Testament scholar and Union Theological Seminary professor Marvin Vincent: "'Healing through the prayer of faith,' says Mr. Gordon, 'stands on an entirely different basis from such miracles as raising the dead, turning the water into wine, and *speaking with unknown tongues*.' But in Mark [16] the promise, 'they shall speak with new tongues,' is given, *on Mr. Gordon's own expressed admission, to them that believe*, as an inheritance for all time." Taking the logic of Gordon's exegesis "a little further," Vincent pointedly noted "this miracle of speaking with tongues . . . is nevertheless included in the promise to *all* believers."[26] Indeed, the appeal of Gordon and other radical evangelicals to the promise of physical healing in Mark 16:18, the "gift of healing" in 1 Corinthians 12:9, and other New Testament passages virtually forced them to argue for the availability of the gift of tongues as well.

Expectancy of tongues surfaced again when three members of the Cambridge Seven of athletic fame in England arrived in China in 1885 to serve with J. Hudson Taylor's China Inland Mission. Sailing with Taylor up the Han River, C. T. Studd and Cecil and Arthur Polhill-Turner set aside their Chinese grammar books and prayed for the Pentecostal gift of the Mandarin language. After they reached Hanzhong, they encouraged two young missionary women to do the same. By this time infuriated with their behavior, Taylor scolded them: "How many and subtle are the devices of Satan to keep the Chinese ignorant of the gospel. If I could put the Chinese language into your brains by one wave of the hand I would not do it."[27]

"We waited on the Lord, believing He would teach us, as He taught the 120 at Pentecost, and fulfill in us Mark xvi. 17, 18," confessed Studd, but "He has now, after some time, shown us that at present He means us to study; they did not understand us at all at first at [Hanzhong]—thought us idle fanatics, I fancy— but the Lord has now removed the misunderstanding, praise God."[28] As they began their arduous lessons in Mandarin, Studd and the Polhill-Turner brothers would probably have agreed with the sentiment expressed by another veteran missionary at the 1891 SVM conference, "The romance of missionary life will not last very long."[29]

IRVING REVISITED

The possible restoration of the gift of tongues also arose in 1888-1889 during an uproar over whether the instructions of Jesus in Matthew 10:9-10 established the sole divinely commanded paradigm for Christian missions. An American missionary to North Africa, E. F. Baldwin, had submitted a series of seventeen articles to *The Christian*, a prominent British weekly reflecting Keswick views on Christian spirituality. Printed under the banner "The Question of the Hour— Foreign Missions," he wrote them in response to an earlier article entitled "Can Pentecost Be Regained?" and directed his attention to the mission dynamics of the early church.[30]

"Ah! that was the golden age of missions," sighed Baldwin, standing proudly on his soapbox of thinly veiled contempt for denominational hierarchies and traditional methods as he looked at the New Testament.[31] "The heralds consulted not with flesh and blood. They knew neither committee nor comity. . . . They and their Divine Master were not in need of the patronage of the great. These power-filled heralds could not have wrought on lines marked out by human wisdom."[32] Passionately arguing for a return to the simpler apostolic methods of first-century Christianity, he contended that better results would come from missionaries who modeled their lifestyles after the disciples and prayed for miracles.[33] The ensuing debate over his proposals and the possibility of miracles churned for more than a year, drawing the notice of other periodicals, as well as a chorus of supporters such as Arthur Pierson and Andrew Murray, and an array of opponents.[34]

Among Baldwin's readers, London doctor James Maxwell, secretary of the Medical Missionary Association, took exception not only to the notion that miracles of healing might accompany evangelism, but that such an open-ended restoration of apostolic power might prompt some to look forward to the reappearance of the gift of tongues. In the Acts of the Apostles, the latter represented a "wonder, associated especially with new ingatherings of believers, and indicated . . . the purpose of the Spirit, not only that every believer should be a confessor and witness for Christ, but also that the Gospel should be diffused among all peoples, and in every tongue."[35] Although Baldwin had sidestepped the issue of tongues, Maxwell charged him with looking for "faith-tongues and faith-healings" at the very moment when the "present methods," including medical missions, had been "crowned . . . in heathendom with ever-increasing tokens of [God's] blessing."[36] Obviously, Baldwin, like Gordon, could not escape the logical implications of his appeal to Mark 16 without making him responsible for "folly and fanaticism" in the eyes of his critics.[37]

Ironically, his most strident adversary proved to be Fanny Guinness, editor of *Regions Beyond*. She and her husband, H. Grattan Guinness, had been leaders in the faith missions movement and co-founded the Regions Beyond Missionary Union.[38] In her estimation, Baldwin's extremely ascetic application of faith missions, which he personally modeled, smacked of the controversial proposals that Irving had laid before the London Missionary Society in 1824. Both Guinness and Eugene Stock, editorial secretary of the Church Missionary Society, grimaced at the similarity of views. The linkage of Baldwin with Irving—"a fanatic and a heretic"—meant that he had "gone quite off Evangelical and Scriptural lines," in the opinion of Stock.[39]

Guinness alleged that Irving's interpretation of Matthew 10:9-10 was "closely connected" to "his later faith in modern miracles, and in the revival of the gift of tongues."[40] Regrettably, "craving after the supernatural, so common in the Church just now" had stirred the recent interest. "Good people" could be led astray because of an unhealthy curiosity in "claims [of] direct inspiration or the gift of tongues, or miraculous interpositions, or even miracle-working power, in a way that Scripture does not warrant *nor experience justify*."[41]

Though not a party to the squabble with Baldwin, church historian Philip Schaff pointedly addressed the "Miracle of Pentecost" and the gift of tongues in the third edition of his *History of the Christian Church*, published in 1889, while the debate still roiled. "[The gift of tongues] passed away gradually with the other extraordinary or strictly supernatural gifts of the apostolic age," he wrote, but people later misunderstood it to mean the "miraculous and permanent gift of *foreign* languages for *missionary* purposes." Schaff then declared that the "whole history of missions furnishes no clear example of such a gift for such a purpose." Interestingly, he had listened to "Corinthian glossolalia" ("unknown tongues") on one occasion at an "Irvingite congregation" in New York City. "The words were broken, ejaculatory and unintelligible, but uttered in abnormal, startling sounds, in a state of apparent unconsciousness and rapture, and without any control over the tongue, which was seized as it were by a foreign power." His friend and colleague at Union Seminary, Charles Briggs, had noticed the same phenomenon when visiting the main Irvingite church in London a decade earlier.[42] In these instances, tongues did not relate to missions.

THE SEVERE LOGIC

Another failed restoration of the gift of tongues occurred shortly after in 1890 when members of the Kansas-Sudan movement reached Sierra Leone.[43] Encouraged by George Fisher, a YMCA mission enthusiast inspired by the preaching of Grattan Guinness at a summer Bible conference, nine young Kansans dedicated their lives to African missions. Arriving on the East Coast, they stayed at A. B. Simpson's missionary hostel in New York City before they boarded the *City of Chicago* for Africa.[44] Their confidence in the faith principle and anticipation of physical healings reflected that of other radical evangelicals. Sadly, several died within a few weeks of reaching their destination, having refused to take quinine.[45] Had they taken the medicine, it would have signaled their lack of faith in God's power to heal them. Even so, headlines about young men and women dedicating their lives to missions and then dying as a result of their embrace of faith healing embarrassed leaders of the faith missions.

Virtually all the articles written about the outcome of the Kansas-Sudan movement focused on the tragedy and the extreme view of healing.[46] Yet one contemporary observer of the mission scene and a noted linguist, Robert Needham Cust, reported they had initially assumed they would be given the gift of tongues. Such bizarre behavior could only be attributed to "hare-brained excited young men, full of so-called zeal, empty of all experience, [and] ready to adopt the last new hallucination, such as Faith-healing, Pentecostal gift of vernacular languages, *claiming* a sick person of God, and talking of their work being *owned by God.*"[47]

Some laid the blame for their deaths at the doorstep of Simpson, an accusation likely based more on suspicion than fact. In their opinion, the Kansans had left Topeka without belief in faith healing and then embraced it while they resided at his hostel.[48] Probably troubled by Fisher's connection to the ministry of her husband, disturbed by the teachings of the healing movement, angered over the recent tragic events, and recognizing the same radical ideas that Baldwin had proposed, Guinness now adjusted her editorial sights and took aim at Simpson's "foolish, false, and mischievous doctrines."[49] "Dr. Simpson," she charged, "thinks we need these 'signs,' and asks, 'What right have we to go to the unbelieving world and demand their acceptance of our message *without* these signs?'" Lamentably, "he thinks too, like Irving before him, that we may expect, and are even beginning to see, a restoration of the gift of tongues." She then quotes him as saying, "Instances are not wanting now of its apparent restoration in missionary labours both in India and Africa." To Guinness, such statements lacked any foundation: "[Simpson] does not cite any instance of this, nor are we acquainted with any! We did indeed hear of a dear young enthusiast who tried to learn Chinese by prayer and faith without study, but we heard also that he did not succeed, and that, perceiving his mistake, he soon adopted the usual course."[50]

It is true that Simpson had endorsed—in fact, "cheerfully accept[ed]"—the "severe logic" of Mark 16: "If you expect the healing of the sick, you must also include the gift of tongues and the power to overcome malignant poisons. . . . We cannot afford to give up one of the promises." Hence, "We see no reason why a humble servant of Christ, engaged in the Master's work, may not claim in simple faith the power to resist malaria and other poisons and malignant dangers. To a greater or less extent the gift of tongues has been continuous in the Church of Christ, and along with many counterfeits has undoubtedly been realized in the present generation."[51] With expectant faith, "these signs [would] accompany those who believe."

Despite Guinness's rebuke, interest in tongues persisted in the Alliance. In an article published in February 1892, he referred to "much earnest inquiry into the real meaning of this apostolic gift, and not a few intending missionaries are hoping and praying, and even believing for the bestowal of this gift upon them, to enable them to preach the Gospel to the heathen."[52] Among them were William Simpson (no relation to A. B. Simpson) and William Christie, graduates of Simpson's training school for missionaries, who landed in China in May, intent on evangelizing Tibet. Like Studd and the Polhill brothers, their exuberant trust in Mark 16:17 prompted their prayers for Mandarin and Tibetan.[53]

Several months later at the Alliance's New York convention, Simpson told the faithful, "We believe that it is the plan of the Lord to pour out His Spirit not only in the ordinary, but also in the extraordinary gifts and operations of His power, in proportion as His people press forward to claim the evangelization of the entire world." Confident of the biblical promises, he added, "We are praying for the special outpouring of the Spirit in connection with the acquiring of foreign languages." But, perhaps bruised by Guinness's censure and thinking of the failure of the two missionary recruits (Simpson and Christie) to miraculously obtain the languages, he cautioned against the "dangers of Irvingism," aware that "every little while [the idea] is so easily taken up that some persons are called even in these days to a kind of apostolic ministry, and to receive some sort of personal gift."[54]

Simpson openly wondered if missionaries had the right to expect foreign languages for preaching the gospel without diligent study. Yet, both in the early church and the modern church, God had given individuals this gift for preaching, "but this did not become a permanent gift, and we advise our dear friends to be fully persuaded in their own minds before they commit themselves to a theory which might bring to them great disappointment."[55] Though he cited no examples of such remarkable occurrences, he did speak of missionaries in China who, through divine enablement in their study of Mandarin, had been able to preach within a few months.

Because God conceivably could do anything for the seeker who "claimed the promises" with robust confidence, Simpson struggled to resolve the dilemma that his radical stance on faith had engendered: "Should God give [the language] immediately to the faith of any of them, by the miraculous answer to prayer, we should greatly rejoice and should not question it, but we do not feel authorized to encourage them uniformly to expect it."[56] Wanting to avoid the dangers of "excess and fanaticism," and once again distancing himself and the Alliance from Irving, he contended several weeks after the convention closed that one could still find the "middle ground of supernatural reality and power, where we may safely stand, as far on one side from the excesses of Irvingism as it is on the other from the coldness of unbelief."[57]

By 1898—six years later—his certainty that in rare instances and with sufficient faith some missionaries might receive the languages had waned, knowing of missionaries who "have been saved from this error." With language instruction and heaven's blessing, they quickly mastered and preached in the language. Those who proposed that the Alliance "should send our missionaries to the foreign field under a sort of moral obligation to claim this gift, and to despise the ordinary methods of acquiring a language," did not foresee that the results would surely lead to "wild fanaticism and bring discredit upon the truth itself."[58] Less than a decade later, Simpson again would face turbulence in the Alliance over the gift of tongues, resulting in differences of opinion that would have far-ranging effects on the organization and the Pentecostal movement.

ASTONISHING CLAIMS

Those looking for a success story of someone actually having a gift of language cheered at the news of Jennie Glassey, upon whom the Holy Spirit purportedly had bestowed a dozen African dialects and several other languages.[59] What is more, reports circulated that her proficiencies had been corroborated by knowledgeable bystanders. Glassey was born in 1877 into the Scottish Presbyterian family of William and Elizabeth Glassey, residents of St. Louis.[60] In the early 1890s, the family moved to a farm near Cuba, Missouri, approximately eighty miles southwest of St. Louis, to live among an extended family.[61]

The Glasseys attended the Presbyterian Church in Cuba, located close by the rail line that connected the town to St. Louis. Two visiting evangelists—John Stewart and Walter Black—traveling there by train met the seventeen-year-old Jennie when they held revival services in the Presbyterian Church in 1894. Stewart, a renegade Presbyterian minister, recently had been defrocked by the Synod of Illinois of the United Presbyterian Church. A graduate of Indiana University at Bloomington, he had prepared for a career in law. After practicing law for several years, he entered Xenia Theological Seminary in Ohio and received ordination from the Chicago Presbytery in 1884. Following a pastorate in Nebraska, he became an evangelist and at some point began preaching that "the age of miracles is not past, but that the people are at fault in not exercising true faith in God."⁶² As a result of this turn in his ministry, the Presbytery of Monmouth, Illinois, with which he was then affiliated, pressed charges against him and conducted a church trial in October 1893 for his preaching of faith healing, rejecting the authority of church leaders, and "by claiming to impart the Holy Ghost by the laying on of hands, as did the disciples of old."⁶³ The presbytery subsequently defrocked him and while a synodical commission considered his appeal, Stewart and his friend Daniel Warner, founder of the holiness "Evening Light Saints" (Church of God [Anderson, Indiana]), conducted "salvation and healing" meetings in the same city, an action that did little to endear him with denominational officials reviewing his appeal.⁶⁴ Stewart then moved to St. Louis and became pastor of Full Gospel Tabernacle, the local branch of the Christian and Missionary Alliance.⁶⁵

In November 1894, he and his congregation hosted the national convention of the Alliance in St. Louis, an event that afforded him the opportunity to hear Stephen Merritt preach on the "Fourfold Gospel" ("Jesus Christ our Savior, Sanctifier, Healer and Coming King")⁶⁶ and to meet and hear A. B. Simpson.⁶⁷ In due course, he left the congregation to found First Full Bible Church in a former saloon at the corner of Twenty-third Street and Washington Avenue, the name denoting the recovery of radical holiness and healing teachings that had been absent in the mainline churches.⁶⁸ His friend, the Canadian Walter Black, then followed him as pastor of Full Gospel Tabernacle. Born in Nova Scotia, he graduated from Acadia College (now University) in Wolfville in 1889 and from Newton Theological Institution (now Andover Newton Theological School) in Newton Centre, Massachusetts, three years later. Before he and his wife, Frances, moved to St. Louis, they had pastored Baptist churches in Massachusetts and Minnesota.⁶⁹ The shared radical faith of these two university and seminary graduates, one a Presbyterian and the other a Baptist, enabled Stewart and Black to work together. Unlike the faith missionaries that Bainbridge encountered in China, well-educated clergy also could thrive on the left wing of popular evangelicalism.

According to the available information, when Stewart preached in Cuba in March 1894, Glassey "was converted and sought for sanctification and a full gospel." On March 23, she went into a trance in which God appeared to her and said, "Go."⁷⁰ With the call directing her to Africa, she "pleaded her inability, her lack of means, her ignorance of the language," and when "all these were promised her . . . she consented to go."⁷¹ Later in the summer, the Blacks preached in the vicinity of Cuba and likely encouraged Glassey to obey the call. In January 1895 and against the opposition of her family, she left for St. Louis and stayed with the Blacks; there she received "Bible training" with others. Black baptized her by immersion on July 5, 1895, and four days later she received the promised languages. The West African dialects Housa, Croo, and "Khoominar" (?) came to her in a vision. "The Spirit," as a newspaper article reported, "unrolled before her eyes [a] long scroll covered with strange characters. These were in the Croo language. The [S]pirit read them most rapidly, and she read after him. First the psalms, for she was reared a psalm-singing Scottish Presbyterian, then the Bible.

So rapid was the reading that she feared she could not remember all, but has done so, and speaks the Croo language with grace and fluency." Verification of Khoominar came through revelation ("because the Lord said it was")[72] and the testimonies of an African who had traveled in Sierra Leone and an old seaman who had sailed along the West African coast and been held captive by a tribe at some point in his journeys. After he recognized the language that Glassey spoke, "the power of God settled upon him, and then and there he broke down, confessed his sins, and became a Christian."[73] What better proof than the conversion of an unbeliever through a miracle of language?

Glassey shared her story publicly and answered questions at the August "faith-healing camp meeting," sponsored by First Full Bible Church in the Hodiamont Avenue area of St. Louis, at the time an affluent white middle-class neighborhood. She told of receiving even more languages including German, French, Latin, and Greek.[74] When someone asked Glassey how her expenses for going to Africa would be met, she responded by saying that "she did not have one cent, and had no earthly guarantee of support, but she was confident that the promises of God were sufficient and that she would not starve."[75] Stewart confirmed to reporters his confidence in her claims and then "ridiculed the idea of missionaries having to study for years to learn foreign languages no faster than a heathen could learn English. The right way was to seek the gift of tongues and preach [in] it at once." Furthermore, "he was seeking it, and if he obtained it, he was going to India to preach."[76]

All the same, the events at the camp meeting, along with their pastor's enthusiastic involvement, shocked the faithful at Full Gospel Tabernacle. "These manifestations are not sanctioned by the Alliance and are believed to emanate from the Evil Spirit who is seeking to throw discredit on the true religion," charged Clara Ely, one of the founders of the church.[77] Dismissed as pastor, Black moved to First Full Bible Church and became the acting assistant pastor. Once again, a commotion had arisen in the Alliance over the gift of tongues.

Late in the fall, the Blacks too received Khoominar, sometime after Stewart and members of his congregation laid hands on them in prayer in fulfillment of Mark 16:17. While they could converse with Glassey in the language and answer her questions, they curiously lacked the "power of interpretation" and did not understand what was spoken. Nonetheless, the experience brought them a call to Africa as well.[78] Like the faith missionaries that Bainbridge met, they depended on directives from the Lord to guide their movements. Hence, two weeks after Frances Black and Glassey left St. Louis, Walter finally received divine confirmation—"I could not go till He said the word";[79] he then met them in New York City. From there, they headed to Connecticut and then on to Amherst, Nova Scotia, where their recently attained notoriety furnished them the opportunity to share their testimonies and plans to an overflow crowd at the YMCA on December 8. During their brief visit, Glassey received the "Chinese language" and visited two "Celestials" (Chinese) at a local laundry whose expressions were taken as recognition of the language.[80] (Within a few years, Pentecostals would be visiting Chinese laundries for the same purpose.[81])

Traveling as "faith missionaries," the Blacks with their infant daughter and

Glassey sailed to Liverpool, England, and arrived there in January 1896, with plans to book passage for Sierra Leone. As it happened, they remained there for two years due to insufficient funds and resided at the home of W. H. Archer, an English evangelist who directed the Bethel Mission.[82] Though discouraged by their long delay, they accepted it as a time of testing of their faith and preparation for an even more difficult ministry in Africa. "[God] has led us by signs, wonders, miracles, healings, tongues, and prophecy," declared Walter Black, "and the end is not yet."[83] He later sent a letter to assure family and friends in Cuba, Missouri, that Jennie had genuinely received many African dialects, "scores of African tunes," and the gifts of prophecy, discerning of spirits, and tongues. The local newspaper, the *Crawford County Telephone*, printed the letter with its sensational claims on the front page of its edition for April 2, 1897.[84] A local girl had achieved fame in an unlikely way.

In the meantime, several American periodicals branded their miraculous claims as fraudulent, a charge not easily dismissed after Glassey refused to allow her languages to be examined by a representative sent to England by a Christian organization in America. "It is no wonder the Lord would not permit me to verify the gift of tongues when there were so many volumes of prayer ascending to God for us," she wrote in a letter to Frank Sandford, founder of the Shiloh community near Durham, Maine. "Do you know while [the representative] was trying to compel me to do as *he* said, I felt as if I was held by such an unseen force I dare not move." Apparently God would not allow an outsider to verify or disprove the marvel of the gift of languages. Yet, opposition—"We have met so few who have any sympathy with us"—did not deter their confidence in miracles.[85] In fact, Glassey received more amazing gifts: seventeen new teeth, including "*five fullgrown* [sic] white teeth [that] filled old vacancies during a half hour's heavy sleep"; handicraft skills, especially "practical needle work"; and newfound ability in instrumental music.[86] "Those who know how unproficient she was in all those things when she left her home," said Walter Black of the hapless Glassey, "need no further proof that she has been divinely taught, for all these gifts are as unnatural to her as the gift of tongues."[87]

The story of this unusual missionary party might have died in obscurity had not Sandford printed their letters in his *Tongues of Fire* newspaper. "Such is the account of the Pentecostal method of learning foreign languages for the proclamation of the gospel," he declared. Christians who had the faith to try the "purely Holy Ghost machinery" of Mark 16:17-18 could achieve quickly the Great Commission, since neither "20,000 nor 100,000 missionaries of the common sanctified type will [ever] evangelize this globe."[88] He received a personal confirmation of these happenings from their former pastor, John Stewart, who had visited them in Liverpool while traveling in England. Returning to North America through the port of Halifax, Stewart then stopped at Shiloh on his way home to St. Louis.[89]

Sandford became acquainted personally with Glassey and the Blacks in Liverpool, and they chose to join him on his way to Jerusalem to announce the restoration of the kingdom of God.[90] For whatever reason, they abandoned their immediate plans for Sierra Leone and disembarked for Palestine at the beginning of July 1898. Little is known about their activities there except that the connection with Sandford ended shortly after their arrival.[91] Though the Blacks had returned to Canada by 1904, Glassey showed the mettle of her missionary calling by remaining and working for fourteen years.[92] She became a member of the Alliance church in Jerusalem and evangelized Muslims with the help of a native woman who probably served as an interpreter. Because of her "hearty spirit and efficient service in the isolation and discouragements of [sharing the gospel in] Hebron and Beersheba," she received the status of "associate worker" from the Alliance board of missions.[93]

PENTECOST ON BEULAH HILL, 1900

Interest in the gift of tongues existed for several years at Shiloh, all part of the supernatural signs and wonders that Sandford and the faithful anticipated would come with the advancement of Christ's kingdom.[94] Though having downplayed the importance of tongues—knowing critics would cry *"Irvingism! Irvingism! Irvingism!"*—he described the early days of 1900 as "a real Pentecost" at Shiloh.[95] Beginning with the New Year's Eve service, prayer sessions in the following days lasted from mid-morning to past midnight. In an interview, he said that "real gifts of the Spirit" had been manifested. "I have heard during these past ten days persons stand there in the temple and deliver as truly prophetic utterances as were ever given to the world," he remarked, and "the gift of tongues has descended also."[96] Looking around the chapel, he counted 120 people in attendance, exactly the number present at the first Pentecost and suggestive of this as a momentous happening in the end times. Seventy people subsequently went forth two-by-two to crisscross the nation preaching the gospel— traveling by faith—"without staff or scrip" (Matt 10:9-10 [AV]).[97]

Charles Parham, who would help chart the course of Pentecostalism and Pentecostal missions, met Sandford in the summer of 1900.[98] After attending Southwest Kansas College in Winfield to prepare for the ministry, he had served as a supply pastor at the Methodist Church in Eudora, Kansas. At the annual Southwest Kansas district conference in 1895, he surrendered his license to preach and "left denominationalism forever."[99] Denouncing Methodism as spiritually bankrupt, he now had a "world-wide parish," free of the "confines of a pastorate, with a lot of theater-going, card-playing, wine-drinking, fashionable, unconverted Methodists."[100] Three years later, he moved his independent holiness and healing ministry to Topeka, where he established Beth-El Healing Home and enlarged his activities to include a placement service for orphans and an employment bureau, among other initiatives. But by the spring of 1900, these operations had declined and he faced a personal crisis about his future ministry.

Information about Glassey gleaned from a St. Louis periodical (information derived from Sandford's *Tongues of Fire*) had caught Parham's attention. With the story reprinted in his *Apostolic Faith* newspaper in 1899, readers learned that she "could read and write, translate and sing the language while out of the trance or in a normal condition, and can until now. Hundreds of people can

testify to the fact, both saint and sinner, who heard her use the language."[101] In
April 1900, he announced that a "Bro. and Sister Hamaker are now in Beth-El
to labor for Jesus until He gives them an heathen tongue, and then they will
proceed to the missionary field."[102] Residing at the heart of his operation in
Topeka and devoting themselves to prayer for the conferral of a language, the
Hamakers surely heightened his interest in the gift.[103] Whether through reading
about Glassey or rubbing shoulders with the Hamakers, Parham stood primed
for the Pentecostal outpouring of the Spirit and end-times missionary evangelism. However, he struggled to find the true meaning of the baptism in the Holy
Spirit. Was it the Wesleyan-holiness experience of sanctification? Or the "special
anointing" that the disciples received when Jesus breathed on them and said,
"Receive the Holy Spirit" (John 20:22)?[104]

Two months later on the weekend of June 8-9, he traveled from Topeka to
Kansas City to attend special services at the home of George Barton, who was
hosting two of the seventy students that had been sent out from Shiloh. Parham,
the two students, and four others soon joined the Sandford party on its way eastward by rail from Tacoma.[105] "The bond of union Sunday afternoon which had
united three leaders of three great movements, one in the extreme west [Nathan
Harriman of the Ecclesia Mission], another in the extreme east [Sandford] and
the third in the centre of our vast country [Parham]," wrote Sandford jubilantly,
"must have brought rejoicing among the angels, and especially to the heart of
Him who prayed so long ago that we might be 'one.'"[106]

Parham too had pondered how Christian unity could be achieved: "For years
the thought of my Lord's prayer that we all might be one, has burned itself upon
my heart." Though having doubted that it could ever be accomplished, two
weeks at Shiloh convinced him of its reality and he sang its praises. Sandford
believed the Holy Spirit would lead the restored New Testament church into all
truth, free from the human restraints of denominationalism and energized for
world conquest.[107] "Here I found the church of my heart's desire in active and
perfect operation," bubbled Parham, "and learned that God demanded central-
ized force, divine order and authority." Yet, with an obvious measure of inner
struggle, he added: "I was led to see God's hand in selecting our able Brother
Sandford to the leadership in apostolic order in these last days, and I was pleased
to slip into my place in the body of my Lord, so nothing would be lacking, or
any part weakened through any over-act of individualism on my part." God
would use "this mighty movement," with Shiloh as its headquarters, to bring
"every true child of God into perfect unity, and the world shall yet know that
Jesus came out from the Father."[108] For Sandford, Parham's enlistment would
add Topeka to the movement's list of external centers.[109]

During his stay at Shiloh, Parham may have learned more about Jennie
Glassey, as well as the occurrences of the gifts of prophecy and tongues there
in the previous January. But more importantly, he discovered that the gift of
tongues had been received by some of the future missionaries in this spiritually
charged atmosphere, having heard tongues-speech for the first time when several
students came down from their vigils in one of the prayer towers.[110] His expectations of Mark 16:17 and Acts 2:4 ("All of them were filled with the Holy Spirit

and began to speak in other tongues as the Spirit enabled them"), the reports about Glassey, the anticipation of the Hamakers, and what he observed and heard at Shiloh must have deeply impressed him. He also accepted Sandford's conviction that consecrated believers could receive a special Spirit baptism and miraculous gifts—including that of language—for world evangelism.[111] But for Sandford's claim as Elijah the Restorer and the subsequent de-emphasis and departure from speaking in tongues at Shiloh (he never spoke in tongues himself), many American Pentecostals might have traced their roots directly back to the Pentecost on Beulah Hill in January 1900.[112]

On July 18, Parham joined Sandford and seventeen others on a trip to Winnipeg for one month of evangelistic meetings. All of them enjoyed the train ride across the country into Canada, traveling in a first-class compartment through the kindness of the conductors, an act of generosity perceived to be a reward for their willingness to go on the journey trusting in God entirely for their financial needs. On the return trip four weeks later, however, a breach became evident when Parham left the Sandford party after the train made a stop in Kansas City. He boasted to a reporter that on the trip he had "lived like a king" and returned home with more money than when he left. God miraculously had provided the necessary funds several times through strangers who walked up to him and gave him cash. While one can wonder about how they learned of his needs, it reconfirmed to him the importance of the life of faith in Christian ministry.[113]

Though from the Shiloh perspective, Parham had fallen "into a snare by breaking away," he generously praised Sandford and the great work on Beulah Hill.[114] Nevertheless, he failed to mention the rupture in their relationship, and his tune notably had changed: the extended trip to major holiness centers in the Northeast had left him with the "profound conviction that no one in these days was really enjoying the power of a personal Pentecost, while many were anointed above measure."[115] Both men had left denominations and poured contempt on church hierarchies and contemporary mission practices, bristling at the notion of submitting to any human authority in the work of God. Parham later penned these words, no doubt while reflecting on Shiloh: "Bible unity cannot be accomplished in concentration camps . . . [with the] crushing out [of] all personal views and each one yielding to the standard view . . . as infallible."[116] As time would prove, however, he would be no less certain than Sandford in his opinions, and the later rise of other independent-minded leaders in the Pentecostal movement would frustrate him.

In October 1900, Parham opened Bethel Bible School, modeled on Shiloh's Holy Ghost and Us Bible School, to prepare his own cadre of Spirit-filled missionaries who would leave for the ends of the earth. By this point his re-conceptualizing of Spirit baptism had fully matured with the uniquely added "Bible evidence" of speaking in tongues. The reception of the global languages would mark the actual onset of the end times,[117] the sealing of the bride of Christ, and provide the means for the speedy evangelization of the world.[118] Beginning on January 1, 1901, the anticipation became a reality for him and his students. The first to speak in tongues, Agnes Ozman, said she received the Chinese language. "We will not have to wait until we master the foreign languages," Parham told a reporter from the *Kansas City Times*, because "God will give us the power to speak so that we will be understood."[119] This mighty baptism of power would make God's "saints" into "world-wide powers for good" to the effect that the gospel would be preached in all the world, in effect "[removing] the covering cast over all the face of the earth, for we believe this to be the will of God, and the accomplishment of the same well pleasing in His sight."[120] Parham had learned more from Sandford than he would acknowledge publicly.

MISSIONAL INFLUENCE

To nineteenth-century radical evangelicals, physical healings and the gift of tongues would signify that God still performed miracles. When the latter failed to happen, missionaries such as C. T. Studd and William Simpson simply returned to their books. Their confidence had not been built on Spirit baptism, but on faith in God's promise, especially Mark 16:17. Neither they, nor Gordon and Simpson, nor even Jennie Glassey suggested that God intended for every believer to have such languages; tongues were for missionaries. While agreeing with Sandford about the importance of the Pentecostal baptism and gifts for evangelization, Parham's linkage of tongues with Spirit baptism added a dramatically innovative dimension to what might be restored. By insisting that every believer should have this experience, he pressed the case for the importance of tongues much farther, even past the "severe logic" to which Simpson had referred. Thus, at Bethel Bible School, housed in a large mansion complete with a tower turned into a prayer room and where everyone lived by faith, the Spirit had re-established the original "Apostolic Faith" in Parham's estimation. Just a year after the unusual happenings on Beulah Hill and under its shadow, the Pentecost at Topeka in January 1901 would forever shape the theological and missiological contours of Pentecostalism.

The long quest for the full restoration of the Spirit's power had finally produced the most unusual phenomenon of all: the divine bestowment of unlearned languages. Naturally, for early Pentecostals like Parham, tongues could be empirically verified. After all, they were supposed to be human languages. Yet, this pragmatic solution to the problem of acquiring languages blurred naiveté with exuberant faith in God's power to accomplish what appeared to be impossible. More than any other "shortcut" conceived to hasten the evangelization of the world, such as faith missions and Bible institutes, the missional nature of tongues set Pentecostals apart from their radical evangelical parents, though spiritual ecstasy would readily appear in their DNA.

5

Diverging Currents of the Spirit's Work

This Conference recommends the holding of special Conventions of Indian and Ceylon Christians and Missionaries, to seek for a real spiritual uplift and a true Pentecostal Baptism, in consequence of which Christian obedience and service will become a delight, and the Churches will become purer, stronger, and more fruitful, to the glory of God.[1]

Resolution at the Fourth Decennial
Indian Missionary Conference, 1902

A . . . hindrance to the Holy Spirit's accomplishing all that he might is a widespread misapprehension as to what the principal work of the Holy Spirit is . . . to infer from the second chapter of Acts that the principal kind of witnessing which the Holy Spirit will empower Christians to give is some kind of preaching about Jesus Christ, attended by some remarkable signs corresponding to the tongues of fire upon the heads of the disciples, and accompanied with some unusual power of utterance like the gift of tongues.[2]

American Board missionary Robert Hume, 1905

God is solving the missionary problem, sending out new-tongued missionaries on the Apostolic Faith line, without purse or scrip, and the Lord is going before them to prepare the way.[3]

Apostolic Faith newspaper, Azusa Street Revival, 1906

Hundreds of correspondents, including missionaries, native Christian workers and leaders of the missionary activities on the home field, while they have differed on nearly all questions pertaining to plans, means, and methods, have been absolutely united in the expressed conviction that the world's evangelization is a Divine enterprise, that the Spirit of God is the great Missioner, and that only as He dominates the work and workers can we hope for success in the undertaking to carry the knowledge of Christ to all people.[4]

Report of Commission I, World Missionary Conference,
Edinburgh, 1910

Three thousand people gathered in the little New England hamlet of Williamstown, Massachusetts, in the fall of 1906 to celebrate the centenary of the Haystack Prayer Meeting, an event that led to the founding of the first foreign missions society in the new republic, the American Board of Commissioners for Foreign Missions. They had come to honor Samuel Mills and four other students of Williams College, who on a hot Saturday afternoon in August 1806 walked out to the maple grove near Sloan's Meadow for their twice-weekly time of prayer.[5] When a thunderstorm arose, they found shelter from the wind and rain on the lee side of a big haystack. Reflecting on their studies and the need for "missions to the heathen," they began to pray and consecrated their lives to foreign missions.[6] The influence of the young men and mounting interest in missions prompted the General Association of Congregational Ministers of Massachusetts to establish the American Board in 1810 and ordain Adoniram Judson, Gordon Hall, Samuel Nott, Samuel Newell, and Luther Rice for service in India. Years later, American Board secretary Rufus Anderson said the prayer meeting at Williams College represented more than "any and all other places, the *Antioch* of our Western Hemisphere" (Acts 13:1-3), alluding to the port on the Syrian coast where Christians commissioned Paul, Silas, and John Mark for their first missionary journey.[7]

On the second day of the centennial, the program began with a sunrise prayer meeting around the monument dedicated to the five students. As happened one hundred years before, an unexpected rainstorm disrupted the plans; the five hundred people present found shelter in one of the college buildings for their prayer service. Before leaving, they repeated in unison the famous motto of Mills: "We can do it if we will."[8] A special highlight came in the afternoon with testimonies of converts from Africa, Bohemia, Ceylon, China, Hawaii, India, Japan, Mexico, and Turkey. "Many hearts in the audience were deeply stirred," said one in attendance.[9] "This great and glorious day," gushed Howard Bridgman, editor of *The Congregationalist and Christian World*, "revealed anew the hold which the foreign missions have upon varied elements in our churches—the highly intellectual, as typified by the college presidents assembled; the plain everyday people everywhere in evidence; the students now in our colleges—some of them—so ardent and persistent in their missionary impulses."[10]

Yet, despite the heavy clouds of nostalgia and optimism that hovered over the celebration, the winds of transition were blowing swiftly across the mission establishment and the mission lands. Biting criticisms of the movement had grown unabatedly, moving the Board's foreign secretary, James Barton, to write a book-length treatise, *The Missionary and His Critics* (1906), to ward off the snipers.[11] For some time, the winds also had been affecting the Congregational churches and their premier theological school, Andover Theological Seminary. Having long provided missionaries for the Board, it had shifted to a progressive theological orientation, triggering the "Andover controversy" of 1886. In that year, the seminary board allowed professors to teach "future probation": the belief that non-Christians who die without hearing the gospel will be given a chance in the future life to accept or reject the message of Christ before facing the final judgment of God.[12] Twenty years later, even this had lost its relevance.[13]

Then, just months before the centennial, the Board's Prudential Committee voted against sending out any new missionaries, held back those who recently had been appointed, and cut back on other plans due to major financial short-falls.[14] One mission editor lamented that "few 'Signs of the Times' are to us more alarming than the fact that one of the greatest missionary societies of the world . . . has felt constrained to take such backward steps."[15] In the following years, the American Board slowly declined, with its supporting churches and missionaries losing the sense of urgency in "saving the lost" that had originally characterized the endeavor; missionaries consequently became less evangelistic and more institutional and humanitarian in their undertakings.

Others, however, were heartened by the number of widely reported revivals in many parts of the world, representing in their opinion "a multiplied modern Pentecost."[16] Missionaries utilized Pentecostal imagery from the New Testament to describe the events and their phenomena, punctuated with references to the fulfillment of Joel's prophecy, the book of Acts, and other Scriptures, in this way showing the heightened anticipation of the Spirit's empowerment in the final years of Kenneth Scott Latourette's "Great Century" in missions. The moment of the great end-time harvest of souls seemed to have arrived at long last.

In this chapter, we examine how the radical evangelicals, mainstream evangelicals, and theological progressives all registered interest in what the Spirit might accomplish in church and mission, though in crucial respects they had strikingly different expectations. Despite the outward unity of the mission enterprise, it slowly fell to pieces. Noticeable cracks appeared almost immediately in the pavement leading up to the 1910 World Missionary Conference at Edinburgh. A decade later and due in no small part to concerns about the theological integrity of missionaries, the fundamentalist/modernist controversy began to rumble through the Protestant establishment in America, especially among the Northern Baptists and Northern Presbyterians, eventually destroying the ecumenical missionary consensus built by nineteenth-century evangelical architects.[17] Holiness and Anabaptist missions, however, continued to grow largely unaffected by these events.[18] The year of the Haystack Centennial—1906—also signaled the beginning of Pentecostal missions, a young plant that proponents contended was nourished by "latter rain," but critics suspected had been bottled in hell.[19]

DECADE OF REVIVALS

The Prayer Meeting revival of 1857-1858 that spread across the northern tier of the United States and then inspired revivals in the British Isles and in far parts of the world and the ones that took place after the turn of the twentieth century served as bookends to a remarkable period of evangelical prominence, social activism, transoceanic contacts, international and regional missionary conferences, and growth in missions.[20] Newspapers and other channels of communication carried stories of revivals around the world; word of these happenings spurred believers in other places to pray for the same in their own localities.

The promotion of prayer in mission circles intensified as the century drew to a close. Believers petitioned God for renewal in the churches and the Pentecostal baptism for divine enablement for witnessing to non-Christians. Calls to prayer echoed back and forth across the continents. When revivals occurred, insiders invariably attributed them to the intercession of the faithful to the exclusion of other factors. Still, because of their local or regional dimensions, many considered them to be the "early showers" preceding the promised cloudburst of the Spirit's end-time outpouring. Thus, after an unusual revival in 1906 at the Dohnavur Mission in South India, Amy Carmichael felt obliged to admit, "We have not had Revival in anything like the full sense of the word, but in our own compound the change is very marked."[21] To others, like the crowds gathering at the Apostolic Faith Mission on Azusa Street in Los Angeles in the same year, something of a far greater magnitude had been launched, worldwide in scope and with all the exhilaration of eschatological fulfillment. But in general, the "Great Revival" came in a kaleidoscope of local revivals with some highlighted by spiritual gifts and in certain instances, speaking in tongues. The insistence that tongues-speech accompany Spirit baptism, however, distinguished the stream coming from Azusa Street.

A major revival stirred churches in Australia in 1902-1903, inspired by the preaching tour of the American evangelist R. A. Torrey, accompanied by the popular gospel singer Charles Alexander. "God's people were in earnest," wrote one in attendance, "the Holy Spirit was given His way and sway, and believers greeted each other with: 'The big revival has begun, Glory to God!'"[22] Expectations of an awakening had been building for some years: Four ministers had formed the "Band of Prayer" in 1889 and met every Saturday for eighteen years to pray two hours for the coming of the "Great Revival."[23] Two years later, the Keswick Convention in England authorized George Grubb and three others to travel abroad as "Keswick missionaries." Grubb subsequently held several weeks of fruitful meetings across Australia.[24] The success of Torrey and Alexander, however, eclipsed that of the Grubb campaign and brought visitors from nearby countries to see firsthand the events there. Two came from the Mukti Mission at Kedgaon in South India, missionary Minnie Abrams and Manoramabai, the daughter of Pandita Ramabai, to "catch the inspiration of the revival fire and form praying-bands for Mukti among the Australian Christians."[25] All of the subsequent revivals had such connections, facilitated through personal visits, newspaper accounts, letters, books written about them, or the translations of those books.

Coming on the heels of the events in Australia, the revival in Wales raised expectations even higher. Taking its cue from Joel 2:28 (AV), the Keswick Convention had inaugurated the "Upon All Flesh" prayer circle in 1902 for the worldwide outpouring of the Spirit. By sponsoring Keswick-like meetings and the Llandrindod Convention in Wales for the deepening of the spiritual life, it contributed to the revival that eventually came. "Upon All Flesh" circles soon flourished in England, North America, India, and elsewhere.[26] "Not mere revival in our churches," avowed Arthur Pierson, one of the circle's four secretaries, "but the Divine and gracious visitation of the millions outside all churches is what this prayer circle seeks."[27] For many like Pierson, prayer, spiritual awakenings, and missions comprised vital ingredients in the recipe for global evangelization.

Having begun in November 1904, the Welsh revival produced more than 35,000 conversions by the following January.[28] This surprising number in such a short period of time generated considerable publicity and attracted many visitors.[29] Ecstatic spiritual experiences in the meetings, reflecting cultural forms of expression, came in fervent and loud spontaneous prayers, intense "singing in the Spirit," personal testimonies, and prophecies.[30] "Is this the beginning of the latter rain?" queried Pierson.[31] Before long, renewal had spread throughout the Welsh diaspora, notably to the Welsh Calvinistic Methodist (Presbyterian) mission stations in northeast India.[32]

After several weeks of touring Wales, Pierson concluded, "It is with a loud, clear voice, rather than a 'murmur of stillness,' such as Elijah heard, that the Holy Spirit is now speaking to all the churches." The message appeared in peoples' confidence in the "Inspired Word of God": the "rationalistic and destructive 'criticism' that has, in our day, been lifting up its ax upon the carved work of the sanctuary, has left the temples of God in Wales almost untouched," an allusion to the increasing friction in denominational and mission circles over the trustworthiness and traditional interpretation of Scripture.[33] It also called attention to the sovereignty of God's divine operations—the revival had occurred in an unlikely place; demonstrated the potential of Spirit-filled local assemblies of believers; and revealed the power of united prayer and sacred song. The unusual supernatural activity of the Holy Spirit heightened the sense of direct spiritual guidance; this particularly impressed him and made the Welsh revival legendary. "There has been something akin to the revival of the *prophetic* Spirit—by which we mean that subtle *sensitiveness to spiritual impression*, often accompanied by marvelous insight into the real state of the hearers . . . even forecasting the course the Spirit would take and the results that would follow in conversion."[34] Another traveler, Joseph Smale, pastor of First Baptist Church in Los Angeles, California, returned home enthused to see the same kind of revival in his city; nineteen weeks of protracted meetings in his church in hope of a Wales-type revival forced his resignation, but influenced the coming of the Azusa Street revival.[35]

The revivals that arose after Wales shared the attributes of confession and repentance, in addition to other manifestations, all being stitched into the seams of an emerging global tapestry of charismatically inclined Christianity that would be apparent to all by the end of the twentieth century. Whether in India, China, Manchuria, Korea, Africa, or Madagascar, some or all of the following dynamics appeared or had been noticeable for some time: the modification and application of indigenous cultural patterns to Christian worship, increased initiative of native leaders, heightening of Christian unity, leveling effect among believers, reports of miracles and gifts of the Spirit (for example, the gift of prophecy in India), dreams and visions, motivation to evangelize non-Christians, and conflicting opinions about such happenings bubbling to the surface among missionaries.

THE INDIAN PENTECOST

The "Indian Pentecost" of 1905-1906 amply illustrates these dimensions.[36] Missionaries and Indian Christians paid close attention to the reports coming out of Wales and those of other revivals.[37] As in Wales, the ground had been prepared through calls to prayer and publications that promoted revival, in addition to the religious culture already in place.[38] When it came, the awakening transcended the normal boundaries separating Anglicans, Baptists, Congregationalists, Danish Lutherans, Methodists, Presbyterians, Quakers, Reformed, YMCA, YWCA, and independent faith missions. It also occurred among the Syrian Christians in Travancore.[39]

In March 1905, the earliest stirrings occurred in the Khassia Hills in the northeast (present-day Meghalaya) at the mission stations of the Calvinistic Methodists,[40] followed by events at the Mukti Mission in South India beginning on June 30. Within twelve months, over five thousand converts had been gained in the Khassia Hills. Before long, stories similar to those in Wales and from the earlier revivals in Tiruneveli and Travancore began to spread. Mission periodicals told of confessions of sin—the extraordinary public admittance of shame in South Asian cultures that place "saving face" on their list of foremost values, reconciliation, restoration of things stolen, visions and dreams, "prayer-storms" (hours spent in intense and often loud prayer), dancing, falling down caused by the Spirit's power, appearances of supernatural lights, confrontations with evil powers and exorcisms, repayment of debts, miraculous provisions of food, and conversions.[41]

Indigenous compositions of music marked the revivals, showing the depth of their impact: In the Khassia Hills, girls sang "The Heavenly Songs" and "The Angels' Hymns," while experiencing visions. "A girl in a state of trance sang a hymn which was jotted down in sol-fa by her brother, but he failed to get the words," according to one report. "When she came to consciousness she had no recollection of it. Some days after, in another trance, she sang the same hymn, and this time her brother caught the words as well. The people soon picked up the words and music, and it became a great favourite."[42]

"I was . . . greatly impressed by the way the missionaries have allowed the Spirit of God to lead them," wrote Calvinistic Methodist missionary J. Pengwern Jones, the best-known publicist of the Khasi revival. "All the missionaries would have condemned this frenzied joy a year ago. . . . *Dancing in the house of the Lord*, the idea would have been repugnant, but the Holy Spirit came, and took His own way of working." Perhaps most notably, "there was a willingness to follow 'the lead' of the Spirit."[43] In an article entitled "This Is That" (taken from Peter's sermon on the Day of Pentecost), he explained, "*This* that you read of today . . . is that which you have often read in the Acts of the Apostles. The similarity is striking."[44]

Still, missionaries felt relief when the "extraordinary phenomena" gave way to routine—albeit renewed—behavior in church life.[45] Some, like Anglican missionary H. D. Buswell, even questioned the need to pray for a fresh outpouring of the Spirit since the Holy Spirit had continued with an abiding presence in the church since the Day of Pentecost. Fortunately, "the Church, now, has a prestige, and a consequent influence for good which it had not when the miraculous gifts were bestowed; an influence which ought to be a more powerful factor in missionary work than signs such as followed the preaching of the Apostles."[46] But, as the well-known secretary for the Student Volunteer Movement and YMCA in India, Sherwood Eddy, explained: "Let us remember that every true Christian has the Spirit, but the Spirit has not full possession of every Christian. We may be 'born of the Spirit' and yet not be 'filled with the Spirit.'"[47] Missionaries themselves told of personal spiritual renewal on the path of "humiliation and confession" that Indian believers had trod. "The Lord has allowed us to pass through the same experiences as the Christians of this country," said a member of the Poona and Indian Village Mission, "so that we may fully sympathize with them and lead them on. At one time their loud crying and tears, their visions and prophesyings were to me the effect of excited nerves; but now I understand more what they mean since I have had to go the same road."[48]

Elsewhere revivals displayed similar phenomena: In Madagascar in late 1904, following several weeks of repentance and reconciliation, revival began and non-Christians came to the faith.[49] American Baptist missionary Carrie Putnam told of two thousand converts among the Karen people of Burma in 1905, with many of them Buddhists.[50] Confessions and repentance marked the Korean "Pyongyang Pentecost" of 1907 and transformed the Protestant churches.[51] In the Chinese and Manchurian revivals, much of the publicity went to the preaching of the Canadian Presbyterian missionary Jonathan Goforth, but other evangelists of renown in China included Dr. Y. S. Lee in central China,[52] and especially Ding Limei in Shandong province, their activities revealing the indigenous character of the movements.[53] At stations of the Rhenish Missionary Society in Borneo, native Christians took the lead in evangelism, resulting in significant growth in the churches.[54] Finally, the leveling effect in cultures that normally repressed the public role of women sometimes enfranchised them for ministry. "One of the peculiar features of the movement," reported the London Missionary Society about the revival in Madagascar, appeared in the ministry of the women: "They are most effective in speaking, praying, and visiting, and in the winning of souls."[55]

In view of the nature and the phenomena of these revivals, it becomes evident that not since the time of the ancient church had there been such a remarkable period of religious awakenings around the globe typified by "Pentecostal" phenomena. It also revealed how differently indigenous Christians and missionaries read their Bibles, particularly in their perception of the ongoing relevance of Jesus as a healer and exorcist. The idea that miracles had ceased with early Christianity had been grown among certain constituencies of Protestant Christians in the West; it was not native to the soils of the mission lands. Indeed, even in North America and Europe, grassroots piety embraced the continuing potential of supernatural interventions.[56] The worldviews of Majority World Christians—closer in important respects to the biblical period than that of the West—also prompted them to pray like their ancient counterparts.

With revivals came a greater indigenization of the faith, already apparent in the growth of self-supporting Presbyterian churches in the Punjab region of India before the dramatic events at the Sialkot Convention in 1905.[57] The conference report jubilantly announced that the impact of the revival had been felt "not only [in] this one district, but many others; not only our own Mission, but the whole Punjab, and, praise God, the whole of India, are being touched with the Pentecostal flame."[58] Such happenings continued for many years among the Presbyterians in the Punjab and led to the "Pentecostal controversy" of 1926 in which several missionaries resigned from the United Presbyterian Church.[59]

For Indian Christians, responsibility for leadership and evangelism increas-

ingly rested on their shoulders; to them, God had conferred dignity and power in
the Spirit's outpouring, not just on the "sons and daughters," but on the "male
and female servants" as well (Joel 2:28-29). This maturation contributed to the
establishment of the interdenominational and Indian-led National Missionary
Society (NMS) in 1905 during the first year of the awakening. Utilizing Pentecostal imagery, leaders issued an "Appeal to Indian Christians" to evangelize their
own nation, stating,

> After two hundred years of Protestant Missionary effort from foreign
> lands, are we not ready to take up our own burden, and live and die for
> our country? . . . The hour of India's opportunity has struck! We shall not
> fail our God in the day of His power.
>
> India is awakening. God is speaking to our age and to our land in the
> mighty reviving work of His Spirit. In Wales we have seen a nation well
> nigh reborn in a day. In Assam we have heard of His mighty power. In
> parts of Northern, Western and Southern India the revival has already
> begun. A revival of whom—and for what? The spirit of Pentecost is arous-
> ing the Church today, not for ecstatic emotions or pleasant feelings as an
> end in themselves, but in order to give service for the unsaved. . . .
>
> *Breathes there a man with soul so dead*
> *Who never to himself hath said,*
> *"This is my own, my native land"?*
>
> Yes, it is our own! . . . in the solemn obligation alike of ownership and
> of opportunity, of sacrifice and responsibility. It is ours! To win or lose; to
> save or to neglect.[60]

The manifesto underscores how Pentecostal concepts could roll from the interpretation of biblical texts into social and political aspirations without the blinking
of an eye. The Spirit's outpouring on the "male and female servants"—peoples
dominated politically, militarily, economically, and ecclesiastically by colonial
masters—signaled that the hour for indigenous leadership had arrived. The revival
helped prepare the churches for national independence, in part, through the raising up of their own leaders, the founding of the NMS, and the later National
Christian Council.[61] Similar effects of indigenization resulted from the revivals
in the Protestant churches of Korea during the Japanese occupation.[62] Hence, the
revivals of the first decade brought much more than spiritual renewal and passionate concern to evangelize non-Christians; the perception of the Spirit's liberating
presence among believers would have long-term and unexpected results.

THE LARGER SCENE IN MISSIONS

Despite the wide publicity given to the revivals, especially in church and mis-
sion-related periodicals, important sectors of the missionary force and mission
churches escaped their influence by choice. Though many evangelicals praised
their results, others remained skeptical, variously from objections to the Wesleyan-holiness and Keswick teachings about the Spirit-filled life that often char-

acterized them, the perceived overemphasis on experiential piety, and the physical "excesses" that occurred, to the attendant millennial speculation about the imminent return of Christ. "This kind of Revival is not consistent with genuine Lutheranism, with the truth of the Holy Scripture as we Lutherans have discerned it," declared Arthur Fehlberg of the Leipzig Evangelical Lutheran Mission in India. "The two only means of grace, Word and Sacraments, 'do not find their right place' in this kind of Revival." "Where [the human] will should be converted in the main," he frowned, "only the feelings are stirred up."[63] Protestant missionaries from traditions that historically had struggled to accept the experiential piety of revivalism shared these sentiments.

Not surprisingly, theological progressives also negatively assessed the revivals, influenced in part by their own declining interest in personal evangelism, dislike of premillennial eschatology, and distrust of emotional religion.[64] Heeding the insights of the nineteenth-century Congregationalist theologian Horace Bushnell, they preferred to consider salvation as a long process of spiritual nurturing instead of the revivalist appeal to "believe and be saved."[65] Without immediate eschatological anticipations, they worked for the long-term advancement of the kingdom of God over evil. "It is matter of experience that the battle begins as soon as there are Christians: ignorance, superstition, cruelty, and even uncleanliness, are recognized as enemies when men are living in Christ," wrote William Newton Clarke, the best-known advocate of the "New Theology." "In this view of missions the endeavor for social betterment takes its place among the natural and necessary endeavors of Christianity, which should be begun at once, and yet which wait for success upon the long operation of the great revolutionary force, the life of God in the soul of man."[66] Because the supernatural permeates the natural realm, "the Holy Spirit, Lord and giver of life, is at work with the truth that Christ reveals."[67] In light of this, contended Theodore Munger, "foreign missions are in the fullest accord with the type of Christianity now developing through science, humanity, and social ethics."[68]

At the turn of the twentieth century, the line between theological progressives such as American Board missionary Robert Hume of Ahmednagar, India, and evangelical missionaries remained sufficiently fuzzy to allow a measure of unity to prevail in the missionary communities.[69] Hume, who had been at the center of the "Andover controversy," did not deny the importance of preaching that Christ had died for the sins of humanity, but challenged such a narrow focus; instead, he pushed for the improvement of the cultures in which the converts lived: "The largest and most promising missionary activity is now considered to be the all round work of spiritual, mental, and physical betterment, because such three-fold comprehensive endeavor best brings men into that abundance of life which God through Jesus Christ desires to give them."[70] Many missionaries before World War I might have agreed with Hume on this point; a wedge between evangelism and social and educational involvement would have diminished the civilizing factor as a valid mission activity.

Gradually, growing respect in theologically progressive (liberal/modernist) circles for the non-Christian religions challenged the importance of traditional gospel preaching and added fuel to the fundamentalist/modernist controversy. "We shall some future time drop the name of 'Christianity' and just say religion, a *life with God*," wrote a contributor to *Dnyanodaya*, the newspaper published by the mission at Ahmednagar, who reflected the new outlook on the meaning of Christ. "The world needs religion, it needs that life with God. It needs Christ. To have religion it must have Christ."[71] Now with esteem for the world religions stamped on their passports, missionaries could most effectively serve in largely educational and humanitarian endeavors.[72]

In addition to the Haystack commemoration, bicentennials and centennials in the first decade included those of the (Anglican) Society for the Propagation of the Gospel in Foreign Parts ([SPG] 1701), Danish-Halle Mission (1705), British and Foreign Bible Society (1804), and the American Board of Commissioners for Foreign Missions (1810). Preaching at the great thanksgiving service for the SPG at St. Paul's Cathedral in London on June 15, 1901, American Bishop William Croswell Doane, looking to the future, remarked: "Centrifugal forces shall become centripetal, and the power that drives us out to the remotest edges shall draw us together to the center of a real union among ourselves."[73] In the nineteenth century, mission leaders had trumpeted the need for comity arrangements among agencies (division of territory for spheres of activity) and for uniting mission churches.[74] Conferences steadily advanced comity and agencies implemented such proposals until the Edinburgh Conference crowned them with a plan for the future. The hope for Christian unity had never been brighter.

The delegates at the China Centenary Missionary Conference, meeting for a whole month in Shanghai in the spring of 1907, reiterated their commitment to evangelical truths as they proposed new levels of cooperation and unity. The preamble to the resolutions on "Evangelistic Work" notably began with the statement:

> By the power of the living God alone can the grace and truth which came by Jesus Christ be adequately set before this great people to their salvation. Therefore, we, representing the great army of missionaries working in China, . . . do now with one accord implore almighty God for His own name's sake, to POUR OUT UPON US THE HOLY SPIRIT.[75]

Recognition of the Spirit's work in church and mission had not been so widespread and intense since the early Christian era, though with less agreement about its meaning.

Under this umbrella of prayer for the Spirit's blessing stood the spectrum of evangelical and the increasing number of theologically liberal missionaries, all part of the mission establishment in China.[76] Declaring that concord on essentials already existed, the conferees resolved to promote unification of the churches.[77] The various Presbyterian groups had already united, reflecting a trend among churches in South Africa, India, the Philippines, Korea, and Japan as well. Accordingly, this would solve the problem of competition, and hopefully before indigenous peoples remove the confusion about the number and varieties of the Protestant denominations, each one having championed the purest form of the faith. Like others at the conference whose optimism outran their discernment of the times, Harlan Beach, professor of missions at Yale Divinity School, applauded the achievement of the China Conference in forming a union organization, the Christian Federation of China, observing that the "prevailing atmosphere of prayer and brotherliness came off victorious." In his estimation, "the indigenous church has now before it a bright future."[78]

EDINBURGH 1910

Christianity witnessed its greatest advance to date in the nineteenth century. Missionaries from Europe and North America had evangelized, planted churches, taught school, translated the Scriptures, educated and assisted women in numerous ways, and operated charitable institutions for the hurting around the world. Untold numbers of Majority World Christians—both clergy and laity, women and men—extended the faith far beyond the range of missionary activities, though usually with limited recognition in mission publications. The 1900 mission census reported 3.6 million Protestant Christians in the mission lands.[79] Ten years later, the World Missionary Conference at Edinburgh, Scotland, would bring this dramatic age to a close with profound confidence as it strategized for the future growth of Christianity in the "Non-Christian World."[80]

Three other international conclaves had preceded Edinburgh: the Conference on Missions at Liverpool in 1860, Centenary Conference on the Protestant Missions of the World at London in 1888, and the Ecumenical Missionary Conference at New York City in 1900. Each one examined the church's self-understanding of mission and the methodologies to be employed. Coming on the eve of World War I and building on the work of its predecessors, Edinburgh went beyond their achievements to launch the modern ecumenical movement through its creation of the Continuation Committee to carry out the dream of united advance on an international scale.

The realization of the prayer of Jesus, "That all of them may be one, Father, just as you are in me and I am in you. May they also be in us so that the world may believe that you have sent me" (John 17:21), now seemed within reach. "The Holy Spirit seems to be impressing men everywhere with deeper convictions of the claims of our Lord Jesus Christ to our undivided loyalty, of the sin and weakness of schism, and of the necessity for union to enable the Church to fulfill her mission, and do her work both at home and abroad," reported the Commission on Co-operation and the Promotion of Unity.[81] For the delegates, the wind of the Spirit was blowing in the direction of Christian unity. In 1921, the Continuation Committee evolved into the International Missionary Council, an agency that forty years later would become a constituent part of the World Council of Churches.[82]

Edinburgh drew considerable interest among radical and other conservative evangelicals, but not without hesitations and even disappointments. "This gathering of missionary experts was a sign of the times in its evidence of the advance toward closer sympathy and more united effort among Christians in promoting the Kingdom of God on earth," wrote Pierson.[83] He applauded the stated goals and declarations: the evangelization of neglected areas of the world, training of native leaders to take the reins of leadership, loyalty to Christ as the only savior of humankind, the Scriptures as revealing the one true way to salvation, the necessity of distinctly Christian instruction in mission schools, the insistence that "Christian" governments in the mission lands not interfere with the progress of the gospel, and the strong desire for more cooperation among missionaries.[84]

At the same time, he and others fretted that the planners had gone too far in making compromises to include the High Church (Anglo-Catholic) Party of the Church of England with its strong leanings toward union with the Roman Catholic Church. Negotiations resulted in the exclusion at the conference of all deliberation of Protestant work among Roman Catholic, Eastern Orthodox, and Oriental Orthodox populations, and allowed for the expression of sympathetic opinions on the need for a warmer relationship with the Catholic Church. Thus, Bishop Charles Brent, the Protestant Episcopal bishop for the Philippines, could voice his hope that "we might be able to love Rome out of its self-satisfied isolation and the Greek Church out of its cold orthodoxy."[85] The agreement also promised the publication of Catholic mission statistics and gave a privileged voting position to the High Church on the Continuation Committee.[86]

Evangelicals found the interest of moving closer to the "Church of Rome" especially galling because of longstanding perceptions and misperceptions of Catholic Christianity dating back to the Protestant Reformation.[87] Most Protestants at the time viewed Roman Catholicism as a threat to the Protestant hegemony in England and North America; for their part, missionaries who confronted Catholicism saw it as a corruption of the Christian faith, functioning at a level barely above the heathen religions.[88]

Nevertheless, interest in the Holy Spirit had been mounting in the Catholic Church as well. On January 1, 1901, in St. Peter's Basilica in Rome, Pope Leo XIII had solemnly intoned the hymn "Come, Holy Ghost (Creator Blest)" in the name of the whole church, denoting renewed attention to the ministry of the Spirit, already evident in his earlier encyclical *Divinum Illud Munus* ("On the Holy Spirit" [1897]). Not done by happenstance, he pronounced this invocation on the first day of the new century at the urging of Elena Guerra, an obscure Italian religious sister, dubbed many years later as the "Apostle of the Holy Spirit" by Pope John XXIII.[89] When he opened the Second Vatican Council in 1962 and prayed for a "New Pentecost," little did he foresee that a Catholic charismatic renewal would arise and encompass over one hundred million of the faithful within forty years, adding strong new emphasis to evangelization and important elements to the inculturation of the local churches around the world.[90] On the pilgrimage of the "people of God"—the church—in the world, charismatic renewal would move alongside other movements, such as Focolare and the Neocatechumenal Way, all attributed to the inspiration of the Spirit.[91]

Though Pierson approved of the conference and what it achieved, Jonathan Goforth, fresh from the revival in China, left Edinburgh profoundly disappointed. He had arrived hoping for a "new Pentecost." Eager that the proceedings move beyond what he considered to be mundane issues, he envisioned it would prompt such a vigorous spiritual awakening that "the home churches, empowered by a mighty Holy Ghost Revival, would send out men fitted as were Paul and Barnabas. With their enormous resources in men and means the world would be evangelized in a generation." Yet, to his displeasure, "of the many who spoke to that great missionary gathering," he later recalled, "not more than three emphasized God the Holy Spirit as the one essential factor in world evangelization. Listening to the addresses . . . one could not but conclude that the giving of the Gospel to lost mankind was largely a matter of better organization, better equipment, more men and women."[92] "Was there ever such an incomparable opportunity for Christian leaders [?]" he asked with sadness. "Alas! It was only a dream."[93]

It remains unclear as to what exactly he anticipated would happen at the conference. Edinburgh in fact affirmed that the hope of taking the gospel to the non-Christian world could not rest principally on human initiatives, whether the resources of mission agencies, time-proven methods, efficiency of organizations, personnel involved, and success in fundraising, but ultimately "upon the Living God dominating, possessing, and using all these factors and influences."[94] Indeed, F. E. Marsh, from the Christian and Missionary Alliance, said that "underneath all [the deliberations] there was the recognition of the Holy Spirit as the Effective Worker."[95]

The conference also approved the study paper "The Superhuman Factor in Carrying the Gospel to All the Non-Christian World," which related the spiritual dynamics of the early church to modern missions. Only the "quickening powers of His Gospel can overthrow or transform systems of error rooted for thousands of years, and entwined with the laws, institutions, customs, and sentiments of peoples of ancient civilizations." Moreover, the record of modern missions revealed that the Spirit of God alone had the power to convict non-Christians of their sin and need of salvation.[96] It then speaks favorably of the recent revivals in China, including Goforth's ministry there, India, Korea, and Japan, as well as the continued need for prayer.[97] "Unless [Christian workers] surrender themselves to Christ and are controlled by His Spirit, unless they work in His power," the documents adds, "they had better turn from this service; for unyielded lives and unspiritual work will only be a hindrance to the enterprise."[98]

The authors, however, had not pinned their text onto the bulletin board of premillennialism. Although this document, as well as others, referred to the gravity of the hour, it failed to mention the need for Christians to receive the baptism in the Holy Spirit for pure living and empowerment in witness, so dear to the hearts of those influenced by the Holiness movement and Keswick. Consequently, it lacked the intense urgency about the soon return of Christ that characterized the concerns of radical evangelicals like Goforth, Pierson, A. J. Gordon, and A. B. Simpson. One eleven-page document focusing on the importance of the Holy Spirit found in nine books of conference papers probably spoke volumes to radical critics about the greater weight that had been placed on "pedestrian" matters. Still, their worry reflected the larger problem threatening the historic evangelical consensus of the missionary movement, namely, the continuing relevance of conversionary evangelism. The evangelical unity at Edinburgh, so highly praised at the time, would unravel in the years that followed.

PENTECOSTALISM

"In the year 1901 the latter rain began to fall in different parts of the world," trumpeted the *Missionary Manual*, published three decades later by the Foreign Missions Department of the Assemblies of God. Most importantly, the evangelistic zeal of "waiting, hungry-hearted people," who had been baptized in the Holy Spirit, signaled the resumption of "the Lord's Pentecostal missionary movement." Halted at the end of the first century when the Holy Spirit was "largely rejected and His position as leader usurped by men," Spirit-led missions then ceased and the Dark Ages commenced.[99] Now, in the remaining days of history, Pentecostals alone would carry the apostolic banner down the parade route of modern missions. Though Pentecostalism was distorted in its interpretation of history and larded with triumphalism, early leaders and missionaries resonated with such sentiments. In reality, this outlook—officially expressed by the largest Pentecostal mission agency—depicted the idealism, if not the isolation in which they found themselves. For them, the Spirit-filled church should resemble a missionary community at home and abroad for saving the lost, witnessing for Christ just days, weeks, or months before the call of the archangel.

Early Pentecostalism arose from the eschatological and missiological concerns raised by radical evangelicals in the nineteenth-century missionary movement. The direct relationship appeared in revivals from 1901 to 1908, after which the Pentecostal movement gradually developed in ways not originally envisioned by the earliest participants: the founding of mission agencies, theological divisions, creedal statements, denominations, church-related institutions of various kinds, alignment of most Pentecostals with conservative evangelicals, the rise of movements in the mission lands with wider screens for spiritual phenomena than tongues-speech, and the unabashedly holistic "progressive Pentecostalism" of a century later.[100]

The revival at Charles Parham's Bethel Bible School in Topeka, Kansas, in January 1901 placed theological and missiological stamps on Pentecostalism that have endured and created a movement that Catholic scholar Kilian McDonnell later described as "Classical Pentecostalism."[101] More than any other factor, including their stalwart belief in faith healing, speaking in tongues distinguished Pentecostals from their radical evangelical parents. In all other respects, with the exception of Oneness Pentecostals, who embraced a modal monarchian view of the Godhead, they bore the family resemblance: the Bible as the primary source of authority, belief in salvation by grace, Spirit baptism as an experience subsequent to conversion, premillennial eschatology, the faith life and faith healing, and distaste for higher biblical criticism and liberal theology.[102]

Surprisingly, between the years 1901 and 1905, Pentecostals did not travel beyond the shores of North America as missionaries, with one possible exception. A similar lapse in time had existed between the Haystack Prayer Meeting of 1806 and the founding of the American Board in 1810, indicating that other factors besides enthusiasm for missions sometimes had to be set in place before missionaries ventured abroad.[103] Yet, Parham maintained that the necessary languages could be "acquired in an hour" from the Holy Spirit and that "students are preparing now for the journey, though they have no visible means of support, and are confident that money will materialize."[104] Lack of finances, biting opposition, and discouragement likely derailed their plans. Further explanations might be that, for whatever reason, Parham himself—like Edward Irving before him—did not become a missionary and was distracted by other interests, such as organizing an expedition to the "Holy Land" to recover the lost Ark of the Covenant and his fascination with the Zionist movement.[105] Thus, he seems to have failed in taking concrete steps toward sending missionaries overseas. But why no one ventured abroad as did the later missionaries from the Azusa Street revival remains a mystery.

Even so, Pentecostals evangelized on the home turf, while adamantly telling of their preparation for missionary service if God called them and "opened the way" by providing the needed funds. Within a few years of the initial broadcast of his influential connection of glossolalia with Spirit baptism, Parham found the stage crowded with an entire cast of enterprising leaders. After all, in their estimation, "There is no man at the head of this movement. God Himself is speaking in the earth."[106]

North American Pentecostalism before 1906 grew from a cluster of early revivals, beginning with Topeka in 1901 and notably afterward in Galena, Kansas, and Houston, Texas. Parham and his followers, under the name "Apostolic Faith movement," focused on evangelism and held protracted meetings in many locations in a Midwestern corridor from Kansas to Texas, though newspapers publicized their activities well beyond the region.[107] During six weeks of meetings in Galena, crowds reaching up to 2,500 people came to hear him preach; hundreds of conversions followed, many told of physical healings, and others of speaking in tongues.[108] The results greatly encouraged him and caused a turnabout in the fortunes of the movement. With renewed confidence, he established in July 1905 a base of operations in Orchard, Texas, near Houston. There he led his followers in holding revival meetings and street meetings in white and black neighborhoods, the business district, and even in places of ill repute.[109] "These disciples, both men and women, made an invasion of the 'Red Light' district," according to a newspaper account published in August. "With banners flying . . . they visited several houses . . . and their conduct attracted a crowd of followers and listeners. It was the first work of the kind done here."[110] Women evangelists took the lead in these efforts. Pentecostals displayed zealous interest in the winning of lost souls to Christ, a priority demonstrating their rootedness in evangelical revivalism. In December 1905, Parham opened another Bible institute that enrolled, among others, the black holiness preacher William Seymour. A few weeks later, Seymour took the message of the Apostolic Faith to Los Angeles and became a major catalyst for the Azusa Street revival.[111] By the next summer, the movement had gathered approximately eight to ten thousand followers, mostly in the Midwest.[112]

Another movement grew in the upper Midwest where tongues-speech had occurred among certain Scandinavian pietist congregations dating back to the 1890s. Since they apparently had no contact with Parham's Apostolic Faith movement, to label them "Pentecostal" becomes problematic since they did not espouse his doctrine of evidential tongues for the Pentecostal baptism. While not "Classical Pentecostal" as the term would later be understood—wrapped with distinct theological, denominational, and cultural connotations—a "Pentecostal" spirituality thrived.[113] In November 1904, Mary Johnson of the Swedish Free Mission in Moorhead, Minnesota, testified to being baptized in the Spirit and speaking in tongues. With veteran missionary Ida Andersson, who would experience tongues several years later, she embarked for Durban, South Africa; they arrived in January 1905 to begin work among the Zulus.[114] Because she associated Spirit baptism with missionary service (and happened to speak in tongues), her actions reflected to a certain degree those of later Pentecostals who left Azusa Street and other revival centers for the mission lands. In this sense, Johnson may deserve the accolade as the first Euroamerican "Pentecostal" missionary of the twentieth century.[115]

Two months later, in Fergus Falls, Minnesota, during a revival conducted by evangelist Carl Hanson,[116] a newspaper stated that young people in attendance had "worked themselves into frenzies, rolling on the floor, trying to climb the walls and talking in strange languages, under the supposition that they have the gift of tongues." Shocked by their daughter's behavior at the meeting, the parents of Olga Nelson prevailed on the local authorities to confine her in the city jail for her own safety; however, she did not immediately improve, "but walks her cell, sings almost constantly and imagines she is going to Africa."[117] Perhaps the several days of incarceration and her parents' opposition kept this potential missionary from leaving the country. A number of Scandinavians like those at Fergus Falls who experienced tongues-speech eventually identified with the broader Apostolic Faith—later Pentecostal—movement that traced its lineage back to early revivals such as the Azusa Street revival and ultimately to Topeka.[118]

EARLY PENTECOSTAL MISSIONS, 1906-1908

The first issue of the *Apostolic Faith* newspaper, published by Clara Lum and William Seymour of the Apostolic Faith Mission on Azusa Street in Los Angeles, sounded the clarion call of Pentecostal fulfillment in September 1906 with the headline "Pentecost Has Come" and the byline "Los Angeles Being Visited by a Revival of Bible Salvation and Pentecost as Recorded in the Book of Acts."[119] With thousands of copies sent across North America and overseas, it appeared to some on the left wing of radical evangelicalism that the "Great Revival" had come at last, attended by the "Bible evidences"—"many being converted and sanctified and filled with the Holy Ghost, speaking in other tongues as they did on the day of Pentecost." Furthermore, the "real revival" had just begun since "God has been working with His children mostly, getting them through to Pentecost, and laying the foundation for a mighty wave of salvation among the unconverted."[120]

Word of these happenings found a ready response among seekers far and wide, facilitated by certain holiness periodicals and many new publications, especially the *Apostolic Faith*, in addition to the *Apostolic Faith* (Houston), *Cloud of Witnesses to Pentecost in India* (Mumbai), *Bridegroom's Messenger* (Atlanta), and *Confidence* (England). Personal visits to Azusa Street by hundreds of individuals who then left to share the news of the "latter rain" accelerated the expansion of the movement; notable among them: Bernt Berntsen (China),[121] Charles Mason

(Memphis),[122] Ivey Campbell (Ohio),[123] William Durham (Chicago),[124] Gaston Cashwell (North Carolina),[125] Abundio and Rosa Lopez (Southern California),[126] and Martin Ryan (Washington). Newspaper articles and letters also figured prominently.[127] When an early issue of the *Apostolic Faith* reached Pandita Ramabai's Mukti Mission in Kedgaon, India, in late 1906, it spurred Indian Christians and missionaries there to seek for tongues, even though reports of glossolalia already had begun to emerge toward the end of the "Indian Pentecost" in the summer of 1906.[128] Similar occurrences took place at mission stations of the Christian and Missionary Alliance in India and China.[129] In September, Parham took the message to John Alexander Dowie's former supporters in Zion City, Illinois, prompting another influential revival in which about two hundred had received Spirit baptism by June 1907 and from which thirty-five "missionaries" went out across the country and overseas within two years.[130]

More than the events at Topeka and Houston, the Azusa Street revival became the boulevard to the international progress of the movement.[131] "This Pentecostal Gospel has been spreading ever since [Topeka], but on the Pacific coast it has burst out in great power and is being carried from here over the world," declared the *Apostolic Faith*. The ripples flowed across North America, reaching Winnipeg, Chicago, Dunn (N.C.), Memphis and Cleveland (Tenn.), Nyack (N.Y.), and innumerable other places, to Europe and global destinations. It impacted existing holiness networks and created an astonishing number of new ones. Alfred Garr, the first to leave Azusa Street as a missionary, wrote from Calcutta: "Reports are coming in from all over the world about how people are speaking in tongues, even before they heard of the Los Angeles meeting. Word comes from Russia, Ontario . . . Eastern and Western United States, Burma, and India."[132] Though a product of Azusa Street, he perceived the Spirit's outpouring to be universal in magnitude without dependence on one particular place of origin.[133]

Like the revivals in Australia, Wales, India, and Korea, the Pentecostal revivals called for confession and repentance; but above all, they resounded with the charismatic dimension of tongues-speech, healing, and the gifts of the Spirit. Other concerns expressed by the faithful centered on the need for unity among the Spirit-baptized, and in some instances racial reconciliation, both marks of the Spirit's work according to New Testament writers.[134] Nevertheless, because Pentecostals heeded the direction of an otherworldly compass, the pursuit of unity inevitably became sidetracked, and concern for racial reconciliation waited until the last half of the twentieth century before attaining wider recognition and interest among important sectors of the movement.[135]

While some successes can be found in this period, Pentecostal missions to 1908 continually teetered on the brink of disaster. A band of thirteen people, notably including blacks and whites—illustrative of how the heat of revival could melt social barriers—left Azusa Street for New York City in the fall of 1906 to embark for Liberia as missionaries, though knowing of its reputation as the "white man's graveyard."[136] Still, "the Lord put His seal upon the departing of the missionaries for Africa," reported the *Apostolic Faith*.[137] In this respect, they resembled the Kansas-Sudan missionaries who had left for West Africa almost two decades earlier, fully confident of faith healing and that God would provide the necessary languages.

One in the party, George Batman, testified that God had given him six languages and instructed him to go to Monrovia. In a vision, "he showed me the town which is on the west coast. I described the town and country to Bro. Mead, [another member of the group and a veteran Methodist] missionary that had been there and he said it was a perfect description."[138] Unfortunately, within weeks, Batman and his wife, Daisy, and their three children and two co-workers died from disease.[139] While many missionaries had died from disease in West Africa, among them several of the Kansas-Sudan missionaries, to Pentecostals this group represented the potential of what Spirit-filled missionaries could achieve in the speedy evangelization of the world. Seven deaths and the relative failure of the party must have profoundly disappointed the faithful at Azusa Street; their doctrine of faith healing did not allow for medicine ("for unbelievers" only) and may have left them little recourse but to conclude that those who died, as well as their colleagues who lived, had lacked sufficient faith for their healing.[140] The *Apostolic Faith* never published the sad news. One of the missionaries, Lucy Farrow, returned home after seven months with the periodical reporting with perhaps misplaced triumph: "The Lord showed her when she went, the time she was to return and sent her the fare in time, brought her home safely, and used her in Virginia and in the South along the way."[141] In fact, Farrow was fortunate to have survived.

On the east coast, another disastrous venture began when five men and twelve young women of the "Holy Ghost Society" left Philadelphia in 1907 for New York City to board ship for London, influenced by Parham's revival in Zion City, possibly news of the Azusa Street revival, and possibly the teachings of Frank Sandford at the Shiloh community in Maine.[142] While staying at an African-American mission in the "Hell's Kitchen" neighborhood of Manhattan, police arrested the party led by Thomas O'Reilly, likely due to parental complaints.[143] No less a public figure than Anthony Comstock, secretary of the New York Society for the Suppression of Vice and dubbed the "Keeper of Public Morals," had intervened unsuccessfully on behalf of the parents of Mabel Collins, a young woman from Philadelphia, to secure her removal from the group. (Collins, however, refused to sign an affidavit attesting to her insanity, a move that prevented Comstock from having her committed to Bellevue Hospital.) When the magistrate at the Tombs Police Court released them, they knelt down in the corridor outside the courtroom and "offered up a brief prayer of thanks and short petitions for the Magistrate, the detective, the lawyers in the case, and for Mr. Comstock."[144] Identifying themselves with the disciples of old, they had suffered persecution for the sake of the gospel.

"We were members of the Holy Ghost sect and we had the gift of tongues and went out to teach the rest of the world the real Christ," Collins recalled. The party divided in London, where one of the leaders, "Mr. McElroy," heard the call to go to India; the others left for Argentina.[145] Traveling by faith, McElroy's party of six nearly starved in Calcutta before they ventured north to Benares, one of the holiest cities of Hinduism, located on the banks of the Ganges River.

Continuing to struggle because of their lack of money, two of the young women (from Zion City) left to marry Indians.[146] "They are now in harems and I can't blame them much," Collins bitterly remarked. "We did not have the real gift and life was far more terrible than I can tell you." Going farther north to Lucknow, "wild hill men . . . rode down and stopped at our camp" and kidnapped Mabel Charles. The remaining three (Collins, Lillie Thomas, and McElroy) then returned to Calcutta, from whence they somehow managed to sail to Buenos Aires to meet up with the others.

In Argentina, they encountered "even harder times," once more stranded without funds. One of the women, May Simes, died in the Pampas on the way to the city of Rosario, two others gained employment in factories, and three of the men ended up laying ties on a South American railroad for income. When her parents pawned "many of [their] household articles to raise the money to bring Mabel home," Collins made it back to Philadelphia disillusioned by the harrowing experience: "Our gift of tongues was not from God. It was from some devil." "Starting away from Philadelphia . . . a pretty girl of eighteen years," wrote an interviewer, "Miss Collins looks today like a woman of fifty."[147]

Others in the Philadelphia group felt called to China and left in June 1908 to walk across the United States—"preaching along the way"—to the West Coast and then board ship to their destination. When asked how they would pay for their food and lodging, they simply said, "God will attend to that."[148] After getting as far as Yeadon in Delaware County on the outskirts of Philadelphia, a fourteen-year-old girl in the group was arrested by police at the request of her father; two weeks in the "House of Detention" influenced her to remain at home. "All I wanted to do was to preach the gospel," she told the judge.[149] Whether any of the party reached the West Coast or China is unknown. Those who read the newspaper accounts or heard the stories of the Liberia missionaries and the East Coast missionaries certainly did not perceive such happenings as the auspicious beginning of a new golden age of missions, as the *Missionary Manual* of the Assemblies of God would later avow.

Happily, some groups fared better, as in the case of Martin Ryan and twenty members of his holiness church in Spokane, Washington, who envisioned evangelizing Japan, China, Korea, and the Philippines, as well as Holland, Norway, and Iceland.[150] The first (and only) contingent led by Ryan left Seattle in September 1907 for Japan and Hong Kong; another member of the congregation went to South America.[151] All maintained confidence in their new-found linguistic abilities and told family and friends they would never see the shores of America again before Christ returned.[152] Despite their frustration at not knowing the languages when they arrived, they persevered and their efforts bore lasting results, at least in Hong Kong and China, and to a very small extent in Japan.[153]

Others who attempted to go as missionaries either never left the country or their activities overseas have yet to be discovered. On the morning after Alice Caulson spoke in tongues at the Open Door Mission in Sioux City, Iowa, believers there interpreted the tongues and told her that "God had commanded [her] to go into the world." While telling the people at the Mission, "I have given up all the ties that have bound me to my other life," a mail carrier arrived with a letter for her that contained a "draft for a large amount [of money]." Caulson, a well-educated young woman who had come from a wealthy Illinois family to work at the Mission,[154] and "Miss Booker" "laughed and wept hysterically over the money." With God's provision—the reward for their faith and obedience— they presumably departed for the regions beyond.[155] At the Church of the Full Gospel in Denver, fifteen young men outfitted with the gift of tongues prepared to leave as missionaries—"Most of them understand no foreign language, but they will leave in the faith that this difficulty will be overcome through divine aid."[156] Clearly everyone who received Spirit baptism could be called by God to ministry and missions, whether black, white, Hispanic, male or female, rich or poor, old or young, it made no difference. Education, finances, language study, and other human resources aside, the Holy Spirit supernaturally would provide all the necessary means to help them bring closure to the Great Commission; it simply required the Pentecostal baptism and expectant faith. "If you are baptized with the Holy Ghost," advised the *Apostolic Faith*, "it will give you holy boldness to stand before the world without fear."[157]

In observing the mission endeavors of the Pentecostals, A. B. Simpson reported to the 1908 Alliance convention: "Without preparation, without proper leadership, and without any reasonable support, several of these parties have gone out to heathen lands only to find themselves stranded upon some foreign shore without the ability to speak any intelligible tongue, without the means of support, or even of return." Tragically, left to the charity of strangers, they had returned home after considerable difficulty, "disappointed, perplexed and heart-broken."[158] Among others, he likely had in mind the party that left Philadelphia, from which Mabel Collins may have been the only one to return home. While Simpson challenged the wisdom of such undertakings, he did not question the sincerity of the participants.

Less charitably, S. C. Todd, who worked with the Bible Missionary Society in Macau, discerned a satanic conspiracy in the activities of the Pentecostal Holiness missionary Thomas McIntosh, when he led a brief revival there.[159] His judgment also fell on Alfred Garr and the other Pentecostal missionaries in Hong Kong.[160] "To my mind there seems to be a dual movement—one from heaven, the other from hell," he suspected. "Not simply wrong doctrines and mistakes, but a real spirit of evil, personal demons, sweeping down upon God's children, marked as an angel of light—but who comes from the pit."[161] Yet, interestingly, McIntosh's ministry in Macau directly contributed to the later revival at the Alliance mission station in Wuzhu, China, in October 1907 where missionary Robert Jaffray reported: "I have never received such a spiritual uplift as when . . . I received this blessed Baptism and spoke in tongues."[162] Even so, fears of satanic "counterfeits" had been coiling across the evangelical movement for some time.[163]

Despite the problems and criticisms, bright spots appeared on the landscape with the efforts of certain individuals that brought long-term successes, even though some did not stay long enough to become permanent missionaries; among many others, these included John and Jennie Lake, Thomas Hezmalhalch, Charles and Emma Chawner, and Henry and Anna Turney in South

Africa;[164] Thomas and Annie McIntosh in Macau; Ansel and Henrietta Post in Egypt;[165] and Alfred and Lillian Garr, May Law, and Thomas Junk in Hong Kong.[166] Pentecostals also cheered when veteran missionaries joined their ranks: In India—Minnie Abrams (Methodist, independent), Susan Easton (Woman's Union Missionary Society),[167] George Berg (independent holiness), Max Wood Moorhead (Presbyterian, YMCA), Walter Norton (independent holiness), Kate Knight (CMA), Maud Orlebar and Agnes Hill (YWCA),[168] Christian and Violet Schoonmaker (CMA);[169] China—Harold and Josephine Baker (Disciples of Christ), Bernt and Magna Berntsen (independent Norwegian missionaries), Antoinette Moumau (Presbyterian), Nellie Clark [Bettex] (London Missionary Society); Argentina—Alice Wood (Friends, CMA), and more. The majority of veterans who received Spirit baptism with tongues served in India—sixty in number representing fifteen mission agencies; however, the majority remained within their organizations.[170]

THE WIND OF GOD

"We have depended too much on man, too little on God," confessed Presbyterian missionary John Nevius to the Shanghai Missionary Conference in 1890. "We have rested too much on human agencies and methods and too little on the direct power of the Holy Spirit."[171] Four years later at the Japan Missionary Conference, Barclay Buxton of the Church Missionary Society told the delegates: "The only hope for Japan is that the workers shall be filled with the Holy Ghost: so that their eyes shall see spiritual sights which others do not see, and their ears hear the crying of famishing hearts, till they feel as if they could go and do anything that sinners might be saved."[172] Nevius and Buxton had every right to be concerned; the Protestant churches in both countries represented only tiny percentages of the populations.[173] It seemed that only the renewing work of the Spirit could energize the churches, and the holiness and Keswick movements had done their part in sowing the seed.

At Edinburgh, the conferees did not risk jeopardizing their hard-won solidarity to give paramount attention to the revivalist agenda. Though not blind to the surge of interest in the Holy Spirit among missionaries and native Christian constituencies, they chose the safer—and in their minds the more strategic—objective of addressing the pressing problems of the Western missionary enterprise: cooperation, means of evangelism, recruitment, fundraising, education, literature, medical missions, the growing hostility of the non-Christian religions, and the pursuit of mission in socially and politically volatile contexts. The younger churches planted by the older mission boards also needed their encouragement. Missionaries and mission agencies could have ignored these concerns, but only at the peril of their long-range goals.

But far outside the corridors of the conference hall, reports of unusual happenings indicated that indigenous Christians did not measure the empowering acts of the Spirit by the Western yardstick of hesitation: The "apostles" in Madagascar were evangelizing and casting out demons; William Wadé Harris, who later trekked across Ivory Coast and Ghana in a remarkable preaching tour, was sitting in a Liberian prison cell where he would receive from the Angel Gabriel (during a trance visitation) an "anointing" of the Holy Spirit to evangelize as a "prophet of the last times";[174] thousands of converts joined the Batak Protestant Christian Church on the island of Nias (Indonesia) when people were "convulsively shaken" and confessed their sins;[175] and revivals continued in countries from China to Nyasaland (Malawi). Pentecostal missionaries—little more than an annoyance to other missionaries at the time—were traveling in ever-greater numbers to the mission lands with a spirituality that uniquely connected to the worldviews and needs of their hearers.

With these new advances stirred by the impact of Bible translations, interest in supernatural demonstrations of power, the teachings of radical evangelicalism, and the spiritual energy of revivals, observers wondered if all caution about the restoration of charismatic gifts and New Testament offices in the church had been cast aside. The fourteen hundred representatives at Edinburgh could not foresee the future magnitude of the Pentecostal revivals and the charismatically inclined Christian movements emerging in the Majority World. The younger mission churches, along with new and vigorous movements tagged by Pentecostal phenomena, would contribute to the gradual shift of the center of Christianity southward.[176]

"[God] gave the former rain moderately at Pentecost," declared Azusa Street's *Apostolic Faith* in its inaugural September 1906 edition, "and He is going to send upon us in these latter days the former ["early"] and latter rain. There are greater things to be done in these last days of the Holy Ghost."[177] Two months later, James Barton, on behalf of the American Board, sent a letter to its missionaries in India encouraging them to pray for the Spirit's outpouring. "The great aim of all our effort is to bring the nations of the earth into the Kingdom and make them know Jesus Christ as a personal redeemer and Lord," he wrote. While institutions and money had their values, "external means" such as these "must lamentably fail unless we have with us the presence and power of the Holy Spirit."[178] Notwithstanding the differing perceptions of the Azusa faithful and the officers of the American Board about what the outpouring would bring, history has shown that all those with fixed opinions on the acts of the Holy Spirit in God's mission in the world have eventually discovered—frequently to their dismay—that the "wind blows wherever it pleases" (John 3:8).

"In foreign missions the superhuman and divine character of Christianity appears clearly," wrote Swedish Lutheran Archbishop Nathan Söderblom to the International Missionary Council meeting at Jerusalem in 1928. "In the work of missions it is impossible to rely upon human calculations. Missions are the proof that God's foolishness is wiser than men (I Corinthians 1:25)."[179] Perhaps, but other Western observers uttered doubts about the supposed clarity of the Spirit's activities as they witnessed the appearance of ever more restorationist forms of the faith.

Part II

APOSTOLIC POWER AND MISSIONS

6

The Source of Missional Power

I do not question the reality of those who are manifesting this gift of tongues in Calcutta, but I feel they are in great danger, and if they yield to a trace of self it will mean satanic manifestations of the tongues, without their knowing the change of the source![1]

British author Jessie Penn-Lewis, 1907

It is sad beyond all expression, that God's children, who have been praying for years for an outpouring of the Holy Spirit upon all flesh, should now, when God is beginning to answer their prayer, be so hasty in judging and picking their fellow Christians to pieces.[2]

Indian Christian leader Pandita Ramabai, 1907

I have seen several preachers of various denominations and some missionaries baptized with the Holy Ghost, and the joy and glory of such an hour is indescribable. . . . How their hearts burn for the salvation of the lost, for the glory of Jesus and the purifying of His Church![3]

Norwegian Pentecostal pioneer Thomas Barratt, 1909

The . . . great need of our organized work is a tremendous revival which will bring the power of the Holy Spirit into our hearts. We have splendid machinery but not enough power for it.[4]

Chilean Methodist bishop Roberto Elphick (who had condemned the Pentecostal movement in his denomination) at the Panama Congress, 1916

The facts are that hundreds of the greatest soul-winners of the whole Christian era, without the gift of tongues, have had a much greater enduement of power and have been used to accomplish a much greater and deeper work than Mr. Parham.[5]

Evangelist F. F. Bosworth, 1918

"We wanted power from on high to help save the world," declared Charles Parham matter-of-factly to a newspaper reporter as he reviewed the events of the January 1901 revival at his Bethel Bible School in Topeka, Kansas. "We prayed for it; we received it."[6] It was all heady stuff for this little band of radical evangelicals, gaining the full restoration of the Spirit's power ahead of others who had sought unsuccessfully for the Pentecostal blessing or thought they already had it without speaking in tongues. More Pentecostal revivals came in the succeeding years, though the hope of heralding the Apostolic Faith around the globe took longer than initially expected.

Histories of Pentecostalism have recounted how early North American adherents anticipated preaching in their newfound languages until disappointing reports from missionaries trickled home.[7] In 1908, Alfred Garr wrote to the British periodical *Confidence* and announced to the Pentecostal world that he had "not seen any one who is able to preach to the natives in their own tongue with the languages given with the Holy Ghost."[8] But despite the disappointment, tongues remained central to their perception of Spirit baptism.[9] It has been assumed that with some embarrassment they returned to the New Testament to discover what it meant. However, careful scrutiny of published testimonies and other information about tongues-speech at home and abroad paints a different picture, namely, one of theological and spiritual continuity. In the early years, many Pentecostals saw the values of glossolalic utterances to include not only languages for preaching, but "prayer in the Spirit," revealing an embryonic entwining of deed and doxology that would long characterize Pentecostalism. They also recognized the importance of love in the Spirit-filled life, wrestled with questions that grew around the gift of interpretation, and identified their experiences as a modern-day continuation of the Acts narrative.

When the failure of tongues as a missio-linguistic tool became apparent, Pentecostals consequently retained their confidence in praying in tongues as the source of missional power, an approach both biblical and already familiar to them. Instead of this letdown traumatizing the self-understanding of the movement and blunting its growth, the fledgling diaspora of Pentecostal ministers and missionaries steadily increased decade after decade. Though the psychological and social factors of speaking in tongues and the theologies of important early leaders have been carefully explored,[10] we will examine the earliest Pentecostal descriptions of Spirit baptism and how they believed tongues empowered them. Finally, some questioned the ironclad requirement of speaking in tongues, a troublesome dispute given the ramifications for missional empowerment, but even so, the emphasis on tongues distinguished the movement from its beginning.

RECEPTION OF SPIRIT BAPTISM

Judging by their testimonies, Pentecostals knew that speaking in tongues—"prophesying" (preaching) according to Joel 2:28—afforded them the absolute certainty of Spirit baptism and the ability to miraculously communicate in unlearned languages.[11] Hence, at Topeka, Agnes Ozman claimed to receive

Chinese, Howard Stanley spoke the "language of the East Indians, the Hindoos," while others gained Turkish, Yiddish, Zulu, and many more.[12] Languages announced at the later Azusa Street revival in Los Angeles, which began in April 1906, included German, Italian, Japanese, Bengali, Chippewa, and Eskimo, among others.[13] Early Pentecostals often identified them by the familiar sounds of the utterance, by the testimony of hearers who said they recognized the language,[14] through the assistance of a vision of a foreign country when speaking in tongues, or direct confirmation from God.[15] Those not identified were simply "unknown tongues," as was the case with John Lake, who received his Spirit baptism at Zion City, Illinois, and later journeyed to South Africa as a missionary.[16] But in Alliance, Ohio, when critics decried the tongues-speech they heard at the Pentecostal camp meeting as gibberish and not resembling any known language, Levi Lupton insisted that "somewhere on earth are people who speak these tongues and [those] who receive the gift are bound to seek out the people speaking the language and carry the message from the Holy Ghost," though he offered no hints about how to begin the search.[17]

But tongues brought them much more than divinely given language proficiency. In British India, Max Wood Moorhead, a Presbyterian who served with the YMCA, marveled that in Spirit baptism, "God has brought one into the sphere of the supernatural, the sphere of the Holy Ghost who can now work in and through one's being much more effectually."[18] Another Presbyterian-turned-Pentecostal working in China, Alfred Street, known for his pamphlet *Intercessory Prayer Missionaries*, said it "brings into a man the entire range of workings of the Holy Spirit Himself who is thus ready to work in all His completeness all the nine [gifts]."[19] In the estimation of one Azusa participant, "It is a greater light than when you were sanctified. It is the full blessing of Christ."[20]

The dynamics included new levels of rapturous joy and love; control of the "unruly member"—the tongue (Jas 3:8-10);[21] heightened sensitivity to the promptings of the Holy Spirit in personal prayer, corporate worship, and ministry; invigorated boldness to witness for Christ; the facility to cast out demons;[22] and the "gateway" to the charismatic gifts (1 Cor 12:7-11). In fact, Parham claimed that he and his followers had "received all the gifts that Christ conferred upon His earliest disciples."[23] While holiness believers had similarly identified many of these features in their own encounters with the Spirit, what distinguished Pentecostals and also alienated them from their radical evangelical parents was the pivotal role of tongues in producing such enablement.[24]

Pentecostals combed the English language for metaphors to describe the blessing that came with languages they had never learned. "Great floods of laughter came into my heart," recalled Lilian Thistlethwaite when hands were laid on her at Bethel Bible School to receive Spirit baptism, "so I just let the praise come as it would in the new language given, with the floodgates of glory wide open."[25] Tom Anderson at Azusa Street felt the Holy Spirit "pulling the rope which rings the joybells of heaven in my heart."[26] Blanche Appleby told the Atlanta-based *Bridegroom's Messenger* that "the waves of glory that flowed through my soul were like the turbulent Niagara that flows over the precipice to the rocks beneath," leaving "a joy that remaineth, a power that does not yield to the flesh in the hour of temptation, and a heart, mind, and body dedicated to God, perfectly willing to go where He wants me to go."[27] Appleby later sailed for East Asia as a missionary and spent twenty-five years in China and the Philippines.[28]

With the impending close of history in view and wondering how the gospel could be preached "in the whole world as a testimony to all nations" (Matt 24:14), Parham and other Pentecostals had daringly looked at Acts 2 as the precedent for Spirit baptism and preaching in divinely bestowed languages.[29] In describing his own Spirit baptism, he said, "a glory fell over me . . . and I began to worship God in the Swedish tongue, which later changed to other languages and continued so until the morning."[30] "The Holy Ghost knows all the languages of the world," he told a Kansas City reporter, "and all we have to do is to yield ourselves wholly to God . . . and power will be given us so that we can have such control of our vocal chords, that we can enter any country on earth and talk and understand [the] language."[31]

Pentecostals could embrace the two components of language proficiency and prayer and worship in Spirit baptism because they read of the disciples "declaring the wonders of God" on the Day of Pentecost (Acts 2:11) and "praising God" in tongues in the home of Cornelius (Acts 10:46). It thus constituted Spirit-inspired speech as when Parham "began to *worship* God in the Swedish tongue." Paul's statement in 1 Corinthians 14:2 took on great importance: "For those who speak in a tongue do not speak to other people but to God. Indeed, no one understands them; they utter mysteries by the Spirit." It is here that the published testimonies—the voices of insiders, though lacking the precision of formal theological exposition—show that Pentecostals had discovered in Spirit baptism an avenue of joyful adoration in glossolalic utterance not restored extensively since the time of the ancient church. The charismatic dimension of spirituality then notably changed their perception of the Holy Spirit. No longer regarding the Third Person of the Trinity as an "influence or a blessing," Evangelist Carl Hanson now saw the Spirit "as a person, [who] took possession of His Temple, speaking in other tongues."[32]

Because the exceptional feature of tongues-speech as a missio-linguistic tool drove the notoriety of the new movement, the concomitant role of prayer and worship was obscured. Nevertheless, it steadily gained more attention. After hearing Parham preach at a meeting in Joplin, Missouri, people buzzed that tongues brought "not only a . . . crown of rejoicing to us who have received, but gives us power to witness for our Master."[33] In the summer of 1905, Parham's *Apostolic Faith* (Melrose, Kans.) newspaper announced that when the glossolalic utterances of the newly Spirit baptized were interpreted at the revival in Orchard, Texas, the meaning was "always in praise or supplication to God."[34]

Commenting on criticisms about unknown tongues at their meetings, as well as the intent of 1 Corinthians 14:2, Warren Carothers, a lieutenant of Parham, explained it even more forthrightly: "Tongues . . . are praises to God in language, peculiarly acceptable to Him for the reason that He forms the words, and there is abundant use for the tongue whether any man understands him or not, in fact the inevitable inference from St. Paul's statement is that it is not primarily intended that any man should understand the tongues."[35] Others shared a similar outlook: In early 1907 in Calcutta, when unable to preach in the language he claimed to have gotten at Azusa Street, Garr, who still believed he prayed in but could not preach in Bengali, retained belief in prayer and praise in tongues as the fountain of Pentecostal power. "Oh! the blessedness of His presence when those foreign words flow from the Spirit of God through one's soul, and then are delivered back to God in praise to Him or in edification to others or in prophecy."[36] In Wales, just a few months before Garr published his opinion, Catherine Price expressed the same idea, looking upon "these languages . . . as avenues or doors by which I was led in and out of heaven."[37] The spiritual ecstasy confirmed the reality of the restored doctrine of Spirit baptism.

Pentecostals also coupled Romans 8:26b-27 with tongues where Paul says: "We do not know what we ought to pray for, but the Spirit himself intercedes for us through wordless groans. And he who searches our hearts knows the mind of the Spirit, because the Spirit intercedes for God's people in accordance with the will of God." Lillian Garr professed a greater "burden on my heart for India's hungry souls. The Spirit has groaned through my soul for hungry ones until the pain was like travail."[38] Revealing the nexus of pneumatology, eschatology, and the urgent summons of the Great Commission in their thinking, Pentecostals identified such intercessory "prayer in the Spirit" as essential to the Lord's work.[39] Although periodicals continued to tell of its appearance as a "sign . . . for unbelievers" (1 Cor 14:22),[40] the hope of tongues as a gift of language for preaching had begun to diminish by 1908.[41] Yet, as late as 1912, the following story circulated on the wire services: "The gift of tongues has been acquired by a St. Louis teacher of art by three days of prayer and fasting; so she says. She has resigned her position in the Teachers' college to do missionary work among foreigners. It is to be hoped that the newly acquired languages can be understood as well as spoken."[42]

In a related development and in contrast to the notion that tongues always represented unlearned human languages, some began to identify tongues as the languages of angels (1 Cor 13:1), a phenomenon that also highlighted adoration. This surfaced as early as February 1904 in Audubon, Minnesota, where A. O. Morken described the tongues heard in revival meetings there as "Angel Language."[43] Three years later, Alfred Garr concluded that unknown tongues could be either recognizable languages or those of angels.[44] This helped resolve the problem of sounds that did not resemble the syllables of languages they had heard being spoken. In this event, only God could provide the meaning through bestowing the gift of interpretation; others present would not be able to recognize it. Alexander Boddy said that speaking in tongues "may be the tongue of men or of angels, or changing swiftly and unmistakably from language to language, until three or more languages have been used. Sometimes with interpretation—more often at first no interpretation. But it is Divine worship indeed."[45] The belief that tongues operated primarily for prayer meant that Spirit-inspired speakers were "setting forth the mysteries of God."[46] "It is like a message from heaven to your own spirit," said another, "and your spirit is edified though your understanding may be unfruitful."[47]

EMPOWERED THROUGH LOVE

Like their evangelical and holiness counterparts, Pentecostals understood love to be indispensable to Christian integrity and noted Paul's emphasis on it in relation to the Spirit-filled life (Gal 5:22; 1 Cor 13). Tongues-speech could not be separated from the core value of Christian love for their new-found view of Spirit baptism to be biblically valid. Therefore, pioneer evangelist Howard Goss considered love the "most necessary accompaniment which the Spirit freely confers."[48] Because the disciples "were all with one accord in one place" (Acts 2:1 [AV]) on the Day of Pentecost, Pentecostals took this to mean that love and unity had to prevail among them—the result of sanctification or consecration—in preparation for the Spirit's outpouring and their work in the vineyard of the Lord. At Topeka, "all moved in harmony" in spiritual expectancy,[49] and whether Methodists, Friends, "holiness," or independents, the students prayed collectively, though "only white persons [were] present at the first Pentecostal shower."[50] After their reception of tongues, they "began to sing together [with] each one singing in [their] own new language in perfect harmony," according to Thistlethwaite, symbolizing the supernatural concord of love among them.[51]

The solidarity lived beyond Topeka. A newspaper article on the 1903 revival in Galena, Kansas, expressed surprise that "[Parham's meetings have] brought about conditions that were never before witnessed in this section." In observing the audience, the writer commented on the leveling effect: "Here the man of prominence and position clasps hands with the uneducated son of toil or oft times with those who have a prison record back of them. Here women who have formerly lived for society and gaiety kneel beside some fallen sister and endeavors [*sic*] to point her heavenward and here the 'followers' receive what they term 'the Pentecost.'" The revival services were apparently open to all races, including Native Americans.[52]

At the same time, however, Pentecostals seldom gave quarter to opponents, or those they perceived to be enemies. Sometimes their rhetoric could be strident. On occasion, certain ones appeared to have a "gift" for alienating people, as when Parham publicly denounced other Christians in Galena as "'hypocrites,' 'Pharisees,' 'old dry bones,' 'selfish,' 'dishonest,' 'deceivers of the people,'" and then scornfully rendered the ultimate insult: "If Christ was to come to Galena, these ministers and members of the organized churches would join to put him to death."[53] In Calcutta, Garr managed to offend both the Anglican and Methodist establishments with his scoldings and contention that "there is no baptism of the Holy Spirit without the sign of speaking with tongues."[54] In Ohio—especially vulnerable to the divine wrath—Claude McKinney announced that the "Day of the Lord is at hand" and Akron would be destroyed by an earthquake because of local hostility, negative press coverage, and denunciations of the meetings at his church.[55] In the northwestern part of the state, Ralph Mackin and his wife, Seventh-Day Adventists who received Spirit baptism, were arrested and jailed for two weeks for "giving 'tongues demonstrations' on the streets" in Toledo and Clyde. Mrs. Mackin prophesied that a hurricane from Lake Erie would strike Toledo on September 30, 1908, and a "disaster" would overcome

Clyde on October 10.[56] For Pentecostals, there were no gray areas when it came to what they considered to be issues of eternal importance, be they membership in denominations that appeared to deny the power of the Holy Spirit or doubting God's willingness to spiritually enable contemporary Christians in the same way as he did for the disciples on the Day of Pentecost.[57] Even so, when answering the question, "What is the real evidence that a man or woman has received the baptism with the Holy Ghost?" a writer in the *Apostolic Faith* responded by saying, "Divine love . . . in their daily walk and conversation; and the outward manifestations; speaking in tongues and the signs following: casting out devils, laying hands on the sick and the sick being healed, and the love of God for souls increasing in their hearts."[58]

An early sign of gender equality and racial deference in ministry denoting confidence in the Spirit's outpouring highlighted the large Apostolic Faith convention in Houston in August 1906. In addition to other events, it offered a short-term ministerial training school; four of the ten instructors were women, including Millicent McClendon, who taught aspiring evangelists how to preach.[59] One of the other notable speakers at the convention was Lucy Farrow. "Although a Negro . . . [she] was received as a messenger of the Lord to us, even in the deep south of Texas," remembered Howard Goss.[60]

A more spectacular demonstration of mutual love and respect happened at Azusa Street, where one participant said, "the 'color line' was washed away in the blood,"[61] and another declared that "Pentecost means to live right in the 13th chapter of First Corinthians, which is the standard. . . . [It] makes us love Jesus more and love our brothers more. It brings us all into one common family."[62] The revival had begun when several African-Americans began speaking in tongues on April 9, 1906 at a private home on North Bonnie Brae Street in Los Angeles under the pastoral leadership of William Seymour. In a short time, they rented the former Stevens African Methodist Episcopal Church located on Azusa Street in the industrial part of the city, adopting the name Apostolic Faith Mission. As word of the events spread, the small African-American congregation welcomed increasing crowds of seekers to its services, a development that added a multi-racial and multi-cultural flavor as whites, Hispanics, and persons of other ethnic backgrounds attended.[63]

In another unusual display of unity, a wide swath of Pentecostals said that as the Spirit's "overcoming power" came upon them, they began singing in tongues, an occurrence that virtually video-streamed them into the adoration of the Lamb in heaven (Rev 19:6-9).[64] "Oh, it was like bursting clear through the earthly into the heavenly," hummed Kate Knight, serving with the Christian and Missionary Alliance in Bombay. "The music is all new and seems to transport my soul into the choir of the angels."[65] In nearby Kedgaon, Minnie Abrams sang a "hymn of praise to the Triune Jehovah in Hebrew, and she knows no Hebrew."[66] Someone else said, "The Lord drops down sweet anthems from the paradise of God, electrifying every heart," a marvel eliminating the need for song books and musical instruments since the "Holy Ghost plays the piano in all our hearts."[67] For "Brother Burke" in Anaheim a "music band of a thousand instruments was set up within me" that left him singing days afterward.[68] To Church of God in

Christ founder Charles Mason, "It was the sweetest thing to have [the Holy Spirit] sing through me."[69] But when the whole congregation sang in tongues, reported Susan Duncan on the revival in Rochester, New York, the immanent presence of the Spirit transformed them into a "heavenly choir" with its voice "sounding out like a great oratorio of angelic voices."[70] Frank Bartleman called this group experience at Azusa Street a "gift of God of high order," sovereignly bestowed by the Holy Spirit and bringing a "heavenly atmosphere, as though the angels themselves were present and joining with us."[71] Such an encounter was nothing less than one's spirit being ushered "into the throne room of God," insisted Alfred Street who received Spirit baptism in Chicago.[72]

At a Swiss Pentecostal meeting, an interpretation of tongues announced the "Spirit would sing." Immediately, a young woman (a soprano) began to sing in tongues shortly before another young woman (an alto) followed suit. "The blending of the two was like celestial music," penned Madame Seifer, "for the Holy Spirit was singing through them in a strange yet very soft and musical language," while the congregation listened in silence with rapt attention.[73] Though in this instance only two voices were heard, the audience participated in the theater of the event. The harmony that emanated by way of such happenings involved far more than music: it united Pentecostals together from many backgrounds, appeared to sweep them up into the eschatological worship of heaven—pulling back the curtain briefly to let them glimpse the divine love for humankind,[74] and thereby energized them to enlist in the mission of God. "We would have messages [in tongues] and interpretations and we would sing by the power of the Holy Ghost in the Heavenly Choir, and weep for a lost world," remembered William Booth-Clibborn about the early Pentecostal revivals in Germany.[75]

The bonding of Spirit baptism with the Christian world mission appeared as well in comments like the following from the pages of the *Apostolic Evangel*: "This baptism puts more love in us for God and His people and for the lost than anything that has ever come to this world."[76] Church of God founder Ambrose Tomlinson observed that Joel's prophecy indicated that believers would receive visions in the last days. He knew something of this himself because when he began speaking in tongues, a vision transported him to Central America to see the plight of the masses, resulting in a "paroxysm of suffering [that] came over me as I seemed to be in soul travail for their salvation." From there the vision took him to other countries as he spoke in their languages.[77] The Methodist Thomas Barratt of Oslo "could easily distinguish the different languages by the . . . difference in the sound of the words," as he saw the nations in his vision.[78] Barratt soon traveled across Europe and to India to promote the Pentecostal message. Minnie Draper, an associate of A. B. Simpson, also experienced a vision at Spirit baptism and "spoke of train men going through the [passenger] cars, saying, 'Last call for dinner,' and the Spirit was showing His children that now the last call is going out to the world."[79] Others viewed Christ suffering on the cross for the salvation of the world and were moved to action.[80]

The Pentecostal baptism with its component of languages inspired women and men to reach over ethnic and cultural barriers. "God makes no difference in nationality," said one Azusa enthusiast, "Ethiopians [African-Americans],

Chinese, Indians, Mexicans, and other nationalities worship together."[81] They also freely disclosed how the "fullness" of the Holy Spirit altered their attitudes. Carrie Judd Montgomery, a well-known advocate of faith healing living in California and a promoter of missions, told of gaining a "remarkable love" for the Chinese people, "something different—an outgoing of the Spirit in divine love toward them, an intercession which was wonderful."[82] In India, two women missionaries "came into such a measure of the joy of the Lord in their immersion in the Holy Ghost that their hearts overflowed in love and longing to have their native brothers and sisters in the adjoining district share the great blessing [of the baptism in the Holy Spirit]."[83]

Tasting the ideal of equality in Christ, however, both gratified and challenged the faithful. During the revival at the Alliance orphanage in Kaira (Gujarat State) in which missionaries and Indian Christians received Spirit baptism, Sarah Coxe remembered that "one little Indian girl was so happy after she was baptized that she laughed and laughed and finally went up to Mrs. Schoonmaker . . . and said: 'God loves me as well as He does you. I'm black, you're white, but He has given me the Baptism too.'"[84] The promise of God's conferral of spiritual gifts "also upon the servants and upon the handmaids" (Joel 2:29 [AV]) in places of social and political oppression explains in part why Pentecostalism has been so easily contextualized around the world.[85]

While the fledgling movement professed an idealized unity among the Spirit-baptized, autonomy reigned in Pentecostal revivals.[86] Assisted by their dogged activism and readiness to face human and even what they considered to be satanic opposition, the early Pentecostals persevered and growth often followed, though not uniformly.[87] When young women evangelists of the Mukti Mission (at Kedgaon in Maharashtra State) went out to preach in the villages, they stayed "unmoved and fearless by the power of the Holy Ghost," in spite of being "despised, evil spoke against [and] stones, dirt, and all manner of things thrown at them." Hearing the stories of what Jesus had done for these evangelists and what he could do for them, "the people are often wonder-struck and cannot understand by what power these girls can speak in such a way."[88] Such accounts reminded Pentecostals of first-century Christianity and affirmed the legitimacy of their endeavors.

THE GIFT OR THE GIVER?

After hearing reports about Pentecostal meetings or gleaning information directly from firsthand contact, bystanders grimly warned "of many instances where the alleged gift of tongues led the subjects and the audiences into the wildest excesses and were accompanied with voices and actions more closely resembling wild animals than rational beings, impressing all unprejudiced observers that it was the work of the devil." "Indeed," lamented Alliance founder A. B. Simpson, "the worst feature of the whole thing is the tendency to seek some special gift rather than the Giver Himself," though ironically certain of his oldest and most trusted colleagues would join the new movement.[89]

The charged atmosphere of Pentecostal meetings produced widely varied emotional responses, with nervous onlookers scandalized by the "emotional mania" and the "wildest [kind of] fanaticism."[90] To them, the "freedom in the Spirit" that Pentecostals trumpeted sounded more like the percussion of hysteria or the counterpoint of malevolent influence on human emotions. In Minnesota, Carl Hanson vigorously rejected allegations of hypnotic manipulation by declaring that regardless of the ecstasy of charismatic encounter, Pentecostals "know exactly what they are doing at all times."[91]

Pentecostals themselves wasted little time in condemning the shortcomings of those who erred in their thinking and conduct and were guilty of "excesses." "The devil plays football," growled Daniel Opperman, with offenders who "grieve the Holy Spirit" and forget that "Holy Ghost baptism was given that we might have power to witness for Jesus in a sinful world."[92] "If you get angry, or speak evil, or backbite," huffed one Pentecostal, "I care not how many tongues you may have, you have not the baptism with the Holy Spirit. You have lost your salvation."[93] In their minds, they had been raised up by God to evangelize the world in the end times; too much was at stake to tolerate the misdeeds of those who might betray the good testimony of the movement.

Nonetheless, the judgment pronounced by Simpson and others became a stereotype of Pentecostal seekers long used by their critics. That rational thinking and prescribed cultural decorum in worship should distinguish Christian behavior reflected a widespread conviction in the larger evangelical community, particularly with "satanic counterfeits" on the loose, such as Theosophy, Christian Science, and Spiritualism now threatening to undermine the spiritual security of believers. "God's work of grace is ever paralleled by another force energizing a contrary spirit," trembled Alliance writer Kenneth Mackenzie.[94] But the issue really centered on glossolalic utterances more than the emotional demonstrations in Pentecostal meetings, phenomena long seen on the trail of American revivalism, and their uncompromising stand that this manifestation had to occur at Spirit baptism for persons to consider themselves to be "Pentecostal" in the New Testament sense.[95] Those who scaled over the wall of respectable piety by engaging in what critics branded as the irrational act of tongues-speech would land in the devil's domain, not in some newly restored dimension of biblical spirituality.[96] Stories that Mormons spoke in tongues and demons did the same in exorcisms in China did little to sanction the Pentecostal cause.[97] Consequently, recognition that Pentecostals had waded farther than others into the charismatic currents of New Testament Christianity and the Christian spiritual tradition would not find acceptance for many years to come.[98]

Despite the accusations of their opponents, Pentecostals readily professed that Christ—the "Giver"—stood at the heart of their faith, disclosing their pedigree in the Christocentrism of the evangelical movement and refusal to condone spiritual claims that detracted from it.[99] Virtually all subscribed to the theme of the "Full Gospel" or "Fourfold Gospel," popular in holiness circles, albeit with their own distinctive view of Spirit baptism: Jesus Christ as Savior, Sanctifier (and/or Baptizer in the Holy Spirit), Healer, and Coming King. Hence, "The baptism with the Holy Ghost gives us power to testify to a risen, resurrected

Saviour," declared Seymour. "Our affections are in Jesus Christ, the Lamb of God that takes away the sin of the world."[100]

THE GIFT OF INTERPRETATION

Even as Pentecostals affirmed the twofold usage of speaking in tongues, they struggled with how the gift of interpretation worked.[101] Their quandary stemmed in part from distinguishing the perceived personal function of tongues in the Lukan literature (Acts 2:4; 10:46; 19:6), denoting that Spirit baptism had occurred and remained in the life of the seeker, from the Pauline requirement that a manifestation of the gift of tongues in a church service necessitated interpretation (1 Cor 14:13).[102] Questions naturally arose: Should the personal utterance of tongues be interpreted? Does the public use of the interpretive gift, expressed when people are gathered in worship, parallel the gift of prophecy in a way that makes their purposes virtually identical? The faithful generally answered "yes" to both questions. In England, the Anglican pastor and influential editor of *Confidence*, Alexander Boddy, explained: "Speaking in tongues when there is interpretation can be 'prophecy' ('forthtelling') and more. Peter on the Day of Pentecost says of the speaking in tongues: 'This is that,' quoting Joel, who said that they should 'prophesy' (Acts 11:17)."[103]

Pentecostals frequently heard interpretations of tongues. For example, in paying tribute to "some of the finest singers in the world baptized with the Holy Ghost" at Azusa Street, Seymour happily noted, "The Holy Spirit sings through [them] and some interpret right along while singing is going on."[104] But this was not the case everywhere: "I believe that the next thing that our Father is going to give us, is the gift to interpret," wished E. G. Murrah in a letter to the *Bridegroom's Messenger*.[105] In certain contexts, only one person received the gift of interpretation as happened at the Calcutta revival.[106] However, as Agnes Ozman contended, "This is the privilege of all who speak in tongues." God would generously allow anyone to have the interpretation of their own tongues or those of others,[107] a view in vogue in some quarters over a century later.[108]

The content of the interpretations varied from warnings of the soon return of Christ, common across the Pentecostal movement for many years;[109] to calls for sinners to repent;[110] to the reciting of "Scripture passages, praises to God, [and] exaltation of Christ";[111] to stringent calls for clean living;[112] and even personal direction for another individual.[113] Indeed, such reports "from all quarters" about "utterances of tongues . . . attended with interpretations full of the praises of Jesus and of the shed blood . . . precludes the assumption that they could be from the devil," avowed E. A. Spence with obvious relief in the *New Acts*.[114]

If they believed prospective missionaries had been miraculously equipped to preach in the native languages, Pentecostals also pondered how this phenomenon related to the growing number of Spirit-filled believers who did not travel overseas as missionaries and to their audiences in the homeland. In the period under study, and in light of their observation of the meaning of tongues in

Acts 2:11 and 10:46, the frequent hortatory nature of interpretations, and the close association of that gift with the gift of prophecy, many concluded that a preacher could speak in tongues before an audience and expect a Spirit-inspired interpretation to follow.

In her reflection on the Topeka revival, Lilian Thistlethwaite recalled that on one occasion during a sermon, Charles Parham began speaking in tongues at length. When he finished, a man stood and said, "I am healed of my infidelity; I have heard in my own tongue the 23rd Psalm that I learned at my mother's knee."[115] Parham justified this style of preaching on Paul's appeal to a prophecy of Isaiah: "For with stammering lips and another tongue will he speak to this people"(Isa 28:11; 1 Cor 14:21 [AV]).[116] Therefore, "God intends to use the speaking in other tongues in preaching to our people."[117]

In Houston, leaders and students of the Bible Training School founded by Parham and later reopened by his followers preached in tongues, conducted with the gift of interpretation as a "clearly supernatural 'sign to unbelievers.'"[118] "In such preaching the Spirit does not theorize, argue, or reason with men," according to the *Apostolic Faith* (Houston), "but simply announces with authority God's truth, and then commands or exhorts [sinners] to flee to Christ for refuge."[119] Evangelist Mabel Smith would "preach in tongues and interpret right along, all the way through the sermon," remembered one listener.[120] Proponents pointed to the marked success of this divine dictation in street meetings, gathering "vast throngs and held what would otherwise have been a mob, spellbound, as they, like the people on the day of Pentecost, heard the 'wonderful works of God.'"[121] These scenes were repeated twenty years later during a revival in China, though the young preachers who engaged in such "prophetic preaching" probably knew nothing about the events in Houston.[122]

After the decline of the Bible Training School in Houston, one of the leaders of the Apostolic Faith movement in the region, Daniel Opperman, conducted short-term Bible schools in various locations. Not just the means of "governing" the schools but the primary method of instruction rested on the use of tongues and interpretation. In December 1913, complaints prompted the leaders to persuade Opperman to discontinue the practice and operate on "Bible lines." A subsequent announcement stated: "We trust that the minds and hearts of the students will be filled with the word of God and then that both they and this truth shall be set on fire from heaven by the mighty power of the Holy Ghost."[123]

While this specific approach to preaching and teaching declined,[124] forms of it continued for many years with preachers occasionally interrupting their sermons with spontaneous expressions of tongues and interpretation or allowing others to do so. British leader Donald Gee remembered this occurring during sermons of Smith Wigglesworth, the first "world evangelist" of the movement, when he "would often become tangled in long, involved sentences. Then he would relieve the audience's perplexity by speaking angelically in tongues which he always interpreted himself. It was all part of the sermon."[125]

But with the line of demarcation between clergy and laity less pronounced in the earlier decades of Pentecostalism, especially when it came to participation of the latter in worship services, the sermon could be a shared production. In keeping with Paul's instruction in 1 Corinthians 14:26 ("When you come together, each of you has a hymn, or a word of instruction, a revelation, a tongue or an interpretation"), some maintained that "if anyone is speaking or delivering a message or preaching the gospel, and the Holy Spirit desires to reveal something by prompting someone to speak in tongues and someone to interpret the same, or to prophesy, giving light at that point in the message," wrote E. N. Bell, the first general superintendent of the Assemblies of God, "then this is scriptural, and it would be scriptural for the speaker of the regular message to stop for the promptings of the Holy Ghost to be brought forth."[126] Another author said that "when the Holy Spirit can work unhindered, the message in the tongue and its interpretation . . . becomes, and is, a part of the sermon being preached."[127] In one memorable instance at a General Assembly of the Church of God convened in Cleveland, Tennessee, four messages in tongues and interpretations interrupted the sermon of evangelist J. W. Buckalew. "This speaking forth in ecstasy was by no means unusual but was rather the expected nature of the services since glossolalia was prevalent, not only in the [General] Assemblies, but also in the local worship services," according to historian Charles Conn.[128] Although this practice could be found in wide sectors of Pentecostalism, it too decreased as worship and preaching became increasingly structured and manifestations of the vocal gifts (especially tongues, interpretation, and prophecy) became less prevalent.[129]

NEW WORLD OF REALITIES

Pentecostals consciously strove to model the spirituality of first-century Christians and hem their own experiences within the borders of Scripture, though the spiritual and missiological unity they shared did not hinder the surfacing of different perspectives on the linguistic nature of tongues, prayer in the Spirit, and the gift of interpretation. The early literature exhibits a more textured theology of Spirit baptism than previously acknowledged, focused not just on "doing," but on "being" as well. Even as first-century Christians received divine power to speak the "wonders of God" in "other tongues," Pentecostals believed prophetic speech as a charism would increase their Christlikeness through individual prayer and corporate worship. Precisely here in their vulnerability of stepping beyond the rational into the Christian mystical arena of speaking glossolalic utterances, they told of an augmented intuition in the spiritual currents of their hearts to obey the Spirit's promptings as God bestowed gifts for the building of his church, re-forming them into being "partners with the Holy Spirit."[130] "It is being in the Spirit," attested Alexander Boddy, "mightily under His control."[131] As one missionary to the Tibetans in the region of Darjeeling, India, put it, "*Now* we have the witness of things *seen* and *heard* and *known* in the spiritual world, that were utterly beyond our [range of vision] when we were content to walk without the Baptism of the Holy Ghost."[132]

After the students at Topeka had begun to sing together in tongues such familiar songs as "All Hail the Power of Jesus' Name," remembered Thistlethwaite, Parham entered the room and expressed surprise at what he saw and heard. Kneeling down, "he thanked God for the scene he was allowed to witness" and asked that should it be God's will that he "stand for the baptism of the Holy Spirit . . . to give him the Bible evidence."[133] Though Parham had previously heard tongues in the "Pentecostal-charged" atmosphere at Shiloh, Frank Sandford and his community had moved in a different direction and the gift faded.[134] Now with reception of the vocal utterance wrapped around the conferral of Spirit baptism, the last days actually had begun. The return of the apostolic power meant one could hear the "whirring" of the Clock of Time as it readied to strike the last hour; and with that, the presence of the Spirit apparent in the glossolalic singing and accompanying unity had lifted the students' consciousness into the celestial realm. There, above the cultures that have divided mortals since the dispersion at Babel, it seemed they could join in the victory song of the redeemed in heaven, while receiving their marching orders for the battle in the here and now. Hence, "it is a mistake to think that the outward signs . . . are the most important part," mused Alfred Street. "The real wonder is the *new world of realities in which we live . . .* the new possibilities that arise from our spirit being restored to its proper place under the guidance of the Holy Spirit."[135]

That Pentecostals had not arrived at this understanding of tongues-speech by themselves becomes evident in the writings of Simpson, who ironically criticized their insistence on tongues for Spirit baptism. Nonetheless, he believed the genuine gift of tongues could appear in the last days and said he knew of such instances.[136] In looking at the New Testament church, he found that the phenomenon "appears to have been a divine ecstasy, which lifted the soul above the ordinary modes and expressions of reason and utterance." Unwittingly in harmony with Street, Garr, Carothers, and other early Pentecostals who increasingly saw the focus of tongues as prayer in the Spirit, he wrote that "tongues appeared to overleap the mind altogether and find its expression in speech, quite unintelligible to the person himself and yet truly expressing the higher thought and feeling of the exalted spiritual state of the subject. It may be a human tongue, or it may be a heavenly tongue"; in any event, it served as a "channel of direct worship and adoration."[137] This interesting concord on the meaning of the experience demonstrates his restorationist approach to the study of the New Testament and marked another milestone on his long-time journey of reflection on the gift of tongues and its missional purpose.[138] All the same, Simpson's voice soon got lost in the chorus of condemnation, but his explanation became in fact what Pentecostals largely would come to believe about tongues.[139]

THUS SAITH THE LORD?

Without hesitation, Pentecostals professed that the breadth of the apostolic power had been made available to them through Spirit baptism. As George Taylor of the Pentecostal Holiness Church contended, it opened the way into the "full enjoyment of being the Bride of Christ" and all the gifts of the Holy

Spirit. It fills "the spirit and soul and body of the recipient, and completely envelops the entire being with power and glory."[140] Critics naturally asked how their insistence on tongues, obviously fundamental to their understanding of the experience, could lack an explicit "Thus saith the Lord" (a clear statement or command) in Scripture to establish it as a doctrine and, moreover, how they could explain the zeal and success of other Christians—past and present—who had not spoken in tongues?[141]

Like others who have sought for the restoration of New Testament Christianity, Pentecostals appealed to a precedent in Acts—in their case, to the stories of glossolalia, and then offered an interpretation of Christian history wherein their reception of this experience positioned them at the forefront of God's present activity in the world.[142] Luke the Evangelist had written, not just as a historian, but as a theologian through his emphasis on the actions of the Spirit in the empowerment of believers.[143] By turning to the narrative of the early church, Pentecostals followed the hermeneutical grid of their holiness and Keswick predecessors in explaining how Spirit baptism as portrayed among the disciples signified the fulfillment of Joel's prophecy.[144] That they looked to Luke as a theologian in his own right and refused to "subordinate" his writings to those of Paul—the usual approach in theological methodology—put them ahead of their time in the development of biblical interpretation in the twentieth century.[145]

From this vantage, Luke's recording of the "pattern" of Spirit baptisms with the accompaniment of tongues (Acts 2:4; 10:46; 19:6; and by two inferences to tongues: 8:15-17; 9:17-19), not only depicted the experience of the apostolic church, but established a spiritual and doctrinal norm. In effect, Pentecostals pressed the utility of the phenomenon farther than their holiness teachers, who interpreted the "tongues of fire" (Acts 2:3) as primarily for purification or consecration for Christian service, but which they recognized as languages for contemporary preaching in the mission lands and prayer in the Spirit. Since Peter had announced on the Day of Pentecost, "The promise [of Spirit baptism] is for you and your children and for all who are far off—for all whom the Lord our God will call" (Acts 2:39), this meant that all believers should receive glossolalia. Although not limiting the citation of biblical passages in support of this doctrine to Acts alone (for example, 1 Cor 14:4-5), their use of Acts for bonding Spirit baptism with tongues-speech proved to be indispensable. In later years, exegetical expositions became more sophisticated, with Pentecostal scholars placing greater attention on the theology of the Spirit in both the Gospel of Luke and Acts, and bringing more nuances to the understanding of the doctrine.[146] Dependence on Mark 16:17 ("they will speak in new tongues") as a supporting text notably declined among Pentecostal exegetes.[147]

The elevation of direct or probable implications of Scripture to the same level of authority as explicit declarations marked a departure from the interpretive procedure advocated by Lutheran and Reformed theologians since the sixteenth century.[148] "Each passage [of Scripture] must be interpreted in the light of the context in which it stands," wrote Lutheran theologian Henry Eyster Jacobs just a year before the Azusa Street revival. "The central and fixed point for the treatment of each doctrine is to be found in those parts of Holy Scripture which explicitly and fully discuss it . . . all incidental allusions in other texts are to be subordinated."[149] Jacobs and other conservative theologians in the historic churches, indebted to scholasticism for their methodology, obviously lived in a parish apart from the Pentecostals and other restorationist Christians who ardently championed the revival of neglected doctrines and practices.[150] But even with the guidelines offered by theologians for the proper study of the Bible, virtually all Christians—Protestants as well as Catholics and Orthodox— have buttressed certain beliefs on their discovery of patterns from the life of the ancient church. In the Majority World, Christians have not labored under the methodological burden of Western theology in their application of biblical insights, but instead have found direct relevance in much of what the Scriptures say and illustrate for their circumstances: real-life issues of poverty and hunger, demonic oppression, gender and racial discrimination, and state tyranny and oppression.[151]

Lutherans and Reformed churches called for the return of what they considered essential biblical truth and early Christian practice in the sixteenth century. Martin Luther claimed to recover the true meaning of the gospel through his espousal of the forensic nature of justification by faith.[152] In Zurich, Huldrych Zwingli disallowed the use of musical instruments in the liturgy and removed all forms of art work from the Great Minster church to restore primitive purity to the worship of the faithful.[153] In the Genevan churches, John Calvin established four orders of office (pastors, doctors [teachers], elders, deacons) which he maintained Christ had instituted to govern his church.[154] While the Reformers sustained these views from selected passages in Scripture, all three endorsed infant baptism, a custom not mentioned or illustrated anywhere in the New Testament, but partially supported by later tradition, appeal to the Old Testament covenant sign of male circumcision as precedent, that in the Bible God deals with families instead of individuals, and claims that accounts of "household baptisms" in Acts must surely imply the inclusion of infants (10:46-48; 16:15; 16:33).[155]

On the radical fringe of the Reformation, Anabaptists such as the Swiss Brethren and the Mennonites called for "believer's baptism" to replace infant baptism, along with other changes in the form of the church, to adhere more closely to the apostolic model. The followers of Jacob Hutter embraced communal living after the example of the Jerusalem church (Acts 2:44-45), though not called for or illustrated anywhere else in Acts or the New Testament.[156] More than a century later, evangelical revivalism, known as "pietism," began to spread among Lutheran and Reformed congregations in Germany. Prominent leaders such as Philipp Jakob Spener and August Hermann Francke addressed the meaning of regeneration in the life of the believer and reform in the church. By promoting the recovery of first-century spiritual dynamics, the movement naturally cultivated restorationist tendencies: varying appeals to paradigms of primitive Christianity that complemented instructions from the Gospels and Epistles.[157]

An important application of a pattern emerged in the pietistic Renewed Unitas Fratrum (Moravian Church) under the leadership of Nikolaus von Zinzendorf. At the Moravian "Pentecost" on August 13, 1727, participants were "baptized by the Holy Spirit Himself to one love" and "forged into an effective fellowship of faith and mission."[158] Afterward, they successfully implemented a revolutionary model of the church that diminished barriers between clergy and laity, allowing opportunities for everyone to minister.[159] In part through Moravian influence, revivalism arose in England through John and Charles Wesley and George Whitefield. Although they never left the Church of England, the Wesleys effectively evangelized the masses and organized Christians into small groups of "class meetings" for the enhancement of discipleship training, a practice reminiscent of the gatherings of early Christians (Acts 2:46).[160]

Restorationism also became a powerful force on the American scene, with each advocate professing some distinctive insight either in doctrine and/or rite dependent to some degree on a model found in Acts. "Re-discoveries" included the essential "order of salvation" in conversion (faith, repentance, confession, water baptism by immersion, forgiveness of sins, and the gift of the Holy Spirit) and weekly reception of the Lord's Supper in the "restoration movement" of Barton Stone and Thomas and Alexander Campbell; the Wesleyan-holiness teaching on entire sanctification; and various brands of church governance. To these could be added the faith healing promoted by Charles Cullis for whom "the treasures hidden in the word of God were more and more fully opened to his view."[161] Each one represented a unique return to a reputed feature of New Testament Christianity. Not surprisingly, restorationists of different stripes have sharply disagreed over what legitimately may be restored; for the Pentecostals, however, the issue ultimately settled on whether the Spirit's ministry changed after the Apostolic Age.

Pentecostals understood themselves to be the strategically placed last renewal movement before the coming of Christ, an assumption of self-importance shared by previous movements.[162] "Thousands have claimed the Baptism of the Holy Ghost for years," declared Taylor, "but now greater light has come, and it is clearly showing who have been honest and who are willing to sacrifice theory in order to go every step of the way."[163] Daniel Kerr, a pioneer figure in the Assemblies of God, offered a similar version of history after reviewing the contributions of Luther (justification), Wesley (sanctification), and Johann Christoph Blumhardt, Dorothea Trudel, and Simpson (healing): "During the past few years God has enabled us to discover and recover this wonderful truth concerning the Baptism in the Spirit as it was given at the beginning." Then, looking back on previous innovative movements through the centuries, he concluded: "We have all that the others got, and we have got this too. We see all they see, but they don't see what we see."[164] Applicable to Taylor's and Kerr's interpretation of history, missiologist Klaus Fiedler observes: "Revival leaders usually (and mistakenly) claim to teach nothing new, but only to revise what always was the teaching of the church." Hence, "they do not expect a new revival . . . to come after their own and, when it does come, they themselves or their successors are not usually happy about it."[165] As it turned out, Classical Pentecostals would feel keenly the threat of later renewal movements marked by charismatic phenomena.[166]

Notwithstanding the spiral staircase of past renewal movements and its handrail of doctrinal continuity, Pentecostals faced the awkwardness of explaining to critics why such luminaries as Jonathan Edwards, John Fletcher, Charles Finney, J. Hudson Taylor, and Dwight Moody could have accomplished so much for the gospel without having spoken in tongues. "How can you say that they did not have the Baptism of the Holy Ghost?" they demanded.[167] Taylor retorted, "No other man is my standard; I am building on the Word. When God gives light, I have no right to ask if others walked in it or are walking in it until I walk in it myself."[168] But the quarrel could not be so easily resolved since the underlying issue centered on how the work of the Holy Spirit differed in the lives of believers who spoke in tongues and those who did not, a theological question with which Pentecostal theologians still wrestle.[169] Finally, charges that Pentecostalism lacked "luminary" evangelists were premature, as subsequent events would show.[170]

Early Pentecostal beliefs about glossolalia reveal a consistently held role for adoration and prayerful intercession that enabled the faithful to withstand the impact of changes in their understanding of the experience, a spiritual phenomenon that represented the peak of the nineteenth-century radical evangelical quest for a deeper experience of the Holy Spirit.[171] Praying in the Spirit in the languages of the world glued their missional calling to personal fortitude. More than other explanations offered for the cause of glossolalic utterances—satanic counterfeit,[172] psychological dysfunction,[173] or the emotional distress of social dislocation[174]—this best explains why they were willing to forsake all and go to the regions beyond.

7

The Search for Order

The Apostolic Faith movement is not an organization or controlled by man in any way, but is under the direct control and supervision of the Holy Ghost.[1]

Editorial note in The Pentecost, 1908

While in Hong Kong, we found some dear Pentecostal missionaries, and had some blessed times of refreshing in meetings, which they were holding among the Chinese. Quite a number of Chinese people had received the Latter Rain outpouring of the Holy Spirit, and it was precious to come in touch with them in their simple faith and humility, and to realize that in the blessed outpourings of His Spirit, God is no respecter of persons.[2]

Pentecostal editor Carrie Judd Montgomery
after her tour in Asia and the Middle East, 1909

The vast majority of Pentecostal missionaries that went out on [the faith] line from 1907 to 1912 have proved failures, and their work is lost. I followed in their tracks, and found it so. Yea, I found some to be real destroyers of God's work in foreign fields. Still others I found to be frauds, deceiving the people in the homeland by misrepresentation in order to secure support.[3]

Pentecostal Holiness leader Joseph King
after his tour in Asia and the Middle East, 1910-1912

Often the Spirit would awaken her in the night, with the name of a worker in a distant land and cause her to mightily intercede until she prevailed. A burning love for souls in every heathen land possessed her and no personal sacrifice was too great in order to have more money to send to the foreign fields.[4]

From a eulogy at the funeral of Minnie Draper, 1921

"Our people are tired, sick, and ashamed of traveling, sight-seeing experimenting missionaries, who expect to make a trip around the world and come home," wrote an exasperated E. N. Bell, editor of the *Word and Witness*, published in Malvern, Arkansas. "We want missionaries who go out to live and die on foreign fields . . . to settle down to learn the language, to establish assemblies of saved people, to stay with these, teaching them and using them to reach their own people."[5] Did he have in mind Alfred and Lillian Garr, the first missionaries out of Azusa Street, who made several trips to India and Hong Kong and never stayed in either place for very long? Or Thomas and Annie McIntosh, the first Pentecostal missionaries to China, who spent only a few months in any one location and also ministered in Palestine?[6] He may also have been thinking about the peripatetic Martin Ryan, who led members of his congregation from Spokane, Washington, to Japan and China, and the itinerant missionary-evangelist Lucy Leatherman.[7] To farsighted Pentecostals, the "frequent traveling to and fro of missionaries" represented just one cause of concern about the health of their mission enterprise.[8]

By the time Bell penned these words, the impetuous nature of the earliest Pentecostal missions (1906-1908) had begun to give way to reasoned calls for stability, predictable means of support, and notably language study; some even considered organized missional structures for cooperation. Permanent residences and training converts increasingly appeared on the agenda. As we will explore in this chapter, these suggestions led to the formation of several agencies in North America that took their inspiration from the established faith missions such as the China Inland Mission, and especially the Christian and Missionary Alliance.[9] All the same, the women and men who connected to these agencies viewed themselves as independent faith missionaries working under the direct guidance of the Holy Spirit; affiliations provided camaraderie and wider contacts with like-minded believers, but little actual supervision.

NO COLLECTIONS TAKEN

"When Pentecostal lines are struck, Pentecostal giving commences," boasted the *Apostolic Faith* in explaining how the faithful at Azusa Street supported missionaries. "Hundred of dollars have been laid down for the sending of missionaries and thousands will be laid down. No collections are taken . . . no begging for money."[10] But large donations did not represent the norm. After the reading of a letter from Robert and Ida Evans, pioneer missionaries to the Bahamas, at the sixth General Assembly of the Church of God in Cleveland, Tennessee, in 1911, delegates prayed and received an offering for them, "amid tears and groans one after another came forward and laid their offering on the Bible till finally it was counted and found to amount to $21.05."[11] Still, the expectant faith of early Pentecostals inclined them to believe that one could freely do what God commanded without human interference, because he would always provide; after all, the "silver and gold are His own to carry on His own work."[12] However, in practice, as with other independent missionaries, this meant that only the hardiest of individuals survived, persons who could financially maintain their activities through writing letters to family, friends, supporting congregations, and editors of Pentecostal periodicals; withstand privation and disease in the mission lands; and endure rejection from other missionaries.[13]

Even so, the problems grew: "Is there no middle ground where the missionary will have full liberty to work as God leads, and an exercise for his faith, without being compelled to take a stand beyond that to which God has called him?" queried Anna Reiff, editor of the *Latter Rain Evangel*. "We feel the leaders of the Pentecostal Movement should realize the need of an effective systematic arrangement so that faithful, tried missionaries will not suffer for the common necessities of life."[14] Finding the "middle ground" in a movement where people prized individual directives from the Holy Spirit would not be easily—if ever— accomplished.

Before the organization of mission agencies, individuals either left on their own for the regions beyond, as in the case of Mabel Collins and the ill-fated party from Philadelphia, or went abroad through the encouragement of local churches and gatherings of believers at revival campaigns and camp meetings. These included the Apostolic Faith Mission on Azusa Street in Los Angeles,[15] Hebden Mission in Toronto,[16] North Avenue Mission in Chicago, and meetings in Dunn, North Carolina,[17] and Alliance, Ohio, among many others. Because William Durham's influence at North Avenue had extended into Chicago's ethnic mix, he gave his blessing to several individuals who traveled overseas and played major roles in the shaping of world Pentecostalism: Giacomo Lombardi left for Italy in 1908, Luigi Francescon to Argentina in 1909, Daniel Berg and Adolf Vingren to Brazil in 1910, and Andrew Urshan to Persia in 1914.[18] Durham also ordained Robert and Aimee Semple [McPherson], who went to Hong Kong in 1910 where they met Thomas McIntosh and the missionaries who had come with Ryan.[19]

Despite the celebration of missionary triumphs—variously by accounts of conversions, physical healings, exorcisms, and providential provisions—that continuously received coverage in Pentecostal periodicals, the turnover in personnel lessened the potential, reflecting a problem faced by Protestant missions in general.[20] The records remain too incomplete to know the exact number of Pentecostal missionaries or even all their names. The missionary roster of the Assemblies of God, an early Pentecostal denomination with the largest number of personnel serving abroad, showed dramatic instability in the years from the organization's founding in 1914 to 1921, presumably due to the tolls from death, disillusionment, lack of resources, sundry other factors, and perhaps anti-organizational sentiments.[21] Turnover appeared on a smaller scale with the personnel of the Pentecostal Holiness Church shrinking in number from about fifteen missionaries in 1913 to six in 1915, with many of those who left preferring to work independently.[22]

While editors mentioned and lamented the deaths of missionaries, they gave little if any notice to those who had given up and gone home in defeat. Missionary Fannie Van Dyck simply divided the early recruits into two camps: those who had genuine calls to missions and those who didn't. "Although some went with no special training in the Word, but were really filled with the Spirit, they have made good missionaries." Yet, "others went only because they were heard speaking in the language of a certain country, but having no definite call from the Lord have made shipwreck."[23] While the circumstances of turnover reveal more complexity than her assessment suggests, the discovery on the part of some that the gift of tongues had not enabled them to preach in the language of their hearers undoubtedly affected their morale.[24]

Apart from local supporters in the homeland, some of their most important friends sat in offices editing periodicals intended for readerships that stretched from a few hundred to thousands, publicizing their activities and forwarding donations their way. Clara Lum and William Seymour edited the *Apostolic Faith*, undoubtedly the publication with the largest circulation in the three years of its existence; E. N. Bell of the "Old Apostolic Faith movement" (formerly led by Charles Parham) published *Word and Witness* in Malvern, Arkansas; William Piper and later Anna Reiff produced *Latter Rain Evangel* from the Stone Church in Chicago. Other publications included *Word and Work,* edited by Samuel Otis of the Christian Workers Union in Framingham, Massachusetts; *Triumphs of Faith,* by Carrie Judd Montgomery in Oakland; *New Acts,* by Levi Lupton in Alliance, Ohio; *Bridegroom's Messenger,* by Gaston Cashwell and Elizabeth Sexton in Atlanta; *Apostolic Evangel,* by Joseph King in Falcon, North Carolina; *Church of God Evangel,* by Ambrose Tomlinson in Cleveland, Tennessee; *Apostolic Light,* by Martin Ryan in Spokane, Washington, and later in Japan; *Confidence,* by Alexander Boddy in England; and *Cloud of Witnesses to Pentecost in India,* by Max Wood Moorhead. These editors and many more created a broad sense of unity by linking Pentecostals together through supplying a steady stream of inspirational articles, testimonies, news stories, commentary, announcements, and letters from missionaries.

On another level, behind the emerging efforts to form Pentecostal agencies in the United States and Canada stand individuals who had been associated in one way or another with the Christian and Missionary Alliance: Alfred Ward, George Fisher, John Boddy, Carrie Judd Montgomery, Minnie Draper, Frank Casley, J. Roswell Flower, E. B. Nichols, Philip Wittich, and Etta Wurmser, to name just a few. They worked variously to establish and administer mission agencies, disburse funds, provide assistance to missionaries, or contribute to their educational preparation. Though largely forgotten today, all of them had been attracted to the Alliance. When they recognized the ambivalence in the organization over the importance of tongues-speech, they allied themselves with the Pentecostal movement, but did not alter their commitment to missions. In contrast to the attitude of many Pentecostals who had left or been forced out of their former churches and then touted their freedom from all ecclesiastical attachments, their experiences in the Alliance led them to retain confidence in the value of cooperative endeavors and formal training.[25] Two of them, Montgomery and Wurmser, kept one foot in each camp, reflecting the fluidity of boundaries among these radical evangelicals: for Montgomery, the Alliance and the Assemblies of God;[26] and for Wurmser, the Alliance and the National and International Pentecostal Missionary Union. In the African-American wing of the movement, John Houston, E. B. Nichols, and Henry Fisher brought the mission zeal of the Alliance into the United Holy Church of America.[27]

APOSTOLIC FAITH ASSOCIATION

The first known attempt by Pentecostals to establish a mission agency occurred in June 1907 at a camp meeting in Ohio, sponsored by the holiness-Quaker evangelist-turned Pentecostal, Levi Lupton. The conservative Ohio Yearly Meeting of Friends could hardly have been prepared for his meteoric rise as an evangelist among them and his penchant for controversy, for which he eventually rivaled John Alexander Dowie and Frank Sandford in getting negative press coverage. His adoption of Pentecostalism further aggravated the relationship.

Ordained a minister by the East Goshen Monthly Meeting (a local congregation) in northeast Ohio, he traveled as an evangelist on the revival circuit,[28] preaching salvation, faith healing, entire sanctification as a post-conversion experience of purification, along with the eschatological teachings of premillennialism. God had authorized his people, averred Lupton, "who have seen [the] deeper truths to spare no efforts to spread holiness over every civilized land and proclaim it throughout the world."[29]

Recognizing the need for a Friends' meeting house in the nearby city of Alliance, he conducted revival services there beginning on May 1, 1900 and established a permanent congregation. In the following summer, Lupton sponsored what became an annual holiness camp meeting. Later, he acquired twelve acres on the outer edge of the city and constructed a large, three-story, wood-framed building that housed the headquarters for his evangelistic ministry, a center he dubbed the "Missionary Home."[30] Eventually this accommodated a training school designed "to Scripturally teach and train laborers on radical, Apostolic lines . . . seeking under God to lead them into the deepest spiritual life and to the use of the best possible methods of work for the Master."[31]

Lupton and his associates wanted to press beyond the restraints of the Friends and expand their efforts into a broader international ministry, prompting them to organize the World Evangelization Company (WEC) in 1904 "expressly for the purpose of devising and using every possible means for the preaching of the full Gospel to every possible person it can by any means reach." Like other radical evangelicals disenchanted by the slow progress of the older mission boards, they believed the "commands and promises of the Great Head of the church" warranted its establishment.[32] WEC then commenced publication of the *New Acts*, a periodical named after Arthur Pierson's 1893 Duff Missionary Lectureship in Scotland in its published form, *The New Acts of the Apostles*.

In November 1904, Lupton and a party of six set out for Africa to open a mission station in Nigeria. The officers of the Damascus Quarterly Meeting (the district in which he ministered) took a dim view of the enterprise, stating, "We do not as a meeting see our way to endorse . . . an individual and independent work of the character and magnitude proposed."[33] Since the Ohio Yearly Meeting primarily supported mission work in China and India, Lupton may have felt he had no recourse but to skirt their disapproval. "He had little use for committees that came to criticize his work," observed his biographer. "Time after time these committees dealt with Lupton as an offender of the discipline of the Friends Church. These made little impression upon the new preacher ensconced behind [his determination to] 'Mind God.'"[34]

Traveling on the "faith principle" popularized by George Müller, the band of missionaries left Ohio with eight dollars in cash and the necessary railroad and steamship tickets.[35] They raised funds along the way from the United States to England and eventually to West Africa. "Faith opened the Red Sea before Israel, and closed it upon Pharaoh's host," lauded William Smith, Lupton's associate, when comparing their venture to those of the "heroes of faith" mentioned in Hebrews 11. "Who shall dare say what other exploits faith will not do yet, exercised by others of those for whom God has provided some better thing in order to perfect what He did in them by faith?"[36]

After settling the five other members of the group at a village on the Benue River in eastern Nigeria, Lupton and Smith returned to America confident that the work would carry on. As would be true of Lupton's other projects, the effort struggled due to poor planning, financial insecurity, and also illness in this case; the five returned home after little more than a year in Africa. However, before this happened, Smith had glowingly described the endeavor in *Chapters from the New Acts: An Account of the First Missionary Journey of the World Evangelization Company to Africa—1904-5.* For Lupton, the trip and the book put him in the limelight as an advocate of foreign missions and the director of a mission agency. Nonetheless, the severe financial condition of the World Evangelization Company and his other activities provoked the Quarterly Meeting to appoint an oversight committee to monitor the finances in the spring of 1906.[37] The *New Acts* ceased publication in October, the training school closed, and Lupton's dreams faded.

News of the outpouring of the Spirit at Azusa Street, however, breathed life back into his aspirations and introduced him to a new and vibrant movement. Lupton traveled to Akron, Ohio, in December 1906 to hear evangelist Ivey Campbell, recently from Los Angeles, preach at South Street Church, a "branch" of the Christian and Missionary Alliance, pastored by Claude McKinney, a former missionary to the Belgian Congo.[38] Impressed by what he heard and saw in the meetings, he returned to the Missionary Home and conducted prayer meetings for the Pentecostal baptism. "I began to speak in other tongues. The dear Lord had taken my jaws and vocal organs and moved them in His own peculiar manner, as witnessed by many of those who stood by," he said about his own experience on December 30. "I wish to have it well understood that I was not seeking the gift of tongues, but the gift of the Holy Ghost."[39] And adding to the drama of the occasion, his wife, Laura, noticed that "a halo lit upon his brow."[40]

Not having seen the halo themselves, the members of the Quarterly Meeting reacted quickly and dismissed him in February.[41] A month later, Edward Mott, the clerk of the Ohio Yearly Meeting, branded those who sought after the gift of tongues as "fanatics, deluded men and women who imagined the days of miracles not yet ended and that they could be endowed with supernatural power such as came upon those of old."[42] The influence of Lupton and the Pentecostal revival among the Ohio Friends, however, could not be so easily exorcised and played a crucial role in the growing division between "modernists" and conservatives in American Quakerism.[43]

With the assistance of McKinney and Campbell, he revived his annual camp meeting, this time renamed the "Pentecostal Camp Meeting" and scheduled it to meet in June 1907. It proved to be a roaring success, possibly the largest gathering of this nature for Pentecostals east of the Mississippi to date, attracting approximately six hundred to eight hundred persons from twenty-four states, and even a few from Canada, the West Indies, South America, and Australia,[44] assembling a virtual "who's who" of emerging leaders.[45] While Lupton served as the host and nominal leader, Frank Bartleman, fresh from the revival in Los Angeles arrived as one of the featured speakers and preached on "Jesus Christ, in World-wide Evangelism, in the Power of the Holy Ghost."[46] Reflecting the Quaker heritage of Lupton and his associates, as well as the leveling effect of early Pentecostalism, the ninety-five tents of the whites and blacks were intermingled and blacks participated in the services.[47]

The enthusiasm at the camp renewed the dream of the now-defunct World Evangelization Company. Denoting the intensified atmosphere of restorationism, a new mission agency—the Apostolic Faith Association (AFA)—came into being on June 25 with Lupton as director. In a vision, God commanded him to make the city of Alliance the world headquarters of the Pentecostal movement, the new "Zion"—a "Pentecostal city which would surpass Jerusalem in its greatest glory and would eclipse the Zion City founded by the late prophet [John] Alexander Dowie."[48] What's more, the AFA would "have charge" of it all. "It was an interdenominational association, and did not require one to sever his connection with the church to which he belonged," recalled Joseph King. "The prospect for a great work to be accomplished throughout the world seemed to be held out before this representative body."[49] The other officers included McKinney (first vice-president) from Akron, George Davis (secretary) from Pennsylvania, and Oscar Courtney (treasurer) from Beloit, Ohio; and board members George Fisher (Toronto), Bartleman (Los Angeles), William Elliott and L. C. Grant (Cleveland), and King (North Carolina).[50] One journalist said that leaders "commanded" the faithful at the camp "to sell their jewelry and give the proceeds and all the old gold and silver they have," limit their food intake to one meal a day, and wear inexpensive clothes in order to provide for the expenses of the missionaries.[51] Otherworldliness ruled the day, but not without an offering plate.

Other plans included the sponsorship of the missionary training school by the AFA and the editing of the recently revived *New Acts* by King.[52] For these left-wing radical evangelicals who thrived on independence, this signified a remarkable turn of events, demonstrating their practical nature in regard to the goal of world evangelization and also respect for the voices of those in attendance who valued cooperation: King from the Pentecostal Holiness Church, and McKinney, Fisher, Elliott, and Davis from the Alliance.

The selection of Lupton as director, however, did not occur without fireworks;

in fact, the AFA may have functionally imploded before the camp ended. In Lupton's vision, God had commissioned him to be the leader and conferred upon him the apostolic office, making him the "Apostle Levi," seemingly like Paul, an apostle "born out of due time" (1 Cor 15:8 [AV]). Trouble brewed immediately when McKinney and Bartleman next received visions designating them as the leaders. Whether the appointments of McKinney as vice-president and Bartleman to the board represented a compromise or not, the situation did not improve. "Angered by differences, a delegation of fifty abandoned the camp," according to a newspaper account. "The colony also is divided on doctrine, many asserting that the pentecostal blessing should be made the prime principle, instead of the gift of tongues." Further undercutting the plans for the AFA, "gifts of money and jewelry to Rev. Mr. Lupton have fallen off."[53] Competition for the top leadership post and a key theological difference over the necessity of tongues for Spirit baptism apparently figured more prominently in the failure of the agency than any anti-organizational sentiments that may have lingered on the grounds. Nevertheless, the 1907 Alliance camp meeting and its ensuing regional and global impact soon rivaled that of Azusa Street.

Once more, efforts progressed toward the formation of a mission agency at the next annual camp meeting; the faithful approved the following declaration, the first of its kind in North American Pentecostalism:

Pentecostal Manifesto

Evangelists, Pastors, and Workers present at the Pentecostal Camp Meeting held at Alliance, Ohio, June 1908, meeting in conference and prayer to consider means to mutually advance the work of God, send greeting:

Forasmuch as we have heard that *certain which went out from us have troubled you*, it seemed good to us, and we trust to the Holy Spirit, being assembled with one accord to write you after this manner.

(1) We believe that the formation of any ruling body would not meet the approval of God's baptized people, but that such an affiliation of Pentecostal Missions is desirable as will preserve and increase the tender sweet bond of love and fellowship now existing and guard against abuse of legitimate liberty.

(2) We would urge all those baptized with the Holy Spirit, who believe they are called to be missionaries, either at home or on the foreign field, *not to be hasty in going forth*, but to tarry until very clearly shown that it is the Lord's time; and that they seek such preparation, both in Bible study and practical work, enabling them to go forth with the necessary equipment, being thus prepared as much as possible.

(3) That *workers going out into the field should obtain from their home body papers of recognition and approval*, showing that like Peter and John, Paul and Barnabas, they have been sent out by the assembly. Acts 8:14; 13:1-4; 15:22-28.

(4) That Assemblies be exceedingly careful to lay hands suddenly on no man, but follow the example of the early church, as shown in the above passages; that no one be recognized as workers, but those who have shown themselves well grounded in the truth, in love and in doctrine, and to have received, at least in some measure, suitable gifts and equipment of the Spirit.

(5) Exercising great care and prudence, yet under necessity, to notify one another of those *travelling false apostles*, who are bringing such injury to the work of God. Rom. 16:17-18; 2 Cor. 11:13; 1 Tim. 1:18, 20; 1 Cor. 5:1-2; 2 Pet. 2:1-3; 1 John 4:1.[54]

The call for mature Christian workers—persons of doctrinal soundness, backed by the encouragement and support of their home congregations, and with levelheaded judgment about their calling as missionaries—would enable Pentecostals to distinguish them from others less responsible, especially the "travelling false apostles," and provide a certain measure of accountability. Characteristic of Pentecostal reasoning, this perceptive analysis of ills afflicting the mission enterprise denoted common sense at work within a spiritually charged atmosphere where "every person in [the] camp looks forward to the repetition of miracles recorded in the Bible."[55] The Missionary Training School in Alliance would do its part; students left for Africa and India beginning in 1908.[56] The instructors for the fall and winter terms included evangelist and later missionary Daniel Awrey; Lillian Denney from India; John Harrow, a former Methodist missionary from Liberia; Grace Davis; and "Miss Michener," a teacher formerly at the Missionary Training Institute at Nyack, New York.[57]

INTERIOR MISSION, LIBERIA

The nine missionaries of the Interior Mission, the first successful Pentecostal mission society, landed at Garraway, Liberia, on Christmas Day in December 1908, two years after an ill-fated missionary party had left Azusa Street for Monrovia. They described themselves as a "band of disciples of our Lord and Saviour Jesus Christ, who have been led by the Holy Spirit to sanctify their lives for the propagation of the Gospel among the native tribes in the interior regions of Liberia, West Africa."[58] Former Methodist missionaries, John Harrow, the superintendent, and John Perkins had been inspired by Bishop William Taylor. While home on furlough in 1907, they both received Spirit baptism during a Pentecostal revival in Toronto, probably at the Hebden Mission.[59] Resigning from the Methodist Board of Foreign Missions, they returned to Liberia, displaying the same reliance on personal faith and maverick inclination as Taylor.[60]

Nearly a decade later in 1916, thirty missionaries, mostly Canadians and Americans along with two from Scotland, served with the Interior Mission. "We represent Methodist, Presbyterian, Congregational, Baptist, Dunkard, Mennonite, Quakers, Pentecostal Holiness, Mission People and Gospel Workers," wrote Harrow. "So you see we are sort of a mixture, but no dispute has ever arisen in our ranks. We make the Bible the chief book, and strive to live simple Christian lives."[61] The diversity included the African-Americans Isaac and Martha Neeley, who stood equally with the other missionaries. The Mission appears to have been a field-based association of independent missionaries, though the details of its operation and whether a North American office existed remains unknown. The death toll from disease was staggering: twenty missionaries during the first decade.[62] Eventually, the work of the Interior Mission came under the auspices of the Pentecostal Assemblies of Canada and the Assemblies of God (U.S.A.), but interdenominational cooperation continued with other Pentecostal missionaries who entered the country.[63]

PENTECOSTAL MISSIONARY UNIONS

A broader endeavor originated in England in January 1909 at the urging of Cecil Polhill,[64] one of the famous "Cambridge Seven," and Alexander Boddy, editor of *Confidence* and Anglican rector of All Saints Church in Sunderland, the earliest site of Pentecostal activity in England.[65] Polhill fashioned the Pentecostal Missionary Union for Great Britain and Ireland (PMU) after J. Hudson Taylor's China Inland Mission of which he had been a missionary.[66] In the premier issue of the PMU's *Flames of Fire*, a magazine devoted entirely to mission, Polhill underlined Spirit baptism as an indispensable qualification for effective service, "so that not only your love, and all the Graces of the Spirit given you on conversion are quickened, developed, nourished, strengthened, gloriously fertilized; not only this *but* that over and above this you have received 'power for testimony.'"[67]

Even with the clear Pentecostal identification of the agency and shared aims in evangelization, it ironically differed in major ways from others that formed in its wake. While the PMU emphasized the role of faith in its operation, Polhill generously contributed to its expenses from his private fortune. With his upper-class background and training in a hierarchically based British Public School (Eton), as well as service in the British Army, he maintained an authoritarian control over the organization and its missionaries until it became the missionary arm of the newly formed Assemblies of God of Great Britain and Ireland in 1925.[68] "Are you willing to work in harmony with those who may be placed over you in the Lord should you be ultimately accepted for foreign service?" asked the application for candidates.[69] Attempting to curb the propensity of Pentecostal missionaries to be led too freely by the Spirit in the course of their work created friction within the ranks, and represented an anomalous policy among European Pentecostal mission efforts—usually driven by congregational church polity without bureaucratic structures—and those of North American agencies.[70] Nonetheless, the vision of the PMU inspired others to band together for cooperation in mission.

Five months after the founding of the British PMU, a camp meeting in Eastern Canada convened near Stouffville, Ontario, on June 10-20, 1909. Missionary evangelists Alfred and Lillian Garr gave reports of their activities in Hong Kong and India, and leaders took up an offering to cover their travel expenses back to India. One of the speakers, Alfred Ward, an evangelist in Western Canada and director of the Alliance mission in Winnipeg when he received Spirit baptism with tongues, took the occasion to press on the audience and the ministers the need to create a Pentecostal Missionary Union for Canada, following the precedent set in England.[71] In this, they received encouragement from an important visitor, Alexander Boddy, who had just begun his tour of Pentecostal centers in North America. George Fisher, a pastor in Toronto and sometime speaker at conventions of the Christian and Missionary Alliance, became the chairman, and Ward, the secretary.[72] The fledgling agency announced its intention to serve the movement by endeavoring "to cooperate in all possible ways with Pentecostal workers who may go to mission fields independently, or as representing local Pentecostal missions in Canada."[73]

Notwithstanding the good intentions, the organizers ultimately could not buck the reprimands from James and Ellen Hebden, the pioneer Pentecostal leaders in Ontario, who allowed "absolutely no room for incorporated Presbyteries, Boards, Synods or Pentecostal Missionary Unions."[74] "Rather than engage in a controversy, and thus endanger the spiritual state of this new Movement," recalled Ward in his memoirs, "we decided not to lay any stress upon the infant organization."[75] Whatever operations the PMU (Canada) may have put into effect, it ceased to exist within a year or two of its founding, marking the second failed effort in North America at forming a permanent agency, once more involving members of the Alliance.

In Ohio, the "Pentecostal Manifesto" had set the stage for the launching of a similar venture at Lupton's camp meeting on June 17-27, which overlapped with the gathering in Stouffville. The establishment of the British PMU had not only inspired the Canadian Pentecostals, but provided the paradigm for another namesake. An organizational meeting took place at the Missionary Home on June 23.[76] The presence of members or former members of the Alliance—John Boddy, William Gillies, George Fisher, S. A. Renicks, David McDowell, veteran missionaries George and Annie Murray (Palestine), and others—to help in the formation of a new agency marked the third such effort among Pentecostals in the Alliance.

"It was a remarkable scene as we gathered on that broad upper verandah," reflected Alexander Boddy, who had traveled from Stouffville to attend the meeting. "They all had their views on every point, too, and meant to speak them out. But the Lord beautifully ruled and over-ruled, and they were generously willing to be counseled a little by the Englishman who had come amongst them." In his estimation, they had done the right thing in organizing "for the purpose of sending out and helping and advising Pentecostal Missionaries in the dark places of Heathenism . . . the great need today."[77] Seven members were elected to the council with three of them forming an executive board (Lupton, John Boddy—a pastor from Pittsburgh—and an unnamed person). He observed an interesting balance in the top leadership: "The two who will most easily meet together are men of such different temperaments, one so quick and eager to act for the Master [Lupton], the other so careful and reserved [Boddy], both so blessedly welded into one in the Holy Ghost that we can indeed see the Master's Hand in the choice."[78]

Divine sanction came in the evening when the "Holy Ghost fell upon us, melting us into such tender, joyful unity, as some had never experienced before, and one could not keep back the tears as He, in Whom we were one, was worshipped and loved and adored." The council then spent the remaining days of the camp meeting examining fifty candidates who presented themselves for missionary service, a significant number (far more than in the British PMU) reflecting the missional vitality of early Pentecostalism and indicating their recognition of the need to connect with other Spirit-filled believers.[79] Among the candidates, eleven had pledged themselves for China, eleven for India, twenty for Africa, three for South America, two for the West Indies, one for Egypt, and two for Switzerland.[80] Still, some Pentecostals took a dim view of this development: "These self-appointed Popes and Archbishops, who would 'lord it over God's heritage' under the guise of protection, [should] vacate the offices which they have assumed and . . . lay aside the authority which they have arrogated to themselves," grumbled Harry Van Loon in the Los Angeles-based *Gospel Witness*.[81]

How many missionaries the PMU (U.S.A.) actually commissioned between 1909 and 1910 and the extent to which they received funds through the organization is unknown, as well as the number that studied at the Training School. Even though lacking oversight authority once they left the campground, it still commissioned people who then operated as independent missionaries. The agency maintained some level of contact, probably through correspondence and the circulation of the *New Acts*, with seventy-five Pentecostal missionaries; among them, veterans like Albert Norton and Minnie Abrams (India), and more recent recruits: Martin Ryan (Japan), Lillian Trasher (Egypt), Robert Massey (India), and May Law (China). Doubtless, these individuals viewed themselves as directly under the guidance of the Spirit; the PMU represented just one of the increasing formal and informal networks among Pentecostals, albeit an early one that braved the prevailing distrust of organization.

Lupton continued to travel extensively, speaking in Pentecostal circles and preaching at camp meetings and conventions.[82] In December 1910, the PMU unexpectedly collapsed with his admission of an extramarital affair; he was "gently, yet firmly deposed" from leadership by John Boddy.[83] For Lupton's associates, his dynamic leadership could not trump the requirement of conventional moral standards. But despite his failings, he had made more progress than any other North American Pentecostal toward convincing a noteworthy contingent of leaders that broad cooperation could help them achieve their shared objective of world evangelization; in this, he had received ready assistance from erstwhile members of the Alliance.

The annual camp meetings now under the direction of Boddy, John Float, and other former associates of Lupton flourished at Homestead Park in Pittsburgh in the years that followed.[84] Notable among those who attended the 1910 meeting were missionary George Brelsford (Egypt), who had received his missionary call at the Alliance camp meeting two years before, and the twenty-three-year-old Lillian Trasher, who would sail to Egypt four months later on a shoestring budget and found what would become a world-famous orphanage at Asyut.[85] A year later, the speakers included James Hebden from Toronto and missionary George Berg, with the crowds reaching three thousand in attendance.[86] The significance of the Alliance, Ohio, and Homestead meetings for the advancement of Pentecostalism in the Mideast and Northeast and for Pentecostal missions has yet to be fully explored.

PENTECOSTAL MISSION IN SOUTH AND CENTRAL AFRICA

In the same year, the efforts of four women members of the Christian and Missionary Alliance led to the founding of the Pentecostal Mission in South and Central Africa ("Pentecostal Mission"). The close friendships of Minnie Draper, Mrs. Alice Thompson, Mrs. Lewis B. Heath, and Mary Stone resulted in partnerships in mission: the Ossining Gospel Assembly in Ossining, New York; and Bethel Pentecostal Assembly, Bethel Bible Training School, and the Pentecostal Mission, all in Newark, New Jersey.

Draper, the best known among them, was born in Waquit, Massachusetts, in 1858 and grew up in Ossining, New York, a small community across the Hudson River not far from Nyack, where the family attended a local Presbyterian church. She never married and for a time supported herself and her mother through teaching. But when the strain of overwork broke her health, she lived as an invalid for nearly four years. Hearing about the doctrine of faith healing, she visited A. B. Simpson's Gospel Tabernacle in New York City where she received the anointing of oil and prayer for healing. She testified not only to a miraculous recovery, but said the Lord "definitely sanctified and anointed her with the Holy Ghost and power."[87] With Simpson's encouragement, she became an evangelist and assisted him at conventions held at Old Orchard Beach, Maine; Rocky Springs Park in Pennsylvania; New York City; and elsewhere.[88] Draper also worked in the ministry of healing with Sarah Lindenberger at Berachah Home and served on the board of Wilson Memorial Academy, both located in Nyack. Her range of activities extended northward to Shiloh, Maine, where for a short time she spoke at conferences sponsored by Frank Sandford, whose wife, Helen [Kinney], and her family hailed from Ossining.[89]

With her assistance, a small group of believers started an Alliance branch in Ossining. "The work was sealed by the instantaneous healing, in answer to prayer, of a very sick woman who had been in great agony for three days," she reported in her capacity as secretary. In addition, "a missionary spirit is rapidly growing in this little band of twenty-one, who have pledged $300 for the support of a missionary for the year 1894."[90] Mary Stone, a daughter of Sumner Stone, a wealthy banker who lived in Ossining with substantial property holdings, became a benefactor to the church. A Methodist, she also served as an officer of the interdenominational Woman's Union Missionary Society founded by Sarah Doremus in New York City in 1861, the first foreign mission society in America established and operated solely by women.[91] In another important development, Alice Thompson, a member of the Gospel Tabernacle in New York City, founded the branch in Newark, New Jersey, in 1907, with Draper giving her the first ten dollars as a "token from God toward its support."[92]

Beginning in 1906, tensions arose in the Alliance over speaking in tongues, particularly over the insistence of some that it had to accompany Spirit baptism; ultimately the conflict would lead to the formation of the Pentecostal Mission.[93] Like others who sought for a greater dimension of the Spirit's power in their lives, Draper viewed with cautious interest the news of the Azusa Street revival. Before long, however, she told of the Lord appearing to her in a vision in which "hours elapsed wherein she saw unutterable things and when she finally came to herself she heard her tongue talking fluently in a language she had never learned."[94] As it happened, negative sentiments in the Alliance marginalized her and the Pentecostals therein who avowed the necessity of tongues for the Spirit-filled life.[95] Though an increasing number of them chose to exit, she stayed until submitting her resignation in 1912.[96]

Both the Ossining and Newark branches experienced Pentecostal revivals beginning in 1907; the majorities of members later left to found independent congregations.[97] Those in Ossining established the Ossining Gospel Assembly in 1913 with Draper, Stone, and Christian Lucas, the first pastor, among the charter members. Before long, the congregation erected a church on land donated by the Stone family. Next door they built a hostel for visiting missionaries, underwritten by an original endowment of $75,000 through the generosity of Mary Stone.[98]

While the exact chronology of events in Newark remains fuzzy, Thompson, who retained her membership in the Alliance, died in 1910 while pastoring the independent Bethel Pentecostal Assembly, started in the preceding year.[99] The leadership of the church then passed to Draper (she did not serve as pastor), though she resided in Ossining and served on the church board there.[100] The Newark church incorporated in 1910 under the name Executive Council of the Bethel Pentecostal Assembly, Inc., with the Pentecostal Mission fitting beneath this legal canopy. The next year, Allan Swift, who had just finished his studies at Nyack, became the first full-time pastor.[101] With Draper's board membership at Ossining and tenure as board chair in Newark, the two congregations naturally cooperated. The Council's mission statement provided a worldwide vision for the congregation by its plan "to maintain and conduct a general evangelistic work in the State of New Jersey, in all other states of the United States and any and all foreign countries."[102]

The Pentecostal Mission possessed several unique features: the sponsorship of a local church (famous for the largest offerings taken for missions in the Pentecostal movement—sometimes seven to eight thousand dollars in a single offering) and its own training institution—the Bethel Bible Training School, established in 1916. [103] It also enjoyed the patronage of wealthy Pentecostals on the executive council (Stone, Joseph Potter, Mr. and Mrs. Lewis B. Heath, and Mrs. William R. Schoenborn), who invested the mission endowment on the stock market to generate more income. As a structured agency, it maintained a field office and superintendent in South Africa and produced the first known periodical among North American Pentecostals devoted exclusively to missions, the *South and Central African Pentecostal Herald* (later *Full Gospel Missionary Herald*).[104] With obvious parallels to Alliance institutions, one might conclude that the Pentecostals at Ossining and Newark ranked among Simpson's best students.

Sending its missionaries primarily to South Africa, the Pentecostal Mission also supported personnel in China, India, and South America.[105] The "Central Africa" portion of the name allowed the British Pentecostal William Burton to legally enter the Belgian Congo as its representative several years before he and James Salter founded the Congo Evangelistic Mission (1919).[106] By 1925, the Pentecostal Mission had an operating budget of $30,150 derived from offerings and interest from the trust fund, making it second only to the General Council of the Assemblies of God in sponsoring, financing, and directing overseas evangelism.[107] The agency later suffered a devastating blow with the loss of its endowment in the stock market crash of 1929; many of its missionary personnel, already affiliated with the Assemblies of God (U.S.A.), chose to work with its mission board.[108] These early missionaries forged enduring legacies in South Africa, embodied today in the Full Gospel Church of God and the Assemblies of God (S.A.).[109]

UNITED FREE GOSPEL AND MISSIONARY SOCIETY

Western Pennsylvania became a hotbed of Pentecostal revival in the Alliance after 1906.[110] As a result, defections climbed as resistance grew. One leader in the Pittsburgh suburb of Turtle Creek, Frank Casley, encouraged several branches under his influence to exit the organization and form the United Free Gospel and Missionary Society in 1916 (now Free Gospel Missions). A native of England, he had founded the Union Gospel Mission at Turtle Creek.[111] His ministry first appears in the *Christian and Missionary Alliance Witness* in 1902 after holding "large and successful tent meetings" at nearby McKeesport.[112]

With the coming of Pentecostalism, Casley and his brother William openly insisted on tongues as an evidence of Spirit baptism in their preaching, despite the position of Alliance leaders that allowed for the gift of tongues, but not as a requirement.[113] Rather than joining the Assemblies of God as John Boddy and David McDowell had done, Casley and his associates founded a new mission agency "to preach the gospel at home and abroad."[114] Within ten years, its missionaries worked in China, Philippines, India, and Guatemala.

BEZALEEL EVANGELISTIC MISSION

Early Pentecostalism had two missionaries, both veterans, already known to the wider missionary community: Cecil Polhill (1860-1938), formerly of the China Inland Mission, and Minnie Abrams (1859-1912), sometime Methodist missionary who served on the staff of Pandita Ramabai's famous Mukti Mission at Kedgaon, about one hundred miles southeast of Bombay. With Polhill's place in history already secured in his lifetime through having been a member of the renowned Cambridge Seven, his identification with the Pentecostal movement proved embarrassing to evangelicals.[115] Abrams preceded him in death by twenty-six years and had an impact on the course of world Pentecostalism, the promotion of women in preaching ministry, and in evangelizing non-Christian peoples.[116] When she died, major mission periodicals eulogized her contributions to missions in India, but neglected to mention her Pentecostal faith.[117]

Born in Wisconsin in 1859, Abrams grew up in Mapleton, Minnesota. Desiring to become a teacher, she graduated from Mankato State Normal School (now Minnesota State University, Mankato), where the suffragette Julia Sears had served as president a few years before her enrollment. Abrams then studied for two years at the University of Minnesota. Inspired by the life of Fidelia Fiske, an early nineteenth-century missionary educator, she committed her life to foreign missions. In 1885, she enrolled in the first class of the Chicago Training School for City, Home, and Foreign Missions. Lucy Rider Meyer, a leading figure in the new Methodist deaconess movement, had founded the school to offer theological and practical training for young women.[118] After graduation, the Minneapolis Branch of the Woman's Foreign Missionary Society commissioned Abrams as a Methodist "deaconess-missionary" before she left for India in 1887.[119]

Arriving in Bombay, she began working at a boarding school designed to provide religious instruction for the daughters of church members. For Abrams and many other women, ministry in a foreign land centered on educational and charitable ministries—a vital component in the nineteenth-century "Woman's Work for Woman" missiology.[120] Before long the protective walls around the compound seemed confining. Etched in her memory was the ride through the streets after her ship reached port. On the way to the school, she saw masses of people living in heartbreaking conditions. Then, under the cover of night, she made her way to opium dens and witnessed the emaciated bodies of people of all ages enslaved by their addictions. "Oh, how my heart cried out," she recounted, "and how I longed to be able to bring the message of life to these people in all their darkness." Despite the presence of missionaries in Bombay, she concluded "they couldn't reach the thousandth part of the people with the sound of the gospel."[121]

After ten years of waiting, Methodist officials gave her permission to become a full-time evangelist. Then, in 1898, Ramabai invited her to assist in administering the Mukti Mission.[122] By now an independent faith missionary, she flourished in this new environment since it afforded her the opportunity to train young women for ministry. Given the immensity of the task in India, the saints at the 1898 Keswick Convention in England responded to the personal appeal of Ramabai and earnestly prayed that God would raise up 100,000 male and 100,000 female Indians "to go up and down the land proclaiming the gospel of Christ."[123] She and Abrams would do their part in recruiting young women to preach in the villages.

When word of the Welsh revival (1904–1905) reached India, revivals began among tribal peoples in the Khassia Hills in the northeast and later at Mukti.

Shortly afterward, Abrams began taking "praying bands" of young women with her in evangelistic endeavors. In the spring of 1906, she penned her widely read *Baptism of the Holy Ghost and Fire* to encourage believers to seek for the post-conversionary experience of Spirit baptism for purity of life and power to evangelize. Occurrences of speaking in tongues came in the summer and at Mukti in December.[124] Originally serialized in articles published in the *Bombay Guardian*, *Christian Patriot*, and the Methodist *Indian Witness*, a second edition with mention of the restoration of tongues—but not as a necessity for Spirit baptism—came out later in the year in book form; the revision then served as a theology of mission for both holiness believers and Pentecostals.[125] It notably helped lay the groundwork for the Chilean Pentecostal revival when she sent a copy to Methodist missionaries Willis and Mary Hoover, the latter a classmate at the Chicago Training School.[126]

Leaving India in 1908 for a two-year promotional tour in the United States, Abrams preached at many important sites of Pentecostal activity. These included Carrie Judd Montgomery's Home of Peace in Oakland; Upper Room Mission in Los Angeles; Stone Church in Chicago; Apostolic Faith Mission in Indianapolis; Elizabeth Baker's Elim Tabernacle and Rochester Bible Training School in Rochester; Bethel Pentecostal Assembly in Newark; the Pentecostal camp meeting at Homestead Park in Pittsburgh; and the headquarters of the Christian Workers Union in Massachusetts.[127]

On her visits around the country, she enlisted several single women to accompany her back to India for frontline evangelism. Like other holiness and Pentecostal women ministers, Abrams believed that the "promise of the Father" (Acts 1:4) gave them equal opportunity with men in preaching. While visiting St. Paul, Minnesota, in 1910 before returning, she attended a Laymen's Missionary Convention where she heard "the evangelization of the world was a man's job." Recalling the revival at Mukti, she said, "the great outpouring of the Spirit came upon us, and today we have 400 Spirit-filled young women, and they are saying, 'Here I am; send me,' and the Lord has opened their lips and He has filled their mouths with a testimony that cannot be gainsaid."[128] In her estimation, the Spirit's calling had once more trumped humanly imposed restrictions on who could preach the gospel.

Ramabai called the new missionaries the "Phillipus Class" because "like the daughters of Philip, they are to be evangelists" (Acts 21:9).[129] Abrams organized the endeavor as the Bezaleel Evangelistic Mission (Exod 31:3: "I have filled [Bezaleel/Bezalel] with the Spirit of God, with wisdom, with understanding, with knowledge and with all kinds of skills"), the only known Pentecostal women's missionary society.[130] She then recommended that other interested women consult with her friend Minnie Draper in Ossining before they journeyed to India.

"We want educated and cultured women, but above all we want women full of love and the Holy Spirit," Abrams announced, "women willing to settle down and plod, and hammer away until the rock breaks . . . who do not know what it is to be defeated in that which they undertake . . . [and] at least thirty years of age for this pioneer work."[131] While two of the women remained at Mukti, Abrams and the rest of the group traveled north to the city of Faizabad and then later to

Uska Bazar near the border of Nepal where the mission centered its activities.[132] Doctrinally, Bezaleel "has always stood for the full Gospel," wrote Ethel King who later joined the group, "and God has done miracles indeed in healing the sick, not only among us as a Christian company, but in the villages as well. The fame of Jesus the Healer has spread in the villages round about."[133]

In an interesting twist, the *Year Book of Protestant Missions in India, Burma and Ceylon: 1912* categorized many of the independent Pentecostal missionaries—the majority of them women—as "Open Brethren," an odd fit given the refusal of the Brethren to approve speaking in tongues.[134] A later directory listed some of them among the twelve missionaries affiliated with Bezaleel: Edith Baugh, Abrams's successor—another alumna of the Chicago Training School and a Student Volunteer;[135] Lillie Doll, Marguerite Flint, Bessie Gager, Anna Helmbrecht, Ethel King, Jennie Kirkland, Bernice Lee, Christine McLeod, Annie Morrison; with two more who previously had served as Alliance missionaries in India, Margaret Felch and Laura Gardner.[136] Abrams died in 1912 from malaria after returning from a trip with her friend Alice Luce, a missionary with the Church Missionary Society who later trained Hispanic pastors and evangelists in America and did more than anyone else to shape the early development of missiology in the Assemblies of God.[137]

After the death of Baugh to malaria in 1920, Bernice Lee followed her as director. All the Bezaleel missionaries joined the Assemblies of God sometime between 1915 and 1923, once more demonstrating the flexibility with which early Pentecostal missionaries viewed affiliations.[138] Former Alliance missionary Christian Schoonmaker and others had organized the Indian Assemblies of God in 1918 at Navapur in Maharashtra State to create a "united company of anointed men and women . . . under which we shall present ourselves as servants of Jesus Christ to the people of India."[139] This arrangement allowed the Bezaleel personnel and others to keep their different connections or independent status while holding membership in the Assemblies of God. The new link also introduced the women to a growing community of missionaries and a larger home base of financial support.

Yet, in the transition from the Bezaleel Evangelistic Mission to the Assemblies of God, Abrams's vision for a women's missionary society died and the participation of the women in formal decision-making processes eventually declined, creating a scenario much like the incorporation of other such agencies into denominational boards controlled by males.[140] "With the passing of the first generation of Pentecostal women," observes historian Dana Robert, "leadership of the movement devolved to the men." They became helpers under the authority of male leaders, "categorized as either 'wife' or 'old maid.'" "The irony was that while faith mission women were throwing the gender-based mission theory of the woman's missionary movement out the front door, second-class status came knocking on the back."[141] Regrettably, the "sisterhood network" of friends: Minnie Abrams, Elizabeth Baker and her sister Susan Duncan, Edith Baugh, Minnie Draper, Mary Stone, Bernice Lee, Anna Reiff,[142] Alice Luce, and Carrie Judd Montgomery, along with others such as Alice Belle Garrigus, the pioneer Pentecostal missionary to Newfoundland;[143] Marie Burgess Brown, pastor

of Glad Tidings Tabernacle in New York City;[144] Christine Gibson, founder of
Zion Bible Institute in East Providence, Rhode Island;[145] Virginia Moss, founder
of Beulah Heights Bible and Missionary Training School in North Bergen, New
Jersey;[146] and Etta Wurmser, founder of Apostolic Bible School in Norwalk,
Ohio—all significant either as missionaries, missiologists, mission promoters,
administrators, and educators of the pioneer generation—would not be recap-
tured with the same magnitude of influence by other women after their deaths.

NATIONAL AND INTERNATIONAL
PENTECOSTAL MISSIONARY UNION

In October 1913 in Norwalk, Ohio, Philip Wittich and his brother Benjamin
from the Mt. Horeb Full Gospel Mission and Detroit Missionary Bible School,
along with Etta Wurmser, ordained to the ministry Esther Bragg [Harvey], the
previously mentioned Anna Helmbrecht, and other students at Wurmser's Apostolic Bible School who were ready to enter the ministry or depart for the mission lands. With a Presbyterian background, Bragg had left Michigan to study
in Norwalk. Helmbrecht studied at Edinboro Normal School (now Edinboro
University of Pennsylvania) and later at Lupton's Missionary Training School.[147]
Two months later in New Bremen, Ohio (about one hundred miles to the southeast of Norwalk), Philip Wittich ordained Harry Waggoner, who with his wife,
Helen, had studied at the Missionary Training Institute at Nyack. Bragg, Helmbrecht, and the Waggoners soon left for India, not knowing initially where they
would go once they disembarked at Bombay, but all would subsequently spend
decades as successful missionaries.

As early as 1913, if not before, Wittich and Wurmser informally had worked
in tandem and with others for the cause of evangelism and world missions. To
say the least, they were opposites. Wittich, a well-educated former Lutheran pastor, had studied at the universities of Stuttgart, Württemberg, and Leipzig prior
to enrolling at Lutheran Theological Seminary in Gettysburg, Pennsylvania. He
then gained considerable pastoral experience in the General Synod of the Evangelical Lutheran Church before he accepted the call in 1906 to St. Paul's Lutheran
Church in New Bremen.[148] Impressed by the holiness and healing movements, he
led the charge for prohibition in the community. His unsuccessful opposition to
a saloonkeeper serving on the church board led to a rupture in the congregation
eleven months later when Wittich and seventy-two families left to found Christ
Church.[149] In the following years, he frequently spoke at the German-language
services held during the annual Central District conventions of the Christian
and Missionary Alliance at Beulah Park, near Cleveland.[150] In 1912, he and his
wife, Emilie, along with many church members, "received the baptism in [the]
Holy Ghost according to Acts 2:4," and Christ Church became known as the
Pentecostal Mission.[151]

In contrast, the indomitable Etta Wurmser, a fiery evangelist, pioneered Alliance churches in northwest Ohio.[152] "Her commands and demands are absolute," quipped one of her critics to a newspaper reporter in Sandusky. "Her

God is a god of war and always fights her battles according to her teachings."[153] Despite the negative press coverage, Wurmser proved to be a farsighted leader, displaying the restorationist impulse and practical orientation of early Pentecostalism. Born Etta Haley in Findlay, Ohio, in 1865, she married photographer and artist Frank Wurmser in 1888. A daughter was born to their union five years later, but the marriage ended in divorce with young Naomi staying with her mother. "How glad I would have been if death had ended those years of crushing sorrow," she said of her life at the time. But during a time of prayer at night, she heard the audible voice of the Lord say, "I have chosen thee out of the furnace of affliction." This transformed her life: "From that moment God began to deal with me, and make me ready for the work whereunto He had called me; . . . He began to tell me what I was to do, and I did it all." [154]

Wurmser joined the Alliance in 1900 and later enrolled at the Missionary Training Institute where she spent a year in study. Having paid close attention to the news about the Welsh revival, she later received the Pentecostal baptism and "found [herself] speaking Chinese and other tongues."[155] She also had modeled the faith life: everything depended on divine provision from her attending the Institute ("I didn't have a dollar to take me to Nyack. . . . The Lord paid every bit of my way"), to her church planting endeavors in Ohio, and finally to establishing Apostolic Bible School in Norwalk in 1911, one of the earliest Pentecostal Bible institutes.[156] When it outgrew the space of a private home, she rented the downtown Maple Hotel.[157] With Norwalk as the base of operations, she pastored the Alliance branch under the title of superintendent, directed and taught in the school, and supervised the advance of the Alliance in that region of the state. "I have a vision that is larger than our school," she remarked. "When the Lord called me to be a missionary around the world He gave me a worldwide vision."[158] She stood among others called to world missions but directed to serve at the home base.

The school and its sixty students moved to Findlay in 1914, the year of the establishment of the General Council of the Assemblies of God with Findlay as the first site of its headquarters.[159] A local pastor who had joined the Council, Thomas Leonard, offered the use of his facilities for office space to Council leaders E. N. Bell (general chairman) and J. Roswell Flower (general secretary), as well as his print shop for publications. Although Wurmser and J. Roswell and Alice Flower had been friends for several years,[160] cooperation with the Council may have been precluded because of the irascible Leonard and the Council's condemnation of divorce, but more likely by Bell's stiff opposition to women clergy.[161] Hence, for several decades two Pentecostal schools existed in the same city: Leonard's Gospel School and Wurmser's renamed Bible and Missionary Training School, supported by different, but overlapping, constituencies.[162]

Within three years of the school moving to Findlay, it had graduated twenty-five more missionaries along with other Christian workers. "All of these students have had to get their own outfits, their own passage money, and have someone in the homeland who would stand back of them in prayer at least, and with some of their gifts, involving thousands of dollars," Wurmser reported. Alliance branches she had founded in Sandusky, Norwalk, and Berlin Heights provided them with assistance.[163] In another wing of the network, Benjamin Wittich's Detroit Missionary Bible School, founded in 1912, "sent out to Africa five adults and four children, while several more only wait the command to go and financial backing which shall thrust them out into Africa, China, and India."[164]

Nevertheless, the need for a broader base of support demanded action, and she announced in 1917, "I have been led to form an Advisory Council in reference to the missionaries going out to the field from this school and others with whom we come in touch. I thought if we could [counsel] and pray together and co-operate our missionaries might be better provided for."[165] This announcement served as a catalyst for the incorporation of the network in 1919 as the National and International Pentecostal Missionary Union with Philip Wittich as president and Wurmser as vice-president "to carry out the command of Our Lord and Master, given in Matt. 28:18-20."[166] With this came a statement of faith, constitution and bylaws, and an official periodical that began circulation in 1923: *Maran-Atha* ("Our Lord Is Coming"). Ten years later, the roster listed 24 pastors, 107 evangelists, and 38 missionaries serving in Brazil, China, India, and Venezuela with ten of them also affiliated either currently or lately with the Assemblies of God. The Union comprised five districts: Chicago, Findlay, Cleveland, Pacific, and Atlantic.[167] Characterized by a high level of gender equality, it functioned as a ministerial association and as a mission agency in the service of autonomous congregations. By mid-twentieth century, however, the Union declined following the deaths of the founders.

The missional vision of Wittich and Wurmser—both with attachments to the Alliance—and a host of other Pentecostal leaders from Maine to New York City to Detroit to the West Coast rested on their understanding of Spirit baptism, anticipation that "signs and wonders" would accompany gospel proclamation, and recognition of the importance of cooperation and training for evangelization in the last days.

DENOMINATIONAL MISSIONS

The Pentecostal Missionary Unions, Pentecostal Mission, United Free Gospel and Missionary Society, Bezaleel Evangelistic Mission, and the National and International Pentecostal Missionary Union all represented attempts after 1908 to find the "middle ground" to resolve the "missionary problem" and did so with varying levels of success. With the demise of the American and Canadian PMUs and Bezaleel, the Interior Mission, Pentecostal Mission, and the emerging networks of congregations forged by Wurmser, Wittich, and Casley remained. Clearly, the Canadian and American (northern and midwestern) independent Pentecostals from the Reformed or Keswick wing of the movement had taken the lead in orchestrating collaborative arrangements, with the exception of the World-Wide Prayer and Mission Band in the South. Others followed suit and resolved to find more structured ways to support missionaries and hold them accountable for their use of funds.

With obvious pride about recent developments in Pentecostal missions that demonstrated their credibility, Martin Ryan reported to the *Chinese Recorder*, the premier periodical for China missionaries, that workers from across North America had met in Hot Springs, Arkansas, in April 1914 and formed the "General Council of the Assemblies of God in the United States, Canada and Foreign Lands."[168] Underlining the practical problems that independent Pentecostal missionaries faced, he noted they "have had to do legal business in the name of some other denominational body because [they] had no legal standing in the homeland and in some instances have been unable to secure ground on which to build mission stations." Relieved that the Council had promised not to "legislate laws of government," "usurp authority," or deprive local assemblies of their "scriptural or local rights," he listed the twelve members of the Missionary Presbytery, pleased that the biblical term "presbytery" had been chosen instead of "committee" or "board," terms that smacked of earthly institutions.[169] Ryan, however, did not join the Council despite its announced intent of "cooperation without ecclesiastical centralization," possibly in order to safeguard himself from any potential human directives.[170]

Several networks and many individuals came together to form the General Council for more reasons than Ryan suggested; in addition to their hope for finding better and more equitable means of supporting missionaries, the more than three hundred delegates desired a greater unity among the churches to conserve the work at home and abroad, encourage local congregations to charter with a biblical name, and start a Bible training school.[171] Leaders had issued a call in December 1913 for "all the Churches of God in Christ [and] to all Pentecostal or Apostolic Faith Assemblies" to meet in Hot Springs in order to find more effective ways to "push the interests of the kingdom of God everywhere."[172] Significantly, J. Roswell Flower, formerly of the Alliance branch in Indianapolis, went to the conclave from another, albeit smaller midwestern network, the Association of Christian Assemblies (1913).[173]

During the first year of its existence, forty missionaries joined the Council. The number mushroomed to 221 six years later with personnel serving largely in the traditional areas of Protestant endeavor: China, Japan, India, Africa, Egypt, Palestine, and a few in Latin America and Russia.[174] Rapid expansion characterized the home base as men and women planted churches and regions of churches formed district councils, even while theological schism traumatized the organization in 1915-1916.[175]

In important respects, the Assemblies of God reflected the inner contradictions of a restorationist movement with a strong practical bent. First, it resisted the label "organization" but incorporated under a national Executive Presbytery (also serving as the "Missionary Presbytery") with general officers situated at a designated headquarters.[176] Second, to retain its evangelical identity, the Council condemned an internal movement supporting a modalistic monarchian position on the Godhead in 1916 through the adoption of a doctrinal summary, the "Statement of Fundamental Truths." Nonetheless, it assured the faithful that it was "not intended as a creed for the Church, nor as a basis of fellowship among Christians, but only as a basis of unity for the ministry alone."[177] Yet, the "Statement" effectively placed a doctrinal boundary around the new organization and helped determine whom it would appoint as missionaries. Third, Council leaders trumpeted the soon return of Christ by issuing "An Appeal to the Pentecostal People Throughout the World to Observe Sunday, Nov. 3rd and Monday, Nov. 4, 1918 in United Prayer Inviting Jesus, Our Heavenly Bridegroom, to Come Back," and established the Missionary Department a year later with Flower as director to better handle the correspondence and the distribution of over $90,000 in offerings to its missionaries.[178] Finally, to gain assistance with matters related to missionary personnel traveling and residing overseas, along with understanding policies of the State Department in Washington, D.C., the Council joined the Foreign Missions Conference of North America in 1920,[179] affording leaders the first official contact of Pentecostal representatives with those of the larger Protestant mission movement.[180] In fact, the Assemblies of God had taken one step into the broader church world, gaining a club membership that ordinarily one would not expect a simple "co-operative fellowship" to hold.[181]

In the early years, leaders set up the undenominational "Missionary Conference" as a forum for discussions on "cooperation in the power of the Spirit between the missionaries on the field, and the Pentecostal people everywhere." Not actually affiliated with the Council, it met several times beginning in 1917 in association with church conventions or General Council gatherings and attracted both Assemblies of God and independent missionaries. Conveners hoped "a better understanding of the great problems which confront us along missionary lines could be had if we could get together for a heart to heart talk concerning these matters."[182] Enthused about their worth, Willa Lowther, a missionary to Sainam, China, remarked, "I am sure there is no body of people [that] suffers so much from disorganization and splits and issues as the missionaries."[183] Delegates discussed a variety of problems, such as fund raising, and passed non-binding resolutions.[184] Independent missionaries sometimes joined the Council because of the positive relationships established at the meetings; as this happened, the conferences gradually outlived their usefulness with the last one convening in 1921.[185]

Two southern Wesleyan-holiness denominations, the Pentecostal Holiness Church and the United Holy Church of America, created missions departments in 1911 and 1918, respectively.[186] The Pentecostal Holiness Church emerged from the union in 1911 of the Fire-Baptized Holiness Church, Holiness Church of North Carolina, and the Tabernacle Presbyterian Church. All three bodies had became Pentecostal as a result of the ministry of Gaston Cashwell, who returned from Azusa Street to Dunn, North Carolina, where he held services in a tobacco warehouse in December 1906.[187] Reflecting on the popularity of the meetings, which also drew people from South Carolina and Georgia, and the number who received Pentecostal baptism, he noted that "all the signs follow me since I received Pentecost."[188] Interest in missions also highlighted the revival with some, like Thomas McIntosh, who said he had received the Chinese language, preparing to leave for the mission lands.

Interest in establishing a mission agency surfaced in the early summer of 1909, shortly before the organization of the PMU (U.S.A.) in Alliance, Ohio. Holiness Pentecostals formed the World-Wide Prayer and Mission Band with headquarters in Columbia, South Carolina, and a field office in Hong Kong.[189] "God's love is planet-wide, the atonement is planet-wide and the commission of Jesus is planet-wide, and if we get all these in us we will be planet-wide Christians," declared Joseph King, who had earlier recognized the value of broader cooperation at Lupton's camp meeting. King served as president with John Pike, editor of the *Way of Faith*, as treasurer.[190] The earliest missionaries came from the Fire-Baptized Holiness Church that had been founded by Benjamin Irwin.[191] Although the details remain sketchy about the activities and effectiveness of the World-Wide Prayer and Mission Band, it soon gave way to the creation of the Foreign Missionary Board of the Pentecostal Holiness Church in 1911, established "to receive mission funds from the local churches and to use these in evangelistic and education work in mission fields."[192]

One of the best-known African-American Pentecostal missionaries, Kenneth Spooner, had been reared in an Anglican family in Barbados and later immigrated to New York City.[193] In 1906, he received his call to be a missionary: "God spoke to me as it were in audible tones: 'I want you to go to Africa.'" Further confirmation came while attending services at Simpson's Gospel Tabernacle. A member there, Mrs. N. A. Caughlin, made arrangements and paid the tuition for him to study at Boydton Institute in southern Virginia, a school founded by Charles Cullis—the well-known advocate of faith healing in Boston and sponsor of charitable endeavors—located on the former campus of Randolph and Macon College.[194] Cullis founded the school to provide for the "higher education of colored people" and as a place to prepare blacks for the ministry.[195] Sometime before he arrived at Lupton's camp meeting in June 1907, Spooner had received Spirit baptism with tongues-speech.[196] There he met the veteran holiness missionary to South Africa Jacob Lehman, who had recently received the same experience.

Spooner's anticipation of going to South Africa, however, dimmed with the knowledge that the British colonial government would not allow Americans of African descent to enter the country; probably for this reason, his friends at the Bethel Pentecostal Assembly in Newark did not attempt to sponsor him as a missionary. Seven years later, when Lehman returned to the United States, he enlisted Spooner and his wife, Geraldine, to serve as missionaries with the Pentecostal Holiness Church. After John Boddy and Liberia missionary John Perkins "laid hands upon me and separated me to the service of our Lord and Savior Jesus Christ," Spooner recalled, he and Geraldine went to the dock in New York City and boarded ship for Cape Town, arriving in January 1915 and surprisingly gaining entry. Before his death in 1937, he had planted sixty churches and helped in the development of the Pentecostal Holiness Church in South Africa.[197] The Assemblies of God also welcomed two African Americans to its missionary roster, Isaac and Martha "Mattie" Neeley, who had gone from the Stone Church in Chicago in 1913 with missionary William Johnson as independent missionaries to serve with the Interior Mission in Liberia.[198]

The affiliation of the Spooners and the Neelyes with white Pentecostal denominations, though notable for the time, stood as exceptions to the norm. It would be the United Holy Church of America, founded in North Carolina in 1886, that would take the lead in foreign missions among African-American Pentecostal organizations.[199] With different historical and cultural roots than those of the networks and denominations previously discussed, it embraced speaking in tongues early in the twentieth century, but without the insistence of glossolalia for Spirit baptism. The missiological and eschatological influence of the Alliance was felt through its operation of the Boydton Institute (with the support of the United Holy Church), and the recommendation to the latter's congregations to send their mission monies to the Alliance.[200]

The missional concerns of prominent leaders Henry Fisher, John Houston, and E. B. Nichols—the last two actually from the Alliance—reveal the close contact of the two organizations in the early years, traced back in part to the "colored work" of the Alliance in the South.[201] When the August 1916 convention of the Central District of the Alliance met at Beulah Park in Cleveland, Ohio, Fisher and Nichols heard an array of Alliance speakers, including A. B. Simpson, as well as ten missionaries and Robert Glover, the foreign missions secretary who had served in China.[202] According to the report in the *Alliance Weekly*, "the Spirit of the meeting was . . . intensely earnest, prayerful, responsive, and overflowing with missionary zeal." At the Sunday afternoon closing "rally," 134 young people stood and committed themselves to become missionaries.[203] The calls for world evangelization deeply stirred Fisher. "I caught the vision of 'Missions' as never before," he remembered. "I saw a world lost in heathen darkness and we, as a church, were responsible to God to give them the light of the Gospel that they might be saved."[204]

Now with an "enlarged vision . . . [of] the earth's wide and white harvest field" and the "millions in heathen darkness, who never heard of Him who came to seek and to save that which was lost, [and] were filling Christless graves," the United Holy Church established the Missionary Department in 1918 with a goal at once global in perspective and holistic in nature.[205] The first missionaries, Isaac and Annie Williams, traveled to Liberia.[206] In 1925, the *World Missionary Atlas* noted the Department aimed "to give the Gospel and establish schools especially among the Negro people in the regions beyond."[207] Three years later, the United Holy Church joined the Foreign Missions Conference of North America, the second Pentecostal agency after the Assemblies of God to do so. E. B. Nichols, the first director of missions, served the cause in the denomination until his death in Liberia in 1937.

FAITH AND MUTUAL EFFORT

"I don't care for a Mission Board to back me up with pledged financial support," wrote former Alliance missionary William Simpson in a letter to a Pentecostal periodical before his return to China in 1918, "but I must have the people of God who are of like precious faith with me, to uphold me with their prayers and fellowship if I am to do the work the Lord expects of me in China."[208] Simpson's first choice for prayer support over secure financial backing, reflecting the outlook of many other missionaries, demonstrated his conviction that the last-days harvest of souls was a time of spiritual conflict. "For our struggle is not against flesh and blood," as Paul had declared, "but [rather] against the rulers, against the authorities, against the powers of this dark world and against the spiritual forces of evil in the heavenly realms" (Eph 6:12). Therefore, the success of God's mission in the world rested not on mission boards, bookkeepers, and the most efficient means of fundraising, but on "Holy Ghost machinery," as radical evangelicals had claimed.[209]

Since all of God's people needed to give their fair share for the evangelization of the world, Simpson said—several paragraphs later—that they "should not curtail their usual offerings." He then itemized his travel costs and daily expenditures, in addition to the funds needed for salaries of local pastors, a Bible institute for Chinese believers, a training center for new missionaries, shipping costs for supplies, and equipment. The expenses, including $3,000 needed to cover his family's steamship tickets to China and supplies for the first year after their return, and Simpson's readiness to announce them publicly showed his willingness to modify George Müller's prized concept of the faith life that focused on presenting financial needs only to the Lord in prayer.[210] Anna Reiff put the challenge bluntly: "There are those who are out on what is termed 'faith lines' who have not a 'George Müller call'"; they too deserved the regular support of the saints at home.[211]

Though defending their freedom to be directed by the Holy Spirit, Pentecostal missionaries increasingly affiliated themselves with networks of like-minded believers who wanted to play their part in the grand drama of the end times. Whether connecting to the Interior Mission, the higher profile Pentecostal Missionary Union (Great Britain and Ireland), Pentecostal Mission, the diminutive Bezaleel Evangelistic Mission, the denominational mission boards, or simply the numberless informal networks among individuals and local churches, they gradually recognized the value of cooperative arrangements and predictable financial backing.[212] But when boarding ship to the regions beyond and walking up the gangplank with luggage in hand, they gave the credit to God alone for their provisions and knew with irrepressible certainty that the Spirit would make up whatever might be lacking for the task ahead. Simpson had assured the readers that his ministry in China rested on unflinching faith, but the public recitation of his expenses revealed his belief in its corporate nature.

Behind most of the early organized expressions of Pentecostal missions, one finds the influence of the Christian and Missionary Alliance. If the news of the outpouring of the Holy Spirit at Azusa Street inspired Pentecostal revivals across the United States, Canada, and overseas, it was the vision of the China Inland Mission in the United Kingdom and the Alliance in North America that provided the scaffolds to enable Pentecostals to labor together in mission. After visiting with A. B. Simpson in New York City on another tour of America in 1914, Alexander Boddy remarked, "It seems quite a pity that there should be a gulf separating the 'Alliance' from many of the earnest Pentecostal workers."[213] The disagreement over tongues-speech could not conceal the missional architecture of the Alliance in the shaping of North American Pentecostal missions.

8

Missionaries and Strategies

It seems we can't get rid of sickness. . . . Though the testing is severe, Jesus will see us through. . . . Oh! Mama, the trials seem so hard at times I just don't know what to do. Sometimes I think we are forsaken by friends and I get quite lonely.[1]

Missionary Cora Fritsch [Falkner] in a letter to her mother, 1912

I cannot tell you how my heart rejoices to know that God has not forgotten the little orphans. Last month when we were nearly out of cash, the Lord sent a Mohammedan man to give me a nice offering. It is wonderful how God sees every need and when we most need help He always sends it from the least expected sources.[2]

Founder of the Asyut orphanage in Egypt, Lillian Trasher, 1915

Let others educate, doctor, do philanthropy . . . avoid also the incubus to the evangelist of day schools, orphanages, and the 101 things which may be accumulated in station life.[3]

President of the Pentecostal Missionary Union Cecil Polhill, 1916

Mr. Henry Turney [a pioneer Pentecostal missionary to South Africa] traveled a lot. He was righteous, but very difficult.[4]

Missionary to South Africa John Richards, ca. 1917

While praying for God to call others, I heard the voice of the Lord calling, "Whom shall I send, and who will go for Me?" . . . At this time I did not know the field God was calling me to labor in, but . . . I was willing to go anywhere.[5]

Lula Boyette at the Holmes Bible and Missionary Institute (S.C.), 1920

Some of these sectarian groups, such as the Pentecostals . . . because they have no established institutions to support, can use all their resources on new evangelistic endeavors.[6]

Church of South India educator J. Russell Chandran, 1953

Apart from the distinctive features of their spirituality, Pentecostal missionaries closely resembled the holiness and evangelical missionaries they encountered abroad. They believed Christ to be the only savior for humankind; saw themselves engaged in the end-time conflict between the victorious Christ and Satan; opposed the teaching of future probation; and shared identical cultural attitudes toward the "heathen." They faced the same issues of living abroad and followed many of the same strategies in mission. In the years after 1908, Pentecostal missions slowly stabilized, and by the 1920s and 1930s their operations had become more predictable. It is to this period that we now turn to examine the missionaries, their struggles, preparation, methods in evangelism, and, finally, their expositions on the Three Selfs—the belief that mission churches should become self-governing, self-supporting, and self-propagating—and to the groundbreaking publication of Melvin Hodges's *Indigenous Church* in 1953.[7] Like the pioneers of other movements, their outlook on the task before them—in this case, the Christian world mission—has special importance for later generations who find their own activities in mission inspired and legitimized by faithful devotion to the original vision. It also shows where they stood in the larger picture of Protestant missions.[8]

MIRACLES AND CHALLENGES

"I will not say anything of the future, but at present it is like drilling away at solid rock," wrote Cora Falkner to her parents about her work in Japan, having arrived just three months before in September 1907 with Martin Ryan's party from Spokane, Washington. Along with her co-workers, she struggled to adjust to life in another culture and faced the resistance of an established religion. Without mentioning the disappointment of their tongues-speech not being the Japanese language, she mentioned that "Bertha [Milligan] and I are learning the language. We find speaking to them in their own language goes so much better than English."[9] Seventeen months later, however, they moved to Hong Kong because the Lord was "leading that way."[10] Falkner and Milligan persevered as missionaries despite the hurdles they encountered—an indication of their determination and their ability to muster resources to support themselves and their activities.

Judging by the letters missionaries sent to Pentecostal periodicals, signs and wonders amply followed their gospel witness: healings, deliverances from chemical addictions, exorcisms, visions and dreams, and other unusual occurrences. Amid the religious skepticism of the modern era, as well as the trials of ministry abroad, demonstrations of supernatural power assured them of the absolute certitude of the gospel they proclaimed. From India, Jennie Kirkland wrote that "by [God's] grace, drunkards, harlots, and heathen have been saved, healed, and baptized in the Spirit."[11] Benno Schoeneich in Nicaragua said that "nearly every day someone gets healed." "Healing is part of the Gospel," he averred. "It not only includes the healing of the soul, but of the body as well."[12] In Brazil, Daniel Berg and Gunnar Vingren "gave all the glory [to the Lord Himself for the] wonderful work in this land . . . in saving souls and baptizing them with the Holy Spirit and with fire, and healing the sick."[13] In the same matter-of-fact way, T. H. Rousseau told of local church leaders in the Shaukiwan area of Hong Kong who regularly prayed for the sick: "At times people from the neighboring villages bring their sick to the mission and God heals them. This is the hook that brings them in."[14] According to Isaac Neeley, who conducted exorcisms in Liberia, "not only has the Lord healed bodies, but there have also been a number of cases of deliverances from demon possession."[15] Indeed, an astonishing number of miracle stories circulated across the expanse of Pentecostal missions, inspiring the faithful at the home base, confirming that "signs will accompany" those who believe, and justifying their continued support of missions.

Consistent with their anticipation of miraculous happenings, Pentecostals generally took a "hands off" approach when revivals occurred, though not without exercising restraint when they considered it appropriate. After children and youth at the Adullam Rescue Home in Yunnan Province in China "wanted to know if they could stay [in the prayer room] and pray instead of going to the garden or to other industrial work," Harold Baker, a former missionary with the Disciples of Christ, immediately granted permission.[16] This led to a "mighty outpouring of the Holy Spirit" with regular activities set aside for more than a week of prayer. Seeking to avoid interfering with the Spirit's "wonderful working," he said the missionaries decided to "open up our hearts that we too might be taken deeper into the heavenly blessings that were falling in such mighty showers."[17] The outcome included repentance, a deepening of personal faith among believers, and the conversion of non-Christians.[18] Though the status of the missionaries and their cultural outlook separated them from their wards in important respects, they believed that the power and gifts of the Spirit transcended such differences. The children and youth also told of visions of events in the life of Christ and future eschatological scenes such as the Great Tribulation, the battle of Armageddon, the coming of Christ with the angels, and the New Jerusalem, all viewed in premillennial cinematography and which nurtured within them greater interest in Bible study.[19] At a revival in Travancore, India, Bertha Cook observed, "Praise and great liberty in the Spirit prevailed after . . . confessions [of sin were made]. During the songs of praise, some were dancing in the Spirit and some clapping their hands or raising them up" and "one brother saw angels over the platform and a dove flying over us."[20] At a deeper level, such happenings illustrated the appeal of Pentecostal spirituality in non-Western cultures.

Letters and other sources from the period paint more details into the picture than miracles, revivals, and conversions: financial stresses, human and demonic opposition, death threats, physical suffering, disappointments, loneliness, natural disasters, the inconvenience of travel, danger from bandits, and the whirlwinds of political instability fill in the spaces on the canvas.[21] "Life on the mission field is something more than preaching," Schoeneich said drolly about the challenges of missionary life.[22] In a relatively rare occurrence, the call to mission itself could be stressful, as when Maria Atkinson and her husband, Mark, separated after he refused to become a Christian and she obeyed the voice of the Spirit heard during a vision and went to Mexico as a missionary.[23] Before leaving

for the Belgian Congo, Julia Richardson spent earnest time in prayer to overcome her fear of snakes.[24] Seasickness in crossing the Atlantic Ocean was only
the beginning of troubles for the P. F. Barnewall and J. F. Carscadden families
on their journey to French West Africa.[25] In Hong Kong, adding to his suffering
from overwork, a high fever and chills, the stomach of John James became "seriously impaired by living a long time on Chinese food."[26] In the interior of Liberia, Macie Boddy (daughter of John Boddy) recounted that "twice I attempted
to eat stewed rat, but failed to succeed very well. Again I endeavored to eat some
highly scented monkey in palm butter, but the odor was quite sufficient and
more than I cared for." But she didn't give up easily: "When native food is fresh
and cooked well it is very palatable, and one can eat with relish when tired and
hungry."[27]

Mission work amid the Quiché Mayan Indians in the mountains of Guatemala slowed to a halt for Charles Furman and Thomas Pullin when rumors
circulated alleging they "secretly caught, killed and ate children," and that the
ghoulish Furman had been observed "coming out of a cemetery one night gnaw-
ing the flesh from a bone." Opposition mounted as merchants refused to sell
them food, ruffians stoned their meeting places, and on occasion people shot at
them.[28] Nevertheless, they slowly built a peaceful and trustful relationship with
the people; persevering in their endeavors, they steadily planted churches.[29]

In China, missionaries fretted over unsanitary conditions, flooding that left
their quarters and clothing covered with green mold, the perils of residing in ram-
shackle housing, and, of course, living with the constant nuisance of mosquitoes
and other insects. In addition to all of this, political unrest and rising anti-Christian
sentiments exacerbated the anxiety of life. Sometimes the toll affected marital
and family bonds: Harland Lawlor abandoned his wife, Emma, and daughter,
Beatrice, in Shanghai, and returned with his son to the United States.[30] They too
had been in the group of missionaries with Martin Ryan, whose own wife later
divorced him. "In [that] heathen country," as Rowena Ryan bitterly related, "she
[Mrs. Ryan] and her children were without food and a proper home, and as a last
resort, she learned the language and finally secured a place as [a] teacher among
the Japanese children." After complaining to her husband about the lack of support sent their way, his advice apparently brought little comfort: "Obey the Lord;
He will provide a home for you and the children."[31]

Sorrows ranging from disease to other life-threatening circumstances followed
in their paths as well. Blanche Appleby described the time of Cora Falkner's
fatal illness: "I was sick in one room with Asiatic diarrhea; [Bertha] Milligan
was sick in another room with malaria, and in the next flat was Mrs. Falkner
with malaria."[32] Because Falkner said the "Lord had so wonderfully kept her for
five years [since arriving in China] that she would trust Him now," she refused
medical treatment.[33] No miracles occurred on that occasion, except perhaps that
Appleby and Milligan recovered. Olive Bolton, a recently arrived missionary to
the Lisu people with her husband, Leonard, died after childbirth at the China
Inland Mission hospital in the city of Ta-li.[34] In northwest China, bandits killed
the young William Ekvall Simpson, son of William Simpson.[35] In India, Christian
Schoonmaker, "because of [his] strong convictions on divine healing, did not feel

free to be vaccinated," died from smallpox, and left a widow and six children.[36] While sailing his small boat in the Caribbean Sea for evangelism in the smaller islands, Church of God in Christ missionary Cornelius Hall drowned when it capsized.[37] In some of these situations, the remaining family members stayed on as missionaries—an indicator of a shared commitment, though in other instances relatives of the bereaved returned home. When Clarence Grothaus and Karl Wittich (nephew of Philip Wittich) died within months after reaching German East Africa (Tanzania), the latter's widow, Marian [Keller], survived illness herself and became a pioneer in Kenya for the Pentecostal Assemblies of Canada.[38] But, rather than such news discouraging the faithful at home, missionary enlistment steadily climbed.

The salvation of "lost souls"—sometimes referred to as "plucking brands from the burning"—kept them at their posts despite the difficulties that confronted them. When the Welsh Presbyterian missionary J. Pengwern Jones met with Alfred and Lillian Garr in Calcutta, he found them to be "earnest Christians" who "have a passion for souls and have the means of bringing many sinners to Christ," though errant in their certainty about speaking in tongues as a proof of Spirit baptism.[39] Pentecostals also listed obedience to Christ and ministry to the hurting among their motives for mission. While reading a report by Sophie Nygaard on her activities in Liberia, Annie Cressman of Elmira, Ontario, reflected: "When the young people of the . . . church read that letter, they'll get ready and go. It seemed that simple. And God said, 'Annie, you go.' And it was never the same again."[40] Countless personal callings of this kind have filled the parade routes of Euroamerican and Majority World Pentecostal missionaries.

FAITH AND MONEY

Pentecostals in North America sent mixed signals about giving to missions, caused by perceptions of the idealized faith life, now severely tested by the never-ending stream of financial appeals. Speaking on world evangelization to the General Assembly of the Church of God in Cleveland, Tennessee, evangelist J. W. Buckalew thundered: "God is looking for men that will go heedless of the cost, trusting Him to supply all the needs," but regrettably, "some will not go unless there is a sack of money tied to the end of their call."[41] Even so, the Church of God soon recommended that treasurers of local congregations take a monthly offering for foreign missions.[42] Stanley Frodsham, missionary treasurer for the Assemblies of God, rhapsodized that "Pentecostal missionaries delight in the life of faith," preferring to trust in God rather than depending on individuals, assemblies, councils, or organizational officers for funds. Then, in a virtual contradiction of his statement, he mentioned that missionaries themselves "admitted that it would be a good thing . . . on the field to have the systematic support of an assembly back of them . . . and agreed they would encourage any efforts on the part of assemblies to take over the support of some missionaries that are not properly cared for."[43] Of course, missionaries felt under great pressure to produce results, as one in India bemoaned, "The Pentecostal people run well for a while, but after one is on the field and can not write such glowing reports he is forgotten."[44]

In an "open letter" to the members of the Pentecostal Holiness Church, T. H. Rousseau forthrightly condemned the "common idea prevailing among people in the homeland that mission work may be successfully carried on with little outlay of cash. They think after the outfit is purchased, the steamer ticket secured, excess baggage paid and a few dollars for the voyage," along with food and clothing after arrival, "[this] constitutes the missionaries' sole needs." But then, to achieve what they had been sent out to do, "a thousand and one other demands for cash" arise, including high rents, hiring of teachers, and purchasing property. Farsighted in his hope to evangelize the Chinese people, he warned that "to barely maintain a work is not sufficient; it needs to grow."[45]

Underscoring the power of expectant belief in God, James Jamieson in the West Indies trumpeted that "faith is heaven's money" and "there are many large things to ask the Lord for these days, especially the opening up of such doors as Nepal, Afghanistan, the East Coast of Africa and many parts of Central Africa."[46] One had to ask for big things, lest God's benevolence be limited by low expectation. Hattie Salyer, who evangelized among Muslim women in Egypt, received a nickel in the first offering taken for her fare and outfit, but "her faith reached up for $250.00 and that was the exact sum she received." Unfortunately, as Frodsham noted, "she afterwards realized that her faith should have reached up for more and the Lord would have provided more."[47] In Liberia, John Harrow glowed, "Our temporal needs have all been bountifully supplied by our Heavenly Father's hand, as we have trusted alone in Him for the support of every missionary and every need on the field." Furthermore, "each missionary trusts God for his own supplies, and also that of the children under their care. We have lacked nothing these eight years [1908-1916], and have gladly helped one another when the load got too heavy."[48] Notwithstanding the testimony of Salyer, Harrow, and many others to the provision of God, the concept of faith in relation to money would remain a problem in the Pentecostal tradition.[49] Given the lack of theological reflection when it came to money—even in the "faith life"—and judging by the broadcasting of needs and projects, one might suspect that to the faithful at home the mission of God through the church in the world would grind to a halt without it. Pentecostal missionaries willingly worked long hours and with little financial security—devoid of conventional salaries, pension plans, guaranteed furloughs home, or even monies reserved for steamship tickets home—because as Jesus had predicted, "Night is coming, when no one can work" (John 9:4). How could God's plan proceed without their efforts?

If they labored with limited resources, the editors of periodicals and church officials who received offerings to be sent their way agonized over the inequity in distribution. Designated funds went directly to the intended recipients, some of whom also received help from other sources, with undesignated monies usually divided to insure that all might receive some assistance. "Not that any have ever received too much, but some of God's worthy servants have received far too little, and for this we grieve," wrote Anna Reiff.[50] In the pages of the *Pentecostal Testimony*, Canadian Pentecostals learned: "It is a known fact . . . that almost all of our missionaries on the field are unable to do a very aggressive work for lack of means to go ahead."[51] Leaders of the Church of God expressed disappointment in 1922 when they discovered that only $891.32 had been received from their 550 churches for foreign missions during the preceding year, an embarrassing sum averaging to only $1.62 per congregation. "Brethren, this ought not to be," declared Z. D. Simpson, chair of the missions committee, though perhaps it reflected in part the economic plight of the faithful in this originally Appalachian-based denomination. "Will we, the Church of God, which have the commission to go into all the world and preach the gospel stand for such a report as this to come to this Assembly next year? Something must be done, and what will it be?"[52] Facing the same problem in the Pacific Northwest, the much smaller Bible Standard movement sent this admonition to its pastors and eight congregations: "Let every church take a missionary offering each month. . . . Your work will grow much faster and prosper more abundantly if you give liberally to missions than if you do not. 'He that watereth shall be watered also himself'" (Prov 11:25 [AV]).[53] Church leaders had cause for concern: For the support of five missionary families in 1928, combined offerings could be as low as $200 a month.[54] During the Great Depression, when mission offerings plummeted in the Pentecostal Church of God, missionary secretary Alfred Worth reminded the faithful that "there is no depression in Heaven and the Lord has told us that the cattle upon a thousand hills belong to Him and whatsoever we ask in faith believing it should be done."[55]

Like the increasing number of other Americans going overseas for various reasons including business and sightseeing, missionaries too enjoyed the sights and sounds of travel and found interest in the wares displayed in the shops. Recounting in detail the hardships and dangers of her trip from Jerusalem through Turkey to Europe in 1917 to flee the war zone in Palestine, Elizabeth Brown's report bubbles over with excitement at what she saw on the way. In one instance, after reaching Damascus, a missionary showed her the "sights of the city," including an old mosque said to be the original temple of the god Rimmon (2 Kgs 5:18) with a tomb inside that contained the head of John the Baptist![56]

But given the gravity of their calling and the otherworldly orientation of the faith life, monies spent on themselves and family members for mundane purposes, pleasure, or even what might be perceived as pleasure by some could scarcely be mentioned to supporters. Brown had nothing to fear because her sightseeing came at no added expense. But for others, caution about discussing finances when writing to the home base did not eliminate vulnerability to criticism. Early in 1911, Lillian Garr shared in a letter to the readers of the *Latter Rain Evangel* the needs of missionaries in China, some of whom had gone without funds for ten months in the previous year, as well as her and her husband's own desire to purchase a house in Hong Kong as a center for ministry.[57] At the very time the edition with her letter went to print, newspapers in the Midwest reported that her husband, Alfred, had managed to purchase a five-foot vase and pay the expense of shipping it all the way from Hong Kong to Anderson, Indiana, as a gift to his sister. As the first genuine Chinese vase ever seen in the area, it sparked considerable interest. "It is exquisite workmanship," reported the *Indianapolis Star*, "having been made by Chinese potters by a process not known in this country."[58] Whatever resources the Garrs may have possessed that could explain the expenditure—and the details are sketchy—they walked a tightrope between two worlds, far higher than the one walked by Pentecostals at home.

From another vantage point, though living simpler lifestyles than they had in America and shorn of many conveniences, Pentecostal missionaries had only a limited perception of the image their own Western affluence conveyed to their audiences.[59] Neither did they understand non-Christian beliefs and related social customs; apart from viewing religious practices in mission lands as demonic in origin, they expressed little interest in gaining a deeper and more accurate knowledge of them. (This slowly began to change; in the late 1940s several missionaries pursued graduate study at the Kennedy School of Missions in Hartford, Connecticut.[60]) In Mongolia, Thomas Hindle placed the blame on the prevailing Buddhism that "over sixty per cent of the male population are not allowed to take wives, but permitted to live the vilest immoral lives, so it is plain to be seen the race is a dying one, and their only salvation is to save them from their religion."[61] Missionaries also refused to accept the more positive reappraisals of the non-Christian religions emerging in some circles. Just months before missionary John Farquhar's *Crown of Hinduism* (1913) rolled off the presses, Max Wood Moorhead, an early leader in the Student Volunteer Movement and missionary to India who joined the Pentecostal movement, already aware of the shifting attitude toward Hinduism, rejected the notion that Christianity could be the "fulfillment" of Hinduism. He based his conclusion on a study of idolatry in the Old Testament to which he compared the function of Hindu idols.[62] As it did for other missionaries, Islam with its monotheism presented a special challenge. "Pray for the Mohammedans," charged the exasperated veteran missionary to Egypt Marie Ericsson. "Do not class them with the heathen. They are not heathen, but they are worse than the heathen and harder to teach."[63] Ironically, in Palestine, Pentecostal missionaries faced the dilemma of having pro-Zionist sympathies—part of the warp and woof of premillennial eschatology—while ministering to Muslims, who, along with the Jews, did not express much interest in their message.[64] In Asyut, Egypt, Lillian Trasher remembered, "Many many missionaries came out here, very capable people, but few stayed."[65]

Squabbling also complicated their lives. Independent and suspicious of organization, the concept of teamwork often fared better in theory than in practice. Ethel Bingeman, who had already served four years with the Interior Mission in Liberia, may have been more honest than most in filling out her application for appointment with the Assemblies of God in 1919. When it asked, "Do you get along well with others?" she could only answer, "fairly."[66] Nevertheless, approval followed. The problem of relationships became more apparent a year later as California pastor Harold Needham toured mission stations in Japan, China, India, Egypt, and Palestine on behalf of the denomination's Missionary Department. In his visits, he discovered "duplications of work, missionaries bumping elbows with each other, chafing under the circumstances and bringing friction between the native constituencies." Furthermore, "wide expanses of territory in surrounding districts were wholly unevangelized and untouched."[67]

In India, after Robert Cook left the Assemblies of God to become independent—later joining the Church of God (Cleveland, Tenn.)—and took the mission property with him, his former colleagues resented what they perceived as a betrayal.[68] Serving in a remote area of KwaZulu-Natal, Fred Burke established a school and correspondence program that trained many aspiring independent African church leaders. Like others of the era, he charted his own course. Having first been appointed by the Pentecostal Mission, Burke eventually joined the Assemblies of God and on more than one occasion exasperated mission executives in America.[69]

Obviously, they were not above brawling among themselves for what they perceived to be righteous causes in the work of God. The idealized unity of the Spirit baptized, so widely voiced among the faithful from the earliest years of the movement, tottered along with a limp, both at home and in the mission lands. With a strong preference for a charismatic style of leadership wherein one received directives from the Holy Spirit for the course of ministry, they often struggled with the notion that a committee could better discern the will of God than an individual. Martha Schoonmaker complained about the growing structure in Assemblies of God foreign missions: "We are so highly organized now . . . that if God were to lead an individual to go to a certain place for evangelistic work, he or she would have to first of all consult with three committees. . . . As a missionary of the Lord Jesus Christ, I want to be allowed to be led by His Spirit and do whatever He may want me to do."[70] While all the reasons for the conflict remain unknown, she subsequently resigned from the denomination; nonetheless, she remained in India as an independent missionary. Her supporters—Assemblies of God pastors and churches—more readily would have believed her side of the story.

In many contexts missionaries did work together well within their denominational affiliations, and occasionally above organizational lines or their independent status in mutual efforts. Examples included the Interior Mission (Liberia); the cooperative arrangement between the Russian and Eastern European Mission and the Assemblies of God;[71] comity arrangements between the Assemblies of God and the Pentecostal Assemblies of Canada;[72] and the informal associations among missionaries in Hong Kong and elsewhere.[73] In an unusual arrangement, the Congo Inland Mission, an agency founded by the Defenseless Mennonites and the Central Conference of Mennonites in 1911, admitted Pentecostals through the encouragement of Alma Doering, a missionary who traveled widely in Pentecostal circles.[74]

PREPARATION FOR THE HARVEST

Many Protestants who served abroad had been educated in universities and colleges with minimal formal theological training; though some attended seminaries, they often lacked the focused training on evangelism found among personnel of the faith missions who increasingly were products of Bible institutes. Pentecostals generally had the same level of education as most Americans at the beginning of the twentieth century, although a small number had attended universities and colleges before heading to the mission lands, including the veteran missionaries who became Pentecostal.[75] But, more commonly, they either went with no special preparation or had attended Bible institutes or similar training schools, including some non-Pentecostal ones such as Brooks Bible Institute (St. Louis), Chicago Training School for City, Home, and Foreign Missions, God's Bible School (Cincinnati), Missionary Training Institute (Nyack), Moody Bible Institute (Chicago), the Vanguard (St. Louis), and Toronto Bible Training School.

Many enrolled in the growing number of Pentecostal schools. Such institutions met certain needs for the preparation of clergy as when Church of God overseer Ambrose Tomlinson proposed the opening of the Bible Training School in Cleveland, Tennessee, to provide a place "where our young people can take a course of Bible and missionary training."[76] The superintendent of the school, Flavius Lee, compared it with the Old Testament schools of the prophets in the days of Samuel and Elijah. It not only supplied students with inspiration and biblical knowledge, but "I firmly believe," he added, "that the Bible school is the greatest thing in the Church of God as it will train the preachers to see eye to eye and preach the same thing."[77]

Originally designed as a "shortcut" into missions, the Bible institute allowed the student to bypass the normal path of four years of college and three years of seminary by offering a program that might last anywhere from several months to three years.[78] While leaders in the mainstream churches challenged the adequacy of such limited preparation, the genius of the institution rested on its fervent spiritual atmosphere, concentrated study of the Bible, emphasis on personal holiness, the importance of a divine calling, corporate experience of students and faculty praying and believing that God would underwrite the expenses, instruction, and assignments in practical ministry while enrolled, and quick entry into Christian service after graduation.[79] At some schools, students received ordination at commencement (for example, at the Apostolic Bible School in Ohio), but many went abroad as "Christian workers" without ministerial credentials. In addition, as Lee keenly observed, it had the opportunity to enhance uniformity in doctrine and unity among the preachers, churches, and their missionaries. Daniel Kerr, an early educator in the Assemblies of God, also looked to the Bible institute to train "laborers, who have passed the 'doubting point' concerning the verbal inspiration of the Bible . . . and the eternal judgment of the wicked," along with other fundamental tenets of the faith, showing his concern about the theological conflicts of the 1920s.[80]

Perhaps most important for foreign missions, Bible institutes resonated with a global outlook. "God strove with me to say 'yes' to a call to open a Pentecostal Missionary Training School," declared "Mother" Virginia Moss, pastor of an independent congregation in North Bergen, New Jersey. "God told me that we, as a mission, were settling down in ourselves and we must have an outlet or our testimony would die out; for the command had been given to testify first 'in Jerusalem, and in all Judea, and in Samaria, and unto the uttermost part of the earth' (Acts 1:8 [AV])."[81] In 1912, she opened Beulah Heights Bible and Missionary Training School, an institution that graduated many early missionaries. Though the curricula of these schools offered few courses in missions—Central Bible Institute in Springfield, Missouri listed just one in 1922—visiting missionaries made up for the lack when they spoke in chapel services.[82] Student prayer groups for different parts of the world usually met every week to read letters from missionaries and pray for the needs presented. Behind this stood the model of A. B. Simpson's Missionary Training Institute, the first Bible institute in America.[83]

In the 1920s and '30s, the Bible institute became dominant in the North American Pentecostal movement for the training of missionaries, though many still went overseas without such instruction. The shortcut with its advantages, however, came at a steep price: Like their fundamentalist and conservative evangelical counterparts who also employed Bible institutes for preparing missionaries, the Pentecostals and their mission executives were left with less education than missionaries in the mainline denominations.[84] While this did not deter them from becoming effective missionaries and administrators, the narrow lens of the curriculum limited their preparation for addressing the larger issues—theological, missiological, and cultural—with which the major Protestant agencies had been wrestling since the late nineteenth century and which they themselves eventually would face. "Left to their own nonreflective, activist proclivities," wrote historian Joel Carpenter, "fundamentalist missions and their leaders exhibited the epitome of what European missions leaders thought was the great fault of the American missionary enterprise: its anti-intellectual, impatient, pragmatic, and technique-oriented outlook."[85] This proved to be no less true of Pentecostal missionaries and their leaders. Nevertheless, as Assemblies of God general superintendent John Welch discovered, conversations with establishment mission leaders would have been difficult given the shifting ground on the traditional interpretation of the Bible and the ultimate claims of the faith in circles of the latter.

Pentecostals started many schools of ministry—all with a conservative theological bent, some of which lasted only a brief time or merged, while others endured for many years. They produced dedicated women and men who were obedient to the divine call and pragmatic in their approach to ministry. The following sampling of twenty schools with their original locations —most of them located in urban areas—represents the many such institutions founded before 1930:

Apostolic Bible School (Norwalk, Ohio)
Berean Bible Institute (San Diego)
Bethel Bible Training School (Newark)
Beulah Heights Bible and Missionary Training School (North Bergen, N.J.)
Bible Standard Training School (Eugene, Ore.)
Bible Training School (Cleveland, Tenn.)
Canadian Pentecostal Bible College (Winnipeg)

Central Bible Institute (Springfield, Mo.)
Detroit Missionary Bible School
Elim Bible Institute (Endwell, N.Y.)
Franklin Springs Institute (Ga.)
Glad Tidings Bible Institute (San Francisco)
Gospel School (Findlay, Ohio)
Holmes Bible and Missionary Institute (Greenville, S.C.)[86]
Latin American Bible Institute (San Antonio)
Lighthouse of International Foursquare Evangelism (Los Angeles)
Missionary Training School (Alliance, Ohio)
Rochester Bible Training School (N.Y.)[87]
Southern California Bible School (Los Angeles)
Zion Bible Institute (East Providence, R.I.)

That women held important posts in most of these schools, variously as
founders, administrators, and teachers, reveals the substantial part they played
in the shaping of early Pentecostal reflection on mission, mission education, and
missionaries.[88] Minnie Draper served as board chair of the Pentecostal Mission
in South and Central Africa when it established the Bethel Bible Training School
in Newark in 1916. In Cleveland, Tennessee, Nora Chambers, the first instructor
at the Bible Training School, had studied at Holmes Bible and Missionary Institute, engaged in evangelism in North Carolina and Georgia with her husband,
and now shared her expertise with the first class of twelve students who enrolled
in January 1918.[89] At Berean Bible Institute in San Diego, Alice Luce taught
Hispanics a Pentecostal version of indigenous church principles that would have
far-reaching effects. In Los Angeles, former missionary Aimee Semple McPherson trained thousands of future leaders at her "Lighthouse." Patterned after the
Bible institutes in North America, the schools created overseas by their graduates and the leadership provided by women missionaries in their operation
represent another part of the legacy of women. Furthermore, women greatly
outnumbered men as missionaries, as they did in the larger Protestant mission
movement.[90] When asked how she had managed to care for so many orphans
without a large church organization bankrolling the expenses, the plucky Lillian
Trasher, a graduate of Holmes Bible and Missionary Institute, said proudly, "An
American girl can do anything, if she tries hard enough."[91]

THREAT OF UNIVERSALISM

One of several thousand who attended the North American Missionary Conference at Washington, D.C., in early 1925—billed as the most important such
gathering on the continent since the Ecumenical Missionary Conference in New
York City twenty-six years earlier—John Welch heard the address by President
Calvin Coolidge and others by prominent mission leaders, including John Mott,
Charles Brent, Robert Speer, E. Stanley Jones, and Samuel Zwemer. Coolidge
may have startled the crusty Welch when he said, "The works of charity and

benevolence of education and enlightenment will best lay the foundation upon which to rear the permanent structure of a spiritual life."[92] But he winced when he heard Canadian Presbyterian J. D. MacRae, dean of the School of Theology at Shantung Christian University (Jinan, China), declare: "Now let no one allow that evangelist with a Bible under his arm, full of zeal and enthusiasm to preach Christ to individuals, get in the way of this great program of the church; for this great program of the church for world-wide Christian education is the true evangelism."[93] A lively round of applause followed. Launching Christian colleges overseas would surely detract from the primary need of preaching the gospel, thought Welch. "I did not imagine that the whole situation had practically turned from the idea of individual salvation into talking now about salvation as a community matter. They have . . . gone so far from the vision of the gospel that they are actually talking boastfully about saving the world through this great brotherhood of man."[94]

His lengthy and largely negative appraisal of the conference in the *Pentecostal Evangel* only confirmed what Pentecostals and other premillennialists suspected about the call for unity and the mounting "apostasy" in the mainline churches, an obvious harbinger of other prophetic fulfillments just around the corner. "Satan's super-man is on the way," he averred, "the modern church along with the nations, unconscious of what they are doing, are [lending] their efforts directly to the establishment of conditions for the antichrist to take supreme control. This 'get-together' idea is nothing other than that."[95] Yet, despite these concerns and amid the rising tide of the fundamentalist/modernist controversy, Welch did not recommend withdrawing from the Foreign Missions Conference of North America, which sponsored the convention and whose members held a wide range of theological views. The practical benefits to Assemblies of God foreign missions far outweighed the threat of the non-binding opinions of the speakers he heard.[96]

Pentecostal leaders generally knew of the changing currents in the historic Protestant churches, as well as the threat of "false leaders and teachers" who influenced people within their own circles. "We have people among us who cannot stand on the rock and endure for Christ. They have to have a tickled feeling and will run after everybody that can find it for them," Welch complained. He may have had in mind the well-known Pittsburgh pastor Charles Pridgeon and the British Pentecostal A. E. Saxby, both of whom espoused a form of Christian universalism that struck at the core objective of evangelism.

The publication in 1920 of Pridgeon's widely circulated *Is Hell Eternal: or, Will God's Plan Fail?* stunned Pentecostals, not because the author came from the liberal ranks of Protestantism, but because of his standing with radical evangelicals.[97] With impeccable credentials—graduate of Lafayette College (Easton, Pa.) and the conservative Princeton Theological Seminary (class of 1889)—he had worked with Dwight Moody in evangelistic campaigns. While pastoring First Presbyterian Church in Canonsburg, Pennsylvania, he received the "fullness of the Holy Spirit" and began praying for the sick, a turn that forced his resignation from the Presbyterian ministry in 1901. He then moved to Pittsburgh and started the independent Wylie Avenue Church and the Pittsburgh Bible Institute for the training of Christian workers. Both institutions operated on "faith lines," with the school not charging tuition.[98] For many years, he had been a speaker at conventions of the Christian and Missionary Alliance where some early Assemblies of God leaders may have met him and heard him speak. His zeal for missions led to the organization of the Evangelization Society for "the propagation of Christianity and the doing of Christian and charitable work at home and abroad in association with and supplementary to the work of the Pittsburgh Bible Institute."[99] Two years later, after attending a McPherson campaign in Dayton, Ohio, he returned home to encourage his students and associates to pray for a Pentecostal revival, which subsequently followed.[100] He himself then spoke in tongues and strongly recommended it as a means of prayer.[101]

Pridgeon had struggled for many years over the question of God's justice in sending men and women to hell who had never made a profession of faith or had the opportunity to hear the gospel message. "I do not believe that evil is eternal as God is eternal," he wrote. "Therefore, I believe that the duration of the place of punishment will be finite and that God will be Victor. I believe in a conscious existence hereafter, both in heaven and in hell, but I believe that God has a loving and corrective purpose, even in punishment."[102] *Is Hell Eternal*, along with Saxby's *God's Ultimate*, drew considerable interest as millions of people still grieved over relatives and friends who died in World War I.[103]

The roots of this Christian universalism, which included a form of "purgatory," can be traced to the writings of certain ancient church fathers.[104] It was labeled the "Larger Hope" theology (in due course, all will be saved either in this life or the next through the redemptive work of Christ), as well as "future probation," "restitution of all things" (Acts 3:21 [AV]) and "ultimate reconciliation" (Col 1:20). With varying interpretations, it became popular in the late nineteenth century among Unitarians, liberal Protestants,[105] the High Church Party of the Church of England, and even gained the endorsement of a prominent voice within the China Inland Mission—Stanley Smith, one of the Cambridge Seven.[106] In American Pentecostalism, a unique form of universalism had arisen by 1914 through the "Yellow Book Series," pamphlets produced by a group of "demon-deluded females in Chicago," obviously not under proper male submission in the opinion of critics (1 Cor 14:34-35).[107] (Interestingly, the women had pronounced on God's behalf that Eve "did no wrong.") They wrote down their teachings—based on information from messages in tongues and interpretations and prophecies—and printed them anonymously. Speaking directly for God, his "word" through the prophetesses announced: "I care not who you are, I am announcing to you that you are UNDER THE BLOOD," and "the story of NO CONDEMNATION covers more than a few earnest people, it gathers in the whole creation."[108] While future probation argued for a period of purification, their concept of universalism appeared to ignore entirely the need for such a process.[109] Uncharacteristic of the way Pentecostals usually thought, both in regard to universalism and the elevation of personal spiritual experience above the authority of Scripture, the Yellow Books and their authors received swift condemnation and their influence seems to have been minuscule.

By 1920, attention had turned to Pridgeon, his book, and the Pittsburgh

Bible Institute. Leading the charge against "Pridgeonism," Max Moorhead noted with alarm: "This erroneous teaching is knocking at Pentecostal doors for admittance; and we deeply regret that it has found admittance in the hearts of some." Recognizing the implication for evangelism, he asked, "If hell is not eternal, why warn men to flee from the wrath to come?"(Luke 3:7).[110] He sent excerpts from an article by William Proctor to the *Pentecostal Evangel* for publication. Originally published in *The Fundamentals*, a collection of ninety essays prepared by conservative evangelicals to affirm orthodox beliefs traditionally held by Protestants, it bore the title "What Christ Teaches about Future Retribution."[111] Proctor argued that "future retribution is not merely an incidental but a fundamental part of the Gospel message. It is the dark background on which its loving invitations . . . are presented, and the Gospel message loses much force when the doctrine is left out." Furthermore, and with direct relevance to mission, "the earnest exhortations to immediate repentance and faith lose their urgency if the ultimate result will be the same if those duties are postponed beyond the present life."[112] Moorhead, though an independent Pentecostal, contributed to the condemnations of the "Pridgeon doctrine" by the Pentecostal Assemblies of Canada in 1923 and the Assemblies of God in 1925, just seven months after Welch returned from the conference.[113] The liberal theology among missionaries in China had turned up the fire under the already boiling fundamentalist/ modernist controversy; Pentecostal leaders wanted to remain faithful to historic doctrine and preserve the urgent mission impulse of their movement.[114]

THE PENTECOSTAL STANDARD

J. Roswell Flower, the first missionary secretary of the Assemblies of God, spoke for many Pentecostals when he published an editorial in 1920 explaining the "Pentecostal standard" in missions, calling on the more than two hundred missionaries in the organization to concentrate their efforts on preaching the gospel. With the coming of the Lord so near, the "heathen in the neglected parts of the earth would scarcely have time to hear before Jesus should come," a prospect reinforced by "messages . . . given in the Spirit" that warned of time running out.[115] Given the eternal worth of the human soul and because of their pivotal role in end-times evangelism, Pentecostals could not afford to build schools, hospitals, and other charitable institutions.[116] Just five years before, the denomination's General Council in session had dedicated itself to Christ "for the greatest evangelism that the world has ever seen," a resolution that both implied proclamation as the paramount priority and unfurled the flag of an intended discontinuity with the way missions had been done in the "Great Century."[117] Flower's "shoot from the hip" announcement precluded further formal discussion on the matter.

Despite the widespread acceptance of the "standard," Flower warned that it stood in jeopardy because missionaries seemed to be too easily distracted by educational and charitable pursuits. In fact, the column in the *Pentecostal Evangel* next to his editorial contains a news note from Niels Thomsen in India wherein he appealed for funds to purchase property for a mission station. "We are living in a native house, and not complaining about it, for we truly praise the Lord for it," said Thomsen, "but there is not a foot of land attached to it so there is no chance of taking in any one who should be needy."[118] The "needy" could not be easily ignored, despite the narrow-gauged standard.

Flower may have suspected that charity had surpassed evangelism at Lillian Trasher's orphanage in Egypt. On her application for appointment with the Assemblies of God, submitted in 1919 after having served in Egypt for nine years, she answered, "I don't know," when asked how many had been converted under her ministry.[119] Trasher kept detailed information about the number of children she cared for and the funds required and received to feed and shelter them, but her lack of knowledge on this point must have looked puzzling. However, the precise time of a child's conversion might have been difficult to determine. Virtually all of the children came from Coptic Christian families. If they had not been baptized, then Trasher baptized them by sprinkling; otherwise without a record of baptism they were automatically classified as Muslims.[120] (When the children grew older and professed their faith, they were baptized again.) Still, the whole effort of caring for so many children and the constant responsibility of procuring monies to support them must have been overwhelming, and evangelism in the popular way of some in America—with emphasis on the counting of converts—did, in fact, take second place.

For American Pentecostals, the standard reflected their commission as the last missionary surge before the close of human history. To Flower—sharing the outlook of A. J. Gordon, A. B. Simpson, Charles Parham, William Seymour, and other radical evangelicals—the priority of gospel proclamation made perfect sense. But to those confronting poverty and hunger in Africa, Asia, and beyond—particularly women—it represented an unworkable criterion. Historically, the contributions of women to mission have been holistic in nature; evangelism and benevolence went hand-in-hand from sheer necessity and respect for human life. "Even in proclamation-oriented evangelical mission agencies, women were the ones to undertake ministries of compassion," according to historian Dana Robert. "Women's mission theory emphasized education, in the nineteenth century as the functional equivalent to preaching, and in the twentieth century for social liberation."[121] This helps to explain why missionaries of the China Inland Mission and the Christian and Missionary Alliance established orphanages, schools, and other institutions in practical defiance of their own missiology.[122] Judging by the complexity of what happened on the ground in Pentecostal missions, those who strictly adhered to the standard may have comprised the minority. The rest had blended ministries, either in projects that took them away from their regular duties for short periods or occupied their attention permanently. Missionaries never united behind the standard in actual practice; in fact, those within the Assemblies of God may have viewed Flower's declaration as presumptuous and an over-stepping of his authority—after all, he had never been a missionary![123] Like their Protestant counterparts, Pentecostals did not achieve a cohesive mission theology, due in part to the North American cultural preference for activism over theorizing.[124]

Illustrative of those who centered their work on proclamation, former Alliance missionaries Victor and Grace Plymire ministered on the Tibetan border and in Tibet. Without changing direction in their activities, they sowed the gospel seed through preaching and distributing tens of thousands of New Testaments, Gospel portions, and tracts on long treks through the mountains and across deserts. (The eldest son in every Tibetan family went to a monastery to learn how to read in order to study the sacred texts.) Certain that Christ would return when the gospel had been preached "in the whole world as a testimony to all nations" (Matt 24:14), they hoped that God "[would] some day cause fruit to spring from [their labors]," since they could not stay long enough in the far-off locations to plant churches because of the brevity of time or even guarantee their return to the areas they had visited.[125] Facing the entrenchment of Tibetan Buddhism, sixteen years passed before they saw their first convert.[126] More converts followed in the years to come, with the Plymires leaving an enduring legacy of churches.[127] In Liberia, United Holy Church missionaries Gladys Poole and Pearl Teasly left their teaching posts at the Georgia mission station in the hinterland to go farther into the bush to evangelize unreached tribes, revealing the commitment of the early missionaries to press forward to the regions beyond.[128]

The means of evangelism varied widely from preaching in the open air to tents and rented halls to other locations and opportunities. Martin Ryan, encountering students from all over East Asia attending Japanese universities, believed their evangelization would be the key to bringing the gospel to the Orient.[129] He also purchased a thirty-foot, two-masted lifeboat for evangelizing the coastal villages.[130] Frank Gray received permission to enter silk factories and preach the gospel, while William and Mary Taylor ministered to women incarcerated in Japanese prisons.[131] Others engaged in conducting street meetings, distributing Bible portions and tracts. Through the work of Chinese colporteurs and their own efforts, William and Orine Turner reported they had sold 12,000 Gospels and given away 24,750 other pieces of Christian literature in just one year, amid their other activities.[132] In South Africa, missionaries preached among the miners, many of whom came from nearby countries for employment in the gold mines; the converts then took their new-found faith back to their homelands.[133] Clarence and Helen Langley went to the prison camps in Hawaii where Filipino prisoners did time at hard labor (as a colonial power, the United States governed the Philippine Islands); spent entire evenings walking up and down the rows of beds in hospitals to give books and tracts to the patients and pray for them; and even ventured into the "basements of hospitals where visitors seldom went, and where the blind, crippled, and maimed received little attention."[134] In Ukraine and Russia, Ivan Voronaeff traveled thousands of miles by train, horse-drawn wagon, and on foot to preach in rented halls, homes, and barns in villages and cities.[135] When Ambrose Tomlinson noticed the Mexican people "who are constantly flowing into the United States," he proposed to the Church of God in 1920 that it begin translating gospel literature into the Spanish language as a means for their conversion.[136]

If their endeavors modeled the Pentecostal standard, then on what basis did missionaries justify other activities? First, charitable ministries had been viewed with favor long before the Pentecostal movement began. The circulation of stories about George Müller and his orphanages in Bristol, England, as well as the heroism of Pandita Ramabai and her care of famine victims in India, had made them legendary in their own lifetimes. As icons of the faith life, they had freely mixed evangelism and compassion together in successful enterprises. Arthur Pierson, who normally insisted on keeping gospel preaching at the forefront of missions, even wrote a popular biography of Müller to promote his work.[137]

Second, institutional work could be authorized by special permission from the Holy Spirit, evidenced by the activities of the early missionaries in Hong Kong and China who had no qualms about starting schools and charitable institutions. "I had God's command to open an 'English School for Boys and Young Men' at [Sainam]," declared May Law after she had "listened with tears, to their stories of cruel treatment by parents, when they accepted the true God."[138] In the same city, Addell Harrison from the hamlet of Lafayette, Oklahoma, prayed, "O God, what can I do for this dark land?" Seeing the terrible shame and poverty suffered by the blind, she and her daughter Golden opened the Orphanage for Blind Girls.[139] At Tianfu, Leslie Anglin, who felt directed to open an orphanage, said, "God gave me such a love for the Chinese until I was sometimes able to go to bed at night hungry that I might be able to feed them. It was easy for me to wear old clothes that those dear little fellows might have something to keep them warm."[140]

Defending the decision to welcome famine victims at the Sharannagar Mission in Nawabganj, India, Esther Harvey wrote in her memoirs: "It was a time of famine in India and people naked and starving came to us for help." She then played the spiritual trump card: "The Lord gave us Isa. 58:4-14" (especially verses 6-7: "Is not this the kind of fasting I have chosen: to loose the chains of injustice and untie the cords of the yoke, to set the oppressed free and break every yoke? Is it not to share your food with the hungry and to provide the poor wanderer with shelter—when you see the naked, to clothe them, and not to turn away from your own flesh and blood?").[141] Missionaries also knew that mercy extended in such circumstances might be instrumental in producing conversions. Thus, when famine struck Mongolia in 1921, Thomas Hindle worked for a time with the United International Relief Committee to provide free shelter, fuel, food and clothing to the victims. "We cannot see these poor people perish before our very eyes," he explained to supporters. "They seem interested in the gospel. This famine may be the means in God's hand of saving many precious souls."[142]

Though Pentecostals usually looked at evil in individual terms and knew of the peril of demonic opposition, some recognized the brutal and evil consequences of exploitation, as when Anna Reiff published information in the *Latter Rain Evangel* on the tragic loss of life among Peruvians due to the harsh conditions on the rubber plantations, as well as the Armenian genocide and the deplorable treatment of women in India.[143] In China, May Law bemoaned the destructive results of the opium trade and the recent efforts of the American Tobacco Company to promote cigarette smoking on a wide scale.[144] In an exceptional way among Pentecostal leaders, editor George Taylor kept his reading audience aware of the larger picture and problems facing missions through frequently reprinting articles in the *Pentecostal Holiness Advocate* from the *Missionary Review of the World*.[145]

Third, providing assistance to people in times of famine or other natural disasters sometimes necessitated relatively short periods of diversion from normal activities. When floods brought disaster to central Japan, Ryan quickly took food to an area of Tokyo where many people faced starvation.[146] For others, it formed part of a seamless daily schedule of ministry. At Taimingfu in North China, Bernt Berntsen and other missionaries conducted a street meeting every morning at 9 A.M. "We . . . have a goodly crowd, for we are feeding the hungry beggars with a little food daily and that has a great effect on the people," reported the cash-strapped Berntsen, "for actions speak better than words." As a result, "they cannot say we are here to get the best of them, and it gives us favor with the people."[147] Along with food assistance, they began to care for orphans.

Fourth, orphanages and schools produced Christian leaders in contexts like China and India where fierce opposition to Christianity often limited traditional evangelistic activities. Jacob Mueller in North India recounted that "not a few of these orphans, trained and developed in our Pentecostal schools, have become excellent Christian workers."[148] Recognition of the need for Bible institutes surfaced early and in many places. At Sainam in 1914, George and Margaret Kelley opened a school for "our converts who wish to be workers for the Lord."[149] At approximately the same time in Venezuela, former Alliance missionary Gerard Bailly founded Hebron Training School.[150] Working among the miners in South Africa, Edgar Pettenger said a Bible training school was the "greatest need of our work at the present time—trained, Spirit-filled, native preachers on fire for God, who will not compromise with the devil."[151] Of course, in some contexts this required that missionaries begin by teaching their students how to read and write in their own languages. One of the most strategically successful schools, the Institute of the Bible, sponsored by the Russian and Eastern European Mission, operated in Gdansk, Poland, until the Nazi invasion of 1939.[152] Many schools, some short-term and others permanent, would be developed in the years ahead, especially in the post–World War II period.

THE INDIGENOUS CHURCH

A survey of Protestant missionaries early in the twentieth century would have found a consensus on the indigenous church as the goal of mission. When a church became self-governing, self-supporting, and self-propagating, it had become essentially capable of sustaining itself. Indigenous church principles—the Three-Selfs—had won a broad hearing in the nineteenth century through the strategies and writings of Henry Venn, chief secretary of the Church Missionary Society; Rufus Anderson, senior secretary of the American Board of Commissioners for Foreign Missions; William Taylor, the Methodist bishop for Africa; Presbyterian missionary John Nevius; and later the Anglican Roland Allen, the latter two serving in China.[153] Regional and international missionary conferences also addressed issues related to the formation of indigenous churches, such as the transitioning of established churches and clergy funded by mission agencies to an indigenous model.[154] Given the level of interest, one can only wonder why missionaries plodded along so slowly toward its realization. Even Pentecostals who touted their unique brand of restorationism as a guarantee for creating "New Testament churches" made only limited progress until after 1950, the notable exceptions being Chile and Brazil—two countries outside the colonial orbit. Among the reasons for both the mainline mission boards and the Pentecostals, there appears the lingering colonial mentality with its cultural prejudices—most Pentecostal missionaries before World War II served in countries under various forms of colonial domination. Other factors included the time required in "civilizing" in preparation for self-governance; the threatened position of the Western missionary; and the penchant for putting native helpers on the mission payroll, thus making them financially dependent on the foreign mission boards.[155]

Like most Westerners who lived abroad, Pentecostal missionaries accepted their racial and cultural superiority as a given. From South Africa, John Lake said missionaries should not come with a lot of "brand new American ideas," and then complained that "one of the curses of [the] American missionaries [he encountered] is that they teach race equality."[156] Pentecostals sprinkled terms like "heathen," "heathenism," "darkness," and "dark land" across their letters and reports home. Henry Turney in South Africa recycled an American racial myth when he said, "We must never forget that the natives are only, after all, grown-up children and require much training and instruction, even after they become Christians."[157] In French West Africa, Arthur Wilson unpacked another myth when he reflected on the intelligence of the Mossi people: "Mentally, they are not the equal of some other tribes, but they are not of such low mentality as some have supposed. They can be trained to a very satisfactory degree."[158] In a commonplace practice among missionaries, Paul and Evelyn Derr in East Africa would not allow their children "to play with natives on account of the fact that disease, filth, etc. are so common."[159] Pearl Loftin looked at every Chinese person she encountered as an "object of pity," while insisting that God had put love in her heart for them. Though "every human being upon which the curse of Adam has fallen is an object of pity, more especially are those who are plodding their way through life in heathen darkness, with nothing to live for, and no promise at the end of the way."[160] Loftin's remark revealed her difficulty in adjusting to a different culture and one that she barely understood. Seemingly, only a divinely bestowed gift of love could make her care for the people. While her comments smack of arrogance and racism, love apparently kept her there; it would have been far easier to return home. Lake, Turney, Wilson, the Derrs, and Loftin remained at their posts, to work for the spiritual and physical welfare of other people.

The accounts of individuals such as Leslie Anglin—"I was sometimes able to go to bed at night hungry that I might be able to feed them"—enlarge the picture. Lillian Trasher ended her engagement to be married to go to Egypt. When asked late in life if she had any regrets about having done so, she responded, "If I had married Tom [Jordan], what would have happened to all these children?"[161]

Missionaries, though largely unschooled in cross-cultural dynamics, generally grew in their understanding and appreciation of the peoples to whom they ministered. As Joseph Blakeney in the Congo reported, "My heart goes out more and more to these people, and greater love than ever is coming into my heart for them."[162] In effect, their actions demonstrated a combination of attitudes: dedication, loving concern, and selflessness wrapped in nurture with the bowknot of a benevolent paternalism. Despite their shortcomings, albeit characteristic of most missionaries at the time, their presentation of the gospel, as well as the comfort and aid they brought, contributed to the unprecedented expansion of Christianity in the twentieth century.

Protestant missionaries had long relegated the possibility of an indigenous church to the distant future because of lengthy educational requirements for native clergy and their need of supervision, though exceptions can be found.[163] Pentecostals also valued training. Hence, Kelley opened a Bible institute because, unlike Christians in America who had been taught the "eternal Word of God . . . from infancy," Chinese converts lacked the preparation to preach the gospel before the public.[164] Preferring the more pragmatic delivery system of the shortcut, Bible institutes—far less expensive to operate than colleges and seminaries—reduced the time of formal training and provided a speedy entry into ministry.[165] This wove the "civilizing" factor into their educational work: In Mossiland (Burkina Faso), missionaries spoke of step-by-step planning to create an indigenous church: reducing the Moré language to writing, Bible translation, preparation of Christian literature, and literacy training.[166]

Though celebrating the outpouring of the Holy Spirit and the distribution of the Spirit's gifts for the building of the church, many Pentecostals struggled to turn over the reins of control. Their status as Westerners in the twilight years of the colonial empires, hesitations about pro-independence movements, the fact that God had called them to serve in particular countries with specific duties to accomplish, and the comparative abundance of their financial resources to those of native Christians, all stood as roadblocks in the path to the indigenous church. Nevertheless, the Assemblies of God *Missionary Manual*, published in 1931, had defined the missionary as an "ambassador for Christ and is sent to represent God to people who have no other means of knowing Him." Furthermore, "he must remember that above all things else he is a servant, should never consider that racial superiority or control of finances entitle him to exercise lordship over the Assemblies. As soon as the native converts manifest gifts of ministry they should be encouraged to take responsibility."[167] Yet, this same spirituality with its belief in the direct conferral of gifts by the Spirit virtually guaranteed schisms from mission churches when younger leaders became frustrated with their missionary mentors and mission board policies.

ADVOCATES OF THE INDIGENOUS CHURCH

The rhetoric of premillennialism unrelentingly warned that believers lived in the very last days of human history with little time to do anything other than preach the gospel; even so, missionaries frequently deflated the urgency of their eschatology to pump up the permanence of their endeavors. Blakeney faced the immediate challenge of constructing buildings in the Belgian Congo before the rainy season commenced. "I have had to use my own hands and saw the timber out of the rough trees by hand," he reported. "One who has never done this in a tropical climate, cannot realize the sweat and toil there is. But I like it and am not complaining."[168] Nurturing converts naturally required them to consider ways of preserving their labors.

The first Pentecostal missionaries gave little thought to mission theory or strategic planning on their way overseas. Their sole responsibility revolved around preaching to whoever would listen; Christ's responsibility was to return (soon!). But upon arrival, the romanticized scenario faded and the realities of mission work appeared: locating or building proper facilities, learning the language, producing gospel literature, discipling converts, starting Bible institutes, caring for the hurting, and securing predictable support from the homeland. Pentecostals benefitted enormously from the foundations laid by earlier missionaries who prepared Bible translations, worked with colonial governments for protection and social improvements, addressed issues facing the churches such as polygamous marriages, and established schools and charitable institutions that served as models.

The earliest Pentecostals to implement indigenous church principles reflected the influence of William Taylor on the Chilean Methodist Pentecostal Church led by Willis Hoover and that of Baptist ecclesiology in the ministries of Daniel Berg and Gunnar Vingren in Brazil.[169] When Pentecostal revival began in 1909 at Valparaiso, it ultimately led to a split within the Methodist Church of Chile, at that time a district within the South American Conference of the Methodist Episcopal Church (U.S.A.).[170] Apart from theological beliefs such as Spirit baptism, the movement grew because it financed itself from the beginning and offered Chileans an authentic non-Catholic indigenous expression of Christianity. "We are just as Methodistic as Wesley," explained Hoover twelve years later. "We have fourteen preaching places outside the central church and a class-meeting is held one night a week in each of those places. . . . Exhorters take turns in preaching. . . . Then we have a great deal of out-door preaching. The brethren form groups and preach on the street-corners, in the market-place, at the fisheries and wharves."[171] As would be true later in many Latin American countries, preaching on the streets and to small groups would be the door to ministry, not the classrooms of the seminaries.

Far from the hierarchical Methodist context in Chile, Berg and Vingren, Swedish Baptist immigrants to America who became Pentecostal in 1909, left for Brazil a year later. Both men felt called to missions but didn't know to what country they should go. During a Saturday night service at the Swedish Baptist Church in South Bend, Indiana, a member of the congregation, Adolf Uldine, prophesied to Vingren that he should go to "Pará" and preach the gospel. Uldine later gave the some prophetic word to Berg. Not knowing the location of Pará, but convinced they had heard from God, they went to the Chicago Public Library where an almanac showed it as a state in Brazil. They boarded a train to New York City and booked passage on a tramp steamer to Belém, a major coastal port and the Pará state capital.[172] The autonomous churches they launched—eventually known as the Assemblies of God of Brazil—depict a Swedish contribution to world Pentecostalism; they had no original link to the later Assemblies of God (U.S.A.).[173] Berg and Vingren and other Swedish Pentecostals who followed them reflected the influence of the Baptist-trained Lewi Pethrus, the father figure of Swedish Pentecostalism. According to their version of Baptist ecclesiology, final authority belongs to the local church and ministerial training should occur within that context and be informal. In Brazil as in Sweden, Pentecostals consequently resisted the notion of permanent Bible institutes that drew students from more than one church. Also coming from the Pentecostal revival in Chicago, the Italian-American Luigi Francescon traveled to Argentina in 1909 and helped in the formation of the Pentecostal movement in the Italian community there; he found greater success a year later in São Paulo, Brazil, where he founded what would become one of the largest Pentecostal bodies in the country, the Congregacioni Christiani.[174]

Rapid growth followed their evangelistic campaigns, with local converts quickly taking the reins of leadership. "We continued from one place to another, distributing Bibles and Testaments and opening up places in the interior," wrote Vingren. After preaching in the state of Ceará, he returned later to find "one church of seventy members and another of thirty members, many baptized in the Holy Ghost," constituting completely self-supporting and self-propagating churches.[175] Baptist (congregational) church polity encouraged the emergence of indigenous Pentecostal churches. Church growth researchers later discovered that in 1911, one year after the arrival of the two missionaries, "a large number of consecrated laymen began to plant churches (without financial assistance from outside Brazil) in main centers on the coast. . . . Within fifty years the Assembléias had established churches in every state in the Republic, eventually becoming the largest Church in most states."[176]

Few treatments of indigenous church principles surface in early Pentecostal literature. Without mentioning the Three Selfs specifically, one of the first expositions appeared in the *Canton Pentecost*, published in China by Paul Bettex. In an article written in 1914, he described three stages of missionary effort: Bible translation and creation of Christian literature; gathering of converts into local churches that become "living centers of light"; and maturation of a "full grown, Spirit-filled church, freed from the childish things of the nursery, filled with the Spirit, reproducing the characteristics of the living New Testament church, leaning on the Word alone as its guide."[177] Echoing Roland Allen, he added that "[Western] financial lines are the leading strings by which that native church is held back. . . . Once the gospel shall run free . . . we will have a Biblical, strong, hardy native church. . . . Until then we are in a certain degree, what a delicate tropical orchid is in a Chicago or London greenhouse—an exotic artificial growth."[178] Building indigenous churches would entail weaning the native clergy and their congregations off the mission subsidy.[179] Bettex's observations and concerns typically represented those of other missionaries in China and beyond.[180]

A year later, Allen's concept of the indigenous church as explained in his famous *Missionary Methods: St. Paul's or Ours?* (1912) gained exposure among Pentecostals when Cecil Polhill published an excerpt that focused on strategy in *Flames of Fire*, the official voice of the Pentecostal Missionary Union. The revolutionary nature of Allen's proposals, however, received more attention in North America with three articles in the *Pentecostal Evangel* written by Alice Luce in 1921, perhaps the most noteworthy statement on missiology penned by a Pentecostal in the first half of the century. A former Anglican serving with the Church Missionary Society, she began evangelizing and later taught Hispanic candidates for ministry in California.[181] Having worked in *zenana* ministry (to women secluded in harems) and educational institutions in India, she read Allen's book with great interest and acknowledged that "it opened my eyes to the diametrical distinction between our methods of working and those of the New Testament."[182] His missiological exposition of the book of Acts naturally interested Pentecostals such as Luce who saw their own approach to mission as an extension of the biblical narrative. Indeed, they were among the few to appreciate his missiological insights.[183]

Despite the biblical framework that Allen offered and the insights of his Spirit-centered ecclesiology for the formation of the indigenous church, Luce went beyond his thinking by calling attention to the vital experience of Spirit baptism and her confidence that miracles would accompany gospel proclamation. Thus, reflecting on her years in India, she asked rhetorically: "When we go forth to preach the Full Gospel, are we going to expect an experience like that of the denominational missionaries, or shall we look for the signs to follow?"[184] Sixteen years later in 1937, the British Assemblies of God leader Donald Gee said much the same in his exposition of the "Indigenous Principle": "The establishing of indigenous churches that conform to the pattern of the New Testament will remain a practical impossibility without that Pentecostal dynamic which can alone account for the existence of a true church anywhere."[185]

In Luce's Pentecostal adaptation of Allen's theory, Spirit baptism offered the means to empower believers for witness and transform relationships necessary for creating indigenous churches. "Love and harmony in the Spirit" would enable missionaries to overcome cultural biases. No longer functioning as "lords over God's heritage" from the throne of cultural and racial superiority, missionaries would supervise temporarily simply "because we are older in the faith and have experienced more of the Spirit's guidance than they have."[186] Finally, with the ascendency of qualified leaders, "what a joy it will be to us to be subject to them, and to let them take the lead as the Spirit Himself shall guide them."[187] Luce's call for the application of the fruit of the Spirit to the interconnection with church leaders, most notably the submission of missionaries to their mature converts, must have startled at least some of her readers. It is interesting to note that her adopted denomination, the Assemblies of God, later preferred the notion of "partnership" as better representing the relationship between Paul and the churches he planted.[188]

As would be true of other Pentecostal advocates of the Three Selfs, Luce reacted against institutional ministries because they offered only a roundabout and uncertain path to the indigenous church: "After 24 years of work as a missionary, I mourn to think of how much time I have spent in serving tables, when I might have been all the time preaching the Gospel."[189] The higher calling of preaching—the Pentecostal standard—meant that others should be left to do works of mercy and philanthropy, lest the "enemy" compromise the proper task of missionaries by diverting "our time and our energies from God's best, viz., the preaching of the glorious Gospel in all its fullness in the little time which yet remains before Jesus comes."[190] When trained leaders had taken their places in the churches, then local deacons would fulfill their prescribed New Testament responsibility of caring for widows and orphans and "all the inevitable 'serving of tables,'" thus freeing the missionary for prayer and preaching.[191]

Not all North American Pentecostals openly embraced the Three Selfs, either because of their doctrine of the church or for other reasons. The Church of God in Christ, as well as the Church of God (Cleveland, Tenn.) and the historically related Church of God of Prophecy, may have been the primary dissenters because of the blending of their ecclesiology and missiology—the latter two organizations each claiming to be "the Church of God of the Bible."[192] The founders of all three denominations viewed church governance through a theocratic lens. With its episcopal form of church government, the Church of God in Christ established the Home and Foreign Mission Board in 1925 and in the next few years sent missionaries to Trinidad, Turks Island, Costa Rica, and Liberia. It then appointed bishops to oversee its churches as they developed in Liberia, Haiti, and South Africa.[193]

Though the exclusive claim of being the one true church faded in the Church of God (Cleveland, Tenn.), leaders perceived that when its missionaries moved into new countries, the church itself advanced in the process.[194] Following a time of inner turmoil and schism in the early 1920s, which paralyzed vital aspects of its development, the next decade witnessed a dramatic expansion through the enterprising James Ingram, who journeyed around the world visiting independent Pentecostal missionaries and their places of activity. His offer of unity with the Church of God promised financial assistance and brought under its tent numerous pioneers, among them Maria Atkinson (Mexico), Robert Cook (India), Charles Furman (Guatemala), and Herman Lauster (Germany).[195] At the South Indian mission station of Robert Cook, the question had arisen: "Where is there a body that would consider the Indians coequal in the work of the church and that would partially help financially?" Upon hearing of Ingram's visit, "the Spirit at once witnessed to Cook: 'Here is your help.'"[196] A later enlargement to the Church of God came in 1951 with the "amalgamation" of the Full Gospel Church in South Africa.[197]

At its International Congress on World Evangelism in 1986, the Church of God officially described itself as "an international communion with vibrant national churches which are sending missionaries to other cultures while effectively evangelizing their own people," but without explicitly mentioning the Three Selfs. Such a reference might have been interpreted as suggesting a lessened role for the church's central hierarchical structure.[198] Nonetheless, as missiologist Warren Newberry discovered, "The various Pentecostal mission bodies, either implicitly or explicitly, have adopted some sort of indigenous church principles into their philosophy or objectives."[199]

TRIUMPH OF THE STANDARD

The years during and immediately after World War II saw important changes in Assemblies of God foreign missions, the largest of the North American Pentecostal agencies and the leader in missiological reflection. Through the influence of Luce's articles on the Pauline mission methods, the General Council—the denomination's highest governing body—approved a lengthy statement on the Three Selfs in 1921.[200] But since the missionaries had made only nominal progress in their implementation by 1929, missionary secretary Noel Perkin pressed them to study Allen's *Missionary Methods* and his later *Spontaneous Expansion of the Church and the Causes Which Hinder It*. "It is very easy to set out for the foreign field and after arrival follow the policy of some old established denomination without stopping to consider whether the methods used are Scriptural or not," he warned.[201] During the war in 1943, with more than a quarter of its personnel at home, the missions department convened a conference in Springfield, Missouri, to plan for the future, one that called for major changes in operation and enabled the top leaders for the first time to chart strategy for the future.[202]

In the following year, Melvin and Lois Hodges returned home from their second term of service in Central America. At the invitation of Perkin, Melvin Hodges began a five-year stint as editor of publications with the apparent request from the mission leadership to press the importance of phasing out the overseas district councils and transitioning the churches to an indigenous status. It came none too soon, as Perkin lamented: "There are many things that we have to learn to overcome when we enter into our life in Christ. There are some things that are so deeply rooted in us that we are hardly conscious of them. One of these is an innate feeling of white superiority. . . . I have seen difference of treatment by our missionaries of those who are colored."[203] Hodges published Perkin's reflection in *Missionary Forum*—Hodges's "bully pulpit"—an in-house publication for missionaries, as well as the letter of an Indian Assemblies of God churchman who bitterly queried: "Are we right in concluding that the same age-old idea which makes the missionary the supreme dictator over a work for which he happens to find the money is also held by the Assemblies of God missionaries?" Moreover, "the entire mission system is based on this unscriptural ground which has produced a set of spoon-fed workers . . . spiritually and financially crippled."[204]

This new direction came in the post-war context of major political realignments, the demise of the colonial empires, and the independence of scores of new nations. As it happened, the mainline Protestant missions and the International Missionary Council had given much more thought to the indigenous character of the "younger churches" in preparation for national independence than had the Pentecostals.[205] Thus, while Hodges and other Assemblies of God leaders carefully studied Allen's writings, they remained unaware or skeptical of conciliar discussions on theology and mission. This came about in part because of the ecclesiastical gerrymandering of the early 1940s in which four Pentecostal denominations—the Assemblies of God, Church of God (Cleveland, Tenn.), Open Bible Standard Churches, and the Pentecostal Holiness Church—joined the conservative National Association of Evangelicals, an action that dampened prospects for discourse with the far larger number of evangelicals in the historic denominations affiliated with the National Council of Churches.

Hodges had come to his position with unique qualifications. The son of a former Methodist pastor-turned-Pentecostal, his ministry began in Greeley, Colorado, where he preached in street meetings and played his trombone. Without formal theological training—perhaps because of limited resources or because of fervent expectancy of Christ's return—he served a succession of pastorates before traveling to El Salvador in 1936 as a missionary.[206] There he worked under the tutelage of Ralph Williams, an understudy of Luce, who had begun to transition the existing Pentecostal churches to an indigenous status. Williams, one of the most influential missionaries to serve in Latin America, had come at the invitation of Francisco Arbizú, with whom he successfully laid the foundations for what they considered to be a model New Testament church.[207] Hodges later moved to Nicaragua, during a time of great political unrest in the country, and founded a Bible institute in Matagalpa for training ministers to reach their own people. Although the work there met with less success than in El Salvador, he reported in 1942 that "the native brethren have decided to withdraw financial help from five of the more established assemblies in order to open new fields."[208] In many respects, he represented the quintessential missionary of earlier Pentecostal missions: someone who lacked formal missiological training but was obedient to the divine call and quick to adapt as a learner when needs arose. In a region where the work of charitable institutions and schools had been a traditional function of the Roman Catholic Church, Williams and Hodges forged their missiology on church planting, free of the encumbrances of orphanages, schools, and relief endeavors that marked Pentecostal missions in India, China, and Africa.[209] The official missiology of the Assemblies of God thus took shape in the nominally Christian contexts of Latin America, not on the frontlines of evangelism in countries dominated by the non-Christian religions.

In 1951, mission leaders invited Hodges to address a special gathering of missionaries. The ensuing lectures formed the basis for his best-known book, *The Indigenous Church*, first printed in 1953 by Gospel Publishing House, the publishing arm of the Assemblies of God. Shortly afterward, it attracted the attention of Moody Press, which gained permission to print it as part of its Colportage Library, along with a crucial abridgement that removed references to miracles, healing of the sick, and the gifts of the Holy Spirit.[210] A clearer demarcation between Pentecostal and evangelical missiology could not have been drawn at the time. Notwithstanding the deletion, the Moody edition reflects the consensus of missiology common to evangelicals and Pentecostals. In important respects, the publication of *The Indigenous Church* signified the triumph of the Pentecostal standard with its undivided attention to the Three Selfs, the training of leaders, and converting existing churches over to a suggested indig-

enous model. The notion of "self-theologizing," however, did not accompany
the objectives of self-governance, self-support, and self-propagation, since in the
minds of the missionaries the doctrines they brought with them did not require
further reflection.

Hodges maintained that the "founding of the indigenous church is the primary objective of missionary activity."[211] The church then should become the
"salt of the earth" and bring social uplift according to Christian principles. In
reference to the popular appeal of charitable ministries and the flow of monies
in that direction, he stressed that "anything which hinders the development of
the Church, no matter how much immediate good it does, should be sacrificed
for the slower but more permanent good achieved through the establishment
of the indigenous church."[212] While the missionary as an individual Christian
would undoubtedly "administer the cup of cold water in Christ's name," the
money must come only from his personal funds. As a missionary, he should
concentrate his energies, activities, and foreign resources on the primary task
of planting the church.[213] Otherwise, the gospel message with its meaning for
personal salvation would become confused with the material by-products of
the faith. When it came to questions of church and society, indigenous Assemblies of God denominations would follow the lead of the politically and socially
conservative missionaries or simply proceed in adapting their faith in ways that
would not be rehearsed in denominational publications in America.[214]

The book came at a time when leaders discerned that Assemblies of God missions stood at a crossroads: either to follow New Testament methods and realize more conversions through the evangelistic activities of indigenous churches
or to see needed funds continue flowing to charitable institutions resulting in
fewer conversions. Perkin already had cautioned missionaries about the growing
expenses of maintaining and enlarging orphanages and similar programs. He
reasoned that "the material and physical need of the people in many lands is
relatively unlimited, so that all available . . . funds could readily be absorbed in
such work."[215] Yet, it proved to be incongruous that while missionaries taught
that salvation and physical healing worked together as components of the gospel, the voices of Hodges, Perkin, and other second-generation Pentecostal leaders consigned additional forms of physical—material—assistance to a second-
ary level of importance. In this respect, they generally mirrored the missiological thinking of conservative evangelicals who championed personal salvation
over social ministries and social action, and who feared the encroachment of the
social gospel.[216]

The Indigenous Church, well received among many evangelicals and Pentecostals, marked a breakthrough for putting into action the Three Selfs; its
impact on church growth has been indisputable. It also became a watershed in
the history of Assemblies of God missions, as Hodges and his associates used it
to retrain the missionary personnel, challenging them to focus on training and
altering their role as supervisors to that of partners with emerging leaders. In
the years following its publication, missionaries founded scores of Bible institutes—eventually hundreds of training schools offering various levels of instruction, depending on the preparedness of students.[217] Missionaries now became

educators, preparing pastors, evangelists, and church officers to evangelize their own nations. Though not immediately evident in the early 1950s, this led to a seismic shift in missionary vocation, a reorientation from the pulpit to the lectern that increasingly withdrew them from the direct evangelism of unreached peoples. It would now be up to trained native leaders with oversight of all the churches to guide them in evangelism.

Meeting a major need at the time and providing a sharper focus to Assemblies of God missions, *The Indigenous Church* excelled for its "how-to" advice, albeit conceptualized from a North American perspective and without a historical lens.[218] The actual implementation, however, led to many divergences of the policy because of inconsistencies in application, changes in mission administrators, as well as the naïve notion that it would fit into all cultural contexts and patterns of authority.[219] Still, in a far-reaching development, Hodges's book became crystallized as the authoritative guide within Assemblies of God foreign missions. In the years following, he reflected more on the church's involvement in society and in helping the hurting, and became one of the earliest Pentecostals to consider the relationship of the advancing kingdom of God with its attendant emphasis on Christian ethical behavior to the mission of the church.[220] "The local church should be encouraged to engage in a program of relief and help to the needy," he later wrote. "They should have their own benevolence fund. Some of the larger churches have established commissaries, schools, and clinics to help first their own members and then the public in general."[221]

Despite the instruction that missionaries received on the Three Selfs, many continued to engage in holistic ministries. "Though the major goal was in theory the salvation of souls," commented missiologist Charles Van Engen, "the missionaries found that as they fell in love with the people to whom they had been sent, they yearned to help them in any way they could and ended up bringing education, medicine, agriculture, translation, and other things."[222] Though speaking generally of evangelical missionaries in the post-war period, Van Engen's observation accurately portrays Pentecostals as well. While the standard offered an idealized vision of mission practice, missionaries, as well as the indigenous church leaders with whom they worked, pared it "as the Spirit led." After all, as Esther Harvey queried, "Could we preach the love of Christ to these and turn them away naked and hungry to die along the roadside? We could not."[223]

9

Healing Movements and Misgivings

There are signs of revival in Christendom. This revival has about it an air of spontaneity. . . . It has not sprung from the clergy, nor has it originated in the Universities. . . . Religion, we are seeing, comes with healing in its wings—health for the soul and health for the body; it is harmony, balance, happiness, peace.[1]
> Vicar of St. Mary-the-Virgin Church (London), Percy Dearmer, 1909

It is this burning zeal of the people who have been healed, and their determination to pass on the gospel of health and salvation to the rest of the world, that is turning the movement into a crusade. In city after city of the United States today the story that Jesus Christ heals is being told by those who say that they have experienced this healing.[2]
> Journalist Mabel Potter Daggett in *Ladies' Home Journal*, 1923

Around this name [Pentecostalism] gathers the story of about everything that is grossly objectionable from a religious standpoint. . . . [But Mr. Hickson,] a consecrated, talented, Church of England layman of London . . . has been used in a remarkable healing ministry in recent years throughout six continents . . . although [he] adopts the more extreme form of the doctrine of healing, namely that the cure of disease is in the Atonement.[3]
> Presbyterian evangelist William Biederwolf, 1939

It would fill a volume to mention all the evils which follow these "healing campaigns."[4]
> Fundamentalist Bible teacher Arno Gaebelein, ca. 1940

As I have been reviewing church growth around the world, I have seen that it frequently correlates with great healing campaigns. . . . Among vast populations, divine healing is one of the ways in which God brings men and women to believe in the Savior.[5]
> Founder of the Church Growth movement, Donald McGavran, 1979

Early in the twentieth century, Pentecostals raced out of the gate with unbridled confidence in God's willingness to save the lost, heal the sick, deliver from chemical addictions, and cast out demons. No one expressed it better than Aimee Semple McPherson in a sermon entitled "Is Jesus Christ the Great 'I AM' or Is He the Great 'I WAS?'"[6] Along with other favorite Scriptures, Pentecostals like McPherson trumpeted Matthew 8:16-17 (Isa 53:4 [LXX] quoted in 17: "He took up our infirmities and bore our diseases"), and Hebrews 13:8 as a guarantee of God's willingness to intervene supernaturally for salvation and physical healing: "Jesus Christ is the same yesterday and today and forever." Such preaching—accompanied by prayer for the sick—drew thousands to their meetings looking for divine aid at a time when many churches had turned to curing the ills of society through programs inspired by the social gospel. "'The Great I AM'—why yes! . . . That's what this old world needs," McPherson preached knowingly, "a Christ who changeth not . . . whose power knows neither lack nor cessation."[7] Yet, perhaps to the surprise of Pentecostals, others had left the gate as well, carrying the message of God's healing power to the nations, but with different trappings.

What appeared to be providential verification that "these signs will accompany those who believe" also arrived with the chance purchase in Cairo of a Greek manuscript by the wealthy American Charles Freer in 1906—coincidental to the beginning of the Azusa Street revival in Los Angeles. It contained the longer ending of the Gospel of Mark (16:9-20), seemingly new evidence that resolved the troublesome textual problem over the legitimacy of the verses. Their credibility or lack thereof had already formed another line of demarcation between newly Spirit-filled believers and "many of the dear holiness people" such as the prominent writer William Godbey, who excluded the verses from his *Commentary on the New Testament*.[8] A writer in the *Apostolic Faith*, previously influenced by his judgment on the matter, said she had changed her mind since attending the "Holy Ghost meetings" at Azusa, having heard the verses repeated "again and again" in the interpretation of tongues, and "seeing them proved true before our eyes." "We have thrown all doubts to the winds and taken to our hearts the whole word of Jesus," she declared.[9] What better proof for authenticity than the occurrence of the very miracles the verses promised?

"In a blessed way God has come forth to confirm the outpouring of the Latter Rain in these last days, with the signs which He said would be manifested, by the discovery of one of the best and oldest manuscripts of the New Testament," wrote Arthur Frodsham. "[It] vindicates those people who take the stand for the Baptism in the Spirit with signs following." With the censure of Pentecostalism in full swing among holiness leaders, fundamentalists, evangelicals, and virtually everyone else, "it was discovered at the very time it was needed."[10] Though overestimating the importance of the manuscript, he correctly identified Pentecostalism's distinctive approach to spirituality, evangelism, and missions: the charismatic enablement of Spirit baptism and miraculous signs and wonders.

Pentecostals never anchored their expectations solely to Mark 16—increasingly conservative biblical scholars doubted the canonical authority of the longer ending[11]—but looked as well to other Gospel passages and Acts to support their claims for the restoration of apostolic power. In their estimation, only unbelief would challenge the relevance of passages such as Acts 5:12 ("The apostles performed many signs and wonders among the people") for contemporary evangelism. Nevertheless, doubts did arise, both as hesitations about some practices and claims, as well as outright rejections by those who put the doctrinal claims of the healing movement in the same basket of religious fanaticism as speaking in tongues.

In this chapter, we turn to consider selected aspects of the international interest in healing in the 1920s, major personalities involved, and conflicts between evangelical mission leaders and Pentecostals over faith healing into the post–World War II era. Indeed, the widespread attraction to healing in the 1920s eclipsed the attention given to the small but growing Pentecostal movement and averted attention away from tongues to miracles of healing. Once again, disagreements over the possibility of supernatural happenings—all commotions coming from the far left wing of evangelicalism—with one noteworthy exception, swirled outside the gates of the Protestant establishment, while encouraging the growth of charismatically inclined Christianity in the Majority World.

THE STRAIN OF THE INCARNATION

Healing has always been associated with the Christian faith. Believers have understood the salvific work of Christ to have soteriological and eschatological dimensions, which means that the work of redemption transcends the present into the future, affecting both soul and body. Thus, after his conversion, Augustine asked his friends to pray with him that God—the "God of health of both soul and body"—would give him relief from a severe toothache; immediately afterward, the pain left.[12] In the sixteenth century, when Philip Melanchthon lay dying, Martin Luther prayed for him and he recovered.[13] Three centuries later, Ethan Otis Allan of Springfield, Massachusetts, laid hands on Sarah Mix and prayed for her healing from tuberculosis. "At that moment I believed I was healed," she recalled, "the room was filled with the glory of God . . . I was so overwhelmed with the power of God, I felt that everything like disease was removed." She lived for another seven years.[14] At the Bethshan Healing Home in London, founded by William Boardman and Elizabeth Baxter in 1880, the South African Reformed pastor Andrew Murray told that after prayer his voice returned from having lost it two years before because of illness.[15] Early in the twentieth century, a German Jesuit missionary to India, George Schurhammer, knelt before the tomb of Francis Xavier in Goa and vowed that should his health be restored, he would write the life of the saint. Subsequently regaining strength, he went on to produce the magisterial biography of Xavier.[16] In Africa, notable movements that featured healing arose among Christians outside the missionary compounds, including the Aladura (Church of the Lord) in West Africa, the Zionist churches in southern Africa, and other African Initiated Churches.[17] The work of healers such as Garrick Briade and Simon Kimbangu revealed the close relationship between the spiritual and physical dimensions of life in African cultures.[18] Such happenings could be multiplied many times over in the history of Christianity.[19] By the beginning of the twentieth century, healing had become a hot topic, apparent in the new healing cults like Christian Science, the miracles at the Catholic shrine of Lourdes, and happenings within the worldwide Anglican Communion.[20]

For their part, Roman Catholics had paid more attention to the physical aspect of healing than Protestants, even though the sacramental rite of anointing and praying for the sick, Extreme Unction, had been applied primarily to the dying.[21] In reacting to the philosophical and religious skepticism of the age, the "Oath Against the Errors of Modernism," imposed on the clergy by the Vatican in 1910, had required them to affirm: "I recognize the exterior proofs of revelation, that is to say, divine works, mainly miracles and prophecies, are sure signs of the divine origin of the Christian religion, and I hold that they are well adapted to the understanding of all ages and of all people, also those of the present time."[22] However, more closely related to grassroots piety, Catholic devotions highlighted the willingness of the resurrected Christ to hear the prayers of the infirm and those of the special intercessors, Mary and the patron saints.[23] In Montreal, Canada, the prayers of Blessed Brother André Bessette— the "miracle-worker of Mount Royal"—and the intercession of St. Joseph purportedly resulted in thousands of healings without medical explanation.[24] Far to the south in Mexico, the activities of folk healers El Niño Fidencio, María Teresa Urrea, and Don Pedrito Jaramillo attracted thousands of Catholics in need of cures.[25]

The scope of healthiness taught by Jesus extended beyond spiritual, emotional, and physical healing to include reconciliation in human relationships and the application of Christian ethical values in social and economic contexts. Nevertheless, "the church's awareness of just how wide-ranging was the nature of Jesus' healing ministry has been fleeting at best," according to theologian Ronald Kydd. In his estimation, the implications for Christian behavior of Christ's coming into the world to transform humanity and society have proven to be intimidating to believers; indeed, "the 'strain of the incarnation' has been too much for Christians to bear."[26] The requirements of love, compassion, egalitarianism, and justice that Jesus modeled and called for have run contrary to human nature, but remain essential to discipleship. Christians often have chosen to focus on the narrower feature of his ministry, namely, the spiritual, emotional, and physical infirmities of humankind rather than on the wider ills of society.[27] Hence, prayer for the sick and the practice of medicine have been perceived as God's chief means of healing, with the latter gaining a marked ascendency in the modern era.

Amid great controversy at the time, the radical evangelicals of the nineteenth century called for the restoration of prayer for the sick and pointed to its relevance in God's mission through the church in the world. By the early 1920s, interest had grown substantially, no doubt influenced by the conditions of thousands of soldiers who returned home injured from the war. The Pentecostal spotlight on healing represented just one part of a far larger trend, wherein proponents employed models for healing that ranged from the thaumaturgical to the sacramental and the therapeutic.[28] Not surprisingly, radical evangelicals and Pentecostals distanced themselves from identification with the Christian Science teachings of Mary Baker Eddy, Elwood Worcester, and the Emmanuel Movement, and other movements they considered to be heretical.[29]

Still, at an unexpected time, cautions about the limits of healing began to surface in that flagship of expectant faith, the Christian and Missionary Alliance, during the same year in which Freer acquired the manuscript. Leaders had struggled for some time over whether missionaries should take medicine for the prevention and treatment of diseases but by 1900 had left this to their discretion, as long as they didn't oppose belief in healing, the third plank in A. B. Simpson's "Fourfold Gospel." "All were finally driven to see that natural law, given and made by God, operates today just as it ever did," contended R. Kelso Carter, who criticized the anti-medical stance of the organization. "Most of the missionaries have used quinine and other remedies freely and all have been and are instructed to observe most carefully the rules of the climate for rest and food and clothing."[30] Much was at stake for the ultimate objective of the Alliance, namely, the evangelization of the world in the shortest possible time. In the Belgian Congo, thirty-three of its missionaries had died between 1884 and 1898, with eighteen of them in their first year of service.[31] Adding to the distress, twelve more died in India in a two-year period (1895-1896) from malaria, typhoid, smallpox, cholera, consumption, and other causes.[32] "God has planted our work in [Africa, India, and China] in crucifixion and sealed it by a missionary tomb," lamented Simpson.[33]

While referring to the "marked feature" of healing in all the Alliance conventions in North America, at the Gospel Tabernacle in New York City, Berachah Home at Nyack, and elsewhere, the annual report for 1905-1906 cautioned against the "many forms of fanaticism and extravagance that the year has brought to light, and the discredit which these exposures have naturally thrown upon this theme," but without offering any specific examples.[34] Did Simpson have in mind the widely publicized trial of Frank Sandford for manslaughter in the untimely death of the fourteen-year-old Leander Bartlett from diphtheria, not having been healed nor having received medical treatment at Shiloh, Maine?[35] Or the extravagant claims of John Alexander Dowie and the "undue preeminence" he gave to healing?[36] Vigilance would be required to maintain the "sane and Scriptural doctrine of Divine Healing as one of the Master's special messages to His people today."[37]

Three years later, while celebrating that "God is continually setting His seal upon the testimony of the Alliance to this present truth," the annual report noted the emphasis on healing had become "less sensational and spectacular and more a matter of habitual experience and normal Christian living."[38] Too many of its missionaries had died despite the "prayer of faith"; hesitations about some practices had arisen, and perhaps with the organization's increasing reaction to Pentecostalism, the position on healing very slowly began to change in the Alliance and among its missionaries.[39]

HEALING AND THE FUNDAMENTALISTS

Pentecostalism represented a small but rapidly growing movement, at first just one chip in the increasing fragmentation of the evangelical movement that began early in the twentieth century. Though shunned by other Christians and considered by some a cult along with Spiritualism, Theosophy, Millennial Dawn (Jehovah's Witnesses), and Mormonism, first- and second-generation Pentecostals and their missionaries forged ahead with firm anticipation of miracles.[40] At the same time, liberal Protestants progressed with redefining the meaning of Christian mission, and older agencies such as the American Board declined. With the liberal "demythologization" of the biblical text that cast doubt on the traditional supernatural framework of the Christian faith, only conservative Protestants, Pentecostals, Roman Catholics, Orthodox Christians, and Christians in Majority World countries retained confidence in the possibility of miracles, with conservative Protestants particularly anxious to defend the credibility of the biblical miracles.[41]

Fears of doctrinal deviation and Pentecostalism, along with increasing trust in the medical profession that provided a scientific approach to physical well-being, led to a decline in the expectation of miracles among some who stood in the ranks of radical evangelicalism.[42] While General Superintendent John Goodwin and other leaders of the holiness Church of the Nazarene (Pentecostal Church of the Nazarene until 1919) attempted to identify with the fundamentalist movement, he wrote *Living Signs and Wonders* (1923), a book that highlighted spiritual integrity, free of extreme teachings. Though celebrating the marvel of the "sanctified life" as a testimony to Christ, he made no reference to the narratives of healings and exorcisms—the "signs and wonders" recorded in Acts.[43] Fundamentalists, however, were a Reformed tribe and took a dim view of Wesleyan encroachment; in the end, the Nazarenes too felt the sting of marginalization.[44]

Unlike the fundamentalists who marshaled rational proofs to defend the historic doctrines of Christianity, Pentecostals—though usually in agreement with such arguments—pointed to physical healings and other demonstrations of supernatural power as evidence of their truthfulness, revealing in a broader sense an apologetic for the faith still found among them. "The young man who sees Divine Healing demonstrated and the Word made life, has no more struggles with infidelity," insisted Anna Reiff in the *Latter Rain Evangel*. Furthermore, "when people realize that the God of the Bible is manifesting Himself today in the same supernatural way as of old, the influence and power of the higher critic is gone."[45]

Despite fundamentalist censures, Pentecostals cheered them on—albeit from the sidelines—as they fought the modernists in the 1920s and '30s.[46] Sounding a cautionary note, however, British Pentecostal leader Donald Gee detected that although fundamentalists defended the biblical miracles, they usually insisted that such miracles had ceased with the early church. "They boldly affirm," he charged, "that the Church has grown beyond the 'childish' need of occasional manifestations of the Spirit in her midst, and assume a development to have taken place that puts them [on the same side as] their Modernist opponents!"[47] But the battlements of fundamentalism could not be so easily plumbed.

Certain fundamentalists—never cozy with left-wing radical evangelicals anyway—wasted little time in expressing their opinions on faith healing and speaking in tongues. The World's Christian Fundamentals Association (WCFA), founded by the Minnesota Baptist pastor William Bell Riley in 1919,[48] weighed in both on the Pentecostal movement and miraculous expectancy at its Chicago convention in 1928, attempting to shield the organization from the charges of modernists who associated it with Pentecostalism:[49]

> WHEREAS, The present wave of Modern Pentecostalism, often referred to as the "tongues movement," and the present wave of fanatical and unscriptural healing which is sweeping over the country today, has become a menace in many churches and a real injury to the sane testimony of Fundamental Christians,
>
> BE IT RESOLVED, That this convention go on record as unreservedly opposed to Modern Pentecostalism, including the speaking with unknown tongues, and the fanatical healing known as general healing in the atonement, and the perpetuation of the miraculous sign-healing of Jesus and His apostles, wherein they claim the only reason the church cannot perform these miracles is because of unbelief.[50]

Notwithstanding the gravity of the condemnation, fundamentalism never entirely achieved a united front against faith healing. When the delegates denounced the "present wave of fanatical and unscriptural healing" and lamented its "real injury to the sane testimony of Fundamental Christians," they likely had in mind the keen embarrassment of John Roach Straton, a stalwart WCFA supporter, sometimes called the "pope of the fundamentalists," and the controversies that had erupted at his New York City church in the two preceding years and covered by newspapers across the country.

Straton, a former Southern Baptist and now pastor of the influential Calvary Baptist Church, had become famous for his resistance to modernism and evolution, debates with the Unitarian pastor Charles Francis Potter, and challenges to denominational policies in the Northern Baptist Convention. He also founded the Fundamentalist League of New York and worked hard for social reform. Despite his close friendship with Riley and other fundamentalist leaders, he became convinced of the truth of healing in the atonement of Christ and dedicated his book *Divine Healing in Scripture and Life* to the memory of A. B. Simpson, "A True Knight and Consecrated Crusader of the Fourfold Gospel."[51]

In 1926, the Interdenominational Evangelistic Committee of Greater New York with the cooperation and recommendation of Straton invited the diminutive fourteen-year-old evangelist Uldine Utley to hold a city-wide campaign at his church in September and October. Five years earlier, she had walked the sawdust trail at a McPherson meeting in Fresno, California, and more recently gained notoriety for her dramatic and effective preaching.[52] She also prayed for the sick in her meetings and emphasized the importance of Spirit baptism, though she was not a Pentecostal.[53] "Because of her deep devotion to God's Word, her unquestioning faith, her complete consecration, her beautiful prayer life, her dauntless courage, her self-sacrificing spirit, her humility and unspoiled sincerity, and her love for the lost," wrote Straton, "I have seen God use her with such manifestations of power that they were evidently supernatural and divine."[54] After packing the church during weeks of meetings, the services then moved to Madison Square Garden where she preached to 14,000 people.[55] Dubbed the "most extraordinary person in America" by Straton and the "Girl 'Billy Sunday'" by the newspapers, Utley now rose to the national limelight,[56] while the reputation of "Sister Aimee"—her model for ministry—ironically took a downturn as a result of her alleged kidnapping.[57] Moreover, Utley's preaching and success appeared to one newspaper writer to reflect the prophet Isaiah's prediction that in the end times "a little child will lead them" (Isa 11:6), the notion that God's truth would prevail through child-like innocence.[58]

The revival that began at Calvary Baptist lingered into 1927 with reports of conversions, healings—Straton's wife Georgia told of miraculous recovery from a hearing loss—and even speaking in tongues.[59] Straton, like others who believed the gift of tongues potentially could be restored, still attempted to distance himself and the events at the church from Pentecostalism. Even so, he affirmed that when his son Warren—a Manhattan Beaux Arts sculpture student—received Spirit baptism and spoke in tongues, he had received a genuine "visitation by the Holy Spirit," his life had been transformed, and his stuttering had ceased.[60] Straton himself continued to pray for the sick in services at the church.[61] However, trouble surfaced when five deacons resigned over the "demonstrations of Pentecostalism."[62] "These 'camp meetin's' in the heart of New York have lasted far into the night," they complained, with "men and women seized with hysteria and cataleptic trances lying on the floor and muttering and screaming unintelligible gibberish which indicates the 'gift of tongues.'"[63] On another front, his Baptist friends denounced his approval of women preachers and invitation to Utley to speak from his pulpit.[64] Nonetheless, he successfully weathered the storms and never wavered on his judgments, but died shortly afterward in 1929.[65]

THE GOSPEL OF HEALING

The founders of the healing movement included Charles Cullis, William Boardman, A. J. Gordon, Otto Stockmayer, Dorothea Trudel, Johann Christoph Blumhardt, Andrew Murray, John Alexander Dowie, Sarah Mix, A. B. Simpson, Maria Woodworth-Etter, and many others.[66] These first-generation leaders had erected the framework for the "gospel of healing" through their many publications and modeling of prayer for the sick, but failed to resolve three nagging questions that dogged their teachings: Is it ever God's will that Christians should suffer from physical maladies? If the redemptive work of Christ in the atonement provides for both spiritual and physical healing, then why isn't everyone healed who prays the "prayer of faith"? Why do believers die if Christ is always willing to heal?

Notable evangelists of the second generation gained international fame through salvation/healing campaigns; among them, Smith Wigglesworth and George Jeffreys from the British Pentecostal movement; and in North America: the Canadian farm-girl-turned-evangelist Aimee Semple McPherson; the British-born and Oxford-educated Congregational pastor Charles Price; Francisco Olazábal—a former Methodist called the "Billy Sunday of the Mexican People";[67] and F. F. Bosworth, the best-known advocate among them in print and one of the most influential popular theologians of the Pentecostal and healing movements from World War I to the 1960s.[68] Bosworth hailed from Dowie's community at Zion City, Illinois, became a Pentecostal, and later left the Assemblies of God to join the Alliance. His book *Christ the Healer* became a principal textbook for the movement and for the post–World War II healing movement.[69] It also was a lightning rod for those who wanted a representative exposition of the doctrine in order to refute it.

Their services attracted thousands who professed conversion, and newspapers reported many healings through the prayer of faith. In the process, however, Spirit baptism (and tongues-speech) typically had limited appearance on center stage, as evident in the McPherson campaign in Canton, Ohio, in 1921 wherein she devoted only one service to the subject in two-and-a-half weeks of meetings.[70] As evangelists, they rarely gained the approval of the larger Christian community, or at least not for very long. For example, after Presbyterian mission leader Robert Speer learned that Olazábal "belonged to the 'tongues' people," he withdrew support for a scheduled evangelistic campaign in Puerto Rico planned with mainline church leaders in 1936.[71] When Christian historians traced the key evangelistic events of the period, they ignored or downplayed Pentecostal contributions.[72] The Pentecostal approach to evangelism did not fit squarely with the preferred manner of favorite revivalists such as Billy Sunday, J. Wilbur Chapman, Bob Jones, Gypsy Smith, and later Billy Graham.

To Pentecostals, like some of the radical evangelicals who preceded them, salvation and physical healing represented two vital aspects of the redemptive work of Christ—a conception of salvation blended with health and healing into an integral whole. Scriptural support came from the Gospel stories of Jesus healing the sick; the linkage of healing to the atonement in Isaiah 53:4-5 and Matthew 8:17; Paul's reference to the charismatic distribution of gifts of healing in 1 Corinthians 12:9; and James 5:13-16 ("Is anyone sick among you? Let him call the elders of the church to pray over them and anoint them with oil in the name of the Lord. And the prayer offered in faith will make them well; the Lord will raise them up. If they have sinned, they will be forgiven").

"In the great Redemption Chapter, the 53rd of Isaiah," wrote Bosworth, "it is *our* sicknesses, as well as *our* sins that Jesus bore, making one privilege as universal as the other."[73] The transformation of the soul would have a physical effect on the new believer, as stated by Paul: "If the Spirit of him who raised

Jesus from the dead is living in you, he who raised Christ from the dead will also give life to your mortal bodies because of his Spirit who lives in you" (Rom 8:11). "Salvation and healing go hand in hand," wrote Anna Reiff. "People are eager to be saved when they realize that God comes down and touches their bodies; that He is not a God that is afar off, but 'a very present help in time of trouble.'"[74] This message resonated with many people in North Atlantic countries, but even more so in the Majority World, as Pentecostal missionary William Turner discovered: "Christians, of all denominations, when they are sick, while they may call for medical help, they will, with the same earnestness, call for prayer. . . . They know and believe that there is power in God, in Christ to bring one out of sickness. The Chinese Church, in this regard is far more apostolic than the Western Churches."[75] In their culture, the physical dimension of life could not be partitioned from the spiritual.

Second-generation evangelists held mass campaigns that Cullis, Gordon, Simpson, and Murray might not have dreamed possible or even proper, from filling Royal Albert Hall in London to civic auditoriums and churches, to large open-air meetings in parks and other places.[76] At Royal Albert Hall, George Jeffreys baptized one thousand converts in water in a single service, an event that left a deep impression on a young South African in attendance, Nicholas Bhengu.[77] Twice that many testified to physical healings on another occasion.[78] In Sweden, Smith Wigglesworth triggered such a furor among medical doctors and clergy of the Lutheran state church that they publicly denounced his practice of praying for the sick. As a result, the government forbade him to lay hands on anyone for prayer. Unworried when a crowd of twenty thousand assembled at an outdoor service, he stayed within the law by telling the sick to stand and lay their hands on their afflicted parts while he prayed for them. Many said they received healings as they did in his campaigns elsewhere.[79] While in Syracuse, New York, after Wigglesworth prayed for a woman and declared her healed, she wavered and said, "If I can only believe." To which he thundered, "There is no 'if' . . . God is all powerful." After laying hands on her once again in prayer, he cast out the "evil spirit" and said, "Now go. You are well."[80] Hesitation simply spelled unbelief. Wigglesworth attributed sickness to the direct activity of Satan and demons, a concept not uniformly taught among Pentecostals.[81]

Thousands likewise came to Christ and told of healings in the ministry of McPherson, one of America's most famous evangelists. As they did with the numbers of healings reported by the other evangelists, critics dismissed her claims as fraudulent, though the results could not be so readily calculated.[82] "It would be convenient if we could find some evidence that Sister Aimee's miraculous healings were faked for the benefit of publicity; but there is no such evidence," wrote the astonished biographer Daniel Epstein. "The documentation is overwhelming: very sick people came . . . by the tens of thousands, blind, deaf, paralyzed. Many were healed, some temporarily, some forever."[83] Based on his study of local newspaper coverage of her campaigns, he found that "no one has ever been credited by secular witnesses with anywhere near the number of healings attributed to Sister Aimee from 1919 to 1922."[84]

THE ANGLICAN COMMUNION

The ministries of Jeffreys, Wigglesworth, McPherson, Price, and Bosworth took place primarily in the Anglophone world, and they became household names among Euroamerican Pentecostals and beyond. Interest in healing, however, had not originated with Pentecostalism nor could be confined within its parameters. In Korea, Pastor Kim Ik Doo, who had been inspired by Mark 16:17 ("these signs will accompany"), conducted revivals and prayed for the sick among the neglected and impoverished lower classes that suffered from rampant disease.[85] With innumerable stories of healing circulating in the churches, the Korean Presbyterian Church dropped its doctrine of cessationism in the early 1920s: Presbyterian Bylaw, Article 1, Chapter 3: "The power of doing miracles has ceased at the present time."[86] According to one source, possibly more than two million conversions occurred under Kim's preaching in his lifetime.[87] Thus, when Pentecostal missionaries arrived overseas and began praying for the sick, they sometimes found indigenous Christians and other missionaries doing the same, all within cultural contexts that embraced various forms of folk healing.

In circles past the reach of Pentecostals, Anglican layman James Moore Hickson took the message of healing around the globe, praying for the sick in Anglican cathedrals and churches, hospitals, asylums, and even leper colonies. Though not familiar to many Pentecostals since he was not one of them, Hickson's "healing missions" became well known in the Anglican Communion and sectors of the Protestant establishment, revealing the desperation of all classes of people when confronted by serious illnesses, as well as the interest in miracles when rapid changes in the culture threatened the comfort of traditional beliefs.[88]

Born the sixth of thirteen children in Broken River, Australia, in 1868, Hickson grew up in an Anglican home where his family often prayed for those struggling with illness. His first accounts of healing occurred at age fourteen when he laid hands on and prayed for two cousins, one suffering from neuralgia and the other from St. Vitus's dance. After these and other miracles of healing, he told how his mother realized that "God was evidently working through me in healing the sick, and that we must pray about it, asking Him to guide me in the right exercise of this ministry." In the years that followed, he continued to pray for the sick, though engaged in secular employment. After moving to London, a turning point came in his life when his uncle, a medical doctor, asked him to pray for a young British officer who had been wounded in the Boer War in South Africa. After Hickson laid hands on him in silent prayer, the pain left within moments, and the man quickly recovered. The uncle then said, "You have no right to be doing anything else, with such a Gift of the Spirit."[89] With that encouragement, he centered his attention on the ministry of healing, while pursuing a certificate in anatomy, physiology, massage, and "medical electricity."

In 1905, Hickson, along with Louis George Mylne, former bishop of Bombay and later of Worcester in England, Prebendary Wilson Carlisle, reportedly healed of a spinal problem before founding the Church of England's Church Army (an agency similar to the Salvation Army) in 1882, Adelaine Duchess of Bedford, Countess Beauchamp, and several others founded the Society of Emmanuel.[90] It served chiefly to "develop the Divine gifts left to His Church by the Master, especially the gift of healing by prayer and laying on of hands, with the object of using these Divine gifts not only for the healing of the body, but as a means of drawing the souls of men nearer to God."[91] He shared this concern with Randall Davidson, the Archbishop of Canterbury, who then commissioned him to move forward "like the patrol of an army and come back and report" and at their parting told Hickson to "lead the main body forward."[92]

In 1908, the society began publication of the monthly magazine *The Healer*, and Hickson wrote his first book, *The Healing of Christ in His Church*, which was distributed and discussed at the fifth Lambeth Conference. In the same year, Hickson addressed the Pan-Anglican Congress in London on the subject of healing. During the sixth Lambeth Conference in 1920, "bishop after bishop arose and told of remarkable cases of healing that had occurred in their own ministry as they had followed the simple injunction in James and prayed for the sick."[93] Among them would have been Arthur Winnington-Ingram, Lord Bishop of London, who also prayed for the sick and later wrote *The Gospel of the Miraculous* (1913).[94]

Another turning point came in 1917 when Hickson went on a spiritual retreat to the Island of Iona off the west coast of Scotland where the sixth-century Irish missionary Columba had established a monastery as a mission center for the evangelization of Scotland. On the way and while at Iona, he prayed for the sick with positive results. Before leaving, he felt "impressed in no uncertain way that I was to go round the world healing the sick and preaching the Gospel of love."[95] After World War I, Hickson commenced a five-year "missionary journey" that took him to North America, China, Japan, Egypt, Palestine, India, Ceylon (Sri Lanka), Union of South Africa, Rhodesia (Zimbabwe), Australia, and New Zealand. In his estimation, "this awakening to the truth of Christ's presence and healing power is a movement of the Holy Spirit in the Church."[96]

Without any advanced planning, but with expectant faith, he sailed to Boston in March 1919. After securing lodging at a hotel, he walked to the Episcopal Cathedral of St. Paul and by happenstance met Archdeacon Grieg of the Diocese of Worcester in England who had arrived in the city on the same day. Knowledgeable of Hickson's ministry in Worcester and believing their meeting to be providential, he commended him to the Episcopal authorities there. "From that moment every Episcopal church opened to me, and the [Archdeacon] went on to New York and Washington preparing the way."[97] In New York City, he received the endorsement of William Manning, the influential rector of Trinity Church on Wall Street and later bishop of New York.

For two years he traveled across the United States and Canada holding healing missions in cathedrals and churches in thirty-five cities, always with the permission and blessing of each diocesan bishop obtained beforehand. His journey came at the very time when the bishops were deliberating on the creation of a rite of "Anointing with Oil and Prayers" for the sick and dying in the *Book of Common Prayer*, in accordance with James 5[98]—an addition supported by many, including Episcopal rector Henry Wilson of Boonton, New Jersey, another advocate of healing, and his Society of the Nazarene.[99] From coast to coast, newspapers blared: "Healing Power of Hickson is Actual Thing,"[100] "5000 Apply for Healing,"[101] "Lame Pack Trinity as 'Healer' Speaks,"[102] "Wounded Yanks Rush Away from Science [Walter Reed Army Medical Center in Washington, D.C.] to Healer's Shrine,"[103] and "Thousands Jam Church to Be Healed,"[104] all unlikely headlines for the sophisticated and staid Episcopal Church in America. In Buffalo, Bishop Charles Brent, former missionary bishop of the Philippines, assisted in the healing services. "He who waives away the healing power of Christ as belonging only to the early New Testament times is not preaching the whole gospel," said Brent. "God was, and is, the Saviour of the body as well as the soul."[105] The presence of bishops and other clergy in the healing missions represented an essential part of the services, which attracted Episcopalians, Baptists, Congregationalists, Disciples, Methodists, Pentecostals, Presbyterians, Roman Catholics, Unitarians, Universalists, Jews, and many others.

It is interesting to note that Hickson did not receive the level of censure given to Pentecostal faith healers, perhaps because his context of healing within the Episcopal Church provided social respectability, posed little threat to conservative evangelical constituencies, and the healing missions took place within church buildings instead of civic auditoriums or the outdoors.[106] Still, the whip of skepticism from Rowland Bingham, founder of the Sudan Interior Mission, flayed at his reputation. He had obtained "unbiased testimony" about the results of Hickson's meetings in Toronto where he prayed for seven thousand people. "There was not a single outstanding case of healing," Bingham announced, though this assertion would have surprised Anglican rector G. F. B. Doherty, who chaired the planning committee and reported on the meetings to the Canadian bishops.[107]

More important for the impact on global Christianity, Hickson left North America in the summer of 1920 for extended travel overseas, again with the warm reception of Anglican bishops and beyond. At the invitation of Damianus, Greek Orthodox Patriarch of Jerusalem, Hickson held a healing service in the chapel of the convent attached to the Church of the Nativity in Bethlehem.[108] In Egypt, William Gairdner of the Church Missionary Society introduced him to Kyrillos V, Pope of the Coptic Orthodox Church, who conferred his blessing on Hickson with permission to minister in his churches.[109] In Travancore in South India, Bishop Charles Gill gained the cooperation of Titus II, Metropolitan Bishop of the Malankara Mar Thoma Syrian Church, to join with him in supporting the healing mission; it proved to be a startling success, drawing crowds upward of twenty thousand people.[110]

In the diocese of Dornakal, he prayed for the sick with the assistance of V. S. Azariah, the first Indian bishop of the Anglican Church; one report stated that seventeen thousand attended the last day of the mission.[111] At Calcutta, as in other places, the mission attracted Parsees, Buddhists, Hindus, Muslims, Jews, and a wide variety of Christians. "People . . . of every rank in life, leveled to the proximity of whatever place was available in that ever-increasing crowd," said an eyewitness. "I saw a Rajah kneeling in line with a Madrasi servant, and the wife of the Governor of a Province sitting on a bench beside a poor Leucoderma patient." With the exorcisms and physical healings that took place ("I have seen the eyes of the blind opened immediately"), "it was as if the clock were put back to the time of the Apostles' first ministry."[112] Revealing the influence on non-Christians, Hickson recalled, "I . . . found that an Indian prince had travelled from a long distance beyond Bombay to Colombo [Sri Lanka] and was awaiting the arrival of my ship, that he might be ministered to in the Name of Jesus Christ, although himself a Mahomedan."[113]

The effect of Hickson's ministry in Delhi in 1921—consistent with the dynamics of his meetings elsewhere—prompted P. N. F. Young of the Cambridge Mission to write:

> We know that Our Lord has been here from the things that have happened. *The sick have been healed.* No sort of record has been possible, but we do know of hearing and sight partially or completely restored, or paralytics healed; we have seen men and women move painfully up to the altar with sticks and crutches and walk away without them.
>
> An even more striking sign of Our Lord's presence was the way in which barriers were broken down and a perfectly wonderful spirit of unity and fellowship created. Who could have believed that in this land so sore with racial bitterness and antagonism, Englishman and Indian, the highest and the lowest, would have so mingled together without a murmur or sign of embarrassment? Yet that happened. All took their turn side by side as equals; among Hindus and [Muslims] the customs of centuries were broken. Englishmen and Englishwomen waited long outside among the poorest, with their sores and their rags, and knelt beside them. . . . Only the Spirit of Christ can do things like this.
>
> We have had, in a word, some foretaste of the Kingdom of God in operation; a new glimpse of what the Church should be like in her life; and, further, to see Hindus and [Muslims] in numbers kneeling at Christ's altar to receive His blessing was an unforgettable vision of the triumph of the Gospel in this land. And it was no unfitting finish when, on the Sunday morning after the Mission, the English and Indian congregations met for a joint act of Communion in St. James's, when some made their Communion for the first time after many years, and all cemented the bonds of fellowship that the week before had forged.[114]

The evangelism, healing emphasis, and social dynamics in such meetings, similar to what had occurred briefly in the Azusa Street revival and at Lupton's camp meeting in Ohio—albeit without revolving around Spirit baptism, tongues-speech, and premillennial eschatology—represented a significant development outside the tent revivals of the Pentecostal movement. Perhaps for this reason, major North American Pentecostal periodicals took little or no notice of Hickson.[115] The insight of Young's reference to the "foretaste of the Kingdom of God" with its implications for holistic ministry, reconciliation, and peace would not enter the missiological exposition of conservative evangelicals and Pentecostals until later in the century.[116]

Commenting on the healing missions in India, China, and Japan, Herbert Pakenham-Walsh, bishop of Assam in British India and noted for his own ministry of praying for the sick, said that Hickson had "set missionaries asking whether it is not the Lord's will today in heathen lands, as in the early days, to 'confirm the Word by signs following.'"[117] The reports of missionaries and other observers to "remarkable and sudden cures, including total blindness, deafness, and dumbness from birth, also of many gradual cures, and above all of spiritual blessing both to the sick and to those who prayed with them" had stirred reflection on the importance of this "new development."[118] Among Chinese Christians, Hunter Yen of the Cathedral in Anking stated that one of the greatest effects of Hickson's mission there came in "bringing to us the realization that there is a wonderful power of God ready for our help and use."[119]

Furthermore, as the later charismatic renewal in the churches would lend legitimacy to aspects of Pentecostal spirituality, so Hickson's missions increased the credibility of Pentecostals. "Once they considered us as reprobates," wrote Verna Barnard from South Africa to the editor of *Word and Work* in Framingham, Massachusetts, "but since Mr. Hickson has been here in the English Churches with such marvelous results in divine healing, all are more ready to hear us. Even in our street meetings the masses stand and listen to us relate the Scriptures on the subject."[120] The long-term effects of the interest of Anglicans in healing on the Pentecostal movement, the later charismatic renewal, and the emergence of charismatically inclined Christianity in the Majority World awaits further exploration.[121] One example of the impact appeared in the work of San Diego Episcopal rector John Gayner Banks and the founding of the International Order of St. Luke the Physician in 1947, an ecumenical organization that has sought to restore the ministry of healing in the worship of the church.[122]

In fundamental respects, Hickson's theology of healing paralleled that of Bosworth and other North Atlantic evangelical and Pentecostal faith healers.[123] All of them emphasized the willingness of God to heal in the present time, the crucial role of prayer and faith, and the provision for spiritual and physical well-being in the atoning work of Christ.[124] They also connected praying for the sick to the celebration of the Lord's Supper. "[It] is more than an ordinance," insisted Bosworth, "because we may partake of Christ while we are partaking of the emblems of His death and the benefits thereof. In Christ there is both bodily and spiritual life, and surely there is no better time for availing ourselves of the privilege of having the 'life also of Jesus . . . made manifest in our mortal flesh' (II Cor. 4:11)."[125] In fact, in the words of another advocate, "You can be healed when you put the bread in your mouth . . . , if not before, by discerning the Lord's body broken for your healing."[126] Similarly, through Hickson's examination of Scripture and the liturgy of the ancient church, he found healing in the Lord's Supper, evidenced by the Eucharistic Prayer: "Furthermore, O Lord, heal the diseases of our souls, cure our bodily weaknesses, O Physician of souls and bodies, Overseer of all flesh, oversee and heal us by Thy salvation."[127] The likeness in views between Bosworth and Hickson gained the notice of the sympathetic Alliance writer Kenneth Mackenzie, who concurred that the "body of the believer as well as his spiritual nature was designed to be a recipient of the correlated results of the crucifixion of our Lord."[128]

Along with points of agreement, important differences appear in Hickson's theology of healing and style of praying for the sick. First, he believed the church should play a central role in healing to accentuate the practical nature of the gospel to the average person—in this way realizing its potential of being "Christ's life-giving body,"[129] and to promote the restoration of Christian unity since divine healing "breaks down all barriers and helps to unite all communions of the Church of Christ."[130] Attending his healing mission at the coastal city of Ningbo, China, with other Protestant missionaries, Pentecostal missionary Nettie Nichols said, "it was a wonderful sight to sit together with many of the dear missionaries and feel conscious of the way God was working to bring about unity in that blessed teaching of Divine Healing."[131] Hickson welcomed all who came regardless of denominational affiliation or religious background. He also normally conducted his healing missions with the assistance of bishops and pastors who gave each seeker their blessing after Hickson laid hands on them in prayer. Before leaving a city, he would urge the faithful to form "Prayer Circles for Spiritual Healing" in local parishes.[132]

Second, Hickson emphasized that healing often occurred gradually in the days, weeks, or months after he anointed seekers with oil and laid hands on them in prayer, an approach that may have reduced the anticipation of instantaneous cures in his quiet and orderly services.[133] His concept of faith focused more attention on God's benevolence than on human effort in achieving sufficient faith for healing, which, as Bosworth insisted: "We never rise above our confession. A negative confession will lower us to the level of that confession. It is what we confess with our lips that really controls us."[134] Hence, as the Australian archbishops and bishops stated in a pastoral letter to their churches after the Hickson meetings in 1923: "Many sufferers, apparently uncured, instead of being 'bitterly disappointed' and 'alienated from a faith which had failed them,' as we were warned they would be, are conscious of a new life within them and a new outlook on all life. Their spirit has been healed of its fear and anxiety."[135] In marked contrast, Pentecostals often struggled with the failure of their faith to receive the promised healing, particularly when evangelists like Wigglesworth would pronounce the immediate healing of a seeker though the symptoms persisted.[136]

Third—and the most striking difference: Hickson affirmed the practice of medicine as a gift of God. He encouraged people to pray the following litany:

> We beseech Thee, Almighty God, that Thou wouldest restore to Thy Church the apostolic gift of healing the bodies as well as the souls of men:
> *Hear us, we beseech Thee.*
> That Thou wouldest bless all doctors and physicians, all nurses and attendants, all who seek to exercise mental and spiritual healing; and grant

unto them knowledge and faith, skill and sympathy, tenderness and
patience:
Hear us, we beseech thee.
That Thou wouldest bless all hospitals and infirmaries, all medical missions among the poor and the heathen, consider the affliction of Thy
people, and forget not thy poor for ever:
Hear us, we beseech Thee.[137]

Hickson welcomed medical doctors to his services; a number of them came
and assisted him.[138] The combination of the prayer of faith with confidence that
God also cured through medical science set him apart from other healing advocates whose teachings routinely contained an anti-medical flavor.

THE MIRACLE GATE

Interest in healing and spiritual gifts in China, evident as early as the mid-
nineteenth-century Taiping Heavenly Kingdom movement, emerged again during the 1920s and '30s in part through the evangelistic work of John Sung (Song
Shangjie), the healing missions of Hickson, and happenings in Shandong province and elsewhere.[139] Prayer for the sick had been practiced by Christians for
some time, among pastors and their congregations and indigenous movements
such as the True Jesus Church and the Jesus Family.[140] J. Herbert Kane, who
served with the China Inland Mission in Anhui province, acknowledged from
firsthand observation that "hundreds of our finest Christians in the Fowyang
field entered the Christian fold by way of the miracle gate. They were driven to
Christ not by a sense of sin, but by a sense of need." The "needs" usually preceded the sense of culpability for sin: "A parent with a sick child, a husband with
a demon-possessed wife, a woman with an opium-smoking husband, a widow
bowed down by oppression, a soldier with an infected foot, a merchant whose
only son had been kidnapped, an aged father with an unfilial son, a bandit serving a prison term."[141] Such happenings also occurred in the mission outposts of
the holiness agencies, the Alliance, the Pentecostals, and many others.[142]

Called variously the "hot gospeler of the East," the "John Wesley of
China," and a "modern-day John the Baptist," Sung was born into the home
of a Methodist pastor in China's Fujian province in 1901.[143] After completing
high school in his homeland, he left for America to attend Ohio Wesleyan
University, where he graduated in 1923. He then pursued graduate work in
chemistry at Ohio State University and received his Ph.D. three years later.
Encouraged to prepare for the ministry, he enrolled at Union Theological Seminary in New York City where he studied under Harry Emerson Fosdick and
possibly Daniel Johnson Fleming, as well as other modernist professors. This
soon triggered a spiritual and psychological crisis that led him for a time into
doubt and religious pluralism.[144]

Given his new interest in various religious expressions, Sung accepted the
invitation of friends to attend the city-wide evangelistic campaign being held

at Straton's Calvary Baptist Church in the early fall of 1926. There, instead of hearing Straton preach, Sung heard Uldine Utley. "Imagine my surprise when I saw a [14]-year-old girl preaching on stage . . . dressed in white from her dress to her shoes and even socks. When she opened the gilded Bible, her delivery of the message was as crisp as it was powerful; the Cross was lifted high and [the] salvation message was thoroughly presented." Recognizing the spiritual presence of the Holy Spirit at work, Sung left "deeply impressed" and went back several times to hear her preach; he then became convinced that every preacher must receive the empowerment of Spirit baptism before they could be effective.[145] As a result, his life was dramatically changed, and he returned to China in the following year.

Sung's evangelistic campaigns led to tens of thousands of converts, not only in China but throughout Southeast Asia. An observer described his pulpit manner as a "mixture of Billy Sunday and Aimee Semple McPherson, the whole flavored by the Oriental."[146] Though not well known in the West, he ranks among the greatest evangelists of the modern era. His fierce denunciation of modernist teachings also gained the appreciation of fundamentalists as the Protestant missionaries in China became bitterly divided.[147] Still, some of his beliefs made conservatives uneasy, namely, speaking in tongues and healing, factors downplayed in a later Moody Press biography.[148] The fact that he prayed in tongues—"On the morning of March 25, [1934], I was praying, when I unconsciously started speaking in tongues, and I felt the power of the Holy Spirit in me"—raised questions, though he disagreed with the Pentecostal insistence on glossolalia with Spirit baptism.[149] More importantly, Sung prayed for the sick and trained his evangelistic teams to do the same. Among a crowd of nearly two thousand at a campaign in Guangzhou province, 783 asked him to lay hands on them and pray; a third of them then testified to receiving healing. "The [three] words, 'In Jesus' Name,' brought me faith," he recorded in his diary.[150] His own study of the Scriptures, Methodist background, and Utley's preaching shaped his spirituality and preaching emphasis on Spirit baptism and healing.

Prayer for the sick featured prominently during the Shandong revival among Presbyterians and Baptists in the years from 1927 to 1937. Mary Crawford reported that the greatest revival in the history of Southern Baptist missions in North China had led to "numbers of Christians and churches . . . being revived; restitution of money is being made . . . sins confessed to God and to those who have been wronged." In addition, the "sick are being healed; devils cast out; men and women, boys and girls are preaching with a power hitherto not known."[151] Missionaries initially embraced the revival, though some later condemned it because of the emotional demonstrations and the ensuing divisiveness it sparked in the churches.[152] "In certain districts where the missionaries and Chinese leaders have been able to keep in sympathetic touch with the Spiritual Gifts movement, considerable good has been done," reported the study committee on China to the International Missionary Council meeting in Madras in 1938. "But . . . their excesses, their bitter criticisms, their arrogant hostility to those who disagree with them, 'preaching love and throwing bricks with both hands,' as one missionary describes it, and their lack of balance in scriptural interpretation, tend

to make them a menace rather than a help to the Church."[153] Indigenous movements of this nature would not be easily corralled inside missionary compounds
or even given a fair hearing for many years to come. But their influence would
endure; as agents of change, they inevitably brought disruption to the routine
of church life.[154]

CHALLENGES TO HEALING

The doctrine and practice of faith healing in the years after World War I drew
negative reactions from certain fundamentalists who enjoyed widespread influence. Among them, three major leaders: R. A. Torrey, a well-known evangelist
and educator; Rowland Bingham, of the Sudan Interior Mission; and Henry
Frost, North American director of the China Inland Mission. All professed support of praying for the sick, had done so themselves, seen people healed, and
believed in the canonical integrity of the longer ending of Mark, but expressed
dismay over what they saw as distortions of biblical teaching. "The land is being
flooded with religious adventurers who are taking advantage of the widespread
interest in this important subject to deceive and rob the people," shuddered Torrey.[155] For his part, Bingham showed little hesitation in branding the culprits—
Dowie, Simpson, McPherson, Bosworth, Price, and Hickson—variously mis-
guided in their beliefs, faulty in their practices of healing, and mistaken about
the results of their meetings.[156]

In *Divine Healing* (1924), Torrey appealed to James 5 as the proper paradigm
for healing. The sick should call for the elders of their local churches, who would
then anoint them with oil and pray for them, rather than turn to "some self-
appointed busy-body who goes about with a little bottle of oil to be used in his
loudly-advertised 'ministry of healing' to which he has been called, or fancies he
has been called." Neither should they "send for some woman who is peculiarly
gifted in prayer, or who thinks she is, and who has a peculiarly psychological or
magnetic or hypnotic personality," an obvious slap at McPherson.[157] Since Jesus
and the apostles did not conduct public meetings "where crowds are instructed
to come to the front and where they are anointed with oil and prayed with,"
such gatherings lacked a scriptural basis.[158] The "skillfully-planned, highly-
emotional music and swaying of the body and passings of the hand and shouts
of hallelujahs, that excite the imagination and thrill the body," only brought
discredit to the legitimate ministry of healing.[159] Along with other complaints—
evangelists robbing the faithful of their money, issuing false claims of healing,
attributing the promise of healing to the atoning work of Christ, and imitating
John Alexander Dowie—Torrey bemoaned that they had placed more emphasis
on physical healing than on saving lost souls. "I have immeasurably more important business to attend to," he avowed. "I would rather be used to save one lost
soul than to heal a thousand sick bodies."[160]

More extensive expositions came from Bingham and Frost, top mission executives of two of the foremost independent faith missions. Looking at the history
of the healing movement, Bingham paid tribute to Gordon and his book *The*

Ministry of Healing for the cautious and balanced approach that it presented, particularly in regard to the provisions of the atonement. In contrast to his usual "authoritative manner," Gordon said that in the atonement, there "*seems* to be a foundation laid for faith in bodily healing," a statement that to Bingham signaled a measure of doubt.[161] Unfortunately, others like Simpson—under whom Bingham had studied—had carried this to an extreme and declared with finality that physical healing had been provided in the atonement, leading him to teach that "natural remedies and human help were unnecessary and were to be deprecated by those who thus took the Lord as their physician."[162] Frost expressed his regard for Gordon and Simpson as well, but held them equally culpable for the erroneous teaching. Moreover, as Bingham and Frost pointed out, the healing theology of Gordon and Simpson had not worked even for themselves as their health declined: Gordon died from bronchitis and pneumonia, and Simpson from arteriosclerosis.[163]

All three writers believed that while God in his mercy sovereignly might choose to heal, the atonement did not encompass physical well-being; his death provided solely for the forgiveness of sin.[164] The body with all of its infirmities ultimately would be transformed in the future resurrection of believers, as Paul had stated in Romans 8:22-23: "We know that the whole creation has been groaning as in the pains of childbirth right up to the present time. Not only so, but we ourselves, who have the firstfruits of the Spirit groan inwardly as we wait eagerly for our adoption, the redemption of our bodies."

The prayer of faith recommended in James 5 also had limited applicability: it represented a "Jewish truth," without pertinence for Gentile Christians. "The instructions of James concerning healing were intended particularly for the church in a condition of a large Jewish membership and at a time when it was emerging from Judaism and was spiritually underdeveloped," Frost insisted, though without the concurrence of either Torrey or Bingham.[165] Miracles had largely served their purpose when Christ offered the "kingdom" to the Jews, thus "they are not so much intended for the church in its present Gentile condition and spiritual maturity," a notion representing one particular school of thought within dispensational premillennialism.[166]

In regard to the connection of miracles with missionary evangelism, Bingham regretted that "unbelief still too often rules God out of the sick chamber . . . whereas God loves to show His divine power and love in the healing of those who may be beyond human help."[167] One could look back to the nineteenth century and find that missionaries had duplicated virtually every scene from the early expansion of the faith recorded in Acts, but "the idea that the presence of healing 'signs' [Mark 16:17] would bring about great spiritual results in the conversion of sinners and the edification of the saints is disproved by facts."[168] Gospel proclamation in the power of the Holy Spirit trumped the need for miracles. The "gospel of healing"—enshrined in Simpson's "Fourfold Gospel"—with its strident claims and dismissal of medicine had simply not worked among missionaries and in bringing lost souls to Christ.[169] Bingham recommended that Christians heed the biblical preventions of disease—the "Six Great Natural Laws"—found in Leviticus and Deuteronomy: sanitation, sterilization (personal cleanliness), quarantine, hygiene and dietetics, exercise, and recuperation (rest). These divine instructions stood in sharp contrast to the teachings of those "who believe that God's way of healing is only by supernatural and instantaneous methods," though this misstated the position of his opponents.[170]

Going a step farther than Bingham, Frost contended in reference to Mark 16 that certain miracles performed by the apostles could not be repeated in the modern era since "no one has heard of any modern saint healing all manner of sickness and disease, cleansing lepers, or raising the dead."[171] Leaning against the wall of Protestant cessationism, he suggested that the apostles represented a "special class of men" whose displays of miraculous power played a unique role in the establishment of the faith.[172] The present "church age" did not constitute an age of miracles, "except as God is pleased to manifest His power to individuals, in exceptional circumstances and for specific purposes."[173] Even in the book of Acts, the frequency of miracles declined. Finally, the statement found in Hebrews 13:8 ("Jesus Christ is the same yesterday and today and forever") had to be approached with caution: "It does not necessarily follow that He will do now all that He did then, or that He will do what he does now in the same way as He did then, for His purposes in some things are different at present from what they were in the past."[174]

With Frost and Bingham serving as directors of major faith missions, their opinions carried considerable weight, not only with their North American readerships, but with the missionaries who worked under them and the believers they shepherded in the mission lands. Along with Torrey and many others, they elevated the spiritual dimension of salvation above the physical in value. In the end, when healings occurred, they might have cataloged them under "acts of special providence."

POST–WORLD WAR II HEALING MOVEMENT

The opinions of Torrey, Bingham, and Frost on healing had more impact on fundamentalists and evangelicals than on Pentecostals. After World War II, an even greater surge in salvation/healing campaigns commenced across North America. William Branham, Oral Roberts, A. A. Allen, and Jack Coe drew massive audiences. Even larger meetings occurred overseas under Tommy Hicks in Buenos Aires, Lester Sumrall in Manila, Clifton Erickson in Rio de Janeiro, and T. L. Osborn in Indonesia.[175] The deaths of McPherson, Price, and Wigglesworth in the mid-1940s had "fired many pure young hearts with a holy desire to pick up the torch of their ministry and carry it forward to new achievements," observed Donald Gee.[176] Their rise to prominence came during a time of crisis in Pentecostalism, when many wondered if the "old-time power" of the movement had waned.[177]

If critics had scolded the earlier evangelists for their showmanship, then the practices, claims, fundraising techniques, and affluent lifestyles of certain prominent third-generation evangelists[178] offered much more ammunition for their fusillades. Presbyterian educator Wade Boggs, Jr., sarcastically queried: "Shall we regard their small amount of blundering success, meager indeed when compared to all the other good work for the relief of human suffering that has been less ostentatiously going on in the regular channels of healing, as the fulfillment of Christ's promise, "Greater works than these will he do?" (John 14:12)[179] Impressed by the views of Frost and Bingham, J. Oswald Sanders, Home Director of the China Inland Mission for Australia and New Zealand, said "'hallucination' is the kindest term to use" in regard to certain features of the movement. "In others, 'racket' best describes their character."[180] Although affirming that genuine miracles of healing still could happen, he argued that results of "impartial and scientific investigation" had proven the claims of the faith healers to be either spurious, disorders cured by auto-suggestion, or sicknesses alleviated through purely natural means.[181] While such complaints merited scrutiny, they more effectively perpetuated a stereotype of faith healers dating from the nineteenth century[182] but gathering new life through the reaction of fundamentalists and evangelicals to Pentecostalism and the problems created by high-profile faith healers.

Yet, despite the condemnations, salvation/healing campaigns significantly led to church growth.[183] The crowds at the Hicks meetings in Argentina in 1954 grew upward from five thousand to two hundred thousand with notable results in conversions, healings, church attendance, and the purchase of Bibles. "The warehouses of the Bible societies have been swept bare, and additional supplies are being rushed to Buenos Aires," reported the editor of the *Christian Century*. Even so, he judged the enthusiastic response to Hicks's promise of healing to be just "one more indication of the seriously disturbed psychic condition of multitudes in all parts of today's world."[184] The rapid growth of Pentecostalism in Brazil, with its strong emphasis on prayer for the sick, and the religious culture of Brazil made possible the mass campaign of Erickson in Rio de Janeiro two years later that attracted fifty thousand people, leading to thousands of conversions, and the distribution of Bibles, books, and tracts.[185] In El Salvador, thirty-three new churches started in one year through the evangelistic campaigns of the lesser-known but highly successful Richard Jeffery, who preached only from one text—Hebrews 13:8—followed by testimonies of persons who had been healed or delivered from demons.[186] Similar happenings occurred in Africa, India, Southeast Asia, the Philippines, and the Caribbean.[187]

However, even more important for evangelism and church growth than the mass meetings of the North American evangelists, which offered high social visibility to Pentecostalism and national mission churches, were the efforts of untold numbers of pastors, evangelists, and laypersons in Majority World countries who prayed for the sick. Among the most notable, the Zulu evangelist Nicholas Bhengu—highlighted in *Time* magazine as the "black Billy Graham"—drew enormous crowds to his Back to God Crusades in southern Africa, which featured salvation, healing, deliverance from demons, and repentance for criminal activities.[188] In West Africa, the Christ Apostolic Church saw significant growth after the Yoruba tribesman Joseph Ayo Babalola (a public works employee), while operating a steamroller, received a vision in which he was called to preach and heal the sick through prayer and the use of holy water.[189]

The controversies that dogged the steps of the healing evangelists did not escape the watchful eyes of Pentecostal leaders, whose concerns ranged from doctrine and ethics to the effects of their overseas campaigns on mission endeavors. The first major challenge from within the Pentecostal movement came from the pen of Donald Gee in his booklet *Trophimus I Left Sick* (1952). "Preachers of Divine healing usually stress that healing should be 'taken' or 'claimed' in the Name of the Lord without question as to it being the will of God to heal," despite the fact that so many seekers did not receive relief from their suffering.[190] Typical of this approach, T. L. Osborn had declared that "Christians need never be sick."[191] But from his study of the New Testament, Gee concluded that evangelism represented the true sphere of miracles both in the first century and the twentieth century. In a sharp jab at the teaching of Bosworth, the other healing evangelists, and in Pentecostal denominations, he argued that guarantees of healing for believers could not be substantiated from Scripture.[192] Furthermore, "to assert that healing for our bodies rests upon an identical authority with healing for our souls in the atoning work of Christ our Saviour can involve serious problems of personal faith and confidence for those weak in the faith if, and when, they see manifest cases where Divine healing, though 'claimed,' has not been received."[193] Paradoxically, he affirmed the availability of physical healing in the atonement and agreed with the statement of the American Assemblies of God that it represented "the privilege of all believers," while qualifying its application by saying that Isaiah 53 still required interpretation in the light of the rest of Scripture.[194] Within the Assemblies of God itself, a significant divergence of opinion on healing had surfaced already by the 1920s with the publication of an official Bible doctrines book that referred to the promise of healing in James 5:14-15, but not to Isaiah 53 and the atonement of Christ.[195] A decade later, two more authorized publications of the same nature appeared, one which affirmed that "divine healing is part and parcel of the gospel," and a larger and more detailed doctrinal study that never linked healing to the atonement.[196]

Weighing in on the unethical practices and strident claims of some evangelists, the leaders of the Assemblies of God lamented that "our precious and wonderful truth of Divine Healing was being wounded in the house of its friends."[197] A more pointed rebuke came from G. H. Montgomery, sometime Pentecostal Holiness Church editor and associate of Oral Roberts, who described them as "Enemies of the Cross." "Some of these same evangelists reported that literally hundreds of deaf people were healed and received their hearing in Jamaica," he reported.[198] But Montgomery's daughter, a missionary there who worked with deaf people, said that neither she nor her colleagues had ever found one person who had been healed of deafness. Noel Perkin, missions director for the Assemblies of God expressed another concern. "The adverse reaction in the thinking of many who crowd to these meetings for healing when disappointed in their hopes is impossible to calculate," and caused him to wonder if in fact healing had replaced the gospel message in the practice of the evangelists. Trying to walk the same tightrope as Gee, he insisted: "The gospel basically is that Christ died for our sins and has risen for our justification." Following conversion, "the life also of Jesus will be made manifest in and through His body in physical benefit as we exercise faith to this end."[199] For these second-generation leaders, salvation and healing had to be kept in proper proportion to one another, though not in equal standing.

Pentecostals practiced healing with a dogmatic conviction that would survive into the twenty-first century in some quarters: the provision for healing in the atonement—always available to those with sufficient faith, with resort to medicine and doctors an implicit sign of unbelief.[200] Yet, over time, a more holistic understanding that saw medical science as a gift from God prevailed as many endeavored to answer the three nagging questions and address the needs of grief-stricken parishioners.[201] Gee's obvious struggle with the biblical basis of the doctrine and its associated problems served as a "shot across the bow" for Pentecostals, a sign of coming changes as Pentecostalism progressed into the second half of the century and adherents embraced medical advances.[202] In January 1978, Oral Roberts broke ground for the City of Faith (hospital) in Tulsa, Oklahoma, to show how belief in miraculous healing with medical treatment could "round out the totality of healing for the whole man," a venture that would have flabbergasted first-generation Pentecostals.[203]

As interest in healing flourished in many parts of the world, passionate debates arose over scriptural warrant and practices. In their reactions, many evangelical Christians (including fundamentalists), though affirming belief in healing, in effect kept one foot on the accelerator and the other firmly on the brake. Pentecostals and Anglicans like Hickson took their foot off the brake. When considering the willingness of God to heal the sick, if the evangelicals felt the Pentecostals and Anglicans anticipated too much, the Pentecostals—having "thrown all doubts to the winds and taken to our hearts the whole word of Jesus"—thought the evangelicals expected too little.

10

Apostolic Faith at the Third Millennium

The Apostolic Faith movement has been uplifted by God for the purpose of restoring primitive Christianity, and the work has been upheld by mighty deeds and wonderful manifestations.[1]

Pentecostal leader Charles Parham, 1905

We are not fighting men or churches, but seeking to displace dead forms and creeds and wild fanaticisms with living, practical Christianity.[2]

Apostolic Faith newspaper, Azusa Street Revival, 1906

We have received many good things from the West, but we are in danger of its evils. . . . I mean the modern Christianity. . . . You Westerners have done a great service to us by bringing back to us our Bible. But please do not mutilate it. If you have modern notions about it, please keep them for yourselves.[3]

Sheik Metry S. Dewairy of Egypt at the
International Missionary Council, Jerusalem, 1928

Much of the Bible teaching on the question of Pentecost and the power of the Holy Spirit of recent years has been colored unduly by a retreat before the tongues people. . . . A revulsion of feeling took place among leaders of Christian thought and it became popular to explain away Pentecost.[4]

Baptist evangelist John R. Rice, 1949

The essential optimism of Christianity is that the Holy Spirit is a force capable of bursting into the hardest paganism, discomfiting the most rigid dogmatism, electrifying the most suffocating organization and bringing the glory of Pentecost.[5]

Assemblies of God mission leader J. Philip Hogan, 1972

To fail to appreciate the multi-dimensional and multi-cultural manner in which the Holy Spirit has worked, and to straitjacket him by an Americo-

centric interpretation of Pentecostalism is to make him less than a God of all nations![6]

Bishop of the Methodist Church in Malaysia Hwa Yung, 2005

American Pentecostals woke up in the latter half of the twentieth century to discover their favored position as the last "wave" of the Spirit's renewal had been overflowed by a tsunami of historic and global proportions steadily rising since the nineteenth century—the tide of large sectors of Christianity embracing charismatic—"Pentecostal"—phenomena in the Majority World.[7] North American Pentecostalism and its mission enterprises have contributed undeniably to this development, but represent a part, not the whole of the picture. Neither can it be said to have originated solely from North America. Movements with Pentecostal traits in the mission lands had begun to surface in the nineteenth century, long before the church world learned about revivals in Topeka, Los Angeles, Toronto, Oslo, Sunderland (England), and Wakkerstroom (South Africa). Bigger than the Pentecostal movement and the charismatic renewals in the mainline Protestant and Roman Catholic churches, this charismatically inclined brand of the faith has taken on dimensions that even the most ardent proponents did not anticipate.

As early as the 1940s, mission scholars began to discern that something momentous was afoot. In a rare tribute to Pentecostals for the time in which it was given, Bishop Stephen Neill of the Anglican Diocese of Tinnevelly in India said they "bear brave and uncompromising witness to one of the fundamental truths of the revelation of God in Christ, that it is the will of God that every Christian should consciously receive and enjoy the witness and power of the Holy Ghost." Reflecting on the historical contributions of renewal movements, he added: "When a doctrine which is the rightful possession of the whole Church is forgotten or allowed to slip into the background or is not duly emphasized, God allows it for a time to become embodied in a sect, which acts as a gadfly to awaken the Church, until the missing doctrine is reabsorbed to the enrichment of the whole of the common life."[8] To which Pentecostals did he refer? Although speaking of them in general, he likely included Indian believers.[9] Years later, another bishop in South India, Lesslie Newbigin, similarly identified "a third stream of Christian tradition. . . . Its central element is the conviction that the Christian life is a matter of the experienced power and presence of the Holy Spirit today."[10]

Interestingly, charismatically inclined Christianity also has risen above the barrier reefs of Protestant, Anglican, and Catholic ecclesiologies to create a revolutionary component in the life of Christians, bringing new vigor to the faith, new churches, and plenty of discomfort to the wary. "Today we are witnessing the upsurge of many and various forms of experience of the Holy Spirit throughout the entire world," wrote Catholic missiologist José Comblin. "They are linked to a deep change in the way Christian people read the Bible, in the way lay people pray, in the vitality of Christian communities."[11] In this last chapter, we will look briefly at the flowering of this development, the present crisis of identity in North American Pentecostalism, how Pentecostal missions fit into the big picture, and the importance of signs and wonders in the historical expansion of Christianity.

CHARISMATICALLY INCLINED CHRISTIANITY

Cultural perceptions of the spirit world and folk healing, Protestant and Catholic missions, the liberating nature of the gospel, revival movements, and Bible translations together have played strategic roles in the emergence of charismatically inclined Christianity.[12] In certain respects, it shows the legacy of the radical evangelicals whose supernaturally charged strategies went from insistence on Spirit baptism to the advocacy of faith missions to faith healing, spiritual warfare, and the gift of languages. Whether considering Edward Irving, A. B. Simpson, Charles Parham, or the later James Moore Hickson and C. Peter Wagner, all have left their mark on the Christian world mission. No less iconoclastic, indigenous leaders such as Justus Joseph, William Wadé Harris, the apostles of Madagascar, and Nicholas Bhengu found charismatic gifts and institutions in Scripture, such as the offices of prophet and apostle, that in their reading could be restored, a possibility not mentioned in the Bible commentaries that missionaries brought from home.

For many contemporary believers, the immanent power and gifts of the Spirit have had more relevance for their lives than upholding the creeds of the Protestant and Catholic traditions. "The Holy Spirit, whom [Christians have] experienced through healings, miracles and empowerment, is also expected to perform miracles and healings," according to Korean theologian Wonsuk Ma. For them, "even the promise of the Lord for supernatural power as recorded in Mark 16:15-18 is understood in the context of mission." Moreover, the belief that "these signs will accompany" cannot be trumped by the misgivings of biblical scholars about the textual authority of one passage of Scripture.[13]

"Pentecostal-charismatic spirituality has a distinct advantage over traditional missiologies in parts of the world where people are familiar with phenomena from the spirit-world," said mission scholar Kirsteen Kim. To those attracted to the faith, the reasons center on the power of the name of Jesus Christ and the work of the Holy Spirit in overcoming sorcery.[14] This helps to explain why Pentecostalism has had special appeal among the poor in regions least influenced by scientific rationalism and secularization, as well as among business and educated elites in countries that have adopted Western ways but where the old cultures light up after business hours.

The sheer magnitude of extraordinary experiences—visions, dreams, prophecies, tongues, healings, exorcisms, and other happenings—prompted one Catholic theologian to describe this outpouring of the Spirit as a universal grace among the divided churches to foster Christian unity,[15] while outside the cloister others have discerned the Spirit's activity in sundry places: the ecumenical movement, civil rights movement, Second Vatican Council, liberation theology, the elevation of women, and the Lausanne movement, among others.[16] Although but one of numerous movements in global Christianity, Pentecostalism in its many expressions and the overlapping growth of charismatically inclined Christianity have been startling and expansive developments. Few could have imagined at mid-twentieth century that Anglican dioceses (Perú and Bolivia) would bill themselves as "catholic, evangelical and charismatic" or that others would be profoundly influenced by the charismatic renewal in the practice of ministry (Anglican Churches of Nigeria, Uganda, and Southeast Asia, among others).[17]

The miracle stories form an extraordinary index of claims in an era when scientific thinking and religious skepticism have monitored the intellectual crossroads of North Atlantic countries. Missionaries such as George Rouse and John Clough, who regretted they lived in an age after miracles had ceased, might have been amazed to discover how "heathen" cultures actually contributed to the responsiveness of non-Christians in receiving the gospel through experiencing and witnessing paranormal phenomena.[18] More recently and from South India, the Vincentian priest Augustine Mundackatt traveled to Mongolia to preach the gospel and pray for the sick. Speaking before a hundred tribal people, he reported, "We prayed for all of them in the name of Jesus. . . . The arm of the tribal chief, paralyzed for years, was healed; the Lord touched a woman who was paralyzed around the waist and she began to walk." Then, linking these events to the spiritual dynamics of the first-century church, he said, "Awe came upon everyone, because many wonders and signs were being done by the apostles" (Acts 2:43).[19] In Kuala Lumpur, Malaysia, actress-turned-evangelist Kong Duen Yee ("Mui Yee") condemned the Chinese gods and goddesses before her audience, provoking a "power encounter" with mediums and gangsters in which she drew attention to the superiority of the Christian God over the spirits worshipped by the Chinese community.[20] In the Muslim world, numbers of converts have told of receiving dreams and visions of Jesus that led them to embrace the Christian faith.[21]

Within nominally Christian countries, miraculous claims have had a similar effect. Thousands of Romani people in Europe have converted to evangelical Christianity, an occurrence traced back in part to a boy's healing from tuberculosis after prayer.[22] Exorcisms and healings have marked the ministries of the Kenyan Charles Omuroka, a lay Orthodox evangelist, and his mentor, the American Greek Orthodox priest Eusebius Stephanou, whose meetings in Greece received the condemnation of the church hierarchy.[23] Far away in Argentina, evangelist Carlos Annacondia began each of his evangelistic campaigns by outwardly rebuking "all spirits of witchcraft, sorcery, mental control, *macumba*, *umbanda*, spiritualism, and other pagan religions" to free people bound by the "chains of Satan."[24] At Templo El Jordán in Mejicanos, El Salvador, "Brother Fidel" [Molina] told his congregation, "The power of Jesus can heal us, it can change our lives completely."[25]

Finally, at an ecumenical pastors' conference, meeting at a teachers' college in northern Tanzania and featuring speakers from the international Lutheran and Anglican charismatic renewals, students—not involved in the conclave—

reported seeing "a light 'brighter than the sun, brighter than daylight' over the building where the pastors were meeting."[26] These accounts, reminiscent of the biblical narratives, as well as the miracle stories recorded by Eusebius of Caesarea and the Venerable Bede, comprise but a handful of the many that appear on the daily spreadsheet of global Christianity, a happening that chagrins those who see this as a step backward from a more enlightened and rational understanding of the faith.[27]

In a noteworthy turn, conservative evangelicals began setting aside their penchant toward cessationism. Even the flag bearer of Southern Baptist fundamentalism, Adrian Rogers, admitted, albeit within a swirl of caution, "I must say that I believe God does heal today—sovereignly, supernaturally, radically, and dramatically."[28] At Fuller Theological Seminary, the course "Signs and Wonders" taught by Pastor John Wimber and Professor Peter Wagner in the early 1980s uproariously disturbed the *status quo* when they began praying for students with illnesses and casting out demons.[29] Critics raised traditional concerns and challenged Wimber's view of "power evangelism."[30] Nevertheless, a new movement—dubbed by Wagner as "the Third Wave of the Holy Spirit"[31] and embodied in the Vineyard Christian Fellowship, had been launched and would have a wide-ranging impact.[32] More voices joined the chorus, including those of Jack Deere of Dallas Theological Seminary, Timothy Warner of Trinity Evangelical Divinity School, Charles Kraft of Fuller Seminary, and Donald Bridge in England, with their ministries and publications exhibiting the ongoing vitality, if not disruptive nature, of radical evangelicalism.[33] In another important development, Mennonite scholars began to explore the nature and issues related to demon possession, adding to the work of conservative evangelical scholars.[34]

Scientists, philosophers, theologians, and historians still dismiss miracle stories for an assortment of reasons, denoting the conflict of worldviews in the present time. From the standpoint of the scientific academy, verification is impossible since causal factors must point in a natural direction and anecdotal evidence to the contrary does not fit into a test tube. With his ordered view of the universe and nature, philosopher David Hume contended that rational people would more readily doubt a miracle than believe it. Since they often experience human deception in various forms, ranging from misunderstanding to exaggeration and to outright falsehoods, they neither expect nor experience the interruption of the natural laws—like gravity, forces that do not change.[35] In this scenario, suspicion then presents the best approach to so-called violations or the supposed setting aside of natural laws. In contrast, Jesus and the New Testament writers urged people to move beyond their doubts and "have faith." "The Christian tradition takes 'miracle' to be principally about God, the agent of the miracles, who has acted in some surprising way . . . to bring about a certain good effect," wrote Catholic theologian Charles Pinches. "Rather than being mainly about strange and anomalous events per se, 'miracle' is a religious description about what the divine power has done or is doing . . . an extraordinary work of God that is to our great benefit."[36] Thus, "only believe . . . all things are possible," words of a popular Christian song, could be heard frequently in Pentecostal healing services.[37] (Even the pronouncement of a miracle by the Medical Bureau of Lourdes finally rests on faith.) Ultimately, the "proof" of a miracle appears in the effect on people—whether or not their lives have changed for the better.[38]

Skepticism also has come from within the Christian tradition: No greater contrast can be found than that between liberal Protestants and Pentecostals. If liberals celebrated the spirit of the age—happily shorn of all superstition, Pentecostals believed the age of the Spirit (the advancing kingdom of God) had come, complete with miracles.[39] The contrast appears on an even larger scale with the charismatically inclined Christians of the Majority World who now represent a far greater constituency than traditional North Atlantic Protestants.[40] Besides the doubts of liberal Protestants, many evangelicals have rejected accounts of healing as fabricated or psychosomatic in nature, rejecting anecdotal evidence to the contrary, in addition to the opinions of Christian medical doctors who have attested to the reality of God's healing power.[41] Complicating the discussion, however, have been the misdeeds of practitioners of healing who have made fraudulent claims, such as the "eyeless vision" act of evangelist Ronald Coyne and the "healings" performed by W. V. Grant, Jr., and Peter Popoff.[42] Others sometimes exercised poor judgment, as when F. F. Bosworth prayed for infants but offered no comfort to the parents when healing did not follow (due to their unbelief);[43] or when Oral Roberts announced that three "medical doctors" had affirmed his healing ministry (none could be identified as medical doctors; one functioned as a "naturopathic physician").[44] In any event, such happenings have brought discredit to others who prayed for the sick.

ALLIANCE WITH EVANGELICALS

The Pentecostal movement marked the first time that a renewal characterized by glossolalia and charismatic gifts had survived long enough to institutionalize and seek to retain these distinctive features. While Pentecostals celebrated the restoration of Spirit baptism and the gifts, in all other beliefs and practices (with the exception of Oneness Pentecostals), they mirrored the evangelical revivalist tradition, which in turn reflected the historic credo of orthodox Christianity. But not surprisingly, their acceptance by evangelicals progressed slowly.[45] After joining the National Association of Evangelicals (NAE) in 1943, the Assemblies of God, Church of God (Cleveland, Tenn.), Open Bible Standard Churches, and the Pentecostal Holiness Church became founding members of the affiliate Evangelical Foreign Missions Association (EFMA), an alternative to the Foreign Missions Conference of North America.[46] When the latter became a constituent part of the National Council of Churches of Christ in the USA in 1950, the Assemblies of God, which had belonged since 1920, dropped its membership but retained status as a "consultative body" until 1961.[47] Meanwhile, the EFMA connection got off to a rocky start when several agencies refused to join because of the inclusion of Pentecostals. In reaction to the resentment, unproven record of assistance, and cost of supporting contributions, the Assemblies of God withdrew from it as well in 1950; at the invitation of EFMA director Clyde Taylor, it rejoined three years later.[48]

In an unprecedented acknowledgment, certain Pentecostals recognized the Holy Spirit at work in the ecumenical movement. In 1952, leaders of the World Pentecostal Conference (WPC) sent the following letter of good will—carried by the secretary, David du Plessis—to the International Missionary Council meeting in Willingen, Germany:

A *Statement by Pentecostal Leaders*

Only by remaining absolutely loyal to itself in Christ can the Pentecostal Movement embody anything of special import in Christian work and witness. That is to say, it must testify particularly to the Baptism in the Holy Spirit with an initial evidence that accords with the New Testament, and to the manifestation of the Spirit through His diversities of supernatural gifts in the churches. It is not distinctive to possess evangelical zeal; neither is it peculiarly "pentecostal" to believe in divine healing. There is nothing whatever Pentecostal in contending for some particular form or idea of church government hoary with age, and already embodied, if not embalmed in more than one existing denomination. The true Pentecostal Revival offers a testimony to a definite spiritual and personal experience, based on the significance and story of the Day of Pentecost. Hence its name, and its only justification for its name. In that distinctive witness lies its strength, its vindication, and its value.

Whatever some of its past local mistakes may have been, the main stream of the Pentecostal Movement sees with gladness the grace of God in all who have believed and turned to the Lord, whose names are written in Heaven by the regenerating power of the Spirit and the Word, and who, therefore, are truly members of the Church, which is Christ's body, the fullness of Him that filleth all in all.

Within Pentecostal ranks there are some honest misgivings concerning some aspects of the ecumenical movement for church unions, but there also is a hearty recognition of a significant moving of the Holy Spirit in recent years to draw all true Christians closer together.

If the Pentecostal Churches now come to give to their sister churches in Christ, they come also to receive. If they dare to believe that on some important lines they can possibly teach, they recognize willingly how much they can learn. They come for fellowship, for the reciprocity of love, for striving together for the faith of the Gospel. In these threatening days Christian ranks must be closed up, and the Pentecostal Churches are ready, please God [!], to step into their place in the army of Emmanuel, bringing with them their own contribution to the equipment of the whole for the good fight of faith. They dare to believe that they are needed, but they also believe that they stand in need.

After nearly half a century of misunderstanding and ostracism, for which they recognize they have not been entirely without blame on their own part, the Pentecostal Churches offer their fellowship in Christ to the whole of His Church in this grave hour of her history. They believe they have something to gain by larger fellowship with all who truly belong to Christ. They are greatly encouraged by many world-wide tokens that old prejudices are melting and a new era of mutual appreciation dawning. Brethren, let us receive one another, as Christ also received us to the glory of God.[49]

The WPC had convened under the topic "Into All the World": "Around this theme will be built the main phases of the Great Commission, '. . . and preach the gospel to every creature.' It is a coming together to unite our efforts to 'go into all the world' with the spoken word of the preacher, the printed word of the writer, the visual aids of the artist, and the far-reaching ministry of the radio, until we have reached every creature," announced du Plessis beforehand.[50] The Statement, however, significantly ventured a step onto unfamiliar turf by looking at the larger developments in world Christianity from the standpoint of Pentecostalism as a renewal movement. A remarkably generous declaration for the time, it struck a posture consistent with the self-perception of first-generation Pentecostals.[51] The measure of humility, obvious confidence in their identity, evangelical zeal, and desire to cooperate for the cause of Christ indicated that a dramatic change in attitude had occurred at least among some of these "Pentecostal evangelicals" toward other Christians. Two years later in 1954, J. Roswell Flower, general secretary of the Assemblies of God, and du Plessis attended the Second Assembly of the World Council of Churches at Evanston, Illinois, and reported favorably on the need for participation.[52]

Nonetheless, mounting criticisms of the NAE and its Pentecostal members by fundamentalists only increased the distance.[53] With the election of Assemblies of God leader Thomas Zimmerman as president of the NAE in 1960, though representing a signal achievement for a Pentecostal leader, the last door closed on contacts with the larger church world. The hopeful possibilities of a renewal movement had been pre-empted by the beneficial alignment with conservative evangelicals, a commanding sense of their basic theological identity, and institutional Pentecostalism's fear of the ecumenical movement, in due course confirmed by increasing theological pluralism in some sectors of the latter. The isolation also resulted from premillennialist fears of growing apostasy in the mainline churches and suspicion that bodies like the National Council of Churches and the World Council foreshadowed a world church that would welcome the Antichrist figure of the book of Revelation.[54] Major Pentecostal denominations had become firmly embedded with evangelicals at this point.[55] Consequently, mission executives virtually had no contact with conciliar agencies whose leaders were sometimes curious about Pentecostalism; in spite of this, students of church growth and ecumenical onlookers investigated the dynamics propelling it.[56] Pentecostals soon constituted the largest constituency in the NAE and formed their own worldwide networks.[57]

When the centenary of Pentecostal missions occurred in 2006 and during celebrations of the Azusa Street revival, leaders noted the outstanding success of the broader movement, purportedly numbering more than half-a-billion adherents, making Pentecostals and charismatics the second-largest family of Christians in the world after Roman Catholics.[58] Based more on phenomenological factors than ecclesiastical and historical parameters, such statistics taken from surveys of global Christianity have presented popular but questionable means for defining "success" and long have been cited to vindicate legitimacy. "This movement of God has resulted in the salvation of hundreds of thousands of sinners, both in so-called Christian lands and in those called heathen; tens of thousands have been healed of various diseases; other hundreds of thousands have received a Pentecostal Baptism in the Holy Spirit," crowed Bennett Lawrence in the first history of the Pentecostal movement published in 1916, just ten years after the beginning of the Azusa Street revival. "Hundreds have felt the missionary zeal of the first evangelists and have gone to the uttermost parts of the earth in one of the most spontaneous and widely spread missionary efforts the world has seen since the days of Pentecost."[59] Apart from the number of missionaries, the other claims are doubtful for the time. (The vendor for Lawrence's statistics has yet to be tracked down.) Decades later, Pentecostal leaders also readily ate the shiny red apple of triumphalism, heralding the statistics and achievements before their constituencies.[60] Unfortunately, the mesmerizing effect of numbers has masked the problems faced by mission agencies, such as missionary turnover; the need for long-range development planning to confront poverty, hunger, and disease in many parts of the world, which elude the effectiveness of short-term mission efforts; duplication of programs; stewardship of money; partisan approaches to evangelism;[61] schisms in national mission churches; and slow progress in some countries and decline in others—for example, in Chile.[62]

CRISIS AND REACTION

By the close of the century and regardless of the glowing statistics, North American Pentecostalism faced an unprecedented crisis of identity. In spirituality, worship, and practice, many churches could not be distinguished from evangelical churches, apart from the posting on the front sign.[63] Pentecostal denominations, though highly organized with well-oiled foreign and home mission enterprises, leveled in domestic growth amid decline in the number of believers receiving Spirit baptism with tongues-speech, as well as other charismatic practices.[64] The once-commanding factor in pressing the urgency of missions—intense eschatological expectation—had peaked with the faithful now endeavoring to transform their culture with Christian values and denominational executives busily planning for the future.[65] Even so, obedience to Christ, saving the lost, and compassion have continued as chief motivations. Leaders subsequently anticipated that a fresh revival would solve the crisis. "Only a vigilant sensitivity to the Holy Spirit can keep the Church marching in step with God's divine purposes on earth," trumpeted Pentecostal Holiness mission director Bernard Underwood.[66]

In light of the experiential nature of revival (renewal), initial dynamics usually last only for one generation; sometimes they may last longer. In any event, the effects shape the generations that follow, which then ordinarily seek to perpetuate it through the creation of new institutions. For Pentecostals, this has presented a particular dilemma since the attempt to legislate the charismatic work of the Holy Spirit by means of doctrinal statements and denominational requirements can encourage but not guarantee the perpetuation of the pre-scribed spirituality. Each generation must experience Pentecostal manifesta-tions for the movement to advance on its idealized trajectory.[67] However, just as culture changes, so certain issues that gave rise to the original revival become increasingly distant to later generations that ask new questions. "[Early Pente-costals] experienced revival in an age that was couched in its own problems and needs," wrote Robert Larden of the Apostolic Church of Pentecost of Canada, "a repeat performance would not answer contemporary needs."[68] In fact, while one may speak of the Pentecostal revival as having marched forward since early in the twentieth century, it may be more accurate to consider that through the years a plurality of revivals have taken place with similar phenomena, but with somewhat different emphases. The progress of Christianity itself has been more of spiraling change than a movement advancing in an unbroken straight line, as if institutional churches and their programs can become perfected as structures over time. "[Christianity] is always in need of re-simplifying, going back to its origins, ridding itself of the excessive superstructure it has acquired through his-tory," observed Comblin.[69] Such have been the jarring effects of renewal move-ments.[70]

Despite the crisis, the vitality for missionary vocation, both full-time and short-term, has shown little sign of dissipating, denoting that mission remains at the heart of the movement.[71] In the same way, interest in the charismatic gifts and tongues-speech, though lessened at times in practice, holds a central place in their conception of the Spirit-filled life. "Glossolalia is not just one of the concomitants of being Spirit-filled, but is the most natural and regular concomi-tant of Spirit-filling involving an invasive or irruptive manifestation of the Spirit in which one's relationship to Jesus Christ is radically and significantly altered," explained Singaporean theologian Simon Chan. "When one experiences the com-ing of the Spirit in such a manner, the most natural and spontaneous response is glossolalia."[72] Harvard scholar Harvey Cox has pointed to the primal nature of speaking in tongues, and adds that the "deeper insight of ecstatic utterance is that . . . human beings can nonetheless speak to God because God makes such speech possible. . . . Our corrupt and inadequate language is transformed by God's love into the tongues of angels."[73] Interest in the spirituality of tongues-speech has continued and with more academic reflection.

Predictable reactions to the crisis have occurred, but not without temporar-ily pushing important questions to the side. As a corrective in the Assemblies of God, leaders re-asserted that Pentecostal identity begins with Spirit baptism and the "initial evidence" of tongues-speech—the "distinctive testimony" the denomination has heralded since 1918, viewed as the key to revival and inspira-tion for church growth.[74] Though helpful, this defines a Pentecostal by a spiri-tual phenomenon, without considering other distinguishing characteristics of the subculture. At the same time, lingering hesitations about the hermeneutical underpinning of the doctrine have taken a heavy toll, although evidence of further development of the doctrine has appeared.[75] Moving in another direction, the International Church of the Foursquare Gospel and Open Bible Churches modified their positions on tongues either in practice (the former) or officially (the latter).[76]

Since the time of Charles Parham, the majority of North American Pentecostals have looked to Spirit baptism as the gateway to the Spirit-filled life. "Pentecostals believe that this baptism is an enduement of power for witnessing and service," declared Canadian leader Gordon Atter in the mid-twentieth century. "They expect frequent 'manifestations of the Spirit' in a fuller and richer measure than could otherwise be possible."[77] Notwithstanding, denominational Pentecostals gradually marginalized related phenomena: dreams and visions; the gifts of tongues, interpretation, and prophecy in corporate worship; rejected the restoration of the offices of prophet and apostle; and even downplayed signs and wonders in evangelism for a variety of reasons, including biblical and practical concerns.[78]

When the *Weekly Evangel*, published by the Assemblies of God, introduced the "Questions and Answers" column in 1916, E. N. Bell listed the "rules" for readers who might wish to send in questions. The second rule stated: "Ask only questions about religious matters that can be answered from the Bible or History; don't ask for interpretation of dreams or visions. We do not have the gift to interpret these."[79] It was an understandable, though telling statement, displaying obvious discomfort with a vital feature of Joel's prediction about the outpouring of the Spirit (Joel 2:28); this reserved attitude eventually would be shared by many American Pentecostals, but form an enduring feature of the spirituality of believers abroad. In Los Angeles, Aimee Semple McPherson, founder of the Foursquare Church, reserved the "utterance gifts" (tongues, interpretation, and prophecy) at her Angelus Temple for meetings held in rooms set aside for prayer; they rarely or never occurred in the carefully orchestrated worship services in the sanctuary, as was customary in Pentecostal churches.[80] Originally absent in the Pentecostal movement, such restrictions have become more common in recent years. This minimizing of spiritual manifestations has stood in stark contrast to the practices of African-American Pentecostals and among overseas constituencies.[81] Elsewhere, Latin American Pentecostals have placed great emphasis on healing—perhaps more than on tongues in some instances—because of the dearth of medical assistance for the poor and their confidence in Jesus as healer.[82]

In the study of global Pentecostalism, the common theme of Spirit baptism readily appears. The Classical Pentecostal version mentioned above, which originated in North America, represents a widely held view on its reception and meaning.[83] Theologian Frank Macchia has suggested, "The challenge . . . for the future of Pentecostal theology is to maintain the focus on Spirit baptism as the chief theological distinctive of Pentecostalism, while leaving 'breathing room' for a diversity of nuances and interpretations among Pentecostal movements globally."[84] Since Pentecostalism no longer fits into a single frame—scholars now speak of "Pentecostalisms," more may be learned from the insights of Pentecostals living in other regions of the world. "By almost any standard," observed historian Everett Wilson, "Pentecostalism presently is not what Charles Fox Parham or any of his successors has pronounced it to be, but rather what contemporary Brazilians, Koreans and Africans demonstrate that it actually is."[85] Indeed, the "progressive Pentecostals" that sociologists Donald Miller and Tetsunao Yamamori studied in different countries heed a less doctrinaire compass on Spirit baptism, exhibit spiritual gifts and enthusiastic worship, and carry a strongly holistic orientation in mission, but are no less evangelical in message.[86]

The core of Pentecostal spirituality revolves around the biblical Jesus, life in the Spirit, and a broad range of charismatic phenomena.[87] Nevertheless, the inclusion of some pneumatically oriented movements in the Majority World under the "Pentecostal" umbrella remains a complicated discussion, one that North Atlantic Pentecostals have generally skirted by dismissing them as syncretistic and lacking an evangelical witness.[88] An important component of the missionary legacy has centered on instruction that combines the cognitive aspects of Bible study with experiential piety in order to avoid potential meandering into theological error and syncretism. "If Pentecostal spirituality is to survive deeper levels of encounter with indigenous cultures and spiritualities," wrote Indian missiologist Ivan Satyavrata, "it must be grounded in the Christ-event as recorded in the biblical account, interpretation of which requires both the guidance of the Spirit and an informed reading of the text."[89]

CROSSCURRENTS IN EVANGELISM

The decline in Pentecostal spirituality and signs and wonders became evident in the ministry of Jimmy Swaggart in the 1970s and 1980s, showing how much American Pentecostals had changed after 1960 and with hardly anyone blinking an eye. Coming to prominence as an Assemblies of God evangelist in the late 1960s, he later transitioned from singing and preaching on the radio to television. A forceful public speaker, his popularity mounted as he preached in packed-out auditoriums across North America and to tens of thousands of people in national stadiums in Africa and Latin America. For large numbers of Pentecostals, Swaggart modeled the ideal evangelist: preaching—"in the power of Christ"—an otherworldly message of salvation and personal holiness before the imminent return of Christ and personal holiness.[90] He became the only nationally known denominational Pentecostal evangelist, though he shared the televangelism spotlight with Jim Bakker of the PTL Club.[91]

In practice, he patterned his evangelistic crusades after those of Billy Graham, with a musical package by Swaggart and his team of vocalists, a simple gospel message, and an invitation to receive Christ as Savior.[92] Differences appeared in the musical and preaching styles, the sometimes blistering rhetoric, and in overseas campaigns a certain level of cultural insensitivity (for example, songs were sung in English before non-English-speaking audiences), as well his ready willingness to publicly criticize the Roman Catholic Church.[93] Apart from a brief prayer for anyone who needed healing, signs and wonders hardly surfaced in his crusades—no individual prayer for the sick, exorcisms, or miracles. If occurring at all, they happened on the periphery of the meetings. (In other contexts, he personally prayed for people.)

Hesitations about healing in the atonement help explain their absence. "Is healing part of the atonement?" Swaggart demanded. "Absolutely and without a doubt!" Still, along with other second- and third-generation leaders, he qualified it by saying that "salvation, while it has its physical aspects, is basically spiritual."[94] His preaching, therefore, elevated the message of personal salvation far above physical healing.[95] R. A. Torrey, Rowland Bingham, and Henry Frost would have concurred, but they hadn't grown up in Pentecostal churches. The minimal emphasis that Swaggart placed on signs and wonders, coupled with his own startling popularity, indicated the ongoing process of the "evangelicalization" of Pentecostalism. But the scarcity of miracles revived questions raised in the nineteenth century about the apostolic character of mission practices, only this time ironically about how Pentecostals did evangelism. As Rufus Anderson had pointed out a century before, those who consider themselves to be the successors of the apostles must exhibit the attendant signs.[96]

Others have continued in the locomotion of the early movement, especially the German evangelist Reinhard Bonnke. The best-known international Pentecostal evangelist at the turn of the twenty-first century, Bonnke has conducted crusades in sub-Saharan Africa with crowds reaching above a million people.[97] Highlighting healings and exorcisms in his services, he has followed the paradigm of earlier evangelists such as Maria Woodworth-Etter, Smith Wigglesworth, Aimee Semple McPherson, and Tommy Hicks. Describing the role of the supernatural, Bonnke said, "When the Holy Spirit and Gospel preaching come together, there is an explosion of power."[98]

Reared in a Pentecostal home, he enrolled at the Bible College of Wales, a school begun by the Welsh revivalist and "prayer intercessor" Rees Howells. Its founding had been inspired by the faith teachings of George Müller; staff and faculty "lived by faith" and did not receive salaries, though the school covered their room and board. This model fit well with Bonnke's Pentecostal faith and independent spirit. "One of the things he cherished was freedom," wrote his biographer, "and he did not take kindly to the shackles of mission boards."[99] After pastoring for seven years in Germany, he went to southern Africa in 1967 and began preaching in Lesotho, eventually taking the name "Christ for All Nations" for his evangelistic ministry. By the 1980s, his impact could be felt across the continent.[100]

Despite the mammoth audiences of Bonnke and other North Atlantic evangelists, as well as the extended coverage their meetings have received on Christian television around the world, their actual impact on church growth at times has been mixed.[101] The linkage of miracles with gospel proclamation has had far greater effect through the long-term activities of countless indigenous evangelists, pastors, and laypersons, a much more crucial factor in the progress of Pentecostalism and charismatically inclined Christianity.[102] Among many contemporary ministries are those of David (Paul) Yonggi Cho (Korea); Joseph Wongsak (Thailand); Kong Hee (Singapore); Jackie Pullinger (Hong Kong); Sharon Lim (Singapore, Africa); Benson Idahosa, William Kumuyi, and Charles Osueke (Nigeria); Ezekiel Guti (Zimbabwe); Margaret Wangare and Margaret Wanjiru (Kenya); Sunday Adelaja (Ukraine); Omar Cabrera and Elvio Canavesio (Argentina); Carlyle Chankersingh (Trinidad); and Mildred Werdini (Jamaica). Across the aisle, Catholic evangelists have included Raniero Cantalamessa, O.F.M. Cap., Preacher to the Papal Household (Italy); Mathew Naickomparambil, V.C. (India); Linda Koontz, S.N.J.M. (Texas); Breige McKenna, O.S.C. (Ireland); Mariano Velarde and Fernando Suarez, C.C. (Philippines); Tom Forrest, C.Ss.R. (Washington D.C.); Ralph Martin (Ann Arbor, Mich.); and Emmanuel Edeh, C.S.Sp., and Archbishop Gabriel Gonsum Ganaka (Nigeria).[103] To their names could be added thousands of other men and women, ranging from those with local ministries—like the layman Julius Mukenzu in Zambia who planted five churches by himself in a six-year period—to those of regional and international magnitudes.[104]

LIMITS OF RESTORATION

Many North American Pentecostals and charismatics outside the denominations have resurrected the overt supernaturalism of the early Pentecostals. Living at the noisy end of the contemporary radical evangelical neighborhood and—not surprisingly—restless about the slow pace of world evangelization, they have proposed new and controversial strategies.[105] Inadvertently following in the footsteps of Arthur Street and Frank Sandford, some have offered innovative approaches to spiritual warfare and promoted the restoration of prophets and apostles, all with the goal of expediting evangelism.[106] Much of the packaging for the spiritual warfare and new apostolic reformation movements has come from North American missiologists, but also from others in Africa, Asia, Australia, and Latin America.[107]

More elaborate in "mapping" satanic forces and their "strongholds" around the world than Street's notion of "intercessory prayer missionaries" and Sandford's "removing the covering," the "strategic-level spiritual warfare" advocated by Peter Wagner, Charles Kraft, and George Otis, Jr., retains the same supernaturalism, but with much more attention to details and methods. "Binding territorial spirits [demons in the satanic archipelago] is a means toward winning the lost," wrote Wagner. "When the strongman is *overcome* . . . or *bound* . . . , only then are the captives released and for the first time they can hear the gospel and then make their personal choices whether they will accept Jesus Christ or not."[108] In many respects, their application of strategy to geography rolls the church growth methodology with its demographical studies onto cosmic terrain where hierarchies of evil powers under Satan's authority negatively influence humanity.[109] To engage in spiritual warfare, one should be amply prepared through prayer and proceed to find the name of the "territorial demon"—perhaps through a revelation or knowledge gained from a demon in an exorcism—over a particular country or area in order to "bind" it so that effective evangelism can proceed (Matt 18:18).[110] While fiercely criticized by some missiologists and theologians as syncretistic,[111] this tactical line of attack has found a warmer reception among Christians in the Majority World who have accommodating world-views.[112] Others, acknowledging the existence of evil powers and the validity of exorcism, question the assumptions supporting this particular approach.[113]

A vexing issue that has historically confronted radical evangelicals, Pentecostals, and charismatics, as well as other restorationists, relates to what more can be recovered from first-century Christianity to apply to the life and teachings of churches today. These could be potentially new insights (or misperceptions) that might call for changes in forms of church leadership and church life, expressions of piety, and the practice of mission. New restorations inevitably create discord within the ranks, while concurrently representing new streams of vitality. In turn, this makes the pursuit of unity among Christians a more difficult goal to achieve since proponents base harmony with other believers on their acceptance of the new insight.[114] The broader understanding of "church" then becomes victim to a sectarian mindset.

To counter "extremes" and maintain a sense of unity, insiders have long attempted to set appropriate boundaries, but not without the risk of causing substantial pain. In 1910, Holiness Pentecostals condemned "Finished Work" Pentecostals who denied sanctification as a second work of grace and appealed to a progressive development in Christian character.[115] When Oneness Pentecostals pushed for baptism in the name of Jesus Christ alone and for a modal monarchian view of the Godhead, the Assemblies of God adopted a Trinitarian statement of faith in 1916, which prompted schism and earned the denomination bitter criticism from those who left and those who condemned the adoption of creeds. For their part, Oneness Pentecostals chimed that they had completely restored the dynamics of the New Testament church by embracing baptism in Jesus' name as prescribed in Act 2:38, while their Trinitarian brothers and sisters had been content simply to restore Acts 2:4 with speaking in tongues.[116] After a group of independent Canadian Pentecostals called for the "impartation" of the gifts of the Spirit through the laying on of hands during the Latter Rain revival of 1948, as well as the notion that God would bestow languages for missionary preaching and appoint new prophets and apostles, they received the condemnation of the Assemblies of God, Pentecostal Assemblies of Canada, and other Pentecostals, not only for biblical reasons, but because of the divisiveness they generated in congregations and among clergy.[117]

The "Statement by Pentecostal Leaders" to the International Missionary Council in 1952 indicated that Pentecostals felt they deserved a seat at the table with other world Christian leaders to jointly address the concerns of the day. Such consultation would come, but only in venues of evangelical cooperation. Nonetheless, their creative and rowdy offspring, always on the lookout for ways to revive the vigor of the New Testament church, rarely receive an R.S.V.P.

THE CHALLENGE OF ROMAN CATHOLICISM

In the first half of the twentieth century, most North American Pentecostal missionaries served in non-Christian countries, the traditional sites of Protestant endeavor: Africa, Middle East, India, China, Japan, and Oceania. Beginning in World War II, increasing numbers went to Latin America, where church growth soon followed. For the first time, a large segment of missionaries now evangelized in nominally Christian countries and followed the conventional Protestant course of disdaining Roman Catholicism. Margaret Wortman referred to the Argentines as these "poor, poor people!" in a letter sent home in 1923. "You simply can't imagine how they live and die," she insisted. "The Roman Church has little to be proud of in this miserable country."[118] Sixteen years later in Nicaragua, Melvin Hodges expressed similar sentiments. "There are no people who walk in deeper darkness than these very ones who seem to proclaim the Christ," he frowned. "Here there is not absence of truth, but truth distorted into falsehood, for there is no religion in the world more adept at 'changing the truth of God into a lie' than Romanism."[119] Certain practices in folk Catholicism astonished Hodges and other missionaries and have remained, to the present, problematic not only for Protestants but for many Catholics as well.[120]

Nevertheless, after the rise of the Catholic charismatic renewal three decades later, Hodges became the first Pentecostal missiologist to publicly discuss the thorny issue of proselytism. "We should extend whatever spiritual help we can to people that are so involved," he wrote in his theology of mission, "encourage them in their progress in the kingdom of God, and trust the Holy Spirit to guide them in their decision about church affiliation."[121] Pentecostals like Hodges who acknowledged the genuineness of the Protestant and Catholic renewal movements concluded that where the fruits and gifts of the Spirit appear, there one finds Christ's church. Hence, this mutually experienced recognition of the Spirit's presence by Catholic charismatics, Protestant charismatics, and some Pentecostals led to a groundbreaking discovery of unity in Christ, one not achieved by ecumenical negotiation.

Even so, the persistence of an inaccurate and monolithic perspective of Roman Catholicism has virtually ruled out contacts even with the renewal in historically Catholic countries, whose members share key elements of their spirituality with Pentecostals and notably make up a sizable portion of the half-billion Pentecostals and charismatics. "[The] charismatic gifts, whether they be the most outstanding or the more simple and widely diffused, are to be received with thanksgiving and consolation," declared the Second Vatican Council, "for they are exceedingly suitable and useful for the needs of the Church."[122] This heightened emphasis on the Holy Spirit added to the foundation for the renewal that followed the Council by two years in 1967.[123] The Council also set in motion the call for a "new evangelization" through the adoption of the "Decree on the Missionary Activity of the Church" (*Lumen Gentium*) and affirmed by two later papal encyclicals: "On the Evangelization of the Modern World" (*Evangelii Nuntiandi*) by Paul VI in 1975, and "On the Permanent Validity of the Church's Missionary Mandate" (*Redemptoris Missio*) by John Paul II in 1990.[124] Reinforced by the charismatic renewal around the world, "the evangelical shift brought about by Vatican II, Paul VI, and [John Paul II] is one of the most dramatic developments in modern Catholicism," commented theologian Cardinal Avery Dulles.[125]

Neither have Pentecostals considered sufficiently the importance of the reforms of the Council, nor the historic agreement on the gift of salvation—the "Joint Declaration on the Doctrine of Justification"—reached by the Catholic Church and the Lutheran World Federation in 1999.[126] Standing almost alone among published Pentecostal missiologists in the 1970s, Hodges acknowledged that the Vatican Council had been responsible for widespread Bible distribution and encouraging its reading by the laity. "This was a radical departure from the situation in Latin America in the 1930s," he remembered. "In contrast, after Vatican II Catholic priests bought and distributed thousands of copies of the New Testament in modern language. It is not surprising that the Word of God has prepared the hearts of the people for a move of His Spirit." He also noted that the official Catholic attitude toward Protestants had changed, transitioning from that of heretics to "separated brethren."[127] Such affirmation of changes in the Catholic Church, however, remained scarce among Pentecostal missionaries and mission executives.[128] Those who worked for better relationships with Catholics could find their voices muffled by in-house pressures.[129]

"But however vigorously Pentecostal movements distance themselves from Catholicism, it often seems easier to understand their religious culture with all its ethical rigorism on the personal plane from within folk Catholicism than from the perspective of the Protestant churches that developed in the nineteenth century [in Latin America]," observed missiologist Rogier van Rossum. "The bridge between Pentecostals and folk Catholicism is a biblicism with affinities with a fundamentalist way of handling the Bible."[130] Despite substantial differences in some areas of doctrine, the appearance of charismatic gifts and healings in both camps demonstrates that Pentecostals and Catholics have far more in common than previously thought.[131] After attending the Sixth International Conference on the Charismatic Renewal in the Catholic Church at Notre Dame University in 1972, Pentecostal Holiness historian Vinson Synan remarked, "I began to see these Bible-carrying, Scripture-quoting, Christ-exalting Catholic [charismatics] as brothers and sisters in Christ. . . . Barriers to fellowship were broken down and walls of ill will and prejudice crumbled in a mighty sweep of love through the power of the Holy Spirit."[132] Before long, progress in understanding between Catholics and Pentecostals began to occur in part through the initiatives of the North American Renewal Service Committee, on which Synan served.[133] It developed at another level through the International Roman Catholic and Classical Pentecostal Dialogue. During the fourth round of meetings, the dialogue fruitfully addressed the sensitive subject of mission under the theme "Evangelization, Proselytism, and Common Witness."[134]

All the same, apart from the World Evangelical Alliance and the Lausanne Committee for World Evangelization, North American denominations generally have not encouraged mission churches to enter into discussions with the broader church world. For example, leaders of the American Assemblies of God failed in their attempt to discourage the Korean Assemblies of God from joining the National Council of Churches of Korea in 1997, a membership that subsequently enhanced its standing in the Korean Christian community, much to the same effect that Pentecostal participation in the NAE had in the United States.[135]

PENTECOSTAL AND CHARISMATIC MISSIONS

At the end of the twentieth century, Pentecostal missionaries generally went overseas with better preparation and more financial support than their predecessors, along with some level of formal or informal instruction in cross-cultural adjustment and often with baccalaureate and even seminary and other graduate degrees. They thought more about the theology of mission, worked toward establishing indigenous churches, and looked more positively at organization, teamwork, and strategic planning. Their fundraising techniques would have amazed and possibly scandalized faith mission advocates such as Edward Irving and J. Hudson Taylor. They also exhibited the same commitment to mission as the pioneers.[136] Pentecostals rightfully merit recognition for their determined and substantial contributions to evangelism, education, ministries of compassion, and establishment of indigenous churches, funded by millions of dollars given by the faithful over the years.[137] They have worked to move beyond paternalism to partnership, though this can remain elusive in practice when one partner comes to the table with most of the resources. Their evangelistic activities have shown a strong pragmatic impulse through the means of tent evangelism, targeting of major population centers for church planting, literature distribution, radio and television programming, evangelism through the Internet, medical clinics, disaster relief, helping victims of human trafficking, and a myriad of innovative projects and programs.[138] One of their signal achievements has been the creation of ministerial training programs around the world, both conventional and non-traditional in format. Leading the way, the Assemblies of God began to multiply its overseas schools in the 1950s as a result of leaders pressing their personnel to train national ministers and turn over the reins of authority. Fifty years later, it assisted mission churches in the support of more than two thousand Bible institutes, Bible colleges, seminaries, and extensions.[139]

The interpretation of the Bible by Pentecostals has directly related to the worldviews of their hearers, a stance undergirded by their affirmation of the entire trustworthiness of Scripture and the uniqueness of Jesus Christ as the only Savior. As one early educator emphasized, a Pentecostal school did not aim "to turn out a lot of dried up students. . . . When men had the Word without the Spirit they were often dead and dull and dry; and when men had the Spirit without the Word there is always a tendency towards fanaticism."[140] Equipped with both, they would meet the apostolic standard in ministry. "As we press the battle against the forces of darkness, we know that Satan will not remain dormant, but will come out in full battle fury. How good to know that we stand in His strength," missionary Wally Lee told his Bible school students in Papua New Guinea. Launching out into evangelism, they told of praying for the sick, healings, and even raising the dead.[141] "After almost a century of expansion," wrote Everett Wilson, "this still not easily categorized religious phenomenon [Pentecostalism] has produced tens of millions of apparently sincere, committed Christian believers, whose personal lives and church communities have inspired renewal and imitation throughout the historic churches."[142]

Yet, like other North American and Majority World missionaries, Pentecostals have carried the features of their culture that frequently clash with cultural patterns in host countries. Though often farsighted in their accomplishments, they have been nearsighted on occasion in what they failed to see about the needs and aspirations of the people to whom they ministered. Always in a hurry, probably a reflection of North American culture as much as their eschatology, and enamored with the potential of the latest technology for evangelism and training, Pentecostals have cherished activism over theorizing. The end results have indicated enormous successes, but also exhibited deficiencies triggered by a sometimes unreflective activism.

A strategic but controversial change arose with the embrace of charitable ministries and social concern as vital components of God's mission through the church—the conveyance of the fullness of life in Jesus Christ to a "hurting, hungry, oppressed, and lost world."[143] Such endeavors long had been viewed with misgivings because the saving of lost souls demanded top priority, even though earlier Pentecostal belief had notably coupled soul and body to the redemptive work of Christ. In his *Sixteen New Testament Principles for World Evangelization,* published in 1988, mission leader Bernard Underwood devoted only a paragraph to "benevolence" and that with a cautionary note.[144] However, a decade later at the Brussels Consultation, sponsored by Assemblies of God World Missions to strategically plan for the twenty-first century, the conveners looked to the advancing kingdom of God (rule of God) in the present and the future as the starting point for articulating a biblically based theology of mission. "Jesus identified his mission, ministry, and message with the inauguration of the kingdom of God," announced the agreed-upon "Brussels Statement on Evangelization and Social Concern." "Miracles, signs and wonders were performed and acts of compassion were practiced in response to human need," as demonstrated in the book of Acts. Leading to the subsequent transformation of individuals and their contexts, "established social and religious orders were challenged and economic, racial and cultural barriers within the community of faith were overcome in a demonstration of the reconciling power of God's reign."[145] Consistent with expositions of evangelical missiology, the document packages holistic ministry in a Pentecostal wrapper.

The "Brussels Statement" clearly revealed that a growing number of influential missionaries and missiologists had begun to explore the wider implications of mission, but without diminishing the importance of conversionary evangelism. Several publications in particular led the way: *The Third Force in Missions* (1985), by Paul Pomerville; *Called & Empowered: Global Mission in Pentecostal Perspective* (1991) and *The Globalization of Pentecostalism: A Religion Made to Travel* (1999), both edited by Murray Dempster, Byron Klaus, and Douglas Petersen; and the latter's *Not by Might Nor by Power: A Pentecostal Theology of Social Concern in Latin America* (1996).[146] Missiological reflection on the non-Christian religions also appeared with *An Introduction to the Theology of Religions: Biblical, Historical & Contemporary Perspectives* (2003), by Veli-Matti Kärkkäinen, and *The Spirit Poured Out on All Flesh: Pentecostalism and the Possibility of Global Theology* (2005), by Amos Yong.[147] It is interesting to note that fewer academic treatments on praying for the sick and power encounters in evangelism have been published, perhaps revealing appreciation for and dependence on Third Wave writers such as John Wimber.[148]

The current involvement of missionaries in educational and charitable endeavors has signaled that a century after the beginning of Pentecostal missions, the majority now function as fraternal workers with church bodies overseas, most of which have been self-governing for some time. Only a minority of denominational missionaries directly evangelize unreached people groups, denoting a radical departure from the pattern of early Pentecostal missionaries.[149] Nevertheless, the major shift in vocational direction shows an enlarged understanding of the missionary's role and the church's mission in the world.[150] Pentecostals had heeded the Great Commission of Jesus in Matthew 28:19; now their attention turned to the ethical implications of "kingdom living" in Matthew 25:40: "The King will reply, 'Truly I tell you, whatever you did for one of the least of these my brothers and sisters of mine, you did for me.'" In their estimation, ministry to the hurting fits under the apostolic banner as well. Notwithstanding, "one looks in vain in this movement for a major work of the Holy Spirit to bring reconciliation between groups in society across racial, cultural, social and class barriers," reflected Anglican missiologist Chris Sugden. "Christians who lead healing crusades do not address the issues of injustice."[151]

Although displaying tremendous potential, independent charismatics in North America experienced tumultuous bumps on the road before they increased their attention to missions. Beginning in the 1970s, conflicts raised by the Shepherding (discipleship) movement and especially the popular "Prosperity Gospel" consumed their energies.[152] "The Holy Spirit emphasized financial prosperity to liberate us from debt and from a poverty mentality," avowed charismatic missiologist David Shibley, "and He raised our level of faith so we could believe Him for increase in our finances."[153] Even so, given the cultural items on the shopping list for prosperity, interest in world missions lagged behind in the check-out line.[154] Shibley and others then pushed the independents to look outward. Though more difficult to track in their endeavors, they have become heavily involved in sending missionaries, establishing training programs, and supporting charitable activities.[155]

As missiologist Edward Pousson observed, they could learn much from the maturity of Pentecostal mission agencies since "they have needlessly repeated virtually every early Pentecostal fiasco: duplication, competition, inadequate training and financial backing for missionaries, lack of structure and the omission of long-term strategy planning."[156] Paradoxically, many congregations in Pentecostal denominations have followed suit by turning the clock back to the rambunctious autonomy of the early movement, unwittingly reflecting American culture in addition to whatever divine directives they might have received. Preferring to be their own agencies, they typically jettison support for career missionaries familiar with the culture and language and replace them with the tourism of short-term missionaries from within their own groups. The notion of consulting veteran missionaries and mission executives still frequently falls by the wayside in a tradition that champions leaders receiving individual directives from the Spirit. "I get my orders from Heaven," charged Ansel Post before an exasperated judge in Pasadena, California, during the summer of 1906. After attempts at negotiation failed, the city council finally took him to court over the loud noise coming from his tent revival where the daily service began at 10 A.M. and lasted late into the night. Post's refusal to cooperate because "this is not the contest of man versus man, but the battle of God versus the devil" reflected a mindset that has continued to blossom in many circles with little or no pruning.[157] If William Bainbridge, the New England Baptist pastor, had toured the missions at the start of the third millennium and met independent charismatic missionaries, he would have noted a marked similarity with the radical evangelicals he encountered in China in the early 1880s.

THE INTRUDING PRESENCE

"It has become almost a convention that those who undertake to write about the Holy Spirit should begin by deploring the neglect of this doctrine in the thought and life of the Church today," said theologian George Hendry wryly.[158] While many reasons could be cited for the neglect—traced back at least to the creed of Nicaea that abruptly ended with the terse, "We believe in the Holy Spirit"[159]— the real cause may center on the "difficulties and obscurities, which baffle the mind, and which no book has yet been able to dispel."[160] After all, as another theologian, Kilian McDonnell, insisted, "the Holy Spirit cannot be objectified and viewed from a distance because, though distinct, the Spirit is not separable from the very faith processes by which an attempt is made to 'define' who the Spirit is."[161] Perhaps because the Spirit represents the living presence and action of God in the world, traditional methods of formulating theology have failed to grasp the mystery they seek to define, and theologians have produced overly circumscribed expositions of the Spirit's ministry.[162] "When the Church tries to bottle up the Spirit within herself she acts contrary both to her own and to His nature," warned missiologist Harry Boer. "For it is the nature of the Church ever to be enlarging her borders, and it is the nature of the Spirit to transmit His life to ever-widening circles."[163] Simply put, Western theology has been a size too small to contain the modern-day claims of the Spirit's miraculous power.

McDonnell also found that "presence [of God the Holy Spirit] is a major category in the charismatic renewal. God is presence: here, now, real, a person, loving, acting. He is not the Great Absent One."[164] It is precisely for this reason that Christians in the Majority World do not read the Bible or even parts of it as fiction. The Old and New Testaments have special appeal to believers who do more than read them, but live them, particularly in corresponding cultures where people fear spiritual and other forces that oppress them. "Many of the unwritten tribal laws of my own people, the Zulus, are identical with the laws of the Old

Testament," wrote evangelist Nicholas Bhengu in South Africa. "They didn't worship any idol, but they knew there was a God in heaven." Then, describing his plan of evangelism, he reported: "We go into a city where there are no Christians, and we just pitch up a tent or rent a hall and publicize our meetings. People begin to be healed, and the revival has started."[165] This sense of divine involvement—the benevolent intruding presence of the Spirit amidst alienation, oppression, and poverty of soul and body—has profoundly altered the terrain of mission; and for many in the West, it has filled the spiritual vacuum left by the demythologization of the Scriptures and the aridity of secularism.[166]

If the Spirit's work baffled Hendry, the emergence of charismatically inclined Christianity has added to the bewilderment of theologians. Reformed missiologist David Bosch barely mentioned the Pentecostal and charismatic movements or the charismatic gifts in his groundbreaking *Transforming Mission: Paradigm Shifts in Theology of Mission* (1991), though he was surrounded by Pentecostals in South Africa.[167] In the United States, Baptist theologian Millard Erickson devoted only two out of sixty chapters to the person and work of the Holy Spirit in his highly acclaimed *Christian Theology* (1998). While affirming the possibility of miracles and charismatic gifts today, but echoing the sentiments of other evangelical and fundamentalist theologians, he challenged their importance: "In the final analysis, whether the Bible teaches that the Spirit dispenses special gifts today is not an issue of great practical consequence. For even if he does, we are not to set our lives to seeking them. He bestows them sovereignly."[168] To Majority World Christians, such passivity seems misplaced. For them, seeking the gifts— as recommended by Paul in 1 Corinthians 12:31—has enormous "practical consequence" in light of everyday challenges and the hope offered by divine action.[169] In this respect, they tenaciously pray like their biblical predecessors who saw God forcefully intervening in history. For David Yonggi Cho and the 800,000 members of the Yoido Full Gospel Church in Seoul, Korea, the reality of supernatural power is a given.[170] Testifying to his healing from tuberculosis following a vision of Christ, he said, "[Jesus] took me when I was dying, saved me, healed me and filled me with His Spirit. The world needs more of that. It needs more than a philosophy, more than a religion. It needs the presence of Jesus Christ."[171] Therefore, when praying for the sick, church leaders drive out the demons of sickness "in the name of Jesus."[172] "Praying through," as Pentecostals have called persistent prayer, continues until the seeker receives divine assurance that the prayer has been answered. Archbishop Ganaka, who led the Catholic charismatic renewal in Nigeria until his death, maintained that charismatic Christianity was one of the good things that had happened to the Catholic Church because it "provided an answer to the contradiction between faith and life and creed and deed."[173] As Stephen Neill had predicted, the Pentecostal gadfly, hatched in the nineteenth century, had awakened the churches to a new awareness of the Spirit's ministry.

It is interesting to note that radical evangelicals and Pentecostals themselves have struggled to comprehend the Spirit's work. When faith healers such as A. B. Simpson and F. F. Bosworth declared that God would surely heal those with sufficient faith, they placed the responsibility for failure on the individual's unbelief, refusing to see that sovereignty frequently shrouds the summit of the

Almighty. As a result, they found themselves constantly on the defensive before an ever-increasing chorus of critics. On the front lines of spiritual warfare, the discernment of specific satanic hierarchies and the discovery of longstanding "curses" over geographical areas have shown a strongly practical approach to biblical interpretation; the subsequent application to mission sets the stage for a highly speculative strategy that may obscure larger issues of evil.[174] Thus, when Jorge Serrano, a Protestant charismatic church member in Guatemala, ran for president in 1990, he called for a national exorcism under the theme of "Jesus is Lord of Guatemala" to lift the curse on the country left by its pre-Christian religion. However, after his election and because of his subsequent governmental policies, accusations of corruption, and questions about his personal morality, Serrano soon found himself exorcised to Panama in political exile.[175]

In regard to Spirit baptism with tongues-speech—the crown jewel of Pentecostal experience—advocates have declared its indispensability for spiritual enablement, though the difference from the Spirit's work in believers who have not spoken in tongues—yet have productive ministries—remains problematic. Beginning to shed their sectarian trappings after mid-century and taking a more charitable view of the contributions of others in missions, Assemblies of God mission leaders notably acknowledged: "Like flashes of light in [the] darkest days of church history gleam the records of individuals who were obviously dedicated to God and filled with His Spirit," specifically including two medieval missionaries: Columba from Ireland and Raymund Lull from Majorca, Spain, the latter martyred in North Africa while preaching to Muslims.[176] In a far-sighted observation from early in the twentieth century, Donald Gee, who otherwise strongly defended Pentecostal doctrines, advised: "In the final analysis, the Baptism in the Spirit is not a doctrine, but an experience, and the test of whether I have received is not a cleverly woven doctrine that will include me within its borders, but whether I know the experience in burning fact in heart and life."[177] That the ministry of the Spirit transcends any one Christian movement explains why the parade lines in the history of missions swell when searching for those who sought for the Spirit's "fire" in their ministries.

In the early years, North Atlantic Pentecostals sought to comprehend the meaning of their charismatic experiences of tongues and discovered it to be prayer in the Spirit. Like other restorationists appealing to a precedent in the Acts narrative, they excluded or downplayed the importance of other patterns.[178] For example, New Testament scholar J. Massyngberde Ford discovered the social and political implications of the miraculous happenings in the early church, remarking that "Luke . . . carefully structured Acts to form a juxtaposition . . . between enthusiastic ministry and social/political revolution."[179] Moreover, Luke "presents a religion which eschews magic and money making, and seeks to embrace all humanity and bring it to its bountiful and merciful Lord and God."[180] Mission scholars have enriched the discussion by looking at the archetypes of mediation within cross-cultural diversity, holistic ministry, evangelistic strategy, and the function of apostles.[181] Christians of many backgrounds continue to appeal to models from the life of the New Testament church as means for bringing about spiritual revitalization and social change. Since expectancy of the Spirit's power and gifts has been the hallmark of Pentecostalism, sociologist Margaret Poloma concluded that the best hope for resolving the crisis of identity may come "through the different waves of the Pentecostal spirit that have refreshed believers and brought in new believers throughout the past century."[182]

Examining stories of the transforming and liberating effects of Pentecostalism, sociologist David Martin found that it "unites theology and social aspiration by anticipating, in hope and trembling, an end to the current world order." For the unlearned and marginalized, it represents a down payment of blessing on the "new order" that will come in the prophetic fulfillment of the last days. Consequently, "when the spiritual gifts include 'tongues' transcending the Babel of conflicting languages, then one has a 'third sacrament' of global aspiration embracing all humankind, and the emergence of a 'new voice' which is both individual and communal." Hence, "Pentecostalism, like Methodism, is about finding your voice, which is why it is sung as much as it is spoken."[183] In the Indian Pentecost of 1905-1906, yearnings for a better life could not be separated from the conferral of gifts and dignity that came with the Spirit's outpouring. Likewise, eight decades later, a group of non-white South African Pentecostal theologians forthrightly denounced the apartheid policy of their government as sinful. They took their inspiration from the Azusa Street revival: "It was here that God called to himself a prophetic movement in an oppressive society that belied the dignity of black people. It was here that God called to himself humble people to be his witnesses in a hostile world. It was here that powerless people were baptized in the Holy Spirit and endued with power to preach the good news of Jesus Christ, with 'signs following.'"[184] The spiritual, intercultural, and interracial dynamics of Azusa Street have offered to many an inspirational model for mission.[185] Today's "new voices" of deliverance and liberation have sounded loudly, though sometimes dissonantly.

MIRACLES AND MISSION IN RETROSPECT

Miracles have been central to the Christian tradition, more so than in any other world religion. For many Christians, the grand drama of redemption sweeps from the miracle of creation to that of the new heavens and the new earth foretold in the book of Revelation. In story after story in the biblical narratives and the Gospels, miracle-workers such as Moses, Samuel, Elijah, Elisha, Peter, and Paul command attention, but pale compared to Jesus, who told his disciples: "Very truly I tell you, all who have faith in me will do the works I have been doing, and they will do even greater things than these." (John 14:12). Reports of paranormal phenomena continued on in the Christian era, not only on the trails of the missionaries, but in local churches as well. In turn, a wide range of Christians have understood such happenings as "glorifying" Christ and his redemptive work (John 16:14). "The Holy Spirit is truly God the evangelist: He brings sinners to conversion. He does this through a variety of means," stated Reformed theologian J. I. Packer before the International Congress on

World Evangelization in 1989 (Lausanne II in Manila).[186] Even the Armenian Apostolic Church, not known for conversionary evangelism, declared in its catechism: "The Holy Spirit communicated to the Apostles the power . . . of working miracles. He taught them perfectly all religious truth and filled their hearts with unconquerable courage in preaching that God is one, and that His only Begotten Son who had risen from the dead is the Savior of all mankind." [187] Accordingly, the legitimate function of miracles draws attention to the gospel message but does not replace it. For early Pentecostals, miraculous deliverances from sickness, chemical addictions, and satanic oppression actually constituted part of the gospel itself.

For both postmillennial and premillennial advocates in the nineteenth century, the outpouring of the Spirit took on great importance as the source of spiritual energy for achieving the evangelization of the world. For its part, premillennialism brought a negative forecast about human progress before the return of Christ. Consequently, radical evangelicals proposed that miracles would not only expedite the effectiveness of gospel proclamation, but serve as witnesses to the reality of God and to the veracity of traditional beliefs in the homelands of Western Christianity where doubts about the faith alarmingly had gained acceptance. Pentecostalism, therefore, initially arose from the nineteenth-century mission movement with the goal of quickly evangelizing the nations in supernatural power. "It's simply a marvelous work of God that when the Pentecostal version of the gospel has been preached all around the world for the past half-century there has been a tremendous harvest," observed Packer. "It's a wonderful work in our time, which we can set against the decline of Christianity in North America and Western Europe."[188]

Despite the growing interest in the Spirit's role in mission, it only gradually earned a prominent place in the study of missiology.[189] With the exceptions of Roland Allen's publications on the Spirit, Harry Boer's *Pentecost and Missions* (1961), Melvin Hodges's *Theology of the Church and Its Mission* (1977), and José Comblin's *Holy Spirit and Liberation* (1989), the subject received surprisingly little exploration until late in the twentieth century.[190] The burgeoning growth of Pentecostalism, however, pushed missiologists to study the dynamics behind it.[191] This brought a "corrective" to missiological reflection on the ministry of the Spirit, a development aided by New Testament scholar Gordon Fee, as well as the work of Third Wave missiologists such as Charles and Marguerite Kraft in their books *Christianity with Power* (1989) and *Understanding Spiritual Power* (1995), respectively; Peter Wagner, *The Third Wave of the Holy Spirit: Encountering the Power of Signs and Wonders Today* (1988); and more recently, Andrew Lord, *Spirit-Shaped Mission—A Holistic Charismatic Missiology* (2005).[192]

THE APOSTOLIC FAITH

When the bishops at the Council of Constantinople (381) appended the Nicene Creed to describe the church as "one, holy, catholic, and apostolic,"

Christianity had by then entered a new and challenging era. The apostolic faith extended far beyond the Roman imperial boundaries and Christians within had gained newfound respectability as Christendom flowered in the Mediterranean world and eventually in Europe. Its expansion took on dimensions that would have inspired and disappointed earlier generations of believers. Through the centuries, confidence that the gospel message would be accompanied by signs and wonders has teeter-tottered on contrasting expectations. But today, miracles play a greater role in the lives of Christians—particularly in the Majority World—and in their witness to the faith than they have at any other time since the ancient church.

At the beginning of the third millennium, Pentecostal versions of the apostolic faith face daunting challenges. While likely to retain their evangelistic emphasis on saving souls from eternal destruction, Pentecostals now must grapple with issues ranging from the need for renewal to biblical interpretation and application; holiness and the quest for spiritual power; poverty, hunger, and disease; the rampaging effects of systemic evils at work in the world; proselytism; and Christian unity. In the past, Pentecostals and charismatics showed substantial fortitude in wrestling with difficulties that came their way, and this suggests hope for the future. Due to the longstanding tension in the movement between "obeying the voice of the Spirit" and "doing what it takes" to advance the gospel, they have become highly successful and well organized, surprising critics who had predicted the early demise of the movement. On the contrary, it has dramatically revived generation after generation, while continually testing the relationship of renewal to institution.[193] Consequently, historians George Rawlyk and Mark Noll have predicted: "If the New Birth defined the essence of evangelicalism during the first century of its history, the emphases of Pentecostalism may well be the defining characteristic of evangelicals in the twenty-first century."[194] How perception of supernatural manifestations will shape mission in the future may open a new chapter in the history of the Christian world movement.

The seventeenth-century Reformed theologian Markus Wendelin, though likely a cessationist, astutely defined a miracle as "an unusual work, surpassing the created powers of the whole of nature, affecting the senses and hustling men into amazement, issued by God to build up faith in His word and to declare His power."[195] Given the current dynamics at work in global Christianity, one may assume that in the building of Christ's church, the divine "hustle" will not end anytime soon.

Notes

1. THE NAGGING COMPARISON

1. Unless otherwise indicated, all Scripture quotations are taken from *Today's New International Version* (TNIV).

2. Alexander Duff, *India, and India Missions* (Edinburgh: John Johnstone, Hunter Square, 1839), xiii.

3. Unnamed missionary, quoted in untitled note in *MRW* 5 (n.s.) (October 1892): 773.

4. Graham Wilmot Brooke, "A Dying Testimony," *MRW* 5 (n.s.) (June 1892): 436.

5. A. T. Pierson, *The New Acts of the Apostles* (New York: Baker and Taylor, 1894), 61.

6. Sir Hiram Maxim, quoted in Eugene Stock, "Missions Fifty Years Ago, and Now," *MRW* 30 (n.s.) (January 1917): 22.

7. "The Constantinopolitan Creed" in *Creeds of the Churches*, 3rd ed., ed. John H. Leith (Atlanta: John Knox, 1982), 33. For an insightful discussion, see Robert J. Scudieri, *The Apostolic Church: One, Holy, Catholic and Missionary* (St. Louis: Lutheran Society of Missiology, 1996); also Thaddeus D. Horgan, ed., *Apostolic Faith in America* (Grand Rapids: Eerdmans, 1988).

8. Thomas Aquinas, *Summa Theologiae*, trans. T. C. O'Brien (New York: McGraw-Hill, 1964), 14: 85-87.

9. David Hume, *An Enquiry Concerning Human Understanding*, Great Books of the Western World, ed. Robert Maynard Hutchins, no. 35: *Locke, Berkeley, Hume* (Chicago: Encyclopaedia Britannica, Inc., 1952), 491. See also Jakub Pawlikowski, "The History of Thinking about Miracles in the West," *SMJ* 100 (December 2007): 1229-35.

10. Mark A. Noll, "The Potential of Missiology for the Crises of History," in *History and the Christian Historian*, ed. Ronald A. Wells (Grand Rapids: Eerdmans, 1998), 113-15.

11. Philip Schaff, *A Companion to the Greek New Testament and the English Version: With Facsimile Illustration of Mss. and Standard Editions of the New Testament* (New York: Harper & Brothers, 1883), 81.

12. Benjamin B. Warfield, *Counterfeit Miracles* (London: Banner of Truth Trust, 1972; originally published in 1918), 23–24; cf. Jon Ruthven, *On the Cessation of the Charismata: The Protestant Polemic on Postbiblical Miracles* (Sheffield: Sheffield Academic Press, 1997), 193.

13. Warfield, *Counterfeit Miracles*, 64.

14. See W. H. C. Frend, "The Place of Miracles in the Conversion of the Ancient World to Christianity," in *Signs, Wonders, Miracles: Representations of Divine Power in the Life of the Church*, Studies in Church History 41, ed. Kate Cooper and Jeremy Gregory (Woodbridge, Suffolk, U.K.: Ecclesiastical History Society and Boydell Press, 2005), 11-21.

15. Eusebius, *Ecclesiastical History*, trans. Christian Frederick Cruse (Grand Rapids: Baker Book House, 1955), 3: xxxvii.

16. Kilian McDonnell and George T. Montague, *Christian Initiation and Baptism in the Holy Spirit: Evidence from the First Eight Centuries* (Collegeville, Minn.: Liturgical Press, 1991), 314.

17. Ramsay MacMullen, *Christianity and Paganism in the Fourth to Eighth Centuries* (New Haven: Yale University Press, 1997), 8-10, 94-97; cf. James E. Bradley, "Miracles and Martyrdom in the Early Church: Some Theological and Ethical Implications," in *All Together in One Place: Theological Papers from the Brighton Conference on World Evangelization*, ed. Harold D. Hunter and Peter D. Hocken (Sheffield: Sheffield Academic Press, 1993), 227-41.

18. Basil, "On the Spirit," in *A Select Library of Nicene and Post-Nicene Fathers of the Christian Church*, second series, vol. 8: *St. Basil: Letters and Select Works*, ed. Philip Schaff and Henry Wace (Grand Rapids: Eerdmans, 1952), 8: 47.

19. Athanasius, *The Life of St. Antony*, trans. R. T. Meyer (New York: Newman, 1978), 78–79.

20. D. M. Lang, ed., *Lives and Legends of the Georgian Saints*, 2d ed. (Crestwood, N.Y.: St. Vladimir's Seminary Press, 1976), 13–19.

21. Walter F. Adeney, *The Greek and Eastern Churches* (New York: Charles Scribner's Sons, 1932), 540-41; Gregory Bishop of Tours, *History of the Franks*, trans. Ernest Brehaut (New York: W. W. Norton, 1969), 38-40; William Young, "Miracles in Church History," *Churchman* 102: (1988): 111-12; Luke Alexander Veronis, *Missionaries, Monks and Martyrs: Making Disciples of All Nations* (Minneapolis: Light and Life, 1994), 60.

22. E. A. Wallis Budge, *The Book of the Saints of the Ethiopian Church: A Translation of the Ethiopic Synaxarium, Made from the Manuscripts Oriental 660 and 661 in the British Museum* (Cambridge: Cambridge University Press, 1928), 1: 1243.

23. For Patrick's own account, see Joseph Duffy, *Patrick: In His Own Words* (Dublin: Veritas, 1972), 12-38.

24. For examples, see Bede, *History of the English Church and People*, trans. Leo Sherley-Price (New York: Penguin Books, 1968), bk. 1, ch. 18, 20; bk. 4, ch. 24; bk. 5, ch. 1, 3-6.

25. Gregory the Great, "The Book of Pastoral Rule and Selected Epistles of Gregory the Great, Bishop of Rome," in *Nicene and Post-Nicene Fathers*, second series, ed. Philip Schaff and Henry Wace (Grand Rapids: Eerdmans, 1969), XII, 7, 30, p. 240.

26. William D. McCready, *Miracles and the Venerable Bede* (Toronto: Pontifical Institute of Mediaeval Studies, 1994), 78.

27. William D. McCready, *Signs of Sanctity: Miracles in the Thought of Gregory the Great* (Toronto: Pontifical Institute of Mediaeval Studies, 1989), 33-64; idem, *Miracles*, 105-6.

28. Eric Waldram Kemp, *Canonization and Authority in the Western Church* (Oxford: Oxford University Press, 1948), 31-35.

29. For example, see Edward Maclagan, *The Jesuits and the Great Mogul* (Gurgaon, Haryana, India: Vintage Books, 1990), 77, 293-95; also Alexandra Walsham, "Miracles in Post-Reformation England," in *Signs, Wonders, Miracles,* ed. Cooper and Gregory, 279-83.

30. Robert Bellarmine, quoted in Robert Bruce Mullin, *Miracles and the Modern Religious Imagination* (New Haven: Yale University Press, 1996), 12.

31. R. Po-chia Hsia, *The World of Catholic Renewal, 1540-1770* (Cambridge: Cambridge University Press, 1998), 130.

32. Sources that provide helpful information and perspectives on the miracles attrib-

uted to Xavier include Anthony Grant, *The Past and Prospective Extension of the Gospel by Missions to the Heathen: Considered in Eight Lectures* (London: Francis & John Rivington, 1845), 145-49, 344-47; cf. Georg Schurhammer, *Francis Xavier: His Life, His Times*, vol. 2, *India, 1541-1545*, trans. M. Joseph Costelloe (Rome: Jesuit Historical Institute, 1977), 389-90.

33. *The Acts and Decrees of the Synod of Diamper, 1599*, ed. Scaria Zacharia (Edamattam, Kerala, India: Indian Institute of Christian Studies, 1994), 34-35.

34. Martin Luther, *Sermons on the Gospel of John: Chapters 14-16*, in *Luther's Works*, ed. Jaroslav Pelikan and Daniel E. Poellet, 55 vols. (St. Louis: Concordia, 1958-1986), 24: 79, 180-81; John Calvin, "Prefatory Address to King Francis," in *Institutes of the Christian Religion*, ed. John T. McNeill, trans. Ford Lewis Battles, 2 vols. (Philadelphia: Westminster, 1960), 1: 14-18. See also Mullin, *Miracles*, 12-13; Ruthven, *Cessation*, 33-35.

35. Walsham, "Miracles," in *Signs, Wonders, Miracles*, 273-74.

36. Calvin, *Institutes*, 1: 16-18.

37. Johannes Wollebius, *Compendium Theologiae Christianae*, in *Reformed Dogmatics: Seventeenth-Century Reformed Theology Through the Writings of Wollebius, Voetius, and Turretin*, ed. John W. Beardslee III (Grand Rapids: Baker Book House, 1977), 141; cf. John Milner, *The End of Religious Controversy, in a Friendly Correspondence between a Religious Society of Protestants and a Roman Catholic Divine* (New York: D. & J. Sadlier, 1818), 156-76.

38. Walsham, "Miracles" in *Signs, Wonders, Miracles*, 278.

39. Seventeenth-century orthodox Lutherans concluded that first-century Christians had fulfilled the Great Commission, evident in the perspectives of the hymn writer Philipp Nicolai; see *Classic Texts in Mission & World Christianity*, ed. Norman E. Thomas (Maryknoll, N.Y.: Orbis Books, 1995), 43-46.

40. Wollebius, *Compendium*, 181 n. 102. Beardslee observes: "The development of missionary concern is one of the great factors differentiating the orthodoxy of [Charles] Hodge's time from that of Wollebius, F. Turretin, and even Voetius, none of whom shows interest in it"; cf. Jan A. B. Jongeneel, "The Missiology of Gisbertus Voetius, the First Comprehensive Protestant Theology of Missions," *CTJ* 26 (April 1991): 47-49.

41. William Carey, *An Enquiry into the Obligations of Christians, to Use Means for the Conversion of the Heathens*, reprinted in Timothy George, *Faithful Witness: The Life and Mission of William Carey* (Birmingham, Ala.: New Hope, 1991), E.5.

42. Mullin, *Miracles*, 14-15, 98-99.

43. G. H. Rouse, "Apostolic and Indian Missions Compared," *IER* 9 (July 1875): 1.

44. Calvin refers to the "foul slander" of "those who object that our doctrine is without miracles" in his *A Harmony of the Gospels: Matthew, Mark and Luke*, ed. David W. Torrance, et al.; trans. A. W. Morrison (Grand Rapids: Eerdmans, 1972), 3: 255.

45. Daniel P. Kidder, a pioneer Methodist missionary in Brazil, and J. C. Fletcher wrote of Anchieta, "His self-denial as a missionary, his labor in acquiring and methodizing a barbarous language, and his services to the State, were sufficient to secure to him an honest fame and a precious memory; but in the latter part of the ensuing century he was made a candidate for saintship, and his real virtues were made to pass for little in comparison with the power by which it was pretended that he had wrought miracles"; see Daniel P. Kidder, *Brazil and the Brazilians, Portrayed in Historical and Descriptive Sketches* (Philadelphia: Childs & Peterson, 1857), 115-16.

46. T. W. M. Marshall, *Christian Missions: Their Agents, and Their Results*, 4th ed. (New York: D. &. J. Sadlier, 1880), 2: 145.

47. Ibid., 2: 143. In the face of continuing post-Enlightenment skepticism, the Catho-

lic Church reaffirmed belief in miracles: The "Dogmatic Constitution on the Catholic Faith" (*Dei Filius*), approved by the First Vatican Council (1869-1870), states: "In order that the obedience of our faith might be in harmony with reason, God willed that to the interior help of the Holy Spirit there should be joined exterior proofs of His revelation, to wit, divine facts, and especially miracles and prophecies, which, as they manifestly display the omnipotence and infinite knowledge of God, are most certain proofs of His divine revelation adapted to the intelligence of all men"; *Dogmatic Canons and Decrees* (Rockford, Ill.: TAN Books, 1912), 224. Beginning in 1967, the Catholic Charismatic Renewal revived the tradition of miracles and the charismatic gifts in Catholic evangelization; see Ralph Martin and Peter Williamson, eds., *John Paul II and the New Evangelization* (San Francisco: Ignatius Press, 1995).

48. Marshall, *Christian Missions,* 2: 146 (Marshall's emphases).

49. Joseph Schmidlin, *Catholic Mission Theory* (Techny, Ill.: Mission Press, S.V.D., 1931), 345.

50. Peter Masten Dunn, *Early Jesuit Missions in Tarahumara* (Berkeley: University of California Press, 1948), 105, 209-10; Jean Charbonnier, "The Catholic Church in China," in *Guide to the Catholic Church in China* (Singapore: China Catholic Communication, n.d.), 13; Carlos Suriá, *History of the Catholic Church in Gujarat* (Anand, Gujarat, India: Gujarat Sahitya Prakash, 1990), 321.

51. Francis X. Weninger, S.J., quoted in Jay P. Dolan, *Catholic Revivalism: The American Experience, 1830-1900* (Notre Dame, Ind.: University of Notre Dame Press, 1978), 146; Gilbert J. Garraghan, *The Jesuits of the Middle United States* (New York: America Press, 1938), 53-65, 57 n. 19; also Kilian McDonnell, *Charismatic Renewal and the Churches* (New York: Seabury, 1976), 11-13.

52. The longer ending of the Gospel of Mark (16:9-20) was not extensively disputed before the publication of the *English Revised Version* (1881-1885); for further information, see Bruce M. Metzger, *A Textual Commentary on the Greek New Testament* (London: United Bible Societies, 1971), 122-26.

53. D. P. Walker, "The Cessation of Miracles," in *Hermeticism and the Renaissance: Intellectual History and the Occult in Early Modern Europe*, ed. Ingrid Merkel and Allen G. Debus (Washington: Folger Shakespeare Library, 1988), 114.

54. For a perceptive study of cessationism, see Willem Berends, "Cessationism," *Vox Reformata* 60 (1995): 44-54.

55. Eve Garnett, *To Greenland's Icy Mountains: The Story of Hans Egede, Explorer, Coloniser, Missionary* (London: Heinemann, 1968), 120-21.

56. Walsham, "Miracles," in *Signs, Wonders, Miracles*, 284-88.

57. For example, see John W. B. Tomlinson, "The Magic Methodists and Their Influence on the Early Primitive Methodist Movement," in *Signs, Wonders, Miracles*, 389-99.

58. For example, A. W. Pitzer, "The Inheritances of Nations Allotted by God," *MRW* 3 (n.s.) (November 1890): 820-26. For insightful discussions, see William R. Hutchison, *Errand to the World: American Protestant Thought and Foreign Missions* (Chicago: University of Chicago Press, 1987), 15-42; and Wilbert R. Shenk, "The 'Great Century' Reconsidered," in *Anabaptism and Mission*, ed. Wilbert R. Shenk (Scottdale, Pa.: Herald, 1984), 158-77.

59. Hereafter, American Board.

60. Sheldon Dibble, *Thoughts on Missions* (New York: American Tract Society, ca. 1845), 72-73; see also D. L. Leonard, "The Anglo-Saxon and the World's Redemption— I," *MRW* 7 (n.s.) (October 1894): 748-54.

61. Herbert Edwardes, untitled address in *Conference on Missions Held in 1860 at Liverpool* (London: James Nesbit, 1860), 337-55.

62. Rev. Dr. [August Wilhelm] Schreiber, "Appendix," *Report of the Centenary Conference on the Protestant Missions of the World, Held in Exeter Hall (June 9th-19th), London, 1888,* ed. James Johnston (New York: Fleming H. Revell, 1888), 2: 558.

63. Quoted in R. C. Bose, "How to Deal with English Speaking Hindus," *Report of the Second Decennial Missionary Conference, Held at Calcutta, 1882-83* (Calcutta: Baptist Mission Press, 1883), 165.

64. An expression used by Rufus Anderson in his *Foreign Missions: Their Relations and Claims* (New York: Charles Scribner, 1869), 2. For a lengthy presentation of providential acts in the history of missions, see *The Missionary World, Being an Encyclopaedia of Information, Facts, Incidents, Sketches, and Anecdotes, Relating to Christian Missions, In All Ages and Countries, and of all Denominations* (New York: Anson D. F. Randolph, 1873), 313-412.

65. William Carey, et al., to Dr. J. T. Vanderkemp, February 14, 1801, reproduced in S. Pearce Carey, *William Carey D.D., Fellow of Linnaean Society* (New York: George H. Doran, 1923), 202.

66. John Aberly, *An Outline of Missions* (Philadelphia: Muhlenberg, 1945), 68-69.

67. N. B. C. Love, *John Stewart: Missionary to the Wyandots* (New York: Missionary Society of the Methodist Episcopal Church, n.d.), 5.

68. Francis Mason, *The Karen Apostle, or Memoir of Ko Thah Byu* (Bassein, Burma: SGAU Karen, 1884), 160.

69. See William A. Spicer, *Miracles of Modern Missions: Gathered Out of the Mission Records* (Washington, D.C.: Review and Herald, 1926).

70. John Clough, quoted in M. C. Mason, "Methods of Mission Work," in *The Assam Mission of the American Baptist Missionary Union* (Calcutta: Baptist Mission Press, 1887), 99.

71. For Catholic and Orthodox perspectives, see William Cardinal O'Connell, "Cardinal O'Connell's Sermon," in *The Great American Catholic Missionary Congresses,* ed. Francis C. Kelley (Chicago: J. S. Hyland, n.d.), 25-27; Nikita Struve, "Macaire Gloukharev: A Prophet of Orthodox Mission," *IRM* 54 (July 1965): 310-14.

72. Joseph Tracy, *History of the Board of Foreign Missions of the General Assembly of the Presbyterian Church in the United States of America, and of Its Missions,* reprinted in *History of American Missions to the Heathen, from their Commencement to the Present Time* (Worcester: Spooner & Howland, 1840), 710.

73. Henry Clark, quoted in *Proceedings of the General Conference on Foreign Missions Held at the Conference Hall, in Mildmay Park, London, in October, 1878* (London: John F. Shaw, 1879), 93.

74. J. M. Thoburn, quoted in *Report of the General Missionary Conference, Held at Allahabad, 1872-73,* ed. J. Barton, et al. (London: Seeley, Jackson, & Halliday, 1873), 85.

75. Edward Irving, *Missionaries after the Apostolical School* (London: Hamilton, Adams, 1825), 118-23.

76. Rufus Anderson, *Foreign Missions: Their Relations and Claims* (New York: Charles Scribner, 1869), 115-16.

77. Ibid., 117.

78. Rouse, "Apostolic and Indian Missions Compared," 2.

79. Ibid., 3.

80. R. C. Mather, "On Bazaar Preaching," *Report of the General Missionary Conference,* 41.

81. W[illiam] Miller, quoted in ibid., 47.

82. Dr. [Arthur] Tidman, quoted in *Conference on Missions Held in 1860*, 53.

83. Rouse, "Apostolic and Indian Missions Compared," 4.

84. F. F. Ellinwood, *The "Great Conquest"; or, Miscellaneous Papers on Missions* (New York: William Rankin, 1876), 22.

85. Robert Stewart, *Apostolic and Indian Missions Compared* (Calcutta: Baptist Mission Press, 1903), 27-28; also Miron Winslow, *A Sketch of Missions; or History of the Principal Attempts to Propagate Christianity Among the Heathen* (Andover: Flagg & Gould, 1819), 13-29.

86. H[erman] N. Barnum, quoted in "Another Eloquent Appeal," *MRW* 2 (n.s.) (December 1889): 943.

87. R. C. Mather, "On Bazaar Preaching," *Report of the General Missionary Conference*, 41.

88. Chalmers Martin, *Apostolic and Modern Missions* (New York: Fleming H. Revell Co., 1898), 46.

89. The "Resolution on the Native Church," passed at the 1879 Missionary Conference for South India and Ceylon; *The Missionary Conference: South India and Ceylon, 1879* (Madras: Addison, 1880), 1: 402. For a later discussion of "native agents," see John L. Nevius, "Historical Review of Missionary Methods—Past and Present—in China, and How Far Satisfactory," *Records of the General Conference of the Protestant Missionaries of China. Held at Shanghai, May 7-20, 1890* (Shanghai: American Presbyterian Mission Press, 1890), 171-76.

90. For insightful discussions on the optimism of the "Great Century" in Christian missions, see Kenneth Scott Latourette, *A History of the Expansion of Christianity*, vol. 4, *The Great Century: Europe and the United States* (New York: Harper & Row, 1969; reprint, Grand Rapids: Zondervan, 1970), 9-21; Hutchison, *Errand to the World*, 43-61.

91. A. T. Pierson, *The New Acts of the Apostles* (New York: Baker and Taylor, 1894), 298-99.

92. A. T. Pierson, *The Modern Mission Century: Viewed as a Cycle of Divine Working* (New York: Baker and Taylor, 1901), 452.

93. A[rthur] Wenger, *Report of the General Missionary Conference*, 325.

94. Pierson, *Modern Mission Century*, 452.

95. Walter R. Lambuth, M.D., "The Scriptural Claims and Spiritual Ends of Medical Missions," in *The Student Missionary Appeal: Addresses at the Third International Convention of the Student Volunteer Movement for Foreign Missions Held at Cleveland, Ohio, February 23-27, 1898* (New York: Student Volunteer Movement for Foreign Missions, 1898), 506; Pierson, *New Acts*, 382-85; also the papers presented on "Medical Missions," in *Report of the Centenary Conference*, 2: 101-7.

96. Ellinwood, *"Great Conquest,"* 23-24.

97. Jonathan J. Bonk, "'And They Marveled': Mammon as Miracle in Western Missionary Encounter," in *Evangelical, Ecumenical, and Anabaptist Missiologies in Conversation: Essays in Honor of Wilbert R. Shenk*, ed. James R. Krabill, Walter Sawatsky, and Charles E. Van Engen (Maryknoll, N.Y.: Orbis Books, 2006), 86.

98. Frederick Trestrail, "On Native Churches," *Conference on Missions Held in 1860*, 279.

99. Joseph Angus, "Duty of the Churches in Relation to Missions," in *History, Essays, Orations, and Other Documents of the Sixth General Conference of the Evangelical Alliance, Held in New York, October 2-12, 1873*, ed. Philip Schaff and S. Irenaeus Prime (New York: Harper & Brothers, 1874), 583-87.

100. Royal G. Wilder, quoted in Hutchison, *Errand to the World*, 99.

101. James Johnston, "A Century of Protestant Missions," *MRW* 9 (o.s.) (October 1886): 383.

102. Dana L. Robert, *Occupy until I Come: A. T. Pierson and the Evangelization of the World* (Grand Rapids: Eerdmans, 2003), 147-56; C. Howard Hopkins, *John R. Mott, 1865-1955* (Grand Rapids: Eerdmans, 1979), 24-30.

103. Joh[annes] Warneck, *The Living Christ and Dying Heathenism*, trans. Neil Buchanan (New York: Fleming H. Revell, 1909), 17.

104. Rouse, "Apostolic and Indian Missions," 12.

105. John Ross, quoted in *Report of the Centenary Conference*, 1: 238.

106. Irving, *Missionaries*, 125.

107. F. Max Müller, *On Missions* (New York: Scribner, Armstrong, 1874), 52-53; cf. "The Faith of Max Muller," *Dnya*, August 29, 1907, 1.

108. E. Arno Lehmann, *It Began at Tranquebar: A History of the First Protestant Mission in India* (Madras: Christian Literature Society, 1956), 68-76.

109. John S. Moffat, *The Lives of Robert and Mary Moffat*, 12th ed. (London: T. Fisher Unwin, n.d.), 184.

110. Lucius E. Smith, ed., *Heroes and Martyrs of the Modern Missionary Enterprise* (Hartford: Brockett, 1854), 135-36.

111. Carey to Vanderkemp, 202.

112. Marshall Broomhall, *Robert Morrison: A Master-Builder* (London: Student Christian Movement, 1927), 197.

113. General Minutes of the South India Conference of the M.E. Church, January 1889, 114, quoted in Robert E. Speer, *George Bowen of Bombay* (n.p.: By the author, 1938), 347; address by Appaji Bapuji summarized in *Second Decennial*, 312.; cf. Wade Crawford Barclay, *History of Methodist Missions*, part 2: *The Methodist Episcopal Church, 1845-1939*, vol. 3: *Widening Horizons, 1845-95* (New York: Board of Missions of the Methodist Church, 1957), 3: 529. Barclay refers to converts under Bowen's ministry, but only after the arrival of the Methodist evangelist William Taylor.

114. J. B. Lightfoot, *Historical Essays* (London: Macmillan, 1895), 72.

115. For example, see the various endeavors reported in the collected histories and surveys of mission agencies working in China contained in D. MacGillivary, ed., *A Century of Protestant Missions in China (1807-1907) Being the Centenary Conference Historical Volume*, 2 vols. (Shanghai: American Presbyterian Mission Press, 1907).

116. See Timothy P. Weber, *Living in the Shadow of the Second Coming: American Premillennialism, 1875-1925* (New York: Oxford University Press, 1979), 65-72; also Dana L. Robert, "'The Crisis of Missions': Premillennial Mission Theory and the Origins of Independent Evangelical Missions," in *Earthen Vessels: American Evangelicals and Foreign Missions, 1880-1980*, ed. Joel A. Carpenter and Wilbert R. Shenk (Grand Rapids: Eerdmans, 1990), 29-46.

117. The "warning sound of the Clock of Time" was a popular metaphor among premillennialists; see R. C., "Brunner, Texas, October 9, 1905," *AF* (Melrose, Kans.), October-November 1905 (pages not numbered); A. B. Simpson, "The Clock of Time," *LT*, June 1907, 313-320.

118. A. T. Pierson, "Are We Nearing the End of the Age?" *MRW* 12 (n.s.) (December 1899): 882. Curiously, nineteen years had already elapsed when Pierson wrote this, leaving only twenty-one years for the anticipated prophetic fulfillment.

119. For information on Theodore T. Munger, see David Everett Swift, "Conservative Progressive Orthodoxy in Latter 19th Century Congregationalism," *CH* 16 (March 1947): 22-31; Grant Wacker, *Augustus H. Strong and the Dilemma of Historical Consciousness*

(Macon, Ga.: Mercer University Press, 1985), 149-52. For an example of the "tourism" that Munger described, see "Pilgrimage to Foreign Lands. Wealthy Contributors to Missions Plan a Tour of Inspection," *St. Louis Post-Dispatch*, December 11, 1895, 7.

120. For an extensive defense of missionaries against their detractors, including "tourists," see James L. Barton, *The Missionary and His Critics*, 3d ed. (New York: Fleming H. Revell, 1906). On the negative effect of criticisms on the work of British Wesleyan Methodist missionaries in India, see G. G. Findlay and W. W. Holdsworth, *History of the Wesleyan Methodist Missionary Society* (London: Epworth, 1921), 1: 140.

121. Dr. [Theodore T.] Munger, "The 'Critics of Missions,'" *MRW* 2 (n.s.) (August 1889): 611; this is an excerpt from an article by Munger published in *Forum*, June 1889.

122. Cyrus Hamlin, "Characteristics of the Recent Adverse Criticisms upon Missions," *MRW* 2 (n.s.) (September 1889): 696, 699.

123. Munger, "Critics," 611.

124. B. C. Henry, *The Cross and the Dragon or Light in the Broad East* (New York: Anson D. F. Randolph, 1885), 412-13.

125. Edward W. Blyden, *Christianity, Islam and the Negro Race*, 2d ed. (Baltimore: Black Classics, 1994; originally published in 1888), 18; cf. J. T. Gracey, "The Relative Progress of Christianity," *MRW* 1 (n.s.) (July 1888): 499-502. See also Kwame Bediako, *Christianity in Africa: The Renewal of a Non-Western Religion* (Maryknoll, N.Y.: Orbis Books, 1995), 6-14.

126. Carey, *Enquiry*, in George, *Faithful Witness*, E.21-E.44.

127. Gordon Hall and Samuel Newell, *The Conversion of the World: Or the Claims of Six Hundred Millions and the Ability and Duty of the Churches Respecting Them* (Andover: American Board of Commissioners for Foreign Missions, 1818), 18, 24-25.

128. John Calvert, "The Work among the Fiji Islands," *MRW* 1 (n.s.) (September 1888): 658 (Calvert's emphasis).

129. Robert E. Speer, *Missionary Principles and Practice* (New York: Fleming H. Revell, 1902), 501; cf. Hutchison, *Errand to the World*, 99-100. For the results of the worldwide mission census (1900), see Harlan Page Beach, *A Geography and Atlas of Protestant Missions: Their Environment, Forces, Distribution, Methods, Problems, Results and Prospects at the Opening of the Twentieth Century*, vol. 2: *Statistics and Atlas* (New York: Student Volunteer Movement for Foreign Missions, 1906).

130. Unnamed traveler, quoted in E. P. Thwing, "The Accelerated Momentum of Truth," in *Records of the General Conference of the Protestant Missionaries of China, Held at Shanghai, May 7-20, 1890* (Shanghai: American Presbyterian Mission Press, 1890), 30. According to the census for 1900, there were 204,672 Protestant communicants and adherents out of a total population of 350 to 386 million; see Beach, *Geography*, 2: 19.

131. Statistic cited in Isaac Taylor, "The Great Missionary Failure," *FR* 44 (October 1, 1888): 490.

132. Ibid., 488-500.

133. Isaac Taylor, "The Great Missionary Failure," *EM*, December 1888, 853.

134. Ibid., 857.

135. "Islam and Christian Missions," *MRW* 2 (n.s.) (August 1889): 561-77.

136. "The Progress of Islam," *New York Times*, November 25, 1887, 4; "Missionary Needs," *Daily Northwestern* (Oshkosh, Wis.), December 20, 1888, 2.

137. "Foreign Missions Attacked," *The Constitution* (Atlanta, Ga.), January 2, 1889, 4.

138. For example, Hamlin, "Characteristics of the Recent Adverse Criticism," 696-700.

139. Edwin M. Bliss, "Criticisms upon Foreign Missions," *MRW* 2 (n.s.) (March 1889): 187.

140. "Islam and Christian Missions," *577*; S. M. Zwemer, *Arabia: The Cradle of Islam* (New York: Fleming H. Revell, 1900), 391.

141. For example, see William F. Bainbridge, *Around the World Tour of Christian Missions: A Universal Survey* (Boston: D. Lothrop, 1882).

142. William McKinley, address in *Ecumenical Missionary Conference, New York, 1900: Report of the Ecumenical Conference on Foreign Missions, Held in Carnegie Hall and Neighboring Churches, April 21 to May 1* (New York: American Tract Society, 1900), 1: 39-40.

143. Some radical evangelicals speculated that Christ would return in 1900; for example, see the comments of A. B. Simpson in *Report and Retrospect of the Work of the Christian and Missionary Alliance, 1896-1897*, 26, Annual Reports, http://www.cmalliance.org/resources/archives/annual-report.

144. Frank W. Sandford, "An Introduction of the Editor to His Readers," *EG*, January 1, 1901, 2.

2. THE GREAT OUTPOURING

1. Martin Luther, "A Mighty Fortress Is Our God," *The Hymnal of the Protestant Episcopal Church in the United States of America* (New York: Church Pension Fund, 1940), #551.

2. Christian David and Nikolaus von Zinzendorf, quoted in A. J. Lewis, *Zinzendorf: The Ecumenical Pioneer* (Philadelphia: Westminster, 1962), 59.

3. H. E. Scudder, *Life and Letters of David Coit Scudder* (New York: Hurd & Houghton, 1864), 225.

4. J. R. Stillwell, "Leadership in Revivals," *BMR* 13 (May 1907): 194-95.

5. Pandita Ramabai, "Showers of Blessing," *MPB*, September 1907, 10.

6. John H. Morrison, "On Prayer for the Outpouring of the Holy Spirit," *Report of the General Missionary Conference, Held at Allahabad, 1872-73*, ed. J. Barton, et al. (London: Seeley, Jackson, and Halliday, 1873), 2 (Morrison's emphasis).

7. Griffith John, "The Holy Spirit in Connection with Our Work," *Records of the General Conference of the Protestant Missionaries of China, Held at Shanghai, May 10-24, 1877* (Shanghai: Presbyterian Mission Press, 1878), 32; see also Jas. H. Ballagh, "Sermon" ["The Need and Promise of the Power of the Holy Spirit in Our Work as Missionaries"], *Proceedings of the General Conference of the Protestant Missionaries of Japan, Held at Osaka, Japan, April, 1883* (Yokohama: R. Meiklejohn, 1883), 1-20.

8. For example, J. L. P., "Hints on Revival," *IER* 12 (April 1876): 443-45.

9. A. T. Pierson, "Missionary Quickenings of the Century," *MRW* 13 (n.s.) (April 1900): 241 (Pierson's emphasis).

10. C. I. Scofield, *Plain Papers on the Doctrine of the Holy Spirit* (Greenville, S.C.: Gospel Hour, 1969; originally published in 1899), 9.

11. A. T. Pierson, "The Pentecostal Movement—Pilkington of Uganda," *MRW* 12 (n.s.) (May 1899): 321.

12. Martin Luther, *Small Catechism*, in *Book of Concord: The Confessions of the Evangelical Lutheran Church*, ed. Theodore G. Tappert (Philadelphia: Fortress, 1959), 345. For helpful insights on the Reformers' attitudes toward mission, see David J. Bosch, *Transforming Mission: Paradigm Shifts in Theology of Mission* (Maryknoll, N.Y.: Orbis Books, 1991), 239-61.

13. John Calvin, *Institutes of the Christian Religion*, ed. John T. McNeill; trans. Ford Lewis Battles (Philadelphia: Westminster, 1960), III, I, 3.

14. Martin Luther, *Luther's Works*, vol. 18, *Lectures on the Minor Prophets*, ed. Hilton C. Oswald (St. Louis: Concordia, 1975), 107-8.

15. John Calvin, *Commentaries on the Twelve Minor Prophets*, vol. 2: *Joel, Amos, Obadiah* (Grand Rapids: Eerdmans, 1950), 102-3; L. Berkhof, *History of Christian Doctrines* (Edinburgh: Banner of Truth Trust, 1937), 262-64. For an analysis of amillennial eschatology, the view traditionally ascribed to Luther and Calvin, see Millard J. Erickson, *Contemporary Options in Eschatology: A Study of the Millennium* (Grand Rapids: Baker Book House, 1977), 73-89.

16. Luther, *Works*, vol. 18, *Lectures on the Minor Prophets*, 106.

17. Ibid., 107.

18. For selected documents on the Reformers' views on the evangelization of non-Christians, see Norman E. Thomas, ed., *Classic Texts in Mission & World Christianity* (Maryknoll, N.Y.: Orbis Books, 1995), 32-49; cf. D. H. W. Gensichen, "Were the Reformers Indifferent to Missions?" in *History's Lessons for Tomorrow's Mission* (Geneva: World's Student Christian Federation, 1960), 119-27.

19. Thomas, *Classic Texts*, 34-35, 38-39; cf. Philip E. Hughes, "John Calvin: Director of Missions," in *Heritage of John Calvin*, ed. John H. Bratt (Grand Rapids: Eerdmans, 1973), 40-54.

20. Thomas, *Classic Texts*, 41-43.

21. James A. Scherer, ed., *Justinian Welz: Essays by an Early Prophet of Mission* (Grand Rapids: Eerdmans, 1969), 49-54.

22. For example, Balthasar Hubmaier, "On the Christian Baptism of Believers," in *Anabaptist Beginnings (1523-1533): A Source Book*, ed. William R. Estep, Jr. (Nieuwkoop: B. De Graaf, 1976), 78-83; Wolfgang Schäufele, "The Missionary Vision and Activity of the Anabaptist Laity," in *Anabaptism and Mission*, ed. Wilbert R. Shenk (Scottdale, Pa.: Herald, 1984), 70-87.

23. *Canons and Decrees of the Council of Trent*, trans. H. J. Schroeder (Rockford: TAN Books, 1978), 32-33; also Pope Paul III, *Sublimus Dei* (1537).

24. Gustav Warneck, *Outline of a History of Protestant Missions from the Reformation to the Present Time*, 3rd ed. (New York: Fleming H. Revell, 1906), 53; also Bosch, *Transforming Mission*, 277-81.

25. Andrew F. Walls, "Missions and Historical Memory: Jonathan Edwards and David Brainerd," in *Jonathan Edwards at Home and Abroad: Historical Memories, Cultural Movements, Global Horizons*, ed. David W. Kling and Douglas A. Sweeney (Columbia: University of South Carolina Press, 2003), 248-49.

26. Richard Lovelace, "Baptism in the Holy Spirit and the Evangelical Movement," in *Faces of Renewal: Studies in Honor of Stanley M. Horton Presented on His 70th Birthday*, ed. Paul Elbert (Peabody, Mass.: Hendrickson, 1988), 209-33.

27. Cotton Mather, quoted in Ernst Benz, "Pietist and Puritan Sources of Early Protestant World Missions (Cotton Mather and A. H. Francke)," *Church History* 20 (June 1951): 335.

28. Timothy L. Smith, "Righteousness and Hope: Christian Holiness and the Millennial Vision in America, 1800-1900," *AQ* 31 (Spring 1979): 21.

29. Jonathan Edwards, *An Humble Attempt to Promote Explicit Agreement and Visible Union of God's People in Extraordinary Prayer for the Revival of Religion and the Advancement of Christ's Kingdom on Earth*, ed. Stephen J. Stein, *Works of Jonathan Edwards*, vol. 5 (New Haven: Yale University Press, 1977), 329. Alexander Duff later wrote that the application of "pure Apostolic Christianity" in the evangelization of the

world "would re-paradise the earth, and replenish the heaven of heavens with myriads of the ransomed and the saved"; *Evangelistic Theology: An Inaugural Address* (Edinburgh: Andrew Elliot, 1868), 18. See also Grant Wacker, "The Holy Spirit and the Spirit of the Age in American Protestantism, 1880-1910," *JAH* 72 (June 1985): 45-62.

30. Samuel Hopkins, *A Treatise on the Millennium* (New York: Arno, 1972; originally published in 1793), 152-54.

31. David W. Kling, "The New Divinity and the Origins of the American Board of Commissioners for Foreign Missions," in *North American Foreign Missions, 1810-1914: Theology, Theory, and Policy*, ed. Wilbert R. Shenk (Grand Rapids: Eerdmans, 2004), 24.

32. For an insightful discussion, see W. R. Ward, *Early Evangelicalism: A Global Intellectual History, 1670-1789* (Cambridge: Cambridge University Press, 2006), 85-98.

33. For example, Cotton Mather, John Morrison, and the Methodist theologian John Fletcher referred to the era of church history in which they lived as the "dispensation of the Spirit": Mather, "Pietist," 47; Morrison, "On Prayer," 5; John Fletcher, *Works of the Reverend John Fletcher, Vicar of Madeley* (reprint edition, Salem, Ohio: Schmul, 1974), 3: 166-69. On John Wesley's attitude toward millenarianism, see Henry D. Rack, *Reasonable Enthusiast: John Wesley and the Rise of Methodism* (Philadelphia: Trinity Press International, 1989), 382, 491.

34. On the theology of the "New Divinity" and its proponents, see E. Brooks Holifield, *Theology in America: Christian Thought from the Age of the Puritans to the Civil War* (New Haven: Yale University Press, 2003), 135-49.

35. Richard Lee Rogers, "'A Bright and New Constellation': Millennial Narratives and the Origins of American Foreign Missions," in Shenk, ed., *North American Foreign Missions*, 44.

36. William Carey, *An Enquiry into the Obligations of Christians, to Use Means for the Conversion of the Heathens* (1792), reprinted in Timothy George, *Faithful Witness: The Life and Mission of William Carey* (Birmingham, Ala.: New Hope, 1991), E.52-E53 (Carey's emphasis).

37. Morrison, *On Prayer*, 4.

38. John, "Holy Spirit," 32.

39. Ibid., 39.

40. [J.] B. Whiting, "On the Best Means of Exciting and Maintaining a Missionary Spirit," in *Conference on Missions Held in 1860 at Liverpool* (London: James Nisbet, 1860), 59.

41. Edwards, *Humble Attempt*, 321.

42. John Greenfield, *Power from on High: The Story of the Great Moravian Revival of 1727*, 5th ed. (Bethlehem: Moravian Church in America, 1977), 26.

43. The Prayer Union of India listed four objectives: "It is proposed that the children of God should be asked to plead with Him for a general outpouring of the Holy Spirit— 1st. Upon all the clergy, ministers, and missionaries, that the Word preached may be with power, and effectual; 2nd. Upon all *truly* converted people, that the coldness we now have to mourn over may be removed, and that *fresh life* may be given; 3rd. Upon the unconverted Europeans and Eurasians in this land; and 4th. Upon the vast masses of heathen, that they may be delivered from the darkness in which they are now sunk, and enabled to cast aside their idols and come to Jesus. Many of them see the falseness of their religion, but turn to infidelity instead of Christianity." "A Prayer Union," *TC*, October 13, 1881, 17.

44. Pope Gregory XVI, *Probe Nostis* (On the Propagation of the Faith), September 18, 1840; Joseph Schmidlin, *Catholic Mission Theory* (Techny, Ill.: Mission Press, S.V.D., 1931), 341-47.

45. Eliza G. Jones, *Memoir of Mrs. Eliza G. Jones: Missionary to Burmah and Siam* (Philadelphia: American Baptist Publication Society, 1853), 42 (Jones's emphasis).

46. Ibid., 44.

47. James Gilmour, *James Gilmour of Mongolia: His Diaries, Letters, and Reports*, ed. Richard Lovett (London: Religious Tract Society, 1895), 59.

48. John Hewlett, "Training of Workers," in *Report of the Centenary Conference on the Protestant Missions of the World. Held in Exeter Hall (June 9th-19th), London, 1888*, ed. James Johnston (New York: Fleming H. Revell, 1888), 2: 376.

49. Rufus Anderson, *Foreign Missions: Their Relations and Claims* (New York: Charles Scribner, 1869), 309. See also A. T. Pierson, "Spiritual Movements of the Half Century—The Revival of the Prayer-Spirit," *MRW* 11 (n.s.) (January 1898): 1-8.

50. A. T. Pierson, "Missionary Quickenings of the Century," *MRW* 13 (n.s.) (April 1900): 241.

51. Ibid., 242.

52. Ibid.

53. Ibid., 243-44. For example, James Burns, *Revivals: Their Laws and Leaders* (London: Hodder and Stoughton, 1909).

54. For example, John Clough said he had "witnessed many precious outpourings of the Holy Spirit"; quoted in Ada C. Chaplin, *Our Gold-Mine: The Story of American Baptist Missions in India* (Boston: W. G. Corthell, 1877), 355.

55. See C. W. Forman, "Preaching to the Heathen," *Report of the Second Decennial Missionary Conference Held at Calcutta, 1882-83* (Calcutta: Baptist Mission Press, 1883), 4-10.

56. For example, Edith L. Blumhofer and Randall Balmer, eds., *Modern Christian Revivals* (Urbana: University of Illinois Press, 1993); Kathryn Long, *Revival of 1857-58: Interpreting an American Religious Awakening* (Oxford: Oxford University Press, 1998); Andrew F. Walls, *The Missionary Movement in Christian History: Studies in the Transmission of Faith* (Maryknoll, N.Y.: Orbis Books, 1996); Charles Yrigoyen, Jr., ed., *The Global Impact of the Wesleyan Traditions and Their Related Movements*, Pietist and Wesleyan Studies 14 (Lanham, Md.: Scarecrow, 2002); J. Edwin Orr, *Evangelical Awakenings in Africa* (Minneapolis: Bethany Fellowship, 1975).

57. "Shensi, China," *MRW* 9 (n.s.) (March 1896): 228.

58. Miron Winslow, *Memoir of Mrs. Harriet L. Winslow, Thirteen Years a Member of the American Mission in Ceylon* (New York: American Tract Society, 1840), 299.

59. Ibid., 312.

60. Ibid., 309.

61. Amanda Smith, *An Autobiography: The Story of the Lord's Dealings with Mrs. Amanda Smith, the Colored Evangelist* (Chicago: Meyer & Brother, 1893), 366; see also "Bishop William Taylor, World Evangelist," *MRW* 15 (n.s.) (August 1902): 609-13.

62. Titus Coan, *Life in Hawaii: An Autobiographic Sketch* (New York: Anson D. F. Randolph, 1882), 42-50; also J. Edwin Orr, *Evangelical Awakenings in the South Seas* (Minneapolis: Bethany Fellowship, 1976), 27-42.

63. Richard Lovett, *History of the London Missionary Society, 1795-1895* (London: Henry Frowde, 1899), 2: 381.

64. Ibid., 2: 385.

65. Winslow, *Memoir*, 407.

66. See John Wesley, *A Plain Account of Christian Perfection*, in *The Works of the Rev. John Wesley*, ed. Thomas Jackson (London: John Mason, 1872), 11: 366-446.

67. E. T. Wells, "Does the Holy Spirit Witness to the Experience of Entire Sanctification?" in *Proceedings of Holiness Conferences Held at Cincinnati, November 26th, 1877,*

and at New York, December 17th, 1877 (Philadelphia: National Publishing Association for the Promotion of Holiness, 1878), 42; see also Melvin Easterday Dieter, *Holiness Revival of the Nineteenth Century*, 2d ed. (Lanham, Md.: Scarecrow, 1996), 3-4; Wallace Thornton, Jr., "The Revivalist Movement and the Development of a Holiness/Pentecostal Philosophy of Missions," *WTJ* 38 (Spring 2003): 160-86.

68. Wilson Thomas Hogue, *G. Harry Agnew: A Pioneer Missionary* (Chicago: Free Methodist Publishing House, 1905), 137-38. See also John Parker, "Holiness as Related to the Conversion of the World," in *Proceedings of Holiness Conferences*, 188-203. For the work of Vivian Dake, see Ida Dake Parsons, *Kindling Watch-Fires: Being a Brief Sketch of the Life of Rev. Vivian A. Dake* (Chicago: Free Methodist Publishing House, 1915).

69. Asa Mahan, *Baptism with the Holy Ghost. The Enduement of Power* by Charles G. Finney (London: Elliot Stock, 1880); reprinted as *Baptism of the Holy Spirit;* includes *God's Provision of Power* (Clinton, N.Y.: Williams, n.d.), 44-49, 183-85. See also Donald W. Dayton, *Discovering an Evangelical Heritage* (Peabody, Mass.: Hendrickson, 1976), 35-43.

70. For an example of the Keswick teaching, see [Clement] Clemance, "The Baptism of the Holy Ghost," *TC*, September 11, 1884, 26-27. On the Keswick conferences, see Steven Barabas, *So Great Salvation: The History and Message of the Keswick Convention* (London: Marshall, Morgan & Scott, 1952).

71. Finney in Mahan, *Baptism with the Holy Ghost*, 183.

72. Dwight L. Moody, *Moody: His Words, Work, and Workers*, ed. W. H. Daniels (New York: Nelson & Phillips, 1877), 397. See also David W. Bebbington, *The Dominance of Evangelicalism: The Age of Spurgeon and Moody* (Downers Grove, Ill.: InterVarsity, 2005), 200-214.

73. Charles F. Harford-Battersby, *Pilkington of Uganda* (London: Marshall Brothers, 1898), 222, 225.

74. Pierson, "Pentecostal Movement," 321-31.

75. See A. T. Pierson, *Forward Movements of the Last Half Century* (New York: Funk & Wagnalls, 1905), 24-50; G[eorge] Bowen, "The Promotion of Spiritual Life and Enthusiasm in the Churches of India," *Report of the Second Decennial Missionary Conference*, 85-90. See also Luther Jeremiah Oconer, "'Fullness of the Spirit'—The Goal of the Christian Life: The Holiness Advocacy of Bishops James Mills Thoburn and Francis Wesley Warne of India," paper presented to the Oxford Institute of Methodist Theological Studies, Post-Wesley Group, August 12-21, 2007; available at http://www.oxford-institute.org/docs/2007papers/2007-3Oconer.pdf.

76. Hessie Newcombe, "China," in *Official Report of the Missionary Conference of the Anglican Communion on May 28, 29, 30, 31 and June 1, 1894*, ed. George A. Spottiswoode (London: Society for Promoting Christian Knowledge, 1894), 650.

77. Robert P. Wilder, "Power from on High," in *Spiritual Awakenings Among India's Students: Addresses of Six Student Conferences of the Student Volunteer Movement Held at Jaffna, Bombay, Lahore, Lucknow, Calcutta, and Madras* (Madras: Addison, 1896), 30.

78. James Gall, *The Evangelistic Baptism: Indispensable to the Church for the Conversion of the World* (Edinburgh: Gall & Inglis, 1888), 2.

79. Ibid., 56; cf. D. Mullan, "The Pentecostal Baptism," *TC*, April 29, 1886, 4.

80. J. L. P., "Hints on Revival," 441-42. Nonetheless, the author recognized the benefits of religious excitement.

81. A. T. Pierson, "The Keswick Movement," *MRW* 10 (n.s.) (February 1897): 90 (Pierson's emphasis).

82. "Notes and Intelligence," *IER* 12 (October 1876): 246.

83. "Recent Revival among the Zulus," *MRW* 13 (n.s.) (February 1900): 158.

84. [Heinrich] Ritter, *History of Protestant Missions in Japan*, trans. George E. Albrecht (Tokyo: Methodist Publishing House, 1898), 114.

85. Ibid., 117-18.

86. Donald Fraser, "Livingstonia. Revival Scenes at Loudon," *Missionary Record of the United Free Church of Scotland*, December 1910, 544-45 (United Free Church of Scotland, Glasgow; archived in National Library of Scotland); T. Jack Thompson, *Christianity in Northern Malawi: Donald Fraser's Missionary Methods and Ngoni Culture* (Leiden: E. J. Brill, 1995), 143-47.

87. W. C. Wilcox, quoted in "Pentecostal Times in South Africa," *MRW* 11 (n.s.) (January 1898): 45.

88. The term "excess" to describe the potentially negative features of revivals has remained in currency into the twenty-first century. For example, in a press release from the historically Wesleyan Asbury College (Wilmore, Ky.) dated February 8, 2006 that described a campus revival, President Paul Rader reported about the positive effects and then stated: "We have been spared excesses." http://www.asbury.edu/press/chapeldaytwo06.

89. Amy Wilson-Carmichael, "Need We Tell God How to Work?" *MRW* 20 (n.s.) (January 1907): 52.

90. See Andrew F. Walls, *The Missionary Movement in Christian History: Studies in the Transmission of Faith* (Maryknoll, N.Y.: Orbis Books, 1996), 79-101.

91. Frank W. Warne, *The Revival in the Indian Church* (New York: Board of Foreign Missions, Methodist Episcopal Church, 1907), 29-30. See also J. E. Robinson, "Days of Power and Blessing at Asansol," *IW*, December 21, 1905, 803-4.

92. William Brown, quoted in "The Religious Awakening in Travancore," *IER* 4 (April 1874): 407.

93. Ibid., 397.

94. The telegraph clerks in India refused to send the message according to W. J. Richards, "The 'Six Years' Party' in Travancore," *CMIR* 7 (n.s.) (November 1882): 663-64; "Notes and Intelligence," *IER* 6 (January 1876): 383; W. J. Richards, "Church Missionary Society. Travancore and Cochin," *Missionary Conference: South India and Ceylon, 1879* (Madras: Addison, 1880), 2: 167. For Joseph's letters in which he talks about his belief in the urgency of the hour and the need to warn people of the coming of Christ in 1881, see Joseph Chakko Kurundamannil, "Yuomayam: A Messianic Movement in Kerala, India" (D.Miss. diss., Fuller Theological Seminary, 1978), 56-58.

95. Hugald Grafe, *History of Christianity in India*, vol. 4, part 2: *Tamilnadu in the Nineteenth and Twentieth Centuries* (Bangalore: Church History Association of India, 1990), 69.

96. Richards, "Church Missionary Society," 164-65.

97. "Madras and South-India Mission," *Proceedings of the Church Missionary Society for Africa and the East*, 1861-1862, 141.

98. "Tinnevelly," *Proceedings of the Church Missionary Society for Africa and the East, 1860-1861*, 125.

99. Ibid., 127.

100. *Annual Report of the American Board of Commissioners for Foreign Missions, 1861*, 96.

101. For the activities of Rhenius and Groves, see Stephen Neill, *A History of Christianity in India, 1707-1858* (Cambridge: Cambridge University Press, 1985), 218-22, 408-9.

102. Robert Bernard Dann, *Father of Faith Missions: The Life and Times of Anthony Norris Groves (1795-1853)* (Bath, U.K.: Authentic Paternoster, 2004), 267-75, 405-7.

103. G. H. Lang, *The History and Diaries of an Indian Christian (J. C. Aroolappen)* (London: Thynne, 1939), 144-45. See also "The Revival in North Tinnevelly," *CMI* 11 (August 1860): 180.

104. Anthony Norris Groves, *Memoir of Anthony Norris Groves, Compiled Chiefly from His Journals and Letters*, 3rd ed. (London: James Nisbet, 1869), 313-14.

105. Ibid., 625.

106. Ibid., 140.

107. Ibid., 151, 186.

108. Dibb's comment appeared in the *Indian Watchman*, February 1861, and is quoted in *Memoir of Anthony Norris Groves*, 616.

109. Unnamed missionary, quoted in *IW*, June 1861, reprinted in Lang, *History and Diaries*, 199.

110. "Tinnevelly," *Proceedings, 1860-1861*, 131-32. "Animal excitement" refers to an excitable nature and passionate outbursts.

111. Ashton Dibb, "The Revival in North Tinnevelly," *CMR* 5 (n.s.) (August 1860): 178 (Dibb's emphasis).

112. "Tinnevelly," *Proceedings, 1860-1861*, 134-35.

113. For helpful information on the revival in Tiruneveli, see J. Edwin Orr, *Evangelical Awakenings in India* (New Delhi: Christian Literature Institute, 1970), 29-38.

114. The names of the family members are found in Eugene Stock, *History of the Church Missionary Society* (London: Church Missionary Society, 1899), 2:539. For Joseph Peet's account of their conversion, see "Mavelikara," *CMR* 7 (n.s.) (September 1862): 285-88.

115. Stock, *History of the Church Missionary Society* , 2:539. See also Kurundamannil, "Yuomayam," 50-51.

116. Oomen Mamen, "Allepie," *CMR* 7 (n.s.) (September 1862): 283.

117. "Religious Awakening," *IER* 4, 400.

118. Ibid.

119. The achievements, however, were limited despite the best intentions of the CMS missionaries; see C. M. Agur, *Church History of Travancore* (Madras: S.P.S., 1903), 120-28; Neill, *History of Christianity in India*, 241-54; Cyril Bruce Firth, *An Introduction to Indian Church History* (Madras: Christian Literature Society, 1961), 171-72.

120. Richards, "Six Years' Party," 661. On the disregard of caste, see "Notes and Intelligence," 109.

121. Richards, "Six Years' Party," 661. Others wrote new lyrics or hymns as well; examples are provided in J. M. Speechly, "Narrative of a Short Tour up the Rani River by the Rev. J. M. Speechly," *CMI* 11 (n.s.) (March 1875): 92-96. (Reprinted from *MCMR*). Speechly, who had been principal of the Cambridge Nicholson Institution in Kottayam and served as one of Justus Joseph's teachers, received appointment as the first bishop of the newly formed diocese of Travancore and Cochin in 1879.

122. David Fenn, "South India Mission," *CMR* 4 (n.s.) (April 1874): 90-96.

123. Richards, "Church Missionary Society," 166.

124. Kurundamannin, "Yuomayam," 55.

125. Agur, *Church History*, 950-52.

126. Richards, "Six Years' Party," 662.

127. W. J. Richards, "Journal Notes by Rev. W. J. Richards," *MCMR* 45 (March 1878): 105.

128. Richards, "Six Years' Party," 663.

129. Samuel Mateer, quoted in "Six Years People," *IER* 11 (July 1881): 129.

130. Ibid.

131. Richards, "Six Years' Party," 664.

132. Ibid., 663.

133. Ibid., 664.

134. Joseph Pothen, "Report of the Puthupalli Pastorate," *MCMR* 45 (September 1878): 303.

135. Kurundamannil, "Yuomayam," 145-46.

136. "Mavelikara," *Proceedings of the Church Missionary Society for Africa and the East, 1875-76*, 149. See also Orr, *Evangelical Awakenings in India*, 37, where he follows the assessment of the missionaries that Justus Joseph "made the usual mistake of confusing the human response to the Spirit's working with the working of the Holy Spirit himself. There had been emotional outbursts in some of the meetings, so he tried ardently to conserve all the emotional patterns. This led to the sheerest emotionalism, which meant a sheer manipulation of emotion."

137. "Notes and Intelligence," *IER*, 248.

138. "South India," *CMR* 4 (n.s.) (October 1874): 287. For Joseph's responses on the issue of correct biblical interpretation, see Kurundamannil, "Yuomayam," 59-61. I am indebted to Dr. Kurundamannil for making many of the translated letters of Joseph available in his dissertation.

139. Richards, "Six Years' Party," 666.

140. Justus Joseph to J. H. Bishop, reprinted in Kurundamannil, "Yuomayam," 63.

141. For the later development of Joseph's "Revival Church," see Kurundamannil, "Yuomayam," 77-138.

142. Stock, *History of the Church Missionary Society*, 3: 182.

143. Kurundamannil, "Yuomayam," 4.

144. M. E. Pechin, "The 'Apostles' of Madagascar," *MRW* 17 (August 1904): 617; Sutarman Soediman Partonadi, *Sadrach's Community and Its Contextual Roots: A Nineteenth Century Javanese Expression of Christianity* (Amsterdam: Rodopi, 1990), 63-96.

145. Philip Jenkins, *The New Faces of Christianity: Believing the Bible in the Global South* (Oxford: Oxford University Press, 2006), 177.

146. Graham Duncan and Ogbu U. Kalu, "*Bakuzufu*: Revival Movements and Indigenous Appropriation in African Christianity," in *African Christianity: An African Story*, ed. Ogbu U. Kalu (Trenton, N.J.: Africa World Press, 2007), 245-69.

3. EXPECTANT FAITH

1. Anthony Norris Groves, *Memoir of Anthony Norris Groves, Compiled Chiefly from His Journals and Letters*, 3rd ed. (London: James Nisbet, 1869), 313-14.

2. Elizabeth Baxter, quoted in *Record of the International Conference on Divine Healing and True Holiness Held at the Agricultural Hall, London, June 1 to 5, 1885* (London: J. Snow, 1885), 87.

3. Jennie Fuller, "India Work for November," *CAMW*, February 10, 1893, 91.

4. J. Hudson Taylor, quoted in "Some Nuggets of Thought Gathered from the 'Ecumenical' Mines," *MRW* 13 (n.s.) (July 1900): 505.

5. Andrew Murray, *The Key to the Missionary Problem*, 2d ed. (London: James Nisbet, 1901), 131.

6. Minnie F. Abrams, "Mukti Mission," *MPB*, September 1907, 18.

7. Theodore Christlieb, *Modern Doubt and Christian Belief* (New York: Scribner, Armstrong, 1874), 337.

8. H. Grattan Guinness, "The Approaching End of the Age," *TC*, March 11, 1886, 18.

9. See A. B. Simpson, "The Days of Heaven," *CAMW*, January 3, 1890, 6-7.

10. A. T. Pierson, *The Crisis of Missions; or, The Voice out of the Cloud* (London: James Nisbet, 1886), 11-17.

11. The uneasiness within the Protestant mission establishment over the success of the enterprise appear in "The Wide Work and Great Claims of Modern Protestant Missions," Appendix I, *Proceedings of the General Conference on Foreign Missions Held at the Conference Hall, in Mildmay Park, London, in October, 1878* (London: John F. Shaw, 1879), 407-13.

12. A. J. Gordon, "The Holy Spirit in Missions," in *Student Mission Power: Report of the First International Convention of the Student Volunteer Movement for Foreign Missions, Held at Cleveland, Ohio, U.S.A., February 26, 27, 28 and March 1, 1891* (Pasadena, Calif.: William Carey Library, 1979), 19.

13. For an insightful essay on how the Wesleyan-holiness movement impacted Pentecostal missions, see Jay R. Case, "And Ever the Twain Shall Meet: The Holiness Missionary Movement and the Birth of World Pentecostalism, 1870-1920," *RAC* 16 (Summer 2006): 125-59. A postmillennial outlook on missions appears in C. S. Eby, "Basal Ideas in Missions," *MRW* 12 (n.s.) (April 1899): 288-91.

14. Randall J. Stephens, *The Fire Spreads: Holiness and Pentecostalism in the American South* (Cambridge, Mass.: Harvard University Press, 2008), 161-85.

15. According to Irwin, believers should receive three and even more experiences of grace, beginning with salvation, followed by sanctification and later the baptism of fire; he employed chemical names for the experiences beyond the baptism of fire: "dynamite," "lyddite," and "oxidite." See Martin H. Schrag, "The Spiritual Pilgrimage of the Reverend Benjamin Hardin Irwin," *BCHL* 4 (June 1981): 3-29.

16. Benjamin H. Irwin, "What God Hath Wrought," *LCF*, December 29, 1899, 4.

17. Joseph H. King, "History of the Fire-Baptized Holiness Church," *PHA*, April 7, 1921, 10-11; also B. H. Irwin, "My Pentecostal Baptism—A Christmas Gift," *TF*, May 1907, 114-17.

18. Grant Wacker, *Heaven Below: Early Pentecostals and American Culture* (Cambridge, Mass.: Harvard University Press, 2001), 2.

19. Ibid., 26.

20. "Conference on Unfulfilled Prophecy," *TC*, November 9, 1882, 16.

21. "A Missionary" [E. F. Baldwin], "The Question of the Hour—Foreign Missions," *TC*, February 8, 1889, 110.

22. C. I. Scofield, ed., *Scofield Reference Bible* (New York: Oxford University Press, 1909), 1170. For "dispensationalism," a popular form of premillennialism, see Millard J. Erickson, *Contemporary Options in Eschatology: A Study of the Millennium* (Grand Rapids: Baker Book House, 1977), 109-24. For the perspective of A. T. Pierson, see Dana L. Robert, *Occupy until I Come: A. T. Pierson and the Evangelization of the World* (Grand Rapids: Eerdmans, 2003), 136-37, 154.

23. William Owen Carver, *Missions in the Plan of the Ages: Bible Studies in Missions* (New York: Fleming H. Revell, 1909), 254.

24. Ashbel Green, *Presbyterian Missions*, with supplemental notes by John C. Lowrie (New York: Anson D. F. Randolph, 1893), 138.

25. A. T. Pierson, "Editorial Notes on Current Topics," *MRW* 5 (n.s.) (November 1892): 863.

26. Ibid., 864.

27. A. J. Gordon, "Education and Missions," *MRW* 6 (n.s.) (August 1893): 585.

28. Edward Irving, *Missionaries after the Apostolical School* (London: Hamilton, Adams, 1825), xv; also Meade C. Williams, "Edward Irving," *PTR* 1 (January 1903): 8-9.

29. Ibid., xvi.

30. Irving, *Missionaries*, xix.

31. Robert Needham Cust, "Thoughts on the Methods of Evangelization," *TGAL*, March 1890, 119.

32. Irving, *Missionaries*, xvii.

33. Ibid., 113.

34. Sheridan Gilley, "Edward Irving: Prophet of the Millennium," in *Revival and Religion since 1700*, ed. Jane Garnett and Colin Matthew (London: Hambledon, 1993), 98. For Arthur Pierson's endorsement of Irving's appeal to Matthew 10, see "Great Missionary Appeals of the Last Century—II," *MRW* 15 (n.s.) (March 1902): 173-77.

35. For the Albury Circle, see Timothy C. F. Stunt, *From Awakening to Secession: Radical Evangelicals in Switzerland and Britain, 1815-35* (Edinburgh: T & T Clark, 2000), 135-37.

36. D. W. Bebbington, *Evangelicalism in Modern Britain: A History from the 1730s to the 1980s* (Grand Rapids: Baker Book House, 1989), 76, 79-81, 92-94.

37. Charles H. Spurgeon, "Preparing the Way," in *Missionary Sermons: A Selection from the Discourses Delivered on Behalf of the Baptist Missionary Society on Various Occasions* (London: Carey, 1924), 16.

38. Arthur T. Pierson called Johannes Evangelista Gossner the "father of faith-missions," in *Forward Movements of the Last Half Century* (New York: Funk & Wagnalls, 1905), 93; cf. Klaus Fiedler, *The Story of Faith Missions: From Hudson Taylor to Present Day Africa* (Oxford: Regnum Books International, 1994), 11-22.

39. A. T. Pierson, *George Müller of Bristol and His Witness to a Prayer-Hearing God* (New York: Baker and Taylor, 1899), 72.

40. Ibid., 211-12.

41. George Müller, quoted in ibid., 405 (Müller's emphasis).

42. David W. Bebbington, *The Dominance of Evangelicalism: The Age of Spurgeon and Moody* (Downers Grove, Ill.: InterVarsity, 2005), 185-86.

43. Anthony Norris Groves, *Christian Devotedness, or The Consideration of Our Saviour's Precept, "Lay not up for yourselves treasures upon earth,"* 2d ed. (London: James Nisbet, 1829).

44. Groves, *Memoir*, 357-58. See also Robert Bernard Dann, *Father of Faith Missions: The Life and Times of Anthony Norris Groves (1795-1853)* (Bath, U.K.: Authentic Paternoster, 2004), 248.

45. G. H. Lang, *The History & Diaries of an Indian Christian (J. C. Aroolappen)* (London: Thynne, 1939), 128-34.

46. Fiedler, *Story of Faith Missions*, 24-25. For the influence of Müller on Arthur Pierson, see Robert, *Occupy until I Come*, 103-7.

47. Unnamed missionary, quoted in Robert Needham Cust, *Notes on Missionary Subjects* (London: Elliot Stock, 1889), 108.

48. William F. Bainbridge, *Around the World Tour of Christian Missions* (Boston: D. Lothrop, 1882), 226 (Bainbridge's emphasis).

49. F. F. Ellinwood, "The Monthly Concert of Missions," *MRW* 3 (n.s.) (December 1890): 948-49.

50. Cust, *Notes on Missionary Subjects*, 107.

51. Robert A. Hume, "The Natural and the Supernatural," *Dnya*, July 11, 1907, 2.

52. Robert A. Hume, "Is There Demoniacal Possession?" *Dnya*, December 12, 1907, 1.

53. Timothy C. F. Stunt, "Trying the Spirits: Irvingite Signs and the Test of Doctrine," in *Signs, Wonders, Miracles: Representations of Divine Power in the Life of the Church*, ed. Kate Cooper and Jeremy Gregory (Woodbridge, Suffolk, U.K.: Ecclesiastical History Society and Boydell Press, 2005), 400.

54. Mrs. H. Grattan (Fanny) Guinness, "Missionaries According to Matt. X," *RB*, April 1889, 109-10.

55. Christlieb, *Modern Doubt*, 332.

56. Ibid.

57. A. J. Gordon, *The Ministry of Healing: Miracles of Cure in All Ages* (Harrisburg, Pa.: Christian Publications, n.d.; originally published in 1881), 116.

58. Johannes Warneck, *The Living Christ and Dying Heathenism*, 3rd ed. (New York: Fleming H. Revell, n.d.), 175-82; Martin E. Lehmann, *A Biographical Study of Ingwer Ludwig Nommensen (1834-1918), Pioneer Missionary to the Bataks of Sumatra* (Lewiston, N.Y.: Edwin Mellen, 1996), 105-40.

59. Ibid., 181-82.

60. In volume one Pierson pays warm tribute to Christlieb, whose insights inspired the title of his books. See A. T. Pierson, *The Miracles of Missions: Modern Marvels in the History of Missionary Enterprise*, first series (New York: Funk & Wagnalls, 1891), v-vii.

61. Pierson, *Forward Movements*, 393.

62. For Pierson's own healing and his views on faith healing, see Dana L. Robert, "Arthur Tappan Pierson and Forward Movements of Late-Nineteenth-Century Evangelicalism" (Ph.D. diss., Yale University, 1984), 345-46.

63. William Taylor, *Christian Adventures in South Africa* (New York: Phillips & Hunt, 1880), 275-76.

64. Case, "And Ever the Twain," 134-35.

65. Taylor, *Christian Adventures*, 276-77.

66. Popular defenses of the canonicity of the passage included Gordon, *Ministry of Healing*, 245-46; "Notes on Scripture.—17," *TC*, November 6, 1884, 9.

67. Robert Needham Cust, quoted in James Johnston, ed., *Report of the Centenary Conference on the Protestant Missions of the World. Held in Exeter Hall (June 9th-19th), London, 1888* (New York: Fleming H. Revell, 1888), 2: 116.

68. A. B. Simpson, *The Gospel of Healing*, rev. ed. (Harrisburg, Pa.: Christian Publications, 1915), 13-14.

69. Ibid., 44; "Faith Convention at Old Orchard," *TC*, October 5, 1882, 8.

70. Gordon, *Ministry of Healing*, 198.

71. John Alexander Dowie, "God's Way of Healing," *LH*, August 31, 1894, 5.

72. See Grant Wacker, et al., "John Alexander Dowie: Harbinger of Pentecostal Power," in *Portraits of a Generation: Early Pentecostal Leaders*, ed. James R. Goff, Jr. and Grant Wacker (Fayetteville: University of Arkansas Press, 2002), 3-19.

73. Helpful studies on the healing movement include Raymond J. Cunningham, "From Holiness to Healing: The Faith Cure in America, 1872-1892," *Church History* 43 (December 1974): 499-513; Paul Gale Chappell, "The Divine Healing Movement in America" (Ph.D. diss., Drew University, 1983); Ronald A. N. Kydd, *Healing through the Ages: Models for Understanding* (Peabody, Mass.: Hendrickson, 1998); Nancy A. Hardesty, *Faith Cure: Divine Healing in the Holiness and Pentecostal Movements* (Peabody, Mass.: Hendrickson, 2003).

74. "Faith Convention," 8.

75. Ibid.

76. See Edith L. Blumhofer, "Life on Faith Lines: Faith Homes and Early Pentecostal Values," *AGH* 10 (Summer 1990): 10-12, 22; idem, "Life on Faith Lines" (Part 2: Zion Faith Homes), *AGH* 10 (Fall 1990): 5-7, 21-22.

77. W. E. Boardman, "The Call to the International Conference on Divine Healing and True Holiness," in *Record of the International Conference*, iv.

78. [William] Lockhart, "On Medical Missions in China," in *Conference on Missions Held in 1860 at Liverpool* (London: James Nisbet, 1860), 100. For the historical development of medical missions, see Christoffer H. Grundmann, *Sent to Heal! Emergence and Development of Medical Missions* (Lanham, Md.: University Press of America, 2005).

79. J. G. Kerr, "Essay. Medical Missions," in *Records of the General Conference of the Protestant Missionaries of China, Held at Shanghai, May 10-24, 1877* (Shanghai: Presbyterian Mission Press, 1878), 114-15.

80. See the discussion on medical missions in Johnston, *Report of the Centenary Conference*, 1: 379-96.

81. M. C. Mason, "Methods of Mission Work," in *The Assam Mission of the American Baptist Missionary Union. Papers and Discussions of the Jubilee Conference Held in Nowgong. December 18-29, 1886* (Guwahati, Delhi: Spectrum Publications, 1992), 100.

82. Ibid., 111-12.

83. Mrs. S. G. Weems, "Our God is a Prayer-Hearing and Prayer-Answering God," *MRW* 5 (n.s.) (September 1892): 681.

84. Cf. Green, *Presbyterian Missions*, 239-40.

85. A. B. Simpson, "Missions and the Lord's Coming," *CAMW*, May 2, 1890, 282; cf. Franklin Arthur Pyles, "The Missionary Eschatology of A. B. Simpson," in *The Birth of a Vision*, ed. David F. Hartzfeld and Charles Nienkirchen (Beaverlodge, Alberta: Buena Book Services, 1986), 29-48.

86. Ibid., 283.

87. A. B. Simpson, quoted in *Record of the International Conference*, 69.

88. A. B. Simpson, "The New Testament Standpoint of Missions," *CAFMW*, December 16, 1892, 389.

89. A. B. Simpson, "A Gross Misrepresentation," *CAMW*, November 15, 1889, 241-42; "Correspondence and General Intelligence," *MRW* 1 (n.s.) (April 1888): 289; Robert L. Niklaus, John S. Sawin, Samuel J. Stoesz, *All for Jesus: God at Work in the Christian and Missionary Alliance over One Hundred Years* (Camp Hill, Pa.: Christian Publications, 1986), 83-84, 87-88.

90. Simpson, *Gospel of Healing*, 57, 77-79, 183. See also Andrew Walls, "The Evangelical Revival, the Missionary Movement, and Africa," in *Evangelicalism: Comparative Studies of Popular Protestantism in North America, the British Isles, and Beyond, 1700-1990*, ed. Mark A. Noll, David W. Bebbington, George A. Rawlyk (New York: Oxford University Press, 1994), 310-30.

91. Grace Stephens, *Triumphs of the Cross* (Baltimore: Williams & Wilkins, 1901), 107.

92. For an example of the latter opinion, see A. Andrew, "Exorcism," *HF*, April 1890, 361-67.

93. "Pastor Blumhardt and His Work," *TC*, December 1, 1881, 20-21; Kydd, *Healing through the Ages*, 37-42.

94. References to Theodore Christlieb and an article published by Robert C. Cardwell in *Contemporary Review* are mentioned in John L. Nevius, *Demon Possession and Allied Themes* (New York: Fleming H. Revell, 1894), 95, 110. For an example of the interest among radical evangelicals, see Mary E. Guptill and Marea E. Tonneson, "Demonology in Ancient and Modern Times," *TFire*, August 1, 1897, 115-21.

95. Nevius, *Demon Possession*, 135.

96. Alvyn Austin, *China's Millions: The China Inland Mission and Late Qing Society, 1832-1905* (Grand Rapids: Eerdmans, 2007), 260-64.

97. Nevius, *Demon Possession*, 135-36.

98. Ibid., 140.

99. C. H. Robertson, "The 'People's Alphabet' as Developed by the Late Rev. A. E. Street," *CR*, May 1923, 301-2.

100. Alfred E. Street, *Intercessory Foreign Missionaries: Practical Suggestions from a Missionary to Earnest Christians* (Boston: American Advent Mission Society, n.d.), 4. It was reprinted by the American Advent Mission Society and many years later by Moody Press under the title *How to Pray for Missionaries*. The original printing by the Student Volunteer Movement probably appeared sometime in 1903-1905.

101. Ibid., 6.

102. Ibid., 8-10.

103. Ibid., 10.

104. Alfred E. Street, "Intercessory Foreign Missionaries," *MRW* 18 (n.s.) (November 1905): 840-45.

105. The three major works on the life of Frank W. Sandford include William C. Hiss, "Shiloh: Frank W. Sandford and the Kingdom: 1893-1948" (Ph.D. diss., Tufts University, 1978); Frank S. Murray, *The Sublimity of Faith: The Life and Work of Frank W. Sandford* (Amherst, N.H.: Kingdom, 1981); Shirley Nelson, *Fair, Clear and Terrible: The Story of Shiloh* (Latham, N.Y.: British American Publishing, 1989).

106. F. W. Sandford, *Around the World*, no. 3: *My Visit to China* (Great Falls, N.H.: F. L. Shapleigh, 1891), 115.

107. Frank W. Sandford, *Seven Years with God* (Mont Vernon, N.H.: Kingdom, 1957), 12.

108. Frank W. Sandford, "The First Editorial," *TFire*, December 1 and 15, 1900, 210.

109. Sandford, *Seven Years with God*, 12.

110. G. P. Pardington, *Twenty-five Wonderful Years, 1889-1914* (New York: Christian Alliance, 1914), 123.

111. Frank W. Sandford, "The Everlasting Gospel," *TFire*, March 1, 1897, 44; idem, "The History of the World's Evangelization Crusade on Apostolic Principles," *TFire*, January 1895, 2-3; idem, *Seven Years with God*, 94-132; idem, "Defends Himself: Evangelist Sandford Talks of Miracles at Shiloh," *Bangor Daily Whig and Courier*, December 18, 1889, 8.

112. Frank W. Sandford, "The Second Annual Convention of the World's Evangelization Crusade on Apostolic Principles," *TFire*, October 1895, 1; idem, "Thanksgiving for the Doors of Hope," *TFire*, November 15, 1898, 173-74.

113. "A Queer Connecticut Sect," *New York Times*, October 26, 1897, 4; E. Sisson, "Pentecostal Truths," *Trust*, January 1913, 15-18.

114. E. V. Baker, "A Miracle of Healing," *TFire*, August 1895, 12-13; Gary B. McGee, "Three Notable Women in Pentecostal Ministry," *AGH* 6 (Spring 1986): 3-5, 12, 16.

115. Murray, *Sublimity of Faith*, 172. For a description of Shiloh as a "Mighty Prayer Center," see N. H. Harriman, "Shiloh," *EG*, January 29 to February 2, 1901, 51-52.

116. Ibid., 178-87.

117. Victor P. Abram, "Foreword," in Frank W. Sandford, *The Golden Light upon the Two Americas* (Amherst, N.H.: Kingdom, 1974), 8.

118. Ibid., 65.

119. Murray, *Sublimity of Faith*, 406.

120. Ibid., 396-483; cf. Nelson, *Fair, Clear, and Terrible*, 285-333.

121. Condemnation of both Dowie and Sandford appears in "The Downfall of Religious Despots," *MRW* 20 (n.s.) (May 1907): 321-22.

122. Edith L. Blumhofer, "The Christian Catholic Apostolic Church and the Apostolic Faith: A Study in the 1906 Pentecostal Revival," in *Charismatic Experiences in History*, ed. Cecil M. Robeck, Jr. (Peabody, Mass.: Hendrickson, 1985), 129-35.

123. Andrew Walls, "Globalization and the Study of Christian History," in *Globalizing Theology: Belief and Practice in an Era of World Christianity*, ed. Craig Ott and Harold A. Netland (Grand Rapids: Baker Academic, 2006), 71.

124. For example, C. Peter Wagner, "Territorial Spirits and World Missions," *EMQ* 25 (July 1989): 278-88; idem, *Confronting the Powers* (Ventura, Calif.: Regal Books, 1996); idem, ed., *The Queen's Domain: Advancing God's Kingdom in the 40/70 Window* (Colorado Springs: Wagner Publications, 2000); idem and F. Douglas Pennoyer, eds., *Wrestling with Dark Angels: Toward a Deeper Understanding of the Supernatural Forces in Spiritual Warfare* (Ventura, Calif.: Regal Books, 1990). For a less sensational approach, see Marguerite G. Kraft, *Understanding Spiritual Power: A Forgotten Dimension of Cross-Cultural Mission and Ministry* (Maryknoll, N.Y.: Orbis Books, 1995).

125. The personnel of the China Inland Mission (CIM) came from a wide variety of evangelical backgrounds. The missionaries that Bainbridge encountered represented just one sector, albeit a major one, in the CIM.

126. Bainbridge, *Around the World Tour*, 221.

127. Ibid., 227-28.

128. Ibid., 222.

129. Ibid., 225.

130. Ibid.

131. Ibid., 227.

132. Ibid., 228.

133. For the trouble in Basutoland caused by an independent "missionary free-lance," who described himself as "half Salvation Army . . . and half Dowieite," see "Editorials," *MRW* 18 (n.s.) (November 1905): 858-59.

134. See Edvard P. Torjesen, *Fredrik Franson: A Model for Worldwide Evangelism* (Pasadena, Calif.: William Carey Library, 1983).

135. J. Hudson Taylor, "Sermon," in *Records of the General Conference of the Protestant Missionaries of China. Held at Shanghai, May 7-20, 1890* (Shanghai: American Presbyterian Mission Press, 1890), 9.

136. George M. Stephenson, *The Religious Aspects of Swedish Immigration: A Study of Immigrant Churches* (Minneapolis: University of Minnesota Press, 1932), 126; Austin, *China's Millions*, 319-20.

4. THE SHORTCUT TO LANGUAGE PREPARATION

1. John Wesley, *Explanatory Notes upon the New Testament* (London: Epworth, 1966; originally published in 1754), 396.

2. David Greene, "The Gift of Tongues," *CQ* 9 (January 1865): 123.

3. Orson Pratt, quoted in Lee Copeland, "Speaking in Tongues in the Restoration Churches," *DJMT* 24 (Spring 1991): 22.

4. J. M. Thoburn, *Missionary Addresses* (Cincinnati: Cranston & Curts, 1894), 179.

5. [Herbert] Goodenough, "Babel at Johannesburg," *MRW* 13 (n.s.) (January 1900): 78.

6. Reprinted from *The Christian* as "The Gift of Tongues for Missionary Service" in *IMN*, April 1, 1891, 58. This article came on the heels of the debate discussed in the pages below. It would have been published sometime between January 1890 and March 1891, before it was reprinted in *IMN*. Unfortunately, issues of *The Christian* for the years 1890-1893 were unavailable.

7. Ibid., 59. At a time when aids for language study were limited and few missionary language schools existed, the means of attaining such preparation received increasing attention. For example, see J. C. R. Ewing, "The Intellectual and Practical Preparation of the Volunteer," *The Student Missionary Appeal: Addresses at the Third International Convention of the Student Volunteer Movement for Foreign Missions Held at Cleveland, Ohio, February 23-27, 1898* (New York: Student Volunteer Movement for Foreign Missions, 1898), 70-71.

8. Mrs. J. N. (Ellen) Cushing, quoted in *Student Mission Power: Report of the First International Convention of the Student Volunteer Movement for Foreign Missions, Held at Cleveland, Ohio, U.S.A., February 26, 27, 28 and March 1, 1891*, 157 (reprinted by William Carey Library, Pasadena, Calif., n.d.).

9. A. T. Pierson, *The New Acts of the Apostles* (New York: Baker and Taylor, 1894), 382. Pierson wrote: "In the Acts of the Apostles, two great aids were granted to the witnessing Church: first, the gift of *tongues*, which fitted the heralds to reach strange peoples without the slow mastery of a foreign speech; and, secondly, the gift of *healing*, which made even opponents favourably disposed toward the herald who first brought such help to the body. In a natural way, the lack of these supernatural gifts is now compensated. Christian scholarship has so far outrun the best learning and training of those earlier days, that grammars and dictionaries of all the leading languages and dialects can be supplied to the student. . . . Within the hundred years past, at least one hundred tongues that had before no literature, not even an alphabet, have by missionaries been reduced to writing. And the Word of God, in over three hundred dialects, now, like a perpetual Pentecost, speaks to the nations, so that each man may in his own tongue read the wonderful works of God. This reduction of the world's languages to a written form, to a scientific form, is God's modern gift of tongues" (Pierson's emphasis).

10. Edward A. Lawrence, *Modern Missions in the East: Their Methods, Successes, and Limitations* (New York: Harper & Brothers, 1895), 147; see also "Letter from Mr. Rugh," *Newark Daily Advocate* (Ohio), March 17, 1904, 8.

11. See A. J. Gordon, "Pre-Millennialism and Missions," *Watch*, April 1886, 30-35; cf. Pierson, *New Acts*, 298-99.

12. As in the case of Jonathan Goforth, see Rosalind Goforth, *Goforth of China* (Minneapolis: Bethany Fellowship, n.d.; originally published in 1937), 87-88.

13. Conyers Middleton, *A Free Inquiry into the Miraculous Powers, Which Are Supposed to Have Subsisted in the Christian Church, From the Earliest Ages through Several Successive Centuries* (London: R. Manby and H. S. Cox, 1749), xx-xxii, 121-22; William Dodwell, *Free Answer to Dr. Middleton's Free Inquiry Into the Miraculous Powers of the Primitive Church*, 2d ed. (London: S. Birt, 1749), 88-92. For a Catholic response to Middleton, see John Milner, *The End of Religious Controversy in a Friendly Correspondence Between a Religious Society of Protestants, and a Roman Catholic Divine* (New York: D. & J. Sadlier, 1818), 156-76. For a valuable study on the gift of tongues in Christian history, see George H. Williams and Edith Waldvogel, "A History of Speaking in Tongues and Related Gifts," in *The Charismatic Movement*, ed. Michael P. Hamilton (Grand Rapids: Eerdmans, 1975), 61-113.

14. T. W. M. Marshall, *Christian Missions: Their Agents, and Their Results* (New York: D. & J. Sadlier, 1865), 1: 211; cf. James Brodrick, *Saint Francis Xavier (1506-1552)*

(New York: Wicklow, 1952), 132. Pentecostal writers included Charles F. Parham, *A Voice Crying in the Wilderness*, 2d ed. (Baxter Springs, Kans.: Apostolic Faith Bible College, 1910; originally published in 1902), 29; B. F. Lawrence, *The Apostolic Faith Restored* (St. Louis: Gospel Publishing House, 1916), 34; Stanley H. Frodsham, *With Signs Following: The Story of the Latter Day Pentecostal Revival* (Springfield, Mo.: Gospel Publishing House, 1926), 231; Carl Brumback, *What Meaneth This? A Pentecostal Answer to a Pentecostal Question* (Springfield: Gospel Publishing House, 1947), 92; Vessie D. Hargrave, "Glossolalia: Reformation to the Twentieth Century," in *The Glossolalia Phenomenon*, ed. Wade H. Horton (Cleveland, Tenn.: Pathway, 1966), 92; Paul H. Walker, *The Baptism with the Holy Ghost and the Evidence* (Cleveland, Tenn.: Church of God Publishing House, ca. 1935), 34. Walker qualifies his reference to the Roman Catholic Francis Xavier by describing him as "a truly converted man and was a most remarkable missionary."

15. John Ryland, quoted in S. Pierce Carey, *William Carey, D.D., Fellow of Linnaean Society* (New York: George H. Doran, 1923), 50.

16. David W. Dorries, "West of Scotland Revival," *New International Dictionary of Pentecostal and Charismatic Movements*, ed. Stanley M. Burgess and Eduard Van Der Maas, rev. and exp. ed. (Grand Rapids: Zondervan, 2002).

17. Cited from a letter of Mary Campbell in Robert Herbert Story, *Memoir of the Life of the Rev. Robert Story* (London: Macmillan, 1862), 202; see also Timothy C. F. Stunt, *From Awakening to Secession: Radical Evangelicals in Switzerland and Britain, 1815-35* (Edinburgh: T&T Clark, 2000), 230-35.

18. D. L. Leonard, quoted in "The Religious World," *Daily Gazette* (Colorado Springs), October 12, 1884, 2. Leonard is remembered for his *Missionary Annals of the Nineteenth Century* (Cleveland: F. M. Barton, 1899), and *A Hundred Years of Missions: The Story of Progress since Carey's Beginning* (New York: Funk & Wagnalls, 1903).

19. Titus Coan, *Life in Hawaii: An Autobiographical Sketch* (New York: Anson D. F. Randolph, 1882), 101-2.

20. Copeland, "Speaking in Tongues," 22; for an example of "singing in tongues," see "Mormon Conference in Ohio," *Helena Independent* (Mont.), April 13, 1883, 1; on Brigham Young receiving the gift of tongues, see George Q. Cannon, "The Dead Prophet," *Defiance Democrat* (Ohio), September 13, 1877, 1; on Mormon beliefs, "The Mormon Church," *Stevens Point Gazette* (Wis.), April 28, 1888, 9; in an obituary on Mrs. Zina D. Young, favorite wife of Brigham Young, who had received the gift of tongues and interpretation during a vision, see "Gone to Be a Celestial Bride," *Grand Rapids Tribune* (Wis.), October 19, 1901, 3.

21. On the Highways and Hedges Mission, see Miss C. M. Reade, "Punrúti Mission," *The Missionary Conference: South India and Ceylon, 1879* (Madras: Addison, 1880), 421-23. The Highways and Hedges Mission, founded by Reade's father, had close ties to the Christian Brethren.

22. "A Gift of Tongues," *NZCR*, April 14, 1881, 11. North American Pentecostal writers seem to have been unaware of the story, probably because of its publication in New Zealand. J. E. Worsfold of the Apostolic Church of New Zealand refers to it in his *History of the Charismatic Movements in New Zealand* (Bradford, Yorks, England: Julian Literature Trust, 1974), 82.

23. A. J. Gordon, *The Ministry of Healing: Miracles of Cure in All Ages* (Harrisburg, Pa.: Christian Publications, 1881), 22; cf. George W. Dollar, "Church History and the Tongues Movement," *BS,* 120 (October-December, 1963): 316-21.

24. Gordon, *Ministry of Healing*, 55.

25. Ibid., 22.

26. Marvin R. Vincent, "Modern Miracles," *PR* 15 (July 1883): 484-85 (Vincent's emphasis).

27. J. Hudson Taylor, quoted in A. J. Broomhall, *Hudson Taylor and China's Open Century*, Book 6 (London: Hodder & Stoughton, 1988), 375-76.

28. C. T. Studd, "Trumpet Calls to Britain's Sons," in *The Evangelisation of the World, a Missionary Band: A Record of Consecration, and an Appeal*, 3rd ed., ed. B. Broomhall (London: Morgan & Scott, 1889), 53.

29. Ella J. Newton, quoted in *Student Mission Power*, 157.

30. "M.," "Can Pentecost be Regained?" *TC*, November 23, 1888, 1086-87; for an important editorial explanation, see "Notes and Comments," *TC*, November 30, 1888, 1107, col. 2.

31. E. F. Baldwin, a Southern Baptist minister from North Carolina, and his wife and eleven children went to North Africa in 1884 under the auspices of the (English) Kabyle Mission after his application to the Board of Foreign Missions had been turned down and his appeal had failed before the Southern Baptist Convention meeting in Baltimore earlier in the year. The Convention stated: "We regret that neither our Board or that of the Missionary Union could see its way clear to undertake just now a mission to the Kabyles"; quoted in Willy Normann Heggoy, "Fifty Years of Evangelical Missionary Movement in North Africa, 1881-1931" (Ph.D. diss., Hartford Seminary Foundation, 1960), 70-71. For more information, see E. F. Baldwin, "My Call to Foreign Mission Work, My Journey, My Support," *TGAL*, April 1885, 160, 162-64; idem, "Evangelization of North Africa," *TGAL*, April 1885, 155, 157-60; idem, "The Jews of Morocco," *MRW* 1 (n.s.) (September 1888): 692-93.

32. "A Missionary" [E. F. Baldwin], "The Question of the Hour—Foreign Missions," *TC*, January 11, 1889, 26.

33. "A Missionary" [E. F. Baldwin], "The Question of the Hour—Foreign Missions," *TC*, January 4, 1889, 12-13; "A Missionary" [E. F. Baldwin], "The Question of the Hour—Foreign Missions," *TC*, February 8, 1889, 10-11.

34. In an editorial, Pierson stated, "Without giving our endorsement to every sentiment of Mr. Baldwin in those letters, we confess to a large measure of sympathy with his general position"; "Editorial Notes on Current Topics," *MRW* 4 (n.s.) (January 1891): 71; see also A. T. Pierson, untitled note, *MRW* 2 (n.s.) (July 1889): 548. For a reference to Murray's "warm appreciation" of the articles, see "Editorial Note," *TC*, July 26, 1889, 664.

35. James L. Maxwell, M.D., "Modern Medical Missions: In Reply to 'A Missionary,'" *TC*, March 1, 1889, 177.

36. Ibid.

37. Mrs. H. Grattan (Fanny) Guinness, "Missionaries According to Matt. X," *RB*, September and October 1889, 283. Baldwin also defended the disputed longer ending of Mark in "The Question of the Hour—Foreign Missions," *TC*, February 15, 1889, 132.

38. Klaus Fiedler, *The Story of Faith Missions: From Hudson Taylor to Present Day Africa* (Oxford: Regnum Books International, 1994), 34-40, 43.

39. Stock noted, "In 1889, a series of articles appeared in *The Christian*, which turned out to be in the main a reproduction of Irving's sermon [to the London Missionary Society]. They had a similar effect on many minds, for a time." Eugene Stock, *History of the Church Missionary Society* (London: Church Missionary Society, 1899-1916), 1: 282n; idem, "Foreign Missions in the New Testament," *CMIR* 14 (n.s.) (May 1889): 296-305. Stock also wrote a series of articles in *The Christian* in response to Baldwin, beginning with the article "The Question of the Hour—Foreign Missions," April 5, 1889, 290-91.

40. Guinness, "Missionaries According to Matt. X," September and October 1889, *RB*, 280.

41. Mrs. H. Grattan (Fanny) Guinness, "Missionaries According to Matt. X," *RB*, April 1889, 111 (Guinness's emphasis).

42. Philip Schaff, *History of the Christian Church*, vol. 1: *Apostolic Christianity*, 3rd ed. (New York: Charles Scribner's Sons, 1889), 1: 237 (Schaff's emphasis).

43. Robert Needham Cust, *Essay on the Prevailing Methods of the Evangelization of the Non-Christian World* (London: Luzac, 1894), 107. For a recent discussion on the Kansas-Sudan movement, see Dana L. Robert, *Occupy until I Come: A. T. Pierson and the Evangelization of the World* (Grand Rapids: Eerdmans, 2003), 178-81.

44. News note, *BGBA*, September 6, 1890, 3-4. See also J. M. S., "The Soudan Missionary Movement," *MRW* 3 (n.s.) (July 1890): 555; "Missions," *CAMW*, August 15, 1890, 92-93.

45. F. F. Ellinwood, "The Faith Element in Missions," *MRW* 3 (n.s.) (December 1890): 944-49.

46. True not only in mission periodicals, but also in the coverage of New York City and Kansas newspapers. For example, in the reprinting of an article from the *New York Sun* (August 17, 1890) in the *Topeka Daily Capital* (August 20, 1890), the new title reads: "A Sad History: The Experiences of Our Topeka Missionaries."

47. Cust, *Essay on the Prevailing Methods*, 197 (Cust's emphasis).

48. For his rebuttal to the charge, see A. B. Simpson, "Editorial," *CMAW*, November 7, 1890, 274-275.

49. Mrs. H. Grattan (Fanny) Guinness, "Faith-Healing and Missions," *RB*, January 1891, 32.

50. Ibid., 31. Guinness does not cite the source for Simpson's statement, but a similar remark appears in his book *The Gospel of Healing*, rev. ed. (Harrisburg, Pa.: Christian Publications, 1915; first published in 1885), 57. Simpson may have had in mind the story of Miss C. M. Reade. The "young enthusiast" might have been C. T. Studd since the Guinnesses had close ties to J. Hudson Taylor and the China Inland Mission.

51. Simpson, *Gospel of Healing*, 57.

52. A. B. Simpson, "The Gift of Tongues," *CAMW*, February 12, 1892, 98.

53. W. W. Simpson, "Letter from Shanghai, China," *CAMW*, July 1, 1892, 13-14; idem, "A Seeker in the Border of Thibet in China," *CWPI*, July 1910, 21-23. They also appealed to Mark 13:11: "Whenever you are arrested and brought to trial, do not worry beforehand about what to say. Just say whatever is given you at the time, for it is not you speaking, but the Holy Spirit."

54. A. B. Simpson, "Connection between Supernatural Gifts and the World's Evangelization," *CAMW*, October 7 and 14, 1892, 227.

55. Ibid.

56. Ibid. Simpson then noted, "Even in the early church an interpreter was frequently required . . . when the gift of tongues was exercised."

57. A. B. Simpson, "The New Testament Standpoint of Missions," *CAMW*, December 16, 1892, 389.

58. A. B. Simpson, "The Worship and Fellowship of the Church," *CAFMW*, February 9, 1898, 126; also idem, "The Supernatural Gifts and Ministries of the Church," *CAFMW*, January 19, 1898, 53-54, 67.

59. "Tarry Until," *TFire*, March 1, 1897, 38.

60. Division of Health of Missouri, "Standard Certificate of Death" (Jennie Glassey), September 12, 1952.

61. Gregory A. Boyd, *Family Maps of Crawford County, Missouri* (Norman, Okla.: Arphax, 2006), 100-105.

62. "Evangelist Stewart on Trial," *Daily Northwestern* (Oshkosh, Wis.), October 12, 1893, 1.

63. "Cured by Miracles," *Chicago Daily*, November 22, 1893, 3; "Rev. J. G. Stewart, a Presbyterian Preacher, Shut Out," *Decatur Weekly Republican* (Decatur, Ill.), October 19, 1893, 2.

64. Ibid.

65. A. B. Simpson, "Editorials," *CAFMW*, November 23, 1894, 482-83.

66. Though on this occasion Merritt preached on the Fourfold Gospel, Simpson had coined the term in 1890; see Charles W. Nienkirchen, *A. B. Simpson and the Pentecostal Movement* (Peabody, Mass.: Hendrickson, 1992), 2.

67. "Christian Alliance Convention," *Colorado Springs Gazette*, November 16, 1894, 5.

68. *Historical Encyclopedia of Illinois and History of Warren County*, vol. 2, Part 2: City of Monmouth, 775. According to this source, "The First Full Bible Church was organized November 22, 1896, by Rev. J. G. Stewart, its distinctive doctrine being that of divine healing. There are twenty-six members, and H. Herbert was chosen clerk. Rev. J. G. Stewart is pastor. The church has no regular meeting place." However, a news article mentions the existence of the church a year earlier: "The Power of Faith," *Daily Republican* (Decatur, Ill.), August 16, 1895, 1.

69. Edward Watson Kirkconnell, ed., *The Acadia Record (1838-1953)*, rev. ed. (Wolfville, N.S.: Acadia University, 1953), 34.

70. "Faith-Healers' Camp-Meeting," *St. Louis Post-Dispatch*, August 15, 1895, 2; reprinted using the byline as "Miss Glassey's Great Gift," *Crawford Weekly Mirror* (Crawford County, Mo.), August 22, 1895, 1.

71. "Mission Work," *Amherst Daily News* (Amherst, N.S.), December 9, 1895, 1.

72. Ibid. I have not been able to identify the "Khoominar" language.

73. "Tarry Until," 38; also "Mission Work," 1.

74. "Faith-Healers' Camp Meeting," 2; cf. "The Passing Show," *St. Louis Post-Dispatch*, August 18, 1895, 4.

75. "Miss Glassey's Claim," *St. Louis Post-Dispatch*, August 17, 1895, 2.

76. "Power of Faith," 1.

77. "Emanate from the Devil: Reasons Why W. E. [*sic*] Black was Removed from His Pastorate," *St. Louis Post-Dispatch*, August 21, 1895, 1.

78. "Mission Work," 1.

79. W. S. Black, "Apostolic," *TFire*, March 15, 1897, 46.

80. From a news item published in the *St. John (N.B.) Daily Sun*, December 30, 1895, reprinted in "Tongues of Fire. Other Tongues," *TFire*, April 15, 1896, 59.

81. For example, "Chicago Girl Talks Chinese under Spells," *Gazette and Bulletin* (Williamsport, Pa.), May 7, 1908, 4.

82. Frances F. Black, "God Also Bearing Them Witness," *TFire*, June 15, 1897, 98.

83. Black, "Apostolic," 46.

84. Untitled letter, *Crawford County Telephone* (Crawford County, Mo.), April 2, 1897, 1.

85. M. Jennie Glassey, "Going on Still," *TFire*, April 1, 1897, 54.

86. Black, "God Also Bearing Them Witness," 97-98.

87. Letter from Walter S. Black to Frank W. Sandford, quoted in "Commit Thy Way," *TFire*, June 15, 1898, 93. Sandford's associate Willard Gleason reported hearing Glassey "sing a part of the ninth Psalm in an African tongue," after meeting her in England. In addition, "Sister Glassey has at different times spoken while in the Spirit, in Greek,

French, Latin, German, Hebrew, Italian, Japanese, Chinese . . . [and] has written many letters of the Greek and Hebrew alphabet." See Willard Gleason, "Notes from My Journal While En Route for The City of The Great King," *TFire*, July 15, 1898, 107. The quotation comes from his entry for May 31, 1898.

88. "Tongues of Fire. Other Tongues," 58-59.

89. Frank W. Sandford in "Tarry Until," 38.

90. Shirley Nelson, *Fair, Clear and Terrible: The Story of Shiloh* (Latham, N.Y.: British American Publishing, 1989), 101-5. Frank S. Murray suggests that the Blacks and Glassey visited Shiloh on their way from St. Louis to Amherst, Nova Scotia, in *The Sublimity of Faith: The Life and Work of Frank W. Sandford* (Amherst, N.H.: Kingdom, 1981), 180. While this may have happened, the correspondence with the Blacks and Glassey, which Sandford published, indicates they were not personally acquainted; for example, see "Tongues of Fire. Other Tongues," 58.

91. Sandford returned to the United States in August 1898. The tenure of the Blacks in Palestine possibly lasted until 1904. In that year, Walter Black once more began pastoring Baptist churches: Moscow and Black Foot, Idaho; Innisfall, Alberta; New Westminster, British Columbia; Redlands, Calif.; and Calgary, Alberta. His last pastorate was a small mission in Los Angeles, Calif., where he died in 1929. "Deaths," *Los Angeles Times*, May 7, 1929, 24. There is no available evidence to suggest that the Blacks or Glassey ever identified with the Pentecostal movement. The funeral for Jennie Glassey was held in the Methodist Church in Cuba, Mo.

92. "Jennie Glassey Passed Away," *Crawford Mirror* (Crawford County, Mo.), September 4, 1952, 1.

93. "Annual Report of the Palestine Mission of the Christian and Missionary Alliance, 1912," *AW*, May 3, 1913, 72. See also "Annual Report," *AW*, July 20, 1912, 248; Mabel E. Best, "Fifteenth Annual Conference of the Christian and Missionary Alliance in Jerusalem," *AW*, March 8, 1913, 360. Glassey and Anna Gummoe pioneered the Alliance mission in Beersheba; see *The Sixteenth Annual Report, 1912-1913*, 14. Her return to America in 1912 or 1913 explains why her name does not appear in Alliance publications after 1913. For a brief account of the Palestine Mission, see G. P. Pardington, *Twenty-five Wonderful Years, 1889-1914* (New York: Christian Alliance, 1914), 108-11.

94. See also William C. Hiss, "Shiloh: Frank W. Sandford and the Kingdom: 1893-1948" (Ph.D. diss., Tufts University, 1978), 101-4, 158-63.

95. "Morning Lessons in the Classroom at the Bible School," *TFire*, February 1, 1899, 38 (Sandford's emphasis). The relationship of Sandford and Shiloh to Pentecostalism is discussed in Shirley and Rudy Nelson, "Frank Sandford: Tongues of Fire in Shiloh, Maine," in *Portraits of a Generation: Early Pentecostal Leaders*, ed. James R. Goff, Jr. and Grant Wacker (Fayetteville: University of Arkansas Press, 2002), 68-69. See also Murray, *Sublimity of Faith*, 927 n. 14; 932 n. 31.

96. "Exodus of the Seventy from Shiloh's Temple," *Lewiston Evening Journal* (Maine), January 6, 1900, 2-3.

97. "Seventy Start," *Bangor Daily Whig and Courier*, January 8, 1900, 3. The reports in Sandford's *Tongues of Fire* primarily highlight the journey of the Sandford party by rail; see Frank W. Sandford, "From the Atlantic to the Pacific," *TFire*, July 1 and 15, 1900, 109-12; idem, "Off for the Great Northwest," *TFire*, August 1, 1900, 125-28.

98. For other connections to Shiloh, see Harold D. Hunter, "Beniah at the Apostolic Crossroads: Little Noticed Crosscurrents of B. H. Irwin, Charles Fox Parham, Frank Sandford, A. J. Tomlinson," *CPCR* (1997), http://www.pctii.org/cyberj/cyberj1/hunter.html.

99. Charles F. Parham, *A Voice Crying in the Wilderness*, 2d ed. (Baxter Springs, Kans.: Apostolic Faith Bible College, 1910; originally published in 1902), 19.

100. Charles F. Parham, *The Everlasting Gospel* (Baxter Springs, Kans.: Apostolic Faith Bible College, n.d.), 7.

101. Charles F. Parham, "The Gift of Tongues," *AF* (Topeka), May 3, 1899, 5. Parham's source was an article in *EG*, published in St. Louis, Mo., by H. W. Peffley. Thus, he may not have read the letters published by Sandford in *Tongues of Fire*.

102. News note, *AF* (Topeka), April 1, 1900, 7, col. 2.

103. James R. Goff, Jr., *Fields White unto Harvest: Charles F. Parham and the Missionary Origins of Pentecostalism* (Fayetteville: University of Arkansas Press, 1988), 73.

104. Parham, *A Voice Crying in the Wilderness*, 29-30.

105. On the rail line eastward, the party stopped in Chicago, Cleveland, and New York City. This enabled Parham to visit the holiness and healing centers of John Alexander Dowie, J. Walter Malone, and A. B. Simpson, respectively. See Goff, *Fields White unto Harvest*, 59-60, 195 n. 81.

106. Frank W. Sandford, "From the Atlantic to the Pacific," *TFire*, July 1 and 15, 1900, 111.

107. F. W. Sandford, "The Church," *TFire*, April 1, 1898, 51-56.

108. Charles F. Parham, "The Unity of the Body," *TFire*, July 1 and 15, 1900, 122.

109. For the list of external centers in 1902, see "Various Centers for This Movement," *EG*, December 13-January 1, 1902, 319. Topeka is not included.

110. C. W. Shumway, "A Critical Study of 'The Gift of Tongues'" (A.B. thesis, University of Southern California, 1914), 165. Information based on Shumway's interview of Parham.

111. Goff, *Fields White unto Harvest*, 59-61.

112. Nelson, "Frank Sandford," 68.

113. "Prays for Aid and Gets It," *Nebraska State Journal*, November 7, 1900, 7. The article was originally published in the *Kansas City Star*.

114. Murray, *Sublimity*, 927 n. 14; "Prays for Aid," 7.

115. Parham, *Voice Crying in the Wilderness*, 31.

116. Ibid., 62. The imagery of the "concentration camp" came from the recent brutal incarceration of Afrikaaner women and children by British forces in South Africa during the Second Boer War (1899-1902).

117. Charles Nienkirchen discusses the historical vision of early Pentecostals in "Conflicting Visions of the Past: Prophetic Use of History in the Early American Pentecostal-Charismatic Movements," in *Charismatic Christianity as a Global Culture*, ed. Karla Poewe (Columbia: University of South Carolina Press, 1994), 119-33.

118. Goff, *Fields White unto Harvest*, 78.

119. Parham, quoted in "Story of His Belief. Rev. Charles Parham Tells How He Learned His Religion," *Kansas City Times*, February 4, 1901; reprinted in *The Topeka Outpouring of 1901*, rev. ed., ed. Larry E. Martin (Joplin, Mo.: Christian Life Books, 2000), 252.

120. Parham, *Voice Crying in the Wilderness*, 13.

5. DIVERGING CURRENTS OF THE SPIRIT'S WORK

1. "Development of Christian Life and Character," *Report of the Fourth Decennial Indian Missionary Conference, Held in Madras, December 11th-18th 1902* (London: Christian Literature Society, 1903), 23.

2. Robert A. Hume, "Some Hindrances to the Spirit's Work," *CCW*, March 4, 1905, 285.

3. Untitled news note, *AF* (L.A.), November 1906, 2, col. 4.

4. "The Superhuman Factor in Carrying the Gospel to All the Non-Christian World," in *Report of Commission I: Carrying the Gospel to All the Non-Christian World, World Missionary Conference, 1910* (Edinburgh: Oliphant, Anderson & Ferrier, 1910), 351.

5. Kenneth Scott Latourette, *A History of the Expansion of Christianity*, vol. 4, *The Great Century: Europe and the United States* (Grand Rapids: Zondervan, 1970), 80; Sherwood Eddy, *Pathfinders of the World Missionary Crusade* (New York: Abingdon-Cokesbury, 1945), 37-40.

6. Edward Warren Capen, "The Significance of the Haystack Centennial," *BS* 63 (October 1906): 703-23; also *The One Hundredth Anniversary of the Haystack Prayer Meeting, Celebrated at the Ninety-Second Annual Meeting of the American Board in North Adams and by the Haystack Centennial Meetings in Williamstown, Mass., October 9-12, 1906* (Boston: American Board of Commissioners for Foreign Missions, 1907).

7. Rufus Anderson, quoted in Clifton Jackson Phillips, *Protestant America and the Pagan World: The First Half Century of the American Board of Commissioners for Foreign Missions, 1810-1860* (Cambridge, Mass.: East Asian Research Center, Harvard University, 1969), 319 (Anderson's emphasis).

8. Howard A. Bridgman, "The Haystack Centennial—A Memorial and a Prophecy," *MRW* 19 (n.s.) (December 1906): 889-890.

9. S. H. Littell, "The Haystack Centennial," *LT*, December 1906, 742.

10. Bridgman, "Haystack Centennial," 894.

11. James L. Barton, *The Missionary and His Critics* (New York: Fleming H. Revell, 1906). The Student Volunteer Movement published a book with a similar purpose: J. Lovell Murray, *The Apologetic of Modern Missions* (New York: Student Volunteer Movement, 1909).

12. John von Rohr, *The Shaping of American Congregationalism, 1620-1957* (Cleveland: Pilgrim, 1992), 372-76.

13. William R. Hutchison, *Errand to the World: American Protestant Thought and Foreign Missions* (Chicago: University of Chicago Press, 1987), 102-5. Note the following editorials by A. T. Pierson: "Missions and Rationalistic Criticism," *MRW* 23 (n.s.) (November 1910): 816-19; "Liberal Christianity and Missionary Zeal," *MRW* 23 (n.s.) (December 1910): 10.

14. On the financial woes of the American Board, see Valentin H. Rabe, *The Home Base of American China Missions, 1880-1920* (Cambridge, Mass.: Harvard University Press, 1978), 113-14, 137-40.

15. "Backward Steps," *MRW* 19 (n.s.) (May 1906): 323.

16. "God's Revival Fires," *MRW* 19 (n.s.) (May 1906): 322-23.

17. James Alan Patterson, "The Loss of a Protestant Missionary Consensus: Foreign Missions and the Fundamentalist-Modernist Controversy," in *Earthen Vessels: American Evangelicals and Foreign Missions, 1880-1980*, ed. Joel A. Carpenter and Wilbert R. Shenk (Grand Rapids: Eerdmans, 1990), 73-91; also George M. Marsden, *Fundamentalism and American Culture: The Shaping of Twentieth-Century Evangelicalism: 1870-1925* (New York: Oxford University Press, 1980), 164-70.

18. See James C. Juhnke, *A People of Mission: A History of General Conference Mennonite Overseas Missions* (Newton, Kans.: Faith and Life Press, 1979); Edmund George Kaufman, *The Development of the Missionary and Philanthropic Interest among the Mennonites of North America* (Berne, Ind.: Mennonite Book Concern, 1931).

19. Jessie Penn-Lewis, with Evan Roberts, *War on the Saints* (New York: T. E. Lowe,

1973), 52-53; Alma White, *Demons and Tongues* (Bound Brook, N.J.: Pentecostal Union, 1910), 33-47; W. B. Godbey, *Tongue Movement, Satanic* (Zarephath, N.J.: Pillar of Fire, 1918); cf. E. Beyerhaus, "A Demon-Attack on 'Pentecost,'" *Conf*, February 1912, 38-39.

20. Kathryn Teresa Long, *The Revival of 1857-58: Interpreting an American Religious Awakening* (New York: Oxford University Press, 1998), 127-36.

21. Amy Wilson-Carmichael, "Need We Tell God How to Work?" *MRW* 20 (n.s.) (January 1907): 50.

22. W. Warren, "The Genesis of the Australian Revival," *MRW* 16 (n.s.) (March 1903): 203; R. A. Torrey, "The Story of Australia's Revival," *Fort Wayne Sentinel* (Ind.), December 5, 1903, 14.

23. Warren, "Genesis of the Australian Revival," 201.

24. E. C. Millard, *What God Hath Wrought: An Account of the Mission Tour of the Rev. G. C. Grubb, M.A. (1889-1890)* (London: E. Marlborough, 1891), 169-87.

25. Helen S. Dyer, *Pandita Ramabai: Her Vision, Her Mission and Triumph of Faith* (London: Pickering & Inglis, 1923), 99.

26. Dana L. Robert, *Occupy until I Come: A. T. Pierson and the Evangelization of the World* (Grand Rapids: Eerdmans, 2003), 259.

27. A. T. Pierson, "The Welsh Pentecost and God's Signals," *MRW* 18 (n.s.) (March 1905): 166.

28. Editorial item from *London Methodist Times,* cited in S. B. Shaw, *The Great Revival in Wales* (Chicago: S. B. Shaw, 1905), 74; "Welshmen in Frenzy," *Washington Post*, December 2, 1904, 12.

29. See Edward J. Gitre, "The 1904-05 Welsh Revival: Modernization, Technologies, and Techniques of the Self," *CH* 73 (December 2004): 792-827.

30. Shaw, *Great Revival in Wales*, 49-51; A. T. Fryer, "The Revival in Wales," *TEW* 3 (April 1905): 174-87.

31. Pierson, "Welsh Pentecost," 163.

32. John Hughes Morris, *The History of the Welsh Calvinistic Methodists' Foreign Mission: To the End of 1904* (Delhi: Indus, 1996; originally published in 1910), 323-26.

33. A. T. Pierson, "The Voice of the Holy Spirit in the Welsh Revival," *MRW* 18 (n.s.) (October 1905): 728.

34. Ibid., 731.

35. "Echoes of the Welsh Revival," *MRW* 19 (n.s.) (July 1906): 482-83.

36. Helen S. Dyer, comp., *Revival in India* (New York: Gospel Publishing House, 1907), 87.

37. For example, "The Revival in the West," *CP*, March 18, 1905, 5. In January 1905, the Methodist Press in Madras (Chennai) published a booklet in English entitled *The Great Revival*, with translations in Tamil, Telugu, and (later) Kannada, languages of South India.

38. Dyer, *Revival in India*, 28-29.

39. Delavan A. Pierson, "The Syrian Christians in India," *RCW* 25 (March 1906): 169-70.

40. "The Revival in Assam," *BGBA*, April 29, 1905, 11-12.

41. J. Pengwern Jones, "The Revival in the Khassia Hills," *IW*, May 11, 1905, 291; idem, "The Revival in the Khassia Hills," *IW*, June 7, 1906, 358-59; T. Walker, "Present Religious Awakenings in the Church in India," *CMRev* 58 (May 1907): 280-90; J. Pengwern Jones, "The Revival in the Lushai Hills," *BMR* 12 (June 1906): 233-37; see also J. H. Lorrain, "Revival in Lushailand," *MH*, October 1907, 331-33.

42. Dyer, *Revival in India*, 81.

43. J. Pengwern Jones, "The Revival at Cherrapoonjee," *IW*, July 20, 1905, 459

(Jones's emphasis). He also remarked: "Perhaps we might understand better had we greater capacity for spiritual gifts in our own hearts. Clearly these plain hill-folk of Assam, but yesterday pagans and demon-worshipers, have attained an insight respecting Gospel truth, a hearty self-surrender, a perception of the love of Jesus Christ, which Christians everywhere would fain share. Let this marvelous movement among the Khasi people be an occasion for fervent prayer for them—and for our own selves" (Jones, quoted in "The Revival in Assam," *MRW* 18 [n.s.] [September 1905]: 714). For the thoughts of a Baptist missionary on the revival phenomena, see W. C. Owen, "The Atmakur Revival," *CML*, April 1906, 128.

44. J. Pengwern Jones, "This is That," *IW*, June 28, 1906, 404.

45. Walker, "Present Religious Awakenings," 283-88.

46. H. D. Buswell, "The Conditions of the Spirit's Indwelling," *CMI* 30 (n.s.) (June 1905): 410.

47. G. S. Eddy, "The Filling of the Spirit," *YMI* 18 (May 1907): 62.

48. Unnamed missionary, quoted in Dyer, *Revival in India*, 152-53.

49. "A Revival in Madagascar," *MRW* 18 (n.s.) (November 1905): 878; James Sibree, *Fifty Years in Madagascar: Personal Experiences of Mission Life and Work* (London: George Allen & Unwin, 1924), 172-74; Charles W. Forman, "A Study in the Self-Propagating Church: Madagascar," in *Frontiers of the Christian World Mission since 1938: Essays in Honor of Kenneth Scott Latourette*, ed. Wilber C. Harr (New York: Harper & Brothers, 1962), 115-70.

50. "The Revival in Burma," *MRW* 18 (n.s.) (December 1905): 953.

51. Myung Soo Park, "'The Korean Pentecost': A Study of the Great Revival of 1903-1910 in Relationship to Contemporary Worldwide Holiness Revival Movements," in *The Global Impact of the Wesleyan Traditions and Their Related Movements*, ed. Charles Yrigoyen, Jr. (Lanham, Md.: Scarecrow, 2002), 185-200.

52. Y. S. Lee, "A Remarkable Chinese Evangelist," *LT* 7 (June 1907): 336-45; Daniel H. Bays, "Christian Revival in China, 1900-1937," in *Modern Christian Revivals*, ed. Edith L. Blumhofer and Randall Balmer (Urbana: University of Illinois Press, 1993), 161-79. For Manchuria, see James Webster, *The Revival in Manchuria* (London: Morgan & Scott, 1910).

53. William N. Brewster, "The Recent Revivals in China," *MRW* 24 (n.s.) (February 1911): 87-90; "The Revival of 1910 in I-Chow-Fu," *MRW* 23 (n.s.) (June 1910): 403-4; also "Awakening in Shantung," *MRW* 19 (n.s.) (September 1906): 643.

54. "Signs of Revival in Borneo," *MRW* 19 (n.s.) (September 1906): 644-645.

55. "The Spirit's Power in Madagascar," *MRW* 19 (n.s.) (August 1906): 566. For insights on how revivalism creates opportunities for normally disenfranchised persons to engage in public ministry, see Klaus Fiedler, *The Story of Faith Missions: From Hudson Taylor to Present Day Africa* (Oxford: Regnum Books International, 1994), 112-21.

56. For example, in the ministry of the Methodist evangelist Lorenzo Dow, see Nathan O. Hatch, *The Democratization of American Christianity* (New Haven: Yale University Press, 1989), 36-40, 58.

57. On the revival in the Punjab and the annual Sialkot Convention, see Emma Dean Anderson and Mary Jane Campbell, *In the Shadow of the Himalayas: A Historical Narrative of the Missions of the United Presbyterian Church of North America as conducted in the Punjab, India, 1855-1940* (Philadelphia: United Presbyterian Board of Foreign Missions, 1942), 136-55, 198-204; also Emma Dean Anderson, "The Supernatural in India," *NA*, April 1907, 2.

58. William B. Anderson and Charles R. Watson, *Far North in India: A Survey of the Mission Field and Work of the United Presbyterian Church in the Punjab* (Philadelphia:

Board of Foreign Missions of the United Presbyterian Church of North America, 1909), 260.

59. Bernice C. Lee, "Pentecost among the Presbyterians in India," *LRE*, July 1924, 6-8; Alfred A. Blakeney, "A Pentecostal Interdenominational Convention," *FGMH*, July 1925, 10-11; Frederick and Margaret Stock, *People Movements in the Punjab: With Special Reference to the United Presbyterian Church* (South Pasadena, Calif.: William Carey Library, 1975), 197; Robert W. Cummings, *Unto You Is the Promise: A Personal Testimony* (Springfield, Mo.: Gospel Publishing House, n.d.); idem, "Golden Opportunity in West Pakistan," August 16, 1963; the latter source available at editorial office files, Assemblies of God World Missions, Springfield, MO 65802.

60. "An Appeal to Indian Christians by the Founders of the National Missionary Society" (1905), in *History of Christianity in India*, ed. M. K. Kuriakose (Madras: Christian Literature Society, 1982), 292-93.

61. Donald Fossett Ebright, "The National Missionary Society of India, 1905-1942" (Ph.D. diss., University of Chicago, 1944); cf. Frank W. Warne, *The Revival in the Indian Church* (New York: Board of Foreign Missions, Methodist Episcopal Church, 1907), 27-30; J. Edwin Orr, *Evangelical Awakenings in India in the Early Twentieth Century* (New Delhi: Christian Literature Institute, 1970), 145-58.

62. Martha Huntley, *Caring, Growing, Changing: A History of the Protestant Mission in Korea* (New York: Friendship, 1984), 131-39.

63. Arthur Fehlberg, "The Revival in India. A Critical View," *HF* 17 (April 1906): 147-48. In contrast, the pietistic missionaries of the Danish Lutheran Mission (Danish-Halle Mission) in Tirukoilur, Tamil Nadu recognized the benefits of the revival; see "The Revival in India," *BGBA*, September 16, 1905, 11-12.

64. The report on the revival at the American Board Mission at Ahmednegar, India in 1906 implies relief about the brevity of the event: "About a year ago there was a quiet but most real season of spiritual blessing and refreshment among the high school boys. . . . The praying went on for about fifteen minutes, and the increase in attention and spiritual power was most noticeable. . . . Then quietly we dispersed." *Ninety-Seventh Annual Report of the American Board of Commissioners for Foreign Missions, 1907*, 86-87.

65. Hutchison, *Errand to the World*, 104; Horace Bushnell, *Christian Nurture* (New York: Charles Scribner's Sons, 1916), 62-64.

66. William Newton Clarke, *A Study of Christian Missions* (New York: Charles Scribner's Sons, 1901), 72; cf. A. T. Pierson, "New Theology and Higher Criticism," *MRW* 23 (n.s.) (October 1910): 780.

67. Ibid., 230; also John Bascom, "The Supernatural," *BS* 59 (April 1902): 240.

68. Theodore T. Munger, "Why I Believe in Foreign Missions," *MRW* 18 (n.s.) (June 1905): 453-54; see also Grant Wacker, "Second Thoughts on the Great Commission: Liberal Protestants and Foreign Missions, 1890-1940," in *Earthen Vessels*, 281-300.

69. Patterson, "Loss of a Protestant Missionary Consensus," 85.

70. Robert A. Hume, *Missions from the Modern View* (New York: Fleming H. Revell, 1905), 38; idem, "Closing Addresses," *Report of the Fourth Decennial*, 210-11; idem, "The Indian Church: Its Future Mission," *MRW* 23 (n.s.) (April 1910): 290-94. Note his progressive position in "The Meaning of Salvation," *Dnya*, June 6, 1907, 2. Hume had been defended before the officers of the American Board by Theodore Munger; untitled news note, *New York Times*, November 4, 1887, 4.

71. H. G. B., "Christ and the World's Religious Life," *Dnya*, January 17, 1907, 2. For the tension such opinions created in mission circles, see E. N. Harris, "How Should We Preach to the Heathen?" *MRW* 15 (n.s.) (April 1902): 264-71.

72. For the impact of the modern outlook on selected missionaries, see Lian Xi, *The Conversion of Missionaries: Liberalism in American Protestant Missions in China, 1907-1932* (University Park: Pennsylvania State University Press, 1997).

73. William Croswell Doane, quoted in E. P. Sketchley, "The Bicentenary of the Society for the Propagation of the Gospel," *MRW* 14 (n.s.) (April 1901): 262.

74. R. Pierce Beaver, *Ecumenical Beginnings in Protestant World Mission: A History of Comity* (New York: Thomas Nelson & Sons, 1962), 42-80.

75. *China Centenary Missionary Conference Records: Report of the Great Conference Held at Shanghai, April 5th to May 8th, 1907* (New York: American Tract Society, 1907), 522. The emphasis appears in the text of the document.

76. The following news report by Harlan P. Beach reveals the broader currents at work in mission from revivals to the unification of mission churches in 1906: "The Great Missionary Events of 1906," *MRW* 20 (n.s.) (January 1907): 11-18.

77. "The Shanghai Statement," *MRW* 20 (n.s.) (September 1907): 703-4; for the resolution, see *China Centenary Mission Conference Records*, 719-21; for the follow-up conference in West China to the Shanghai Conference and its expressed concern for uniting the Protestant churches, see *West China Missionary Conference* (Chentu: Canadian Methodist Mission Press, 1908), 61-63.

78. Harlan P. Beach, "The Great Theme at Shanghai," *MRW* 20 (n.s.) (August 1907): 632; cf. Kevin Xiyi Yao, "At the Turn of the Century: A Study of the China Centenary Missionary Conference of 1907," *IBMR* 32 (April 2008): 65-68, 70. On later events in China, see idem, *The Fundamentalist Movement among Protestant Missionaries in China, 1920-1937* (Dallas: University Press of America, 2003).

79. Harlan Page Beach, *A Geography and Atlas of Protestant Missions: Their Environment, Forces, Distribution, Methods, Problems, Results and Prospects at the Opening of the Twentieth Century*, vol. 2: *Statistics and Atlas* (New York: Student Volunteer Movement for Foreign Missions, 1906), 19.

80. See Brian Stanley, "Twentieth-Century World Christianity: A Perspective from the History of Missions," in *Christianity Reborn: The Global Expansion of Evangelicalism in the Twentieth Century*, ed. Donald M. Lewis (Grand Rapids: Eerdmans, 2004), 52-83. Stanley discusses "The Prophetic View from Edinburgh, 1910."

81. *Report of Commission VIII: Co-operation and the Promotion of Unity* (Edinburgh: Oliphant, Anderson & Ferrier, 1910), 8.

82. Kenneth Scott Latourette, "Ecumenical Bearings of the Missionary Movement and the International Missionary Council," in *A History of the Ecumenical Movement: 1517-1948*, 2d ed., ed. Ruth Rouse and Stephen Charles Neill (Philadelphia: Westminster, 1967), 353-402; also Dana L. Robert, "The First Globalization: The Internationalization of the Protestant Missionary Movement Between the World Wars," *IBMR* 26 (April 2002): 50-66.

83. A. T. Pierson, "Signs of the Times," *MRW* 23 (n.s.) (August 1910): 561.

84. Ibid., 562.

85. Charles Brent, quoted in F. E. Marsh, "The World's Missionary Conference," *CMAW*, July 23, 1910, 1.

86. Pierson, "Signs of the Times," 561-62. For an overview of the conference, see Delavan Leonard Pierson, "The Edinburgh Missionary Conference," *MRW* 23 (n.s.) (September 1910): 645-64.

87. Roswell D. Hitchcock, "Romanism in the Light of History," in *History, Essays, Orations, and Other Documents of the Sixth General Conference of the Evangelical Alliance, Held in New York, October 2-12, 1873*, ed. Philip Schaff and S. Irenaeus Prime

(New York: Harper & Brothers, 1874), 436-37; cf. A. T. Pierson, "The Outlook: Some Signs of the Times," *MRW* 9 (n.s.) (January 1896): 3-6; idem, "Signs," 562; Fiedler, *Story of Faith Missions*, 128-29, 152 n. 44, 152 n. 45.

88. A representative opinion appears in H. Grattan Guinness, "Roman Catholic Missions," *RB*, December 1890, 447-56.

89. Val Gaudet, "A Woman and the Pope," in *The Spirit and the Church*, ed. Ralph Martin (New York: Paulist, 1976), 45, 47.

90. Gabriel Gonsum Ganaka, "Evangelization in the Church of Jos, Nigeria," in *Pope John Paul II and the New Evangelization*, ed. Ralph Martin and Peter Williamson (San Francisco: Ignatius Press, 1995), 101-10; George E. Griener, "Come, Holy Spirit! The Divine Spirit and Evangelization," in *The New Catholic Evangelization*, ed. Kenneth Boyack (New York: Paulist, 1992), 191-201; Tom Forrest, "Evangelization 2000: A Global View," in Boyack, *New Catholic Evangelization*, 214-27.

91. Charles Whitehead, "The Role of the Ecclesial Movements and New Communities in the Life of the Church," in *New Religious Movements in the Catholic Church*, ed. Michael A. Hayes (London: Burns & Oates, 2005), 15-29; also Joseph Ratzinger, *New Outpourings of the Spirit* (San Francisco: Ignatius Press, 2006), 19-61.

92. Jonathan Goforth, *By My Spirit* (Minneapolis: Bethany Fellowship, 1942), 137.

93. Ibid., 137-38.

94. "Superhuman Factor," 352.

95. F. E. Marsh, "Impressions from the World's Missionary Conference," *CMAW*, July 30, 1910, 282.

96. "Superhuman Factor," 354.

97. Ibid., 355; cf. Lin Shao-Yang, *A Chinese Appeal to Christendom Concerning Christian Missions* (New York: G. P. Putnam's Sons, 1911).

98. "Superhuman Factor," 359.

99. *Missionary Manual of General Council of the Assemblies of God* (Springfield, Mo.: Foreign Missions Department, ca. 1931), 7. Although the authorship remains unknown, it was published under the direction of Noel Perkin, Missionary Secretary of the Assemblies of God (1927-1959). The *Manual's* historical prologue, "History of the Pentecostal Movement," may represent the first such interpretation devoted solely to Pentecostal mission produced in North America.

100. Everett A. Wilson, "They Crossed the Red Sea, Didn't They? Critical History and Pentecostal Beginnings," in *The Globalization of Pentecostalism: A Religion Made to Travel*, ed. Murray W. Dempster, Byron D. Klaus, Douglas Petersen (Oxford: Regnum Books International, 1999), 108-10; Donald E. Miller and Tetsunao Yamamori, *Global Pentecostalism: The New Face of Christian Social Engagement* (Berkeley: University of California Press, 2007), 1-5.

101. Kilian McDonnell, "Holy Spirit and Pentecostalism," *Comm*, November 8, 1968, 198-204.

102. Robert Mapes Anderson, *Vision of the Disinherited: The Making of American Pentecostalism* (New York: Oxford University, 1979), 28-46.

103. In "The 'Haystack Meeting' a 'Failure,'" a writer in the *MRW* (13 [n.s.] [November 1900]: 896), commented: "How strange that of the men who, in 1806, gathered under the haystack near Williams College for prayer, and so brought the American Board and American missions into being, only one actually set his foot upon heathen soil, while his career was but brief and unnoteworthy."

104. "New Sect in Kansas Speaks with Strange Tongues," *St. Louis Post-Dispatch*, January 26, 1901; reprinted in *The Topeka Outpouring of 1901: 100th Anniversary Edition*, ed. Larry Martin (Joplin: Christian Life Books, 2000), 235.

105. "To Find the Ark," *Marion Daily Star* (Ohio), February 8, 1902, 2; "The Apostolic Faith," *Galveston Daily News*, November 20, 1905, 8; also W. R. Quinton, "Meeting in Alabama," *WW*, July 1908, 217; "Parnham [*sic*] Will Speak Tonight on Zionism," *San Antonio Gazette*, July 11, 1907, 7.

106. Untitled note, *AF* (L.A.), October-January 1908, 1, col. 4.

107. For example, after Parham announced a summer school in Topeka for seekers to receive tongues for missionary evangelism, the story went out from Topeka on a newspaper wire service across the country. Local editors added their own commentary as evident in "New Kind of Missionaries," *Hawaiian Gazette* (Honolulu), May 31, 1901, 10; "The Gift of Tongues," *Anaconda Standard* (Mont.), June 9, 1901, 20.

108. "All Night Session," *Galena Evening Times* (Kans.), January 1, 1904, 3; "Claim to Be 'Cured,'" *Galena Evening Times* (Kans.), January 4, 1904, 1. C. W. Harvey, editor of the *Galena Evening Times* (Kans.), refuted Parham's theology in three articles: "Faith Healing," November 20, 1903, 2; "Speaking with Tongues," December 7, 1903, 2; "The Romance of Doctrine," December 11, 1903, 2.

109. James R. Goff, Jr., *Fields White unto Harvest: Charles F. Parham and the Missionary Origins of Pentecostalism* (Fayetteville: University of Arkansas Press, 1988), 107-10.

110. "News from Houston," *Galveston Daily News* (Tex.), August 14, 1905, 5.

111. Frank Bartleman, *Azusa Street: The Roots of Modern-day Pentecost* (South Plainfield, N.J.: Bridge, 1980), 41-66; Cecil M. Robeck, Jr., *The Azusa Street Mission & Revival* (Nashville: Nelson Reference & Electronic, 2006), 53-86.

112. Goff, *Fields White unto Harvest*, 115.

113. Darrin J. Rodgers, *Northern Harvest: Pentecostalism in North Dakota* (Bismarck: North Dakota District Council of the Assemblies of God, 2003), 4-17.

114. Naemi Reinholdz, "A Plowwoman for God: Mary Johnson's Life and Work," transcription of an oral translation by Darrin Rodgers, 1999. I am indebted to Rodgers, Director of Flower Pentecostal Heritage Center in Springfield, Missouri, for sharing this information with me.

115. See P. B. Thompson, "A Pentecostal Outpouring of Thirty-four Years Ago," *PE*, November 27, 1937, 8.

116. *NIDPCM*, 2002 ed., s.v. "Hanson, Carl M.," by Darrin J. Rodgers.

117. "Claim to Have Gift of Tongues," *Galveston Daily News* (Tex.), April 9, 1905, 22; "Fined $35," *Fergus Falls Daily Journal* (Minn.), March 11, 1905, 3.

118. Rodgers, *Northern Harvest*, 16-17; "The Old Time Pentecost," *AF* (L.A.), September 1906, 1, col. 2.

119. Edith L. Blumhofer and Grant Wacker, "Who Edited the Azusa Mission's *Apostolic Faith?*" *AGH* 21 (Summer 2001): 15-21.

120. "Pentecost Has Come," *AF* (L.A.), September 1906, 1, col. 1.

121. B. Berntsen, "Came from China to America for Pentecost," *AF* (L.A.), January 8, 1908, 3, col. 4.

122. Mary Mason, comp., *The History and Life Work of Elder C. H. Mason, Chief Apostle, and His Co-Laborers* (n.p., 1924), 26-30.

123. Robeck, *Azusa Street Mission*, 228-34.

124. Edith L. Blumhofer, "William H. Durham: Years of Creativity, Years of Dissent," in *Portraits of a Generation: Early Pentecostal Leaders*, ed. James R. Goff, Jr., and Grant Wacker (Fayetteville: University of Arkansas Press, 2002), 123-42.

125. Doug Beacham, *Azusa East: The Life and Times of G. B. Cashwell* (Franklin Springs, Ga.: LifeSprings Resources, 2006), 45-55.

126. "Spanish Receive the Pentecost," *AF* (L.A.), October 1906, 4, col. 3; "From Los Angeles to Home and Foreign Fields," *AF* (L.A.), December 1906, 4, col. 1.

127. Thomas Ball Barratt, *When the Fire Fell and an Outline of My Life* (Oslo: n.p., 1927), 108-9.

128. Gary B. McGee, "'Latter Rain' Falling in the East: Early-Twentieth-Century Pentecostalism in India and the Debate over Speaking in Tongues," *CH* 68 (September 1999): 648-65.

129. A. B. Simpson, *Annual Report of the Christian and Missionary Alliance, 1907-1908*, 41, 140, 143; Charles W. Nienkirchen, *A. B. Simpson and the Pentecostal Movement* (Peabody, Mass.: Hendrickson, 1992), 73-100.

130. J. A. Spicer, "Strange Things Come from Zion," *Evening Tribune* (Marysville, Ohio), June 29, 1907, 2, 4; Bro. Opperman, "Wayside Notes, " *AF* (Houston), October 1908, 8; Edith Blumhofer, "A Pentecostal Branch Grows in Dowie's Zion," *AGH* 6 (Fall 1986): 3-5; also Gordon P. Gardiner, *Out of Zion into All the World* (Shippensburg, Pa.: Companion, 1990).

131. "History of Pentecost," *FS*, October 1922, 9. The writer refers to the impact of the Azusa Street revival, as well as the revival at Pandita Ramabai's Mukti Mission, as "The Shout Heard Round the World."

132. A. G. Garr, "Tongues. The Bible Evidence to the Baptism with the Holy Ghost," *PP*, March 1907, 4. On tongues-speech in Russia, see W. R. Morfill, "The Russian Sects," *ET* 17 (October 1905-September 1906): 402-3.

133. See *NIDPCM*, 2002 ed., s.v. "Bibliography and Historiography of Pentecostalism in the United States," by Augustus Cerillo, Jr., and Grant Wacker; also Joe Creech, "Visions of Glory: The Place of the Azusa Street Revival in Pentecostal History," *CH* 65 (September 1996): 405-24.

134. Grant Wacker, *Heaven Below: Early Pentecostals and American Culture* (Cambridge, Mass.: Harvard University Press, 2001), 103-5; see also Byron D. Klaus, ed., *We've Come This Far: Reflections on the Pentecostal Tradition and Racial Reconciliation* (*Encounter*: The Pentecostal Ministry Series 2) (Springfield, Mo.: Assemblies of God Theological Seminary, 2007); the chapter entitled "Spiritual Union," in T. B. Barratt, *In the Days of the Latter Rain* (London: Simpkin, Marshall, Hamilton, Kent, 1909), 221-24; and Harold D. Hunter, "A Journey Toward Racial Reconciliation: Race Mixing in the Church of God of Prophecy," in *The Azusa Street Revival and Its Legacy*, ed. Harold D. Hunter and Cecil M. Robeck, Jr. (Cleveland, Tenn.: Pathway, 2006), 277-96.

135. For a comparison of perspectives by insiders, see David J. du Plessis, "Golden Jubilees of Twentieth-Century Pentecostal Movements," *IRM* 47 (April 1958): 193-202; cf. Anthea Butler, "Constructing Different Memories: Recasting the Azusa Street Revival," in Hunter and Robeck, eds., *Azusa Street Revival*, 193-201. See also Harold D. Hunter and Peter D. Hocken, eds., *All Together in One Place: Theological Papers from the Brighton Conference on World Evangelization* (Sheffield: Sheffield Academic Press, 1993).

136. "En Route to Africa," *AF* (L.A.), December 1906, 4, col. 1.

137. Untitled news note, *AF* (L.A.), October 1906, 3, col. 4.

138. "Bro. G. W. Batman's Testimony," *AF* (L.A.), December 1906, 4, col. 1.

139. Robeck, *Azusa Street Revival*, 266-73.

140. "Salvation and Healing, " *AF* (L.A.), December 1906, 2, col. 1; "Questions Answered," *AF* (L.A.), October to January 1908, 2, cols. 1-2.

141. Untitled news note, *AF* (L.A.), Oct. to Jan. 1908, 1, col. 4.

142. Charles Shumway in his A.B. thesis at the University of Southern California writes in regard to this missionary party: "In *The Evangelical Messenger* for December 23, 1908, appears the testimony of Miss Mabel Collins. She, together with Lillie Thomas, ten other women, a Mr. McElroy and four other men, all members of Frank

Sandford's 'Holy Ghost and Us' congregation at Shiloh, Maine, thought they had been given the gift of several of the languages of India together with the divine direction to go there on a tour of evangelization." The article, however, lists them as being members of the "Holy Ghost Society" (without mentioning its location), not the name "Holy Ghost and Us" or "Holy Ghost and Us Society" that Sandford and the newspapers usually cited in reference to the community at Shiloh. Neither the article in the *Evangelical Messenger* (published by the Evangelical Association), nor the one Shumway refers to in *Literary Digest* draws a connection to Sandford. Given the considerable negative press coverage of Sandford's activities at the time, it seems reasonable that newspapers would have held him responsible for what happened to the party, but I have yet to find a newspaper account that does so. Nevertheless, many people visited Shiloh, as they did at the Apostolic Faith Mission on Azusa Street, and stayed only for a short time without becoming permanent members of the community. Since Shumway's reference notes are quite limited, he may have had access to more information than appeared in the two periodicals previously mentioned that he cited as references; C. W. Shumway, "A Critical Study of 'The Gift of Tongues'" (A.B. thesis, University of Southern California, 1914), 43-44; "The Fruit of Fanaticism," *EMes*, December 23, 1908, 1; "The False 'Gift of Tongues,'" *LD*, January 9, 1909, 55-56. It should also be noted that Sandford later condemned the Pentecostal movement; see Shirley and Rudy Nelson, "Frank Sandford: Tongues of Fire in Shiloh, Maine," in *Portraits of a Generation: Early Pentecostal Leaders* (Fayetteville: University of Arkansas Press, 2003), 51-69; Frank S. Murray, *The Sublimity of Faith: The Life and Work of Frank W. Sandford* (Amherst, N.H.: Kingdom, 1981), 927 n. 14, 932 n. 31.

Since one newspaper article refers to them as "Holy Ghosters," there could have been a link to a radical holiness sect in Connecticut with which the former American Board missionary to India and Holiness evangelist Elizabeth Sisson was associated for a time (she later became a Pentecostal). Still, "Holy Ghosters" was a pejorative term used for other sects as well; the Connecticut group was known locally as the "Holiness Band." See "A Queer Connecticut Sect," *New York Times*, October 26, 1897, 4; cf. "'Holy Ghosters' Win Whites and Negroes," *New York Times*, June 8, 1908, 5, cols. 3-4.

143. "'Holy Ghost' Girl Converts Penniless in England," *Oakland Tribune* (Calif.), March 21, 1908, 16.

144. "'Holy Ghosters' Freed," *New York Times*, February 2, 1908, 19.

145. The other leaders were "Prophet" Thomas O'Reilly and a "Brother Anderson"; "Holy Ghosters Are Stranded," *Evening Times* (Cumberland, Md.), November 19, 1908, 1.

146. "Zion City Girls Confined in a Harem," *Eau Claire Daily Leader* (Wis.), March 5, 1909, 3.

147. "Lost Lives in Holy Ghost Sect," *Portsmouth Daily Herald* (N.H.), January 8, 1909, 7; "Fruit of Fanaticism," 1. Collins's account of the trip gained considerable news coverage and resurfaced in newspapers years later; for example, see "Lost Lives in Holy Ghost Sect," *Wellsboro Gazette* (Pa.), August 28, 1913, 8.

148. "Walker to Make Legal Fight for His Children," *Trenton Evening Times* (N.J.), July 16, 1908, 1.

149. "'Holy Ghost' Girl Will be Good," *Trenton Evening Times* (N.J.), August 8, 1908, 3.

150. "With 'Tongues of Fire' They'll Invade Orient," *Anaconda Standard* (Mont.), August 23, 1907, 8; Ryan Leader of Peculiar Sect," *Seattle Post-Intelligencer* (Wash.), September 3, 1907, 4.

151. "'Apostolic Light' Mission," *The Standard* (Ogden, Utah), July 19, 1907, 6.

152. "Bro. Ryan Receives His Pentecost," *AF* (L.A.), November 1906, 3, col. 4.

153. "Languages Not in Repertory," *Evening Gazette* (Cedar Rapids, Iowa), January 6, 1908, 1; see also E. May Law, *Pentecostal Mission Work in South China* (Falcon, N.C.: Falcon, ca. 1916); Cora Fritsch, *Letters from Cora*, comp. Homer and Alice Fritsch (n.p.: By the compilers, 1987). See also Paul Tsuchido Shew, "Pentecostals in Japan," in *Asian and Pentecostal: The Charismatic Face of Christianity in Asia*, ed. Allan Anderson and Edmond Tang (Oxford: Regnum Books International, 2005), 489.

154. "Unknown Tongues at Sioux City," *Des Moines Capital* (Iowa), November 2, 1907, 12.

155. "Child in Trance Tells of Angels," *Waterloo Daily Courier* (Iowa), November 2, 1907, 6.

156. "Claim Gift of Tongues," *Indiana Democrat* (Pa.), December 19, 1906, 3.

157. "A Know-so Salvation," *AF* (L.A.), October 1906, 2, col. 4.

158. A. B. Simpson, *Eleventh Annual Report of the Christian and Missionary Alliance*, May 27, 1908, 11-12.

159. Daniel Woods, "Failure and Success in the Ministry of T. J. McIntosh: The First Pentecostal Missionary to China," *CPCR*, January 2003; http://www.pctii.org/cyberj/cyberj12/woods.html; "Macao, China," *AF* (L.A.), October 1908, 4.

160. Daniel Bays, "The Protestant Missionary Establishment and the Pentecostal Movement," in *Pentecostal Currents in American Protestantism*, ed. Edith L. Blumhofer, Russell P. Spittler, and Grant A. Wacker (Urbana: University of Illinois Press, 1999), 50-67.

161. S. C. Todd, "An Open Letter," 2; idem, "Some Sad Failures of Tongues in Mission Fields," *BA*, January 23, 1908, 1-2.

162. R. A. Jaffray, "'Speaking in Tongues'—Some Words of Kindly Counsel," *CMAW*, March 13, 1909, 396; Philip Hinkey, "A Spiritual Awakening in South China," *BGBA*, July 13, 1907, 9-10; Nienkirchen, *Simpson and the Pentecostal Movement*, 125-28.

163. A fear especially evident in the writings of British author Jessie Penn-Lewis; see her (with Evan Roberts) *War on the Saints* (New York: T. E. Lowe, 1973; originally published in 1912).

164. Allan Anderson, *Spreading Fires: The Missionary Nature of Early Pentecostalism* (Maryknoll, N.Y.: Orbis Books, 2007), 167-73; Peter Watt, *From Africa's Soil: The Story of the Assemblies of God in Southern Africa* (Cape Town: Struik Christian Books, 1992), 19-29.

165. "In Memoriam," *PE*, August 15, 1931, 8.

166. NIDPCM, 2002 ed., s.v. "Junk, Thomas," by Cecil M. Robeck, Jr.

167. Edith L. Blumhofer, "Woman to Woman: Susan Easton's Missionary Vision," *AGH* 4 (Winter 1992-93): 4-8, 26.

168. Lucy M. Moor, *Girls of Yesterday and To-Day: The Romance of the Y.W.C.A.* (London: S. W. Partridge, 1910), 183; Agnes Hill, "Do Foreign Missions Pay? The Transition of India," *LRE*, January 1913, 7-12; idem, "Evangelistic Work among Women in India," in *North American Students and World Advance*, ed. Burton St. John (New York: Student Volunteer Movement for Foreign Missions, 1920), 383-86; Ruth Rouse, *The World's Student Christian Federation: A History of the First Thirty Years* (London: SCM, 1948), 100.

169. See A. C. George, *Trailblazers for God: A History of the Assemblies of God of India* (Kothanur, Bangalore: SABC Publications, 2004), 29-35.

170. "A Late Report from Bombay," *AF* (Portland, Ore.), July/August 1908, 3; McGee, "Latter Rain," 663 n. 63, n. 64.

171. John L. Nevius, "Historical Review of Missionary Methods—Past and Pres-

ent—in China, and How Far Satisfactory," in *Records of the General Conference of the Protestant Missionaries of China. Held at Shanghai, May 7-20, 1890* (Shanghai: American Presbyterian Mission Press, 1890), 168.

172. Barclay F. Buxton, "Devotional Paper," in *Proceedings of the General Conference of Protestant Missionaries in Japan, Held in Tokyo, October 24-31, 1900* (Tokyo: Methodist Publishing House, 1901), 622; also B. Godfrey Buxton, *The Reward of Faith in the Life of Barclay Fowell Buxton, 1860-1946* (London: Lutterworth, 1949).

173. According to the mission census for 1900, there were 204,672 Protestant communicants and adherents in China out of a total population of 350 to 386 million; in Japan, 84,394 out of 46 million; see Beach, *Geography and Atlas of Protestant Missions*, 2: 19.

174. David A. Shank, *Prophet Harris, the "Black Elijah" of West Africa* (Leiden: E. J. Brill, 1994), 105-30.

175. A. Bettin, "The Revival in Nias," in *The Foreign Missions Convention at Washington, 1925*, ed. Fennell P. Turner and Frank Knight Sanders (New York: Foreign Missions Conference of North America, 1925), 309-11.

176. Dana L. Robert, "Shifting Southward: Global Christianity Since 1945," *IBMR* 24 (April 2000): 50-54, 56-58.

177. Untitled note, *AF* (L.A.), September 1906, 4, col. 4.

178. James L. Barton, "A Message from the American Board," *Dnya*, January 3, 1907, 2.

179. Nathan Söderblom, "The Historical Christian Fellowship," in *Jerusalem Meeting of the International Missionary Council, March 24-April 8, 1928*, vol. 3: *The Relation between the Younger and the Older Churches* (New York: International Missionary Council, 1928), 130.

6. THE SOURCE OF MISSIONAL POWER

1. Jessie Penn-Lewis, "Mrs. Penn-Lewis on the True and False in the Revival," *IW*, March 28, 1907, 203.

2. [Pandita] Ramabai, "Showers of Blessing," *MPB*, September 1907, 11.

3. T. B. Barratt, *In the Days of the Latter Rain* (London: Simpkin, Marshall, Hamilton, Kent, 1909), 65.

4. Roberto Elphick, "Chile," in *Christian Work in Latin America* (New York: Missionary Education Movement, 1917), 1: 222; Willis Collins Hoover, *History of the Pentecostal Revival in Chile*, trans. Mario G. Hoover (Lakeland, Fla.: By the translator, 2000), 68-71.

5. F. F. Bosworth, *Do All Speak with Tongues? (1 Cor. 12:30): An Open Letter to the Ministers and Saints of the Pentecostal Movement* (New York: Christian Alliance, 1918; originally published ca. 1917), 5.

6. Charles F. Parham, quoted in "New Religion 'Discovered' at 'Stone's Folly' Near Topeka," *Topeka Mail and Breeze* (Kans.), February 22, 1901; in *The Topeka Outpouring of 1901: 100th Anniversary Edition*, ed. Larry Martin (Joplin, Mo.: Christian Life Books, 2000), 219.

7. Robert M. Anderson, *Vision of the Disinherited: The Making of American Pentecostalism* (New York: Oxford University Press, 1979), 89-92; Vinson Synan, *The Holiness-Pentecostal Tradition: Charismatic Movements in the Twentieth Century* (Grand Rapids: Eerdmans, 1997), 89-92, 101-2; Grant Wacker, *Heaven Below: Early Pentecostals and American Culture* (Cambridge, Mass.: Harvard University Press, 2001), 44-51.

8. A. G. Garr, "A Letter from Bro. Garr," *Conf*, Special Supplement to *Conf*, May

1908, 2; cf. "Fanatic Delusions Have Ruined Many," *Daily Republican-News* (Hamilton, Ohio), January 31, 1908, 2; reprint of article by S. C. Todd in *BA* (Louisville, Ky.). The exception appears to have been Sophie Hansen, a missionary to Shanghai, China, who claimed that beginning on July 26, 1908, she could preach the gospel in the Chinese language: "I can speak it at any time, but the Gospel only. It is not given me to speak earthly things, and I cannot read or write it"; Sophie Hansen, "Gift of the . . . Chinese Language," (tract) (Oakland, Calif.: Triumphs of Faith, n.d.), 4.

9. For example, the well-known British Pentecostal writer Donald Gee ignored the issue entirely by not mentioning the early North American Pentecostal expectancy of preaching in the newly bestowed languages; *The Pentecostal Movement: Including the Story of the War Years (1940-1947)* (London: Elim, 1949), 11-19.

10. Anderson, *Vision of the Disinherited*, 10-27; Wacker, *Heaven Below*, 51-57; Douglas Jacobsen, *Thinking in the Spirit: Theologies of the Early Pentecostal Movement* (Bloomington: Indiana University Press, 2003).

11. While virtually all early Pentecostals valued speaking in tongues, some questioned the exegetical underpinning of requiring this experience of everyone seeking Spirit baptism; for example, W. H. Piper, "Manifestations and 'Demonstrations' of the Spirit," *LRE*, October 1908, 16-20; and especially Bosworth, *Do All Speak with Tongues?* The hermeneutical issue of how to correctly interpret Acts 2, 10, 19 and 1 Corinthians 12 and 14 represented the first theological division in the Pentecostal movement, predating the later Finished Work Controversy on sanctification (1910), which divided the movement between "Holiness-Pentecostals" and "Reformed evangelical Pentecostals," and the New Issue on the nature of the Godhead (1914) (Trinitarian versus modal monarchian), both of which took permanent form in organized Pentecostalism.

12. For Howard Stanley, see Larry Martin, ed., *The Topeka Outpouring of 1901*, rev. ed. (Joplin: Christian Life Books, 2000), 215; references to other languages on pp. 235, 244, 247.

13. News note, *AF* (L.A.), September 1906, 1, col. 4.

14. For example, A. E. Doering, "An African Tongue," *Conf*, July 1913, 143-44.

15. For example, "Have the 'Gift of Tongues,'" *Saturday Evening Telegraph* (Alton, Ill.), February 2, 1901, 1; "Woman Claims Great Gift," *Fresno Morning Republican* (Calif.), September 15, 1906, 3; "Strange Language," *Oakland Tribune* (Calif.), September 29, 1906, 10.

16. Diary of John G. Lake, entry for October 1907, 5-6. Available at Flower Pentecostal Heritage Center, Springfield, MO 65802.

17. "Gift of Tongue," *Indiana Progress* (Pa.), June 19, 1907, 6.

18. Max Wood Moorhead, "A Personal Testimony," *CWPI*, September 1907, 38. Moorhead served with the YMCA in Colombo, Ceylon (Sri Lanka), and lived at different times in Bombay (Mumbai), India.

19. A. E. Street, "What Is Pentecost?" *IM*, June 1907, 38.

20. "Salvation According to the True Tabernacle," *AF* (L.A.), September 1907, 3, col. 3.

21. R. A. Jaffray, "'Speaking in Tongues'—Some Words of Kindly Counsel," *CMAW*, March 13, 1909, 396; Ethel E. Goss, *The Winds of God: The Story of the Early Pentecostal Movement (1901-1914) in the Life of Howard A. Goss*, rev. ed. (Hazelwood, Mo.: Word Aflame, 1977), 95.

22. Garfield T. Haywood, "Baptized with the Holy Ghost and Healed," *BM*, December 1, 1908, 3.

23. "New Kind of Missionaries," *Hawaiian Gazette* (Honolulu), May 31, 1901, 10.

See also George F. Taylor, *The Spirit and the Bride* (Falcon, N.C.: By the author, 1907), 128; this was the first book-length treatise of Pentecostal theology.

24. For example, A. M. Hills, *Holiness and Power for the Church and Ministry* (Cincinnati: Revivalist Office, 1897), 297-343. The alienation of Pentecostals from the ranks of the Holiness movement because of tongues is discussed in Taylor, *Spirit and the Bride*, 39-59. See Grant A. Wacker, "Travail of a Broken Family: Radical Evangelical Responses to the Emergence of Pentecostalism in America, 1906-16," in *Pentecostal Currents in American Protestantism*, ed. Edith L. Blumhofer, et al. (Urbana: University of Illinois Press, 1999), 23-49.

25. Lilian Thistlethwaite, "The Wonderful History of the Latter Rain," in Sarah E. Parham, *The Life of Charles F. Parham, Founder of the Apostolic Faith Movement* (Baxter Springs, Kans.: Apostolic Faith Bible College, 1930), 61.

26. "Pentecostal Testimonies," *AF* (L.A.), February-March 1907, 8, col. 1.

27. Blanche Appleby, "A Transformation," *BM*, October 1, 1907, 1.

28. Inez Spence, *With a Song in Her Heart: Blanche Appleby*, Heroes of the Conquest 1 (Springfield, Mo.: Foreign Missions Department of the Assemblies of God, n.d.), 3-14.

29. Alexander Boddy corrected this interpretation: "On the day of Pentecost the Divine ecstasy and the tremendous crying out in snatches of tongues—the praise and adoration—the speaking of the wonderful works of God—this attracted multitudes, but it was *Peter's speech* which was used to convert. The speaking in tongues was not the converting instrument. It *attracted*. The 120 knew that the blessed Holy Ghost was in them because He had taken their mouths and used them to speak through. He testified thus to His presence." A. A. Boddy, "Speaking in Tongues"—2, *TC*, August 8, 1907, 25 (Boddy's emphasis).

30. Charles F. Parham, quoted in Parham, *Life of Charles F. Parham*, 54.

31. Charles F. Parham, quoted in "Story of His Belief: Rev. Charles F. Parham Tells How He Learned His Religion," *Kansas City Times* (Mo.), February 4, 1901; reprinted in Martin, ed., *Topeka Outpouring*, 252.

32. C. M. Hanson, "My Personal Experiences of the Graces of Salvation, Healing and Baptism in the Holy Spirit" (tract) (Dalton, Minn.: By the author, 1906), 4. Hanson's Spirit baptism probably occurred in 1899. I am indebted to Darrin J. Rodgers for sharing this tract and other related materials with me.

33. Mrs. D. M. Preston, quoted in an unnamed Joplin, Missouri, newspaper article reprinted in Parham, *Life of Charles F. Parham*, 111.

34. "Revivals at Orchard and Houston, Texas," *AF* (Melrose, Kans.), August 1905 (pages not numbered); see also "The AF," *AF* (Melrose, Kans.), October-November 1905 (pages not numbered); the ability to "speak and pray in languages unknown" is also mentioned in "News from Houston," *Galveston Daily News* (Tex.), August 14, 1905, 5.

35. Warren F. Carothers, *The Baptism with the Holy Ghost and the Speaking in Tongues* (Zion City, Ill.: n.p., 1906), 21. In contrast, George Taylor recommended that seekers praise God as the means of gaining Spirit baptism and tongues; however, once received, speaking in tongues functioned only for preaching in the mission lands; *Spirit and the Bride*, 134-35.

36. A. G. Garr, "Tongues. The Bible Evidence to the Baptism with the Holy Ghost," *PP*, March 1907, 3. During a Pentecostal meeting in Danville, Virginia, before his voyage to India, Garr told of a man in the audience who was baptized in the Spirit and "spake in tongues and magnified God"; "Pentecost in Danville, Va.," *AF* (L.A.), October 1906, 14, col. 3.

37. Catherine S. Price, quoted in Stanley H. Frodsham, *"With Signs Following": The Story of the Latter Day Pentecostal Revival* (Springfield, Mo.: Gospel Publishing House, 1926), 70.

38. Sister A. G. (Lillian) Garr, "In Calcutta, India," *AF* (L.A.), April 1907, 1, col. 1.

39. For example, Cora Hansen, "Testimony," *IA*, August 1908, 23.

40. Referring to his conversion during Parham's meetings in Galena, Kansas in 1903, Howard Goss said: "I feel that I owe my conversion to Christianity to hearing people speak in other tongues. The 14th Chapter of 1 Corinthians tells us that tongues are a sign to the 'unbelievers.' Today, I still thank God that I heard and saw His own sign from heaven." Goss, *Winds of God*, 37. Alexander Boddy described similar happenings in England in "A Visit to Kilsyth," *Conf*, April 1908, 9. Pentecostals continued to be enamored with anecdotes of people being converted through hearing someone speaking in their own language, though the person speaking had never studied it; see Frodsham, *With Signs Following*, 208-29; Ralph W. Harris, *Spoken by the Spirit: Documented Accounts of "Other Tongues" from Arabic to Zulu* (Springfield, Mo.: Gospel Publishing House, 1973).

41. In November 1906, Warren Carothers expressed hesitation about Pentecostal missionaries being able to preach in unlearned languages: "Just what part the gift of tongues is to fill in the evangelization of heathen countries is [a] matter for faith as yet. It scarcely seems from the evidence at hand to have had much to do with foreign mission work in New Testament times, and yet, in view of the apparent utility of the gift in that sphere and of the wonderful missionary spirit that comes with Pentecost, we are expecting the gift to be copiously used in the foreign field. We shall soon know." Carothers, *Baptism with the Holy Ghost*, 21; also Thomas G. Atteberry, "Tongues," *AT*, December 1906, 7-8.

42. "Gleanings of News," *The Agitator* (Wellsboro, Pa.), July 24, 1912, 6.

43. A. O. Morken, "From Our Own Learning Circle," trans. Erik L. Williamson, *Folke-Vennen* ("The People's Friend"), February 25, 1904, 4. Rodgers writes, "I did not find any evidence that the Scandinavians from Minnesota and the Dakotas had contact with Parham's AF band, which operated primarily in Kansas, Missouri, and Texas. Parham's group did not grow significantly until 1905, well after Pentecostal congregations had formed on the northern Great Plains" (Darrin J. Rodgers, *Northern Harvest: Pentecostalism in North Dakota* [Bismarck: North Dakota District Council of the Assemblies of God, 2003], 16).

44. Garr, "Tongues," 3.

45. A. A. Boddy, "Speaking in Tongues"—1, *TC*, August 1, 1907, 23.

46. Ibid.

47. "Questions and Answers," *BM*, November 1, 1908, 2.

48. Howard Goss, quoted in Goss, *Winds of God*, 96.

49. Thistlethwaite, "History," in Parham, *Life of Charles F. Parham*, 59.

50. Ibid., 63.

51. Ibid., 61.

52. "Three Months of Religious Fervor," *Joplin Daily News Herald* (Mo.), January 24, 1904, 11; the writer refers to an "Indian who had come from the Pawnee reservation that day to attend the services." For the reference to a "Peoria Indian preacher" receiving Spirit baptism, see B. F. Lawrence, *The Apostolic Faith Restored* (St. Louis: Gospel Publishing House, 1916), 60; also James R. Goff, Jr., *Fields White unto Harvest: Charles F. Parham and the Missionary Origins of Pentecostalism* (Fayetteville: University of Arkansas Press, 1988), 107-11.

53. Charles F. Parham, quoted in C. W. Harvey, "The Romance of Doctrine," *Galena*

Evening Times (Mo.), December 11, 1903, 2. Wacker discusses the temperament of early Pentecostals in *Heaven Below*, 18-34.

54. F. B. Price, "Manifestations Genuine and Counterfeit," *IW*, April 18, 1907, 252.

55. "Akron Will Fall by Earthquake," *Lima Daily News* (Ohio), January 12, 1907, 3.

56. "A Long Trip," *Van Wert Daily Bulletin* (Ohio), October 3, 1908, 4. For the conversation of the Mackins with Ellen G. White over their charismatic experiences, see Arthur G. White, "The Ralph Mackin Story" (Part 1), *RH*, August 10, 1972; "The Word—Not Feeling" (Part 2), August 17, 1972; "Calculated to Lead Astray" (Part 3), August 24, 1972.

57. Wacker, *Heaven Below*, 23-25.

58. "Questions Answered," *AF* (L.A.), October to January 1908, 2, col. 1.

59. "The Apostolic Faith," *Galveston Daily News* (Tex.), August 6, 1906, 7. The other women instructors during the two-week training school, which concluded with the ordination and assignments of the graduates, included Mrs. W. R. Quinton, who spoke on "Healing—Visiting and Prayer for the Sick"; Miss Bird on "Altar Work"; and Mrs. Mabel Smith on "Unity and Obedience." Smith, Mrs. [Anna] Hall, and Lucy Farrow, along with Parham and Carothers, spoke in the general services. For a newspaper report on Smith's preaching, see "Apostolic Faith Meetings," *Galveston Daily News* (Tex.), August 10, 1906, 6. Nonetheless, not everyone in the Apostolic Faith movement in the Midwest agreed that women should be allowed to teach or hold office in the church, notably Warren F. Carothers: "What the Movement Teaches," *AF* (Houston), October 1908, 7.

60. Howard Goss, quoted in Goss, *Winds of God*, 98; cf. Goff, *Fields White unto Harvest*, 109. Farrow had returned from the Azusa Street revival in Los Angeles to attend the convention on her way to the East Coast to embark as a missionary to Liberia.

61. Frank Bartleman, *Azusa Street: The Roots of Modern-Day Pentecost* (S. Plainfield, N.J.: Bridge, 1980; originally published in 1925 as *How Pentecost Came to Los Angeles*), 54.

62. Untitled note, *AF* (L.A.), May 1908, 3, col. 2.

63. Cecil M. Robeck, Jr., *The Azusa Street Mission & Revival: The Birth of the Global Pentecostal Movement* (Nashville: Nelson Reference & Electronic, 2006), 137; cf. Bartleman, *Azusa Street*, 145.

64. Untitled note, *AF* (L.A.), September 1907, 3, col. 4.

65. Kate Knight, "For His Glory," *CMAW*, January 25, 1908, 274.

66. Rachael Nalder, "Miracles of Salvation, Healing, Provision and Protection," *LRE*, November 1908, 10; "The Dhond Revival," *TF*, September 1908, 197.

67. Untitled note, *AF* (L.A.), December 1906, 2, col. 5.

68. Bro. Burke, "The Holy Ghost from Heaven," *AF* (L.A.), November 1906, 3, col. 2.

69. C. H. Mason, "Tennessee Evangelist Witnesses," *AF* (L.A.), February-March 1907, 7, col. 2.

70. Susie [*sic*] A. Duncan, quoted in Frodsham, *With Signs Following*, 53.

71. Bartleman, *Azusa Street*, 56. Bartleman referred to it as the "heavenly chorus." Other accounts include Marie E. Brown, "I Remember," *PE*, March 15, 1964, 20-21; Ruth Carter, "An Unusual Experience in the Upper Room Mission," *PE*, August 7, 1966, 9; Alice Reynolds Flower, "The Ministry of 'Brother Tom,'" *PE*, June 12, 1966, 23. In the Chilean Pentecostal revival that began in 1909, Willis C. Hoover said people described the phenomenon variously as the "Heavenly Anthem," "Heavenly Choir," and "Song of the Lord." Willis Collins Hoover, *History of the Pentecostal Revival in Chile*, trans. Mario G. Hoover (Lakeland, Fla.: By the translator, 2000), 154-55.

72. A. E. Street, "The Way to Perfect Satisfaction," *IM*, January 1908, 63.

73. Madame Seifer, "The Work of the Holy Ghost in Switzerland," *CWPI*, March 1908, 27.

74. Carothers connected singing in tongues with the song of the 144,000 (Rev 14:3) in *Baptism with the Holy Ghost*, 24. Others related it to the "wedding song of the Lamb" in Rev 19:9; see "Notes by Two Visitors," *Conf*, June 30, 1908, 14.

75. William Booth-Clibborn, quoted in Frodsham, *With Signs Following*, 111.

76. "Some Infallible Evidences," an article reprinted from *Apostolic Evangel* in *CWPI*, September 1907, 55. Chicago pastor William Durham said that as a result of his Spirit baptism, "I had a depth of love and sweetness in my soul that I had never even dreamed of before, and a holy calm possessed me, and a holy joy and peace, that is deep and sweet beyond anything I ever experienced before, even in the sanctified life." W. H. Durham, "A Chicago Evangelist's Pentecost," *AF* (L.A.), February-March 1907, 4, cols. 2-3.

77. A. J. Tomlinson, *The Last Great Conflict* (Cleveland, Tenn.: Walter E. Rodgers, 1913), 212.

78. T. B. Barratt, "The Seal of My Pentecost," *LT*, December 1906, 737; Gee, *Pentecostal Movement*, 14-15.

79. S. G. Otis, "Work in Boston and Vicinity," *WW*, June 1907, 178.

80. For example, the vision that accompanied the Spirit baptism of Marguerite Fell at the Rochester, New York, revival; Elizabeth V. Baker, et al., *Chronicles of a Faith Life*, 2d ed. (Rochester, N.Y.: Elim, ca. 1926), 135; also that of Christian H. Schoonmaker in India: "My Baptism in the Holy Spirit," *CWPI*, November 1908, 2.

81. "The Same Old Way," *AF* (L.A.), September 1906, 3, col. 2; also Bartleman, *Azusa Street*, 43-66.

82. Carrie Judd Montgomery, quoted in Frodsham, *With Signs Following*, 213.

83. Max Wood Moorhead, quoted in ibid., 130.

84. Sarah Coxe, quoted in ibid., 135.

85. David Martin, *Pentecostalism: The World Their Parish* (Oxford: Blackwell, 2002), 167-72.

86. Unity continued in some contexts: Levi R. Lupton, "Work in New York," *WW*, April 1908, 115; "'Holy Ghosters' Win Whites and Negroes," *New York Times*, June 8, 1908, 5; cf. "'Holy Ghoster' Now Behind Bars," *Trenton Evening Times* (N.J.), February 11, 1910, 7. A rare theological unity between some who believed and others who did not believe that tongues must accompany Spirit baptism continued at the Mukti Mission in India; see Minnie Abrams, "India," *Conf*, September 15, 1908, 14.

87. Wacker, *Heaven Below*, 1-14. For one unnamed Pentecostal's perception of satanic opposition, see "Speaking with Tongues," *MRW* 21 (January 1908): 61.

88. Miss K. Steele, "Tongues in Pandharpur," *CWPI*, March 1908, 6. Affiliated with the Poona and Indian Village Mission, Steele also reported that most of the young women "pray at times in 'tongues,'" and "are . . . lost in praise and prayer. . . . They are indeed speaking to God."

89. A. B. Simpson, "Editorial," *CMAW*, February 2, 1907, 1; cf. "Editorials," *IA*, June 1908, 138-39; see also Charles W. Nienkirchen, *A. B. Simpson and the Pentecostal Movement* (Peabody, Mass.: Hendrickson, 1992), 107-22. Taylor responds to criticism that Pentecostals "exalt the 'gifts' above the 'Giver'" in *Spirit and the Bride*, 45-46.

90. A. T. Pierson, "Speaking in Tongues"—II, *MRW* 20 (n.s.) (September 1907): 683; for a Pentecostal response to Pierson's arguments, see E. A. Spence, "Speaking with Tongues," *NA*, March 1908, 4-6.

91. "Fined $35," *Fergus Falls Daily Journal* (Minn.), March 11, 1905, 3.

92. Bro. Opperman, "Wayside Notes," *AF* (Houston), October 1908, 8.

93. "To the Baptised Saints," *AF* (L.A.), June-September 1907, 2, col. 1.

94. Kenneth Mackenzie, Jr., *Anti-Christian Supernaturalism* (New York: Christian Alliance, 1901), 11; also Jessie Penn-Lewis, with Evan Roberts, *War on the Saints* (New York: T. E. Lowe, 1973; originally published in 1912).

95. Ann Taves, *Fits, Trances, & Visions: Experiencing Religion and Explaining Experience from Wesley to James* (Princeton: Princeton University Press, 1999), 328-41.

96. For an insightful study of the reaction of holiness believers to early Pentecostalism in England, see Tim Walsh, "'Signs and Wonders that Lie': Unlikely Polemical Outbursts Against the Early Pentecostal Movement in Britain," in *Signs, Wonders, Miracles: Representations of Divine Power in the Life of the Church*, ed. Kate Cooper and Jeremy Gregory (Woodbridge, Suffolk, U.K.: Ecclesiastical History Society and Boydell Press, 2005), 410-22.

97. On Mormons and speaking in tongues, see Lee Copeland, "Speaking in Tongues in the Restoration Churches," *DJMT* 24 (Spring 1991): 13-33; "The Mormon Services and Habits," *Fort Wayne Daily Democrat* (Ind.), October 3, 1870, 1; "The Religious World," *Daily Gazette* (Colorado Springs, Colo.), October 12, 1884, 3; "Prophecy Delivered in an Unknown Tongue," *Ogden Standard* (Utah), April 13, 1908, 8; cf. "Speaking in Tongues as a Modern Religious Mania," *LD*, March 9, 1907, 379. On demons and tongues, see John L. Nevius, *Demon Possession and Allied Themes* (New York: Fleming H. Revell, 1896), 46-47, 58-59.

98. Simon Chan offers insights in *Pentecostal Theology and the Christian Spiritual Tradition* (Sheffield: Sheffield Academic Press, 2000); also Kilian McDonnell, ed., *Presence, Power, Praise: Documents on the Charismatic Renewal*, 3 vols. (Collegeville, Minn.: Liturgical Press, 1980).

99. For example, Charles Hodge, "The Unity of the Church Based on Personal Union with Christ," in *History, Essays, and Other Documents of the Sixth General Conference of the Evangelical Alliance, Held in New York, October 2-12, 1873*, ed. Philip Schaff and S. Irenaeus Prime (New York: Harper & Brothers, 1874), 139-44. See also David W. Bebbington, *The Dominance of Evangelicalism: The Age of Spurgeon and Moody* (Downers Grove, Ill.: InterVarsity, 2005), 85-86; Wacker, *Heaven Below*, 87-89.

100. W. J. Seymour, "River of Living Water," *AF* (L.A.), November 1906, 2, col. 2.

101. For example, [Susan A. Duncan], "The Field," *Trust*, September 1908, 15.

102. For example, G. B. Cashwell, "Speaking in Other Tongues," *BM*, November 1, 1907, 2.

103. Boddy, "Speaking in Tongues"—2, 25. For later writers, see Ralph M. Riggs, *The Spirit Himself* (Springfield, Mo.: Gospel Publishing House, 1949), 162-68; cf. Anthony D. Palma, *The Holy Spirit: A Pentecostal Perspective* (Springfield, Mo.: Gospel Publishing House, 2001), 227-32.

104. W. J. Seymour to "Brother Carothers," July 12, 1906. Available at Flower Pentecostal Heritage Center, Springfield, MO 65802.

105. E. G. Murrah, "The Unaskable and the Unthinkable Blessing," *BM*, November 1, 1907, 3.

106. Max Wood Moorhead, "Pentecost at Calcutta," *CWPI*, March 1908, 10.

107. Agnes N. O. LaBerge, *What God Hath Wrought: Life and Work of Mrs. Agnes N. O. LaBerge* (Chicago: Herald, n.d.), 33. Ozman cautiously added, "as God wills." Similarly, William Seymour wrote: "Beloved, if you do not know the language that you speak, do not puzzle yourself about it, for the Lord did not promise us He would tell us what language we were speaking, but He promised us the interpretation of what we speak." W. J. Seymour, "The Baptism with the Holy Ghost," *AF* (L.A.), February-March 1907, 7, col. 1. See also Dagmar Gregersen, "Sister Dagmar Gregersen (interpreted by Mrs. Beruldson)," *Conf*, June 30, 1908, 16. In India, Pandita Ramabai, director of the

Mukti Mission, reported: "The girls, who have received the gift of tongues, are not using them for delivering scripture messages, except those who have received the gift of interpretation." Ramabai, "Showers of Blessing," 5; also Minnie F. Abrams, "Mukti Mission," *MPB*, September 1907, 19.

108. For example, Oral Roberts, *Unleashing the Power of Praying in the Spirit!* (Tulsa, Okla.: Harrison House, 1993), 48-53.

109. For example, Addie M. Otis, "The AF Movement," *WW*, February 1907, 51; untitled note, *AF* (L.A.), May 1907, 3, col. 4; J. Roswell Flower, "The Pentecostal Commission," *PE*, June 12, 1920, 12.

110. Mrs. G. R. (Wilhelmine) Polman, quoted in Frodsham, *With Signs Following*, 208.

111. Untitled note, *AF* (L.A.), December 1906, 4, col. 3.

112. Moorhead, "Pentecost at Calcutta," 10.

113. For example, [Mrs.] C. Beruldsen, "A Testimony from Edinburgh," *Conf*, April 1908, 12; also Hoover, *History of the Pentecostal Revival*, 53; S. P. Hamilton, "More About Revival," *IA*, June 1908, 137.

114. Spence, "Speaking with Tongues," 5.

115. Thistlethwaite, "Wonderful History," in Parham, *Life of Charles F. Parham*, 62; also "Tongues Convict Sinners," *AF* (L.A.), September 1907, 4, col. 2.

116. Parham continued this practice of preaching; see "Houstonians Witness the Performance of Miracles," *Houston Chronicle*, August 13, 1905, 6.

117. Charles F. Parham, *A Voice Crying in the Wilderness*, 2d ed. (Baxter Springs, Kans.: AF Bible College, 1910; originally published in 1902), 31; cf. Cashwell, "Speaking in Other Tongues," 2.

118. For the decline of Parham's influence, see Lawrence, *Apostolic Faith Restored*, 67-68; Goff, *Fields White unto Harvest*, 128-46.

119. "The Bible Training School in Houston, Texas," reprinted from an issue of the *AF* (Houston) (date not mentioned) in *CWPI*, August 1909, 11.

120. Henry G. Tuthill, quoted in "History of Pentecost," *FS*, July 1922, 12.

121. "Bible Training School," 11. The writer states: "Even the clerks in closed banks stopped their work and crowded to the doors to hear God's call for repentance . . . while others crowded the second story windows in buildings near enough to hear the Word of God. By such preaching in tongues, a clearly supernatural 'sign to unbelievers,' God is giving people in the closing days of this age a warning of the soon coming of His Son and leaving such as do not repent without excuse." For another reference to the practice, see "Lebow Quit Faith," *Galveston Daily News*, July 8, 1906, 11. Cf. Cashwell, "Speaking in Other Tongues," 2.

122. H. A. Baker, "An Amazing Pentecostal Outpouring in Western China," *LRE*, June 1929, 5.

123. H. A. Goss and E. N. Bell, "Bible Schools," *WWit*, December 20, 1913, 2.

124. Evident in W. F. Carothers, "The Gift of Interpretation," *LRE*, October 1910, 7-10; this article originally appeared in the *AF* (Houston).

125. Donald Gee, "Smith Wigglesworth," *RT*, March 13, 1964, 5-6.

126. E. N. Bell, *Questions and Answers* (Springfield, Mo.: Gospel Publishing House, 1923), 81.

127. Frank Lindblad, *The Spirit Which Is from God* (Springfield, Mo.: Gospel Publishing House, 1928), 174.

128. Charles W. Conn, *Like a Mighty Army: A History of the Church of God, 1886-1976*, rev. ed. (Cleveland, Tenn.: Pathway, 1977), 136-37.

129. For an insightful case study of the tension between charisma and routinization

within Pentecostalism, see Margaret M. Poloma, "Charisma and Structure in the Assemblies of God: Revisiting O'Dea's Five Dilemmas," in *Church, Identity, and Change: Theology and Denominational Structures in Unsettled Times*, ed. David A. Roozen and James R. Nieman (Grand Rapids: Eerdmans, 2005), 45-96.

130. Untitled note, *AF* (L.A.), May 1908, 2, col. 2.

131. Boddy, "Speaking with Tongues"—2, 25. See also "Odd Words by Prayer," *Massillon Independent Semi-Weekly* (Ohio), November 29, 1906, 2.

132. J. Kelly, "A Thibetan Missionary's Experience," *CWPI*, July 1910, 5 (Kelly's emphasis). Kelly served with the Tibetan Mission, a small faith mission agency headquartered in Darjeeling, India.

133. Thistlethwaite, "Wonderful History," in Parham, *Life of Charles F. Parham*, 61.

134. Rudy and Shirley Nelson, "Frank Sandford: Tongues of Fire in Shiloh, Maine," in *Portraits of a Generation: Early Pentecostal Leaders*, ed. James R. Goff, Jr., and Grant Wacker (Fayetteville: University of Arkansas Press, 2002), 51-69.

135. Alfred Street, "To Our Readers," *Intercessory Missionary* 1, no. 4 (January 1908): 50; also Hanson, "My Personal Experiences," 5-6 (Street's emphasis).

136. A. B. Simpson, "Editorial," *CMAW*, June 8, 1907, 205.

137. A. B. Simpson, "Gifts and Grace," in *The Signs of the Times or God's Message for To-day* (New York: Alliance Press, 1907), 105-6; cf. "For Strangers, Who Are We?" *WWit*, May 1914, 1. In what amounts to a proposed statement of faith for the AF movement, Warren Carothers wrote: "Baptized persons are used by the Spirit as the instruments of His will in edifying the body and convincing the world, speaking through us as He wills, communing with our spirits in language unutterable without spiritual interpretation, and manifesting His presence and power and working His will through us in the charismatic gifts of the Spirit." W. F. Carothers, "What the Movement Teaches," *AF* (Houston), October 1908, 6.

138. Nienkirchen, *A. B. Simpson*, 131-55.

139. Evident in Myer Pearlman, *Knowing the Doctrines of the Bible* (Springfield, Mo.: Gospel Publishing House, 1937), 327; Guy P. Duffield and Nathaniel M. Van Cleave, *Foundations of Pentecostal Theology* (Los Angeles: L.I.F.E. Bible College, 1983), 323. For an important later statement on speaking in tongues by Alliance leaders, see Board of Managers, The Christian and Missionary Alliance, "Seek Not—Forbid Not!" (Adopted April 4, 1963) in McDonnell, *Presence, Power, Praise*, 3: 63-67; cf. Nienkirchen, *A. B. Simpson*, 139-40.

140. Taylor, *Spirit and the Bride*, 22-23.

141. See Gordon D. Fee, "Hermeneutics and Historical Precedent—A Major Problem in Pentecostal Hermeneutics," in *Perspectives on the New Pentecostalism*, ed. Russell P. Spittler (Grand Rapids: Baker Book House, 1976), 118-32.

142. See Charles Nienkirchen, "Conflicting Visions of the Past: The Prophetic Use of History in the Early American Pentecostal-Charismatic Movements," in *Charismatic Christianity as a Global Culture*, ed. Karla Poewe (Columbia: University of South Carolina Press, 1994), 119-33.

143. For an insightful study, see Dana L. Robert, "Encounter with Christ: Luke as Mission Historian for the Twenty-first Century," in *Evangelical, Ecumenical, and Anabaptist Missiologies in Conversation*, ed. James R. Krabill, Walter Sawatsky, and Charles E. Van Engen (Maryknoll, N.Y.: Orbis Books, 2006), 19-27.

144. For example, see E. T. Wells, "Does the Holy Spirit Witness to the Experience of Entire Sanctification?" in *Proceedings of Holiness Conferences Held at Cincinnati, November 26th, 1877, and at New York, December 17th, 1877* (Philadelphia: National

Publishing Association for the Promotion of Holiness, 1877), 32-48; R. A. Torrey, *The Baptism with the Holy Spirit* (New York: Fleming H. Revell, 1897), 9-36; cf. Wilber T. Dayton, "The Divine Purification and Perfection of Man," in *A Contemporary Wesleyan Theology*, ed. Charles W. Carter (Grand Rapids: Zondervan, 1983), 1:542.

145. See Gary B. McGee, "Early Pentecostal Hermeneutics: Tongues as Evidence in the Book of Acts," in *Initial Evidence: Historical and Biblical Perspectives on the Pentecostal Doctrine of Spirit Baptism*, ed. Gary B. McGee (Eugene, Ore.: Wipf & Stock, 2008), 96-118; William W. Menzies and Robert P. Menzies, *Spirit and Power: Foundations of Pentecostal Experience* (Grand Rapids: Zondervan, 2000), 47-61; also I. Howard Marshall, *Luke: Historian and Theologian* (Grand Rapids: Zondervan, 1971); C. H. Talbert, *Literary Patterns, Theological Themes, and the Genre of Luke-Acts* (Missoula, Mont.: Society of Biblical Literature and Scholars Press, 1974); R. F. O'Toole, *The Unity of Luke's Theology*, Good News Studies 9 (Wilmington, Del.: Michael Glazier, 1984).

146. For example, see Robert P. Menzies, "Evidential Tongues: An Essay on Theological Method," in McGee, *Initial Evidence*, 219-33.

147. John Christopher Thomas and Kimberly Ervin Alexander have pointed to the historic canonical authority of the longer ending of Mark (until the nineteenth century) and urged its reconsideration for the study of Pentecostal history and theology; "'And the Signs Are Following': Mark 16:9-20—A Journey into Pentecostal Hermeneutics" (paper presented at the annual meeting of the Society for Pentecostal Studies, Lakeland, Florida, March 14-16, 2002).

148. For the different kinds of theological statements in the Bible and their "appropriate degree of authority," see Millard J. Erickson, *Christian Theology*, 2d ed. (Grand Rapids: Baker Book House, 1998), 83-84.

149. Henry Eyster Jacobs, *A Summary of the Christian Faith* (Philadelphia: Board of Publication of the General Council of the Evangelical Lutheran Church in North America, 1905), 9; also Robert D. Preus, *The Theology of Post-Reformation Lutheranism*, vol. 1: *A Study of Theological Prolegomena* (St. Louis: Concordia, 1970), 1: 335-39.

150. For Protestant scholasticism, see Richard A. Muller, *After Calvin: Studies in the Development of a Theological Tradition* (Oxford: Oxford University Press, 2003), 25-46.

151. Philip Jenkins, *The New Faces of Christianity: Believing the Bible in the Global South* (Oxford: Oxford University Press, 2006), 5.

152. *Luther's Works*, vol. 34. *Career of the Reformer* 4, ed. Lewis W. Spitz (Philadelphia: Fortress, 1960), 336-37.

153. Charles Garside, *Zwingli and the Arts* (New Haven: Yale University Press, 1966), 39-52.

154. *Calvin: Theological Treatises*, Library of Christian Classics 22, ed. J. K. S. Reid (London: SCM, 1954), 58-66.

155. Kurt Aland, *Did the Early Church Baptize Infants?* trans. G. R. Beasley-Murray (Philadelphia: Westminster, 1963); cf. Joachim Jeremias, *The Origins of Infant Baptism: A Further Study in Reply to Kurt Aland*, trans. Dorothea M. Barton (Naperville, Ill.: A. R. Allenson, 1963); see also Heinrich Schmid, *The Doctrinal Theology of the Evangelical Lutheran Church, Verified from the Original Sources*, 5th ed., trans. Charles A. Hay and Henry E. Jacobs (Philadelphia: United Lutheran Publication House, 1899), 548; Donald Bridge and David Phypers, *The Water That Divides: The Baptism Debate* (Downers Grove, Ill.: InterVarsity, 1977), 33-70; G. W. H. Lampe, "Christian Theology in the Patristic Period," in *A History of Christian Doctrine*, ed. Hubert Cunliffe-Jones (Philadelphia: Fortress, 1978), 157-62.

156. For an abridged exposition of this belief, see P. Riedemann, "Account of Our Religion," in *The Protestant Reformation*, ed. H. J. Hillerbrand (New York: Harper & Row, 1968), 143-46.

157. F. Ernest Stoeffler, *German Pietism during the Eighteenth Century* (Leiden: E. J. Brill, 1973), 120-28; Franklin H. Littell, "Radical Pietism in American History," in *Continental Pietism and Early American Christianity*, ed. F. Ernest Stoeffler (Grand Rapids: Eerdmans, 1976), 164-82.

158. A. J. Lewis, *Zinzendorf: The Ecumenical Pioneer* (Philadelphia: Westminster, 1962), 59.

159. Robert L. Gallagher, "Zinzendorf and the Early Moravians: Pioneers in Leadership Selection and Training," *Miss* 36 (April 2008): 237-44.

160. Howard A. Snyder, *The Radical Wesley* (Downers Grove, Ill.: InterVarsity, 1980), 125-42.

161. W. H. Daniels, ed., *Dr. Cullis and His Work* (Boston: Willard Tract Repository, 1885), 11.

162. Klaus Fiedler, *The Story of Faith Missions: From Hudson Taylor to Present Day Africa* (Oxford: Regnum Books International, 1994), 113-14; see also Franklin H. Littell, "Radical Pietism in American History," in *Continental Pietism and Early American Christianity*, ed. F. Ernest Stoeffler (Grand Rapids: Eerdmans, 1976), 164-67.

163. Taylor, *Spirit and the Bride*, 42.

164. D. W. Kerr, "The Basis for Our Distinctive Testimony," *PE*, September 2, 1922, 4.

165. Fiedler, *Story of Faith Missions*, 113.

166. For example, see Ray H. Hughes, "The New Pentecostalism: Perspective of a Classical Pentecostal Administrator," in *Perspectives on the New Pentecostalism*, ed. Russell P. Spittler (Grand Rapids: Baker Book House, 1976), 166-80; cf. Edith L. Blumhofer, *Restoring the Faith: The Assemblies of God, Pentecostalism, and American Culture* (Urbana: University of Illinois Press, 1993), 203-41.

167. Taylor, *Spirit and the Bride*, 42; Bosworth, *Do All Speak with Tongues?* 5, 17.

168. Taylor, *Spirit and the Bride*, 42-43.

169. For example, see John W. Wyckoff, "The Baptism in the Holy Spirit," in *Systematic Theology*, rev. ed., ed. Stanley M. Horton (Springfield, Mo.: Gospel Publishing House, 1995), 427-33.

170. In what may be a response to Bosworth's charge about the lack of noted evangelists among Pentecostals, see "History of Pentecost," *FS*, October 1922, 16; see also Edith L. Blumhofer, *Aimee Semple McPherson: Everybody's Sister* (Grand Rapids: Eerdmans, 1993); David Edwin Harrell, Jr., *All Things Are Possible: The Healing and Charismatic Revivals in Modern America* (Bloomington: Indiana University Press, 1975).

171. Reflected in A. J. Gordon, "The Holy Spirit in Missions," in *Student Mission Power: Report of the First International Convention of the Student Volunteer Movement for Foreign Missions, Held at Cleveland, Ohio, U.S.A., February 26, 27, 28 and March 1, 1891* (Boston: T. O. Metcalf, 1891; reprinted by William Carey Library, 1979), 7-20; A. B. Simpson, "The Supernatural Gifts and Ministries of the Church," *CAFMW*, January 19, 1898, 53-54, 67.

172. "Speaking with Tongues as a Modern Religious Mania," *LD*, March 9, 1907, 378-79.

173. George Barton Cutten, *Speaking in Tongues: Historically and Psychologically Considered* (New Haven: Yale University Press, 1927), 157-84.

174. Anderson, *Vision of the Disinherited*, 231.

7. THE SEARCH FOR ORDER

1. Editorial note, *TP*, November 1908, 3.

2. Carrie Judd Montgomery, *"Under His Wings": The Story of My Life* (Oakland, Calif.: Office of Triumphs of Faith, 1936), 177.

3. Joseph H. King and Blanche L. King, *Yet Speaketh: Memoirs of the Late Bishop Joseph H. King* (Franklin Springs, Ga.: Publishing House of the Pentecostal Holiness Church, 1949), 192.

4. Ernest Hooper, "At Home with her Lord," *LRE*, April 1921, 11.

5. E. N. Bell, "A Word to Foreign Missionaries," *WWit*, October 20, 1912, 3; idem, "Too Much Returning. Why Is It? The Remedy," *WWit*, September 20, 1913, 2.

6. "Missionaries to Palestine," *AF* (L.A.), May 1908, 4, col. 1.

7. "Bound for the Orient," *AL*, August 28, 1907, 1; "Alleged Crank in Limelight," *Daily Oregon Statesman* (Salem, Ore.), January 7, 1911, 1, 6; on Leatherman's travels, see Allan Anderson, *Spreading Fires: The Missionary Nature of Early Pentecostalism* (Maryknoll, N.Y.: Orbis Books, 2007), 152-53, 155.

8. Anna C. Reiff, "Things Missionary," *LRE*, March 1913, 15.

9. For the history of the Alliance, see Robert L. Niklaus, John S. Sawin, Samuel J. Stoesz, *All for Jesus: God at work in the Christian and Missionary Alliance over One Hundred Years* (Camp Hill, Pa.: Christian Publications, 1986).

10. Untitled note, *AF* (L.A.), September 1906, 1, col. 3.

11. *Minutes of the Sixth General Assembly of the Church of God, Held at Cleveland, Tennessee, January 3-8, 1911*, 11. For Robert M. and Ida Evans, see Charles W. Conn, *Where the Saints Have Trod: A History of Church of God Missions* (Cleveland, Tenn.: Pathway, 1959), 13-14, 49-55.

12. Untitled note, *AF* (L.A.), September 1906, 1, col. 3.

13. Note the similarity to the guiding principles of the China Inland Mission in Klaus Fiedler, *The Story of Faith Missions: From Hudson Taylor to Present Day Africa* (Oxford: Regnum Books International, 1994), 33.

14. Anna C. Reiff, "Missionary Problems That Confront Us: What Is Our Responsibility?" *LRE*, January 1913, 19. For information on Reiff, see Barbara Liddle Cavaness, "Factors Influencing the Decrease in the Number of Single Women in Assemblies of God World Missions" (Ph.D. diss., Fuller Theological Seminary, 2002), 85-87.

15. Cecil M. Robeck, Jr., *The Azusa Street Mission & Revival* (Nashville: Nelson Reference & Electronic, 2006), 239-44.

16. Irving Alfred Whitt, "Developing a Pentecostal Missiology in the Canadian Context (1867-1944): The Pentecostal Assemblies of Canada" (D.Miss. diss., Fuller Theological Seminary, 1994), 388; Thomas William Miller, "The Canadian Jerusalem: The Story of James and Ellen Hebden and their Toronto Mission," Part 2: "Into All the World," *AGH* 11 (Winter 1991-92): 22-25, 30-31.

17. Doug Beacham, *Azusa East: The Life and Times of G. B. Cashwell* (Franklin Springs, Ga.: LSR Publications, 2006), 59-92.

18. Edith L. Blumhofer, "Portrait of a Generation: Azusa Street Comes to Chicago," *Enri*, Spring 2006, 94-102; idem, "William H. Durham: Years of Creativity, Years of Dissent," in *Portraits of a Generation: Early Pentecostal Leaders*, ed. James R. Goff, Jr., and Grant Wacker (Fayetteville: University of Arkansas Press, 2002), 123-42.

19. Edith L. Blumhofer, *Aimee Semple McPherson: Everybody's Sister* (Grand Rapids: Eerdmans, 1993), 89-92.

20. Fiedler, *Story of Faith Missions*, 78-80, 83; Alvyn Austin, *China's Millions: The*

China Inland Mission and Late Qing Society, 1832-1905 (Grand Rapids: Eerdmans, 2007), 341-42.

21. Gary B. McGee, *This Gospel Shall Be Preached: A History and Theology of Assemblies of God Foreign Missions to 1959* (Springfield, Mo.: Gospel Publishing House, 1986), 88-90.

22. Joseph E. Campbell, *The Pentecostal Holiness Church, 1898-1948: Its Background and History* (Franklin Springs, Ga.: Publishing House of the Pentecostal Holiness Church, 1951), 348, 350.

23. Fannie M. Van Dyck, "History of the Full Gospel Work in Youngstown Since 1890," unpublished mss., n.d., 11. Available at Flower Pentecostal Heritage Center, Springfield, MO 65802.

24. Thomas Atteberry, a Pentecostal editor in Los Angeles, shared Van Dyck's opinion in "Tongues," *AT*, December 1906, 7-8.

25. For major studies on the influence of Simpson and the Christian and Missionary Alliance on Pentecostalism, see Charles W. Nienkirchen, *A. B. Simpson and the Pentecostal Movement* (Peabody, Mass.: Hendrickson, 1992); Paul L. King, *Genuine Gold: The Cautiously Charismatic Story of the Early Christian and Missionary Alliance* (Tulsa, Okla.: Word & Spirit Press, 2006).

26. On the contributions of George and Carrie Judd Montgomery to missions, see Jennifer Stock, "George S. Montgomery: Businessman for the Gospel" (Part 1), *AGH* 9 (Spring 1989): 4-5, 17-18; (Part 2), *AGH* 9 (Summer 1989): 12-14, 20.

27. See Ogbu Kalu, *African Pentecostalism: An Introduction* (Oxford: Oxford University Press, 2008), 48-53.

28. For instance, see "Tent Meetings at Maple City," *Morning Record* (Traverse City, Mich.), August 25, 1897, 2; "Holiness Healing Reported at Marion," *Fort Wayne Evening Sentinel* (Ind.), August 18, 1905, 8; Levi R. Lupton, "Past Experiences of Faith," *NA*, May 31, 1906, 2-3.

29. "'Ye Shall Be Witnesses': An Exhortation to the Holiness Preachers and Evangelists of America," *NA*, May 10, 1906, 1.

30. For further information on Lupton, see Grant Wacker, "Early Pentecostals and the Study of Popular Religious Movements in Modern America," in *The Work of the Spirit: Pneumatology and Pentecostalism*, ed. Michael Welker (Grand Rapids: Eerdmans, 2006), 126-46.

31. "Opening of School," *NA*, October 12, 1905, 1-2.

32. William M. Smith, *Chapters from the New Acts: An Account of the First Missionary Journey of the World Evangelization Company to Africa—1904-5* (Alliance, Ohio: World Evangelization Company, 1905), Appendix, 1.

33. *Minutes of the Alliance Monthly Meeting*, September 1, 1904.

34. C. E. McPherson, *Life of Levi R. Lupton: Twentieth Century Apostle of the Gift of Tongues, Divine Healer, Etc.* (Alliance, Ohio: By the author, 1911), 112.

35. "Brought to Completion," *NA*, February 1, 1906, 1-4; McPherson, *Life of Levi R. Lupton*, 89-96.

36. Smith, *Chapters from the New Acts*, 14.

37. "Rigid Future Faith Policy," *NA*, May 31, 1906, 4-6; "Damascus Quarterly Meeting Minute," *NA*, May 31, 1906, 6.

38. For the ministry of "Sisters [Ivey] Campbell and Hudson from East Liverpool" in Akron, see Pearl Bowen, "Akron Visited with Pentecost," *AF* (L.A.), January 1907, 1, col. 2; Ivey Campbell, "Report from Ohio and Pennsylvania," *AF* (L.A.), February-March, 1907, 5, col. 1; on McKinney, see "Our Heritage" (Akron, Ohio: First Assembly of God, n.d.), 1-6; Harold C. McKinney, "C. A. McKinney," *PE*, February 10, 1940, 7.

39. Levi R. Lupton, "Testimony," *NA*, February 1907, 3; cf. "Claims Gift of Tongues," *Elyria Daily Reporter* (Ohio), January 15, 1907, 8.

40. "Claim Gift of Tongues," *Canton Repository* (Ohio), January 4, 1907, 6.

41. Gary B. McGee, "Levi Lupton: A Forgotten Pioneer of Early Pentecostalism," in *Faces of Renewal: Studies in Honor of Stanley M. Horton Presented on His 70th Birthday*, ed. Paul Elbert (Peabody, Mass.: Hendrickson, 1988), 199.

42. "Tit-a-Tat, Tit-a-Too," *Alliance Daily Review* (Ohio), March 11, 1907, 1.

43. Thomas D. Hamm, *The Transformation of American Quakerism: Orthodox Friends, 1800-1907* (Bloomington: Indiana University Press, 1988), 169-72.

44. "Report of Pentecostal Camp, Alliance, O.," *NA*, July and August 1907, 2; "To Convert All Mankind His Plan," *Lima Daily News* (Ohio), June 18, 1907, 2.

45. These included L. P. Adams, Edith Baugh, George Berg, A. S. Copley, George Fisher, Lizzie Frazier, J. Roswell Flower, Joseph King, Lucy Leatherman, Bernice Lee, Jacob Lehman, Thomas Leonard, Kenneth Spooner, George Taylor, and Alice Wood.

46. Frank Bartleman, *Azusa Street: The Roots of Modern-day Pentecost* (South Plainfield, N.J.: Bridge, 1980), 106.

47. "At the Camp, At the Home," *Alliance Daily Review* (Ohio), June 17, 1907, 1; "'Gift of Tongues' Is Now on Exhibition," *Alliance Daily Review* (Ohio), June 17, 1907, 1, 8; "Fanatics in a Frenzy," *Evening Herald* (Norwalk, Ohio), June 17, 1907, 1; "Days Doings at Camp Lupton," *Alliance Daily Review* (Ohio), June 21, 1907, 1.

48. Lupton, quoted in "Sins, He Asks Pardon World," *News-Palladium* (Benton Harbor, Mich.), December 15, 1910, 1; "Seems to be Imitating Dowie," *Evening Telegram* (Elyria, Ohio), June 25, 1907, 3; "Religious Frenzy Seizes Followers," *Newark Advocate* (Ohio), June 21, 1907, 1.

49. King and King, *Yet Speaketh*, 132.

50. "Apostle Levi, Says Vision," *Alliance Daily Review* (Ohio), June 26, 1907, 1; "Lupton Again," *Alliance Daily Review* (Ohio), June 25, 1907, 1.

51. "Seems to Be Imitating Dowie," 3. In connection with the need to have a simpler lifestyle to support foreign missions, the British Pentecostal periodical *Confidence* reported the following about the American evangelist Elizabeth Sisson: "Now the Pentecostal people are mostly poor, yet God has said to her (Miss Sisson) that He is going to send out hundreds of thousands of Missionaries. It will mean cutting down our butter and sugar, etc."; "The Sunderland Conference," *Conf*, June 1908, 16.

52. I have not been able to discover whether King ever edited the *NA*.

53. "And Your Young Men Shall Dream Dreams," *Fort Wayne News* (Ind.), June 25, 1907, 1; the byline of the article reads: "Over at Alliance, however, the dreams were mighty conflicting." See also "Lupton's Converts Leaving Camp," *Evening Herald* (Norwalk, Ohio), June 25, 1907, 2; "Quarrel over Leadership," *New Castle News* (Pa.), June 26, 1907, 1.

54. "Important Pentecostal Manifesto," *Conf*, August 15, 1908, 9-10 (emphasis within the document).

55. "A Half Bushel of Jewelry and Money," *Marion Weekly Star* (Ohio), June 27, 1908, 3.

56. For the account of John Reid, see the untitled news note, *Conf*, December 15, 1908, 8; Albert Norton, "Boys' Christian Home," *WW*, November 1908, 346; for others who had been trained in Alliance, Ohio, see Anderson, *Spreading Fires*, 170-72.

57. "Summer Bible School," *WW*, August 1908, 247; on Awrey, see *NIDPCM*, 2002 ed., s.v. "Awrey, Daniel P.," by Daniel Woods; on Michener, see William C. Stevens, "Report from the Missionary Training Institute," in A. B. Simpson, *Tenth Annual Report of the Christian and Missionary Alliance*, 1907, 74.

58. *Report of the Liberia Interior Mission, 1908-1916* (Cape Palmas, Liberia: Interior Mission, ca. 1916), 2.

59. See Sister [Ellen] Hebden, "In Toronto, Canada," *AF* (L.A.), April 1907, 1, col. 4; J. M. Perkins, "If I Had Only One Hour to Live," *PE*, May 17, 1941, 4; J. M. L. Harrow, "After Twenty Years' Service for God in Africa," *LRE*, August 1916, 19. For more information on Perkins, see Letter of H. B. Garlock to Rev. E. L. Phillips, July 6, 1968; available at editorial office files, Assemblies of God World Missions, Springfield, MO 65802.

60. See David Bundy, "William Taylor, 1821-1902: Entrepreneurial Maverick for the Indigenous Church," in *Mission Legacies: Biographical Studies of Leaders of the Modern Missionary Movement*, ed. Gerald H. Anderson, et al. (Maryknoll, N.Y.: Orbis Books, 1994), 461-68.

61. *Report of the Liberia Interior Mission*, 4; cf. William H. Johnson and J. M. Perkins, "Interior Mission, Cape Palmas, Liberia," *WE*, August 25, 1917, 12.

62. Thomas William Miller, *Canadian Pentecostals: A History of the Pentecostal Assemblies of Canada* (Mississauga, Ont.: Full Gospel Publishing House, 1994), 229. For the diseases that missionaries faced in Africa, see Joseph F. Conley, *Drumbeats That Changed the World: A History of the Regions Beyond Missionary Union and the West Indies Mission, 1873-1999* (Pasadena, Calif.: William Carey Library, 2000), 77-79.

63. Mary E. Martin, *West Africa: An Open Door* (Springfield, Mo.: Foreign Missions Department of the Assemblies of God, 1943), 10. Other Pentecostal groups represented included the Independent Pentecostal Assemblies and Open Bible Standard Churches, as well as missionaries of the Swedish Pentecostal churches.

64. The children of the Polhill-Turner family later dropped "Turner" from the name; see Peter Hocken, "Cecil H. Polhill—Pentecostal Layman," *Pneuma* 10 (Fall 1988): 116 n. 2.

65. For an insightful study of Boddy, see Darin D. Lenz, "'Visions on the Battlefields': Alexander A. Boddy, Early British Pentecostalism, and the First World War, 1914-1918," *JRH* 32 (September 2008): 281-302.

66. For the organization of the PMU in Great Britain, see "The Pentecostal Missionary Union," *Conf*, January 1909, 13-15; James S. Dennis, et al., eds., *World Atlas of Christian Missions* (New York: Student Volunteer Movement for Foreign Missions, 1911), 38; Peter Kay, "The Pentecostal Missionary Union and the Fourfold Gospel with Baptism in the Holy Spirit and Speaking in Tongues: A New Power for Missions?" *JEPTA* 19 (1999): 89-104; on Polhill, see Hocken, "Cecil H. Polhill," 116-40.

67. "What is the Baptism of the Holy Ghost and Fire?" *FF*, October 1911, 1 (Polhill's emphasis).

68. Kay, "Pentecostal Missionary Union," 91.

69. Cited in ibid., 93.

70. See Cornelis van der Laan, *Sectarian Against His Will: Gerrit Roelof Polman and the Birth of Pentecostalism in the Netherlands* (Metuchen, N.J.: Scarecrow, 1991), 204-5; also David Landin, *Our Foreign Missions: A Biblical Guideline* (Stockholm: Philadelphia Church, 1937); Willis Save, "Pentecost in Sweden," *WP*, June 1971, 19-20.

71. On Ward, see "Fifty Years of Pentecostal Fullness," *PE*, September 8, 1957, 8-9, 22-23; Whitt, "Developing a Pentecostal Missiology," 139-40, 180-83, 277-80.

72. On Fisher, see "Meeting of the Council of the Christian and Missionary Alliance," *CMAW*, May 1, 1899, 183; "The Maritime Provinces," *CMAW*, September 16, 1899, 249.

73. Dennis, et al., eds., *World Atlas*, 16.

74. Ellen Hebden, quoted in Miller, *Canadian Pentecostals*, 106.

75. A. G. Ward, quoted in ibid., 105.

76. A. A. Boddy, "An American P.M.U.," *Conf*, August 1909, 175.

77. Ibid.

78. Ibid. Alexander Boddy described Lupton in 1909 as a "keen, lovable man, about 40 or more, alert, with dark complexion and short beard and mustache, middle-sized, dressed in dark clothes, not clerical dress especially, but like the evangelists and preachers in the States. His manner is perfectly natural, and you feel he is a man of God. He has been in West Africa, and his whole heart goes out in intercession for the heathen and the missionaries." A. A. Boddy, "Across the Atlantic," *Conf*, August 1909, 172.

79. Ibid.

80. "Many Missionaries," *Alliance Review* (Ohio), July 27, 1909, 7.

81. *TGW*, vol. 1, no. 2, 13.

82. On Lupton's participation at a New York gathering, see Albert Weaver, "The New York Convention," *WW*, February 1910, 54-55. For his sermon at the Stone Church in Chicago, see "'Wilt Thou Go with This Man?' A Strong Plea for Heathen Evangelization," *LRE*, June 1910, 18-24. The Missionary Training School continued for a time under the direction of Grace Davis; "Across the Atlantic," *Conf*, September 1909, 197.

83. "Gift of Tongues Sect Likely to Go to Pieces," *Evening Observer* (Dunkirk, N.Y.), December 17, 1910, 11; "Oust Lupton," *New Castle News* (Pa.), December 22, 1910, 3; McPherson, *Life of Levi R. Lupton*, 160-66; "Arrest of Lupton Is Prevented," *Newark Advocate* (Ohio), December 15, 1910, 1, 5; "Find Old Scandal in Lupton's Life," *Cleveland Plain Dealer* (Ohio), December 17, 1910, 1, 9; "Lupton Sorely Tempted Falls," *Evening Tribune* (Marysville, Ohio), December 14, 1910, 1. For information on John T. Boddy, see Stanley H. Frodsham, "Former Editor of *Evangel* with the Lord," *PE*, November 21, 1931, 7; idem, *With Signs Following: The Story of the Latter Day Pentecostal Revival* (Springfield, Mo.: Gospel Publishing House, 1926), 43-47.

84. "Campmeeting Notices," *LRE*, June 1915, 11.

85. "Called by God to Go to Egypt in a Camp Meeting in Alliance Ohio," *BM*, September 1908, 1; Lillian Trasher, "Why I Came To Egypt Thirty-four Years Ago," *PE*, September 23, 1944, 1, 6-7.

86. "Lupton Cult Seeking Gift," *Marion Weekly Star* (Ohio), July 15, 1911, 2; "Costs $2 to Live 2 Months in India," *New Castle News* (Pa.), July 24, 1911, 2; "'Apostolics' Laying Siege to Pittsburg [sic]," *San Antonio Light* (Tex.), July 18, 1911, 5; "Strange Sect Roll, Scream and Kick in Worship," *Fort Wayne Journal-Gazette* (Ind.), July 12, 1911, 5.

87. Christian J. Lucas, "In Memoriam," *FGMH*, April 1921, 3.

88. For example, "Convention Reports," *CAFMW*, August 28, 1896, 174.

89. For Draper's friendship with the Kinney family and her limited participation at Shiloh, see "History of the World's Evangelization Crusade on Apostolic Principles Continued During 1895," *TFire*, January 1, 1897, 8-9. Helen Sandford's father, C. N. Kinney, a close friend of A. B. Simpson, served on the Alliance Board of Managers for many years. In regard to Shiloh, Draper's involvement at Sandford's conferences appears to have ended in 1895 or in 1896; she also wrote a column entitled "Children's Corner" for his *Tongues of Fire* magazine.

90. M. T. Draper, "Work in Sing Sing," *CAFMW*, January 12, 1894, 49; see also "A Missionary Incident as Told by Miss Draper at the Council," *CMAW*, May 18, 1901, 278.

91. Evelyn L. Fish, *The Ossining Heights Methodist Church* (Ossining, N.Y.: By the author, 1959), 2. Fish also states that the second Methodist church in Ossining was organized in the Stone Mansion. On the Woman's Union Missionary Society and Sarah Doremus, see Dana L. Robert, *American Women in Mission: A Social History of Their Thought and Practice* (Macon, Ga.: Mercer University Press, 1996), 115-16.

92. Lucas, "In Memoriam," 4.

93. For the problem created by those seeking Spirit baptism with tongues at the Alliance Convention at Old Orchard Beach, Maine, in 1907, see Bartleman, *Azusa Street*, 108-9. Both Minnie Draper and Alice Belle Garrigus attended the special prayer meetings at the village church and later "in the woods," because they were not allowed to hold them on the campground.

94. Ibid.; see also Gary B. McGee, "Three Notable Women in Pentecostal Ministry," *AGH* 6 (Spring 1985-86): 3-5.

95. Burton K. Janes, *The Lady Who Came: The Biography of Alice Belle Garrigus, Newfoundland's First Pentecostal Pioneer* (St. John's, Newfoundland: Good Tidings Press, 1982), 100-101; Nienkirchen, *A. B. Simpson*, 112-13.

96. Letter of Minnie T. Draper to the secretary of the Christian & Missionary Alliance, April 6, 1912.

97. For the Pentecostal developments and the problems created in the Alliance branch in Newark, see "A Remarkable Testimony," *CMAW*, November 9, 1907, 98; "Newark Meetings," *CMAW*, January 9, 1909, 254; M. H. Cromwell, "New Jersey Prayer Conference," *CMAW*, April 10, 1909, 34.

98. Christian J. Lucas, Harry J. Steil, John Johnson, with Elizabeth Yost, "The Ossining Gospel Assembly, Ossining, New York," unpublished paper, 1974, 2. Available at Flower Pentecostal Heritage Center, Springfield, MO 65802. Incorporated in 1914, the Ossining Gospel Assembly later joined the Assemblies of God.

99. Untitled news note mentioning the death of Alice Thompson, *CMAW*, December 24, 1910, 8. Before going to Newark, Thompson had pastored the Alliance branch in Ossining. For the date of the founding of Bethel Pentecostal Assembly, see "With the Lord," *FGMH*, July 1925, 9; it joined the General Council of the Assemblies of God in 1953 and changed its name to Bethel Assembly of God. Also, *Dedicating unto Our Lord: Bethel Assembly of God: 1913—50th Anniversary—1963* (Newark: Bethel Assembly of God, 1963).

100. Lucas et al., "Ossining Gospel Assembly," 1-2.

101. Allan and Carrie Swift left for China in 1915 to work in Tibet as missionaries under the Pentecostal Missionary Union (Great Britain and Ireland); see "A New Bible School," *FGMH*, April 1921, 17; "Brother Swift Called Home," *PE*, March 15, 1964, 21.

102. Harlan P. Beach and Charles H. Fahs, eds., *World Missionary Atlas* (New York: Institute of Social and Religious Research, 1925), 24.

103. Watson Argue, "The Get Acquainted Page," *LRE*, July 1936, 14.

104. The periodical began in 1917 and ceased publication in 1927; see "Important Notice," *FGMH*, Nov.-Dec. 1927, 4. A later resumption of the publication in 1931 in South Africa took the name *South African Evangel*.

105. For glimpses into the historical development of the Pentecostal Mission in South Africa, see "Kroonstad Conference," *FGMH*, January 1921, 8; Eleanor B. Schoenborn, "Reports from Other Lands," *FGMH*, January 1921, 16. Also, John Richards, "South Africa," unpublished mss., May 11, 1978; available at editorial office files of Assemblies of God World Missions, Springfield, MO 65802.

106. See W. F. P. Burton, *God Working with Them: Being Eighteen Years of Congo Evangelistic Mission History* (London: Victory, 1933).

107. Beach and Fahs, eds., *World Missionary Atlas*, 24.

108. McGee, *This Gospel Shall Be Preached*, 65-67.

109. Peter Watt, *From Africa's Soil: The Story of the Assemblies of God in Southern Africa* (Cape Town: Struik Christian Books, 1992), 19-26.

110. "Wilkinsburg Pentecostal Convention," *NA*, March 1909, 15.

111. "Announcement," *WWit*, June 1915, 8.

112. F. H. Senft, "McKeesport," *CMAW*, April 18, 1903, 10.

113. For example, see F. E. Marsh, "The Gift of Tongues," *LT*, May 1907, 259-64; Nienkirchen, *A. B. Simpson*, 89-96.

114. Beach and Fahs, eds., *World Missionary Atlas*, 24. For the influence of the Casley brothers on Assemblies of God leaders, see Glenn Gohr, "The Ministry of Ben Mahan: A Man of Prayer and Conviction," *AGH* 14 (Winter 1994-95): 6-9, 34-35.

115. A premier evangelical author, John Pollock, ignored Polhill's Pentecostal involvement in *The Cambridge Seven* (London: InterVarsity, 1966), 109.

116. See Gary B. McGee, "Minnie F. Abrams: Another Context, Another Founder," in Goff and Wacker, eds., *Portraits of a Generation*, 87-104.

117. For example, "Missionary and Church News," *BGBA*, December 7, 1912, 3.

118. Lucy Rider Meyer, "Missionary Training for Women," *MRW* 1 (n.s.) (December 1888): 940-44.

119. Effie G. Lindsay, *Missionaries of the Minneapolis Branch of the Woman's Foreign Missionary Society of the Methodist Episcopal Church* (n.p., 1904), 20-23; Frances J. Baker, *The Story of the Woman's Foreign Missionary Society of the Methodist Episcopal Church: 1869-1895* (Cincinnati: Curts & Jennings, 1898), 233.

120. Robert, *American Women in Mission*, 245.

121. Minnie F. Abrams, "The Midnight Darkness of India's Superstition," *LRE*, August 1910, 8.

122. "Writes of Famine Horrors in India," *Monroe Weekly Times* (Wis.), May 24, 1900, 5.

123. S. M. Adhav, ed., *Pandita Ramabai* (Madras: Christian Literature Society, 1979), 216.

124. Max Wood Moorhead, "Pentecost in Mukti, India," *AF* (L.A.), September 1907, 4, cols. 2-3.

125. Minnie F. Abrams, *The Baptism of the Holy Ghost and Fire*, 2d ed. (Kedgaon: Mukti Mission Press, 1906), 69-70. The "first edition" was simply a series of articles in the *Bombay Guardian*, *Indian Witness*, and *Christian Patriot* that were later reproduced in book form—the "second edition"; see "'The Baptism of the Holy Ghost and Fire,'" *Bombay Guardian*, July 28, 1906, 12. Abrams believed that tongues would normally accompany Spirit baptism, but believed there could be exceptions; see Minnie F. Abrams, "The Object of the Baptism in the Holy Spirit," *LRE*, May 1911, 10.

126. Willis Collins Hoover, *History of the Pentecostal Revival in Chile*, trans. Mario G. Hoover (Lakeland, Fla.: By the translator, 2000), 9.

127. "The Homestead (Pa.) Camp Meeting," *LRE*, August 1910, 13. On Elizabeth V. Baker, see McGee, "Three Notable Women," 5, 12.

128. Abrams, "Midnight," 10. For a description of Abrams and a "Prayer Band" in action, see A. L. Wiley, "India," *MW* (n.s.), May 1, 1906, 19-22.

129. "Pentecostal Items," *Conf*, January 1911, 5; Minnie F. Abrams, "A Note of Praise," *LRE*, October 1910, 11; "Missionaries Enroute to India," *LRE*, November 1910, 12. The original party consisted of Abrams, Phinette Bristol, Grace Dempster, Minnie Houck, Edith Baugh, Lillie Doll, Blanche Cunningham, and an eighth person, "Miss MacDonald," who met them when their ship docked at Marseilles.

130. Ethel M. King, "Uska Bazar," *PE*, October 14, 1922, 13.

131. Minnie F. Abrams, "'Whom Shall I Send?'" *WW*, July 1911, 218; also A. W., "Fallen Asleep," *WW*, April 1913, 1.

132. "Prayer Answered in North India," *LRE*, August 1911, 14-16; Anderson, *Spreading Fires*, 100-101.

133. King, "Uska Bazar," 13.

134. J. P. Jones, *Year Book of Missions in India, Burma and Ceylon: 1912* (Madras: Christian Literature Society for India, 1912), 596.

135. D. L. McCarty, "Letter from India," *Cambridge City Tribune* (Ind.), May 27, 1920, 1; see also Edith E. Baugh, "Upon the Handmaidens Will I Pour Out My Spirit," *LRE*, July 1909, 4-6; idem, "Entrance into Heathen Hearts thro' Healing: Taking New Territory for God," *LRE*, April 1918, 15-18; also Gordon P. Gardner, *Out of Zion Into All the World* (Shippensburg, Pa.: Companion, 1990), 275-84.

136. James Inglis, comp., *Protestant Missionary Directory* (Ajmer, Rajputana: Scottish Mission Industries, 1917), 94-95.

137. Everett A. and Ruth Marshall Wilson, "Alice E. Luce: A Visionary Victorian," in *Portraits of a Generation*, 159-76.

138. *Minutes of the General Council of the Assemblies of God, 1927*, 114-15.

139. Violet Schoonmaker, *Christian Schoonmaker: A Man Who Loved the Will of God* (Landour, Mussoorie, India: Hyratt, 1959), 35.

140. See Cavaness, "Factors Influencing the Decrease," 291-304.

141. Robert, *American Women in Mission*, 254.

142. On Reiff, see Cavaness, "Factors Influencing the Decrease," 85-87.

143. For Garrigus, see Janes, *Lady Who Came*; also vol. 2: *The Lady Who Stayed* (St. John's, Newfoundland: Good Tidings Press, 1983).

144. On Brown, see Edith L. Blumhofer, *Pentecost in My Soul: Explorations in the Meaning of Pentecostal Experience in the Early Assemblies of God* (Springfield, Mo.: Gospel Publishing House, 1989), 191-219.

145. See Mary Campbell Wilson, *The Obedience of Faith: The Story of Rev. Christine A. Gibson, Founder of Zion Bible Institute* (Tulsa, Okla.: Victory House, 1993).

146. See Virginia E. Moss, *Following the Shepherd: Testimony of Mrs. Virginia E. Moss* (North Bergen, N.J.: Beulah Heights Assembly and School, ca. 1919).

147. Esther Bragg Harvey, *The Faithfulness of God*, rev. ed. (Battle Creek, Mich.: Grounds Gospel Press and Book Store, 1949), 14-23; Anna Maria Helmbrecht, "Application for Endorsement as Missionary," Foreign Missions Committee of the General Council of the Assemblies of God, n.d. Available at editorial office files, Assemblies of God World Missions, Springfield, MO 65802.

148. "Anniversary," *Mara*, April 1934, 5.

149. "Withdrew from Church," *Mansfield News* (Ohio), July 15, 1907, 2.

150. For example, "Notes from the Home Field," *CMAW*, September 1, 1909, 42.

151. "Anniversary," 5.

152. "With the Lord: Mrs. E. H. Wurmser," *AW*, November 7, 1951, 701. See Larry Lepard, "The Early Christian and Missionary Alliance Mission in Norwalk, Ohio," in *Gospel Tabernacle of the Christian & Missionary Alliance Now Known as Norwalk Alliance Church, Norwalk, Ohio: Her First 75 Years: 1928-2003* (Norwalk, Ohio: Norwalk Alliance Church, ca. 2003), 5.

153. Reinhold Bauer, quoted in "New 'Gift of Tongues' Cult Splits Adams St. Mission," *Sandusky Star Journal* (Ohio), May 30, 1912, 1.

154. Etta Wurmser, "Chosen in the Furnace of Affliction," *LRE*, January 1917, 20.

155. Ibid., 21.

156. Wurmser is listed as a "missionary" in *Directory of the City of Norwalk, Ohio* (Norwalk: W. M. Lawrence, 1907-1908), 74. In "Chosen in the Furnace of Affliction," she does not specify the date of her Spirit baptism (likely in 1906 or 1907). Apostolic Bible School was in operation by 1911 with nine students according to *Directory of the City of Norwalk, Ohio* (Norwalk: W. M. Lawrence, 1911), 96.

157. Wurmser, "Chosen in the Furnace of Affliction," 22.

158. Ibid.

159. "Findlay Property for Bible School," *Morning Republican* (Findlay, Ohio), June 29, 1914.

160. Esther Bragg Harvey, unpublished biographical memoir, May 14, 1979, 1; available at editorial office files, Assemblies of God World Missions, Springfield, MO 65802. The Flowers held meetings at the school in Norwalk in 1911.

161. E. N. Bell, "Some Complaints," *WWit*, January 20, 1914, 2.

162. See Michael G. Owen, "Preparing Students for the First Harvest: Early Ohio Bible Schools," *AGH* 9 (Winter 1989-1990): 3-5, 16-19.

163. Wurmser, "Chosen in the Furnace of Affliction," 22.

164. "Carl Stroh Writes," *Butler County Democrat* (Hamilton, Ohio), April 16, 1914, 6.

165. Wurmser, "Chosen in the Furnace of Affliction," 22.

166. *Constitution of and Rules Governing the National & International Pentecostal Missionary Union*, July 19, 1919, 1.

167. "Latest Official Membership List of the National and International Pentecostal Missionary Union," *Mara*, March 1929, 2-5.

168. The Pentecostal Assemblies of Canada separated from the Assemblies of God (U.S.A.) in 1925; see Whitt, "Developing a Pentecostal Missiology," 185-233.

169. M. L. Ryan, "The Pentecostal Movement," *CR*, May 1915, 322.

170. D. W. Kerr, "Cooperation, Not Ecclesiasticism," *WWit*, May 20, 1914, 2.

171. "General Convention of Saints and Churches of God in Christ," *WWit*, December 20, 1913, 1.

172. "General Convention," 1. See also Darrin J. Rodgers, "The Assemblies of God and the Long Journey toward Racial Reconciliation," *AGH* 28 (2008): 50-61, 66.

173. "A Closer and Deeper Fellowship for the Pentecostal Assemblies of Indiana and the Central States," *CE*, July 19, 1913, 1-2.

174. Cavaness, "Factors Influencing the Decrease," 382.

175. *Minutes of the General Council, 1916*, 8-14; E. N. Bell, "The Sad New Issue," *WWit*, June 1915, 2; cf. Frank J. Ewart, *The Phenomenon of Pentecost* (St. Louis: Pentecostal Publishing House, 1947), 108-20; David A. Reed, *"In Jesus' Name": The History and Beliefs of Oneness Pentecostals* (Blandford Forum, Dorset, U.K.: Deo Publishing, 2008). For the impact of the "New Issue" on Assemblies of God foreign missions, see McGee, *This Gospel Shall Be Preached*, 89, 106. On Oneness Pentecostal missions, see Talmadge L. French, "'The Whole Gospel to the Whole World': A History of Missions of Oneness Pentecostalism," paper presented at the 29th Annual Meeting of the Society for Pentecostal Studies, March 16-18, 2000, at Northwest College, Kirkland, Washington. The *World Missionary Atlas* (1925), edited by Harlan P. Beach and Charles H. Fahs (p. 24), lists the "Foreign Mission of the Pentecostal Assemblies of the World" (PAW), a Oneness denomination, but provides neither a date for its organization nor a mission statement. By 1925, it had missionaries in Japan, China, India, Palestine, Liberia, Kenya, Jamaica, and Hawaii.

176. Later general officers stoutly resisted the term "denomination," preferring to refer to the General Council as the "fellowship"; see Thomas F. Zimmerman, "Fervent in Spirit," *PE*, October 8, 1961, 3, 13, 21, 24.

177. *General Council Minutes*, 1916, 10; cf. J. L. Hall, *The United Pentecostal Church and the Evangelical Movement* (Hazelwood, Mo.: Word Aflame, 1990). In 1927, after the General Council met in Springfield, Missouri, and adopted a constitution and bylaws, the official publication, *PE*, did not mention this signal development in the report on the conference to its readership.

178. "An Appeal to the Pentecostal People Throughout the World to Observe Sunday, Nov. 3rd and Monday, Nov. 4, 1918 in United Prayer Inviting Jesus, Our Heavenly Bridegroom, to Come Back," *CE*, August 24, 1918, 1; McGee, *This Gospel Shall Be Preached*, 109.

179. Kenneth Scott Latourette, "Ecumenical Bearings of the Missionary Movement and the International Missionary Council," in *A History of the Ecumenical Movement, 1517-1948*, 2d ed., ed. Ruth Rouse and Stephen Charles Neill (Philadelphia: Westminster, 1967), 374.

180. *Executive Presbytery Minutes*, April 20, 1920; Cecil M. Robeck, Jr., "The Assemblies of God and Ecumenical Cooperation: 1920-1965," in *Pentecostalism in Context: Essays in Honor of William W. Menzies*, ed. Wonsuk Ma and Robert P. Menzies (Sheffield: Sheffield Academic Press, 1997), 110-20.

181. J. Roswell Flower, "Little Talks with the Office Editor," *WE*, May 13, 1916, 2.

182. D. W. Kerr, "Third Missionary Conference," *CE*, August 10, 1918, 11.

183. Willa B. Lowther, "Approval of the Missionary Conference," *WE*, February 23, 1918, 11.

184. McGee, *This Gospel Shall Be Preached*, 118-20.

185. Stanley H. Frodsham, "The Fourth Missionary Conference," *PE*, October 18, 1919, 1.

186. For the early development of Church of God (Cleveland, Tenn.) foreign missions, see Charles W. Conn, *Where the Saints Have Trod: A History of Church of God Missions* (Cleveland, Tenn.: Pathway, 1959), 11-26.

187. Beacham, *Azusa East*, 59-75.

188. G. B. Cashwell, "Pentecost in North Carolina," *AF* (L.A.), January 1907, 1, col. 4.

189. For the limited work of the earlier mission board of the Pentecostal Holiness Church established in 1904, see George F. Taylor, "Our Church History," *PHA*, February 24, 1921, 9.

190. "World-Wide Mission Band," *AE*, June 1909, 4. The name may have been changed to Pentecostal Missionary Society by 1912; see "Pentecostal Missionary Society, Dunn, N.C.," *AE*, January 1912, 8. Whether the latter continued separately from the Foreign Missionary Board of the Pentecostal Holiness Church remains unclear.

191. George F. Taylor, "Our Church History" (Foreign Missions), *PHA*, April 7, 1921, 8; also Randall J. Stephens, *The Fire Spreads: Holiness and Pentecostalism in the American South* (Cambridge, Mass.: Harvard University Press, 2008), 179-85.

192. Beach and Fahs, eds., *World Missionary Atlas*, 24.

193. Mrs. K. E. M. [Geraldine] Spooner, A. E. Robinson, P. F. Beacham, comp., *Sketches of the Life of K. E. M. Spooner: Missionary, South Africa* (n.p., 1937), 3.

194. Ibid., 86-88.

195. W. H. Daniels, ed., *Dr. Cullis and His Work* (Boston: Willard Tract Repository, 1885), 319-336; Niklaus, *All for Jesus*, 170.

196. Kenneth E. M. Spooner, *A Sketch of Native Life in South Africa* (n.p., ca. 1930), 5-6.

197. Campbell, *Pentecostal Holiness Church*, 349; Frank G. Tunstall, *The Simultaneous Principle: The History of IPHC World Missions: The First 100 Years* (Franklin Springs, Ga.: LSR Publications, 2005), 160-67.

198. Martha A. Neeley, "First Hardships as a Missionary," *LRE*, April 1914, 11-12.

199. Isaac and Martha Neeley, "Mr. and Mrs. Neeley's Report," *Report of the Liberia Mission*, 19. The Church of God in Christ did not organize a foreign missions department until 1925; see Carlis L. Moody, "The Church of God in Christ Movement," *WP* 3, no. 7 (1979): 22.

200. W. H. Chandler, "A Visit to Boydton Institute," *AW*, May 8, 1920, 91-92; William C. Turner, Jr., *The United Holy Church of America: A Study in Black Holiness-Pentecostalism* (Piscataway, N.J.: Gorgias, 2006), 51, 65-66.

201. See "Our Colored Work in the South," *CMAW*, January 14, 1911, 252.

202. "Beulah Park Convention," *AW*, August 5, 1916, 300-301.

203. Untitled news note, *AW*, September 2, 1916, 1.

204. H. L. Fisher, *History of the United Holy Church of America, Inc.* (N.p., n.d.), 18.

205. Ibid.

206. Ibid., 19; Chester W. Gregory, *History of the United Holy Church of America, Inc.: 1886-1986* (Baltimore: Gateway, 1986), 188.

207. Beach and Fahs, eds., *World Missionary Atlas*, 24. For more information on early United Holy Church missionaries in Liberia, as well as the prominent evangelistic role of its women missionaries, see Fisher, *History of the United Holy Church*, 21-22.

208. W. W. Simpson, "Bro. W. W. Simpson's Plans," *WE*, January 5, 1918, 7. On Simpson, see Michael D. Wilson, "Contending for Tongues: W. W. Simpson's Pentecostal Experience in Northwest China," *Pneuma* 29 (2007): 281-298.

209. Frank W. Sandford, "Tongues of Fire. Other Tongues," *TFire*, April 15, 1896, 59. See also F. G. Harrington, "The Holy Spirit and Missions," *BMR* 2 (November 1896): 412-419.

210. Simpson, "Bro. W. W. Simpson's Plans," 7.

211. Reiff, "Missionary Problems," 18.

212. For example, see "A Conference of Pentecostal Workers and Missionaries, Boston, March 5-13, 1913," *LRE*, October 1912, 24.

213. A. A. Boddy, "Westward Ho!" *Conf*, October 1914, 183.

8. MISSIONARIES AND STRATEGIES

1. Cora Fritsch [Falkner], *Letters from Cora*, comp. Homer and Alice Fritsch (n.p.: By the compilers, 1987), 111.

2. Lillian Trasher, "Little Orphans Not Forgotten," *WE*, March 20, 1915, 4.

3. Cecil Polhill, quoted in David Maxwell, "'Networks and Niches': The Worldwide Transmission of the Azusa Street Revival," in *The Azusa Street Revival and Its Legacy*, ed. Harold D. Hunter and Cecil M. Robeck, Jr. (Cleveland, Tenn.: Pathway, 2006), 132.

4. John Richards, "South Africa," May 11, 1978, 1. Available at editorial office files of Assemblies of God World Missions, Springfield, MO 65802.

5. Lula Boyette, "My Call to Africa," *PHA*, December 21, 1922, 6.

6. J. Russell Chandran, "The Christian Mission and the Judgment of History," in *Missions under the Cross: Addresses Delivered at the Enlarged Meeting of the International Missionary Council at Willingen, in Germany, 1952; with Statements Issued by the Meeting*, ed. Norman Goodall (New York: Friendship, 1953), 105.

7. The "Three Selfs" of indigenous church theory brought by missionaries to China became the inspiration for the Three-Self Patriotic Movement, known officially as the National Committee of the Three-Self Patriotic Movement of the Protestant Churches in China, which serves as the government-sanctioned Christian organization for the People's Republic. See Wilbert R. Shenk, "The Origins and Evolution of the Three-Selfs in Relation to China," *IBMR* 14 (January 1990): 28-35.

8. I am grateful to the following students for the contributions they made to this chapter through their historical research in my course, "Early Pentecostal Missions,"

offered in the spring of 2008: Thomas Biro, Ashley Burdette, Steven Campbell, Christopher Craft, Terrence Harris, Alvin Hook, Brad Kesler, Nicholas Malo, Jason Myers, Benjamin Phillips, Sean Silverii, Ronald Van Tilburg, and Joel Wilson.

9. Fritsch, *Letters from Cora*, 26. Fritsch married missionary Homer Falkner in 1912.

10. Ibid., 32.

11. Jennie Etha Kirkland, "Application for Endorsement as Missionary," Foreign Missions Committee of the General Council of the Assemblies of God, n.d., 3. Available at editorial office files of Assemblies of God World Missions, Springfield, MO 65802. See also Nettie Moomau, "The Lord Working with Signs Following in China," *PT*, May 1923, 3.

12. B. A. Schoeneich, "Telling the Gospel Story in Nicaragua," *LRE*, November 1925, 19.

13. "Gunnar Vingren and Daniel Berg," *CE*, August 22, 1914, 4.

14. T. H. Rousseau, "Report of the China Work," *PHA*, March 15, 1923, 5.

15. I. S. Neeley, "Miraculous Deliverances from Demon Possession," *LRE*, August 1919, 10.

16. See H. A. Baker, *Under His Wings* (Taiwan: By the author, n.d.). Available at Flower Pentecostal Heritage Center, Springfield, MO 65802.

17. H. A. Baker, "An Amazing Pentecostal Outpouring in Western China," *LRE*, June 1929, 4.

18. Ibid., 19.

19. Ibid., 5.

20. Bertha N. Cook, quoted in Robert F. Cook, *A Quarter Century of Divine Leading in India* (Chengannur, Travancore State, India: By the author, ca. 1939), 52.

21. For the sorrows faced by early Assemblies of God missionaries, see George O. Wood, "Their Last Full Measure," *Enri*, Fall 1999, 66-71.

22. Schoeneich, "Telling the Gospel Story," 17.

23. Peggy Scarborough, *Maria Atkinson* (Cleveland, Tenn.: Pathway, n.d.), 11-13.

24. Julia Richardson, "Fear Not," *CE*, March 28, 1914, 7.

25. Charles W. Conn, *Where the Saints Have Trod: A History of Church of God Missions* (Cleveland, Tenn.: Pathway, 1959), 24-25.

26. Untitled news note based on letter from Mrs. John James, *LRE*, February 1919, 13.

27. Macie M. Boddy, "Miss Boddy's Report for 1916," in *Report of the Liberia Interior Mission, 1908-1916* (Cape Palmas, Liberia: Liberia Interior Mission, ca. 1916), 17.

28. Conn, *Where the Saints Have Trod*, 133.

29. Everett A. Wilson, "Identity, Community, and Status: The Legacy of the Central American Pentecostal Pioneers," in *Earthen Vessels: American Evangelicals and Foreign Missions, 1880-1980*, ed. Joel A. Carpenter and Wilbert R. Shenk (Grand Rapids: Eerdmans, 1990), 136-39.

30. Fritsch, *Letters from Cora*, 124. "Mother" Emma Lawler and Beatrice remained as missionaries for many years and founded Emmanuel Missionary Society.

31. "Alleged Crank in Limelight," *Daily Oregon Statesman*, January 7, 1911, 1, 6.

32. Blanche Appleby, "Heroism on the Mission Field," *LRE*, June 1918, 20.

33. Fritsch, *Letters from Cora*, 112.

34. Leonard Bolton, *China Call* (Springfield, Mo.: Gospel Publishing House, 1984), 48-49.

35. W. W. Simpson, "'In Remembrance of Me': A Plea for the Unfinished Task," *LRE*, February 1933, 9-10, 23.

36. Violet Schoonmaker, *Christian Schoonmaker: A Man Who Loved the Will of God* (Landour, Mussoorie, India: Hyratt, n.d.), 37. In contrast, China missionary Allan Swift,

also a former member of the Alliance and graduate of the Missionary Training Institute at Nyack, had his young son vaccinated for small pox, appealing to 1 Peter 2:13a: "Submit yourselves for the Lord's sake to every human authority." Allan A. Swift, letter in "Tidings from Tibet and Other Lands," *FF*, July 1915, 6.

37. *From the Beginning of Bishop C. H. Mason and the Early Pioneers of the Church of God in Christ* (Memphis: Church of God in Christ, 1991), 49.

38. "Carl Stroh Writes," *Butler County Democrat* (Ohio), April 16, 1914, 6; Philip Wittich, "Death of Rev. Karl Wittich and Rev. Clarence Grothaus in German East Africa," *CE*, May 9, 1914, 2.

39. J. Pengwern Jones to Jessie Penn-Lewis, July 4, 1907; available at the Donald Gee Centre for Pentecostal and Charismatic Research, Mattersey Hall, Mattersey, U.K. DN10 5HD.

40. Annie Cressman, quoted in Thomas William Miller, *Canadian Pentecostals: A History of the Pentecostal Assemblies of Canada* (Mississauga, Ont.: Full Gospel Publishing House, 1994), 230.

41. J. W. Buckalew, "Evangelization," *Echoes from the General Assembly Held at Cleveland, Tennessee, January 9-14, 1912*, 13-14; on the colorful ministry of Buckalew, see Charles W. Conn, *Like a Mighty Army: A History of the Church of God, 1886-1976*, rev. ed. (Cleveland, Tenn.: Pathway, 1977), 106-10.

42. "Foreign Mission," *Echoes from the Tenth Annual Assembly of the Churches of God Held at Cleveland, Tennessee, November 2-8, 1914*, 28.

43. Stanley H. Frodsham, "The World Wide Missionary Conference," *CE*, June 1, 1918, 2.

44. An unnamed Pentecostal missionary, quoted in Mrs. A. G. [Lillian] Garr, "Missionary Admonitions," *LRE*, February 1912, 23.

45. T. H. Rousseau, "An Open Letter to the Supporters of Missions in China," *PHA*, September 21, 1922, 2.

46. Frodsham, "World Wide Missionary Conference," 3.

47. Ibid. See also J. Elmor Morrison, "Missionary Farewell," *PT*, December 1923, 1.

48. J. M. L. Harrow, "To Our Friends in Christ Jesus," in *Report of the Liberia Interior Mission*, 8.

49. On the concept of prevailing prayer among Pentecostals, see Grant Wacker, *Heaven Below: Early Pentecostals and American Culture* (Cambridge, Mass.: Harvard University Press, 2001), 25-28.

50. Anna C. Reiff, "Missionary Problems That Confront Us: What Is Our Responsibility?" *LRE*, January 1913, 17.

51. "Prospective Missionaries," *PT*, June 1923, 5.

52. Z. D. Simpson, "Report of Committee No. 4, Foreign Missions," *Church of God General Assembly Minutes; Services (continued); Financial Reports; Statistical Report; Constitution; Teachings* (pp. 47-71), 47.

53. An article from the *Bible Standard* (Eugene, Ore.), December 1927, 4, quoted in Robert Bryant Mitchell, *Heritage & Horizons: The History of Open Bible Standard Churches* (Des Moines: Open Bible Publishers, 1982), 105.

54. R. Bryant and Lucille M. Mitchell, *Heritage & Harvests: The History of International Ministries of Open Bible Standard Churches* (Des Moines: Open Bible Publishers, 1995), 15.

55. Alfred L. Worth, quoted in Aaron M. Wilson, *Our Story: The History of the Pentecostal Church of God*, 2d ed. (Joplin, Mo.: Messenger, 2001), 166.

56. A. Elizabeth Brown, "Safe Return from Jerusalem of a Veteran Missionary," *LRE*, October 1917, 21.

57. Garr, "Missionary Admonitions," 24.

58. "Receives a Chinese Vase," *Indianapolis Star*, February 25, 1912, 24.

59. Jonathan J. Bonk, *Missions and Money: Affluence as a Western Missionary Problem* (Maryknoll, N.Y.: Orbis Books, 1991), 28-29.

60. The following completed M.A. degrees at the Kennedy School of Missions, a school within the Hartford Seminary Foundation: Philip Andrew Crouch, "Fundamentals of Faith: A Translation from Kitāb al-arbaīn fī uṣūl al-dīn by Abū Ḥāmid Muḥammad bin Muḥammad bin Muḥammad al-Ghazālī al-Ṭusi" (M.A. thesis, Hartford Seminary Foundation, 1946); Paul DeWitt Schoonmaker, "Mystic Union Examined and Compared in the Apostle Paul and Śrī Śaṇkarāchārya" (M.A. thesis, Hartford Seminary Foundation, 1949); Ruth Agnes Schoonmaker, "Theism of Kabīr and Its Relationship to Bhāgavata and Ṣufi Thought" (M.A. thesis, Hartford Seminary Foundation, 1950).

61. Thomas Hindle, "What Has the Church of Christ Done for Mongolia?" *LRE*, May 1917, 7.

62. Max Wood Moorhead, "Did Christ Come to Fulfil [*sic*] Hinduism?—An Enquiry," *BGBA*, November 16, 1912, 10-11; see also idem, "A Bank Clerk's Conversion: A Personal Testimony," *BGBA*, December 28, 1912, 6-7; on his later assessment of the Student Volunteer Movement and the Young Men's Christian Association, see idem, "The Perils of Bolshevism at Home and Abroad," *PE*, February 7, 1920, 2. On John N. Farquhar, see Eric J. Sharpe, "J. N. Farquhar, 1861-1929: Presenting Christ as the Crown of Hinduism," in *Mission Legacies: Biographical Studies of Leaders of the Modern Missionary Movement*, ed. Gerald H. Anderson, et al. (Maryknoll, N.Y.: Orbis Books, 1994), 290-96.

63. Marie Ericsson, "The Christian's Debt to the Moslem World," *LRE*, March 1926, 4-5.

64. See Eric Nelson Newberg, "The Pentecostal Mission in Palestine, 1906-1948: A Post-colonial Assessment of Pentecostal Zionism" (Ph.D. diss., Regent University, 2008).

65. Lillian Trasher to Christine Carmichael, January 6, 1954. Available at editorial office files, Assemblies of God World Missions, Springfield, MO 65802.

66. Ethel Leah Bingeman, "Application for Endorsement as Missionary," Foreign Missions Committee of the General Council of the Assemblies of God, Springfield, Missouri, October 9, 1919, 1. Available at editorial office files, Assemblies of God World Missions, Springfield, MO 65802.

67. Letter from Harold K. Needham to W. T. Gaston, December 5, 1923. Available at Flower Pentecostal Heritage Center, Springfield, MO 65802.

68. Letter from George and Miriam Cook to the author, September 19, 1985. For Cook's ministry in India, see Cook, *Quarter Century of Divine Leading*, 58, 60-64.

69. Letter from Ruth Burke Rill to Thomas Zimmerman, March 3, 1980; available at editorial office files, Assemblies of God World Missions, Springfield, MO 65802. See also idem, "Blessings and Hardships: Experiences of the Fred Burke Family in Africa," *AGH* 13 (Winter 1993-1994): 4-5, 25; for Burke's autobiography, see Frederic H. Burke, *Portrait of a Pioneer* (Rynfield, R.S.A.: Hebron, 2001).

70. Letter from Martha Schoonmaker to Maynard L. Ketcham and members of the Executive Committee, July 29, 1950; available at editorial office files, Assemblies of God World Missions, Springfield, MO 65802.

71. On the relationship between the Assemblies of God and the Russian and Eastern European Mission, see Gary B. McGee, *This Gospel Shall Be Preached: A History and Theology of Assemblies of God Foreign Missions to 1959* (Springfield, Mo.: Gospel Publishing House, 1986), 152-54.

72. The comity agreement in East Africa between the Assemblies of God and the

Pentecostal Assemblies of Canada later broke down because of the territorialism of missionaries and feelings of mutual mistrust.

73. As evident in George M. Kelley, "A School for Native Workers," *BM*, March 1914, 2.

74. Harlan P. Beach and Charles H. Fahs, eds., *World Missionary Atlas* (New York: Institute of Social and Religious Research, 1925), 23; Alma E. Doering, "Gleanings from Mulheim, Germany," *LRE*, December 1912, 9-11; idem, "Diversities of Operations but the Same Spirit," LRE, July 1913, 13-17; idem, "From One Fighting Zone to Another," *LRE*, January 1915, 19; idem, "Overcomers as God's Business Managers: Bread Cast upon the Waters," *LRE*, October 1915, 21-22; James C. Juhnke, *A People of Mission: A History of General Conference Mennonite Overseas Missions* (Newton, Kans.: Faith and Life Press, 1979), 67-70.

75. Wacker, *Heaven Below*, 208. Among the universities and colleges attended were University of Minnesota, Kansas State University, Denison University, Denver Normal School, Edinboro University of Pennsylvania, Princeton University, McMaster University, Trenton Normal School (present-day College of New Jersey), Amherst College, Asbury College, Hiram College, Houghton College, Maryville College, Meridian College; in the United Kingdom: Bangor University and Cheltenham Ladies College.

76. A. J. Tomlinson, "Overseer's Annual Address," in *Minutes of the Thirteenth Annual Assembly of the Churches of God Held at Harriman, Tenn., November 1-6, 1917*, 20.

77. F. J. Lee, address in *Minutes of the Seventeenth Annual Assembly of the Church of God Held at Cleveland, Tenn., Nov. 1-7, 1922*, 9.

78. Klaus Fiedler, *The Story of Faith Missions: From J. Hudson Taylor to Present Day Africa* (Oxford: Regnum Books International, 1994), 144-48.

79. Joel A. Carpenter, "Propagating the Faith Once Delivered: The Fundamentalist Missionary Enterprise, 1920-1945," in Carpenter and Shenk, eds., *Earthen Vessels*, 102-5.

80. D. W. Kerr, "Bible Schools are Necessary," *PE*, April 15, 1922, 5.

81. Virginia E. Moss, *Following the Shepherd: Testimony of Mrs. Virginia E. Moss* (North Bergen, N.J.: Beulah Heights Assembly and School, ca. 1919), 32.

82. In its first year of operation, Central Bible Institute offered one course in missions entitled "Missions and Missionaries" with the following description: "In this course is covered the history of Christian Missions up to and including the present efforts being made under the various Boards and by independent missionaries on the world-wide field. The Home Mission work necessary in our own land is also given due prominence"; *First Annual Catalog, Central Bible Institute, 1922-23* (Springfield, Mo.: Assemblies of God, ca. 1922), 14.

83. See John H. Cable, *A History of the Missionary Training Institute: The Pioneer Bible School of America* (Nyack: n.p., 1933); for the influence of the Missionary Training Institute on Assemblies of God Bible institutes, see Charles W. Nienkirchen, *A. B. Simpson and the Pentecostal Movement* (Peabody, Mass.: Hendrickson, 1992), 43-46; Lewis Wilson, "The Kerr-Peirce Role in A/G Education: D. W. Kerr and Willard Peirce Worked Together to Help Found Three A/G Schools," *AGH* 10 (Spring 1990): 6-8, 21-22.

84. Carpenter, "Propagating the Faith," 109.

85. Ibid., 126-27.

86. Nickels J. Holmes founded the school in 1898, nine years before Holmes and the entire school accepted the Pentecostal message; Doug Beacham, *Azusa East: The Life and Times of G. B. Cashwell* (Franklin Springs, Ga.: LSR Publications, 2006), 104-5.

87. Elizabeth Baker and her sisters founded the school in 1906, one year before a Pen-

tecostal revival occurred there; Elizabeth V. Baker, et al., *Chronicles of a Faith Life*, 2d ed. (Rochester, N.Y.: Elim, ca. 1926), 132.

88. Dana L. Robert, *American Women in Mission: A Social History of Their Thought and Practice* (Macon, Ga.: Mercer University Press, 1996), 252.

89. Conn, *Like a Mighty Army*, 148-49.

90. W. Richie Hogg, "The Role of American Protestantism in World Mission," in *American Missions in Bicentennial Perspective*, ed. R. Pierce Beaver (South Pasadena, Calif.: William Carey Library, 1977), 380-82; see also Ruth A. Tucker, *Guardians of the Great Commission: The Story of Women in Modern Missions* (Grand Rapids: Zondervan, 1988). For the percentage of women in early Assemblies of God missions, see McGee, *This Gospel . . . to 1959*, 91-92.

91. Lillian Trasher, quoted in Jerome Beatty, "Nile Mother," *AM*, June 1939, 56.

92. "Christians Sometime Harm Other People, President Asserts," *Ogden Standard Examiner* (Utah), January 28, 1925, 1.

93. Welch paraphrased MacRae's remark; for the actual statement, see J. D. MacRae, "Christian Education and Christian Leadership," in *The Foreign Missions Convention at Washington, 1925*, ed. Fennell P. Turner and Frank Knight Sanders (New York: Foreign Missions Conference of North America, 1925), 109.

94. John W. Welch, "The Present Great World Crisis," *PE*, March 28, 1925, 8. See also Cecil M. Robeck, Jr., "The Assemblies of God and Ecumenical Cooperation: 1920-1965," in *Pentecostalism in Context: Essays in Honor of William W. Menzies*, ed. Wonsuk Ma and Robert P. Menzies (Sheffield: Sheffield Academic Press, 1997), 113-15.

95. Welch, "Present Great World Crisis," 2.

96. Kenneth Scott Latourette, "Ecumenical Bearings of the Missionary Movement and the International Missionary Council," in *A History of the Ecumenical Movement, 1517-1948*, 2d ed., ed. Ruth Rouse and Stephen Charles Neill (Philadelphia: Westminster, 1967), 374. The Foreign Missions Conference of North America operated without requiring members to adhere to a common doctrinal statement.

97. The book was reviewed in the *New York Evening Post*, *New York Tribune*, *Pittsburgh Dispatch*, and *The Constitution* (Atlanta), among others; Grace D. Clementson, *Charles Hamilton Pridgeon* (Gibsonia, Pa.: Evangelization Society of the Pittsburgh Bible Institute, 1963), 134.

98. "The Work," series 2, no. 4 (ca. 1910), 1-2; available at Flower Pentecostal Heritage Center, Springfield, MO 65802. The life of faith received a financial boost when Mrs. W. H. Conley gave the Wylie Avenue Church and the Pittsburgh Bible Institute an endowment of nearly half-a-million dollars in 1908; she and her husband had been leaders in the Christian and Missionary Alliance branch in Pittsburgh; E. D. Whiteside, "Mr. and Mrs. W. H. Conley," *CMAW*, November 21, 1908, 131. Curiously, Pridgeon ceased to speak at Alliance conventions in the same year.

99. Beach and Fahs, *World Missionary Atlas*, 27; also "Former Gaines Lady Missionary to China," *Wellsboro Gazette* (Pa.), November 11, 1926, 4.

100. William W. Menzies, *Anointed to Serve: The Story of the Assemblies of God* (Springfield, Mo.: Gospel Publishing House, 1971), 126 n. 9.

101. C. H. Pridgeon, "Benefits of Speaking in Other Tongues," *PT*, June 1922, 2.

102. Charles H. Pridgeon, quoted in Clementson, *Charles Hamilton Pridgeon*, 132.

103. C. H. Pridgeon, "Comfort for the Bereaved," *Indiana Weekly Messenger* (Pa.), July 3, 1919, 7; A. E. Saxby, *God's Ultimate* (London: Stockwell, n.d.); idem, *The Second Death: An Enquiry into Its Meaning and Operation* (pamphlet) (N.p., n.d.); Gordon F. Atter, *The Third Force* (Peterborough, Ont.: College Press, 1962), 137-39; William K. Kay,

Inside Story: A History of British Assemblies of God (Mattersey, U.K.: Mattersey Hall, 1990), 78-79.

104. Charles H. Pridgeon, *Is Hell Eternal: or, Will God's Plan Fail?* 3rd ed. (Pittsburgh: Evangelization Society of the Pittsburgh Bible Institute, 1931), 278-91.

105. Grant Wacker, "Second Thoughts on the Great Commission: Liberal Protestants and Foreign Missions, 1890-1940," in Carpenter and Shenk, eds., *Earthen Vessels*, 281-300.

106. W. W. King and Alvin I. Hobbs, *Theological Discussion Held at Des Moines, June 22, 1868* (Des Moines: Mills, 1868); E. Brooks Holifield, *Theology in America: Christian Thought from the Age of the Puritans to the Civil War* (New Haven: Yale University Press, 2003), 212-214; Alvyn Austin, *China's Millions: The China Inland Mission and Late Qing Society, 1832-1905* (Grand Rapids: Eerdmans, 2007), 224-25, 385-86.

107. A. G. Garr, "That 'Yellow Book,'" *WWit*, April 20, 1914, 3; Robert Mapes Anderson, *Vision of the Disinherited: The Making of American Pentecostalism* (New York: Oxford University Press, 1979), 159.

108. Prophetesses, quoted in E. N. Bell, "Editor's Note," *WWit*, April 20, 1914, 3; A. J. Harley, "Words of Commendation: Words of Thanks," *WWit*, May 20, 1914, 1.

109. Ibid.

110. Max Wood Moorhead, "Pridgeonism," *PT*, November 1923, 7-8.

111. Wm. C. Proctor, "What Christ Teaches Concerning Future Retribution," in *The Fundamentals: A Testimony to the Truth*, ed. R. A. Torrey, A. C. Dixon, et al. (Grand Rapids: Baker Book House, 1972; originally published in 1917), 3: 53-63.

112. Wm. C. Proctor, "What Christ Teaches about Future Retribution," comp. Max Wood Moorhead, *PE*, November 11, 1922, 6.

113. "Heresies Disapproved," *Combined Minutes of the General Council of the Assemblies of God in the United States of America and Foreign Lands—1914-1925*, 38.

114. George M. Marsden, *Fundamentalism and American Culture*, rev. ed. (Oxford: Oxford University Press, 2006), 167-68; Lian Xi, *The Conversion of Missionaries: Liberalism in American Protestant Missions in China, 1907-1932* (University Park, Pa.: Pennsylvania State University Press, 1997), 7-10.

115. J. Roswell Flower, "The Pentecostal Commission," *PE*, June 12, 1920, 12.

116. See L. Grant McClung, Jr., "'Try to Get People Saved': Revisiting the Paradigm of an Urgent Pentecostal Missiology," in *The Globalization of Pentecostalism: A Religion Made to Travel*, ed. Murray W. Dempster, Byron D. Klaus, and Douglas Petersen (Oxford: Regnum Books International, 1999), 30-51.

117. "A Co-operative Evangelism," in *Combined Minutes of the General Council of the Assemblies of God in the United States of America, Canada and Foreign Lands*, 1914, 12.

118. Niels P. Thomsen, "Brother Niels P. Thomsen," *PE*, June 12, 1920, 12.

119. Lillian Hunt Trasher, "Application for Endorsement as Missionary," Foreign Missions Committee of the General Council of the Assemblies of God, Springfield, Missouri, November 18, 1919, 3. Available at editorial office files, Assemblies of God World Missions, Springfield, MO 65802.

120. Telephone interview with Hazel Crouch, missionary to Egypt, with the author, July 15, 2008; Lillian Trasher, "Assiout, Egypt," *CE*, January 25, 1919, 10; Beatty, "Nile Mother," 56.

121. Robert, *American Women in Mission*, xviii-xix.

122. *The Story of the Christian and Missionary Alliance* (Nyack, N.Y.: Alliance, 1900), 10; cf. 36, 42, 46, 50, 62; Austin, *China's Millions*, 76, 150, 149, 167.

123. For Flower's somewhat controversial tenure as missionary secretary, see McGee, *This Gospel . . . to 1959*, 109-14.

124. Wilbert R. Shenk, "The Role of Theory in Anglo-American Mission Thought and Practice," *MS* 11-2 (1994): 155.

125. Victor Plymire, "Reaping among the Tibetans," *LRE*, March 1924, 11.

126. David V. Plymire, *High Adventure in Tibet: The Life and Labors of Pioneer Missionary Victor Plymire*, rev. ed. (Springfield, Mo.: Gospel Publishing House, 1997), 67.

127. Mrs. Victor G. [Ruth] Plymire, "Did the Lord of the Harvest Make a Mistake?" *PE*, October 8, 1949, 11; George O. Wood, "Prologue," in Plymire, *High Adventure*.

128. H. L. Fisher, *History of the United Holy Church of America, Inc.* (N.p., n.d.), 21-22.

129. M. L. Ryan, "Japan a Gateway," *TP*, April-May 1909, 4-5.

130. M. L. Ryan, "Yokohama, Japan," *WW*, November 1908, 345.

131. Frank Gray, "An Open Door in Japan," *LRE*, March 1917, 15; W. J. Taylor, "From Sunrise Land," *FF*, February 1915, 7.

132. W. H. Turner, "Dear Readers of The Manual," *PHA*, March 15, 1923, 11. See also William T. Purinton, "W. H. Turner and the Chinese Pentecost," *WTJ* 38 (Spring 2003): 226-41.

133. Edgar D. Pettenger, "Natives of the Witwatersrand Gold Fields," *FGMH*, July 1924, 6-7; Mabel Anderson Pettenger, "Mining for Precious Souls among the Gold Miners," *FGMH*, July 1924, 15.

134. Mitchell, *Heritage & Harvests*, 10-11.

135. Paul Voronaeff, *My Life in Soviet Russia* (Tulsa, Okla.: Christian Crusade, 1969), 10.

136. A. J. Tomlinson, "Overseer's Annual Address," *Minutes of the Fifteenth Annual Assembly of the Church of God Held at Cleveland, Tenn., Nov. 3-9, 1920*, 25-27.

137. A. T. Pierson, *George Müller of Bristol and His Witness to a Prayer-hearing God* (New York: Baker & Taylor, 1899).

138. E. May Law, *Pentecostal Mission Work in South China: An Appeal for Missions* (Falcon, N.C.: Falcon, 1916), 8.

139. Ibid., 26.

140. L. M. Anglin, "Baptism of the Spirit Transforms a Baptist Missionary," *LRE*, April 1921, 3.

141. Esther B. Harvey, *The Faithfulness of God* (Battle Creek, Mich.: Grounds Gospel Press and Book Store, ca. 1949), 38.

142. Thomas Hindle, "Gashatay, Mongolia," *PE*, April 30, 1921, 12.

143. Anna C. Reiff, "Rubber Is Death: 30,000 Lives for 4,000 Tons of Rubber," *LRE*, November 1912, 6-7; idem, "Bleeding Armenia Extinguished as a Nation: One Million Driven to Die in Desert," *LRE*, November 1916, 14-16; idem, "Wrongs of Indian Womanhood," October 1924, 20-21.

144. E. May Law, "A Plea for China," *LRE*, August 1917, 13.

145. For example, see "Mission to the Aristocracy of India," *PHA*, April 5, 1923, 10-12; "True and False Democracy in India," *PHA*, April 5, 1923, 12.

146. "Misery and Desolation," *Evening Standard* (Ogden City, Utah), September 3, 1910, 1.

147. B. Berntsen, "Letter from China," *BM*, May 15, 1908, 2.

148. J. J. Mueller, *With Our Missionaries in North India* (Springfield, Mo.: Foreign Missions Department of the Assemblies of God, 1937), 16.

149. Geo. M. and Margaret Kelley [sic], "Days of Blessing," *CE*, January 23, 1915, 4.

150. Gerard Bailly, "Bro. Gerard Bailly," *WWit*, August 1915, 7; idem, "Gerard A. Bailly," *WWit*, May 1915, 6.

151. Pettenger, "Natives of the Witwatersrand Gold Fields," 7.

152. Tom Salzer, "The Danzig Gdanska Institute of the Bible," (Part 1), *AGH* 8 (Fall 1988): 8-11, 18-19; (Part 2), 8 (Winter 1988-1989): 10-12, 17-18.

153. Shenk, "Origins and Evolution of the Three-Selfs," 28-35.

154. For example, see *Report of the Second Decennial Missionary Conference Held at Calcutta, 1882-83* (Calcutta: Baptist Mission Press, 1883), 251-83; *Ecumenical Missionary Conference, New York, 1900: Report of the Ecumenical Conference on Foreign Missions, Held in Carnegie Hall and Neighboring Churches, April 21 to May 1* (New York: American Tract Society, 1900), 2: 289-324.

155. For example, see Marie Juergensen, *A Call from Japan: An Opportunity for Practical Missionary Work* (Springfield, Mo.: Foreign Missions Department of the Assemblies of God, n.d.), 15-17.

156. John G. Lake, "Important Instructions for Missionaries to South Africa," *TP*, June 1909, 3; cf. idem, "Extracts from a Very Important Letter from Bro. J. G. Lake," *Conf*, March 1909, 74-75; cf. with Kemp Pendleton Burpeau who suggests: "Lake's success among blacks may have been attributable to interracial skills and sensitivities he fostered when mentoring under [William] Seymour" (*God's Showman: A Historical Study of John G. Lake and South African/American Pentecostalism* [Oslo: Refleks, 2004], 80). Also, V. S. Molobi and F. Chikane, eds., *An Oral History of the South African Apostolic Faith Mission: A Missing Link of Black Historical Discourse (1908-1960 Onwards)* (Muckleneuk, Pretoria, S.A.: CB Powell Bible Centre, UNISA, 2008).

157. Henry Turney, "Visiting Famine Sufferers in Africa," *BM*, August 1912, 1.

158. A. E. Wilson, *A Visit to Mosi Land* (Springfield, Mo.: Foreign Missions Department of the Assemblies of God, ca. 1932), 7.

159. Paul K. Derr to "Dear Brother and All," February 9, 1932.

160. Pearl Loftin, "Dear Manual Readers," *PHA*, March 15, 1923, 11.

161. Lillian Trasher, quoted in George O. Wood, "What's Your Mission?" *TPE*, February 17, 2008, 30.

162. Joseph K. Blakeney, "Congo Needs," *PE*, February 4, 1922, 12.

163. See *Minutes of a Missionary Conference, at Which Was Formed the Burmah Baptist Missionary Convention, Held at Rangoon, October 15th-21st, 1865.*

164. Kelley, "School for Native Workers," 2.

165. See Marion M. Mead, "Should the Native Worker Be Trained?" *LRE*, March 1932, 19-20.

166. Arthur E. Wilson, *The Gospel among the Mossi People, French West Africa* (Springfield, Mo.: Foreign Missions Department of the Assemblies of God, ca. 1937), 38; idem, "Developing Native Evangelism in Mossi Land," *PE*, July 14, 1934, 11, 14.

167. *Missionary Manual of the General Council of the Assemblies of God* (Springfield, Mo.: Foreign Missions Department, ca. 1931), 26.

168. Blakeney, "Congo Needs," 12.

169. See David Bundy, "Unintended Consequences: The Methodist Episcopal Missionary Society and the Beginnings of Pentecostalism in Norway and Chile," *Miss* 27 (April 1999): 211-29.

170. On the development of early Chilean Pentecostalism, see Willis Collins Hoover, *History of the Pentecostal Revival in Chile*, trans. Mario G. Hoover (Lakeland, Fla.: By the translator, 2000); cf. J. Tremayne Copplestone, *History of Methodist Missions*, vol. 4: *Twentieth-Century Perspectives (The Methodist Episcopal Church,*

1896-1939) (New York: Board of Global Ministries of the United Methodist Church, 1973), 601-10.

171. W. C. Hoover, "Apostolic Power Brings Apostolic Persecution," *LRE*, February 1921, 16; idem, "The Remarkable Spread of Pentecost in Chile," *PE*, January 5, 1918, 11.

172. "By the Missionaries," *The Apostolic Revival in Brazil: A Short Overview of the Swedish Pentecostal Mission*, trans. Roy Nylin (Stockholm: Philadelphia Publishers, 1934), 33-35; Vinson Synan, *The Holiness-Pentecostal Tradition: Charismatic Movements in the Twentieth Century* (Grand Rapids: Eerdmans, 1997), 134-35.

173. Hannah W. Stewart-Gambino and Everett Wilson, "Latin American Pentecostals: Old Stereotypes and New Challenges," in *Power, Politics, and Pentecostals in Latin America*, ed. Edward L. Cleary and Hannah W. Stewart-Gambino (Boulder, Colo.: Westview, 1997), 228-30.

174. Walter J. Hollenweger, *The Pentecostals* (Peabody, Mass.: Hendrickson, 1972), 85-93.

175. Grunner [*sic*] Vingren, "Preaching the Gospel in the Midst of Mobs," *LRE*, January 1916, 15.

176. William R. Read, Victor M. Monterroso, and Harmon A. Johnson, *Latin American Church Growth* (Grand Rapids: Eerdmans, 1969), 67.

177. Article of Paul Bettex from the *Canton Pentecost* (China), December 1914, reprinted in Stanley H. Frodsham, *Wholly for God: A Call to Complete Consecration Illustrated by the Story of Paul Bettex, a Truly Consecrated Soul* (Springfield, Mo.: Gospel Publishing House, n.d.), 39.

178. Ibid.

179. "Step toward Self-Support," *LRE*, February 1926, 15.

180. Cf. "The Chinese Church," in *China Centenary Missionary Conference: Report of the Great Conference Held at Shanghai, April 5th to May 7th, 1907* (New York: American Tract Society, 1907), 8-18.

181. See Everett A. Wilson and Ruth Marshall Wilson, "Alice E. Luce: A Victorian Visionary," in *Portraits of a Generation: Early Pentecostal Leaders*, ed. James R. Goff, Jr., and Grant Wacker (Fayetteville: University of Arkansas Press, 2002), 159-76.

182. Alice E. Luce, "Paul's Missionary Methods" (Part 1), *PE*, January 8, 1921, 6.

183. See Charles Henry Long and Anne Rowthorn, "Roland Allen, 1868-1947: 'Missionary Methods: St. Paul's or Ours?'" in Anderson, ed., *Mission Legacies*, 387-89.

184. Ibid.

185. Donald Gee, *The Indigenous Principle: An Explanation of a Great Missionary Policy* (London: Redemption Tidings Bookroom, ca. 1937), 15. The booklet originally appeared as two articles in *RT*, July 16, 1937, 1-3; July 30, 1937, 5-6.

186. Alice E. Luce, "Paul's Missionary Methods" (Part 3), *PE*, February 5, 1921, 6.

187. Ibid., 6-7.

188. Morris O. Williams, *Partnership in Mission: A Study of Theology and Method in Mission*, 2d ed. (Springfield, Mo.: By the author, 1986), 160-75.

189. Alice E. Luce, "Paul's Missionary Methods" (Part 2), *PE*, January 22, 1921, 6.

190. Ibid.

191. Luce, "Paul's Missionary Methods" (Part 3), 6.

192. R. G. Robins, *A. J. Tomlinson: Plainfolk Modernist* (Oxford: Oxford University Press, 2004), 167-72; Conn, *Like a Mighty Army*, 281-85.

193. For example, see *Fiftieth Anniversary of the Church of God in Christ of Haiti: 13 January 1929—13 January 1979* (n.p., 1979), 7, 9, 11; "The COGIC in Haiti, Part II," *WT*, April 1979, 3. For an explanation of the limited global expansion of the

Church of God in Christ, see David D. Daniels III, "'Follow Peace with All': Future Trajectories of the Church of God in Christ," in *The Future of Pentecostalism in the United States*, ed. Eric Patterson and Edmund Rybarczyk (Lanham, Md.: Lexington Books, 2007), 179-80.

194. *History of Church of God Missions* (Cleveland, Tenn.: Church of God Mission Board, 1943), 17.

195. For the extensive travels and contributions of Ingram, see Peggy Scarborough, *J. H. Ingram: Missionary Dean* (Cleveland, Tenn.: Pathway, 1966).

196. Cook, *Quarter Century of Divine Leading*, 61.

197. Conn, *Where the Saints Have Trod*, 279-81. It subsequently changed its name to Full Gospel Church of God. See also J. Herbert Walker, Jr., "Reaping the Harvest," in *The Promise and the Power: Essays on the Motivations, Developments, and Prospects of the Ministries of the Church of God*, ed. Donald N. Bowdle (Cleveland, Tenn.: Pathway, 1980), 53-83.

198. "A Covenant on World Evangelization," in *Azusa Street and Beyond: Pentecostal Missions and Church Growth in the Twentieth Century*, ed. L. Grant McClung, Jr. (South Plainfield, N.J.: Bridge, 1986), 171.

199. Warren Bruce Newberry, "Major Missiological Motifs in North American Classical Pentecostal Missions" (D.Th. diss., University of South Africa, 1999), 149-50.

200. *Combined Minutes of the General Council of the Assemblies of God in the United States of America, Canada and Foreign Lands, 1914-1923*, 61-64.

201. Noel Perkin, "Preparation for Missions Service," *PE*, September 14, 1929, 10.

202. McGee, *This Gospel . . . to 1959*, 165-68.

203. Noel Perkin, "Racial Superiority," *MF* 12 (n.d.), 3.

204. "As Others See Us," *MF* 1 (1948), 1.

205. See *The World Mission of the Church: Findings and Recommendations of the Meeting of the International Missionary Council, Tambaram, Madras, India, Dec. 12-29, 1938* (New York: International Missionary Council, 1939), 29-32, 36-41; Goodall, ed., *Missions under the Cross*, 195-207.

206. Melvin and Lois Hodges, "Hodges Arrives in Central America," *PA*, June 1936, 4.

207. Wilson, "Identity, Community, and Status," 143-46; on Williams, see Lois Williams, *Hands That Dug the Well* (Springfield, Mo.: RDM, 1997).

208. Melvin L. Hodges, "Great Sacrifice in Nicaragua," *PE*, January 31, 1942, 11.

209. Joseph Schmidlin, *Catholic Mission History* (Techny, Ill: Mission Press, S.V.D., 1933), 424-25; idem, *Catholic Mission Theory* (Techny, Ill.: Mission Press, S.V.D., 1931), 435-40.

210. Melvin L. Hodges, *The Indigenous Church* (Springfield, Mo.: Gospel Publishing House, 1953), 132-33. The Moody Press edition was entitled *On the Mission Field: The Indigenous Church* (Chicago: Moody, 1953).

211. Ibid., 112.

212. Ibid., 115.

213. Ibid., 116.

214. See Harvey Cox, *Fire from Heaven: The Rise of Pentecostal Spirituality and the Reshaping of Religion in the Twenty-First Century* (Reading, Mass.: Addison-Wesley, 1995), 311-12.

215. Noel Perkin, "Support of Benevolent Institutions," *MF* 12 (n.d.), 2. For another critique of institutional ministries, see Frances P. Jones, "The Lessons of a Failure," *MF* 15 (n.d.), 1-2.

216. Arthur F. Glasser, "The Evolution of Evangelical Mission Theology since World War II," *IBMR* 9 (January 1985): 11.

217. Gary B. McGee, *This Gospel Shall Be Preached: A History and Theology of Assemblies of God Foreign Missions since 1959* (Springfield, Mo.: Gospel Publishing House, 1989), 67-70.

218. Wilbert R. Shenk, "The Contribution of the Study of New Religious Movements to Missiology," in *Exploring New Religious Movements: Essays in Honour of Harold W. Turner*, ed. A. F. Walls and Wilbert R. Shenk (Elkhart, Ind.: Mission Focus Publications, 1990), 189. For the influence of Hodges on Pentecostal Holiness missions, see Frank G. Tunstall, *The Simultaneous Principle: The History of IPHC World Missions: The First 100 Years* (Franklin Springs, Ga.: LSR Publications, 2005), 380.

219. Newberry, "Major Missiological Motifs," 149-52.

220. Douglas Petersen, "Missions in the Twenty-First Century: Toward a Methodology of Pentecostal Compassion," *Transformation* 16 (April/June): 55-57; Melvin L. Hodges, "Mission—and Church Growth," in *The Church's Worldwide Mission*, ed. Harold Lindsell (Waco, Tex.: Word Books, 1966), 141, 145; idem, *Grow Toward Leadership* (Chicago: Moody, 1960), 30.

221. Melvin L. Hodges, *A Theology of the Church and Its Mission: A Pentecostal Perspective* (Springfield, Mo.: Gospel Publishing House, 1977), 103.

222. Charles E. Van Engen, "A Broadening Vision: Forty Years of Evangelical Theology of Mission, 1946-1986," in Carpenter and Shenk, eds., *Earthen Vessels*, 211.

223. Harvey, *Faithfulness of God*, 38.

9. HEALING MOVEMENTS AND MISGIVINGS

1. Percy Dearmer, *Body and Soul: An Enquiry into the Effect of Religion upon Health, With a Description of Christian Works of Healing from the New Testament to the Present Day* (New York: E. P. Dutton, 1909), 1, 4.

2. Mabel Potter Daggett, "Are There Modern Miracles?" *LHJ*, June 1923, 166.

3. William Edward Biederwolf, *Whipping-Post Theology or Did Jesus Atone for Disease?* (Grand Rapids: Eerdmans, 1934), 198, 210-11.

4. Arno Clemens Gaebelein, "Preface," in May Wyburn Fitch, *The Healing Delusion* (New York: Loizeaux Brothers, n.d.), 5-6.

5. Donald McGavran, "Divine Healing and Church Growth," *RJ* 17, no. 1 (2001): 1. McGavran presented this address before a conference of the Christian and Missionary Alliance in 1979.

6. Aimee Semple McPherson, *This Is That: Personal Experiences, Sermons and Writings* (Los Angeles: Echo Park Evangelistic Association, 1923), 704-12.

7. Ibid., 707.

8. W. B. Godbey, *Commentary on the New Testament* (Cincinnati: God's Revivalist Office, 1896-1900), 7: 496-97.

9. "Shall We Reject Jesus' Last Words?" *AF* (L.A.), October 1906, 3, col. 1.

10. Arthur W. Frodsham, "The Sixteenth Chapter of Mark: How God Vindicates His Word in the Last Days," *PE*, April 28, 1923, 9; cf. Bruce M. Metzger, *The Text of the New Testament: Its Transmission, Corruption, and Restoration*, 2d ed. (New York: Oxford University Press, 1968), 56-57.

11. For example, F. F. Bruce, "The End of the Second Gospel," *EQ* 17 (July 1945): 169-81; cf. Stanley M. Horton, "Is Mark 16:9-20 Inspired?" *Para* 4 (Winter 1970), 7-12. For a recent examination of the longer ending, see James A. Kelhoffer, *Miracle and Mis-*

sion: The Authentication of Missionaries and Their Message in the Longer Ending of Mark (Tübingen: Mohr Siebeck, 2000).

12. Saint Augustine, *Confessions*, trans. Henry Chadwick (Oxford: Oxford University Press, 1991), IX, iv (12), 163.

13. J. Stenson Hooker, *The Higher Medicine* (London: Celtic, 1907), 125-26.

14. Sarah Mix, quoted in Nancy A. Hardesty, *Faith Cure: Divine Healing in the Holiness and Pentecostal Movements* (Peabody, Mass.: Hendrickson, 2003), 10.

15. Paul Gale Chappell, "The Divine Healing Movement in America" (Ph.D. diss., Drew University, 1983), 214-15.

16. M. Joseph Costelloe, "In Memoriam: Georg Otto Schurhammer, S.J. (1882-1971)," in Georg Schurhammer, *Francis Xavier: His Life, His Times*, vol. 1: *Europe: 1506-1541*, trans. M. Joseph Costelloe (Rome: Jesuit Historical Institute, 1973), 1: xviii.

17. Allan H. Anderson, *African Reformation: African Initiated Christianity in the 20th Century* (Trenton, N.J.: Africa World Press, 2001), 74-86, 93-120.

18. Lamin Sanneh, *West African Christianity: The Religious Impact* (Maryknoll, N.Y.: Orbis Books, 1983), 180-84; Anderson, *African Reformation*, 125-30.

19. For example, see Rosemary Moore, "Late Seventeenth-Century Quakerism and the Miraculous: A New Look at George Fox's 'Book of Miracles,'" in *Signs, Wonders, Miracles: Representations of Divine Power in the Life of the Church*, ed. Kate Cooper and Jeremy Gregory (Woodbridge, Suffolk, U.K.: Ecclesiastical History Society and Boydell Press, 2005), 335-44.

20. Robert Bruce Mullin, *Miracles and the Modern Religious Imagination* (New Haven: Yale University Press, 1996), 181; Thomas A. Kselman, *Miracles & Prophecies in Nineteenth-Century France* (New Brunswick, N.J.: Rutgers University Press, 1983), 189-200.

21. Ludwig Ott, *Fundamentals of Catholic Dogma*, trans. Patrick Lynch (Rockford, Ill.: TAN Books, 1974; originally published in English in 1955), 445-50; cf. *Sacrosanctum, Concilium* (The Constitution on the Sacred Liturgy) in *Vatican Council II*, vol. 1: *The Conciliar and Post Conciliar Documents*, rev. ed., ed. Austin Flannery (Northport, N.Y.: Costello, 1975), 22.

22. "Oath Against the Errors of Modernism" reprinted in Jacques Dupuis, ed., *The Christian Faith in the Doctrinal Documents of the Catholic Church*, 7th ed. (Bangalore: Theological Publications in India, 2004), 52.

23. Ronald A. N. Kydd, *Healing through the Centuries: Models for Understanding* (Peabody, Mass.: Hendrickson, 1998), 82-129; also Cherian Thunduparampil, *The Role of Miracle in the Process of Canonization: A Study of the Current Legislation* (Bangalore: Dharmaram Publications, 2003), 125-220.

24. Kydd, *Healing*, 82-99.

25. See Eliseo "Cheo" Torres, with Timothy L. Sawyer, Jr., *Curandero: A Life in Mexican Folk Healing* (Albuquerque: University of New Mexico Press, 2005).

26. Kydd, *Healing*, xvi.

27. Ibid., xvi-xvii.

28. Mullin, *Miracles*, 240.

29. For example, A. B. Simpson, "The Mind Cure," *WWW*, December 1, 1885, 349-50; Dorothy Ruth Miller, "False and True Emmanuelism," *CMAW*, October 1, 1910, 4-5; A. A. Boddy, "Christian Science," *Conf*, July 1911, 165-66; see also Dale H. Simmons, *E. W. Kenyon and the Postbellum Pursuit of Peace, Power, and Plenty* (Lanham, Md.: Scarecrow, 1997).

30. R. Kelso Carter, *Faith Healing Reviewed: After Twenty Years* (Boston: Christian Witness, 1897), 113-14. Rowland Bingham, founder of the Sudan Interior Mission cor-

roborated Kelso's observation when he wrote more than two decades later: "Let us say then that to us it seems a great inconsistency that they [the Alliance] should believe that healing is a part of their four-fold Gospel, and at the same time send out men to the foreign mission field who make no pretence of being able to live up to their theories. . . . Today, practically all their workers in the tropics use quinine, as all other missions and Government officials have done"; Rowland V. Bingham, *The Bible and the Body: Healing in the Scriptures*, 4th ed. (Toronto: Evangelical Publishers, 1952; originally published in 1921), 100-101.

31. Hardesty, *Faith Cure*, 137.

32. Fred W. Schelander, "The Gods Have Heavy Ears," in *Alliance Missions in India, 1892-1972*, comp. William F. Smalley (N.p., 1973), 1: 931.

33. "Circular to the Friends of the Evangelical Missionary Alliance," *CA*, September 1888, 144.

34. *President's Annual Report of the Christian and Missionary Alliance, 1905-6*, 7.

35. "Holy Ghoster is Guilty," *New York Times*, May 27, 1904, 5; "Mistrial for Holy Ghoster," *New York Times*, October 8, 1905, 7; Shirley Nelson, *Fair, Clear and Terrible: The Story of Shiloh* (Latham, N.Y.: British American Publishing, 1989), 227-42.

36. A. B. Simpson, "The Collapse of Dowieism," *LT*, June 1906, 327.

37. *President's Annual Report*, 7. Simpson wrote in 1905: "Every new truth is especially liable to be parodied and counterfeited by the charlatan and the fanatic. The truth of Divine Healing has much need to be saved from its friends. The absurdities of Christian Science, the extravagances of Dowieism and Sanfordism [*sic*], the imitations of magnetic healing and hypnotism and the more terrible and devilish delusions of Spiritualism may well make us cautious and conservative"; A. B. Simpson, "Divine Healing and Its Counterfeits," *LT*, August 1905, 443.

38. *Twelfth Annual Report of the Christian and Missionary Alliance, 1908-09*, 10-11.

39. Hardesty, *Faith Cure*, 137, 144-45; Paul L. King, *Genuine Gold: The Cautiously Charismatic Story of the Early Christian and Missionary Alliance* (Tulsa, Okla.: Word & Spirit Press, 2006), 196-97, 298-303; cf. David J. Fant, ed., *Modern Miracles of Healing* (Harrisburg, Pa.: Christian Publications, 1943).

40. For a response to the charge that Pentecostalism was a cult, see Albert Henley, "Contending for the Faith," *LRE*, April 1928, 8-9.

41. Mullin, *Miracles*, 265.

42. Grant A. Wacker, "Travail of a Broken Family: Radical Evangelical Responses to the Emergence of Pentecostalism in America, 1906-16," in *Pentecostal Currents in American Protestantism*, ed. Edith L. Blumhofer, Russell P. Spittler, Grant A. Wacker (Urbana: University of Illinois Press, 1999), 33.

43. John W. Goodwin, *Living Signs and Wonders* (Kansas City: Nazarene Publishing House, 1923), 67-85.

44. Timothy L. Smith, *Called unto Holiness: The Story of the Nazarenes: The Formative Years* (Kansas City: Nazarene Publishing House, 1962), 319-20. For the anti-Wesleyan posture of fundamentalism, see Lewis Sperry Chafer, "Sanctification," in *God Hath Spoken: Twenty-five Addresses Delivered at the World Conference on Christian Fundamentals, May 25-June 1, 1919* (Philadelphia: Bible Conference Committee, 1919), 263-79.

45. Anna C. Reiff, "The Remedy for Higher Criticism," *LRE*, December 1921, 13.

46. Anna C. Reiff, "A Marked Division Imminent," *LRE*, September 1921, 9-11; Stanley H. Frodsham, "Disfellowshiped!" *PE*, August 18, 1928, 7.

47. Donald Gee, *Why Pentecost?* (London: Victory, 1944), 28.

48. C. Allyn Russell, *Voices of American Fundamentalism: Seven Biographical Studies* (Philadelphia: Westminster, 1976), 79-106.

49. William Bell Riley, "Fundamentalism Knows No Relation to Pentecostalism," *TCFSC*, January-March 1926, 31.

50. "'Tongues' Movement," *CF*, June 1928, 9. For the purpose and beliefs of the organization, see W. B. Riley, "World's Christian Fundamentals Association," in *Religions and Philosophies in the United States of America*, comp. Julius A. Weber (Los Angeles: Wetzel, 1931), 177-79; Ernest R. Sandeen, *The Roots of Fundamentalism: British and American Millenarianism, 1800-1930* (Chicago: University of Chicago Press, 1970), 243-47.

51. John Roach Straton, *Divine Healing in Scripture and Life* (New York: Christian Alliance Publishing House 1927), 3, 109-27. For an insightful study of Straton, see Russell, *Voices*, 47-78.

52. Uldine Utley, *Uldine Utley: Why I Am a Preacher: Excerpts from Her Book and "Petals" Newsletters, Child & Teen Preacher Series*, comp. T. J. Lavigne (Kissimmee, Fla.: Cloud of Witnesses Publishing, 2006), 9-22.

53. Edith L. Blumhofer, "'A Little Child Shall Lead Them': Child Evangelist Uldine Utley," in *The Contentious Triangle: Church, State, and University: A Festschrift in Honor of Professor George Huntston Williams*, ed. Rodney L. Petersen and Calvin Augustine Pater (Kirksville, Mo.: Thomas Jefferson University Press, 1999), 312. In Utley's three-week campaign in Atlanta, Georgia, combined attendance reached 65,000; "Child Evangelist at Bible Session," *Morning News Review* (Florence, S.C.), February 25, 1926, 8.

54. Straton, *Divine Healing*, 8.

55. Utley, *Why I Am a Preacher*, 60-64.

56. "Youthful Oklahoma Girl Gives Up Movie Career to Work for the Divine Master," *Aiken Standard* (S.C.), July 9, 1926, 7; "Girl 'Billy Sunday' will Hold Big N.Y. Meeting in Fall," *Times* (Hammond, Ind.), July 22, 1926, 9.

57. Edith L. Blumhofer, *Aimee Semple McPherson: Everybody's Sister* (Grand Rapids: Eerdmans, 1993), 281-300.

58. "Youthful Oklahoma Girl," 7; see also Virginia Swain, "Pulpit Prodigy is Giggler, Too; Wears Hair Bobbed, Skirts Short," *Bee* (Danville, Va.), July 7, 1926, 9.

59. "Deacons in Fashionable New York Baptist Church Quit When Queer Religious Rites Are Introduced," *Abilene Daily Reporter* (Tex.), June 24, 1927, 8.

60. "'Vision' Claimed by Dr. Straton for Pastor-Son," *Modesto News-Herald* (Calif.), June 26, 1927, 2; "Straton's Son to Tell How He Was 'Visited' by Holy Ghost," *Charleston Gazette* (W.V.), June 26, 1927, 1; "With Christ," *PE*, May 29, 1966, 31. For a brief reflection on Uldine Utley by Straton's other son, see Hillyer Hawthorne Straton, *Preaching the Miracles of Jesus* (New York: Abingdon-Cokesbury, 1950), 59-60.

61. Anna C. Reiff, "With Persecution," *LRE*, February 1927, 12-13.

62. Marian Hale, "Religious 'Strange Tongues' Fluster Famous Church; Pretty Girl Blamed," *Portsmouth Daily Times* (Ohio), June 28, 1927, 11.

63. "Deacons in Fashionable New York Baptist Church Quit," 8.

64. Lee Canipe, "The Unlikely Argument of a Baptist Fundamentalist: John Roach Straton's Defense of Women in the Pulpit," *BHH* 38 (Spring 2005): 64-76.

65. "Dr. John Roach Straton Is Dead at 54," *Syracuse Herald* (N.Y.), October 29, 1929, 1.

66. For Andrew Murray, see his *Divine Healing* (New York: Christian Alliance Publishing, 1900).

67. "Two-Day Continuous Funeral Service Held for 'Billy Sunday of Mexicans,'" *El Paso Herald-Post* (Tex.), June 25, 1937, 1; Gastón Espinosa, "Francisco Olazábal: Charisma, Power, and Faith Healing in the Borderlands," in *Portraits of a Generation: Early*

Pentecostal Leaders, ed. James R. Goff, Jr., and Grant Wacker (Fayetteville: University of Arkansas Press, 2002), 184, 189.

68. I base this on the wide-ranging impact of Bosworth's *Do All Speak with Tongues?* (ca. 1917) and *Christ the Healer* (1924).

69. On Bosworth's association with the Alliance, see King, *Genuine Gold*, 196-97; also David Edwin Harrell, Jr., *All Things Are Possible: The Healing and Charismatic Revivals in Modern America* (Bloomington: Indiana University Press, 1975), 14-15.

70. McPherson, *This Is That*, 373-82; cf. Edward Thornton Heald, *History of Stark County*, vol. 3: *Industry Comes of Age, 1901-1917* (Canton, Ohio: Stark County Historical Society, 1946-1963), 596-607. Her ministry in Canton was supported by Albert Edward Day, a prominent Methodist clergyman and pastor of First Methodist Church, who authored *Letters on the Healing Ministry* (Nashville: Methodist Evangelistic Materials, 1964).

71. Espinosa, "Francisco Olazábal," 190.

72. For example, Paulus Scharpff, *History of Evangelism: Three Hundred Years of Evangelism in Germany, Great Britain, and the United States of America*, trans. Helga Bender Henry (Grand Rapids: Eerdmans, 1966). Scharpff fails to mention Pentecostal evangelists and, in his few brief references to the Pentecostal movement, places it in a distinctly negative light. A similar orientation appears in Gerald Ira Gingrich, *Protestant Revival Yesterday and Today: A Historical Study of the Characteristics of Twelve Revival Movements and of Their Application in the Mid-Twentieth Century* (New York: Exposition, 1959). For attempts to include Pentecostals, see Earle E. Cairns, *An Endless Line of Splendor: Revivals and Their Leaders from the Great Awakening to the Present* (Wheaton, Ill.: Tyndale House, 1986), 181-83, 229; and notably several books by J. Edwin Orr, including *The Flaming Tongue: Evangelical Awakenings, 1900—*, 2d ed. (Chicago: Moody, 1975), 177-84.

73. F. F. Bosworth, *Christ the Healer* (Old Tappan, N.J.: Fleming H. Revell, 1973; originally published in 1924), 45 (Bosworth's emphasis).

74. Reiff, "Remedy for Higher Criticism," 14. For an insightful study, see Miroslav Volf, "Materiality of Salvation: An Investigation in the Soteriologies of Liberation and Pentecostal Theologies," *JES* 26 (1989): 447-67.

75. W. H. Turner, *Christ the Great Physician* (Franklin Springs, Ga.: Publishing House of the Pentecostal Holiness Church, 1941), 113-14.

76. For the meetings of George Jeffreys in Royal Albert Hall in 1927 and 1928, see Ernest C. W. Boulton, *George Jeffreys: A Ministry of the Miraculous* (London: Elim, 1928), 229-44, 317-36.

77. Nicholas Bhengu, "Taking South Africa for God," *PE*, March 6, 1955, 4.

78. Boulton, *George Jeffreys*, 319.

79. Stanley Howard Frodsham, *Smith Wigglesworth: Apostle of Faith* (Springfield, Mo.: Gospel Publishing House, 1972), 107-8; see also Desmond Cartwright, *The Real Smith Wigglesworth: The Man, the Myth, the Message* (Tonbridge, Kent, U.K.: Sovereign World, 2000).

80. "18 Persons Claim Miraculous Faith Cures Here," *Syracuse Herald* (N.Y.), March 12, 1925, 6.

81. See O. Offler, "The Message of Healing," *PT*, March 1922, 2, 4; also Kimberly Ervin Alexander, *Pentecostal Healing: Models in Theology and Practice* (Blandford Forum, Dorset, U.K.: Deo Publishing, 2006).

82. Bingham challenged the statistics offered by the healing evangelists in *Bible and the Body*, 22-23; also see the criticism of McPherson by W. P. White reproduced in C. E. Putnam, *Modern Religion-Healing: Man's Theories or God's Word?* (Chicago: By the

author, 1924), 160-63; Wade H. Boggs, Jr., *Faith Healing and the Christian Faith* (Richmond, Va.: John Knox, 1956), 31.

83. Daniel Mark Epstein, *Sister Aimee: The Life of Aimee Semple McPherson* (New York: Harcourt Brace, 1993), 111.

84. Ibid., 185.

85. Lee Young-Hoon, "The Korean Holy Spirit Movement in Relation to Pentecostalism," in *Asian and Pentecostal: The Charismatic Face of Christianity in Asia*, ed. Allan Anderson and Edmond Tang (Oxford: Regnum Books International, 2005), 512.

86. "Christian Healing in Pyengyang," *MRW* 14 (March 1921): 246-47; bylaw reprinted in *NIDPCM*, 2002 ed., s.v. "South Korea," by Yeol Soo Eim; see also Lee Young-Hoon, "Korean," 509-26.

87. *DAC*, 2001, s.v. "Kim Ik Doo," by Kim In Soo.

88. Dearmer, *Body and Soul*, 3-4.

89. James Moore Hickson, *Heal the Sick*, 2d ed. (London: Methuen, 1924), 7.

90. The Society of Emmanuel was dissolved in 1921 after Hickson took his healing missions overseas.

91. Hickson, *Heal the Sick*, 8.

92. "James Moore Hickson (Jim)," Hickson Genealogy, http://www.hicksons.org/ByName/healer.html.

93. Missionary Zella Reynolds, quoted in Reiff, "Marked Division Imminent," 10: "Miss Zella Reynolds, writing from Kikungshan, Honan Province, China, where she is spending a few weeks resting, tells us of the awakening in the Episcopal church in China along the line of divine healing through Mr. Hixon [*sic*], the Episcopal layman, whose ministry has been so signally blest along this line on the foreign, as well as in the home-field. She writes: 'You would have been surprised to hear Bishop [William Charles] White of the Episcopal Church here in China speak one morning and tell of the Lambeth Conference in England, where two hundred and fifty-two bishops of the Episcopal Church from various parts of the world freely discussed the subject of Divine Healing and the need of the gift of healing in the ministry of the Church . . . and that they had passed resolutions encouraging the revival of this gift in the church and the study of the Scriptures on the subject with a view to a better understanding of its importance in the presenting of the Gospel.'"

94. Henry B. Wilson, *The Revival of the Gift of Healing* (Milwaukee: Young Churchman, 1917), 36-38.

95. Hickson, *Heal the Sick*, 13.

96. James Moore Hickson, *The Healing of Christ in His Church* (Sydney, NSW, Australia: Church Stores, n.d.), 44.

97. Hickson, *Heal the Sick*, 16.

98. J. W. Ashton, "Healing Power of Hickson is Actual Thing," *Olean Evening Times* (N.Y.), November 24, 1919, 9; cf. Mullin, *Miracles*, 247-48.

99. See Wilson, *Revival*, 39-41.

100. Ashton, "Healing Power," 9-10.

101. "5000 Apply for Healing," *Washington Post*, April 20, 1920, 18.

102. "Lame Pack Trinity as 'Healer' Speaks," *New York Times*, May 10, 1920, 5.

103. "Wounded Yanks Rush Away from Science to Healer's Shrine," *Cumberland Evening Times* (Md.), May 1, 1920, 5.

104. "Thousands Jam Church to Be Healed," *Modesto Evening Times* (Calif.), February 18, 1920, 1.

105. Charles Brent, quoted in Kenneth Mackenzie, "Jesus and Our Mortal Flesh," *AW*, August 19, 1922, 356. For another statement by Brent on healing, see Daggett, "Are There Modern Miracles?" 168, 171.

106. For example, Biederwolf, *Whipping-Post Theology*, 210-11.

107. Bingham, *Bible and the Body*, 24; cf. Doherty's letter reprinted in Hickson, *Heal the Sick*, 43-44; "Miraculous Cure Claimed," *Manitoba Free Press* (Winnipeg), April 5, 1920, 1. See also A. J. Gayner Banks, *The Healing Evangel* (Milwaukee: Morehouse, 1925), 189-201.

108. Ibid., 92-93.

109. Ibid., 47.

110. Ibid., 51; A. A. Boddy, "Divine Healing," *Conf*, April-June 1921, 27.

111. Boddy, "Divine Healing," 27.

112. Hickson, *Heal the Sick*, 64-65. See also "Mr. Hickson in India," *AW*, December 10, 1921, 618.

113. Hickson, *Heal the Sick*, 90.

114. Ibid., 62-63 (Young's emphasis). For an eyewitness description of a Hickson service at an Anglican church in Benares, India, with similar social dynamics, see Mary Norton, "Extracts from Missionary Letters," *TF*, April 1921, 91-92; in America, see Edna B. Kinard, "Many Apply to Hickson for Healing," *Oakland Tribune* (Calif.), March 3, 1920, 1.

115. For example, while Alexander Boddy paid tribute to the work of Hickson in *Confidence*, his name never appears in the *PE*, *PHA*, *PT*, or *Bridal Call Foursquare*; cf. A. A. Boddy, "Divine Life (The Recent Church Mission of Healing)," *Conf*, November-December 1924, 152-53, 156-58. An endorsement came from the former Episcopalian Carrie Judd Montgomery, who attended a Hickson mission at Grace Cathedral in San Francisco: "A Forward Movement," *TF*, March 1920, 60-61. David J. du Plessis, sometime secretary of the Pentecostal World Conference, later paid warm tribute to him as "God's great apostle to restore to the world the reality of divine healing" in *The Spirit Bade Me Go* (Oakland, Calif.: By the author, n.d.), 6.

116. Arthur F. Glasser, "The Evolution of Evangelical Mission Theology since World War II," *IBMR* 9 (January 1985): 9-13; Gary B. McGee, *This Gospel Shall Be Preached: A History and Theology of Assemblies of God Foreign Missions since 1959* (Springfield, Mo.: Gospel Publishing House, 1989), 100-102, 216-20; also Paul Pomerville, *The Third Force in Missions* (Peabody, Mass.: Hendrickson, 1984), 58-62; Paul N. Alexander, "Spirit Empowered Peacemaking: Toward a Pentecostal Peace Fellowship," *JEPTA* 22 (2002): 78-102.

117. H. Pakenham-Walsh, "Divine Healing: A Record of Missionary Study and Experience," *IRM* 11 (1922): 97; on Pakenham-Walsh, see Ernest W. Talibuddin, *The Anglican Church in North-East India (1845-1970): A Missiological Reflection* (Delhi: ISPCK, 2002), 27-28.

118. Pakenham-Walsh, "Divine Healing," 98.

119. Hickson, *Heal the Sick*, 75.

120. Verna B. Barnard, "South Africa," *WW*, June 1923, 13.

121. For an example of Hickson's influence, see John Maillard, *Healing in the Name of Jesus: A Book of Devotion* (New York: Harper & Brothers, 1936), 19-23; idem, *Miracles of Faith* (New York: Harper & Brothers, 1938).

122. "Quiet Healers," *Time*, September 28, 1962, 53; also John Gayner Banks, *Healing Everywhere: A Book of Healing Mission Talks* (San Diego: St. Luke's, 1953), ix-xiv.

123. A helpful analysis of Bosworth's theology appears in Douglas Jacobsen, *Thinking in the Spirit: Theologies of the Early Pentecostal Movement* (Bloomington: Indiana University Press, 2003), 290-313; cf. Paul L. King, *Genuine Gold: The Cautiously Charismatic Story of the Early Christian and Missionary Alliance* (Tulsa, Okla.: Word & Spirit Press, 2006), 235, 242. For the teachings on divine healing by

A. L. Byers, a minister of the non-Pentecostal Church of God (Anderson, Ind.), see his *Two Hundred Instances of Divine Healing: The Doctrine Explained* (Anderson, Ind.: Gospel Trumpet, 1911).

124. Bosworth, *Christ the Healer*, 6-8, 41-42; cf. James Moore Hickson, *The Revival of the Gifts of Healing: Some of the Practical Difficulties Which Hinder the Revival of Spiritual Healing* (New York: Edwin S. Gorham, Publisher, 1920), 4-16.

125. Hickson, *Revival of the Gifts*, 16.

126. Unnamed person (perhaps Bosworth), quoted in Wyburn Fitch, *Healing Delusion* , 61; cf. T. L. Osborn, *Healing the Sick*, 7th ed. (Tulsa, Okla.: T. L. Osborn Evangelistic Association, 1955), 151-56.

127. Hickson, *Heal the Sick*, 260; see also Hickson, *Healing of Christ*, 6-7.

128. Kenneth Mackenzie, "Jesus and Our Mortal Flesh," *AW*, May 13, 1922, 133; also idem, *Our Physical Heritage in Christ* (New York: Fleming H. Revell, 1923).

129. Hickson, *Heal the Sick*, 267; James Hickson, "A Living Church is a Healing Church," *LRE*, May 1920, 9-11.

130. James Moore Hickson, quoted in Mullin, *Miracles*, 241. While Pentecostals touted their interest in Christian unity, few gave attention to the doctrine of the church; an important exception to this was the interest in ecclesiology in the Church of God (Cleveland, Tenn.); see Dale M. Coulter, "The Development of Ecclesiology in the Church of God (Cleveland, Tenn.): A Forgotten Contribution?" *Pneuma* 29, no. 1: 59-85; cf. Joseph H. King, "Our Weekly Sermon: 'Unity,'" *PHA*, August 3, 1922, 2-6.

131. Nettie D. Nichols, "Healing Revival at Ningpo, China," *PE*, July 22, 1921, 2-3.

132. "The Jamaica Diocesan Magazine: March Issue," *The Gleaner* (Kingston, Jamaica), February 28, 1927, 15.

133. "Sick Flock to Faith Healer," *Gettysburg Times* (Pa.), December 16, 1919, 6.

134. Bosworth, *Christ the Healer*, 142; cf. Hickson, *Heal the Sick*, 247-48. For the influence of E. W. Kenyon on Bosworth, see Dale H. Simmons, *E. W. Kenyon and the Postbellum Pursuit of Peace, Power, and Plenty* (Lanham, Md.: Scarecrow, 1997), 294-96; and Bosworth, *Christ the Healer*, 148.

135. "A Pastoral Letter to the People of the Church of England in Australia," reprinted in A. J. Gayner Banks, *Healing Evangel*, 211-18.

136. For the struggle of Charles S. Price to understand why more people were not healed in his campaigns, see Price, *The Real Faith* (Plainfield, N.J.: Logos International, 1972; originally published in 1940), 5-10.

137. J. M. Hickson, *Litany and Prayers for Healing* (Piccadilly, London: Women's Printing Society, n.d.), 5.

138. "Lame," *New York Times*, 5; Kenneth Mackenzie, "Jesus and Our Mortal Flesh," *AW*, May 27, 1922, 165.

139. Lian Xi, "The 'Spiritual Gifts Movement' in War-Torn China" (2007), http://www.calvin.edu/nagel/resources/XiASCH07.pdf.

140. Deng Zhaoming, "Indigenous Chinese Movements," in Anderson and Tang, eds., *Asian and Pentecostal*, 437-66.

141. J. Herbert Kane, *Twofold Growth* (Philadelphia: China Inland Mission, 1947), 106.

142. W. W. Cary, *Story of the National Holiness Missionary Society*, 2d ed. (Chicago: National Holiness Missionary Society, 1941), 48, 85, 123; Alvyn Austin, *China's Millions: The China Inland Mission and Late Qing Society, 1832-1905* (Grand Rapids: Eerdmans, 2007), 241; Daniel H. Bays, "The Growth of Independent Christianity in China," in *Christianity in China: From the Eighteenth Century to the Present*, ed. Daniel H. Bays (Stanford, Calif.: Stanford University Press, 1996), 307-16.

143. *DAC*, 2001, s.v. "Sung, John" by Irene Tay, Hwa Yung, and the China Group.

144. Leslie T. Lyall, *John Sung: Flame for God in the Far East*, rev. ed. (Chicago: Moody, 1964), 35-36.

145. John Sung, *The Journal Once Lost: Extracts from the Diary of John Sung*, comp. by Levi (Singapore: Genesis Books, 2008), 41; cf. John Sung, *The Diaries of John Sung: An Autobiography*, trans. Stephen L. Sheng (Brighton, Mich.: By Luke H. Sheng, M.D. and Stephen L. Sheng, D.D.S., 1995), 14-15; Mrs. D. I. Jeffrey, "Dr. John Sung," *AW*, November 19, 1938, 744. See also Utley, *Why I Am a Preacher*, 60.

146. "Buddhists Hit the Sawdust Trail under Spell of East's 'Billy Sunday,'" *Port Arthur News* (Tex.), January 24, 1937, 14.

147. Kevin Xiyi Yao, *The Fundamentalist Movement among Protestant Missionaries in China, 1920-1937* (Lanham, Md.: University Press of America, 2003), 169-70.

148. See Lyall, *John Sung*.

149. Sung, *Diaries of John Sung*, 29; see also 54; Margaret Kelley, "Where the Flaming Torch Is Lifted High," *LRE*, April 1932, 19.

150. Sung, *Diaries of John Sung*, 47.

151. Mary K. Crawford, *The Shantung Revival* (Shanghai: China Baptist Publication Society, 1933), 26-27. See also Marie Monsen, *The Awakening: Revival in China, A Work of the Holy Spirit*, trans. Joy Guinness (London: China Inland Mission, Overseas Missionary Fellowship, 1961), 54-55; John A. Abernathy, "The Shantung Revival," in *The Church Proclaiming and Witnessing*, ed. Erwin L. McDonald (Grand Rapids: Baker Book House, 1966), 81-92.

152. Margaret Kelley, "Holy Ghost Revival in North China," *LRE*, December 1931, 22; idem, "Great Revival in North China," *LRE*, August 1932, 12, 22.

153. *"The Madras Series": Presenting Papers Based upon the Meeting of the International Missionary Council, at Tambaram, Madras, India, December 12th to 29th, 1938*, vol. 3: *Evangelism* (New York: International Missionary Council, 1939), 3: 163-64.

154. Norman H. Cliff, "Building the Protestant Church in Shandong, China," *IBMR* 22 (April 1998): 67.

155. R. A. Torrey, *Divine Healing* (Grand Rapids: Baker Book House, 1974; originally published in 1924), 12.

156. Bingham, *Bible and the Body*, 21-25.

157. Torrey, *Divine Healing*, 18-19.

158. Ibid., 40.

159. Ibid., 19.

160. Ibid., 63.

161. Bingham, *Bible and the Body*, 58 (my emphasis).

162. Ibid., 19.

163. Ibid., 96-98; Henry W. Frost, *Miraculous Healing: A Personal Testimony and Biblical Study* (Grand Rapids: Zondervan, 1979; originally published in 1931), 49-54.

164. Bingham, *Bible and the Body*, 37.

165. Frost, *Miraculous Healing*, 68; cf. Torrey, *Divine Healing*, 23-24; Bingham, *Bible and the Body*, 87.

166. Alva J. McClain, *The Greatness of the Kingdom: An Inductive Study of the Kingdom of God* (Chicago: Moody, 1968), 402-13; cf. Vern S. Poythress, *Understanding Dispensationalists* (Grand Rapids: Zondervan, 1987), 20-21.

167. Bingham, *Bible and the Body*, 44.

168. Ibid., 66.

169. Ibid., 67, 83-86, 100-104.

170. Ibid., 34; cf. Bosworth, *Christ the Healer*, 182; A. C. Valdez, "Hindrances to Divine Healing," *LRE*, November 1934, 18-20.

171. For an account of raising the dead in Ghana, see Stephen K. Gyermeh, *The Miracles of God: From Heathenism to Christianity* (Lakeland, Fla.: By the author, 1979), 17-18.

172. Frost, *Miraculous Healing*, 72.

173. Ibid., 93-95.

174. Ibid., 108.

175. On the impact of the Osborn campaign in Mombasa, Kenya, see Ronald P. Westbury, "The Nature and Status of Ministry Practices of the Pentecostal Evangelistic Fellowship of Africa" (D.Min. diss., Asbury Theological Seminary, 2002), 33-34.

176. Donald Gee, "The 'Deliverance Campaigns,'" *Pent*, June 1956, 17; Osborn, *Healing the Sick*, 204-8.

177. Richard M. Riss, *Latter Rain: The Latter Rain Movement of 1948 and the Mid-Twentieth Century Evangelical Awakening* (Mississauga, Ont.: Honeycomb Visual Productions, 1987), 60-61.

178. See David Edwin Harrell, Jr., *Oral Roberts: An American Life* (San Francisco: Harper & Row, 1985), 192-95; idem, *All Things Are Possible*, 140-43.

179. Boggs, *Faith Healing*, 31.

180. J. Oswald Sanders, *Heresies: Ancient and Modern* (London: Marshall, Morgan & Scott, 1948), 138.

181. Ibid., 146.

182. J. M. Buckley, *Christian Science and Other Superstitions* (New York: Century, 1899), 1-64.

183. For an insightful discussion, see Bryan Froehle, "Pentecostals and Evangelicals in Venezuela: Consolidating Gains, Moving in New Directions," in *Power, Politics, and Pentecostals in Latin America*, ed. Edward L. Cleary and Hannah W. Stewart-Gambino (Boulder, Colo.: Westview, 1997), 201-25.

184. "But What about Hicks?" *CC*, July 7, 1954, 814-15; cf. Arno W. Enns, *Man, Milieu and Mission in Argentina: A Close Look at Church Growth* (Grand Rapids: Eerdmans, 1971), 76-79.

185. Emilio Conde, "Nearly 50,000 Gather on Easter Sunday," *Pent*, June 1956, 2.

186. Gerald Robeson, as related by Richard Jeffery, *Put the Coffin Back . . . I'm Healed* (Woodburn, Ore.: By the author, 1983); interview with DeLonn Rance, missionary to Central America, May 19, 2008.

187. Harrell, *All Things Are Possible*, 93-96; A. J. Schoeman, "South Africa Stirred," *Pent*, March 1952, 1-3; Julius Stadsklev, *William Branham: A Prophet Visits South Africa* (Minneapolis: n.p., 1952).

188. "The Black Billy Graham," *Time*, November 23, 1959, 69-70; Peter Watt, *From Africa's Soil: The Story of the Assemblies of God in Southern Africa* (Cape Town: Struik Christian Books, 1992), 50-54; Walter H. Hollenweger, *The Pentecostals* (Peabody, Mass.: Hendrickson, 1972), 126-39.

189. J. Kwabena Asamoah-Gyadu, "'Born of Water and the Spirit': Pentecostal/Charismatic Christianity in Africa," in *African Christianity: An African Story*, ed. Ogbu U. Kalu (Trenton, N.J.: Africa World Press, 2007), 344-45. For an insightful study by an African Catholic scholar, see Cécé Kolié, "Jesus as Healer?" in *Faces of Jesus in Africa*, ed. Robert J. Schreiter (Maryknoll, N.Y.: Orbis Books, 1991), 128-50.

190. Donald Gee, *Trophimus I Left Sick: Our Problems of Divine Healing* (London: Elim, 1952), 20.

191. Osborn, *Healing the Sick*, 147.

192. Gee, *Trophimus I Left Sick*, 9-10.

193. Ibid., 21-22.

194. Ibid., 25.

195. S. A. Jamieson, *Pillars of Truth* (Springfield, Mo.: Gospel Publishing House, 1926), 71, 94-96.

196. P. C. Nelson, *Bible Doctrines*, rev. ed. (Springfield, Mo.: Gospel Publishing House, 1971; originally published in 1934), 123; cf. Myer Pearlman, *Knowing the Doctrines of the Bible* (Springfield, Mo.: Gospel Publishing House, 1937), 195-216, 323-24; idem, "The Lord Jesus' Power to Heal," *PE*, February 10, 1934, 13; idem, "The Lord Jesus Responds to Faith," *PE*, March 10, 1934, 9; idem, "Peter Heals a Lame Man," *PE*, February 16, 1935, 13.

197. Ralph M. Riggs, "The Doctrine of Divine Healing Is Being Wounded in the House of Its Friends," *PE*, November 4, 1956, 6.

198. G. H. Montgomery, quoted in Harrell, *All Things Are Possible*, 142. Montgomery was probably referring to T. L. Osborn's evangelistic meetings in Jamaica in 1948 and his claim that 125 deaf persons had been healed; see T. L. Osborn, "The Strategic Issue: Settled for Life," *Diary Notes: Jamaica Crusade*, November 1948, 11, in vol. 1 of *Faith Library in 23 Volumes* (Tulsa, Okla.: OSFO International, 2000).

199. Noel Perkin, "Introduction to the Missions Seminar," *Key*, July-August 1956, 6.

200. For example, Kenneth E. Hagin, *Healing Belongs to Us* (Tulsa, Okla.: Faith Library Publications, n.d.), 11-17; idem, *The Key to Scriptural Healing* (Tulsa, Okla.: Faith Library Publications, 1977), 7-11; cf. D. R. McConnell, *A Different Gospel: Biblical and Historical Insights into the Word of Faith Movement* (Peabody, Mass.: Hendrickson, 1995).

201. For example, see Turner, *Christ the Great Physician*, 126-38.

202. Evident in the position paper adopted in 1974 by the General Council of the Assemblies of God: "Divine Healing: An Integral Part of the Gospel," published in *Where We Stand* (Springfield, Mo.: Gospel Publishing House, 2001), 45-54; "Modern Medicine and the Assemblies of God," http://ag.org/top/Beliefs/contempissues_13_medicine.cfm.

203. Lee Braxton, quoted in Harrell, *Oral Roberts*, 383.

10. APOSTOLIC FAITH AT THE THIRD MILLENNIUM

1. Charles F. Parham, quoted in "The Apostolic Faith," *Galveston Daily News*, November 20, 1905, 8.

2. "The Apostolic Faith Movement," *AF* (L.A.), September 1906, 2, col. 1.

3. Sheik Metry S. Dewairy of Egypt, quoted in *The Jerusalem Meeting of the International Missionary Council, March 24-April 8, 1928*, vol. 3: *The Relation between the Younger and Older Churches* (New York: International Missionary Council, 1928), 3: 126.

4. John R. Rice, *The Power of Pentecost or the Fullness of the Spirit* (Murfreesboro, Tenn.: Sword of the Lord Publishers, 1949), 88-89.

5. J. Philip Hogan, "The Holy Spirit and the Great Commission," *WP* 1 (1972): 4-5.

6. Hwa Yung, "Pentecostalism and the Asian Church," in *Asian and Pentecostal: The Charismatic Face of Christianity in Asia*, ed. Allan Anderson and Edmond Tang (Oxford: Regnum Books International, 2005), 52.

7. In a twenty-year period (1960-1980), denominational "white papers" on the ministry of the Holy Spirit alone filled more than fifteen hundred pages of published text,

amply showing the emerging interest and international theological reflection, but not including those produced by Christian organizations outside the citadels of the religious establishment. See Kilian McDonnell, ed., *Presence, Power, Praise: Documents of the Charismatic Renewal*, 3 vols. (Collegeville, Minn.: Liturgical Press, 1980).

8. Stephen Neill, *Beliefs: Lectures Delivered at the Kodaikanal Missionary Conference, 1937* (Madras: Christian Literature Society for India, 1940), 1.

9. See Michael Bergunder, *The South Indian Pentecostal Movement in the Twentieth Century* (Grand Rapids: Eerdmans, 2008).

10. Lesslie Newbigin, *The Household of God* (New York: Friendship, 1953), 94-95.

11. José Comblin, *The Holy Spirit and Liberation* (Eugene, Ore.: Wipf & Stock, 1989), 7-8.

12. See Paul G. Hiebert, "The Flaw of the Excluded Middle," *Miss* 10 (January 1982): 38-41.

13. Wonsuk Ma, "When the Poor Are Fired Up: The Role of Pneumatology in Pentecostal-Charismatic Mission," *Christian Today* [online Christian news provider in U.K.], May 10, 2005; available at http://www.oikoumene.org/en/resources/documents/wcc-commissions/mission-and-evangelism/cwme-world-conference-athens-2005/plen-10-may-no-4-wonsuk-ma.html. See also Heidi Baker and Rolland Baker, *Expecting Miracles: True Stories of God's Supernatural Power and How You Can Experience It* (Grand Rapids: Chosen Books, 2007).

14. Kirsteen Kim, *The Holy Spirit in the World: A Global Conversation* (Maryknoll, N.Y.: Orbis Books, 2007), 153.

15. Peter Hocken, *The Glory and the Shame: Reflections on the 20th Century Outpouring of the Holy Spirit* (Guildford, Surrey, U.K.: Eagle, 1994), 5.

16. David D. Daniels, III, "The Color of Charismatic Leadership: William Joseph Seymour and Martin Luther King, Jr. as Champions of Interracialism," in *We've Come This Far: Reflections on the Pentecostal Tradition and Racial Reconciliation*, ed. Byron D. Klaus (Springfield, Mo.: Assemblies of God Theological Seminary, 2007), 66-87; Comblin, *Holy Spirit*, 1-42.

17. http://peru.anglican.org/.

18. For example, see Julie C. Ma, *When the Spirit Meets the Spirits: Pentecostal Ministry among the Kankana-ey Tribe in the Philippines* (Frankfurt am Main: Peter Lang, 2000), 213-32.

19. Augustine Mundackatt, V.C., "On the Mongolian Mountains"; available at http://www.datanumeric.com/vlm/12-97/6.htm.

20. Tan Jin Huat, "Pentecostal and Charismatic Origins in Malaysia and Singapore," in Anderson and Tang, eds., *Asian and Pentecostal*, 288.

21. For example, [as told to Sobhi Malek], "Muhammad was My Hero . . . But Jesus Changed My Life," *MM*, December 1984, 12-13; Stuart Robinson, *Mosques & Miracles: Revealing Islam and God's Grace*, 2d ed. (Upper Mt. Gravatt, Qld, Australia: City Harvest Publications, 2004), 263-74.

22. Kenneth Ware, "Revival among the Gypsies," *PE*, October 22, 1961, 8; Sharon E. Mumper, "Gypsies Sing New Song as Revival Spreads Throughout the World," *Pulse*, September 27, 1991, 4.

23. Maria Stethatos, *The Voice of a Priest Crying in the Wilderness: An Authorized Biography of a Greek Orthodox Priest, Father Eusebius Stephanou* (Destin, Fla.: St. Symeon the New Theologian Press, 2007), 181-200, 291, 340-45.

24. Carlos Annacondia, "Power Evangelism, Argentine Style," in *The Rising Revival: Firsthand Accounts of the Incredible Argentine Revival—and How It Can Spread Throughout the World*, ed. C. Peter Wagner and Pablo Deiros (Ventura, Calif.: Renew

Books, 1998), 67 (Annacondia's emphasis). Also, Richard Nicholson, "Argentina's Pentecostal Outpouring," *PE*, February 16, 1986, 10-11.

25. "Brother Fidel," quoted in Philip J. Williams, "The Sound of Tambourines: The Politics of Pentecostal Growth in El Salvador," in *Power, Politics, and Pentecostals in Latin America*, ed. Edward L. Cleary and Hannah W. Stewart-Gambino (Boulder, Colo.: Westview, 1997), 197.

26. Per Anderson, quoted in Larry Christenson, ed., *Welcome, Holy Spirit: A Study of Charismatic Renewal in the Church* (Minneapolis: Augsburg, 1987), 372.

27. Philip Jenkins, *The New Faces of Christianity: Believing the Bible in the Global South* (Oxford: Oxford University Press, 2006), 1-17.

28. Adrian Rogers, *Believe in Miracles but Trust in Jesus* (Wheaton, Ill.: Crossway Books, 1997), 18.

29. Tim Stafford, "Testing the Wine from John Wimber's Vineyard," *CT*, August 8, 1986, 17-22.

30. See John Wimber with Kevin Springer, *Power Evangelism* (San Francisco: Harper & Row, 1986); idem, *Power Healing* (San Francisco: Harper & Row, 1987); cf. Ben Patterson, "Cause for Concern," *CT*, August 8, 1986, 20; Lewis B. Smedes, ed., *Ministry and the Miraculous: A Case Study at Fuller Theological Seminary* (Pasadena, Calif.: Fuller Theological Seminary, 1987); Ken Sarles, "An Appraisal of the Signs and Wonders Movement," *BS* 145 (January-March 1988): 57-82.

31. C. Peter Wagner, *The Third Wave of the Holy Spirit: Encountering the Power of Signs and Wonders Today* (Ann Arbor, Mich.: Servant Publications, 1988), 15-19.

32. Bill Jackson, "A Short History of the Association of Vineyard Churches," in *Church, Identity, and Change: Theology and Denominational Structures in Unsettled Times*, ed. David A. Roozen and James R. Nieman (Grand Rapids: Eerdmans, 2005), 132-40.

33. See Jack Deere, *Surprised by the Power of the Spirit: A Former Dallas Seminary Professor Discovers That God Speaks and Heals Today* (Grand Rapids: Zondervan, 1993); Timothy M. Warner, *Spiritual Warfare: Victory over the Powers of This Dark World* (Wheaton, Ill.: Crossway Books, 1991); Charles H. Kraft, *Christianity with Power: Your Worldview and Your Experience of the Supernatural* (Ann Arbor, Mich.: Vine Books, 1989); Donald Bridge, *Signs and Wonders Today* (Leicester, U.K.: InterVarsity, 1985).

34. Willard M. Swartley, ed., *Essays on Spiritual Bondage and Deliverance* (Elkhart, Ind.: Institute of Mennonite Studies, 1988). Earlier studies included C. Fred Dickason, *Demon Possession & the Christian* (Chicago: Moody, 1987); Merrill F. Unger, *Biblical Demonology: A Study of the Spiritual Forces Behind the Present World Unrest* (Wheaton, Ill.: Van Kampen, 1952).

35. David Hume, *An Enquiry Concerning Human Understanding*, Great Books of the Western World, ed. Robert Maynard Hutchins, no. 35: *Locke, Berkeley, Hume* (Chicago: Encyclopaedia Britannica, 1952), 490-92.

36. Charles Pinches, "Miracles: A Christian Theological Overview," *SMJ* 100 (December 2007): 1240.

37. Paul Rader, "Only Believe," in *Hymns of the Christian Life* (Harrisburg, Pa.: Christian Publications, 1936), #257.

38. Pinches, "Miracles," 1240-42.

39. Robert Bruce Mullin, *A Short World History of Christianity* (Louisville, Ky.: Westminster John Knox, 2008), 212.

40. David B. Barratt, Todd M. Johnson, and Peter F. Crossing, "Missiometrics 2006: Goals, Resources, Doctrines of the 350 Christian World Communions," *IBMR* 30 (January 2006): 28.

41. Thomas R. Edgar, "The Cessation of the Sign Gifts," *BS* 145 (October-December 1988): 371-86; cf. Claude A. Frazier, M.D., ed., *Faith Healing: Finger of God? Or, Scientific Curiosity?* (New York: Thomas Nelson, 1973).

42. For example, see Mrs. R. R. Coyne, *When God Smiled on Ronald Coyne* (Sapulpa, Okla.: By the author, 1954). On Grant and Popoff, see James Randi, *The Faith Healers* (Buffalo, N.Y.: Prometheus, 1987), 99-137, 139-81.

43. May Wyburn Fitch, *The Healing Delusion* (New York: Loizeaux Brothers, n.d.), 46-48.

44. David Edwin Harrell, Jr., *Oral Roberts: An American Life* (San Francisco: Harper & Row, 1985), 163-64.

45. See Donald Grey Barnhouse, "Finding Fellowship with Pentecostals," *Eter*, April 1958, 8-10. Barnhouse had originally opposed the membership of Pentecostals in the NAE.

46. On Pentecostals in the NAE, see Garth M. Rosell, *The Surprising Work of God: Harold John Ockenga, Billy Graham, and the Rebirth of Evangelicalism* (Grand Rapids: Baker Academic, 2008), 93-95.

47. *Foreign Missions Committee Minutes* (Foreign Missions Department of the Assemblies of God), May 26, 1950; November 7, 1951; January 9, 1953; Samuel McCrea Cavert, *Church Cooperation and Unity in America* (New York: Association Press, 1970), 51.

48. *Foreign Missions Committee Minutes* (Foreign Missions Department of the Assemblies of God), December 19, 1950. The other Pentecostal agencies chose to remain in the EFMA; Robert Bryant Mitchell, *Heritage & Horizons: The History of Open Bible Standard Churches* (Des Moines: Open Bible Publishers, 1982), 261.

49. "'A Statement by Pentecostal Leaders,' Issued by the World Conference of International Pentecostal Churches, London, July 5th, 1952," in *Missions under the Cross: Addresses Delivered at the Enlarged Meeting of the Committee of the International Missionary Council at Willingen, in Germany, 1952; with Statements Issued by the Meeting*, ed. Norman Goodall (New York: Friendship, 1953), 249-50. The sending of the statement did not appear in the reports of denominational periodicals on the World Pentecostal Conference: "World Conference of Pentecostal Churches Back Appeal to the United Nations," *PT*, August 1, 1952, 6; "Every Continent Represented at World Conference," *PE*, August 3, 1952, 11-12. The correct title of the association was World Pentecostal Conference, changed to Pentecostal World Conference in 1961. For further information, see David J. du Plessis, *A Brief History of the World Pentecostal Fellowship* (Stamford, Conn.: By the author, n.d.).

50. David J. du Plessis, "Into All the World," *PE*, April 20, 1952, 6-7; also idem, *The Spirit Bade Me Go*, rev. ed. (Oakland, Calif.: By the author, 1963).

51. For example, see "Beginning of World Wide Revival," *AF* (L.A.), January 1907, 1, cols. 1-2.

52. J. Roswell Flower, "A Report Covering the First Week of the Second Meeting of the World Council of Churches, Convened at Northwestern University at Evanston, Illinois, August 14-31, 1954." Available at Flower Pentecostal Heritage Center, Springfield, MO 65802. The noted conservative evangelical leader and editor Donald Grey Barnhouse also attended and spoke favorably of the conference ("Evanston: What it Was," *Eter*, October 1954, 8-9, 38-40). See also Jeffrey Gros, *Pentecostal Engagement in the Wider Christian Community* (Indianapolis: Council on Christian Unity, n.d.).

53. Carl McIntire, *Twentieth Century Reformation*, 3rd ed. (Collingswood, N.J.: Christian Beacon Press, 1946), 202-5; "Resolutions Adopted at Convention Express ACCC's Position on Issues," *CB*, November 6, 1952, 4.

54. Theodore B. Hax, "Signs of the Times," *PE*, January 12, 1958, 5; Edith L. Blumhofer, *Restoring the Faith: The Assemblies of God, Pentecostalism, and American Culture* (Urbana: University of Illinois Press, 1993), 227-32.

55. Cf. J. L. Hall, *The United Pentecostal Church and the Evangelical Movement* (Hazelwood, Mo.: Word Aflame, 1990).

56. See Henry P. Van Dusen, "The Third Force in Christendom," *Life*, June 9, 1958, 113-24; W. D. R., "Pentecost South of the Border," *CT*, July 19, 1963, 31-32; J. S. Murray, "What We Can Learn from the Pentecostal Churches," *CT*, June 9, 1967, 10-12; Alan Walker, "Where Pentecostalism Is Mushrooming," *CC*, January 17, 1968, 81-82; and more recently from a Southern Baptist perspective: Justice C. Anderson, *An Evangelical Saga: Baptists and Their Precursors in Latin America* (Longwood, Fla.: Xulon, 2005), 595-625.

57. These have included the World Assemblies of God Fellowship and the World Fellowship of the International Pentecostal Holiness Church.

58. See *NIDPCM*, 2002, s.v., "Global Statistics," by D. B. Barrett and T. M. Johnson.

59. B. F. Lawrence, *The Apostolic Faith Restored* (St. Louis: Gospel Publishing House, 1916), 11.

60. Harold D. Hunter and Cecil M. Robeck, Jr., "Introduction," in *The Azusa Street Revival and Its Legacy*, ed. Harold D. Hunter and Cecil M. Robeck, Jr. (Cleveland, Tenn.: Pathway, 2006), 13; Barratt, "Missiometrics," 28; Thomas E. Trask and Wayde I. Goodall, *The Blessing: Experiencing the Power of the Holy Spirit Today* (Grand Rapids: Zondervan, 1998), 19-20; Vinson Synan, *The Spirit Said "Grow": The Astounding Worldwide Expansion of Pentecostal & Charismatic Churches* (Monrovia, Calif.: MARC, 1992).

61. Cf. "Evangelizing Together: Ecumenical Issues in Evangelization," in *All Together in One Place: Theological Papers from the Brighton Conference on World Evangelization*, ed. Harold D. Hunter and Peter D. Hocken (Sheffield: Sheffield Academic Press, 1993), 256-61.

62. Jim Grams, "Poorly Kept Secrets: Reflections of a Former Missionary," *Agora* 2 (Winter 1979): 13; John L. Amstutz, "Foursquare Missions: Doing More with Less," *Pneuma* 16 (Spring 1994): 63-80; Edward L. Cleary and Juan Sepúlveda, "Chilean Pentecostalism: Coming of Age," in Cleary and Stewart-Gambino, *Power, Politics, and Pentecostals*, 110-12.

63. See Earl Creps, "Postmodern Pentecostals? Emerging Subcultures among Young Pentecostal Leaders," in Eric Patterson and Edmund Rybarczyk, eds., *The Future of Pentecostalism in the United States* (Lanham, Md.: Lexington Books, 2007), 27-47.

64. Reasons for this decline are offered, albeit from a distinctly North American perspective, in L. John Bueno, "Why Is It Happening?" *TPE*, October 5, 2008, 6-14.

65. Margaret M. Poloma, "Charisma and Structure in the Assemblies of God: Revisiting O'Dea's Five Dilemmas," in Roozen and Nieman, eds., *Church, Identity, and Change*, 45-96.

66. B. E. Underwood, *Sixteen New Testament Principles for World Evangelization* (Franklin Springs, Ga.: Advocate, 1988), 110; on the development of Underwood's missiology, see Elaine Vaden, "'Shooting the Sacred Cows': The Missiological and Theological Perspectives of Bernard E. Underwood" (D.Miss. diss., Fuller Theological Seminary, 2001).

67. The first-generation Pentecostals struggled with the decline of their own revival; see "Is There Declension in the Pentecostal Movement?" *PE*, April 21, 1923, 2-3, 5.

68. Robert A. Larden, *Our Apostolic Heritage* (Calgary, Alberta: Kyle Printing and Stationary, 1971), 191.

69. Comblin, *Holy Spirit*, 60.

70. Klaus Fiedler, *The Story of Faith Missions: From Hudson Taylor to Present Day Africa* (Oxford: Regnum Books International, 1994), 113-14.

71. Byron D. Klaus, "Pentecostalism and Mission," *Miss* 35 (January 2007): 39-54.

72. Simon Chan, *Pentecostal Theology and the Christian Spiritual Tradition* (Sheffield: Sheffield Academic Press, 2000), 58.

73. Harvey Cox, *Fire from Heaven: The Rise of Pentecostal Spirituality and the Reshaping of Religion in the Twenty-First Century* (Reading, Mass.: Addison-Wesley, 1995), 96.

74. *Minutes of the Sixth Annual Meeting of the General Council of the Assemblies of God in the United States, Canada and Foreign Lands*, 1918, 8; Thomas E. Trask and Wayde I. Goodall, *The Blessing: Experiencing the Power of the Holy Spirit Today* (Grand Rapids: Zondervan, 1998), 31-56.

75. Gordon D. Fee, *Gospel and Spirit: Issues in New Testament Hermeneutics* (Peabody, Mass.: Hendrickson, 1991), 83-104; Rick Walston, *The Speaking in Tongues Controversy: The Initial, Physical Evidence of the Baptism in the Holy Spirit Debate* (Longwood, Fla.: Xulon, 2003); cf. Frank D. Macchia, *Baptized in the Spirit: A Global Pentecostal Theology* (Grand Rapids: Zondervan, 2006); William W. Menzies and Robert P. Menzies, *Spirit and Power: Foundations of Pentecostal Experience* (Grand Rapids: Zondervan, 2000); Roger Stronstad, *The Prophethood of All Believers: A Study in Luke's Charismatic Theology* (Sheffield: Sheffield Academic Press, 1999).

76. See Jack W. Hayford, *The Beauty of Spiritual Language: My Journey toward the Heart of God* (Dallas: Word, 1992), 92-95; David Cole, "Heritage and Horizons: The Derivation and Destiny of Open Bible Churches," in Patterson and Rybarczyk, eds., *Future of Pentecostalism*, 165-70.

77. Gordon F. Atter, *The Third Force*, 2d ed. (Peterborough, Ont.: College Press, 1965), 122; cf. Margaret M. Poloma, "The Symbolic Dilemma and the Future of Pentecostalism: Mysticism, Ritual, and Revival," in Patterson and Rybarczyk, eds., *Future of Pentecostalism*, 105-21.

78. For examples of the reductionism, see James L. Slay, "Glossolalia: Its Value to the Individual," in *The Glossolalia Phenomenon*, ed. Wade H. Horton (Cleveland, Tenn.: Pathway, 1966), 217-43; David K. Bernard, *The Oneness of God* (Hazelwood, Mo.: Word Aflame, 1992), 41-54; James K. Bridges, "The Full Consummation of the Baptism in the Holy Spirit," *Enri*, Fall 2000, 92-95.

79. E. N. Bell, "Questions and Answers," *WE*, January 1, 1916, 8.

80. Edith L. Blumhofer, *Aimee Semple McPherson: Everybody's Sister* (Grand Rapids: Eerdmans, 1993), 249-50.

81. See Frederick L. Ware, "The Church of God in Christ and the Azusa Street Revival," in Hunter and Robeck, eds., *Azusa Street Revival*, 243-57.

82. Pablo A. Deiros and Everett A. Wilson, "Hispanic Pentecostalism in the Americas," in *The Century of the Holy Spirit: 100 Years of Pentecostal and Charismatic Renewal, 1901-2001*, ed. Vinson Synan (Nashville: Thomas Nelson, 2001), 315.

83. For example, see Juan Sepúlveda, "Indigenous Pentecostalism and the Chilean Experience," in *Pentecostals after a Century: Global Perspectives on a Movement in Transition*, ed. Allan H. Anderson and Walter J. Hollenweger (Sheffield: Sheffield Academic Press, 1999), 111-34; Walter J. Hollenweger, "Rethinking Spirit Baptism: The Natural and the Supernatural," in Anderson and Hollenweger, eds., *Pentecostals after a Century*, 164-72; J. Kwabena Asamoah-Gyadu, "'Born of Water and the Spirit': Pentecostal/Charismatic Christianity in Africa," in *African Christianity: An African Story*, ed. Ogbu U. Kalu (Trenton, N.J.: Africa World Press, 2007), 339-357.

84. Frank D. Macchia, "Baptized in the Spirit: Towards a Global Pentecostal Theology," in *Defining Issues in Pentecostalism: Classical and Emergent*, ed. Steven M. Studebaker (Eugene, Ore.: Pickwick Publications, 2008), 22-23; also Harold D. Hunter, "Aspects of Initial-Evidence Dogma: A European-American Holiness Pentecostal Perspective," *AJPS* 2 (August 1998): 185-88.

85. Everett A. Wilson, "They Crossed the Red Sea, Didn't They? Critical History and Pentecostal Beginnings," in *The Globalization of Pentecostalism: A Religion Made to Travel*, ed. Murray W. Dempster, Byron D. Klaus, Douglas Petersen (Oxford: Regnum Books International, 1999), 109.

86. Donald E. Miller and Tetsunao Yamamori, *Global Pentecostalism: The New Face of Christian Social Engagement* (Berkeley: University of California Press, 2007), 17-22.

87. Miguel A. Palomino and Samuel Escobar, "Worship and Culture in Latin America," in *Christian Worship Worldwide: Expanding Horizons, Deepening Practices*, ed. Charles E. Farhadian (Grand Rapids: Eerdmans, 2007), 107-30.

88. Ogbu Kalu, *African Pentecostalism: An Introduction* (Oxford: Oxford University Press, 2008), 68-83; Allan H. Anderson, *African Reformation: African Initiated Christianity in the 20th Century* (Trenton, N.J.: Africa World Press, 2001), 106-8; also Edley J. Moodley, "Shembe, Ancestors, or Christ: A Missiological Inquiry into the Status and Role of Jesus Christ in the amaNazaretha Church, Kwa Zulu Natal, South Africa" (Ph.D. diss., Asbury Theological Seminary, 2004).

89. Ivan M. Satyavrata, "Cultural Perspectives on Pentecostalism as a Global Culture: A South Asian View," in Dempster, et al., eds. *Globalization of Pentecostalism*, 215-16.

90. Edith L. Blumhofer, "Divided Pentecostals: Bakker vs. Swaggart," *CC*, May 6, 1987, 430-431.

91. Richard N. Ostling, "Now It's Jimmy's Turn," *Time*, March 7, 1988, 46-48. The ministries of both Swaggart and Bakker waned after their acknowledgment of moral failures within months of each other in 1987-1988.

92. Blan Maurice Stout, "Preaching through Television: An Examination of the Preaching of Jimmy Swaggart Based upon the Aristotelian Triad" (Th.M. thesis, Harvard Divinity School, 1983), 45.

93. Observations based in part on the author's attendance at the Jimmy Swaggart Crusade in Tegucigalpa, Honduras, in January 1988, as well as discussions with Assemblies of God missionaries involved in his crusades elsewhere. Filmed by cameras not far from the platform where the speakers and singers stood, the musical package was sung in English and primarily intended for an American television audience.

94. Jimmy Swaggart with Marvin Solum, *The Balanced Faith Life* (Baton Rouge, La.: Jimmy Swaggart Evangelistic Association, 1981), 38.

95. Appendix I (transcribed interview with Jimmy Swaggart) in Stout, "Preaching through Television," 68-69.

96. Rufus Anderson, *Foreign Missions: Their Relations and Claims* (New York: Charles Scribner, 1869), 115-16.

97. A statistic on the back cover of Reinhard Bonnke, *Evangelism by Fire: Igniting Your Passion for the Lost*, 8th ed. (Frankfurt am Main: Christ for All Nations, 2002), states that crowds have reached upward to 1.6 million people.

98. Bonnke, *Evangelism by Fire*, 98.

99. Ron Steele, *Plundering Hell to Populate Heaven: The Reinhard Bonnke Story* (Tulsa, Okla.: Albury, 1987), 35.

100. Kalu, *African Pentecostalism*, 19.

101. DPCM (1988), s.v. "Church Growth," by C. Peter Wagner.

102. Allan Anderson, "Global Pentecostalism in the New Millennium," in Anderson

and Hollenweger, eds., *Pentecostals after a Century*, 209-23. Euroamerican Pentecostal evangelists sometimes overestimated and/or misinterpreted their successes abroad. This was illustrated in Tommy Hicks's published account of his 1954 campaign in Buenos Aires, Argentina, presumptuously titled *Millions Found Christ* (Los Angeles: Manifest Deliverance and Worldwide Evangelism, 1956); cf. Louie W. Stokes, *The Great Revival in Buenos Aires* (Buenos Aires: Casilla De Correo, 1954).

103. On Cho: see Wonsuk Ma, William W. Menzies, and Hyeon-sung Bae, eds., *David Yonggi Cho: A Close Look at His Theology & Ministry* (Baguio, Philippines: APTS, 2004); on Wongsak: see Joseph C. Wongsak, "Hope of Bangkok Church," in *The New Apostolic Churches*, ed. C. Peter Wagner (Ventura, Calif.: Regal Books, 1998), 271-79; on Kong: see http://en.wikipedia.org/wiki/Kong_Hee; on Pullinger: see Miller and Yamamori, *Global Pentecostalism*, 99-105; on Idahosa: see Kalu, *African Pentecostalism*, 91; on Kumuyi: see William F. Kumuyi, "Deeper Christian Life Ministry," in Wagner and Deiros, *Rising Revival*, 243-55; on Osueke: see Don Corbin, "Hosanna Celebration Marks Growth of African Fellowship," *PE*, February 4, 2001, 31; on David Maxwell, see *African Gifts of the Spirit: Pentecostalism & the Rise of a Zimbabwean Transnational Religious Movement* (Oxford: James Curry, 2006); on Adelaja: see J. Kwabena Asamoah-Gyadu, "African Initiated Christianity in Eastern Europe: Church of the 'Embassy of God' in Ukraine," *IBMR* 30 (April 2006): 73-75; on Cabrera: see Omar Cabrera, "Vision of the Future," in Wagner and Deiros, *Rising Revival*, 91-105; on Canavesio: see Underwood, *Sixteen New Testament Principles*, 58-61; on Chankersingh: see http://faithcentrett.org/index.php?option=com_frontpage&Itemid=41; on Cantalamessa: see *NIDPCM*, 2002, s.v. "Raniero Cantalamessa," by P. D. Hocken; on Naickomparambil: see Julia Duin, "India's 'Billy Graham' is Catholic," *Char*, November 1994, 86, 88-89; on Koontz: see Linda Koontz, "Evangelizing the Poor," in *John Paul II and the New Evangelization*, ed. Ralph Martin and Peter Williamson (San Francisco: Ignatius Press, 1995), 173-83; on McKenna: see Breige McKenna, with Henry Libersat, *Miracles Do Happen: God Can Do the Impossible* (Ann Arbor, Mich.: Servant Books, 1987); on Suarez: see http://www.fatherfernando.com; on Forrest: see Tom Forrest, "Evangelization 2000: A Global View," in *The New Catholic Evangelization*, ed. Kenneth Boyack (New York: Paulist, 1992), 214-27; on Martin: see http://www.renewal ministries.net; on Ganaka: see Gabriel Gonsum Ganaka, "Evangelization in the Church of Jos, Nigeria," in Martin and Williamson, eds., *John Paul II*, 101-10.

104. Thomas William Miller, *Canadian Pentecostals: A History of the Pentecostal Assemblies of Canada* (Mississauga, Ont.: Full Gospel Publishing House, 1994), 389.

105. For the rise of independent charismatic missions, see Edward K. Pousson, *Spreading the Flame: Charismatic Churches and Missions Today* (Grand Rapids: Zondervan, 1992).

106. See David Cannistraci, *Apostles and the Emerging Apostolic Movement* (Ventura, Calif.: Renew Books, 1997).

107. For example, in North America: Wagner, ed., *New Apostolic Churches*; in Australia: David Cartledge, *The Apostolic Revolution: The Restoration of Apostles and Prophets in the Assemblies of God in Australia* (Chester Hill, NSW, Australia: Paraclete Institute, 2000); in Argentina: Ed Silvoso, *That None Should Perish: How to Reach Entire Cities for Christ through Prayer Evangelism* (Ventura, Calif.: Regal Books, 1994).

108. C. Peter Wagner, *Confronting the Powers: How the New Testament Church Experienced the Power of Strategic-Level Spiritual Warfare* (Ventura, Calif.: Regal Books, 1996), 156-57; also Keith E. Webb, *Overcoming Spiritual Barriers in Japan: Identifying Strongholds and Redemptive Gifts* (Bellevue, Wash.: NextChurch Resources, 1999) (Wagner's emphases).

109. Donald Anderson McGavran, "Homogenous Populations and Church Growth," in *Church Growth and Christian Mission*, ed. Donald A. McGavran (South Pasadena, Calif.: William Carey Library, 1965), 69-86; George Otis, Jr., with Mark Brockman, *Strongholds of the 10/40 Window: Intercessor's Guide to the World's Least Evangelized Nations* (Seattle: YWAM, 1995), 9-10.

110. Wagner, *Confronting the Powers*, 68-71.

111. See Robert J. Priest, Thomas Campbell, and Bradford A. Mullen, "Missiological Syncretism: The New Animistic Paradigm," in *Spiritual Power and Missions: Raising the Issues*, ed. Edward Rommen (Pasadena, Calif.: William Carey Library, 1995), 9-87; cf. Charles H. Kraft, "'Christian Animism or God-Given Authority?" in Rommen, ed., *Spiritual Power and Missions*, 88-136.

112. "Lausanne Consultation Struggles with Spiritual Warfare," *Lausanne Committee for World Evangelization Newsletter*, December 2000, 3; Kwame Bediako, *Christianity in Africa: The Renewal of a Non-Western Religion* (Maryknoll, N.Y.: Orbis Books, 1995), 91-106.

113. A. Scott Moreau, et al., eds., *Deliver Us from Evil: An Uneasy Frontier in Christian Mission* (Monrovia, Calif.: World Vision International, 2002); Michael Pocock, Gailyn Van Rheenen, Douglas McConnell, *The Changing Face of World Missions: Engaging Contemporary Issues and Trends* (Grand Rapids: Baker Academic, 2005), 183-208.

114. See Klaas Runia, "Renewal and the Doctrine of the Church: Issues in Modern European Church History," in *The Church: God's Agent for Change*, ed. Bruce J. Nicholls (Exeter, U.K.: Paternoster, 1986), 263-79.

115. William H. Durham, "Personal Testimony of Pastor Durham," *PT* (L.A.) 2, no. 3 (1912): 1-16.

116. For contrasting perspectives on the nature and consequences of the "New Issue," see William W. Menzies, *Anointed to Serve: The Story of the Assemblies of God* (Springfield, Mo.: Gospel Publishing House, 1971), 106-21; cf. David K. Bernard, "The Future of Oneness Pentecostalism," in Patterson and Rybarczyk, eds., *Future of Pentecostalism*, 123-36.

117. Richard M. Riss, *Latter Rain: The Latter Rain Movement of 1948 and the Mid-Twentieth Century Evangelical Awakening* (Mississauga, Ont.: Honeycomb Visual Productions, 1987), 122-31.

118. Margaret Wortman, "Extract from a Letter from South America," *PT*, December 1923, 6.

119. Melvin Hodges, "Religion without Light," *PE*, December 23, 1939, 9.

120. For example, on the veneration of Mary in Nicaragua, see http://www.nicaraguaphoto.com/essays/update_nicaraguaDec2002.shtml; for the legacy of the late Mexican faith healer Niño Fidencio, see Susan Chadwick, "Impoverished Faith Healer Still Makes a Splash," *Houston Post*, January 16, 1993, F-4.

121. Melvin L. Hodges, *A Theology of the Church and Its Mission: A Pentecostal Perspective* (Springfield, Mo.: Gospel Publishing House, 1977), 96; idem, "The Charismatic Movement in World Evangelism," *Advance*, March 1975, 4-5. It is significant that in his later years Hodges participated in a local informal dialogue in Springfield, Missouri, between Assemblies of God leaders and representatives of the Roman Catholic Diocese of Springfield/Cape Girardeau.

122. "Dogmatic Constitution on the Church," in *The Documents of Vatican II*, ed. Walter M. Abbott (Piscataway, N.J.: New Century, 1966), 30.

123. Comblin, *Holy Spirit*, xii.

124. For the development of Catholic missiology since the Second Vatican Coun-

cil and the meaning of Catholic evangelization, see Karl Müller, *Mission Theology: An Introduction* (Nettetal, Germany: Steyler, 1987).

125. Avery Dulles, "John Paul II and the New Evangelization—What Does It Mean?" in Martin, *John Paul II*, 32.

126. Edward L. Cleary, "Latin American Pentecostalism," in Dempster, et al., eds. *Globalization of Pentecostalism*, 135-36; "Joint Declaration on the Doctrine of Justification"; available at http://www.vatican.va/roman_curia/pontifical_councils/chrstuni/documents/rc_pc_chrstuni_doc_31101999_cath-luth-joint-declaration_en.html.

127. Melvin L. Hodges, "The Charismatic Movement in World Evangelism," *Adva*, March 1975, 4.

128. Relationships with Roman Catholics and aspects of post-Vatican II Catholic missiology are not addressed in a later exposition of Assemblies of God missiology. See John V. York, *Missions in the Age of the Spirit* (Springfield, Mo.: Logion, 2000).

129. Most notably Assemblies of God missionary Jerry L. Sandidge; see his "Journey Toward Ecumenism: A Personal Documentary," unpublished manuscript available at the Flower Pentecostal Heritage Center, Springfield, MO 65802; also personal communication from Thomas F. Zimmerman to Jerry Sandidge, January 21, 1983.

130. R. G. van Rossum, "Latin America: Evangelization on a Christian Continent," in *Missiology: An Ecumenical Introduction*, ed. F. J. Verstraelen, A. Camps, L. A. Hoedemaker, M. R. Spindler (Grand Rapids: Eerdmans, 1995), 350.

131. Kilian McDonnell, *The Charismatic Renewal and Ecumenism* (New York: Paulist, 1978), 76-79; Jeffrey Gros, Harding Meyer, and William G. Rusch, eds., *Growth in Agreement II: Reports and Agreed Statements of Ecumenical Conversations on a World Level, 1982-1998* (Grand Rapids: Eerdmans, 2000), 744-47, 750-51.

132. Vinson Synan, *Charismatic Bridges* (Ann Arbor, Mich.: Word of Life, 1974), 26.

133. Steven Lawson, "The Big Charismatic Get-Together," *Char*, September 1987, 56-58.

134. See "Evangelization, Proselytism, and Common Witness: The Report from the Fourth Phase of the International Dialogue (1990-1997) between the Roman Catholic Church and Some Classical Pentecostal Churches and Leaders," *Pneuma* 21 (Spring 1999): 11-51; Kilian McDonnell, "The Death of Mythologies: The Classical Pentecostal/Roman Catholic Dialogue," *Amer*, March 25, 1995, 14-19.

135. See http://www.oikoumene.org/en/member-churches/regions/asia/south-korea.html.

136. Russell P. Spittler, "Implicit Values in Pentecostal Missions," *Miss* 16 (October 1988): 409-24.

137. Frank G. Tunstall, *The Simultaneous Principle: The History of IPHC World Missions: The First 100 Years* (Franklin Springs, Ga.: LSR Publications, 2005), 395-96.

138. Examples of relief endeavors include: Convoy of Hope, which works in conjunction with the Assemblies of God; the humanitarian relief services of Church of God (Cleveland, Tenn.) World Missions; ERDO (Emergency Relief and Development Overseas) of the Pentecostal Assemblies of Canada; COGIC (Charities of the Church of God in Christ); and Compassion Services International of the United Pentecostal Church International.

139. "AGWM Current Facts & Current Highlights," December 31, 2007; available at www.worldmissions.ag.org.

140. "Opening of the Central Bible Institute," *PE*, October 25, 1924, 8.

141. R. Bryant and Lucille M. Mitchell, *Heritage & Harvests: The History of Inter-*

national Ministries of Open Bible Standard Churches (Des Moines: Open Bible Publishers, 1995), 330, 332-33.

142. Everett A. Wilson, *Strategy of the Spirit: J. Philip Hogan and the Growth of the Assemblies of God Worldwide, 1960-1990* (Oxford: Regnum Books International, 1997), 196.

143. "Brussels Statement on Evangelization and Social Concern," *Trans* 16 (April/June 1999), 41.

144. Underwood, *Sixteen New Testament Principles*, 80.

145. "Brussels Statement," 42.

146. Paul A. Pomerville, *The Third Force in Missions* (Peabody, Mass.: Hendrickson, 1985); Murray W. Dempster, Byron D. Klaus, Douglas Petersen, eds., *Called & Empowered: Global Mission in Pentecostal Perspective* (Peabody, Mass.: Hendrickson, 1991); Dempster, et al., *Globalization of Pentecostalism*; Douglas Petersen, *Not by Might Nor by Power: A Pentecostal Theology of Social Concern in Latin America* (Oxford: Regnum Books International, 1996).

147. Veli-Matti Kärkkäinen, *An Introduction to the Theology of Religions: Biblical, Historical & Contemporary Perspectives* (Downers Grove, Ill.: InterVarsity, 2003); Amos Yong, *The Spirit Poured Out on All Flesh: Pentecostalism and the Possibility of Global Theology* (Grand Rapids: Baker Academic, 2005).

148. See Opal L. Reddin, ed., *Power Encounter: A Pentecostal Perspective*, 2d ed. (Springfield, Mo.: Central Bible College Press, 1999).

149. See Alan R. Johnson, *Apostolic Function in 21st Century Missions* (Pasadena, Calif.: William Carey Library, forthcoming).

150. Arthur F. Glasser, "The Evolution of Evangelical Mission Theology since World War II," *IBMR* 9 (January 1985): 9-13; Murray Dempster, "A Theology of the Kingdom—A Pentecostal Contribution," in *Mission as Transformation*, ed. Vinay Samuel and Chris Sugden (Oxford: Regnum Books International, 1999), 45-75.

151. Chris Sugden, *Seeking the Asian Face of Jesus: The Practice and Theology of Christian Social Witness in Indonesia and India, 1974-1996* (Oxford: Regnum Books International, 1997), 300.

152. See S. David Moore, *The Shepherding Movement: Controversy and Charismatic Ecclesiology* (London: T&T Clark International, 2003); D. R. McConnell, *A Different Gospel: Biblical and Historical Insights into the Word of Faith Movement*, 2d ed. (Peabody, Mass.; Hendrickson, 1995).

153. David Shibley, *A Force in the Earth: The Move of the Holy Spirit in World Evangelization*, 2d ed. (Orlando: Creation House, 1997), 122.

154. For a late attempt by Kenneth E. Hagin to correct the abuses of the Prosperity Gospel, see his *Midas Touch: A Balanced Approach to Biblical Prosperity* (Tulsa, Okla.: Kenneth Hagin Ministries, 2000).

155. See Pousson, *Spreading the Flame*, 85-89.

156. Edward Keith Pousson, "A 'Great Century' of Pentecostal/Charismatic Renewal and Missions," *Pneuma* 16 (Spring 1994): 98.

157. Ansel H. Post, quoted in Grant Wacker, *Heaven Below: Early Pentecostals and American Culture* (Cambridge, Mass.: Harvard University Press, 2001), 24.

158. George S. Hendry, *The Holy Spirit in Christian Theology* (Philadelphia: Westminster, 1956), 11.

159. "The Creed of Nicaea (325)," in *Creeds of the Churches*, 3rd ed., ed. John H. Leith (Atlanta: John Knox, 1982), 31.

160. Hendry, *Holy Spirit in Christian Theology*, 11.

161. Kilian McDonnell, *The Other Hand of God: The Holy Spirit as the Universal Touch and Goal* (Collegeville, Minn.: Liturgical Press, 2003), 213.

162. Hendry, *Holy Spirit in Christian Theology*, 12.

163. Harry R. Boer, *Pentecost and Missions* (Grand Rapids: Eerdmans, 1961), 210.

164. McDonnell, *Presence, Power, Praise*, 1: xx.

165. Nicholas Bhengu, "Taking South Africa for God," *PE*, March 6, 1955, 3.

166. Edward D. O'Connor, *Pentecost in the Modern World* (Notre Dame, Ind.: Ave Maria, 1972), 8-17. See also V. S. Molobi and F. Chikane, eds., *An Oral History of the South African Apostolic Faith Mission: A Missing Link of Black Historical Discourse (1908-1960 Onwards)* (Muckleneuk, Pretoria, S.A.: CB Powell Bible Centre, UNISA, 2008).

167. David J. Bosch, *Transforming Mission: Paradigm Shifts in Theology of Mission* (Maryknoll, N.Y.: Orbis Books, 1991), 516.

168. Millard J. Erickson, *Christian Theology*, 2d ed. (Grand Rapids: Baker Books, 1998), 896.

169. Gordon D. Fee, *God's Empowering Presence: The Holy Spirit in the Letters of Paul* (Peabody, Mass.: Hendrickson, 1994), 195-97.

170. See "O Come All Ye Faithful," *Econ*, November 1, 2007; available at http://www.economist.com/specialreports/displaystory.cfm?story_id=10015239&CFID=25385374.

171. David Yonggi Cho, "When Buddha Didn't Answer," in *Sacrifice & Triumph: A Timeless Treasure of Missions Stories*, ed. Joyce Wells Booze and Cathy Ketcher (Springfield, Mo.: Assemblies of God World Missions, 2003), 177.

172. Kim, *Holy Spirit in the World*, 154.

173. Gabriel Gonsum Ganaka, quoted in *DACB*, s.v. "Gabriel Gonsum Ganaka," by Musa A. B. Gaiya.

174. C. Peter Wagner, *Spreading the Fire: A New Look at Acts—God's Training Manual for Every Christian* (Ventura, Calif.: Regal Books, 1994), 12; for example, idem, *Confronting the Queen of Heaven*, rev. ed. (Colorado Springs: Wagner Publications, 2001).

175. Paul Freston, *Evangelicals and Politics in Asia, Africa and Latin America* (Cambridge: Cambridge University Press, 2001), 274-76.

176. Noel Perkin and John Garlock, *Our World Witness: A Survey of Assemblies of God Foreign Missions* (Springfield, Mo.: Gospel Publishing House, 1963), 17-18.

177. Donald Gee, untitled note, *PE*, August 11, 1923, 3.

178. For example, see Jesse K. Moon, "Understanding and Applying the Word," in *Conference on the Holy Spirit Digest*, ed. Gwen Jones, 2 vols. (Springfield, Mo.: Gospel Publishing House, 1983), 1: 74-75.

179. J. Massyngberde Ford, "The Social and Political Implications of the Miraculous in Acts," in *Faces of Renewal: Studies in Honor of Stanley M. Horton Presented on His 70th Birthday*, ed. Paul Ebert (Peabody, Mass.: Hendrickson, 1988), 155.

180. Ibid., 158.

181. Young Lee Hertig, "Cross-cultural Mediation: From Exclusion to Inclusion," in *Mission in Acts: Ancient Narratives in Contemporary Context*, ed. Robert L. Gallagher and Paul Hertig (Maryknoll, N.Y.: Orbis Books, 2004), 59-72; Evvy Hay Campbell, "Holistic Ministry and the Incident at the Gate Beautiful," in Gallagher, ed., *Mission in Acts*, 37-44; Roger S. Greenway, "Success in the City: Paul's Urban Mission Strategy," in Gallagher, ed., *Mission in Acts*, 183-95.

182. Poloma, "Symbolic Dilemma," in Patterson and Rybarczyk, eds., *Future of Pentecostalism*, 115.

183. David Martin, *Pentecostalism: The World Their Parish* (Oxford: Blackwell, 2002), 168.

184. *A Relevant Pentecostal Witness* (Durban, S.A.: Relevant Pentecostals, 1988), 3-4.

185. For example, see Japie LaPoorta, "Unity or Division: A Case Study of the Apostolic Faith Mission of South Africa," in Dempster, et al., eds. *Globalization of Pentecostalism*, 151-69.

186. J. I. Packer, "The Work of the Holy Spirit in Conviction and Conversion," in *Proclaim Christ Until He Comes: Calling the Whole Church to Take the Whole Gospel to the Whole World* (Minneapolis: World Wide Publications, 1990), 100.

187. Khoren Narbey, *A Catechism of Christian Instruction According to the Doctrine of the Armenian Church*, 6th ed., trans. Ter Psack Hyrapiet Jacob (N.p.: Armenian Church, ca. 1898), 69.

188. J. I. Packer, "Knowing God Is a Lifelong Process," interview in *TPE*, March 23, 2008, 15.

189. Robert L. Gallagher, "The Forgotten Factor: The Holy Spirit and Mission in Protestant Missiological Writings from 1945-95," in *Footprints of God: A Narrative Theology of Mission*, ed. Charles Van Engen, Nancy Thomas, Robert L. Gallagher (Monrovia, Calif.: MARC, 1999), 199-214. Missiological and historical studies still occasionally neglect or barely mention Pentecostalism and the emergence of charismatically inclined Christianity in the Majority World; for a recent example, see Martin I. Klauber and Scott M. Manetsch, eds., *The Great Commission: Evangelicals and the History of World Missions* (Grand Rapids: B &H, 2008).

190. See Roland Allen, *The Ministry of the Spirit: Selected Writings of Roland Allen*, ed. David M. Paton (Grand Rapids: Eerdmans, 1962); Harry R. Boer, *Pentecost and Missions* (Grand Rapids: Eerdmans, 1961), 130-33.

191. See Pomerville, *Third Force in Missions*, 79-104.

192. Gordon D. Fee, "The Kingdom of God and the Church's Global Mission," in *Called & Empowered: Global Mission in Pentecostal Perspective*, ed. Murray W. Dempster, Byron D. Klaus, Douglas Petersen (Peabody, Mass.: Hendrickson, 1991), 7-21; Charles H. Kraft, *Christianity with Power: Your Worldview and Your Experience of the Supernatural* (Ann Arbor, Mich.: Vine Books, 1989); Marguerite G. Kraft, *Understanding Spiritual Power: A Forgotten Dimension of Cross-Cultural Mission and Ministry* (Maryknoll, N.Y.: Orbis Books, 1995); Andrew Lord, *Spirit-Shaped Mission—A Holistic Charismatic Missiology* (Bletchley, Milton Keynes, U.K.: Paternoster, 2005).

193. See Ray H. Hughes, "The New Pentecostalism: Perspective of a Classical Pentecostal Administrator," in *Perspectives on the New Pentecostalism*, ed. Russell P. Spittler (Grand Rapids: Baker Book House, 1976), 167-80. Also, General Presbytery of the Assemblies of God, "Endtime Revival—Spirit-Led and Spirit-Controlled: A Response Paper to Resolution 16," August 11, 2000; available at http://ag.org/top/Beliefs/Position_Papers/pp_downloads/pp_endtime_revival.pdf.

194. George A. Rawlyk and Mark A. Noll, eds., *Amazing Grace: Evangelicalism in Australia, Britain, Canada, and the United States* (Grand Rapids: Baker Books, 1993), 18.

195. Markus Friedrich Wendelin, quoted in Heinrich Heppe, *Reformed Dogmatics: Set Out and Illustrated from the Sources* (Grand Rapids: Baker Book House, 1978), 265.

Index

Abrams, Minnie, 97, 133-36
Agnew, G. Harry, 29-30
Alexander, Charles, 80
Allen, A. A., 194
Allen, Roland, 164, 167, 168, 170, 222
Alliance. *See* Christian and Missionary
   Alliance; Scandinavian Alliance
Anderson, Rufus, 12, 78, 163, 210
Anderson, Tom, 103
Andersson, Ida, 92
Anglicans: and healing, 184-90
Anglin, Leslie, 164
Angus, Joseph, 14-15
Annacondia, Carlos, 201
Antony (desert father): and miracles, 5
Apostolic Bible School, 137, 138, 154, 155
apostolic faith, 222-23
Apostolic Faith Association, 123-27
Apostolic Faith Mission, 80, 92, 107, 121,
   135
Apostolic Faith movement, 91, 92, 102,
   107, 112, 119, 122, 198
apostolic power, 4, 27, 114, 176; and mis-
   sions, 4-6
Appleby, Blanche, 103, 104
Archer, W. H., 72
Arulappan, John Christian, 35, 36, 37, 47
Assemblies of God, 90, 95, 113, 117, 121,
   122, 128, 133, 136, 138, 139, 140, 141,
   142, 143, 149, 152, 153, 154, 155, 157,
   158, 159, 160, 165, 167, 168, 170, 171,
   172, 173, 182, 196, 198, 203, 205, 207,
   208, 209, 212, 214, 215, 216, 220
Athanasius, 5
Augustine of Canterbury, 6, 176
Azusa Street, 77, 80, 81, 91, 92, 93, 94, 98,
   103, 105, 107, 108, 111, 115, 120, 121,
   124, 126, 127, 132, 141, 144, 175, 187,
   198, 205, 206, 221

Babalola, Joseph Ayo, 195
Bainbridge, William, 48, 59, 60, 218
Baker, Elizabeth, 58
Baker, Harold, 147; and Josephine, 97
Bakker, Jim, 209
Baldwin, E. F., 43-44, 65, 66
baptism: believer's, 116; evangelistic,
   29-31; of fire, 42; infant, 116; Spirit,
   29-31, 36, 57, 60, 75, 76, 80, 90, 91,
   92, 93, 96, 97, 102, 103, 104, 105, 106,
   108, 109, 110, 111, 113, 114, 115, 126,
   127, 128, 129, 132, 133, 135, 139, 142,
   143, 149, 166, 168, 175, 181, 182, 187,
   191, 200, 203, 206, 207, 208, 209, 220;
   Spirit: objections to, 31-32; Spirit, with
   tongues-speech, 102-6, 115, 142, 206,
   220
Barnum, Herman, 13
Barratt, Thomas, 108
Bartleman, Frank, 125, 126
Barton, George, 74
Barton, James, 78, 98
Basil of Cappadocia, 5
Batman, George, 94
Baugh, Edith, 136
Beach, Harlan, 86
Bede, Venerable, 6, 202
Bellarmine, Robert, 6-7
Bell, E. N., 113, 120, 138, 208
Berg, Daniel, 121, 146, 166, 167
Berg, George, 97, 131
Berntsen, Bernt, 92, 163; and Magna, 97
Bertrand, Louis, 63
Bethel Bible Training School, 62, 75, 76,
   90, 102, 103, 131, 132, 155, 156
Bethel Mission, 72
Bethel Pentecostal Assembly, 131, 132,
   135, 142
Bettex, Paul, 167

318